THIS BIBLE BELONGS TO:

GIVEN BY:

DATE:

OCCASION:

"**How** can a **young [man]** live a **pure life?** **By obeying your word.**" — Psalm 119:9

REFUEL 2

THE COMPLETE NEW TESTAMENT

www.myfaithandlife.com

NCV
NEW CENTURY VERSION

NELSON BIBLES
A Division of Thomas Nelson Publishers
Since 1798
www.thomasnelson.com

TRANSIT
A Division of Thomas Nelson, Inc.
www.ThomasNelson.com

REFUEL 2
THE COMPLETE NEW TESTAMENT

For media inquiries, contact Thomas Nelson, Inc., at:
P.O. Box 141000
Nashville, TN 37214-1000
1-800-251-4000

Managing Editor: Sean Fowlds
Cover Design: Anderson Thomas Design
Interior Design: Anderson Thomas Design
Contributors: Sean Fowlds, Dennis Hensley, Kevin Johnson, Adam Palmer, Matthew Turner, Ken Walker

4 5 6 7 8 9 10 — 11 10 09 08 07

introduction

Life is a trip, and this is your road map. Before you head out on any road trip, you must first get directions to where you're going. And on the journey called life, the Bible not only points you in the right direction, it also identifies the potholes to avoid and suggests rest stops for refueling. By using this guide and following its directions, you'll be well on your way to arriving at your final destination safely and securely.

This Bible covers the territory between the New Testament books of Matthew and Revelation. The text reveals the story of how God has rescued us from the dominion of the devil through the death, burial, and resurrection of God's Son, Jesus Christ. It also will give you awesome insight into what Jesus did for us while he lived here on earth, including how he came to forgive your sins, heal your wounds, and bless your life.

Actually, the Bible is divided into two major sections—the Old Testament and the New Testament. There is a very simple dividing point that distinguishes the two: The Old Testament is compiled of all the stories that took place *before* the birth of Jesus Christ; and the New Testament tells about what life was like *after* his birth.

For more about some of the awesome stories in the Old Testament, check out *Refuel: Epic Battles of the Old Testament*. It covers the books of Joshua through Nehemiah and concentrates on the exploits of powerful rulers, mighty warriors, and other men of God. Reading it will give you the strength you need to fight the daily battles of life and win.

The *Refuel* BibleZine you hold in your hands is the passport for your journey with Jesus. It is specially written in a user-friendly format and includes lots of cool features that address the types of issues you face in life. Each book has an

Introduction written specifically to help answer the questions you are asking. There are also several other special features that supply the fuel you need.

Experts Answer Your Questions deals with a variety of topics important to your daily life. *Count On It* highlights the promises of God to you. *Radical Faith* challenges you to trust God with abandon. *Ways to Walk the Walk* gives you practical ideas for practicing your faith. *Men of the Sword* tells the stories of biblical guys who braved battles like you do. *Fight the Fight* features lessons you can learn from the lives of other men of God. *Class Act* shows you how to become a knight in shining armor. *Guard Your Heart* equips you with weapons for fighting temptation.

There is a ton of info here for you to learn from. Whether you find yourself cruising at the moment or are in need of a pit stop, remember to refuel your spirit daily. The more familiar you become with the owner's manual, the better prepared you are for the trip ahead of you. God bless you on your journey!

table of contents

A Note about the
New Century Version®...

God never intended the Bible to be too difficult for his people. To make sure God's message was clear, the authors of the Bible recorded God's word in familiar everyday language. These books brought a message that the original readers could understand. These first readers knew that God spoke through these books. Down through the centuries, many people wanted a Bible so badly that they copied different Bible books by hand!

Today, now that the Bible is readily available, many Christians do not regularly read it. Many feel that the Bible is too hard to understand or irrelevant to life.

The *New Century Version* captures the clear and simple message that the very first readers understood. This version presents the Bible as God intended it: clear and dynamic.

A team of scholars from the World Bible Translation Center worked together with twenty-one other experienced Bible scholars from all over the world to translate the text directly from the best available Greek and Hebrew texts. You can trust that this Bible accurately presents God's Word as it came to us in the original languages.

Translators kept sentences short and simple. They avoided difficult words and worked to make the text easier to read. They used modern terms for places and measurements. And they put figures of speech and idiomatic expressions ("he was gathered to his people") in language that even children understand ("he died").

Following the tradition of other English versions, the New Century Version indicates the divine name, *Yahweh*, by putting LORD, and sometimes GOD, in capital letters. This distinguishes it from *Adonai*, another Hebrew word that is translated *Lord*.

We acknowledge the infallibility of God's Word and yet our own frailty. We pray that God will use this Bible to help you understand his rich truth for yourself.

To God be the glory.

— From the Editors of *Refuel 2: The Complete New Testament*

THE
NEW
TEST
AM
ENT

MATTHEW

THE LIFE OF CHRIST

Harry Potter may cast enchanting spells, but he's no match for the miracle worker Jesus. In this book you will meet the man known as the Son of God and the Savior of humanity. As the world's greatest healer, ailments such as leprosy, blindness, deformity, and paralysis (even death) are no problem for Christ. Miracles such as feeding multitudes with a boy's lunch and walking on water are commonplace.

Think of the Book of Matthew as the thrilling introduction to the life of Christ. Jesus is revealed as the supreme teacher, giving messages crammed with tips on how to live. He loves people unconditionally and treats the poor with compassion. Instead of bowing down to the rich and famous,

Christ aims his harshest criticisms at powerful religious leaders. While these holy men knew the law, Jesus called them hypocrites for failing to follow it.

Like action plots? Matthew has them! There's the dramatic escape of Jesus as a baby from King Herod's assassination attempt. Later, as an adult, there is his resistance of the devil's temptations in the wilderness. In a bold move, Jesus calls a dozen close followers and tells them to go out and do the same things he has done. Christ winds up dying on a cross between a couple of common criminals. But in the end, he rises from the grave, making him the only Lord worth following.

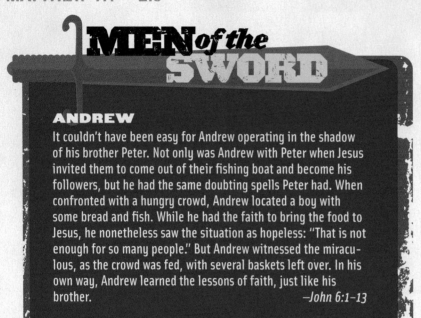

MEN of the SWORD

ANDREW

It couldn't have been easy for Andrew operating in the shadow of his brother Peter. Not only was Andrew with Peter when Jesus invited them to come out of their fishing boat and become his followers, but he had the same doubting spells Peter had. When confronted with a hungry crowd, Andrew located a boy with some bread and fish. While he had the faith to bring the food to Jesus, he nonetheless saw the situation as hopeless: "That is not enough for so many people." But Andrew witnessed the miraculous, as the crowd was fed, with several baskets left over. In his own way, Andrew learned the lessons of faith, just like his brother.
—John 6:1–13

THE FAMILY HISTORY OF JESUS

1 This is the family history of Jesus Christ. He came from the family of David, and David came from the family of Abraham.

2 Abraham was the father[n] of Isaac. Isaac was the father of Jacob. Jacob was the father of Judah and his brothers. 3 Judah was the father of Perez and Zerah.
(Their mother was Tamar.)
Perez was the father of Hezron. Hezron was the father of Ram. 4 Ram was the father of Amminadab. Amminadab was the father of Nahshon. Nahshon was the father of Salmon. 5 Salmon was the father of Boaz.
(Boaz's mother was Rahab.)
Boaz was the father of Obed.
(Obed's mother was Ruth.)
Obed was the father of Jesse. 6 Jesse was the father of King David. David was the father of Solomon.
(Solomon's mother had been Uriah's wife.)
7 Solomon was the father of Rehoboam. Rehoboam was the father of Abijah. Abijah was the father of Asa.[n] 8 Asa was the father of Jehoshaphat. Jehoshaphat was the father of Jehoram. Jehoram was the ancestor of Uzziah. 9 Uzziah was the father of Jotham. Jotham was the father of Ahaz. Ahaz was the father of Hezekiah. 10 Hezekiah was the father of Manasseh. Manasseh was the father of Amon. Amon was the father of Josiah. 11 Josiah was the grandfather of Jehoiachin[n] and his brothers.
(This was at the time that the people were taken to Babylon.)
12 After they were taken to Babylon: Jehoiachin was the father of Shealtiel. Shealtiel was the grandfather of Zerubbabel. 13 Zerubbabel was the father of Abiud. Abiud was the father of Eliakim. Eliakim was the father of Azor. 14 Azor was the father of Zadok. Zadok was the father of Akim. Akim was the father of Eliud. 15 Eliud was the father of Eleazar.

Eleazar was the father of Matthan. Matthan was the father of Jacob. 16 Jacob was the father of Joseph. Joseph was the husband of Mary, and Mary was the mother of Jesus. Jesus is called the Christ.

17 So there were fourteen generations from Abraham to David. And there were fourteen generations from David until the people were taken to Babylon. And there were fourteen generations from the time when the people were taken to Babylon until Christ was born.

THE BIRTH OF JESUS CHRIST

18 This is how the birth of Jesus Christ came about. His mother Mary was engaged[n] to marry Joseph, but before they married, she learned she was pregnant by the power of the Holy Spirit. 19 Because Mary's husband, Joseph, was a good man, he did not want to disgrace her in public, so he planned to divorce her secretly.

20 While Joseph thought about these things, an angel of the Lord came to him in a dream. The angel said, "Joseph, descendant of David, don't be afraid to take Mary as your wife, because the baby in her is from the Holy Spirit. 21 She will give birth to a son, and you will name him Jesus,[n] because he will save his people from their sins."

22 All this happened to bring about what the Lord had said through the prophet: 23 "The virgin will be pregnant. She will have a son, and they will name him Immanuel,"[n] which means "God is with us."

24 When Joseph woke up, he did what the Lord's angel had told him to do. Joseph took Mary as his wife, 25 but he did not have sexual relations with her until she gave birth to the son. And Joseph named him Jesus.

WISE MEN COME TO VISIT JESUS

2 Jesus was born in the town of Bethlehem in Judea during the time when Herod was king. When Jesus was born, some wise men from the east came to Jerusalem. 2 They asked, "Where is the baby who was born to be the king of the Jews? We saw his star in the east and have come to worship him."

3 When King Herod heard this, he was troubled, as were all the people in Jerusalem. 4 Herod called a meeting of all the leading priests and teachers of the law and asked them where the Christ would be born. 5 They answered, "In the town of Bethlehem in Judea. The prophet wrote about this in the Scriptures:

6 'But you, Bethlehem, in the land of Judah, are not just an insignificant village in Judah.

WAYS to WALK the WALK

MATTHEW 1:1–17

WORD: Your history is important.
WALK IT: Trace your ancestry to see what notable things have occurred in your family's past. You'll discover important traits, and you may gain additional clues as to why you are the way you are.

★ 1:2 father "Father" in Jewish lists of ancestors can sometimes mean grandfather or more distant relative. 1:7 Asa Some Greek copies read "Asaph," another name for Asa (see 1 Chronicles 3:10). 1:11 Jehoiachin The Greek reads "Jeconiah," another name for Jehoiachin (see 2 Kings 24:6 and 1 Chronicles 3:16). 1:18 engaged For the Jewish people an engagement was a lasting agreement, which could only be broken by a divorce. If a bride-to-be was unfaithful, it was considered adultery, and she could be put to death. 1:21 Jesus The name "Jesus" means "salvation." 1:23 "The virgin . . . Immanuel" Quotation from Isaiah 7:14.

A ruler will come from you
who will be like a shepherd for my
people Israel.' "   *Micah 5:2*

[7]Then Herod had a secret meeting with the wise men and learned from them the exact time they first saw the star. [8]He sent the wise men to Bethlehem, saying, "Look carefully for the child. When you find him, come tell me so I can worship him too."

[9]After the wise men heard the king, they left. The star that they had seen in the east went before them until it stopped above the place where the child was. [10]When the wise men saw the star, they were filled with joy. [11]They came to the house where the child was and saw him with his mother, Mary, and they bowed down and worshiped him. They opened their gifts and gave him treasures of gold, frankincense, and myrrh. [12]But God warned the wise men in a dream not to go back to Herod, so they returned to their own country by a different way.

JESUS' PARENTS TAKE HIM TO EGYPT

[13]After they left, an angel of the Lord came to Joseph in a dream and said, "Get up! Take the child and his mother and escape to Egypt, because Herod is starting to look for the child so he can kill him. Stay in Egypt until I tell you to return."

[14]So Joseph got up and left for Egypt during the night with the child and his mother. [15]And Joseph stayed in Egypt until Herod died. This happened to bring about what the Lord had said through the prophet: "I called my son out of Egypt."[n]

Pornography is everywhere. As a young man you will more than likely be tempted sometime in your life to look at images that will only distort your God-intended understanding of women and sex. However, the Bible assures us that when we decide to resist such temptations, God always gives us a way of escape.

HEROD KILLS THE BABY BOYS

[16]When Herod saw that the wise men had tricked him, he was furious. So he gave an order to kill all the baby boys in Bethlehem and in the surrounding area who were two years old or younger. This was in keeping with the time he learned from the wise men. [17]So what God had said through the prophet Jeremiah came true:

[18]"A voice was heard in Ramah
of painful crying and deep sadness:
Rachel crying for her children.
She refused to be comforted,
because her children are dead."
Jeremiah 31:15

JOSEPH AND MARY RETURN

[19]After Herod died, an angel of the Lord spoke to Joseph in a dream while he was in Egypt. [20]The angel said, "Get up! Take the child and his mother and go to the land of Israel, because the people who were trying to kill the child are now dead."

[21]So Joseph took the child and his mother and went to Israel. [22]But he heard that Archelaus was now king in Judea since his father Herod had died. So Joseph was afraid to go there. After being warned in a dream, he went to the area of Galilee, [23]to a town called Nazareth, and lived there. And so what God had said through the prophets came true: "He will be called a Nazarene."[n]

THE WORK OF JOHN THE BAPTIST

3 About that time John the Baptist began preaching in the desert area of Judea. [2]John said, "Change your hearts and lives because the kingdom of heaven is near." [3]John the Baptist is the one Isaiah the prophet was talking about when he said:

"This is a voice of one
who calls out in the desert:
'Prepare the way for the Lord.
Make the road straight for him.' "
Isaiah 40:3

2:15 "I called . . . Egypt." Quotation from Hosea 11:1.   2:23 Nazarene A person from the town of Nazareth. Matthew may be referring to Isaiah 11:1, where the Hebrew word translated "branch" sounds like "Nazarene."

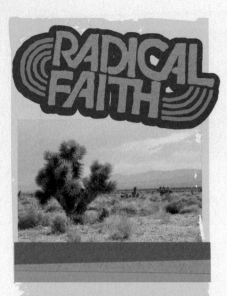

MATTHEW 4:1–11

Even though Jesus was tempted in every way that human beings are, he never caved in to sin (Hebrews 4:15). As a genuine man he felt the lure of evil, so he knows exactly what you suffer when you're tugged to disobey God. He sympathizes with your plight, so he's ready to help you battle whatever onslaught you face (Hebrews 4:16). This episode in Matthew displays Jesus' supreme tactics for fighting off temptation. Just before Jesus began his ministry of preaching, he spent forty days fasting in the desert. Satan himself showed up to tempt Jesus. He prodded the Lord to make bread to fill his stomach, told Jesus to win fans by diving off the roof of the Temple, and offered Jesus all the kingdoms of the world in exchange for bowing before him. In each case, Jesus beat back temptation by quoting Scripture. He fought lies with the truth of God's Word. That's the same strategy you can use to avoid giving in to wrong. When you think that an evil act looks appealing, remind yourself that God's commands are totally right—and his promises are absolutely reliable. Choose to live by God's truth instead of Satan's lies.

[4]John's clothes were made from camel's hair, and he wore a leather belt around his waist. For food, he ate locusts and wild honey. [5]Many people came from Jerusalem and Judea and all the area around the Jordan River to hear John. [6]They confessed their sins, and he baptized them in the Jordan River.

[7]Many of the Pharisees and Sadducees came to the place where John was baptizing people. When John saw them, he said, "You are snakes! Who warned you to run away from God's coming punishment? [8]Do the things that show you really have changed your hearts and lives. [9]And don't think you can say to yourselves, 'Abraham is our father.' I tell you that God could make children for Abraham from these rocks. [10]The ax is now ready to cut down the trees, and every tree that does not produce good fruit will be cut down and thrown into the fire.[n]

[11]"I baptize you with water to show that your hearts and lives have changed. But there is one coming after me who is greater than I am, whose sandals I am not good enough to carry. He will baptize you with the Holy Spirit and fire. [12]He will come ready to clean the grain, separating the good grain from the chaff. He will put the good part of the grain into his barn, but he will burn the chaff with a fire that cannot be put out."[n]

JESUS IS BAPTIZED BY JOHN

[13]At that time Jesus came from Galilee to the Jordan River and wanted John to baptize him. [14]But John tried to stop him, saying, "Why do you come to me to be baptized? I need to be baptized by you!"

[15]Jesus answered, "Let it be this way for now. We should do all things that are God's will." So John agreed to baptize Jesus.

[16]As soon as Jesus was baptized, he came up out of the water. Then heaven opened, and he saw God's Spirit coming down on him like a dove. [17]And a voice from heaven said, "This is my Son, whom I love, and I am very pleased with him."

THE TEMPTATION OF JESUS

4 Then the Spirit led Jesus into the desert to be tempted by the devil. [2]Jesus fasted for forty days and nights. After this, he was very hungry. [3]The devil came to Jesus to tempt him, saying, "If you are the Son of God, tell these rocks to become bread."

[4]Jesus answered, "It is written in the Scriptures, 'A person lives not on bread alone, but by everything God says.' "[n]

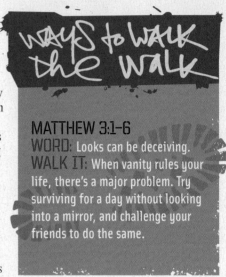

MATTHEW 3:1-6
WORD: Looks can be deceiving.
WALK IT: When vanity rules your life, there's a major problem. Try surviving for a day without looking into a mirror, and challenge your friends to do the same.

[5]Then the devil led Jesus to the holy city of Jerusalem and put him on a high place of the Temple. [6]The devil said, "If you are the Son of God, jump down, because it is written in the Scriptures:

DO pick your date up at the door.

DO greet your date's parents with respect.

DO act like a gentleman toward your date.

DO treat your date as though she's special.

DON'T honk the car horn for your date.

DON'T criticize your date's appearance.

DON'T forget to open doors for your date.

DON'T poke fun at your date's expense.

 3:10 The ax . . . fire. This means that God is ready to punish his people who do not obey him.   3:12 He will . . . out. This means that Jesus will come to separate good people from bad people, saving the good and punishing the bad.   4:4 'A person . . . says.' Quotation from Deuteronomy 8:3.

'He has put his angels in charge of you.
They will catch you in their hands
so that you will not hit your foot on a
rock.'" *Psalm 91:11–12*

[7]Jesus answered him, "It also says in the Scriptures, 'Do not test the Lord your God.' "[n]

[8]Then the devil led Jesus to the top of a very high mountain and showed him all the kingdoms of the world and all their splendor. [9]The devil said, "If you will bow down and worship me, I will give you all these things."

[10]Jesus said to the devil, "Go away from me, Satan! It is written in the Scriptures, 'You must worship the Lord your God and serve only him.' "[n]

[11]So the devil left Jesus, and angels came and took care of him.

JESUS BEGINS WORK IN GALILEE

[12]When Jesus heard that John had been put in prison, he went back to Galilee. [13]He left Nazareth and went to live in Capernaum, a town near Lake Galilee, in the area near Zebulun and Naphtali. [14]Jesus did this to bring about what the prophet Isaiah had said:

[15]"Land of Zebulun and land of Naphtali
along the sea,
beyond the Jordan River.
This is Galilee where the non-Jewish
people live.
[16]These people who live in darkness
will see a great light.
They live in a place covered with the
shadows of death,
but a light will shine on them."
Isaiah 9:1–2

Relationships

"So when you offer your gift to God at the altar, and you remember that your brother or sister has something against you, leave your gift there at the altar. Go and make peace with that person, and then come and offer your gift" (Matthew 5:23–24). Believe it or not, having right relationships with others is an important aspect of worship to God. The interesting thing about this verse is that if someone else is mad at *you*, it's *your* job to make it right. Doesn't seem fair, does it? Nevertheless, it's for your own good, so work to mend relationships, even if the break isn't your fault.

JESUS CHOOSES SOME FOLLOWERS

[17]From that time Jesus began to preach, saying, "Change your hearts and lives, because the kingdom of heaven is near."

[18]As Jesus was walking by Lake Galilee, he saw two brothers, Simon (called Peter) and his brother Andrew. They were throwing a net into the lake because they were fishermen. [19]Jesus said, "Come follow me, and I will make you fish for people." [20]So Simon and Andrew immediately left their nets and followed him.

[21]As Jesus continued walking by Lake Galilee, he saw two other brothers, James and John, the sons of Zebedee. They were in a boat with their father Zebedee, mending their nets.

Jesus told them to come with him. [22]Immediately they left the boat and their father, and they followed Jesus.

JESUS TEACHES AND HEALS PEOPLE

[23]Jesus went everywhere in Galilee, teaching in the synagogues, preaching the Good

fight the fight

Matthew 4:1-11

Jesus has often been pictured as a gentle soul, wearing flowing robes and gathering little children around him. But such images don't reveal the whole truth. To see strength in action, read this passage in Matthew. Christ successfully faced down the devil, who tried clever temptations to make the Son of God turn his back on God. Jesus overcame each one of them by quoting Scripture, setting an example for each believer who follows him. The devil also will try to convince you with deceitful arguments to do something wrong. But follow Jesus' example and use the Word of God to overcome temptations.

 4:7 'Do . . . God.' Quotation from Deuteronomy 6:16. 4:10 'You . . . him.' Quotation from Deuteronomy 6:13.

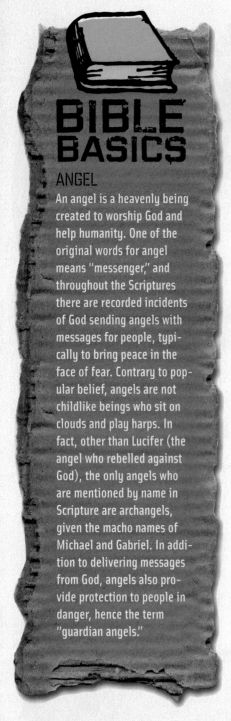

BIBLE BASICS

ANGEL

An angel is a heavenly being created to worship God and help humanity. One of the original words for angel means "messenger," and throughout the Scriptures there are recorded incidents of God sending angels with messages for people, typically to bring peace in the face of fear. Contrary to popular belief, angels are not childlike beings who sit on clouds and play harps. In fact, other than Lucifer (the angel who rebelled against God), the only angels who are mentioned by name in Scripture are archangels, given the macho names of Michael and Gabriel. In addition to delivering messages from God, angels also provide protection to people in danger, hence the term "guardian angels."

News about the kingdom of heaven, and healing all the people's diseases and sicknesses. [24]The news about Jesus spread all over Syria, and people brought all the sick to him. They were suffering from different kinds of diseases. Some were in great pain, some had demons, some were epileptics,[n] and some were paralyzed. Jesus healed all of them. [25]Many people from Galilee, the Ten Towns,[n] Jerusalem, Judea, and the land across the Jordan River followed him.

JESUS TEACHES THE PEOPLE

5 When Jesus saw the crowds, he went up on a hill and sat down. His followers came to him, [2]and he began to teach them, saying:

[3]"They are blessed who realize their
spiritual poverty,
for the kingdom of heaven belongs to
them.
[4]They are blessed who grieve,
for God will comfort them.
[5]They are blessed who are humble,
for the whole earth will be theirs.
[6]They are blessed who hunger and thirst
after justice,
for they will be satisfied.
[7]They are blessed who show mercy to
others,
for God will show mercy to them.
[8]They are blessed whose thoughts are pure,
for they will see God.
[9]They are blessed who work for peace,
for they will be called God's children.
[10]They are blessed who are persecuted for
doing good,
for the kingdom of heaven belongs to
them.

[11]"People will insult you and hurt you. They will lie and say all kinds of evil things about you because you follow me. But when they do, you will be blessed. [12]Rejoice and be glad, because you have a great reward waiting for you in heaven. People did the same evil things to the prophets who lived before you.

YOU ARE LIKE SALT AND LIGHT

[13]"You are the salt of the earth. But if the salt loses its salty taste, it cannot be made salty again. It is good for nothing, except to be thrown out and walked on.

[14]"You are the light that gives light to the world. A city that is built on a hill cannot be hidden. [15]And people don't hide a light under a bowl. They put it on a lampstand so the light shines for all the people in the house. [16]In the same way, you should be a light for other people. Live so that they will see the good things you do and will praise your Father in heaven.

THE IMPORTANCE OF THE LAW

[17]"Don't think that I have come to destroy the law of Moses or the teaching of the prophets. I have not come to destroy them but to bring about what they said. [18]I tell you the truth, nothing will disappear from the law until heaven and earth are gone. Not even the smallest letter or the smallest part of a letter will be lost until everything has happened.

[19]Whoever refuses to obey any command and teaches other people not to obey that command will be the least important in the kingdom of heaven. But whoever obeys the commands and teaches other people to obey them will be great in the kingdom of heaven. [20]I tell you that if you are no more obedient than the teachers of the law and the Pharisees, you will never enter the kingdom of heaven.

JESUS TEACHES ABOUT ANGER

[21]"You have heard that it was said to our people long ago, 'You must not murder anyone.'[n] Anyone who murders another will be judged.' [22]But I tell you, if you are angry with a brother or sister,[n] you will be judged. If you say bad things to a brother or sister, you will be judged by the council. And if you call someone a fool, you will be in danger of the fire of hell.

[23]"So when you offer your gift to God at the altar, and you remember that your brother or sister has something against you, [24]leave your gift there at the altar. Go and make peace with that person, and then come and offer your gift.

[25]"If your enemy is taking you to court, become friends quickly, before you go to court. Otherwise, your enemy might turn you over to the judge, and the judge might give you to a guard to put you in jail. [26]I tell you the truth, you will not leave there until you have paid everything you owe.

JESUS TEACHES ABOUT SEXUAL SIN

[27]"You have heard that it was said, 'You must not be guilty of adultery.'[n] [28]But I tell you that if anyone looks at a woman and wants to sin sexually with her, in his mind he has already done that sin with the woman. [29]If your right eye causes you to sin, take it out and

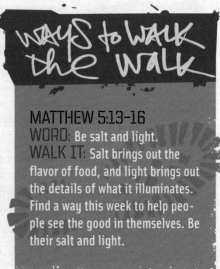

WAYS to WALK the WALK

MATTHEW 5:13–16

WORD: Be salt and light.
WALK IT: Salt brings out the flavor of food, and light brings out the details of what it illuminates. Find a way this week to help people see the good in themselves. Be their salt and light.

 4:24 epileptics People with a disease that causes them sometimes to lose control of their bodies and maybe faint, shake strongly, or not be able to move. **4:25 Ten Towns** In Greek, called "Decapolis." It was an area east of Lake Galilee that once had ten main towns. **5:21 'You . . . anyone.'** Quotation from Exodus 20:13; Deuteronomy 5:17. **5:22 sister** Some Greek copies continue, "without a reason." **5:27 'You . . . adultery.'** Quotation from Exodus 20:14; Deuteronomy 5:18.

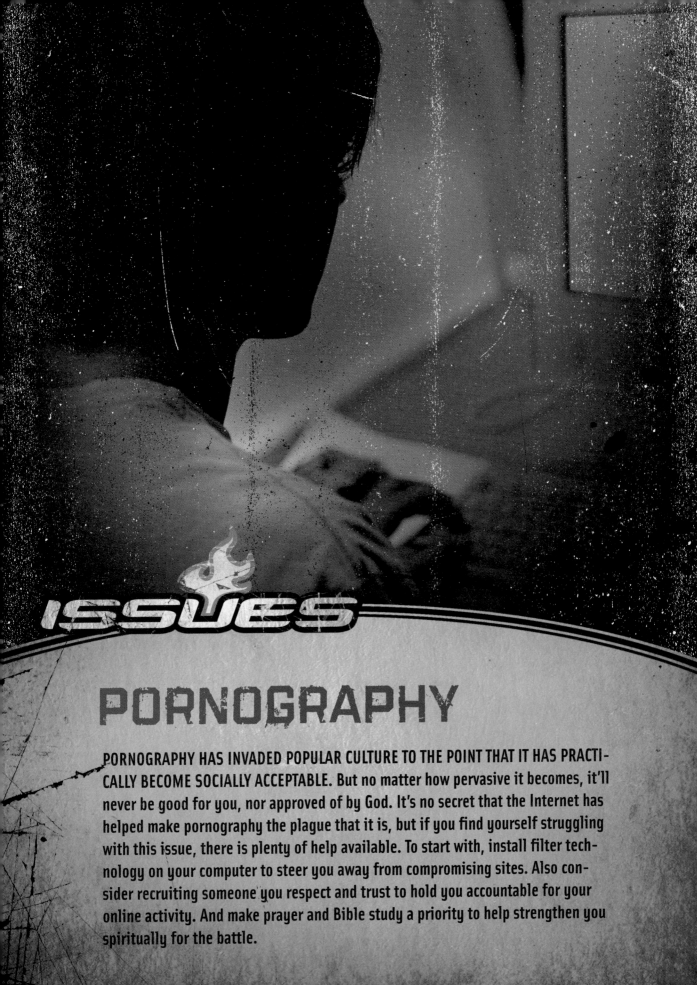

ISSUES

PORNOGRAPHY

PORNOGRAPHY HAS INVADED POPULAR CULTURE TO THE POINT THAT IT HAS PRACTI-CALLY BECOME SOCIALLY ACCEPTABLE. But no matter how pervasive it becomes, it'll never be good for you, nor approved of by God. It's no secret that the Internet has helped make pornography the plague that it is, but if you find yourself struggling with this issue, there is plenty of help available. To start with, install filter technology on your computer to steer you away from compromising sites. Also consider recruiting someone you respect and trust to hold you accountable for your online activity. And make prayer and Bible study a priority to help strengthen you spiritually for the battle.

MATTHEW 5:13

People back in Bible times used salt to flavor food. They also scattered small amounts on their fields as fertilizer. But salt's big use was as a preservative. In an age without refrigerators or ice makers, rubbing salt into meat prevented it from rotting. So, when Jesus called his followers "the salt of the earth," he was saying that they were a preservative to the people around them. They prevented decay by the example of their lives, showing what real goodness looked like. By conforming to God's standards, they helped keep society from falling apart. But there's a problem. Old-school salt was gathered from marshes, and it often contained impurities. Impure salt lost its power as a preservative, so it was tossed out on the ground. The point? When you compromise your moral purity, you lose one of your key functions in the world. You stop benefiting the people around you, who are watching you to discover the way to real life. So strive to guard your integrity in order that your influence on others will be a positive experience and never a negative one.

throw it away. It is better to lose one part of your body than to have your whole body thrown into hell. [30]If your right hand causes you to sin, cut it off and throw it away. It is better to lose one part of your body than for your whole body to go into hell.

JESUS TEACHES ABOUT DIVORCE

[31]"It was also said, 'Anyone who divorces his wife must give her a written divorce paper.'[n] [32]But I tell you that anyone who divorces his wife forces her to be guilty of adultery. The only reason for a man to divorce his wife is if she has sexual relations with another man. And anyone who marries that divorced woman is guilty of adultery.

MAKE PROMISES CAREFULLY

[33]"You have heard that it was said to our people long ago, 'Don't break your promises, but keep the promises you make to the Lord.'[n] [34]But I tell you, never swear an oath. Don't swear an oath using the name of heaven, because heaven is God's throne. [35]Don't swear an oath using the name of the earth, because the earth belongs to God. Don't swear an oath using the name of Jerusalem, because that is the city of the great King. [36]Don't even swear by your own head, because you cannot make one hair on your head become white or black. [37]Say only yes if you mean yes, and no if you mean no. If you say more than yes or no, it is from the Evil One.

DON'T FIGHT BACK

[38]"You have heard that it was said, 'An eye for an eye, and a tooth for a tooth.'[n] [39]But I tell you, don't stand up against an evil person. If someone slaps you on the right cheek, turn to him the other cheek also. [40]If someone wants to sue you in court and take your shirt, let him have your coat also. [41]If someone forces you to go with him one mile, go with him two miles. [42]If a person asks you for something, give it to him. Don't refuse to give to someone who wants to borrow from you.

LOVE ALL PEOPLE

[43]"You have heard that it was said, 'Love your neighbor[n] and hate your enemies.' [44]But I say to you, love your enemies. Pray for those

who hurt you.[n] [45]If you do this, you will be true children of your Father in heaven. He causes the sun to rise on good people and on evil people, and he sends rain to those who do right and to those who do wrong. [46]If you love only the people who love you, you will get no reward. Even the tax collectors do that. [47]And if you are nice only to your friends, you are no better than other people. Even those who don't know God are nice to their friends. [48]So you must be perfect, just as your Father in heaven is perfect.

JESUS TEACHES ABOUT GIVING

6 "Be careful! When you do good things, don't do them in front of people to be seen by them. If you do that, you will have no reward from your Father in heaven.

[2]"When you give to the poor, don't be like the hypocrites. They blow trumpets in the synagogues and on the streets so that people will see them and honor them. I tell you the truth, those hypocrites already have their full reward. [3]So when you give to the poor, don't let anyone know what you are doing. [4]Your giving should be done in secret. Your Father can see what is done in secret, and he will reward you.

JESUS TEACHES ABOUT PRAYER

[5]"When you pray, don't be like the hypocrites. They love to stand in the synagogues and on the street corners and pray so people will see them. I tell you the truth, they already have their full reward. [6]When you pray, you should go into your room and close the door and pray to your Father who cannot be seen. Your Father can see what is done in secret, and he will reward you.

[7]"And when you pray, don't be like those people who don't know God. They continue saying things that mean nothing, thinking that God will hear them because of their many words. [8]Don't be like them, because your Father knows the things you need before you ask him. [9]So when you pray, you should pray like this:

'Our Father in heaven,
    may your name always be kept holy.

 5:31 'Anyone . . . divorce paper.' Quotation from Deuteronomy 24:1.   5:33 'Don't . . . Lord.' This refers to Leviticus 19:12; Numbers 30:2; Deuteronomy 23:21.   5:38 'An eye . . . tooth.' Quotation from Exodus 21:24; Leviticus 24:20; Deuteronomy 19:21.
5:43 'Love your neighbor.' Quotation from Leviticus 19:18.   5:44 you Some Greek copies continue, "Bless those who curse you, do good to those who hate you." Compare Luke 6:28.

8

january

NATIONAL BLOOD DONOR MONTH

"Success is the ability to go from one failure to another with no loss of enthusiasm."
-WINSTON CHURCHILL

1 Write down your goals for the year.	2 Catch up on laundry today.	3 Today is Nichole Nordeman's birthday.	4
5 Write thank-you cards to the people who gave you Christmas gifts.	6	7 Sign up to donate blood.	8
9 Dave Matthews's birthday is today. Pray for his band.	10	11	12 Today is Jars of Clay's Dan Haseltine's birthday.
13	14 Offer to clean out the garage.	15 Martin Luther King Jr. was born on this day in 1929.	16 Spend some quality time with your grandparents.
17	18 Volunteer to help your youth pastor this week.	19	20 Start thinking about a summer mission project.
21	22	23 Pray for your future wife.	24
25	26 Kirk Franklin's birthday is today.	27	28
29	30 Plan a Super Bowl party!	31 Talk to your family about sponsoring a needy child.	

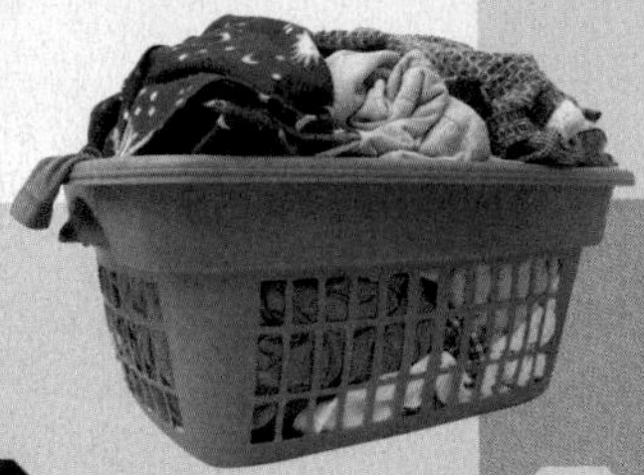

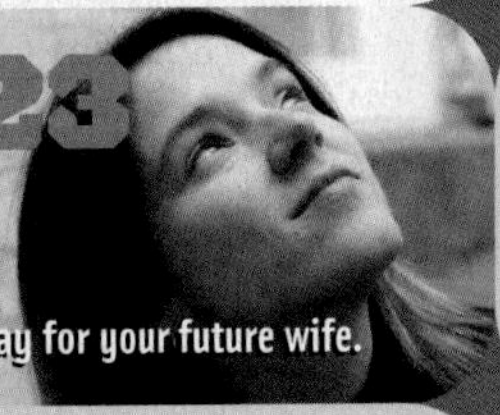

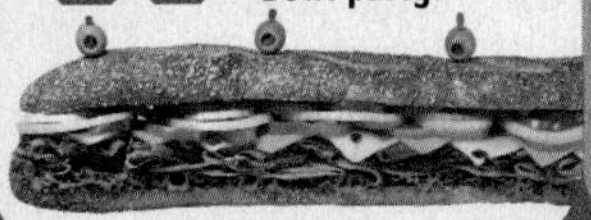

COUNT ON IT

MATTHEW 6:25

Don't think of God as your personal banker opening his wallet to supply your every whim. He has sworn, however, to meet your every need. Whatever you require in life, you can rely on God to provide it in the right time and the right way. That includes the most basic necessities of life, like what you eat and what you wear. When you know that God sees exactly what you need, you can focus your mind on life's important things, like doing what God wants. That's crucial, because when you put God first, then "all your other needs will be met as well" (Matthew 6:33). Keep working hard as you know he wants you to do, because God usually delivers what you need through normal channels like parents and jobs. Yet, you don't have to worry, because he watches over your life.

[10]May your kingdom come
and what you want be done,
here on earth as it is in heaven.
[11]Give us the food we need for each day.
[12]Forgive us for our sins,

just as we have forgiven those who sinned against us.
[13]And do not cause us to be tempted, but save us from the Evil One.' [The kingdom, the power, and the glory are yours forever. Amen.][n]

[14]Yes, if you forgive others for their sins, your Father in heaven will also forgive you for your sins. [15]But if you don't forgive others, your Father in heaven will not forgive your sins.

JESUS TEACHES ABOUT WORSHIP

[16]"When you fast,[n] don't put on a sad face like the hypocrites. They make their faces look sad to show people they are fasting. I tell you the truth, those hypocrites already have their full reward. [17]So when you fast, comb your hair and wash your face. [18]Then people will not know that you are fasting, but your Father, whom you cannot see, will see you. Your Father sees what is done in secret, and he will reward you.

GOD IS MORE IMPORTANT THAN MONEY

[19]"Don't store treasures for yourselves here on earth where moths and rust will destroy them and thieves can break in and steal them. [20]But store your treasures in heaven where they cannot be destroyed by moths or rust and where thieves cannot break in and steal them. [21]Your heart will be where your treasure is.

[22]"The eye is a light for the body. If your eyes are good, your whole body will be full of light. [23]But if your eyes are evil, your whole body will be full of darkness. And if the only light you have is really darkness, then you have the worst darkness.

[24]"No one can serve two masters. The person will hate one master and love the other, or will follow one master and refuse to follow the other. You cannot serve both God and worldly riches.

DON'T WORRY

[25]"So I tell you, don't worry about the food or drink you need to live, or about the clothes you need for your body. Life is more than food, and the body is more than clothes. [26]Look at the birds in the air. They don't plant or harvest or store food in barns, but your heavenly Father feeds them. And you know that you are worth much more than the birds. [27]You cannot add any time to your life by worrying about it.

[28]"And why do you worry about clothes? Look at how the lilies in the field grow. They don't work or make clothes for themselves.

[29]But I tell you that even Solomon with his riches was not dressed as beautifully as one of these flowers. [30]God clothes the grass in the field, which is alive today but tomorrow is thrown into the fire. So you can be even more sure that God will clothe you. Don't have so little faith! [31]Don't worry and say, 'What will we eat?' or 'What will we drink?' or 'What will we wear?' [32]The people who don't know God keep trying to get these things, and your Father in heaven knows you need them. [33]Seek first God's kingdom and what God wants. Then all your other needs will be met as well. [34]So don't worry about tomorrow, because tomorrow will have its own worries. Each day has enough trouble of its own.

BE CAREFUL ABOUT JUDGING OTHERS

7 "Don't judge others, or you will be judged. [2]You will be judged in the same way that you judge others, and the amount you give to others will be given to you.

[3]"Why do you notice the little piece of dust in your friend's eye, but you don't notice the big piece of wood in your own eye? [4]How can you say to your friend, 'Let me take that little piece of dust out of your eye'? Look at yourself! You still have that big piece of wood in your own eye. [5]You hypocrite! First, take the wood out of your own eye. Then you will see clearly to take the dust out of your friend's eye.

[6]"Don't give holy things to dogs, and don't throw your pearls before pigs. Pigs will only trample on them, and dogs will turn to attack you.

WAYS to WALK the WALK

MATTHEW 6:16–18

WORD: Don't be a hypocrite.
WALK IT: Doing something good for God? Don't make a big show of it; that's what hypocrites do. Instead, relax and know that God sees what you're doing, and he will reward you in his time.

6:13 The . . . Amen. Some Greek copies do not contain the bracketed text.   6:16 fast The people would give up eating for a special time of prayer and worship to God. It was also done to show sadness and disappointment.

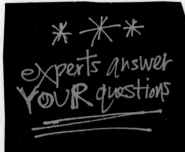

experts answer YOUR questions

Q: How can I forgive people who hurt me?

A: Forgiving others can be difficult. But Jesus made it clear: we owe forgiveness to those who wrong us—not because of anything they've done, but because of what God has done for us. When we consider how much God has forgiven us for, it becomes easier to let go of the pain that others have caused us.

Q: Does God want me to give all my money away?

A: God doesn't ask people to give all their money away. However, he does ask all of us to give sacrificially to those who are in need—not just our money but our time and talents, as well.

ASK GOD FOR WHAT YOU NEED

⁷"Ask, and God will give to you. Search, and you will find. Knock, and the door will open for you. ⁸Yes, everyone who asks will receive. Everyone who searches will find. And everyone who knocks will have the door opened.

⁹"If your children ask for bread, which of you would give them a stone? ¹⁰Or if your children ask for a fish, would you give them a snake? ¹¹Even though you are bad, you know how to give good gifts to your children. How much more your heavenly Father will give good things to those who ask him!

THE MOST IMPORTANT RULE

¹²"Do to others what you want them to do to you. This is the meaning of the law of Moses and the teaching of the prophets.

THE WAY TO HEAVEN IS HARD

¹³"Enter through the narrow gate. The gate is wide and the road is wide that leads to hell, and many people enter through that gate. ¹⁴But the gate is small and the road is narrow that leads to true life. Only a few people find that road.

PEOPLE KNOW YOU BY YOUR ACTIONS

¹⁵"Be careful of false prophets. They come to you looking gentle like sheep, but they are really dangerous like wolves. ¹⁶You will know these people by what they do. Grapes don't come from thornbushes, and figs don't come from thorny weeds. ¹⁷In the same way, every good tree produces good fruit, but a bad tree produces bad fruit. ¹⁸A good tree cannot produce bad fruit, and a bad tree cannot produce good fruit. ¹⁹Every tree that does not produce good fruit is cut down and thrown into the fire. ²⁰In the same way, you will know these false prophets by what they do.

²¹"Not all those who say 'You are our Lord' will enter the kingdom of heaven. The only people who will enter the kingdom of heaven are those who do what my Father in heaven wants. ²²On the last day many people will say to me, 'Lord, Lord, we spoke for you, and through you we forced out demons and did many miracles.' ²³Then I will tell them clearly, 'Get away from me, you who do evil. I never knew you.'

TWO KINDS OF PEOPLE

²⁴"Everyone who hears my words and obeys them is like a wise man who built his house on rock. ²⁵It rained hard, the floods came, and the winds blew and hit that house. But it did not fall, because it was built on rock. ²⁶Everyone who hears my words and does not obey them is like a foolish man who built his house on sand. ²⁷It rained hard, the floods came, and the winds blew and hit that house, and it fell with a big crash."

²⁸When Jesus finished saying these things, the people were amazed at his teaching, ²⁹because he did not teach like their teachers of the law. He taught like a person who had authority.

JESUS HEALS A SICK MAN

8 When Jesus came down from the hill, great crowds followed him. ²Then a

RADICAL FAITH

MATTHEW 7:15

Jesus might sound more than a tad intolerant. But he's giving you a crucial "heads up." He's pointing out that the world is full of people who will lie to you and attempt to fool you about spiritual things. These "false prophets" look appealing, as meek as sheep. To spread their untrue messages they pass themselves off as great people, but they are really ravenous wolves. Jesus says you can unmask these fakes by looking at the fruit they produce. You can measure their teachings against the Bible to see where they fall short. And you can look at what they do, the results of their words. Unbiblical teachings might look good in the short run or even benefit a few people. God's truth aims at the long-term good of all, including you, your neighbor, and strangers on the other end of the planet. His real message produces fruit that is undeniably good. This warning against false prophets doesn't just apply to professors who dismiss God or cultists who get in your face. Friends and others around you can persuade you to buy into harmful lies to develop attitudes that may lead you far from God. Be on guard against their false words, too.

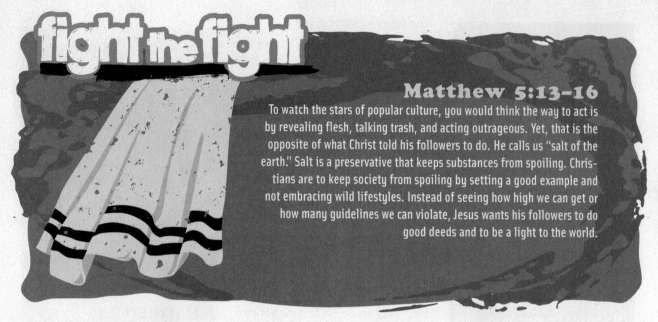

fight the fight

Matthew 5:13–16

To watch the stars of popular culture, you would think the way to act is by revealing flesh, talking trash, and acting outrageous. Yet, that is the opposite of what Christ told his followers to do. He calls us "salt of the earth." Salt is a preservative that keeps substances from spoiling. Christians are to keep society from spoiling by setting a good example and not embracing wild lifestyles. Instead of seeing how high we can get or how many guidelines we can violate, Jesus wants his followers to do good deeds and to be a light to the world.

man with a skin disease came to Jesus. The man bowed down before him and said, "Lord, you can heal me if you will."

[3]Jesus reached out his hand and touched the man and said, "I will. Be healed!" And immediately the man was healed from his disease. [4]Then Jesus said to him, "Don't tell anyone about this. But go and show your-self to the priest[n] and offer the gift Moses commanded[n] for people who are made well. This will show the people what I have done."

JESUS HEALS A SOLDIER'S SERVANT

[5]When Jesus entered the city of Capernaum, an army officer came to him, begging for help. [6]The officer said, "Lord, my servant is at home in bed. He can't move his body and is in much pain."

[7]Jesus said to the officer, "I will go and heal him."

[8]The officer answered, "Lord, I am not worthy for you to come into my house. You only need to command it, and my servant will be healed. [9]I, too, am a man under the authority of others, and I have soldiers under my command. I tell one soldier, 'Go,' and he goes. I tell another soldier, 'Come,' and he comes. I say to my servant, 'Do this,' and my servant does it."

[10]When Jesus heard this, he was amazed. He said to those who were following him, "I tell you the truth, this is the greatest faith I have found, even in Israel. [11]Many people will come from the east and from the west and will sit and eat with Abraham, Isaac, and Jacob in the kingdom of heaven. [12]But those people who should be in the kingdom will be thrown outside into the darkness, where people will cry and grind their teeth with pain."

[13]Then Jesus said to the officer, "Go home. Your servant will be healed just as you believed he would." And his servant was healed that same hour.

JESUS HEALS MANY PEOPLE

[14]When Jesus went to Peter's house, he saw that Peter's mother-in-law was sick in bed with a fever. [15]Jesus touched her hand, and the fever left her. Then she stood up and began to serve Jesus.

[16]That evening people brought to Jesus many who had demons. Jesus spoke and the demons left them, and he healed all the sick. [17]He did these things to bring about what Isaiah the prophet had said:

"He took our suffering on him
  and carried our diseases."   *Isaiah 53:4*

PEOPLE WANT TO FOLLOW JESUS

[18]When Jesus saw the crowd around him, he told his followers to go to the other side of the lake. [19]Then a teacher of the law came to Jesus and said, "Teacher, I will follow you any place you go."

[20]Jesus said to him, "The foxes have holes to live in, and the birds have nests, but the Son of Man has no place to rest his head."

[21]Another man, one of Jesus' followers, said to him, "Lord, first let me go and bury my father."

[22]But Jesus told him, "Follow me, and let the people who are dead bury their own dead."

JESUS CALMS A STORM

[23]Jesus got into a boat, and his followers went with him. [24]A great storm arose on the lake so that waves covered the boat, but Jesus was sleeping. [25]His followers went to him and woke him, saying, "Lord, save us! We will drown!"

[26]Jesus answered, "Why are you afraid? You don't have enough faith." Then Jesus got up and gave a command to the wind and the waves, and it became completely calm.

[27]The men were amazed and said, "What kind of man is this? Even the wind and the waves obey him!"

JESUS HEALS TWO MEN WITH DEMONS

[28]When Jesus arrived at the other side of the lake in the area of the Gadarene[n] people, two men who had demons in them met him. These men lived in the burial caves and were so dangerous that people could not use the road by those caves. [29]They shouted, "What do you want with us, Son of God? Did you come here to torture us before the right time?"

WAYS to WALK the WALK

MATTHEW 8:18–22

WORD: Follow Jesus with abandon.
WALK IT: Some people have conditions for following Jesus, but he wants us to follow him unconditionally. Do you have anything holding you back? Pray and ask him to help you let it go.

 8:4 show . . . priest The Law of Moses said a priest must say when a Jewish person with a skin disease was well.   **8:4 Moses commanded** Read about this in Leviticus 14:1–32.   **8:28 Gadarene** From Gadara, an area southeast of Lake Galilee. The exact location is uncertain and some Greek copies read "Gergesene"; others read "Gerasene."

³⁰Near that place there was a large herd of pigs feeding. ³¹The demons begged Jesus, "If you make us leave these men, please send us into that herd of pigs."

³²Jesus said to them, "Go!" So the demons left the men and went into the pigs. Then the whole herd rushed down the hill into the lake and were drowned. ³³The herdsmen ran away and went into town, where they told about all of this and what had happened to the men who had demons. ³⁴Then the whole town went out to see Jesus. When they saw him, they begged him to leave their area.

JESUS HEALS A PARALYZED MAN

9 Jesus got into a boat and went back across the lake to his own town. ²Some people brought to Jesus a man who was paralyzed and lying on a mat. When Jesus saw the faith of these people, he said to the paralyzed man, "Be encouraged, young man. Your sins are forgiven."

³Some of the teachers of the law said to themselves, "This man speaks as if he were God. That is blasphemy!"ⁿ

⁴Knowing their thoughts, Jesus said, "Why are you thinking evil thoughts? ⁵Which is easier: to say, 'Your sins are forgiven,' or to tell him, 'Stand up and walk'? ⁶But I will prove to you that the Son of Man has au-

GUARD YOUR HEART

If you're already looking at pornography or perhaps you're addicted to pornography, don't lose hope. Confess your sin to God. Then find someone you trust to share this issue with—a friend, a youth pastor, or perhaps a parent. Tell him about your struggle. It will be difficult, but accountability paves the path to freedom.

thority on earth to forgive sins." Then Jesus said to the paralyzed man, "Stand up, take your mat, and go home." ⁷And the man stood up and went home. ⁸When the people saw this, they were amazed and praised God for giving power like this to human beings.

JESUS CHOOSES MATTHEW

⁹When Jesus was leaving, he saw a man named Matthew sitting in the tax collector's booth. Jesus said to him, "Follow me," and he stood up and followed Jesus.

¹⁰As Jesus was having dinner at Matthew's house, many tax collectors and "sinners" came and ate with Jesus and his followers. ¹¹When the Pharisees saw this, they asked Jesus' followers, "Why does your teacher eat with tax collectors and sinners?"

¹²When Jesus heard them, he said, "It is not the healthy people who need a doctor, but the sick. ¹³Go and learn what this means: 'I want kindness more than I want animal sacrifices.'ⁿ I did not come to invite good people but to invite sinners."

JESUS' FOLLOWERS ARE CRITICIZED

¹⁴Then the followers of Johnⁿ came to Jesus and said, "Why do we and the Pharisees often fastⁿ for a certain time, but your followers don't?"

¹⁵Jesus answered, "The friends of the bridegroom are not sad while he is with them. But the time will come when the bridegroom will be taken from them, and then they will fast.

¹⁶"No one sews a patch of unshrunk cloth

*REVIEWS MUSIC

KRYSTAL MEYERS:
KRYSTAL MEYERS

If you're sitting around thinking, *I just wish that Avril Lavigne would sing about Jesus*, your wish might have been answered in the person of Krystal Meyers. The teen, guitar-holding rocker who even comes with her own "Christian" version of rock-n-roll attitude, may be a newbie to the field of Christian music, but her sound is classic. On her self-titled debut, she unleashes her voice with near-perfect control, slams her guitar with eloquence, and shows off the musical influence of Lavigne. Her lyrical content is purely God-focused, with "My Savior" and "The Way to Begin" being her strongest works.

WHY IT ROCKS:

THIS MUSICAL FIRECRACKER DEBUTS WITH A BANG.

krystal meyers

9:3 blasphemy Saying things against God or not showing respect for God.   9:13 'I want . . . sacrifices.' Quotation from Hosea 6:6.   9:14 John John the Baptist, who preached to people about Christ's coming (Matthew 3, Luke 3).   9:14 fast The people would give up eating for a special time of prayer and worship to God. It was also done to show sadness and disappointment.

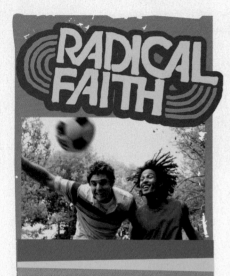

RADICAL FAITH

MATTHEW 9:35–38

No one can dodge this truth: all people are born into sin and are in need of salvation. So Jesus came to the world as a man, to fix humanity's relationship with God. You might assume the first step in that plan would be to launch into a rant about how wretchedly bad people are. Jesus, however, took a different approach. He felt pained to the core as he observed human suffering, and he responded with radical compassion. As he wandered throughout cities and villages, he entered the local centers of worship and preached the truth about God's life-altering kingdom. He miraculously healed the injured and diseased. In every encounter, he was moved by human need. Jesus saw that human beings were like scattered sheep—a slow, weak herd without a leader to keep them from danger. The need was vast. So he invited his followers to help him spread God's care to the planet. He made them his co-workers, harvesters of people ripe to become friends with God. And he wants you to join the venture (see Matthew 28:18–20).

over a hole in an old coat. If he does, the patch will shrink and pull away from the coat, making the hole worse. [17]Also, people never pour new wine into old leather bags. Otherwise, the bags will break, the wine will spill, and the wine bags will be ruined. But people always pour new wine into new wine bags. Then both will continue to be good."

JESUS GIVES LIFE TO A DEAD GIRL AND HEALS A SICK WOMAN

[18]While Jesus was saying these things, a leader of the synagogue came to him. He bowed down before Jesus and said, "My daughter has just died. But if you come and lay your hand on her, she will live again." [19]So Jesus and his followers stood up and went with the leader.

[20]Then a woman who had been bleeding for twelve years came behind Jesus and touched the edge of his coat. [21]She was thinking, "If I can just touch his clothes, I will be healed."

[22]Jesus turned and saw the woman and said, "Be encouraged, dear woman. You are made well because you believed." And the woman was healed from that moment on.

[23]Jesus continued along with the leader and went into his house. There he saw the funeral musicians and many people crying. [24]Jesus said, "Go away. The girl is not dead, only asleep." But the people laughed at him. [25]After the crowd had been thrown out of the house, Jesus went into the girl's room and took hold of her hand, and she stood up. [26]The news about this spread all around the area.

JESUS HEALS MORE PEOPLE

[27]When Jesus was leaving there, two blind men followed him. They cried out, "Have mercy on us, Son of David!"

[28]After Jesus went inside, the blind men went with him. He asked the men, "Do you believe that I can make you see again?"

They answered, "Yes, Lord."

[29]Then Jesus touched their eyes and said, "Because you believe I can make you see again, it will happen." [30]Then the men were able to see. But Jesus warned them strongly, saying, "Don't tell anyone about this." [31]But the blind men left and spread the news about Jesus all around that area.

[32]When the two men were leaving, some people brought another man to Jesus. This man could not talk because he had a demon in him. [33]After Jesus forced the demon to leave the man, he was able to speak. The crowd was amazed and said, "We have never seen anything like this in Israel."

[34]But the Pharisees said, "The prince of demons is the one that gives him power to force demons out."

[35]Jesus traveled through all the towns and villages, teaching in their synagogues, preaching the Good News about the kingdom, and healing all kinds of diseases and sicknesses. [36]When he saw the crowds, he felt sorry for them because they were hurting and helpless, like sheep without a shepherd. [37]Jesus said to his followers, "There are many people to harvest but only a few workers to help harvest them. [38]Pray to the Lord, who owns the harvest, that he will send more workers to gather his harvest."[n]

JESUS SENDS OUT HIS APOSTLES

10 Jesus called his twelve followers together and gave them authority to drive out evil spirits and to heal every kind of disease and sickness. [2]These are the names of the twelve apostles: Simon (also called Peter) and his brother Andrew; James son of Zebedee, and his brother John; [3]Philip and Bartholomew; Thomas and Matthew, the tax collector; James son of Alphaeus, and Thaddaeus; [4]Simon the Zealot and Judas Iscariot, who turned against Jesus.

[5]Jesus sent out these twelve men with the following order: "Don't go to the non-Jewish people or to any town where the Samaritans live. [6]But go to the people of Israel, who are like lost sheep. [7]When you go, preach this: 'The kingdom of heaven is near.' [8]Heal the sick, raise the dead to life again, heal those who have skin diseases, and force demons out of people. I give you these powers freely, so help other people freely. [9]Don't carry any money

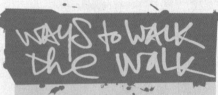

WAYS TO WALK the WALK

MATTHEW 10:16

WORD: Be clever and innocent.
WALK IT: Don't bludgeon people with the Good News. Instead, find common ground with people conversationally, and then think of a way to bring Jesus into what you're discussing. Remember that God cares more about people than programs.

 9:37–38 "There are . . . harvest." As a farmer sends workers to harvest the grain, Jesus sends his followers to bring people to God.

with you—gold or silver or copper. ¹⁰Don't carry a bag or extra clothes or sandals or a walking stick. Workers should be given what they need.

¹¹"When you enter a city or town, find some worthy person there and stay in that home until you leave. ¹²When you enter that home, say, 'Peace be with you.' ¹³If the people there welcome you, let your peace stay there. But if they don't welcome you, take back the peace you wished for them. ¹⁴And if a home or town refuses to welcome you or listen to you, leave that place and shake its dust off your feet.ⁿ

In 2004, the nation's 33 million teenagers accounted for $169 billion in spending, or an average of $91 per week per teen.

—Teenage Research Unlimited

¹⁵I tell you the truth, on the Judgment Day it will be better for the towns of Sodom and Gomorrahⁿ than for the people of that town.

JESUS WARNS HIS APOSTLES

¹⁶"Listen, I am sending you out like sheep among wolves. So be as clever as snakes and as innocent as doves. ¹⁷Be careful of people, because they will arrest you and take you to court and whip you in their synagogues. ¹⁸Because of me you will be taken to stand before governors and kings, and you will tell them and the non-Jewish people about me. ¹⁹When you are arrested, don't worry about what to say or how to say it. At that time you will be given the things to say. ²⁰It will not really be you speaking but the Spirit of your Father speaking through you.

²¹"Brothers will give their own brothers to be killed, and fathers will give their own children to be killed. Children will fight against their own parents and have them put to death. ²²All people will hate you because you follow me, but those people who keep their faith until the end will be saved. ²³When you are treated badly in one city, run to another city. I tell you the truth, you will not finish going through all the cities of Israel before the Son of Man comes.

²⁴"A student is not better than his teacher, and a servant is not better than his master. ²⁵A student should be satisfied to become like his teacher; a servant should be satisfied to become like his master. If the head of the family is called Beelzebul, then the other members of the family will be called worse names!

FEAR GOD, NOT PEOPLE

²⁶"So don't be afraid of those people, because everything that is hidden will be shown. Everything that is secret will be made known. ²⁷I tell you these things in the dark, but I want you to tell them in the light. What you hear whispered in your ear you should shout from the housetops. ²⁸Don't be afraid of people, who can kill the body but cannot kill the soul. The only one you should fear is the one who can destroy the soul and the body in hell. ²⁹Two sparrows cost only a penny, but not even one of them can die without your Father's knowing it. ³⁰God even knows how many hairs are on your head. ³¹So don't be afraid. You are worth much more than many sparrows.

TELL PEOPLE ABOUT YOUR FAITH

³²"All those who stand before others and say they believe in me, I will say before my Father in heaven that they belong to me. ³³But all who stand before others and say they do not believe in me, I will say before my Father in heaven that they do not belong to me.

³⁴"Don't think that I came to bring peace to the earth. I did not come to bring peace, but a sword. ³⁵I have come so that

'a son will be against his father,
    a daughter will be against her mother,
a daughter-in-law will be against her
        mother-in-law.
³⁶   A person's enemies will be members of
        his own family.'   Micah 7:6

³⁷"Those who love their father or mother more than they love me are not worthy to be my followers. Those who love their son or daughter more than they love me are not worthy to be my followers. ³⁸Whoever is not willing to carry the cross and follow me is not worthy of me. ³⁹Those who try to hold on to their lives will give up true life. Those who give up their lives for me will hold on to true life. ⁴⁰Whoever accepts you also accepts me, and whoever accepts me also accepts the One who sent me. ⁴¹Whoever meets a prophet and accepts him will receive the reward of a prophet. And whoever accepts a good person because that person is good will receive the reward of a good person. ⁴²Those who give one of these little ones a cup of cold water because they are my followers will truly get their reward."

How to Land a Jet

Extras:

It happens in the movies all the time: the pilot is incapacitated for some reason (illness, bullet wound, etc.) and some noble average guy like you has to land the plane. Here's how to do it. First, get the pilot out of the seat and try to get someone to give him medical attention. Next, put on the headset and use the radio to call for help. Look for the radio control button (usually on the plane's steering mechanism or on the instrument panel), depress it, and say "Mayday!" twice. Release the button and listen for a response. If no one responds, tune the radio to 121.5, the emergency channel, and try again. Once you get someone on the line, tell him what happened, where you're headed, and the call numbers of the plane. They'll be able to talk you down from there. And when you encounter emergencies in life, remember God's emergency channel—prayer—is always available.

 10:14 shake . . . feet A warning. It showed that they had rejected these people.   10:15 Sodom and Gomorrah Two cities that God destroyed because the people were so evil.

15

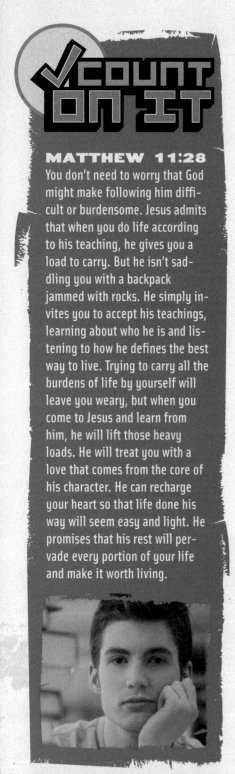

✓ COUNT ON IT

MATTHEW 11:28

You don't need to worry that God might make following him difficult or burdensome. Jesus admits that when you do life according to his teaching, he gives you a load to carry. But he isn't saddling you with a backpack jammed with rocks. He simply invites you to accept his teachings, learning about who he is and listening to how he defines the best way to live. Trying to carry all the burdens of life by yourself will leave you weary, but when you come to Jesus and learn from him, he will lift those heavy loads. He will treat you with a love that comes from the core of his character. He can recharge your heart so that life done his way will seem easy and light. He promises that his rest will pervade every portion of your life and make it worth living.

JESUS AND JOHN THE BAPTIST

11 After Jesus finished telling these things to his twelve followers, he left there and went to the towns in Galilee to teach and preach.

[2]John the Baptist was in prison, but he heard about what the Christ was doing. So John sent some of his followers to Jesus. [3]They asked him, "Are you the One who is to come, or should we wait for someone else?"

[4]Jesus answered them, "Go tell John what you hear and see: [5]The blind can see, the crippled can walk, and people with skin diseases are healed. The deaf can hear, the dead are raised to life, and the Good News is preached to the poor. [6]Those who do not stumble in their faith because of me are blessed."

[7]As John's followers were leaving, Jesus began talking to the people about John. Jesus said, "What did you go out into the desert to see? A reed[n] blown by the wind? [8]What did you go out to see? A man dressed in fine clothes? No, those who wear fine clothes live in kings' palaces. [9]So why did you go out? To see a prophet? Yes, and I tell you, John is more than a prophet. [10]This was written about him:

'I will send my messenger ahead of you,
who will prepare the way for you.'

Malachi 3:1

[11]I tell you the truth, John the Baptist is greater than any other person ever born, but even the least important person in the kingdom of heaven is greater than John. [12]Since the time John the Baptist came until now, the kingdom of heaven has been going forward in strength, and people have been trying to take it by force. [13]All the prophets and the law of Moses told about what would happen until the time John came. [14]And if you will believe what they said, you will believe that John is Elijah, whom they said would come. [15]Let those with ears use them and listen!

[16]"What can I say about the people of this time? What are they like? They are like children sitting in the marketplace, who call out to each other,

[17]'We played music for you, but you did not dance;
we sang a sad song, but you did not cry.'

[18]John came and did not eat or drink like other people. So people say, 'He has a demon.' [19]The Son of Man came, eating and drinking, and people say, 'Look at him! He eats too much and drinks too much wine, and he is a friend of tax collectors and sinners.' But wisdom is proved to be right by what she does."

JESUS WARNS UNBELIEVERS

[20]Then Jesus criticized the cities where he did most of his miracles, because the people did not change their lives and stop sinning. [21]He said, "How terrible for you, Korazin! How terrible for you, Bethsaida! If the same miracles I did in you had happened in Tyre and Sidon,[n] those people would have changed their lives a long time ago. They would have worn rough cloth and put ashes on themselves to show they had changed. [22]But I tell you, on the Judgment Day it will be better for Tyre and Sidon than for you. [23]And you, Capernaum,[n] will you be lifted up to heaven? No, you will be thrown down to the depths. If the miracles I did in you had happened in Sodom,[n] its people would have stopped sinning, and it would still be a city today. [24]But I tell you, on the Judgment Day it will be better for Sodom than for you."

JESUS OFFERS REST TO PEOPLE

[25]At that time Jesus said, "I praise you, Father, Lord of heaven and earth, because you have hidden these things from the people who are wise and smart. But you have shown them to those who are like little children. [26]Yes, Father, this is what you really wanted.

[27]"My Father has given me all things. No one knows the Son, except the Father. And no one knows the Father, except the Son and those whom the Son chooses to tell.

[28]"Come to me, all of you who are tired and have heavy loads, and I will give you rest. [29]Accept my teachings and learn from me, because I am gentle and humble in spirit, and you will find rest for your lives. [30]The burden that I ask you to accept is easy; the load I give you to carry is light."

JESUS IS LORD OF THE SABBATH

12 At that time Jesus was walking through some fields of grain on a Sabbath day. His followers were hungry, so they began to pick the grain and eat it. [2]When the Pharisees saw this, they said to Jesus, "Look! Your followers are doing what is unlawful to do on the Sabbath day."

[3]Jesus answered, "Have you not read what David did when he and the people with him were hungry? [4]He went into God's house, and he and those with him ate the holy bread, which was lawful only for priests to eat. [5]And have you not read in the law of Moses that on every Sabbath day the priests in the Temple break this law about the Sabbath day? But the priests are not wrong for doing that. [6]I tell you that there is something here that is greater than the Temple. [7]The Scripture says, 'I want kindness more than I want animal sacrifices.'[n] You don't really know what those words mean. If you understood them, you would not judge those who have done nothing wrong.

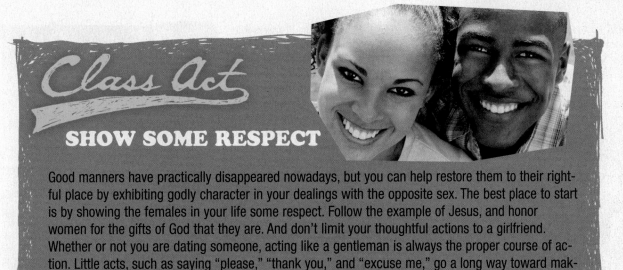

Class Act

SHOW SOME RESPECT

Good manners have practically disappeared nowadays, but you can help restore them to their rightful place by exhibiting godly character in your dealings with the opposite sex. The best place to start is by showing the females in your life some respect. Follow the example of Jesus, and honor women for the gifts of God that they are. And don't limit your thoughtful actions to a girlfriend. Whether or not you are dating someone, acting like a gentleman is always the proper course of action. Little acts, such as saying "please," "thank you," and "excuse me," go a long way toward making a big impression.

[8]"So the Son of Man is Lord of the Sabbath day."

JESUS HEALS A MAN'S HAND

[9]Jesus left there and went into their synagogue, [10]where there was a man with a crippled hand. They were looking for a reason to accuse Jesus, so they asked him, "Is it right to heal on the Sabbath day?"[n]

[11]Jesus answered, "If any of you has a sheep, and it falls into a ditch on the Sabbath day, you will help it out of the ditch. [12]Surely a human being is more important than a sheep. So it is lawful to do good things on the Sabbath day."

[13]Then Jesus said to the man with the crippled hand, "Hold out your hand." The man held out his hand, and it became well again, like the other hand. [14]But the Pharisees left and made plans to kill Jesus.

JESUS IS GOD'S CHOSEN SERVANT

[15]Jesus knew what the Pharisees were doing, so he left that place. Many people followed him, and he healed all who were sick. [16]But Jesus warned the people not to tell who he was. [17]He did these things to bring about what Isaiah the prophet had said:

[18]"Here is my servant whom I have chosen.
 I love him, and I am pleased with him.
 I will put my Spirit upon him,
 and he will tell of my justice to all people.
[19]He will not argue or cry out;
 no one will hear his voice in the streets.
[20]He will not break a crushed blade of grass
 or put out even a weak flame
 until he makes justice win the victory.
[21] In him will the non-Jewish people find hope."   *Isaiah 42:1–4*

JESUS' POWER IS FROM GOD

[22]Then some people brought to Jesus a man who was blind and could not talk, because he had a demon. Jesus healed the man so

fight the fight

Matthew 5:22-24

Whether the brawl is broadcast on national networks or erupts at a local ballfield, bad behavior in sports is just one example of the problem our society has with anger. It's so common it may seem the macho way is to slug it out with your enemy. But that isn't what the Bible says. Jesus warned that those who are angry with others and call them names face judgment for their actions. Instead, Christ advises working it out and making peace. That may not get you acclaim on the street corner, but it is the manly thing to do.

✳ 12:10 Is it right . . . day? It was against Jewish Law to work on the Sabbath day.

that he could talk and see. ²³All the people were amazed and said, "Perhaps this man is the Son of David!"

²⁴When the Pharisees heard this, they said, "Jesus uses the power of Beelzebul, the ruler of demons, to force demons out of people."

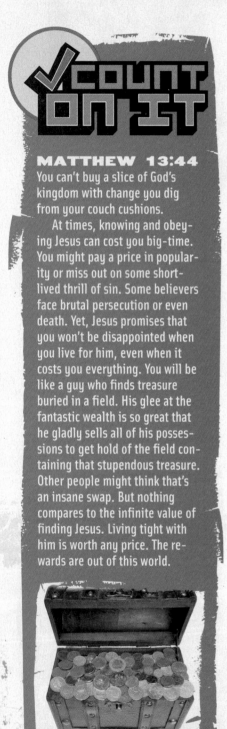

COUNT ON IT

MATTHEW 13:44

You can't buy a slice of God's kingdom with change you dig from your couch cushions.

At times, knowing and obeying Jesus can cost you big-time. You might pay a price in popularity or miss out on some short-lived thrill of sin. Some believers face brutal persecution or even death. Yet, Jesus promises that you won't be disappointed when you live for him, even when it costs you everything. You will be like a guy who finds treasure buried in a field. His glee at the fantastic wealth is so great that he gladly sells all of his possessions to get hold of the field containing that stupendous treasure. Other people might think that's an insane swap. But nothing compares to the infinite value of finding Jesus. Living tight with him is worth any price. The rewards are out of this world.

²⁵Jesus knew what the Pharisees were thinking, so he said to them, "Every kingdom that is divided against itself will be destroyed. And any city or family that is divided against itself will not continue. ²⁶And if Satan forces out himself, then Satan is divided against himself, and his kingdom will not continue. ²⁷You say that I use the power of Beelzebul to force out demons. If that is true, then what power do your people use to force out demons? So they will be your judges. ²⁸But if I use the power of God's Spirit to force out demons, then the kingdom of God has come to you.

²⁹"If anyone wants to enter a strong person's house and steal his things, he must first tie up the strong person. Then he can steal the things from the house.

³⁰"Whoever is not with me is against me. Whoever does not work with me is working against me. ³¹So I tell you, people can be forgiven for every sin and everything they say against God. But whoever speaks against the Holy Spirit will not be forgiven. ³²Anyone who speaks against the Son of Man can be forgiven, but anyone who speaks against the Holy Spirit will not be forgiven, now or in the future.

PEOPLE KNOW YOU BY YOUR WORDS

³³"If you want good fruit, you must make the tree good. If your tree is not good, it will have bad fruit. A tree is known by the kind of fruit it produces. ³⁴You snakes! You are evil people, so how can you say anything good? The mouth speaks the things that are in the heart. ³⁵Good people have good things in their hearts, and so they say good things. But evil people have evil in their hearts, so they say evil things. ³⁶And I tell you that on the Judgment Day people will be responsible for every careless thing they have said. ³⁷The words you have said will be used to judge you. Some of your words will prove you right, but some of your words will prove you guilty."

THE PEOPLE ASK FOR A MIRACLE

³⁸Then some of the Pharisees and teachers of the law answered Jesus, saying, "Teacher, we want to see you work a miracle as a sign."

³⁹Jesus answered, "Evil and sinful people are the ones who want to see a miracle for a sign. But no sign will be given to them, except the sign of the prophet Jonah. ⁴⁰Jonah was in the stomach of the big fish for three days and three nights. In the same way, the Son of Man will be in the grave three days

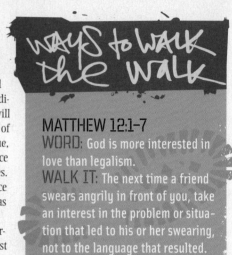

WAYS to WALK the WALK

MATTHEW 12:1–7

WORD: God is more interested in love than legalism.
WALK IT: The next time a friend swears angrily in front of you, take an interest in the problem or situation that led to his or her swearing, not to the language that resulted.

and three nights. ⁴¹On the Judgment Day the people from Nineveh[n] will stand up with you people who live now, and they will show that you are guilty. When Jonah preached to them, they were sorry and changed their lives. And I tell you that someone greater than Jonah is here. ⁴²On the Judgment Day, the Queen of the South[n] will stand up with you people who live today. She will show that you are guilty, because she came from far away to listen to Solomon's wise teaching. And I tell you that someone greater than Solomon is here.

PEOPLE TODAY ARE FULL OF EVIL

⁴³"When an evil spirit comes out of a person, it travels through dry places, looking for a place to rest, but it doesn't find it. ⁴⁴So the spirit says, 'I will go back to the house I left.' When the spirit comes back, it finds the house still empty, swept clean, and made neat. ⁴⁵Then the evil spirit goes out and brings seven other spirits even more evil than it is, and they go in and live there. So the person has even more trouble than before. It is the same way with the evil people who live today."

JESUS' TRUE FAMILY

⁴⁶While Jesus was talking to the people, his mother and brothers stood outside, trying to find a way to talk to him. ⁴⁷Someone told Jesus, "Your mother and brothers are standing outside, and they want to talk to you."[n]

⁴⁸He answered, "Who is my mother? Who are my brothers?" ⁴⁹Then he pointed to his followers and said, "Here are my mother and my brothers. ⁵⁰My true brother and sister and

12:41 Nineveh The city where Jonah preached to warn the people. Read Jonah 3. 12:42 Queen of the South The Queen of Sheba. She traveled a thousand miles to learn God's wisdom from Solomon. Read 1 Kings 10:1–13. 12:47 Someone . . . you." Some Greek copies do not have verse 47.

18

mother are those who do what my Father in heaven wants."

A STORY ABOUT PLANTING SEED

13 That same day Jesus went out of the house and sat by the lake. [2]Large crowds gathered around him, so he got into a boat and sat down, while the people stood on the shore. [3]Then Jesus used stories to teach them many things. He said: "A farmer went out to plant his seed. [4]While he was planting, some seed fell by the road, and the birds came and ate it all up. [5]Some seed fell on rocky ground, where there wasn't much dirt. That seed grew very fast, because the ground was not deep. [6]But when the sun rose, the plants dried up, because they did not have deep roots. [7]Some other seed fell among thorny weeds, which grew and choked the good plants. [8]Some other seed fell on good ground where it grew and produced a crop. Some plants made a hundred times more, some made sixty times more, and some made thirty times more. [9]Let those with ears use them and listen."

WHY JESUS USED STORIES TO TEACH

[10]The followers came to Jesus and asked, "Why do you use stories to teach the people?"

[11]Jesus answered, "You have been chosen to know the secrets about the kingdom of heaven, but others cannot know these secrets. [12]Those who have understanding will be given more, and they will have all they need. But those who do not have understanding, even what they have will be taken away from them. [13]This is why I use stories to teach the people: They see, but they don't really see. They hear, but they don't really hear or understand. [14]So they show that the things Isaiah said about them are true:

'You will listen and listen, but you will not
    understand.
  You will look and look, but you will not
    learn.
[15]For the minds of these people have become
    stubborn.
  They do not hear with their ears,
  and they have closed their eyes.
Otherwise they might really understand
  what they see with their eyes
  and hear with their ears.
They might really understand in their
    minds
  and come back to me and be healed.'
                                    Isaiah 6:9–10

GUARD YOUR HEART

God desires to protect us from poor choices. But sometimes we disobey. When you've made a bad choice—whether sexually or otherwise—don't thrash yourself with guilt or run away from the presence of God. Instead, run toward God. He promises to accept the humble and to help the broken-hearted.

[16]But you are blessed, because you see with your eyes and hear with your ears. [17]I tell you the truth, many prophets and good people wanted to see the things that you now see, but they did not see them. And they wanted to hear the things that you now hear, but they did not hear them.

JESUS EXPLAINS THE SEED STORY

[18]"So listen to the meaning of that story about the farmer. [19]What is the seed that fell by the road? That seed is like the person who hears the message about the kingdom but does not understand it. The Evil One comes and takes away what was planted in that person's heart. [20]And what is the seed that fell on rocky ground? That seed is like the person who hears the teaching and quickly accepts it with joy. [21]But he does not let the teaching go deep into his life, so he keeps it only a short time. When trouble or persecution comes because of the teaching he accepted, he quickly gives up. [22]And what is

Get out there

The Rightnow Campaign proclaims a simple purpose: help connect people to ministry opportunities, recapturing the interest of young adults who have left the church yet who yearn for authentic faith and service. To fulfill that goal, this Dallas-based ministry maintains a network of 80 mission-sending organizations and Christian service groups. In 2004, it launched Fusion Conferences, working with hundreds of churches in a specific area to challenge people to serve through a church or one of Rightnow's partners. The ministry also offers one-day training seminars. It boasts more than 3,000 opportunities to make a difference around the world.

To check one out,
visit www.rightnow.org.

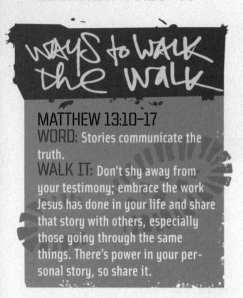

ways to walk the walk

MATTHEW 13:10-17

WORD: Stories communicate the truth.

WALK IT: Don't shy away from your testimony; embrace the work Jesus has done in your life and share that story with others, especially those going through the same things. There's power in your personal story, so share it.

the seed that fell among the thorny weeds? That seed is like the person who hears the teaching but lets worries about this life and the temptation of wealth stop that teaching from growing. So the teaching does not produce fruit[n] in that person's life. 23But what is the seed that fell on the good ground? That seed is like the person who hears the teaching and understands it. That person grows and produces fruit, sometimes a hundred times more, sometimes sixty times more, and sometimes thirty times more."

A STORY ABOUT WHEAT AND WEEDS

24Then Jesus told them another story: "The kingdom of heaven is like a man who planted good seed in his field. 25That night, when everyone was asleep, his enemy came and planted weeds among the wheat and then left. 26Later, the wheat sprouted and the heads of grain grew, but the weeds also grew. 27Then the man's servants came to him and said, 'You planted good seed in your field. Where did the weeds come from?' 28The man answered, 'An enemy planted weeds.' The servants asked, 'Do you want us to pull up the weeds?' 29The man answered, 'No, because when you pull up the weeds, you might also pull up the wheat. 30Let the weeds and the wheat grow together until the harvest time. At harvest time I will tell the workers, "First gather the weeds and tie them together to be burned. Then gather the wheat and bring it to my barn." ' "

STORIES OF MUSTARD SEED AND YEAST

31Then Jesus told another story: "The kingdom of heaven is like a mustard seed that a man planted in his field. 32That seed is the smallest of all seeds, but when it grows, it is one of the largest garden plants. It becomes big enough for the wild birds to come and build nests in its branches."

33Then Jesus told another story: "The kingdom of heaven is like yeast that a woman took and hid in a large tub of flour until it made all the dough rise."

34Jesus used stories to tell all these things to the people; he always used stories to teach them. 35This is as the prophet said:

"I will speak using stories;
   I will tell things that have been secret
      since the world was made."

Psalm 78:2

JESUS EXPLAINS ABOUT THE WEEDS

36Then Jesus left the crowd and went into the house. His followers came to him and said, "Explain to us the meaning of the story about the weeds in the field."

37Jesus answered, "The man who planted the good seed in the field is the Son of Man. 38The field is the world, and the good seed are all of God's children who belong to the kingdom. The weeds are those people who belong to the Evil One. 39And the enemy who planted the bad seed is the devil. The harvest time is the end of the age, and the workers who gather are God's angels.

40"Just as the weeds are pulled up and burned in the fire, so it will be at the end of the age. 41The Son of Man will send out his angels, and they will gather out of his kingdom all who cause sin and all who do evil. 42The angels will throw them into the blazing furnace, where the people will cry and grind their teeth with pain. 43Then the good people will shine like the sun in the kingdom of their Father. Let those with ears use them and listen.

STORIES OF A TREASURE AND A PEARL

44"The kingdom of heaven is like a treasure hidden in a field. One day a man found the treasure, and then he hid it in the field again. He was so happy that he went and sold everything he owned to buy that field.

45"Also, the kingdom of heaven is like a man looking for fine pearls. 46When he found a very valuable pearl, he went and sold everything he had and bought it.

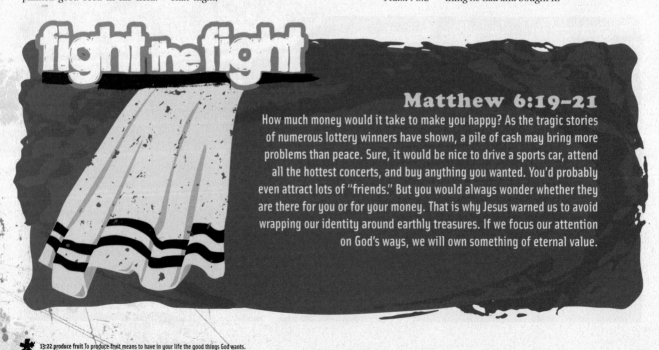

fight the fight

Matthew 6:19-21

How much money would it take to make you happy? As the tragic stories of numerous lottery winners have shown, a pile of cash may bring more problems than peace. Sure, it would be nice to drive a sports car, attend all the hottest concerts, and buy anything you wanted. You'd probably even attract lots of "friends." But you would always wonder whether they are there for you or for your money. That is why Jesus warned us to avoid wrapping our identity around earthly treasures. If we focus our attention on God's ways, we will own something of eternal value.

13:22 **produce fruit** To produce fruit means to have in your life the good things God wants.

A STORY OF A FISHING NET

47"Also, the kingdom of heaven is like a net that was put into the lake and caught many different kinds of fish. 48When it was full, the fishermen pulled the net to the shore. They sat down and put all the good fish in baskets and threw away the bad fish. 49It will be this way at the end of the age. The angels will come and separate the evil people from the good people. 50The angels will throw the evil people into the blazing furnace, where people will cry and grind their teeth with pain."

51Jesus asked his followers, "Do you understand all these things?"

They answered, "Yes, we understand."

52Then Jesus said to them, "So every teacher of the law who has been taught about the kingdom of heaven is like the owner of a house. He brings out both new things and old things he has saved."

JESUS GOES TO HIS HOMETOWN

53When Jesus finished teaching with these stories, he left there. 54He went to his home-town and taught the people in the synagogue, and they were amazed. They said, "Where did this man get this wisdom and this power to do miracles? 55He is just the son of a carpenter. His mother is Mary, and his brothers are James, Joseph, Simon, and Judas. 56And all his sisters are here with us. Where then does this man get all these things?" 57So the people were upset with Jesus.

But Jesus said to them, "A prophet is honored everywhere except in his hometown and in his own home."

58So he did not do many miracles there because they had no faith.

HOW JOHN THE BAPTIST WAS KILLED

14 At that time Herod, the ruler of Galilee, heard the reports about Jesus. 2So he said to his servants, "Jesus is John the Baptist, who has risen from the dead. That is why he can work these miracles."

3Sometime before this, Herod had arrested John, tied him up, and put him into prison. Herod did this because of Herodias, who had been the wife of Philip, Herod's brother. 4John had been telling Herod, "It is not lawful for you to be married to Herodias." 5Herod wanted to kill John, but he was afraid of the people, because they believed John was a prophet.

6On Herod's birthday, the daughter of Herodias danced for Herod and his guests, and she pleased him. 7So he promised with an oath to give her anything she wanted. 8Herodias told her daughter what to ask for, so she said to Herod, "Give me the head of John the Baptist here on a platter." 9Although King Herod was very sad, he had made a promise, and his dinner guests had heard him. So Herod ordered that what she asked for be done. 10He sent soldiers to the prison to cut off John's head. 11And they brought it on a platter and gave it to the girl, and she took it to her mother. 12John's followers came and got his body and buried it. Then they went and told Jesus.

MORE THAN FIVE THOUSAND FED

13When Jesus heard what had happened to John, he left in a boat and went to a lonely place by himself. But the crowds heard about it and followed him on foot from the towns. 14When he arrived, he saw a great crowd waiting. He felt sorry for them and healed those who were sick.

15When it was evening, his followers came to him and said, "No one lives in this place, and it is already late. Send the people away so they can go to the towns and buy food for themselves."

DO's AND Don'ts

DO try out for sports you like.

DO work hard to improve your game.

DO practice good sportsmanship.

DO treat the officials with respect.

DON'T gripe about your playing time.

DON'T overdo your love of the game.

DON'T cut corners during training.

DON'T try to win at all costs.

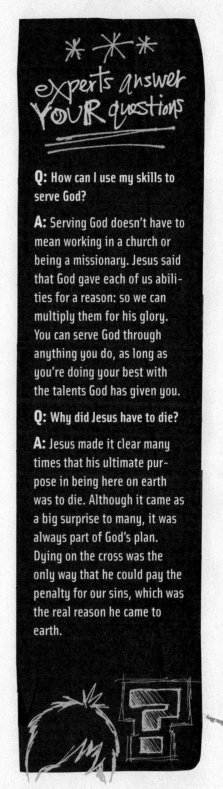

experts answer YOUR questions

Q: How can I use my skills to serve God?

A: Serving God doesn't have to mean working in a church or being a missionary. Jesus said that God gave each of us abilities for a reason: so we can multiply them for his glory. You can serve God through anything you do, as long as you're doing your best with the talents God has given you.

Q: Why did Jesus have to die?

A: Jesus made it clear many times that his ultimate purpose in being here on earth was to die. Although it came as a big surprise to many, it was always part of God's plan. Dying on the cross was the only way that he could pay the penalty for our sins, which was the real reason he came to earth.

16But Jesus answered, "They don't need to go away. You give them something to eat."

17They said to him, "But we have only five loaves of bread and two fish."

18Jesus said, "Bring the bread and the fish

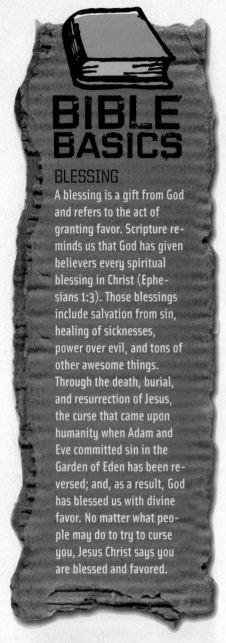

BIBLE BASICS

BLESSING

A blessing is a gift from God and refers to the act of granting favor. Scripture reminds us that God has given believers every spiritual blessing in Christ (Ephesians 1:3). Those blessings include salvation from sin, healing of sicknesses, power over evil, and tons of other awesome things. Through the death, burial, and resurrection of Jesus, the curse that came upon humanity when Adam and Eve committed sin in the Garden of Eden has been reversed; and, as a result, God has blessed us with divine favor. No matter what people may do to try to curse you, Jesus Christ says you are blessed and favored.

to me." [19]Then he told the people to sit down on the grass. He took the five loaves and the two fish and, looking to heaven, he thanked God for the food. Jesus divided the bread and gave it to his followers, who gave it to the people. [20]All the people ate and were satisfied. Then the followers filled twelve baskets with the leftover pieces of food. [21]There were about five thousand men there who ate, not counting women and children.

JESUS WALKS ON THE WATER

[22]Immediately Jesus told his followers to get into the boat and go ahead of him across the lake. He stayed there to send the people home. [23]After he had sent them away, he went by himself up into the hills to pray. It was late, and Jesus was there alone. [24]By this time, the boat was already far away from land. It was being hit by waves, because the wind was blowing against it.

[25]Between three and six o'clock in the morning, Jesus came to them, walking on the water. [26]When his followers saw him walking on the water, they were afraid. They said, "It's a ghost!" and cried out in fear.

[27]But Jesus quickly spoke to them, "Have courage! It is I. Do not be afraid."

[28]Peter said, "Lord, if it is really you, then command me to come to you on the water."

[29]Jesus said, "Come."

And Peter left the boat and walked on the water to Jesus. [30]But when Peter saw the wind and the waves, he became afraid and began to sink. He shouted, "Lord, save me!"

[31]Immediately Jesus reached out his hand and caught Peter. Jesus said, "Your faith is small. Why did you doubt?"

[32]After they got into the boat, the wind became calm. [33]Then those who were in the boat worshiped Jesus and said, "Truly you are the Son of God!"

[34]When they had crossed the lake, they came to shore at Gennesaret. [35]When the people there recognized Jesus, they told people all around there that Jesus had come, and they brought all their sick to him. [36]They begged Jesus to let them touch just the edge of his coat, and all who touched it were healed.

OBEY GOD'S LAW

15 Then some Pharisees and teachers of the law came to Jesus from Jerusalem. They asked him, [2]"Why don't your followers obey the unwritten laws which have been handed down to us? They don't wash their hands before they eat."

[3]Jesus answered, "And why do you refuse to obey God's command so that you can follow your own teachings? [4]God said, 'Honor your father and your mother,'[n] and 'Anyone who says cruel things to his father or mother must be put to death.'[n] [5]But you say a person can tell his father or mother, 'I have something I could use to help you, but I have given it to God already.' [6]You teach that person not to honor his father or his mother. You rejected what God said for the sake of your own rules. [7]You are hypocrites! Isaiah was right when he said about you:

[8]'These people show honor to me with
  words,
  but their hearts are far from me.
[9]Their worship of me is worthless.
  The things they teach are nothing but
    human rules.' "   *Isaiah 29:13*

[10]After Jesus called the crowd to him, he said, "Listen and understand what I am saying. [11]It is not what people put into their mouths that makes them unclean. It is what comes out of their mouths that makes them unclean."

[12]Then his followers came to him and asked, "Do you know that the Pharisees are angry because of what you said?"

[13]Jesus answered, "Every plant that my Father in heaven has not planted himself will be pulled up by the roots. [14]Stay away from the Pharisees; they are blind leaders.[n] And if a blind person leads a blind person, both will fall into a ditch."

[15]Peter said, "Explain the example to us."

[16]Jesus said, "Do you still not understand? [17]Surely you know that all the food that enters the mouth goes into the stomach and then goes out of the body. [18]But what people say with their mouths comes from the way they think; these are the things that make people unclean. [19]Out of the mind come evil thoughts, murder, adultery, sexual sins, stealing, lying, and speaking evil of others. [20]These things make people unclean; eating with unwashed hands does not make them unclean."

JESUS HELPS A NON-JEWISH WOMAN

[21]Jesus left that place and went to the area of Tyre and Sidon. [22]A Canaanite woman from that area came to Jesus and cried out, "Lord, Son of David, have mercy on me! My daughter has a demon, and she is suffering very much."

[23]But Jesus did not answer the woman. So his followers came to Jesus and begged him, "Tell the woman to go away. She is following us and shouting."

[24]Jesus answered, "God sent me only to the lost sheep, the people of Israel."

[25]Then the woman came to Jesus again and bowed before him and said, "Lord, help me!"

[26]Jesus answered, "It is not right to take the children's bread and give it to the dogs."

[27]The woman said, "Yes, Lord, but even the dogs eat the crumbs that fall from their masters' table."

[28]Then Jesus answered, "Woman, you have great faith! I will do what you asked." And at that moment the woman's daughter was healed.

JESUS HEALS MANY PEOPLE

[29]After leaving there, Jesus went along the shore of Lake Galilee. He went up on a hill and sat there.

[30]Great crowds came to Jesus, bringing with them the lame, the blind, the crippled, those who could not speak, and many others. They

 15:4 'Honor . . . mother.' Quotation from Exodus 20:12; Deuteronomy 5:16.   15:4 'Anyone . . . death.' Quotation from Exodus 21:17.   15:14 leaders Some Greek copies continue, "of blind people."

put them at Jesus' feet, and he healed them. [31]The crowd was amazed when they saw that people who could not speak before were now able to speak. The crippled were made strong. The lame could walk, and the blind could see. And they praised the God of Israel for this.

MORE THAN FOUR THOUSAND FED

[32]Jesus called his followers to him and said, "I feel sorry for these people, because they have already been with me three days, and they have nothing to eat. I don't want to send them away hungry. They might faint while going home."

[33]His followers asked him, "How can we get enough bread to feed all these people? We are far away from any town."

[34]Jesus asked, "How many loaves of bread do you have?"

They answered, "Seven, and a few small fish."

[35]Jesus told the people to sit on the ground. [36]He took the seven loaves of bread and the fish and gave thanks to God. Then he divided the food and gave it to his followers, and they gave it to the people. [37]All the people ate and were satisfied. Then his followers filled seven baskets with the leftover pieces of food. [38]There were about four thousand men there who ate, besides women and children. [39]After sending the people home, Jesus got into the boat and went to the area of Magadan.

THE LEADERS ASK FOR A MIRACLE

16 The Pharisees and Sadducees came to Jesus, wanting to trick him. So they asked him to show them a miracle from God.

[2]Jesus answered,[n] "At sunset you say we will have good weather, because the sky is red. [3]And in the morning you say that it will be a rainy day, because the sky is dark and red. You see these signs in the sky and know what they mean. In the same way, you see the things that I am doing now, but you don't know their meaning. [4]Evil and sinful people ask for a miracle as a sign, but they will not be given any sign, except the sign of Jonah."[n] Then Jesus left them and went away.

GUARD AGAINST WRONG TEACHINGS

[5]Jesus' followers went across the lake, but they had forgotten to bring bread. [6]Jesus said to them, "Be careful! Beware of the yeast of the Pharisees and the Sadducees."

[7]His followers discussed the meaning of this, saying, "He said this because we forgot to bring bread."

[8]Knowing what they were talking about, Jesus asked them, "Why are you talking about not having bread? Your faith is small. [9]Do you still not understand? Remember the five loaves of bread that fed the five thousand? And remember that you filled many baskets with the leftovers? [10]Or the seven loaves of bread that fed the four thousand and the many baskets you filled then also? [11]I was not talking to you about bread. Why don't you understand that? I am telling you to beware of the yeast of the Pharisees and the Sadducees." [12]Then the followers understood that Jesus was not telling them to beware of the yeast used in bread but to beware of the teaching of the Pharisees and the Sadducees.

PETER SAYS JESUS IS THE CHRIST

[13]When Jesus came to the area of Caesarea Philippi, he asked his followers, "Who do people say the Son of Man is?"

[14]They answered, "Some say you are John the Baptist. Others say you are Elijah, and still others say you are Jeremiah or one of the prophets."

[15]Then Jesus asked them, "And who do you say I am?"

[16]Simon Peter answered, "You are the Christ, the Son of the living God."

[17]Jesus answered, "You are blessed, Simon son of Jonah, because no person taught you that. My Father in heaven showed you who I am. [18]So I tell you, you are Peter.[n] On this rock I will build my church, and the power of death will not be able to defeat it. [19]I will give you the keys of the kingdom of heaven; the things you don't allow on earth will be the things that God does not allow, and the things you allow on earth will be the things that God allows." [20]Then Jesus warned his followers not to tell anyone he was the Christ.

JESUS SAYS THAT HE MUST DIE

[21]From that time on Jesus began telling his followers that he must go to Jerusalem, where the Jewish elders, the leading priests, and the teachers of the law would make him suffer many things. He told them he must be killed and then be raised from the dead on the third day.

[22]Peter took Jesus aside and told him not to talk like that. He said, "God save you from those things, Lord! Those things will never happen to you!"

[23]Then Jesus said to Peter, "Go away from me, Satan![n] You are not helping me! You don't

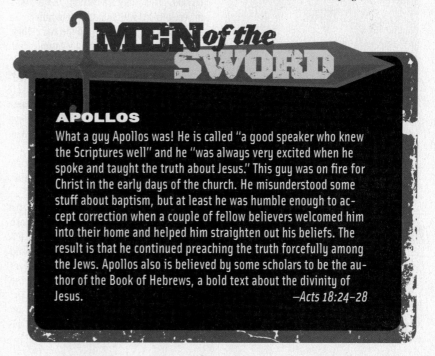

MEN of the SWORD

APOLLOS

What a guy Apollos was! He is called "a good speaker who knew the Scriptures well" and he "was always very excited when he spoke and taught the truth about Jesus." This guy was on fire for Christ in the early days of the church. He misunderstood some stuff about baptism, but at least he was humble enough to accept correction when a couple of fellow believers welcomed him into their home and helped him straighten out his beliefs. The result is that he continued preaching the truth forcefully among the Jews. Apollos also is believed by some scholars to be the author of the Book of Hebrews, a bold text about the divinity of Jesus.

—Acts 18:24–28

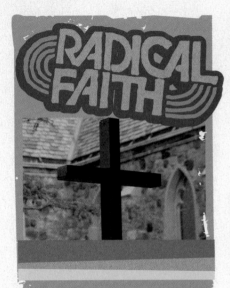

MATTHEW 16:24–26

At first glance, Jesus' words barely make sense: "If people want to follow me, they must give up the things they want. They must be willing even to give up their lives to follow me." But how could you ever mimic what Jesus did—and be willing to die for him? After all, he endured history's most grotesque form of execution, a practice now long extinct. Besides that, his death was one-of-a-kind, taking the blame for human sin and suffering the full penalty of every wrong that people have ever committed (1 Peter 3:18). So no believer can ever do exactly what Jesus did. What your Lord wants you to imitate, however, is his total devotion to God's purposes, the allegiance that caused him to ditch self-centered ambition and stick to God's plan. You take up the cross every time you deny your sinful desires, choosing right over wrong, good over evil, God's way over your way. That's what it means to follow him. If that cost sounds too high to pay, consider this: If you cling to your way of doing life, your dreams will slip through your fingers. If you trust and obey Jesus, you will gain real life.

care about the things of God, but only about the things people think are important."

²⁴Then Jesus said to his followers, "If people want to follow me, they must give up the things they want. They must be willing even to give up their lives to follow me. ²⁵Those who want to save their lives will give up true life, and those who give up their lives for me will have true life. ²⁶It is worthless to have the whole world if they lose their souls. They could never pay enough to buy back their souls. ²⁷The Son of Man will come again with his Father's glory and with his angels. At that time, he will reward them for what they have done. ²⁸I tell you the truth, some people standing here will see the Son of Man coming with his kingdom before they die."

JESUS TALKS WITH MOSES AND ELIJAH

17 Six days later, Jesus took Peter, James, and John, the brother of James, up on a high mountain by themselves. ²While they watched, Jesus' appearance was changed; his face became bright like the sun, and his clothes became white as light. ³Then Moses and Elijah[n] appeared to them, talking with Jesus.

⁴Peter said to Jesus, "Lord, it is good that we are here. If you want, I will put up three tents here—one for you, one for Moses, and one for Elijah."

⁵While Peter was talking, a bright cloud covered them. A voice came from the cloud and said, "This is my Son, whom I love, and I am very pleased with him. Listen to him!"

⁶When his followers heard the voice, they were so frightened they fell to the ground. ⁷But Jesus went to them and touched them and said, "Stand up. Don't be afraid." ⁸When they looked up, they saw Jesus was now alone.

⁹As they were coming down the mountain, Jesus commanded them not to tell anyone about what they had seen until the Son of Man had risen from the dead.

¹⁰Then his followers asked him, "Why do the teachers of the law say that Elijah must come first?"

¹¹Jesus answered, "They are right to say that Elijah is coming and that he will make everything the way it should be. ¹²But I tell you that Elijah has already come, and they did not recognize him. They did to him whatever they wanted to do. It will be the same with the Son of Man; those same people will make the Son of Man suffer." ¹³Then the followers understood that Jesus was talking about John the Baptist.

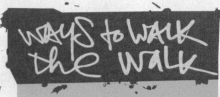

MATTHEW 16:13-20
WORD: Declare who Jesus is.
WALK IT: Wear your faith out in the open. It's sometimes easy to downplay the faith you have in Christ. Instead, let others know who he is and what he means to you.

JESUS HEALS A SICK BOY

¹⁴When Jesus and his followers came back to the crowd, a man came to Jesus and bowed before him. ¹⁵The man said, "Lord, have mercy on my son. He has epilepsy[n] and is suffering very much, because he often falls into the fire or into the water. ¹⁶I brought him to your followers, but they could not cure him."

¹⁷Jesus answered, "You people have no faith, and your lives are all wrong. How long must I put up with you? How long must I continue to be patient with you? Bring the boy here." ¹⁸Jesus commanded the demon inside the boy. Then the demon came out, and the boy was healed from that time on.

¹⁹The followers came to Jesus when he was alone and asked, "Why couldn't we force the demon out?"

²⁰Jesus answered, "Because your faith is too small. I tell you the truth, if your faith is as big as a mustard seed, you can say to this mountain, 'Move from here to there,' and it will move. All things will be possible for you. [²¹That kind of spirit comes out only if you use prayer and fasting.]"[n]

JESUS TALKS ABOUT HIS DEATH

²²While Jesus' followers were gathering in Galilee, he said to them, "The Son of Man will be handed over to people, ²³and they will kill him. But on the third day he will be raised from the dead." And the followers were filled with sadness.

JESUS TALKS ABOUT PAYING TAXES

²⁴When Jesus and his followers came to Capernaum, the men who collected the Temple tax came to Peter. They asked, "Does your teacher pay the Temple tax?"

 17:3 Moses and Elijah Two of the most important Jewish leaders in the past. God had given Moses the Law, and Elijah was an important prophet. 17:15 epilepsy A disease that causes a person sometimes to lose control of his body and maybe faint, shake strongly, or not be able to move. 17:21 That . . . fasting. Some Greek copies do not contain the bracketed text.

²⁵Peter answered, "Yes, Jesus pays the tax."

Peter went into the house, but before he could speak, Jesus said to him, "What do you think? The kings of the earth collect different kinds of taxes. But who pays the taxes—the king's children or others?"

²⁶Peter answered, "Other people pay the taxes."

Jesus said to Peter, "Then the children of the king don't have to pay taxes. ²⁷But we don't want to upset these tax collectors. So go to the lake and fish. After you catch the first fish, open its mouth and you will find a coin. Take that coin and give it to the tax collectors for you and me."

WHO IS THE GREATEST?

18 At that time the followers came to Jesus and asked, "Who is greatest in the kingdom of heaven?"

²Jesus called a little child to him and stood the child before his followers. ³Then he said, "I tell you the truth, you must change and become like little children. Otherwise, you will never enter the kingdom of heaven. ⁴The greatest person in the kingdom of heaven is the one who makes himself humble like this child.

⁵"Whoever accepts a child in my name accepts me. ⁶If one of these little children believes in me, and someone causes that child to sin, it would be better for that person to have a large stone tied around the neck and be drowned in the sea. ⁷How terrible for the people of the world because of the things that cause them to sin. Such things will happen, but how terrible for the one who causes them to happen! ⁸If your hand or your foot causes you to sin, cut it off and throw it away. It is better for you to lose part of your body and live forever than to have two hands and two feet and be thrown into the fire that burns forever. ⁹If your eye causes you to sin, take it out and throw it away. It is better for you to have only one eye and live forever than to have two eyes and be thrown into the fire of hell.

A LOST SHEEP

¹⁰"Be careful. Don't think these little children are worth nothing. I tell you that they have angels in heaven who are always with my Father in heaven. [¹¹The Son of Man came to save lost people.]ⁿ

¹²"If a man has a hundred sheep but one of the sheep gets lost, he will leave the other ninety-nine on the hill and go to look for the lost sheep. ¹³I tell you the truth, if he finds it he is happier about that one sheep than about the ninety-nine that were never lost. ¹⁴In the same way, your Father in heaven does not want any of these little children to be lost.

Relationships

"Jesus answered, 'Surely you have read in the Scriptures: When God made the world, he made them male and female'" (Matthew 19:4). It seems simplistic, but it's a truth we often forget: God made men and women completely different. And our differences extend beyond terminology and anatomy—men and women think differently, feel differently, interact differently. This key principle is easy to forget in the midst of your relationships with girls, but you have to remember that they're way different from you. Try to approach them on their terms instead of your own, and you'll be well on your way toward understanding each other.

fight the fight

Matthew 6:25–30

When your grandparents were youngsters, cable television was in its infancy and most homes had only one television instead of one set per room. The Internet was still a figment of someone's imagination. But in some ways, things haven't changed a bit. People back then worried about whether they had enough food, fashionable clothes, a nice house, and the newest car on the block. That is exactly what Jesus tells us to avoid. We don't need to be concerned about such worldly needs. Our Father knows we need food, clothing, and shelter. So don't make running after material goods the priority of your life.

 18:11 The . . . people. Some Greek copies do not contain the bracketed text.

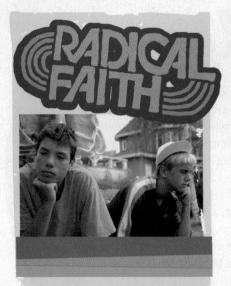

RADICAL FAITH

MATTHEW 18:15-17

Jesus doesn't say, "When someone wrongs you, school him with a good thrashing." He tells you to talk it out. But he doesn't just repeat the advice your mama has been giving you since you were a toddler, saying, "Just use your words." Instead, Jesus sets out a calm step-by-step process for repairing shredded relationships. When you feel wronged, you don't punch your friend's lights out. You don't run off and tell the world. You also don't play tough by stuffing your hurt inside and acting like everything's okay. You go straight to the source of your wound and tell that person why you're irate. If that doesn't work, you take a witness or two to back up your claim and help referee the dispute. Then you pull in an authority figure like a teacher, pastor, or parent. And if none of those steps brings you back together, then you spend some time apart. You don't have to stay in a spot where you get used again. One more thing: whether or not you can make things right with your friend, it's still your job to forgive.

WHEN A PERSON SINS AGAINST YOU

15"If your fellow believer sins against you,[n] go and tell him in private what he did wrong. If he listens to you, you have helped that person to be your brother or sister again. 16But if he refuses to listen, go to him again and take one or two other people with you. 'Every case may be proved by two or three witnesses.'[n] 17If he refuses to listen to them, tell the church. If he refuses to listen to the church, then treat him like a person who does not believe in God or like a tax collector.

18"I tell you the truth, the things you don't allow on earth will be the things God does not allow. And the things you allow on earth will be the things that God allows.

19"Also, I tell you that if two of you on earth agree about something and pray for it, it will be done for you by my Father in heaven. 20This is true because if two or three people come together in my name, I am there with them."

AN UNFORGIVING SERVANT

21Then Peter came to Jesus and asked, "Lord, when my fellow believer sins against me, how many times must I forgive him? Should I forgive him as many as seven times?"

22Jesus answered, "I tell you, you must forgive him more than seven times. You must forgive him even if he wrongs you seventy times seven.

23"The kingdom of heaven is like a king who decided to collect the money his servants owed him. 24When the king began to collect his money, a servant who owed him several million dollars was brought to him. 25But the servant did not have enough money to pay his master, the king. So the master ordered that everything the servant owned should be sold, even the servant's wife and children. Then the money would be used to pay the king what the servant owed.

26"But the servant fell on his knees and begged, 'Be patient with me, and I will pay you everything I owe.' 27The master felt sorry for his servant and told him he did not have to pay it back. Then he let the servant go free.

28"Later, that same servant found another servant who owed him a few dollars. The servant grabbed him around the neck and said, 'Pay me the money you owe me!'

29"The other servant fell on his knees and begged him, 'Be patient with me, and I will pay you everything I owe.'

30"But the first servant refused to be patient. He threw the other servant into prison until he could pay everything he owed. 31When the other servants saw what had hap-

WAYS to WALK the WALK

MATTHEW 18:15-17
WORD: Confront others when they wrong you.
WALK IT: Restoration of a broken relationship is a process, but it is up to you to pursue that restoration. The next time you're wronged, take every possible step to restore the relationship.

pened, they were very sorry. So they went and told their master all that had happened.

32"Then the master called his servant in and said, 'You evil servant! Because you begged me to forget what you owed, I told you that you did not have to pay anything. 33You should have showed mercy to that other servant, just as I showed mercy to you.' 34The master was very angry and put the servant in prison to be punished until he could pay everything he owed.

35"This king did what my heavenly Father will do to you if you do not forgive your brother or sister from your heart."

JESUS TEACHES ABOUT DIVORCE

19 After Jesus said all these things, he left Galilee and went into the area of Judea on the other side of the Jordan River. 2Large crowds followed him, and he healed them there.

3Some Pharisees came to Jesus and tried to trick him. They asked, "Is it right for a man to divorce his wife for any reason he chooses?"

4Jesus answered, "Surely you have read in the Scriptures: When God made the world, 'he made them male and female.'[n] 5And God said, 'So a man will leave his father and mother and be united with his wife, and the two will become one body.'[n] 6So there are not two, but one. God has joined the two together, so no one should separate them."

7The Pharisees asked, "Why then did Moses give a command for a man to divorce his wife by giving her divorce papers?"

8Jesus answered, "Moses allowed you to divorce your wives because you refused to accept God's teaching, but divorce was not allowed in the beginning. 9I tell you that anyone who divorces his wife and marries another

18:15 against you Some Greek copies do not have "against you." 18:16 'Every . . . witnesses.' Quotation from Deuteronomy 19:15. 19:4 'he made . . . female' Quotation from Genesis 1:27 or 5:2. 19:5 'So . . . body.' Quotation from Genesis 2:24.

26

woman is guilty of adultery.[n] The only reason for a man to divorce his wife is if his wife has sexual relations with another man."

[10]The followers said to him, "If that is the only reason a man can divorce his wife, it is better not to marry."

[11]Jesus answered, "Not everyone can accept this teaching, but God has made some able to accept it. [12]There are different reasons why some men cannot marry. Some men were born without the ability to become fathers. Others were made that way later in life by other people. And some men have given up marriage because of the kingdom of heaven. But the person who can marry should accept this teaching about marriage."[n]

JESUS WELCOMES CHILDREN

[13]Then the people brought their little children to Jesus so he could put his hands on them[n] and pray for them. His followers told them to stop, [14]but Jesus said, "Let the little children come to me. Don't stop them, because the kingdom of heaven belongs to people who are like these children." [15]After Jesus put his hands on the children, he left there.

A RICH YOUNG MAN'S QUESTION

[16]A man came to Jesus and asked, "Teacher, what good thing must I do to have life forever?"

[17]Jesus answered, "Why do you ask me

GUARD YOUR HEART

As a teenager, it's easy to let your emotions rule your life. But with so much of your life yet to be lived, don't sell yourself short by getting into a serious relationship with a girl when you are too young. In due time, God will show you his perfect will for your life, but don't rush him.

about what is good? Only God is good. But if you want to have life forever, obey the commands."

[18]The man asked, "Which commands?"

Jesus answered, " 'You must not murder anyone; you must not be guilty of adultery; you must not steal; you must not tell lies about your neighbor; [19]honor your father and mother;[n] and love your neighbor as you love yourself.' "[n]

[20]The young man said, "I have obeyed all these things. What else do I need to do?"

[21]Jesus answered, "If you want to be perfect, then go and sell your possessions and give the money to the poor. If you do this, you will have treasure in heaven. Then come and follow me."

[22]But when the young man heard this, he left sorrowfully, because he was rich.

[23]Then Jesus said to his followers, "I tell you the truth, it will be hard for a rich person to enter the kingdom of heaven. [24]Yes, I tell you that it is easier for a camel to go through the eye of a needle than for a rich person to enter the kingdom of God."

[25]When Jesus' followers heard this, they were very surprised and asked, "Then who can be saved?"

[26]Jesus looked at them and said, "For people this is impossible, but for God all things are possible."

[27]Peter said to Jesus, "Look, we have left everything and followed you. So what will we have?"

[28]Jesus said to them, "I tell you the truth, when the age to come has arrived, the Son of Man will sit on his great throne. All of you who followed me will also sit on twelve thrones, judging the twelve tribes of Israel. [29]And all those who have left houses, brothers, sisters,

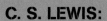

*REVIEWS BOOKS

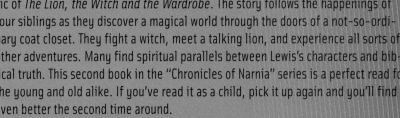

C. S. LEWIS:
THE LION, THE WITCH AND THE WARDROBE

Lewis's creative storytelling and imaginary genius comes to life in the fictional classic of *The Lion, the Witch and the Wardrobe*. The story follows the happenings of four siblings as they discover a magical world through the doors of a not-so-ordinary coat closet. They fight a witch, meet a talking lion, and experience all sorts of other adventures. Many find spiritual parallels between Lewis's characters and biblical truth. This second book in the "Chronicles of Narnia" series is a perfect read for the young and old alike. If you've read it as a child, pick it up again and you'll find it even better the second time around.

WHY IT ROCKS:

A SUPER STORY WITH CHARACTERS WHO COME TO LIFE.

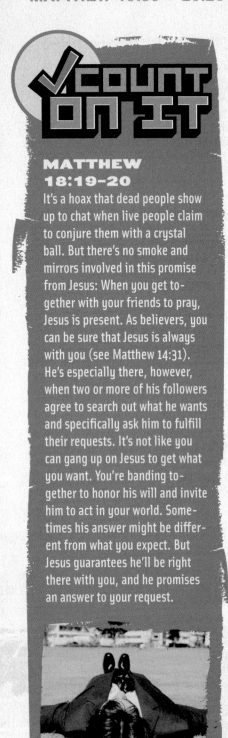

COUNT ON IT

MATTHEW 18:19-20

It's a hoax that dead people show up to chat when live people claim to conjure them with a crystal ball. But there's no smoke and mirrors involved in this promise from Jesus: When you get together with your friends to pray, Jesus is present. As believers, you can be sure that Jesus is always with you (see Matthew 14:31). He's especially there, however, when two or more of his followers agree to search out what he wants and specifically ask him to fulfill their requests. It's not like you can gang up on Jesus to get what you want. You're banding together to honor his will and invite him to act in your world. Sometimes his answer might be different from what you expect. But Jesus guarantees he'll be right there with you, and he promises an answer to your request.

A STORY ABOUT WORKERS

20 "The kingdom of heaven is like a person who owned some land. One morning, he went out very early to hire some people to work in his vineyard. [2]The man agreed to pay the workers one coin[n] for working that day. Then he sent them into the vineyard to work. [3]About nine o'clock the man went to the marketplace and saw some other people standing there, doing nothing. [4]So he said to them, 'If you go and work in my vineyard, I will pay you what your work is worth.' [5]So they went to work in the vineyard. The man went out again about twelve o'clock and three o'clock and did the same thing. [6]About five o'clock the man went to the marketplace again and saw others standing there. He asked them, 'Why did you stand here all day doing nothing?' [7]They answered, 'No one gave us a job.' The man said to them, 'Then you can go and work in my vineyard.'

[8]"At the end of the day, the owner of the vineyard said to the boss of all the workers, 'Call the workers and pay them. Start with the last people I hired and end with those I hired first.'

[9]"When the workers who were hired at five o'clock came to get their pay, each received one coin. [10]When the workers who were hired first came to get their pay, they thought they would be paid more than the others. But each one of them also received one coin. [11]When they got their coin, they complained to the man who owned the land. [12]They said, 'Those people were hired last and worked only one hour. But you paid them the same as you paid us who worked hard all day in the hot sun.' [13]But the man who owned the vineyard said to one of those workers, 'Friend, I am being fair to you. You agreed to work for one coin. [14]So take your pay and go. I want to give the man who was hired last the same pay that I gave you. [15]I can do what I want with my own money. Are you jealous because I am good to those people?'

[16]"So those who are last now will someday be first, and those who are first now will someday be last."

JESUS TALKS ABOUT HIS OWN DEATH

[17]While Jesus was going to Jerusalem, he took his twelve followers aside privately and said to them, [18]"Look, we are going to Jerusalem. The Son of Man will be turned over to the leading priests and the teachers of the law, and they will say that he must die. [19]They will give the Son of Man to the non-Jewish people to laugh at him and beat him with whips

and crucify him. But on the third day, he will be raised to life again."

A MOTHER ASKS JESUS A FAVOR

[20]Then the wife of Zebedee came to Jesus with her sons. She bowed before him and asked him to do something for her.

[21]Jesus asked, "What do you want?"

She said, "Promise that one of my sons will sit at your right side and the other will sit at your left side in your kingdom."

[22]But Jesus said, "You don't understand what you are asking. Can you drink the cup that I am about to drink?"[n]

The sons answered, "Yes, we can."

[23]Jesus said to them, "You will drink from my cup. But I cannot choose who will sit at my right or my left; those places belong to those for whom my Father has prepared them."

[24]When the other ten followers heard this, they were angry with the two brothers.

[25]Jesus called all the followers together and said, "You know that the rulers of the non-Jewish people love to show their power over the people. And their important leaders love to use all their authority. [26]But it should not be that

TOP TEN 10

random ways to fly

1. Go skydiving.
2. Flip on a trampoline.
3. Go hang gliding.
4. Jump off a diving board.
5. Go bungee jumping.
6. Lease a hot air balloon.
7. Go parasailing.
8. Cruise in a helicopter.
9. Go pole vaulting.
10. Leap in the air.

father, mother,[n] children, or farms to follow me will get much more than they left, and they will have life forever. [30]Many who are first now will be last in the future. And many who are last now will be first in the future.

 19:29 mother Some Greek copies continue, "or wife." **20:2 coin** A Roman denarius. One coin was the average pay for one day's work. **20:22 drink . . . drink** Jesus used the idea of drinking from a cup to ask if they could accept the same terrible things that would happen to him.

way among you. Whoever wants to become great among you must serve the rest of you like a servant. [27] Whoever wants to become first among you must serve the rest of you like a slave. [28] In the same way, the Son of Man did not come to be served. He came to serve others and to give his life as a ransom for many people."

JESUS HEALS TWO BLIND MEN

[29] When Jesus and his followers were leaving Jericho, a great many people followed him. [30] Two blind men sitting by the road heard that Jesus was going by, so they shouted, "Lord, Son of David, have mercy on us!"

[31] The people warned the blind men to be quiet, but they shouted even more, "Lord, Son of David, have mercy on us!"

[32] Jesus stopped and said to the blind men, "What do you want me to do for you?"

[33] They answered, "Lord, we want to see."

[34] Jesus felt sorry for the blind men and touched their eyes, and at once they could see. Then they followed Jesus.

JESUS ENTERS JERUSALEM AS A KING

21 As Jesus and his followers were coming closer to Jerusalem, they stopped at Bethphage at the hill called the Mount of Olives. From there Jesus sent two of his followers [2] and said to them, "Go to the town you can see there. When you enter it, you will quickly find a donkey tied there with its colt. Untie them and bring them to me. [3] If anyone asks you why you are taking the donkeys, say that the Master needs them, and he will send them at once."

[4] This was to bring about what the prophet had said:

[5] "Tell the people of Jerusalem,
  'Your king is coming to you.
He is gentle and riding on a donkey,
  on the colt of a donkey.' "

Isaiah 62:11; Zechariah 9:9

[6] The followers went and did what Jesus told them to do. [7] They brought the donkey and the colt to Jesus and laid their coats on them, and Jesus sat on them. [8] Many people spread their coats on the road. Others cut branches from the trees and spread them on the road. [9] The people were walking ahead of Jesus and behind him, shouting,

"Praise[n] to the Son of David!
God bless the One who comes in the name
  of the Lord!   *Psalm 118:26*
Praise to God in heaven!"

[10] When Jesus entered Jerusalem, all the city was filled with excitement. The people asked, "Who is this man?"

[11] The crowd said, "This man is Jesus, the prophet from the town of Nazareth in Galilee."

JESUS GOES TO THE TEMPLE

[12] Jesus went into the Temple and threw out all the people who were buying and selling there. He turned over the tables of those who were exchanging different kinds of money, and he upset the benches of those who were selling doves. [13] Jesus said to all the people there, "It is written in the Scriptures, 'My Temple will be called a house for prayer.'[n] But you are changing it into a 'hideout for robbers.' "[n]

[14] The blind and crippled people came to Jesus in the Temple, and he healed them. [15] The leading priests and the teachers of the law saw that Jesus was doing wonderful things and that the children were praising him in the Temple, saying, "Praise[n] to the Son of David." All these things made the priests and the teachers of the law very angry.

[16] They asked Jesus, "Do you hear the things these children are saying?"

Jesus answered, "Yes. Haven't you read in the Scriptures, 'You have taught children and babies to sing praises'?"[n]

[17] Then Jesus left and went out of the city to Bethany, where he spent the night.

THE POWER OF FAITH

[18] Early the next morning, as Jesus was going back to the city, he became hungry.

fight the fight

Matthew 20:25-28

Before what was likely the last fight of Mike Tyson's career, he bragged about how he was going to easily whip his opponent. Instead, the former heavyweight champion failed to answer the bell for the final round. You could exchange names and circumstances and still come up with plenty of examples of macho men who bragged they were the toughest guys alive. But Christ spoke of a better way. Rather than trying to be the king of the hill, he said those who want to be great should serve others. No matter how loudly someone boasts, remember the perfect role model set a much different example.

21:9, 15 Praise Literally, "Hosanna," a Hebrew word used at first in praying to God for help. At this time it was probably a shout of joy used in praising God or his Messiah.   21:13 'My Temple . . . prayer.' Quotation from Isaiah 56:7.   21:13 'hideout for robbers' Quotation from Jeremiah 7:11.   21:16 'You . . . praises.' Quotation from the Septuagint (Greek) version of Psalm 8:2.

GUARD YOUR HEART

Just because you're a teenager doesn't mean you are incapable of falling in love. However, just because you feel love for a young woman doesn't necessarily mean that the timing is right. Put those desires into the hands of God, and he will give you the wisdom to know when to awaken love for a lifetime.

¹⁹Seeing a fig tree beside the road, Jesus went to it, but there were no figs on the tree, only leaves. So Jesus said to the tree, "You will never again have fruit." The tree immediately dried up.

²⁰When his followers saw this, they were amazed. They asked, "How did the fig tree dry up so quickly?"

²¹Jesus answered, "I tell you the truth, if you have faith and do not doubt, you will be able to do what I did to this tree and even more. You will be able to say to this mountain, 'Go, fall into the sea.' And if you have faith, it will happen. ²²If you believe, you will get anything you ask for in prayer."

LEADERS DOUBT JESUS' AUTHORITY

²³Jesus went to the Temple, and while he was teaching there, the leading priests and the elders of the people came to him. They said, "What authority do you have to do these things? Who gave you this authority?"

²⁴Jesus answered, "I also will ask you a question. If you answer me, then I will tell you what authority I have to do these things. ²⁵Tell me: When John baptized people, did that come from God or just from other people?"

They argued about Jesus' question, saying, "If we answer, 'John's baptism was from God,' Jesus will say, 'Then why didn't you believe him?' ²⁶But if we say, 'It was from people,' we are afraid of what the crowd will do because they all believe that John was a prophet."

²⁷So they answered Jesus, "We don't know."

Jesus said to them, "Then I won't tell you what authority I have to do these things.

A STORY ABOUT TWO SONS

²⁸"Tell me what you think about this: A man had two sons. He went to the first son and said, 'Son, go and work today in my vineyard.' ²⁹The son answered, 'I will not go.' But later the son changed his mind and went. ³⁰Then the father went to the other son and said, 'Son, go and work today in my vineyard.' The son answered, 'Yes, sir, I will go and work,' but he did not go. ³¹Which of the two sons obeyed his father?"

The priests and leaders answered, "The first son."

Jesus said to them, "I tell you the truth, the tax collectors and the prostitutes will enter the kingdom of God before you do. ³²John came to show you the right way to live. You did not believe him, but the tax collectors and prostitutes believed him. Even after seeing this, you still refused to change your ways and believe him.

A STORY ABOUT GOD'S SON

³³"Listen to this story: There was a man who owned a vineyard. He put a wall around it and dug a hole for a winepress and built a tower. Then he leased the land to some farmers and left for a trip. ³⁴When it was time for the grapes to be picked, he sent his servants to the farmers to get his share of the grapes. ³⁵But the farmers grabbed the servants, beat one, killed another, and then killed a third servant with stones. ³⁶So the man sent some other servants to the farmers, even more than he sent the first time. But the farmers did the same thing to the servants that they had done before. ³⁷So the man decided to send his son to the farmers. He said, 'They will respect my son.' ³⁸But when the farmers saw the son, they said to each other, 'This son will inherit the vineyard. If we kill him, it will be ours!' ³⁹Then the farmers grabbed the son, threw him out of the vineyard, and killed him. ⁴⁰So what will the owner of the vineyard do to these farmers when he comes?"

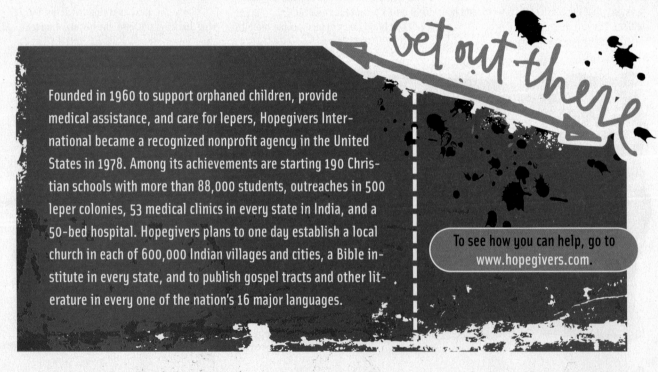

Get out there

Founded in 1960 to support orphaned children, provide medical assistance, and care for lepers, Hopegivers International became a recognized nonprofit agency in the United States in 1978. Among its achievements are starting 190 Christian schools with more than 88,000 students, outreaches in 500 leper colonies, 53 medical clinics in every state in India, and a 50-bed hospital. Hopegivers plans to one day establish a local church in each of 600,000 Indian villages and cities, a Bible institute in every state, and to publish gospel tracts and other literature in every one of the nation's 16 major languages.

To see how you can help, go to www.hopegivers.com.

[41]The priests and leaders said, "He will surely kill those evil men. Then he will lease the vineyard to some other farmers who will give him his share of the crop at harvest time."

[42]Jesus said to them, "Surely you have read this in the Scriptures:

'The stone that the builders rejected
    became the cornerstone.
The Lord did this,
    and it is wonderful to us.'
                    Psalm 118:22–23

[43]"So I tell you that the kingdom of God will be taken away from you and given to people who do the things God wants in his kingdom. [44]The person who falls on this stone will be broken, and on whomever that stone falls, that person will be crushed."[n]

[45]When the leading priests and the Pharisees heard these stories, they knew Jesus was talking about them. [46]They wanted to arrest him, but they were afraid of the people, because the people believed that Jesus was a prophet.

A STORY ABOUT A WEDDING FEAST

22 Jesus again used stories to teach them. He said, [2]"The kingdom of heaven is like a king who prepared a wedding feast for his son. [3]The king invited some people to the feast. When the feast was ready, the king sent his servants to tell the people, but they refused to come.

[4]"Then the king sent other servants, saying, 'Tell those who have been invited that my feast is ready. I have killed my best bulls and calves for the dinner, and everything is ready. Come to the wedding feast.'

[5]"But the people refused to listen to the servants and left to do other things. One went to work in his field, and another went to his business. [6]Some of the other people grabbed the servants, beat them, and killed them. [7]The king was furious and sent his army to kill the murderers and burn their city.

[8]"After that, the king said to his servants, 'The wedding feast is ready. I invited those people, but they were not worthy to come. [9]So go to the street corners and invite everyone you find to come to my feast.' [10]So the servants went into the streets and gathered all the people they could find, both good and bad. And the wedding hall was filled with guests.

[11]"When the king came in to see the guests, he saw a man who was not dressed for a wedding. [12]The king said, 'Friend, how were you allowed to come in here? You are not dressed for a wedding.' But the man said nothing. [13]So the king told some servants, 'Tie this man's hands and feet. Throw him out into the darkness, where people will cry and grind their teeth with pain.'

[14]"Yes, many are invited, but only a few are chosen."

IS IT RIGHT TO PAY TAXES OR NOT?

[15]Then the Pharisees left that place and made plans to trap Jesus in saying something wrong. [16]They sent some of their own followers and some people from the group called Herodians.[n] They said, "Teacher, we know that you are an honest man and that you teach the truth about God's way. You are not afraid of what other people think about you, because you pay no attention to who they are. [17]So tell us what you think. Is it right to pay taxes to Caesar or not?"

[18]But knowing that these leaders were trying to trick him, Jesus said, "You hypocrites! Why are you trying to trap me? [19]Show me a coin used for paying the tax." So the men showed him a coin.[n] [20]Then Jesus asked, "Whose image and name are on the coin?"

[21]The men answered, "Caesar's."

Then Jesus said to them, "Give to Caesar the things that are Caesar's, and give to God the things that are God's."

[22]When the men heard what Jesus said, they were amazed and left him and went away.

SOME SADDUCEES TRY TO TRICK JESUS

[23]That same day some Sadducees came to Jesus and asked him a question. (Sadducees believed that people would not rise from the dead.) [24]They said, "Teacher, Moses said if a married man dies without having children, his brother must marry the widow and have children for him. [25]Once there were seven brothers among us. The first one married and died. Since he had no children, his brother married the widow. [26]Then the second brother also died. The same thing happened to the third brother and all the other brothers. [27]Finally, the woman died. [28]Since all seven men had married her, when people rise from the dead, whose wife will she be?"

[29]Jesus answered, "You don't understand, because you don't know what the Scriptures say, and you don't know about the power of God. [30]When people rise from the dead, they will not marry, nor will they be given to someone to marry. They will be like the angels in heaven. [31]Surely you have read what God said to you about rising from the dead. [32]God said, 'I am the God of Abraham, the God of Isaac, and the God of Jacob.'[n] God is the God of the living, not the dead."

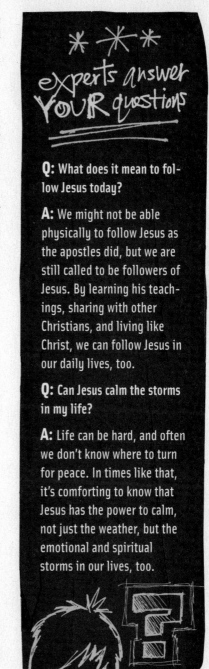

experts answer YOUR questions

Q: What does it mean to follow Jesus today?

A: We might not be able physically to follow Jesus as the apostles did, but we are still called to be followers of Jesus. By learning his teachings, sharing with other Christians, and living like Christ, we can follow Jesus in our daily lives, too.

Q: Can Jesus calm the storms in my life?

A: Life can be hard, and often we don't know where to turn for peace. In times like that, it's comforting to know that Jesus has the power to calm, not just the weather, but the emotional and spiritual storms in our lives, too.

[33]When the people heard this, they were amazed at Jesus' teaching.

THE MOST IMPORTANT COMMAND

[34]When the Pharisees learned that the Sadducees could not argue with Jesus' answers to them, the Pharisees met together. [35]One Pharisee, who was an expert on the law of Moses, asked Jesus this question to test him: [36]"Teacher, which command in the law is the most important?"

21:44 The . . . crushed. Some Greek copies do not have verse 44.　**22:16 Herodians** A political group that followed Herod and his family.　**22:19 coin** A Roman denarius. One coin was the average pay for one day's work.　**22:32 I am . . . Jacob.** Quotation from Exodus 3:6.

31

MATTHEW 22:37–39

Mastering the mechanics of following Jesus might feel like you're trying to solve a math problem that locks up your brain every time. That is, until you realize Jesus boils down his expectations to two key points: "Love the Lord your God with all your heart, all your soul, and all your mind," and "Love your neighbor as you love yourself." When Jesus says you should love God above all else, he isn't dissecting your innards into heart, soul, and mind. He's telling you to love God with your whole being, making nothing in life more important than him. When he says to love your neighbor just as you love yourself, he certainly isn't promoting self-centeredness. He figures that you already know how to care for yourself, so if you treat others as well as you treat yourself, you will keep his command. When you need a re-minder of what it means to live all-out for God, those are the two items to keep in mind. They sum up every other *do* or *don't* that God wants you to obey.

[37]Jesus answered, " 'Love the Lord your God with all your heart, all your soul, and all your mind.'[n] [38]This is the first and most important command. [39]And the second command is like the first: 'Love your neighbor as you love yourself.'[n] [40]All the law and the writings of the prophets depend on these two commands."

JESUS QUESTIONS THE PHARISEES

[41]While the Pharisees were together, Jesus asked them, [42]"What do you think about the Christ? Whose son is he?"

They answered, "The Christ is the Son of David."

[43]Then Jesus said to them, "Then why did David call him 'Lord'? David, speaking by the power of the Holy Spirit, said,

[44]"The Lord said to my Lord,
  'Sit by me at my right side,
    until I put your enemies under your
      control.' '   *Psalm 110:1*

[45]David calls the Christ 'Lord,' so how can the Christ be his son?"

[46]None of the Pharisees could answer Jesus' question, and after that day no one was brave enough to ask him any more questions.

JESUS ACCUSES SOME LEADERS

23 Then Jesus said to the crowds and to his followers, [2]"The teachers of the law and the Pharisees have the authority to tell you what the law of Moses says. [3]So you should obey and follow whatever they tell you, but their lives are not good examples for you to follow. They tell you to do things, but they themselves don't do them. [4]They make strict rules and try to force people to obey them, but they are unwilling to help those who struggle under the weight of their rules.

[5]"They do good things so that other people will see them. They enlarge the little boxes[n] holding Scriptures that they wear, and they make their special prayer clothes very long. [6]Those Pharisees and teachers of the law love to have the most important seats at feasts and in the synagogues. [7]They love people to greet them with respect in the marketplaces, and they love to have people call them 'Teacher.'

[8]"But you must not be called 'Teacher,' because you have only one Teacher, and you are all brothers and sisters together. [9]And don't call any person on earth 'Father,' because you have one Father, who is in heaven. [10]And you should not be called 'Master,' because you have only one Master, the Christ. [11]Whoever is your servant is the greatest among you. [12]Whoever makes himself great will be made humble.

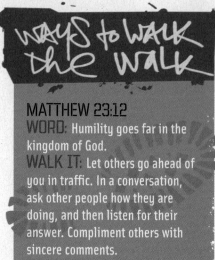

MATTHEW 23:12
WORD: Humility goes far in the kingdom of God.
WALK IT: Let others go ahead of you in traffic. In a conversation, ask other people how they are doing, and then listen for their answer. Compliment others with sincere comments.

Whoever makes himself humble will be made great.

[13]"How terrible for you, teachers of the law and Pharisees! You are hypocrites! You close the door for people to enter the kingdom of heaven. You yourselves don't enter, and you stop others who are trying to enter. [[14]How terrible for you, teachers of the law and Pharisees. You are hypocrites. You take away widows' houses, and you say long prayers so that people will notice you. So you will have a worse punishment.][n]

[15]"How terrible for you, teachers of the law and Pharisees! You are hypocrites! You travel across land and sea to find one person who will change to your ways. When you find that person, you make him more fit for hell than you are.

[16]"How terrible for you! You guide the people, but you are blind. You say, 'If people swear by the Temple when they make a promise, that means nothing. But if they swear by the gold that is in the Temple, they must keep that promise.' [17]You are blind fools! Which is greater: the gold or the Temple that makes that gold holy? [18]And you say, 'If people swear by the altar when they make a promise, that means nothing. But if they swear by the gift on the altar, they must keep that promise.' [19]You are blind! Which is greater: the gift or the altar that makes the gift holy? [20]The person who swears by the altar is really using the altar and also everything on the altar. [21]And the person who swears by the Temple is really using the Temple and also everything in the Temple. [22]The person who swears by heaven is also using God's throne and the One who sits on that throne.

[23]"How terrible for you, teachers of the law

22:37 'Love . . . mind.' Quotation from Deuteronomy 6:5. **22:39** 'Love . . . yourself.' Quotation from Leviticus 19:18. **23:5 boxes** Small leather boxes containing four important Scriptures. Some Jews tied these to their foreheads and left arms, probably to show they were very religious. **23:14 How . . . punishment.** Some Greek copies do not contain the bracketed text.

32

and Pharisees! You are hypocrites! You give to God one-tenth of everything you earn—even your mint, dill, and cumin.ⁿ But you don't obey the really important teachings of the law—justice, mercy, and being loyal. These are the things you should do, as well as those other things. ²⁴You guide the people, but you are blind! You are like a person who picks a fly out of a drink and then swallows a camel!ⁿ

²⁵"How terrible for you, teachers of the law and Pharisees! You are hypocrites! You wash the outside of your cups and dishes, but inside they are full of things you got by cheating others and by pleasing only yourselves. ²⁶Pharisees, you are blind! First make the inside of the cup clean, and then the outside of the cup can be truly clean.

²⁷"How terrible for you, teachers of the law and Pharisees! You are hypocrites! You are like tombs that are painted white. Outside, those tombs look fine, but inside, they are full of the bones of dead people and all kinds of unclean things. ²⁸It is the same with you. People look at you and think you are good, but on the inside you are full of hypocrisy and evil.

²⁹"How terrible for you, teachers of the law and Pharisees! You are hypocrites! You build tombs for the prophets, and you show honor to the graves of those who lived good lives. ³⁰You say, 'If we had lived during the time of our ancestors, we would not have helped them kill the prophets.' ³¹But you give proof that you are descendants of those who murdered the prophets. ³²And you will complete the sin that your ancestors started.

³³"You are snakes! A family of poisonous snakes! How are you going to escape God's judgment? ³⁴So I tell you this: I am sending to you prophets and wise men and teachers. Some of them you will kill and crucify. Some of them you will beat in your synagogues and chase from town to town. ³⁵So you will be guilty for the death of all the good people who have been killed on earth—from the murder of that good man Abel to the murder of Zechariahⁿ son of Berakiah, whom you murdered between the Temple and the altar. ³⁶I tell you the truth, all of these things will happen to you people who are living now.

JESUS FEELS SORRY FOR JERUSALEM

³⁷"Jerusalem, Jerusalem! You kill the prophets and stone to death those who are sent to you. Many times I wanted to gather your people as a hen gathers her chicks under her wings, but you did not let me. ³⁸Now your house will be left completely empty. ³⁹I tell you, you will not see me again until that time when you will say, 'God bless the One who comes in the name of the Lord.' "ⁿ

THE TEMPLE WILL BE DESTROYED

24 As Jesus left the Temple and was walking away, his followers came up to show him the Temple's buildings. ²Jesus asked, "Do you see all these buildings? I tell you the truth, not one stone will be left on another. Every stone will be thrown down to the ground."

³Later, as Jesus was sitting on the Mount of Olives, his followers came to be alone with him. They said, "Tell us, when will these things happen? And what will be the sign that it is time for you to come again and for this age to end?"

⁴Jesus answered, "Be careful that no one fools you. ⁵Many will come in my name, saying, 'I am the Christ,' and they will fool many people. ⁶You will hear about wars and stories of wars that are coming, but don't be afraid. These things must happen before the end comes. ⁷Nations will fight against other nations; kingdoms will fight against other kingdoms. There will be times when there is no food for people to eat, and there will be earthquakes in different places. ⁸These things are like the first pains when something new is about to be born.

⁹"Then people will arrest you, hand you over to be hurt, and kill you. They will hate

Do's AND Don'ts

DO study hard for good grades.

DO concentrate while doing homework.

DO get to school on time.

DO respect your teachers.

DON'T cram for examinations.

DON'T copy other people's work.

DON'T cut classes to be with friends.

DON'T think that school doesn't matter.

Extras:

How to Throw a Fastball

There's no practical use for it, but it's still nice to know how to throw a steamer across the plate. To get a slight rise on your fastball, grip the ball with your index and middle fingers about a half-inch apart, going across the widest point of the seams. If you want the pitch to sink slightly, use the same grip, but at the narrowest point of the seams. Go into your windup to gain power, and throw the ball hard, taking care not to damage your arm in the process. Keep control over the ball by releasing it from your fingertips, then follow your body's natural motion all the way through and watch as the batter swings and misses. It isn't a skill you can develop in a day, but through consistent practice, you'll get there. Consistency counts with Christ, too. Be sure to follow through with your commitments to him, and you'll strike out the enemy every time.

23:23 **mint, dill, and cumin** Small plants grown in gardens and used for spices. Only very religious people would be careful enough to give a tenth of these plants.   23:24 **You . . . camel!** Meaning, "You worry about the smallest mistakes but commit the biggest sin."   23:35 **Abel . . . Zechariah** In the order of the books of the Hebrew Old Testament, the first and last men to be murdered.   23:39 **'God . . . Lord.'** Quotation from Psalm 118:26.

COUNT ON IT

MATTHEW 24:30

After the Resurrection—when Jesus rose from the dead—he ascended into the clouds as his followers watched (Acts 1:9). Before he left, he said he wasn't going away forever. He promised to return. If he seems slow to show up, it's because he's giving the human race time to abandon evil and become friends with him. But rest assured, no one will miss his return. His stunning appearance will cause everyone on the planet to shout out. Jesus will again appear in the clouds, robed in strength and awesome power. His angels will swarm the earth and gather his people. The big question is whether or not you are ready at any time for his return, because he promises not only paradise for those who believe in him (Matthew 25:34), but also punishment for all those who oppose him (Matthew 25:41).

you because you believe in me. ¹⁰At that time, many will lose their faith, and they will turn against each other and hate each other. ¹¹Many false prophets will come and cause many people to believe lies. ¹²There will be more and more evil in the world, so most people will stop showing their love for each other. ¹³But those people who keep their faith until the end will be saved. ¹⁴The Good News about God's kingdom will be preached in all the world, to every nation. Then the end will come.

¹⁵"Daniel the prophet spoke about 'a blasphemous object that brings destruction.'ⁿ You will see this standing in the holy place." (You who read this should understand what it means.) ¹⁶"At that time, the people in Judea should run away to the mountains. ¹⁷If people are on the roofsⁿ of their houses, they must not go down to get anything out of their houses. ¹⁸If people are in the fields, they must not go back to get their coats. ¹⁹At that time, how terrible it will be for women who are pregnant or have nursing babies! ²⁰Pray that it will not be winter or a Sabbath day when these things happen and you have to run away, ²¹because at that time there will be much trouble. There will be more trouble than there has ever been since the beginning of the world until now, and nothing as bad will ever happen again. ²²God has decided to make that terrible time short. Otherwise, no one would go on living. But God will make that time short to help the people he has chosen. ²³At that time, someone might say to you, 'Look, there is the Christ!' Or another person might say, 'There he is!' But don't believe them. ²⁴False Christs and false prophets will come and perform great wonders and miracles. They will try to fool even the people God has chosen, if that is possible. ²⁵Now I have warned you about this before it happens.

²⁶"If people tell you, 'The Christ is in the desert,' don't go there. If they say, 'The Christ is in the inner room,' don't believe it. ²⁷When the Son of Man comes, he will be seen by everyone, like lightning flashing from the east to the west. ²⁸Wherever the dead body is, there the vultures will gather.

²⁹"Soon after the trouble of those days,

'the sun will grow dark,

and the moon will not give its light.

The stars will fall from the sky.

And the powers of the heavens will be shaken.'   *Isaiah 13:10; 34:4*

³⁰"At that time, the sign of the Son of Man will appear in the sky. Then all the peoples of the world will cry. They will see the Son of Man coming on clouds in the sky with great power and glory. ³¹He will use a loud trumpet to send his angels all around the earth, and they will gather his chosen people from every part of the world.

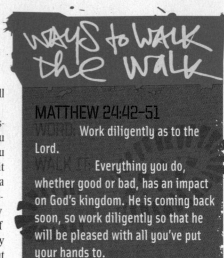

WAYS to WALK the WALK

MATTHEW 24:42–51

WORD Work diligently as to the Lord.

WALK IT Everything you do, whether good or bad, has an impact on God's kingdom. He is coming back soon, so work diligently so that he will be pleased with all you've put your hands to.

³²"Learn a lesson from the fig tree: When its branches become green and soft and new leaves appear, you know summer is near. ³³In the same way, when you see all these things happening, you will know that the time is near, ready to come. ³⁴I tell you the truth, all these things will happen while the people of this time are still living. ³⁵Earth and sky will be destroyed, but the words I have said will never be destroyed.

WHEN WILL JESUS COME AGAIN?

³⁶"No one knows when that day or time will be, not the angels in heaven, not even the Son.ⁿ Only the Father knows. ³⁷When the Son of Man comes, it will be like what happened during Noah's time. ³⁸In those days before the flood, people were eating and drinking, marrying and giving their children to be married, until the day Noah entered the boat. ³⁹They knew nothing about what was happening until the flood came and destroyed them. It will be the same when the Son of Man comes. ⁴⁰Two men will be in the field. One will be taken, and the other will be left. ⁴¹Two women will be grinding grain with a mill.ⁿ One will be taken, and the other will be left.

⁴²"So always be ready, because you don't know the day your Lord will come. ⁴³Remember this: If the owner of the house knew what time of night a thief was coming, the owner would watch and not let the thief break in. ⁴⁴So you also must be ready, because the Son of Man will come at a time you don't expect him.

⁴⁵"Who is the wise and loyal servant that the master trusts to give the other servants their food at the right time? ⁴⁶When the master comes and finds the servant doing his work,

24:15 'a blasphemous object that brings destruction' Mentioned in Daniel 9:27; 12:11 (see also Daniel 11:31).   24:17 roofs In Bible times houses were built with flat roofs. The roof was used for drying things such as flax and fruit. And it was used as an extra room, as a place for worship, and as a cool place to sleep in the summer.   24:36 not even the Son Some Greek copies do not have this phrase.   24:41 mill Two large, round, flat rocks used for grinding grain to make flour.

the servant will be blessed. 47I tell you the truth, the master will choose that servant to take care of everything he owns. 48But suppose that evil servant thinks to himself, 'My master will not come back soon,' 49and he begins to beat the other servants and eat and get drunk with others like him? 50The master will come when that servant is not ready and is not expecting him. 51Then the master will cut him in pieces and send him away to be with the hypocrites, where people will cry and grind their teeth with pain.

A STORY ABOUT TEN BRIDESMAIDS

25 "At that time the kingdom of heaven will be like ten bridesmaids who took their lamps and went to wait for the bridegroom. 2Five of them were foolish and five were wise. 3The five foolish bridesmaids took their lamps, but they did not take more oil for the lamps to burn. 4The wise bridesmaids took their lamps and more oil in jars. 5Because the bridegroom was late, they became sleepy and went to sleep.

6"At midnight someone cried out, 'The bridegroom is coming! Come and meet him!' 7Then all the bridesmaids woke up and got their lamps ready. 8But the foolish ones said to the wise, 'Give us some of your oil, because our lamps are going out.' 9The wise bridesmaids answered, 'No, the oil we have might not be enough for all of us. Go to the people who sell oil and buy some for yourselves.'

10"So while the five foolish bridesmaids went to buy oil, the bridegroom came. The bridesmaids who were ready went in with the bridegroom to the wedding feast. Then the door was closed and locked.

11"Later the others came back and said, 'Sir, sir, open the door to let us in.' 12But the bridegroom answered, 'I tell you the truth, I don't want to know you.'

13"So always be ready, because you don't know the day or the hour the Son of Man will come.

A STORY ABOUT THREE SERVANTS

14"The kingdom of heaven is like a man who was going to another place for a visit. Before he left, he called for his servants and told them to take care of his things while he was gone. 15He gave one servant five bags of gold, another servant two bags of gold, and a third servant one bag of gold, to each one as much as he could handle. Then he left. 16The servant who got five bags went quickly to invest the money and earned five more bags. 17In the same way, the servant who had two bags invested them and earned two more. 18But the servant who got one bag went out and dug a hole in the ground and hid the master's money.

19"After a long time the master came home and asked the servants what they did with his money. 20The servant who was given five bags of gold brought five more bags to the master and said, 'Master, you trusted me to care for

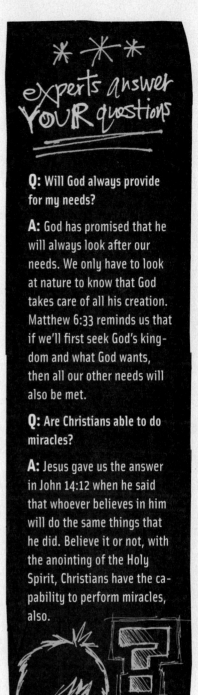

experts answer YOUR questions

Q: Will God always provide for my needs?

A: God has promised that he will always look after our needs. We only have to look at nature to know that God takes care of all his creation. Matthew 6:33 reminds us that if we'll first seek God's kingdom and what God wants, then all our other needs will also be met.

Q: Are Christians able to do miracles?

A: Jesus gave us the answer in John 14:12 when he said that whoever believes in him will do the same things that he did. Believe it or not, with the anointing of the Holy Spirit, Christians have the capability to perform miracles, also.

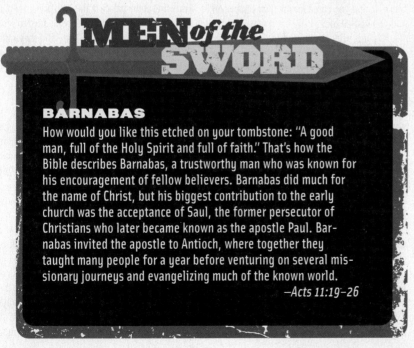

MEN of the SWORD

BARNABAS

How would you like this etched on your tombstone: "A good man, full of the Holy Spirit and full of faith." That's how the Bible describes Barnabas, a trustworthy man who was known for his encouragement of fellow believers. Barnabas did much for the name of Christ, but his biggest contribution to the early church was the acceptance of Saul, the former persecutor of Christians who later became known as the apostle Paul. Barnabas invited the apostle to Antioch, where together they taught many people for a year before venturing on several missionary journeys and evangelizing much of the known world.
—*Acts 11:19–26*

five bags of gold, so I used your five bags to earn five more.' 21The master answered, 'You did well. You are a good and loyal servant. Because you were loyal with small things, I will let you care for much greater things. Come and share my joy with me.'

22"Then the servant who had been given two bags of gold came to the master and said, 'Master, you gave me two bags of gold to care

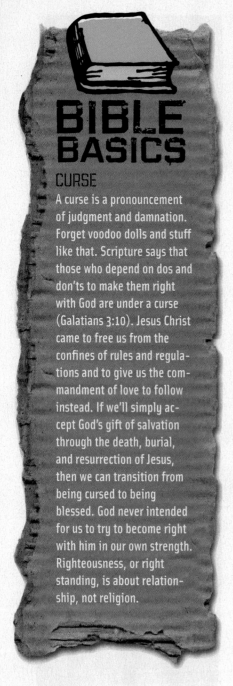

BIBLE BASICS

CURSE

A curse is a pronouncement of judgment and damnation. Forget voodoo dolls and stuff like that. Scripture says that those who depend on dos and don'ts to make them right with God are under a curse (Galatians 3:10). Jesus Christ came to free us from the confines of rules and regulations and to give us the commandment of love to follow instead. If we'll simply accept God's gift of salvation through the death, burial, and resurrection of Jesus, then we can transition from being cursed to being blessed. God never intended for us to try to become right with him in our own strength. Righteousness, or right standing, is about relationship, not religion.

for, so I used your two bags to earn two more.' 23The master answered, 'You did well. You are a good and loyal servant. Because you were loyal with small things, I will let you care for much greater things. Come and share my joy with me.'

24"Then the servant who had been given one bag of gold came to the master and said, 'Master, I knew that you were a hard man. You harvest things you did not plant. You gather crops where you did not sow any seed. 25So I was afraid and went and hid your money in the ground. Here is your bag of gold.' 26The master answered, 'You are a wicked and lazy servant! You say you knew that I harvest things I did not plant and that I gather crops where I did not sow any seed. 27So you should have put my gold in the bank. Then, when I came home, I would have received my gold back with interest.'

28"So the master told his other servants, 'Take the bag of gold from that servant and give it to the servant who has ten bags of gold. 29Those who have much will get more, and they will have much more than they need. But those who do not have much will have everything taken away from them.' 30Then the master said, 'Throw that useless servant outside, into the darkness where people will cry and grind their teeth with pain.'

THE KING WILL JUDGE ALL PEOPLE

31"The Son of Man will come again in his great glory, with all his angels. He will be King and sit on his great throne. 32All the nations of the world will be gathered before him, and he will separate them into two groups as a shepherd separates the sheep from the goats. 33The Son of Man will put the sheep on his right and the goats on his left.

34"Then the King will say to the people on his right, 'Come, my Father has given you his blessing. Receive the kingdom God has prepared for you since the world was made. 35I was hungry, and you gave me food. I was thirsty, and you gave me something to drink. I was alone and away from home, and you invited me into your house. 36I was without clothes, and you gave me something to wear. I was sick, and you cared for me. I was in prison, and you visited me.'

37"Then the good people will answer, 'Lord, when did we see you hungry and give you food, or thirsty and give you something to drink? 38When did we see you alone and away from home and invite you into our house? When did we see you without clothes and give you something to wear? 39When did we see you sick or in prison and care for you?'

40"Then the King will answer, 'I tell you the truth, anything you did for even the least of my people here, you also did for me.'

41"Then the King will say to those on his left, 'Go away from me. You will be punished. Go into the fire that burns forever that was prepared for the devil and his angels. 42I was hungry, and you gave me nothing to eat. I was thirsty, and you gave me nothing to drink. 43I was alone and away from home, and you did not invite me into your house. I was without clothes, and you gave me nothing to wear. I was sick and in prison, and you did not care for me.'

44"Then those people will answer, 'Lord, when did we see you hungry or thirsty or alone and away from home or without clothes or sick or in prison? When did we see these things and not help you?'

45"Then the King will answer, 'I tell you the truth, anything you refused to do for even the least of my people here, you refused to do for me.'

46"These people will go off to be punished forever, but the good people will go to live forever."

THE PLAN TO KILL JESUS

26 After Jesus finished saying all these things, he told his followers, 2"You know that the day after tomorrow is the day of the Passover Feast. On that day the Son of Man will be given to his enemies to be crucified."

> **Matthew 25:31**
> "The Son of Man will come again in his great glory, with all his angels. He will be King and sit on his great throne."

3Then the leading priests and the elders had a meeting at the palace of the high priest, named Caiaphas. 4At the meeting, they planned to set a trap to arrest Jesus and kill him. 5But they said, "We must not do it during the feast, because the people might cause a riot."

PERFUME FOR JESUS' BURIAL

6Jesus was in Bethany at the house of Simon, who had a skin disease. 7While Jesus was there, a woman approached him with an alabaster jar filled with expensive perfume. She poured this perfume on Jesus' head while he was eating.

8His followers were upset when they saw the woman do this. They asked, "Why waste that perfume? 9It could have been sold for a great deal of money and the money given to the poor."

10Knowing what had happened, Jesus said, "Why are you troubling this woman? She did an excellent thing for me. 11You will always have the poor with you, but you will not always have me. 12This woman poured perfume on my body to prepare me for burial. [13]I tell you the truth, wherever the Good News is preached in all the world, what this woman has done will be told, and people will remember her."

JUDAS BECOMES AN ENEMY OF JESUS

[14]Then one of the twelve apostles, Judas Iscariot, went to talk to the leading priests. [15]He said, "What will you pay me for giving Jesus to you?" And they gave him thirty silver coins. [16]After that, Judas watched for the best time to turn Jesus in.

JESUS EATS THE PASSOVER MEAL

[17]On the first day of the Feast of Unleavened Bread, the followers came to Jesus. They said, "Where do you want us to prepare for you to eat the Passover meal?"

[18]Jesus answered, "Go into the city to a certain man and tell him, 'The Teacher says: "The chosen time is near. I will have the Passover with my followers at your house." ' " [19]The followers did what Jesus told them to do, and they prepared the Passover meal.

[20]In the evening Jesus was sitting at the table with his twelve followers. [21]As they were eating, Jesus said, "I tell you the truth, one of you will turn against me."

[22]This made the followers very sad. Each one began to say to Jesus, "Surely, Lord, I am not the one who will turn against you, am I?"

[23]Jesus answered, "The man who has dipped his hand with me into the bowl is the one who will turn against me. [24]The Son of Man will die, just as the Scriptures say. But how terrible it will be for the person who hands the Son of Man over to be killed. It would be better for him if he had never been born."

[25]Then Judas, who would give Jesus to his enemies, said to Jesus, "Teacher, surely I am not the one, am I?"

Jesus answered, "Yes, it is you."

THE LORD'S SUPPER

[26]While they were eating, Jesus took some bread and thanked God for it and broke it. Then he gave it to his followers and said, "Take this bread and eat it; this is my body."

[27]Then Jesus took a cup and thanked God for it and gave it to the followers. He said, "Every one of you drink this. [28]This is my blood which is the new[n] agreement that God makes with his people. This blood is poured out for many to forgive their sins. [29]I tell you this: I will not drink of this fruit of the vine[n] again until that day when I drink it new with you in my Father's kingdom."

ways to WALK the WALK

MATTHEW 26:6-13
WORD: Give Jesus your all.
WALK IT: It could be your car, your girlfriend, or your music. Whatever it is, give it all to Jesus with this simple prayer: "Take this issue and use it as you see fit. I let it go. Amen."

[30]After singing a hymn, they went out to the Mount of Olives.

JESUS' FOLLOWERS WILL LEAVE HIM

[31]Jesus told his followers, "Tonight you will all stumble in your faith on account of me, because it is written in the Scriptures:

'I will kill the shepherd,
 and the sheep will scatter.'

Zechariah 13:7

*REVIEWS MOVIES

STAR WARS, EPISODE III: REVENGE OF THE SITH

The third chapter in this saga of six is arguably the darkest and most violent of the bunch. In *Revenge of the Sith*, we continue to follow Anakin Skywalker as he hands his heart over to the evil Sidious, dives headfirst into the dark side, and eventually murders hundreds of innocent people. This coming-of-age story is where all of the questions get answered, like how do Anakin's twins, Luke and Leah, get separated in the end? Artistically done and packed with spiritual innuendoes, *Revenge of the Sith* probably will become the only new "Star Wars" movie to become a classic.

WHY IT ROCKS:

THE STORYTELLING IS IN A LEAGUE OF ITS OWN.

 26:28 new Some Greek copies do not have this word. Compare Luke 22:20. 26:29 fruit of the vine Product of the grapevine; this may also be translated "wine."

Relationships

" . . . Love your neighbor as you love yourself" (Matthew 22:39b). So how exactly do you love yourself? You take care of yourself. You take pride in a job well done. When your body is run down, you get some rest. When it is empty, you give it food. When it is dirty, you clean it. Take a cue from the way you treat yourself and start treating your family that way. Respect your parents' wishes. Take care of your siblings. When your sister is run down, cheer her up. If your brother is spiritually empty, pray for him. Treat your family the way you would like to be treated.

³²But after I rise from the dead, I will go ahead of you into Galilee."

³³Peter said, "Everyone else may stumble in their faith because of you, but I will not."

³⁴Jesus said, "I tell you the truth, tonight before the rooster crows you will say three times that you don't know me."

³⁵But Peter said, "I will never say that I don't know you! I will even die with you!" And all the other followers said the same thing.

JESUS PRAYS ALONE

³⁶Then Jesus went with his followers to a place called Gethsemane. He said to them, "Sit here while I go over there and pray." ³⁷He took Peter and the two sons of Zebedee with him, and he began to be very sad and troubled. ³⁸He said to them, "My heart is full of sorrow, to the point of death. Stay here and watch with me."

³⁹After walking a little farther away from them, Jesus fell to the ground and prayed, "My Father, if it is possible, do not give me this cup" of suffering. But do what you want, not what I want." ⁴⁰Then Jesus went back to his followers and found them asleep. He said to Peter, "You men could not stay awake with me for one hour? ⁴¹Stay awake and pray for strength against temptation. The spirit wants to do what is right, but the body is weak."

⁴²Then Jesus went away a second time and prayed, "My Father, if it is not possible for this painful thing to be taken from me, and if I must do it, I pray that what you want will be done."

⁴³Then he went back to his followers, and again he found them asleep, because their eyes were heavy. ⁴⁴So Jesus left them and went away and prayed a third time, saying the same thing.

⁴⁵Then Jesus went back to his followers and said, "Are you still sleeping and resting? The time has come for the Son of Man to be handed over to sinful people. ⁴⁶Get up, we must go. Look, here comes the man who has turned against me."

JESUS IS ARRESTED

⁴⁷While Jesus was still speaking, Judas, one of the twelve apostles, came up. With him were many people carrying swords and clubs who had been sent from the leading priests and the Jewish elders of the people. ⁴⁸Judas had planned to give them a signal, saying, "The man I kiss is Jesus. Arrest him." ⁴⁹At once Judas went to Jesus and said, "Greetings, Teacher!" and kissed him.

⁵⁰Jesus answered, "Friend, do what you came to do."

Then the people came and grabbed Jesus and arrested him. ⁵¹When that happened, one of Jesus' followers reached for his sword and pulled it out. He struck the servant of the high priest and cut off his ear.

⁵²Jesus said to the man, "Put your sword back in its place. All who use swords will be killed with swords. ⁵³Surely you know I could ask my Father, and he would give me more than twelve armies of angels. ⁵⁴But it must happen this way to bring about what the Scriptures say."

⁵⁵Then Jesus said to the crowd, "You came to get me with swords and clubs as if I were a criminal. Every day I sat in the Temple teaching, and you did not arrest me there. ⁵⁶But all these things have happened so that it will come about as the prophets wrote." Then all of Jesus' followers left him and ran away.

JESUS BEFORE THE LEADERS

⁵⁷Those people who arrested Jesus led him to the house of Caiaphas, the high priest, where the teachers of the law and the elders were gathered. ⁵⁸Peter followed far behind to the courtyard of the high priest's house, and he sat down with the guards to see what would happen to Jesus.

⁵⁹The leading priests and the whole Jewish council tried to find something false against Jesus so they could kill him. ⁶⁰Many people came and told lies about him, but the council could find no real reason to kill him. Then two people came and said, ⁶¹"This man said, 'I can destroy the Temple of God and build it again in three days.'"

⁶²Then the high priest stood up and said to Jesus, "Aren't you going to answer? Don't you have something to say about their charges against you?" ⁶³But Jesus said nothing.

Again the high priest said to Jesus, "I command you by the power of the living God: Tell us if you are the Christ, the Son of God."

⁶⁴Jesus answered, "Those are your words. But I tell you, in the future you will see the Son of Man sitting at the right hand of God, the Powerful One, and coming on clouds in the sky."

⁶⁵When the high priest heard this, he tore his clothes and said, "This man has said things that are against God! We don't need any more witnesses; you all heard him say these things against God. ⁶⁶What do you think?"

The people answered, "He should die."

⁶⁷Then the people there spat in Jesus' face and beat him with their fists. Others slapped him. ⁶⁸They said, "Prove to us that you are a prophet, you Christ! Tell us who hit you!"

PETER SAYS HE DOESN'T KNOW JESUS

⁶⁹At that time, as Peter was sitting in the courtyard, a servant girl came to him and said, "You also were with Jesus of Galilee."

⁷⁰But Peter said to all the people there that he was never with Jesus. He said, "I don't know what you are talking about."

⁷¹When he left the courtyard and was at the gate, another girl saw him. She said to the

 26:39 cup Jesus is talking about the terrible things that will happen to him. Accepting these things will be very hard, like drinking a cup of something bitter.

GUARD YOUR HEART

Guys sometime rush relationships. Too often we end up saying things (like "I love you" and "I think you're the one") before our hearts and heads have had the time to process them. If you're dating, take your time. Don't rush something as important as love. It isn't meant to be hurried.

people there, "This man was with Jesus of Nazareth."

[72]Again, Peter said he was never with him, saying, "I swear I don't know this man Jesus!"

[73]A short time later, some people standing there went to Peter and said, "Surely you are one of those who followed Jesus. The way you talk shows it."

[74]Then Peter began to place a curse on himself and swear, "I don't know the man." At once, a rooster crowed. [75]And Peter remembered what Jesus had told him: "Before the rooster crows, you will say three times that you don't know me." Then Peter went outside and cried painfully.

JESUS IS TAKEN TO PILATE

27 Early the next morning, all the leading priests and elders of the people decided that Jesus should die. [2]They tied him, led him away, and turned him over to Pilate, the governor.

JUDAS KILLS HIMSELF

[3]Judas, the one who had given Jesus to his enemies, saw that they had decided to kill Jesus. Then he was very sorry for what he had done. So he took the thirty silver coins back to the priests and the leaders, [4]saying, "I sinned; I handed over to you an innocent man."

The leaders answered, "What is that to us? That's your problem, not ours."

[5]So Judas threw the money into the Temple. Then he went off and hanged himself.

[6]The leading priests picked up the silver coins in the Temple and said, "Our law does not allow us to keep this money with the Temple money, because it has paid for a man's death." [7]So they decided to use the coins to buy Potter's Field as a place to bury strangers who died in Jerusalem. [8]That is why that field is still called the Field of Blood. [9]So what Jeremiah the prophet had said came true: "They took thirty silver coins. That is how little the Israelites thought he was worth. [10]They used those thirty silver coins to buy the potter's field, as the Lord commanded me."[n]

PILATE QUESTIONS JESUS

[11]Jesus stood before Pilate the governor, and Pilate asked him, "Are you the king of the Jews?"

Jesus answered, "Those are your words."

[12]When the leading priests and the elders accused Jesus, he said nothing.

[13]So Pilate said to Jesus, "Don't you hear them accusing you of all these things?"

[14]But Jesus said nothing in answer to Pilate, and Pilate was very surprised at this.

PILATE TRIES TO FREE JESUS

[15]Every year at the time of Passover the governor would free one prisoner whom the people chose. [16]At that time there was a man in prison, named Barabbas,[n] who was known to be very bad. [17]When the people gathered at Pilate's house, Pilate said, "Whom do you want me to set free: Barabbas[n] or Jesus who is called the Christ?" [18]Pilate knew that they turned Jesus in to him because they were jealous.

[19]While Pilate was sitting there on the judge's seat, his wife sent this message to him: "Don't do anything to that man, because he is innocent. Today I had a dream about him, and it troubled me very much."

[20]But the leading priests and elders convinced the crowd to ask for Barabbas to be freed and for Jesus to be killed.

[21]Pilate said, "I have Barabbas and Jesus. Which do you want me to set free for you?"

The people answered, "Barabbas."

[22]Pilate asked, "So what should I do with Jesus, the one called the Christ?"

They all answered, "Crucify him!"

[23]Pilate asked, "Why? What wrong has he done?"

But they shouted louder, "Crucify him!"

[24]When Pilate saw that he could do nothing about this and that a riot was starting, he took some water and washed his hands[n] in front of the crowd. Then he said, "I am not guilty of this man's death. You are the ones who are causing it!"

[25]All the people answered, "We and our children will be responsible for his death."

[26]Then he set Barabbas free. But Jesus was beaten with whips and handed over to the soldiers to be crucified.

[27]The governor's soldiers took Jesus into the governor's palace, and they all gathered around him. [28]They took off his clothes and put a red robe on him. [29]Using thorny branches, they made a crown, put it on his head, and put a stick in his right hand. Then the soldiers bowed before Jesus and made fun of him, saying, "Hail, King of the Jews!" [30]They spat on Jesus. Then they took his stick and began to beat him on the head. [31]After they finished, the soldiers took off the robe and put his own clothes on him again. Then they led him away to be crucified.

JESUS IS CRUCIFIED

[32]As the soldiers were going out of the city with Jesus, they forced a man from Cyrene, named Simon, to carry the cross for Jesus. [33]They all came to the place called Golgotha, which means the Place of the Skull. [34]The soldiers gave Jesus wine mixed with gall[n] to drink. He tasted the wine but refused to drink it. [35]When the soldiers had crucified him, they threw lots to decide who would get his clothes.[n] [36]The soldiers sat there and continued watching him. [37]They put a sign above Jesus' head with a charge against him. It said: THIS IS JESUS, THE KING OF THE JEWS. [38]Two robbers were crucified beside Jesus, one on the right and the other on the left. [39]People walked by and insulted Jesus and shook their heads, [40]saying, "You said you could destroy the Temple and build it again in three days. So save yourself!

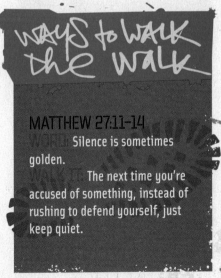

WAYS to WALK the WALK

MATTHEW 27:11-14

WORD Silence is sometimes golden.

WALK IT The next time you're accused of something, instead of rushing to defend yourself, just keep quiet.

 27:9-10 "They . . . commanded me." See Zechariah 11:12–13 and Jeremiah 32:6–9. **27:16-17 Barabbas** Some Greek copies read "Jesus Barabbas." **27:24 washed his hands** He did this as a sign to show that he wanted no part in what the people did. **27:34 gall** Probably a drink of wine mixed with drugs to help a person feel less pain. **27:35 clothes** Some Greek copies continue, "So what God said through the prophet came true, 'They divided my clothes among them, and they threw lots for my clothing.'" See Psalm 22:18.

RADICAL FAITH

MATTHEW 28:18-20

God didn't usher you and every other Christian into a tight friendship with him just so you could hog him for yourself. He intends to spread the Good News about Jesus to the entire world, giving everyone an opportunity to believe in him—the chance to become friends with him now, and to hang in heaven with him forever (John 3:16). God hasn't installed a global surround-sound system to blast this message across the universe. Oddly, he thought the greatest way to spread the news was through ordinary Christians. He commands believers to go to the whole world to help others get to know him. While that's an enormous task, you can do your part. Start with the people right around you. You can offer a message of ultimate truth wrapped in personal experience. In other words, you might find it easiest to start by talking with others about what Jesus has done for you. But even more important is explaining what Jesus has done for everyone—the total truth that Jesus has died for people's sins, and we are made right with God by trusting in him.

Come down from that cross if you are really the Son of God!"

⁴¹The leading priests, the teachers of the law, and the Jewish elders were also making fun of Jesus. ⁴²They said, "He saved others, but he can't save himself! He says he is the king of Israel! If he is the king, let him come down now from the cross. Then we will believe in him. ⁴³He trusts in God, so let God save him now, if God really wants him. He himself said, 'I am the Son of God.' " ⁴⁴And in the same way, the robbers who were being crucified beside Jesus also insulted him.

JESUS DIES

⁴⁵At noon the whole country became dark, and the darkness lasted for three hours. ⁴⁶About three o'clock Jesus cried out in a loud voice, "Eli, Eli, lama sabachthani?" This means, "My God, my God, why have you abandoned me?"

⁴⁷Some of the people standing there who heard this said, "He is calling Elijah."

⁴⁸Quickly one of them ran and got a sponge and filled it with vinegar and tied it to a stick and gave it to Jesus to drink. ⁴⁹But the others said, "Don't bother him. We want to see if Elijah will come to save him."

⁵⁰But Jesus cried out again in a loud voice and died.

⁵¹Then the curtain in the Temple*ⁿ* was torn into two pieces, from the top to the bottom. Also, the earth shook and rocks broke apart. ⁵²The graves opened, and many of God's people who had died were raised from the dead. ⁵³They came out of the graves after Jesus was raised from the dead and went into the holy city, where they appeared to many people.

⁵⁴When the army officer and the soldiers guarding Jesus saw this earthquake and everything else that happened, they were very frightened and said, "He really was the Son of God!"

⁵⁵Many women who had followed Jesus from Galilee to help him were standing at a distance from the cross, watching. ⁵⁶Mary Magdalene, and Mary the mother of James and Joseph, and the mother of James and John were there.

JESUS IS BURIED

⁵⁷That evening a rich man named Joseph, a follower of Jesus from the town of Arimathea, came to Jerusalem. ⁵⁸Joseph went to Pilate and asked to have Jesus' body. So Pilate gave orders for the soldiers to give it to Joseph. ⁵⁹Then Joseph took the body and wrapped it in a clean linen cloth. ⁶⁰He put Jesus' body in a new tomb that he had cut out

of a wall of rock, and he rolled a very large stone to block the entrance of the tomb. Then Joseph went away. ⁶¹Mary Magdalene and the other woman named Mary were sitting near the tomb.

THE TOMB OF JESUS IS GUARDED

⁶²The next day, the day after Preparation Day, the leading priests and the Pharisees went to Pilate. ⁶³They said, "Sir, we remember that while that liar was still alive he said, 'After three days I will rise from the dead.' ⁶⁴So give the order for the tomb to be guarded closely till the third day. Otherwise, his followers might come and steal the body and tell people that he has risen from the dead. That lie would be even worse than the first one."

⁶⁵Pilate said, "Take some soldiers and go guard the tomb the best way you know." ⁶⁶So they all went to the tomb and made it safe from thieves by sealing the stone in the entrance and putting soldiers there to guard it.

JESUS RISES FROM THE DEAD

28 The day after the Sabbath day was the first day of the week. At dawn on the first day, Mary Magdalene and another woman named Mary went to look at the tomb.

²At that time there was a strong earthquake. An angel of the Lord came down from heaven, went to the tomb, and rolled the stone away from the entrance. Then he sat on the stone. ³He was shining as bright as lightning, and his clothes were white as snow. ⁴The soldiers guarding the tomb shook with fear because of the angel, and they became like dead men.

⁵The angel said to the women, "Don't be

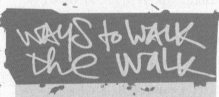

WAYS to WALK the WALK

MATTHEW 28:18-20

WORD: Live a life people will want to follow.

WALK IT: What do people see when you're out in the real world? Model Christ for the people you come in contact with. Internalize the words of Jesus so that you will live them out.

 27:51 curtain in the Temple A curtain divided the Most Holy Place from the other part of the Temple. That was the special building in Jerusalem where God commanded the Jewish people to worship him.

afraid. I know that you are looking for Jesus, who has been crucified. 6He is not here. He has risen from the dead as he said he would. Come and see the place where his body was. 7And go quickly and tell his followers, 'Jesus has risen from the dead. He is going into Galilee ahead of you, and you will see him there.' " Then the angel said, "Now I have told you."

8The women left the tomb quickly. They were afraid, but they were also very happy. They ran to tell Jesus' followers what had happened. 9Suddenly, Jesus met them and said, "Greetings." The women came up to him, took hold of his feet, and worshiped him. 10Then Jesus said to them, "Don't be afraid. Go and tell my followers to go on to Galilee, and they will see me there."

THE SOLDIERS REPORT TO THE LEADERS

11While the women went to tell Jesus' followers, some of the soldiers who had been guarding the tomb went into the city to tell the leading priests everything that had happened. 12Then the priests met with the elders and made a plan. They paid the soldiers a large amount of money 13and said to them, "Tell the people that Jesus' followers came during the night and stole the body while you were asleep. 14If the governor hears about this, we will satisfy him and save you from trouble." 15So the soldiers kept the money and did as they were told. And that story is still spread among the people even today.

stats

Thirty-two percent of teenagers said they had gone further sexually while drinking than they would have sober.

—Teen People

JESUS TALKS TO HIS FOLLOWERS

16The eleven followers went to Galilee to the mountain where Jesus had told them to go. 17On the mountain they saw Jesus and worshiped him, but some of them did not believe it was really Jesus. 18Then Jesus came to them and said, "All power in heaven and on earth is given to me. 19So go and make followers of all people in the world. Baptize them in the name of the Father and the Son and the Holy Spirit. 20Teach them to obey everything that I have taught you, and I will be with you always, even until the end of this age."

MARK

THE MIRACLES OF JESUS

Mark is a book of strong action that packs a lot into a little space. It opens with John the Baptist's call for people to change their hearts, followed by Jesus' baptism, his battles with the devil, and, ultimately, his call to ministry, complete with miracles and healings. He makes it a point to upset religious rulers by ignoring many of their cherished traditions, telling them that other acts—such as helping people—are more important than rules and regulations.

The Book of Mark reviews many of Christ's parables, simple stories that illustrate great truths. In the midst of Jesus' many powerful acts, Mark recalls the hostile reception Christ received in his hometown. Limited to healing a few people of minor ailments, skepticism there prevents Christ from performing miracles. The moral of the story isn't that Jesus lacked power, but that the people lacked faith.

Mark devotes more than a third of his account to the last week of Jesus' life. He points out that even as Christ nears death, he succeeds in leaving a legacy through his teachings. Among the lessons Mark shares are the need for faith when praying and the call to love each other. This book concludes with a radical promise: Those who believe in Jesus will also perform powerful miracles.

JOHN PREPARES FOR JESUS

This is the beginning of the Good News about Jesus Christ, the Son of God,[n] [2]as the prophet Isaiah wrote:

"I will send my messenger ahead of you, who will prepare your way." *Malachi 3:1*

[3]"This is a voice of one who calls out in the desert: 'Prepare the way for the Lord. Make the road straight for him.'"

Isaiah 40:3

[4]John was baptizing people in the desert and preaching a baptism of changed hearts and lives for the forgiveness of sins. [5]All the people from Judea and Jerusalem were going out to him. They confessed their sins and were baptized by him in the Jordan River. [6]John wore clothes made from camel's hair, had a leather belt around his waist, and ate locusts and wild honey. [7]This is what John preached to the people: "There is one coming after me who is greater than I; I am not good enough even to kneel down and untie his sandals. [8]I baptize you with water, but he will baptize you with the Holy Spirit."

JESUS IS BAPTIZED

[9]At that time Jesus came from the town of Nazareth in Galilee and was baptized by John in the Jordan River. [10]Immediately, as Jesus was coming up out of the water, he saw heaven open. The Holy Spirit came down on him like a dove, [11]and a voice came from heaven: "You are my Son, whom I love, and I am very pleased with you."

[12]Then the Spirit sent Jesus into the desert. [13]He was in the desert forty days and was tempted by Satan. He was with the wild animals, and the angels came and took care of him.

JESUS CHOOSES SOME FOLLOWERS

[14]After John was put in prison, Jesus went into Galilee, preaching the Good News from God. [15]He said, "The right time has come. The kingdom of God is near. Change your hearts and lives and believe the Good News!"

[16]When Jesus was walking by Lake Galilee, he saw Simon[n] and his brother Andrew throwing a net into the lake because they were fishermen. [17]Jesus said to them, "Come follow me, and I will make you fish for people." [18]So Simon and Andrew immediately left their nets and followed him.

[19]Going a little farther, Jesus saw two more brothers, James and John, the sons of Zebedee. They were in a boat, mending their nets. [20]Jesus immediately called them, and they left their father in the boat with the hired workers and followed Jesus.

JESUS FORCES OUT AN EVIL SPIRIT

[21]Jesus and his followers went to Capernaum. On the Sabbath day he went to the synagogue and began to teach. [22]The people were amazed at his teaching, because he taught like a person who had authority, not like their teachers of the law. [23]Just then, a man was there in the synagogue who had an evil spirit in him. He shouted, [24]"Jesus of Nazareth! What do you want with us? Did you come to destroy us? I know who you are—God's Holy One!"

[25]Jesus commanded the evil spirit, "Be quiet! Come out of the man!" [26]The evil spirit shook the man violently, gave a loud cry, and then came out of him.

[27]The people were so amazed they asked each other, "What is happening here? This man is teaching something new, and with authority. He even gives commands to evil spirits, and they obey him." [28]And the news about Jesus spread quickly everywhere in the area of Galilee.

JESUS HEALS MANY PEOPLE

[29]As soon as Jesus and his followers left the synagogue, they went with James and John to the home of Simon[n] and Andrew. [30]Simon's mother-in-law was sick in bed with a fever, and the people told Jesus about her. [31]So Jesus went to her bed, took her hand, and helped her up. The fever left her, and she began serving them.

[32]That evening, after the sun went down, the people brought to Jesus all who were sick and had demons in them. [33]The whole town gathered at the door. [34]Jesus healed many who had different kinds of sicknesses, and he forced many demons to leave people. But he would not allow the demons to speak, because they knew who he was.

[35]Early the next morning, while it was still dark, Jesus woke and left the house. He went to a lonely place, where he prayed. [36]Simon and his friends went to look for Jesus. [37]When they found him, they said, "Everyone is looking for you!"

[38]Jesus answered, "We should go to other towns around here so I can preach there too. That is the reason I came." [39]So he went everywhere in Galilee, preaching in the synagogues and forcing out demons.

JESUS HEALS A SICK MAN

[40]A man with a skin disease came to Jesus. He fell to his knees and begged Jesus, "You can heal me if you will."

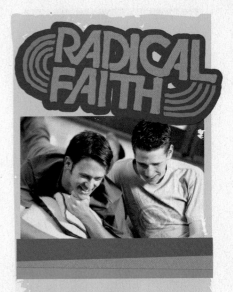

RADICAL FAITH

MARK 1:17

You have to get a clear picture of these first followers of Jesus, Andrew and Simon (also known as Peter). Jesus called them to a radical faith in him, but he didn't enter their lives from nowhere. These guys were already followers of John the Baptist, the cousin of Jesus who was born for the colossal purpose of announcing Christ's arrival as the world's Savior. So don't imagine them as crazed religious fanatics suddenly dropping their fishing nets to follow a stranger. Andrew and Simon answered Jesus' invitation to follow, already knowing more than a slice of who he was (John 1:35–42). That should calm your heart if you have ever questioned whether you really want to trust your entire life to Jesus, deciding to obey his every command without hesitation. Like those first followers, make it your life's top job to learn about Jesus' trustworthy character and to study his complete power. Dig into the Bible and rely on what you discover. The more you know Jesus, the more you will want to follow him. Saying "yes" to following Jesus totally is life's most important commitment, but that decision doesn't always happen without the right information.

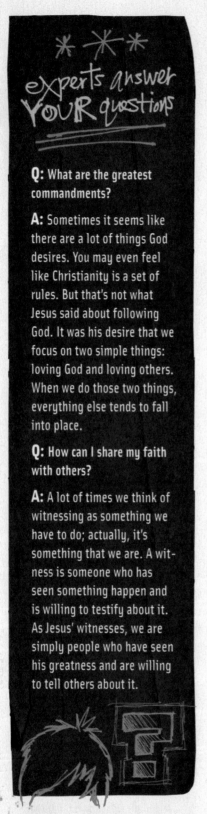

Q: What are the greatest commandments?

A: Sometimes it seems like there are a lot of things God desires. You may even feel like Christianity is a set of rules. But that's not what Jesus said about following God. It was his desire that we focus on two simple things: loving God and loving others. When we do those two things, everything else tends to fall into place.

Q: How can I share my faith with others?

A: A lot of times we think of witnessing as something we have to do; actually, it's something that we are. A witness is someone who has seen something happen and is willing to testify about it. As Jesus' witnesses, we are simply people who have seen his greatness and are willing to tell others about it.

[41]Jesus felt sorry for the man, so he reached out his hand and touched him and said, "I will. Be healed!" [42]Immediately the disease left the man, and he was healed.

[43]Jesus told the man to go away at once, but he warned him strongly, [44]"Don't tell anyone about this. But go and show yourself to the priest. And offer the gift Moses commanded for people who are made well." This will show the people what I have done." [45]The man left there, but he began to tell everyone that Jesus had healed him, and so he spread the news about Jesus. As a result, Jesus could not enter a town if people saw him. He stayed in places where nobody lived, but people came to him from everywhere.

JESUS HEALS A PARALYZED MAN

2 A few days later, when Jesus came back to Capernaum, the news spread that he was at home. [2]Many people gathered together so that there was no room in the house, not even outside the door. And Jesus was teaching them God's message. [3]Four people came, carrying a paralyzed man. [4]Since they could not get to Jesus because of the crowd, they dug a hole in the roof right above where he was speaking. When they got through, they lowered the mat with the paralyzed man on it. [5]When Jesus saw the faith of these people, he said to the paralyzed man, "Young man, your sins are forgiven."

[6]Some of the teachers of the law were sitting there, thinking to themselves, [7]"Why does this man say things like that? He is speaking as if he were God. Only God can forgive sins."

[8]Jesus knew immediately what these teachers of the law were thinking. So he said to them, "Why are you thinking these things? [9]Which is easier: to tell this paralyzed man, 'Your sins are forgiven,' or to tell him, 'Stand up. Take your mat and walk'? [10]But I will prove to you that the Son of Man has authority on earth to forgive sins." So Jesus said to the paralyzed man, [11]"I tell you, stand up, take your mat, and go home." [12]Immediately the paralyzed man stood up, took his mat, and walked out while everyone was watching him.

The people were amazed and praised God. They said, "We have never seen anything like this!"

[13]Jesus went to the lake again. The whole crowd followed him there, and he taught them. [14]While he was walking along, he saw a man named Levi son of Alphaeus, sitting in the tax collector's booth. Jesus said to him, "Follow me," and he stood up and followed Jesus.

[15]Later, as Jesus was having dinner at Levi's house, many tax collectors and "sinners" were eating there with Jesus and his followers. Many people like this followed Jesus. [16]When the teachers of the law who were Pharisees saw Jesus eating with the tax collectors and "sinners," they asked his followers, "Why does he eat with tax collectors and sinners?"

[17]Jesus heard this and said to them, "It is not the healthy people who need a doctor, but the sick. I did not come to invite good people but to invite sinners."

JESUS' FOLLOWERS ARE CRITICIZED

[18]Now the followers of John" and the Pharisees often fasted" for a certain time. Some people came to Jesus and said, "Why do John's followers and the followers of the Pharisees often fast, but your followers don't?"

[19]Jesus answered, "The friends of the bridegroom do not fast while the bridegroom is still with them. As long as the bridegroom is with them, they cannot fast. [20]But the time will come when the bridegroom will be taken from them, and then they will fast.

[21]"No one sews a patch of unshrunk cloth over a hole in an old coat. Otherwise, the patch will shrink and pull away—the new patch will pull away from the old coat. Then the hole will be worse. [22]Also, no one ever pours new wine into old leather bags. Otherwise, the new wine will break the bags, and the wine will be ruined along with the bags. But new wine should be put into new leather bags."

JESUS IS LORD OF THE SABBATH

[23]One Sabbath day, as Jesus was walking through some fields of grain, his followers began to pick some grain to eat. [24]The Pharisees said to Jesus, "Why are your followers doing what is not lawful on the Sabbath day?"

[25]Jesus answered, "Have you never read what David did when he and those with him were hungry and needed food? [26]During the

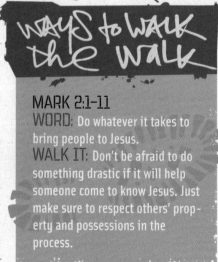

ways to WALK the WALK

MARK 2:1-11
WORD: Do whatever it takes to bring people to Jesus.
WALK IT: Don't be afraid to do something drastic if it will help someone come to know Jesus. Just make sure to respect others' property and possessions in the process.

1:44 Moses . . . well Read about this in Leviticus 14:1–32. **2:18 John** John the Baptist, who preached to the Jewish people about Christ's coming (Mark 1:4–8). **2:18 fasted** The people would give up eating for a special time of prayer and worship to God. It was also done to show sadness and disappointment.

ISSUES

MEDIA

WE'RE CONFRONTED WITH MORE MULTIMEDIA MESSAGES TODAY THAN EVER BEFORE. In order to wade through the "mind field" that faces you, you'll need to consider what types of material you want influencing your life. Just because something looks or sounds cool doesn't mean it is healthy for your soul. If the media that you tune in to doesn't help you become more like Christ, then you are better off unplugging from such ungodly fare. And if you have friends who tend to weigh you down with their media diet, then you need to find others who can help you make wise decisions when it comes to the media you digest.

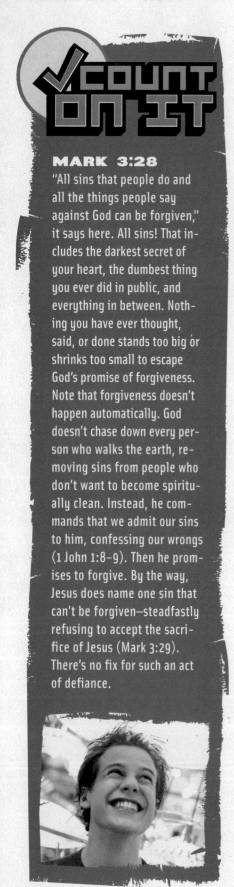

COUNT ON IT

MARK 3:28

"All sins that people do and all the things people say against God can be forgiven," it says here. All sins! That includes the darkest secret of your heart, the dumbest thing you ever did in public, and everything in between. Nothing you have ever thought, said, or done stands too big or shrinks too small to escape God's promise of forgiveness. Note that forgiveness doesn't happen automatically. God doesn't chase down every person who walks the earth, removing sins from people who don't want to become spiritually clean. Instead, he commands that we admit our sins to him, confessing our wrongs (1 John 1:8–9). Then he promises to forgive. By the way, Jesus does name one sin that can't be forgiven—steadfastly refusing to accept the sacrifice of Jesus (Mark 3:29). There's no fix for such an act of defiance.

time of Abiathar the high priest, David went into God's house and ate the holy bread, which is lawful only for priests to eat. And David also gave some of the bread to those who were with him."

[27]Then Jesus said to the Pharisees, "The Sabbath day was made to help people; they were not made to be ruled by the Sabbath day. [28]So then, the Son of Man is Lord even of the Sabbath day."

JESUS HEALS A MAN'S HAND

3 Another time when Jesus went into a synagogue, a man with a crippled hand was there. [2]Some people watched Jesus closely to see if he would heal the man on the Sabbath day so they could accuse him.

[3]Jesus said to the man with the crippled hand, "Stand up here in the middle of everyone."

[4]Then Jesus asked the people, "Which is lawful on the Sabbath day: to do good or to do evil, to save a life or to kill?" But they said nothing to answer him.

[5]Jesus was angry as he looked at the people, and he felt very sad because they were stubborn. Then he said to the man, "Hold out your hand." The man held out his hand and it was healed. [6]Then the Pharisees left and began making plans with the Herodians[n] about a way to kill Jesus.

MANY PEOPLE FOLLOW JESUS

[7]Jesus left with his followers for the lake, and a large crowd from Galilee followed him. [8]Also many people came from Judea, from Jerusalem, from Idumea, from the lands across the Jordan River, and from the area of Tyre and Sidon. When they heard what Jesus was doing, many people came to him. [9]When Jesus saw the crowds, he told his followers to get a boat ready for him to keep people from crowding against him. [10]He had healed many people, so all the sick were pushing toward him to touch him. [11]When evil spirits saw Jesus, they fell down before him and shouted, "You are the Son of God!" [12]But Jesus strongly warned them not to tell who he was.

JESUS CHOOSES HIS TWELVE APOSTLES

[13]Then Jesus went up on a mountain and called to him those he wanted, and they came to him. [14]Jesus chose twelve and called them apostles.[n] He wanted them to be with him, and he wanted to send them out to preach [15]and to have the authority to force demons out of people. [16]These are the twelve men he chose: Simon (Jesus named him Peter), [17]James and John, the sons of Zebedee (Jesus named them Boanerges, which means "Sons of Thunder"), [18]Andrew, Philip, Bartholomew, Matthew, Thomas, James the son of Alphaeus, Thaddaeus, Simon the Zealot, [19]and Judas Iscariot, who later turned against Jesus.

SOME PEOPLE SAY JESUS HAS A DEVIL

[20]Then Jesus went home, but again a crowd gathered. There were so many people that Jesus and his followers could not eat. [21]When his family heard this, they went to get him because they thought he was out of his mind. [22]But the teachers of the law from Jerusalem were saying, "Beelzebul is living inside him! He uses power from the ruler of demons to force demons out of people."

[23]So Jesus called the people together and taught them with stories. He said, "Satan will not force himself out of people. [24]A kingdom that is divided cannot continue, [25]and a family that is divided cannot continue. [26]And if Satan is against himself and fights against his own people, he cannot continue; that is the end of Satan. [27]No one can enter a strong person's house and steal his things unless he first ties up the strong person. Then he can steal things from the house. [28]I tell you the truth, all sins that people do and all the things people say against God can be forgiven. [29]But anyone who speaks against the Holy Spirit will never be forgiven; he is guilty of a sin that continues forever."

[30]Jesus said this because the teachers of the law said that he had an evil spirit inside him.

JESUS' TRUE FAMILY

[31]Then Jesus' mother and brothers arrived. Standing outside, they sent someone in to tell

 3:6 Herodians A political group that followed Herod and his family.   3:14 and called them apostles Some Greek copies do not have this phrase.

him to come out. ³²Many people were sitting around Jesus, and they said to him, "Your mother and brothers* are waiting for you outside."

³³Jesus asked, "Who are my mother and my brothers?" ³⁴Then he looked at those sitting around him and said, "Here are my mother and my brothers! ³⁵My true brother and sister and mother are those who do what God wants."

A STORY ABOUT PLANTING SEED

4 Again Jesus began teaching by the lake. A great crowd gathered around him, so he sat down in a boat near the shore. All the people stayed on the shore close to the water. ²Jesus taught them many things, using stories. He said, ³"Listen! A farmer went out to plant his seed. ⁴While he was planting, some seed fell by the road, and the birds came and ate it up. ⁵Some seed fell on rocky ground where there wasn't much dirt. That seed grew very fast, because the ground was not deep. ⁶But when the sun rose, the plants dried up because they did not have deep roots. ⁷Some other seed fell among thorny weeds, which grew and choked the good plants. So those plants did not produce a crop. ⁸Some other seed fell on good ground and began to grow. It got taller and produced a crop. Some plants made thirty times more, some made sixty times more, and some made a hundred times more."

⁹Then Jesus said, "Let those with ears use them and listen!"

Extras:

How to Order Coffee Like a Connoisseur

We live in an increasingly gourmet coffee-obsessed society, so you might as well learn to sound like you know what you're doing. First, determine what type of coffee-based drink best suits your taste. If you like it strong, go with something containing espresso, like an americano (espresso and hot water) or a macchiato (espresso with foam). Slightly milder are the espresso/milk combinations, like a latte (espresso with steamed milk) or a cappuccino (a latte with foam). Try going a little sweeter with a mocha (a latte with cocoa or chocolate). If you'd prefer less caffeine, order yours "half-caff," which is half-regular, half-decaffeinated. Want more caffeine (or flavor)? Order a "double," "triple," or "quad" for two, three, or four times the espresso. And there's nothing wrong with ordering plain old regular coffee. Everyone has different tastes, but there's no stimulant like God's Word. Check it out for the ultimate buzz!

JESUS TELLS WHY HE USED STORIES

¹⁰Later, when Jesus was alone, the twelve apostles and others around him asked him about the stories.

¹¹Jesus said, "You can know the secret about the kingdom of God. But to other people I tell everything by using stories ¹²so that:

'They will look and look, but they will not learn.

They will listen and listen, but they will not understand.

If they did learn and understand, they would come back to me and be forgiven.'" *Isaiah 6:9–10*

JESUS EXPLAINS THE SEED STORY

¹³Then Jesus said to his followers, "Don't you understand this story? If you don't, how

Get out there

With dozens of "Acquire the Fire" conferences across the nation that attract thousands of youths to each site, Teen Mania is one of the better-known youth ministries in America. However, this 20-year-old ministry goes beyond exciting rallies and extreme summer camps. It also sponsors "Global Expeditions," missions, and relief projects that send teens to nearly 20 countries across the world each year. For example, after the tsunami that devastated Southeast Asia late in 2004, Teen Mania organized trips to the region the following summer. It also sends groups to needy areas in major U.S. cities.

To get involved, see www.teenmania.org.

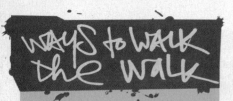

ways to WALK the WALK

MARK 4:21-25

WORD: Use what you have.

WALK IT: What talents has God given you? Give them back to him in ministry. Don't try to be something you aren't; embrace your talents, and pray for new ways to use them.

will you understand any story? [14]The farmer is like a person who plants God's message in people. [15]Sometimes the teaching falls on the road. This is like the people who hear the teaching of God, but Satan quickly comes and takes away the teaching that was planted in them. [16]Others are like the seed planted on rocky ground. They hear the teaching and quickly accept it with joy. [17]But since they don't allow the teaching to go deep into their lives, they keep it only a short time. When trouble or persecution comes because of the teaching they accepted, they quickly give up. [18]Others are like the seed planted among the thorny weeds. They hear the teaching, [19]but the worries of this life, the temptation of wealth, and many other evil desires keep the teaching from growing and producing fruit" in their lives. [20]Others are like the seed planted in the good ground. They hear the teaching and accept it. Then they grow and produce fruit—sometimes thirty times more, sometimes sixty times more, and sometimes a hundred times more."

USE WHAT YOU HAVE

[21]Then Jesus said to them, "Do you hide a lamp under a bowl or under a bed? No! You put the lamp on a lampstand. [22]Everything that is hidden will be made clear and every secret thing will be made known. [23]Let those with ears use them and listen!

[24]"Think carefully about what you hear. The way you give to others is the way God will give to you, but God will give you even more. [25]Those who have understanding will be given more. But those who do not have understanding, even what they have will be taken away from them."

JESUS USES A STORY ABOUT SEED

[26]Then Jesus said, "The kingdom of God is like someone who plants seed in the ground. [27]Night and day, whether the person is asleep or awake, the seed still grows, but the person does not know how it grows. [28]By itself the earth produces grain. First the plant grows, then the head, and then all the grain in the head. [29]When the grain is ready, the farmer cuts it, because this is the harvest time."

A STORY ABOUT MUSTARD SEED

[30]Then Jesus said, "How can I show you what the kingdom of God is like? What story can I use to explain it? [31]The kingdom of God is like a mustard seed, the smallest seed you plant in the ground. [32]But when planted, this seed grows and becomes the largest of all garden plants. It produces large branches, and the wild birds can make nests in its shade."

[33]Jesus used many stories like these to teach the crowd God's message—as much as they could understand. [34]He always used stories to teach them. But when he and his followers were alone, Jesus explained everything to them.

JESUS CALMS A STORM

[35]That evening, Jesus said to his followers, "Let's go across the lake." [36]Leaving the crowd behind, they took him in the boat just as he was. There were also other boats with them. [37]A very strong wind came up on the lake. The waves came over the sides and into the boat so that it was already full of water. [38]Jesus was at the back of the boat, sleeping with his head on a cushion. His followers woke him and said, "Teacher, don't you care that we are drowning!"

[39]Jesus stood up and commanded the wind and said to the waves, "Quiet! Be still!" Then the wind stopped, and it became completely calm.

[40]Jesus said to his followers, "Why are you afraid? Do you still have no faith?"

[41]The followers were very afraid and asked each other, "Who is this? Even the wind and the waves obey him!"

A MAN WITH DEMONS INSIDE HIM

5 Jesus and his followers went to the other side of the lake to the area of the Gerasene" people. [2]When Jesus got out of the boat, instantly a man with an evil spirit came to him from the burial caves. [3]This man lived in the caves, and no one could tie him

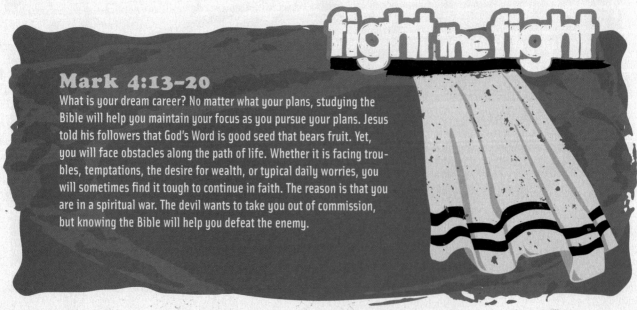

fight the fight

Mark 4:13-20

What is your dream career? No matter what your plans, studying the Bible will help you maintain your focus as you pursue your plans. Jesus told his followers that God's Word is good seed that bears fruit. Yet, you will face obstacles along the path of life. Whether it is facing troubles, temptations, the desire for wealth, or typical daily worries, you will sometimes find it tough to continue in faith. The reason is that you are in a spiritual war. The devil wants to take you out of commission, but knowing the Bible will help you defeat the enemy.

 4:19 producing fruit To produce fruit means to have in your life the good things God wants.　5:1 Gerasene From Gerasa, an area southeast of Lake Galilee. The exact location is uncertain and some Greek copies read "Gergesene"; others read "Gadarene."

february

NATIONAL SNACK FOOD MONTH

> "Attempt something so big that unless God intervenes it is bound to fail."
> —JAMIE BUCKINGHAM

1 It's okay to eat snack foods, but make them healthy ones!

2 It's Groundhog Day, the MOST pointless of all holidays.

3

4 Have your friends over and watch *Napoleon Dynamite*.

5

6

7 Garth Brooks is another year older today.

8

9 Help feed the homeless this week.

10

11 Sheryl Crow celebrates another birthday.

12

13 Believe it or not, today is Man Day, so act like one!

14 Celebrate Valentine's Day by creating a card for your mom.

15 Learn the words to "The Star Spangled Banner."

16

Mom

17 Ask your mailman how you can pray for him.

18

19 Today is Haylie Duff's birthday.

20

21 Take your dad out for a cup of coffee.

22

23 Be nice to your neighbor today.

24

25 It's Sean Astin's birthday.

26

27

28 Straighten up your room without being asked.

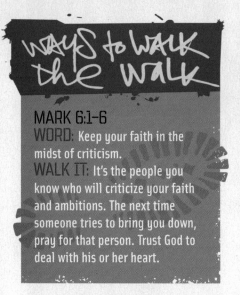

up, not even with a chain. [4]Many times people had used chains to tie the man's hands and feet, but he always broke them off. No one was strong enough to control him. [5]Day and night he would wander around the burial caves and on the hills, screaming and cutting himself with stones. [6]While Jesus was still far away, the man saw him, ran to him, and fell down before him.

[7]The man shouted in a loud voice, "What do you want with me, Jesus, Son of the Most High God? I command you in God's name not to torture me!" [8]He said this because Jesus was saying to him, "You evil spirit, come out of the man."

[9]Then Jesus asked him, "What is your name?"

He answered, "My name is Legion,[n] be-cause we are many spirits." [10]He begged Jesus again and again not to send them out of that area.

[11]A large herd of pigs was feeding on a hill near there. [12]The demons begged Jesus, "Send us into the pigs; let us go into them." [13]So Jesus allowed them to do this. The evil spirits left the man and went into the pigs. Then the herd of pigs—about two thousand of them—rushed down the hill into the lake and were drowned.

[14]The herdsmen ran away and went to the town and to the countryside, telling everyone about this. So people went out to see what had happened. [15]They came to Jesus and saw the man who used to have the many evil spirits, sitting, clothed, and in his right mind. And they were frightened. [16]The people who saw this told the others what had happened to the man who had the demons living in him, and they told about the pigs. [17]Then the people began to beg Jesus to leave their area.

[18]As Jesus was getting back into the boat, the man who was freed from the demons begged to go with him.

[19]But Jesus would not let him. He said, "Go home to your family and tell them how much the Lord has done for you and how he has had mercy on you." [20]So the man left and began to tell the people in the Ten Towns[n] about what Jesus had done for him. And everyone was amazed.

JESUS GIVES LIFE TO A DEAD GIRL AND HEALS A SICK WOMAN

[21]When Jesus went in the boat back to the other side of the lake, a large crowd gathered around him there. [22]A leader of the synagogue, named Jairus, came there, saw Jesus, and fell at his feet. [23]He begged Jesus, saying again and again, "My daughter is dying. Please come and put your hands on her so she will be healed and will live." [24]So Jesus went with him.

A large crowd followed Jesus and pushed very close around him. [25]Among them was a woman who had been bleeding for twelve years. [26]She had suffered very much from many doctors and had spent all the money she had, but instead of improving, she was getting worse. [27]When the woman heard about Jesus, she came up behind him in the crowd and touched his coat. [28]She thought, "If I can just touch his clothes, I will be healed." [29]Instantly her bleeding stopped, and she felt in her body that she was healed from her disease.

[30]At once Jesus felt power go out from him. So he turned around in the crowd and asked, "Who touched my clothes?"

[31]His followers said, "Look at how many people are pushing against you! And you ask, 'Who touched me?'"

[32]But Jesus continued looking around to see who had touched him. [33]The woman, knowing that she was healed, came and fell at Jesus' feet. Shaking with fear, she told him the whole truth. [34]Jesus said to her, "Dear woman, you are made well because you believed. Go in peace; be healed of your disease."

[35]While Jesus was still speaking, some people came from the house of the synagogue leader. They said, "Your daughter is dead. There is no need to bother the teacher anymore."

[36]But Jesus paid no attention to what they said. He told the synagogue leader, "Don't be afraid; just believe."

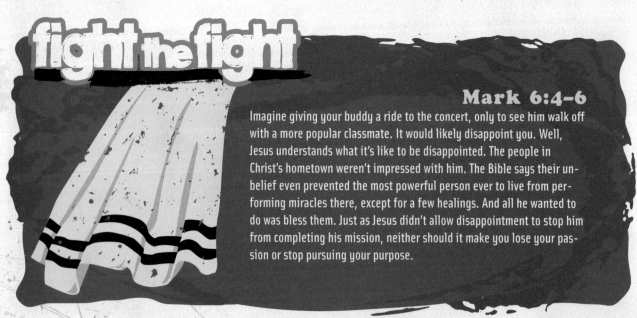

fight the fight

Mark 6:4-6

Imagine giving your buddy a ride to the concert, only to see him walk off with a more popular classmate. It would likely disappoint you. Well, Jesus understands what it's like to be disappointed. The people in Christ's hometown weren't impressed with him. The Bible says their unbelief even prevented the most powerful person ever to live from performing miracles there, except for a few healings. And all he wanted to do was bless them. Just as Jesus didn't allow disappointment to stop him from completing his mission, neither should it make you lose your passion or stop pursuing your purpose.

5:9 Legion Means very many. A legion was about five thousand men in the Roman army.   5:20 Ten Towns In Greek, called "Decapolis." It was an area east of Lake Galilee that once had ten main towns.

50

37Jesus let only Peter, James, and John the brother of James go with him. 38When they came to the house of the synagogue leader, Jesus found many people there making lots of noise and crying loudly. 39Jesus entered the house and said to them, "Why are you crying and making so much noise? The child is not dead, only asleep." 40But they laughed at him. So, after throwing them out of the house, Jesus took the child's father and mother and his three followers into the room where the child was. 41Taking hold of the girl's hand, he said to her, "Talitha, koum!" (This means, "Young girl, I tell you to stand up!") 42At once the girl stood right up and began walking. (She was twelve years old.) Everyone was completely amazed. 43Jesus gave them strict orders not to tell people about this. Then he told them to give the girl something to eat.

JESUS GOES TO HIS HOMETOWN

6 Jesus left there and went to his hometown, and his followers went with him. 2On the Sabbath day he taught in the synagogue. Many people heard him and were amazed, saying, "Where did this man get these teachings? What is this wisdom that has been given to him? And where did he get the power to do miracles? 3He is just the carpenter, the son of Mary and the brother of James, Joseph, Judas, and Simon. And his sisters are here with us." So the people were upset with Jesus.

4Jesus said to them, "A prophet is honored everywhere except in his hometown and with his own people and in his own home." 5So Jesus was not able to work any miracles there except to heal a few sick people by putting his hands on them. 6He was amazed at how many people had no faith.

Then Jesus went to other villages in that area and taught. 7He called his twelve followers together and got ready to send them out two by two and gave them authority over evil spirits. 8This is what Jesus commanded them: "Take nothing for your trip except a walking stick. Take no bread, no bag, and no money in your pockets. 9Wear sandals, but take only the clothes you are wearing. 10When you enter a house, stay there until you leave that town. 11If the people in a certain place refuse to welcome you or listen to you, leave that place. Shake its dust off your feet[n] as a warning to them."[n]

12So the followers went out and preached that people should change their hearts and lives. 13They forced many demons out and put olive oil on many sick people and healed them.

Even though Jesus said nothing about dating relationships, he did give us insight on how we should treat people. His call for kindness, gentleness, peace, faith, and love is the perfect foundation for a healthy dating relationship. So, remember, even though you might not marry the girl you're dating now, treat her well.

HOW JOHN THE BAPTIST WAS KILLED

14King Herod heard about Jesus, because he was now well known. Some people said,[n] "He is John the Baptist, who has risen from the dead. That is why he can work these miracles."

15Others said, "He is Elijah."[n]

Other people said, "Jesus is a prophet, like the prophets who lived long ago."

16When Herod heard this, he said, "I killed John by cutting off his head. Now he has risen from the dead!"

17Herod himself had ordered his soldiers to arrest John and put him in prison in order to please his wife, Herodias. She had been the wife of Philip, Herod's brother, but then Herod had married her. 18John had been telling Herod, "It is not lawful for you to be married to your brother's wife." 19So Herodias hated John and wanted to kill him. But she couldn't, 20because Herod was afraid of John and protected him. He knew John was a good and holy man. Also, though John's preaching always bothered him, he enjoyed listening to John.

21Then the perfect time came for Herodias to cause John's death. On Herod's birthday, he gave a dinner party for the most important government leaders, the commanders of his army, and the most important people in Galilee. 22When the daughter of Herodias[n] came in and danced, she pleased Herod and the people eating with him.

So King Herod said to the girl, "Ask me for anything you want, and I will give it to you." 23He promised her, "Anything you ask for I will give to you—up to half of my kingdom."

24The girl went to her mother and asked, "What should I ask for?"

Her mother answered, "Ask for the head of John the Baptist."

25At once the girl went back to the king and said to him, "I want the head of John the Baptist right now on a platter."

26Although the king was very sad, he had made a promise, and his dinner guests had heard it. So he did not want to refuse what she asked. 27Immediately the king sent a soldier to bring John's head. The soldier went and cut off John's head in the prison 28and brought it back on a platter. He gave it to the girl, and the girl gave it to her mother. 29When John's followers heard this, they came and got John's body and put it in a tomb.

MORE THAN FIVE THOUSAND FED

30The apostles gathered around Jesus and told him about all the things they had done and taught. 31Crowds of people were coming and going so that Jesus and his followers did not even have time to eat. He said to them, "Come away by yourselves, and we will go to a lonely place to get some rest."

Do's and Don'ts

DO exercise discretion with media.

DO tune out objectionable material.

DO limit your exposure to media.

DO use a filter for surfing online.

DON'T lower your media standards.

DON'T pay attention to bad messages.

DON'T allow media to rule your life.

DON'T conform to popular culture.

 6:11 Shake . . . feet A warning. It showed that they were rejecting these people.   6:11 them Some Greek copies continue, "I tell you the truth, on the Judgment Day it will be better for the towns of Sodom and Gomorrah than for the people of that town." See Matthew 10:15.   6:14 Some people said Some Greek copies read "He said."   6:15 Elijah A great prophet who spoke for God and who lived hundreds of years before Christ. See 1 Kings 17.   6:22 When . . . Herodias Some Greek copies read "When his daughter Herodias."

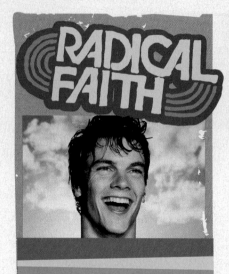

RADICAL FAITH

MARK 7:20–23

The spiritual leaders in Jesus' day were hung up with ceremonial details of religion—topics like the correct ways to worship, what activities were holy enough for the weekly day of rest, and the right foods to eat or not eat in order to please God. They thought the world's most atrocious sins were messing up in these outward matters. Jesus told them to shift their focus to life's actual issues. He said that living for God boils down to two key commands: Love the Lord more than anything else, and love everyone around you as much as you love yourself (Matthew 22:37–39). Jesus even got really specific and said that what matters is breaking free of evil—from sexual sins, theft, and murder to jealousy, badmouthing others, and pride. If Jesus showed up today, he would say that the core of faith doesn't have to do with details like speaking the right religious lingo, advertising your faith on your car's bumper, or wearing a Christian t-shirt every day of the week. It's letting God change your heart so that your life will come clean, too.

[32] So they went in a boat by themselves to a lonely place. [33] But many people saw them leave and recognized them. So from all the towns they ran to the place where Jesus was going, and they got there before him. [34] When he arrived, he saw a great crowd waiting. He felt sorry for them, because they were like sheep without a shepherd. So he began to teach them many things.

[35] When it was late in the day, his followers came to him and said, "No one lives in this place, and it is already very late. [36] Send the people away so they can go to the countryside and towns around here to buy themselves something to eat."

[37] But Jesus answered, "You give them something to eat."

They said to him, "We would all have to work a month to earn enough money to buy that much bread!"

[38] Jesus asked them, "How many loaves of bread do you have? Go and see."

When they found out, they said, "Five loaves and two fish."

[39] Then Jesus told his followers to have the people sit in groups on the green grass. [40] So they sat in groups of fifty or a hundred. [41] Jesus took the five loaves and two fish and, looking up to heaven, he thanked God for the food. He divided the bread and gave it to his followers for them to give to the people. Then he divided the two fish among them all. [42] All the people ate and were satisfied. [43] The followers filled twelve baskets with the leftover pieces of bread and fish. [44] There were five thousand men who ate.

JESUS WALKS ON THE WATER

[45] Immediately Jesus told his followers to get into the boat and go ahead of him to Bethsaida across the lake. He stayed there to send the people home. [46] After sending them away, he went into the hills to pray.

[47] That night, the boat was in the middle of the lake, and Jesus was alone on the land. [48] He saw his followers struggling hard to row the boat, because the wind was blowing against them. Between three and six o'clock in the morning, Jesus came to them, walking on the water, and he wanted to walk past the boat. [49] But when they saw him walking on the water, they thought he was a ghost and cried out. [50] They all saw him and were afraid. But quickly Jesus spoke to them and said, "Have courage! It is I. Do not be afraid." [51] Then he got into the boat with them, and the wind became calm. The followers were greatly amazed. [52] They did not understand about the miracle of the five loaves, because their minds were closed.

[53] When they had crossed the lake, they came to shore at Gennesaret and tied the boat there. [54] When they got out of the boat, people immediately recognized Jesus. [55] They ran everywhere in that area and began to bring sick people on mats wherever they heard he was. [56] And everywhere he went—into towns, cities, or countryside—the people brought the sick to the marketplaces. They begged him to let them touch just the edge of his coat, and all who touched it were healed.

OBEY GOD'S LAW

7 When some Pharisees and some teachers of the law came from Jerusalem, they gathered around Jesus. [2] They saw that some of Jesus' followers ate food with hands that were not clean, that is, they hadn't washed them. [3] (The Pharisees and all the Jews never eat before washing their hands in the way required by their unwritten laws. [4] And when they buy something in the market, they never eat it until they wash themselves in a special way. They also follow many other unwritten laws, such as the washing of cups, pitchers, and pots.[n])

[5] The Pharisees and the teachers of the law said to Jesus, "Why don't your followers obey the unwritten laws which have been handed down to us? Why do your followers eat their food with hands that are not clean?"

[6] Jesus answered, "Isaiah was right when he spoke about you hypocrites. He wrote,

'These people show honor to me with
    words,
  but their hearts are far from me.
[7] Their worship of me is worthless.
The things they teach are nothing but
    human rules.'   *Isaiah 29:13*
[8] You have stopped following the commands of God, and you follow only human teachings."[n]

[9] Then Jesus said to them, "You cleverly ignore the commands of God so you can follow your own teachings. [10] Moses said, 'Honor your father and your mother,'[n] and 'Anyone who says cruel things to his father or mother must be put to death.'[n] [11] But you say a person can tell his father or mother, 'I have something I could use to help you, but it is Corban—a gift to God.' [12] You no longer let that person use that money for his father or his mother. [13] By your own rules, which you teach people, you are rejecting what God said. And you do many things like that."

[14] After Jesus called the crowd to him again, he said, "Every person should listen to me and understand what I am saying. [15] There is nothing people put into their bodies that makes them unclean. People are made unclean by the

7:4 pots Some Greek copies continue, "and dining couches."   **7:8 teachings** Some Greek copies continue, "You wash pitchers and jugs and do many other such things."   **7:10 'Honor . . . mother.'** Quotation from Exodus 20:12; Deuteronomy 5:16.   **7:10 'Anyone . . . death.'** Quotation from Exodus 21:17.

52

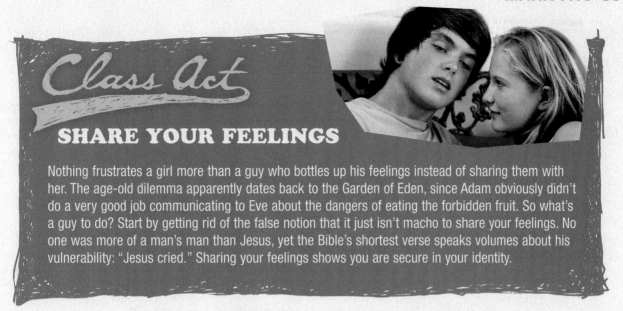

Class Act

SHARE YOUR FEELINGS

Nothing frustrates a girl more than a guy who bottles up his feelings instead of sharing them with her. The age-old dilemma apparently dates back to the Garden of Eden, since Adam obviously didn't do a very good job communicating to Eve about the dangers of eating the forbidden fruit. So what's a guy to do? Start by getting rid of the false notion that it just isn't macho to share your feelings. No one was more of a man's man than Jesus, yet the Bible's shortest verse speaks volumes about his vulnerability: "Jesus cried." Sharing your feelings shows you are secure in your identity.

things that come out of them. [¹⁶Let those with ears use them and listen.]"ⁿ

¹⁷When Jesus left the people and went into the house, his followers asked him about this story. ¹⁸Jesus said, "Do you still not understand? Surely you know that nothing that enters someone from the outside can make that person unclean. ¹⁹It does not go into the mind, but into the stomach. Then it goes out of the body." (When Jesus said this, he meant that no longer was any food unclean for people to eat.)

²⁰And Jesus said, "The things that come out of people are the things that make them unclean. ²¹All these evil things begin inside people, in the mind: evil thoughts, sexual sins, stealing, murder, adultery, ²²greed, evil actions, lying, doing sinful things, jealousy, speaking evil of others, pride, and foolish living. ²³All

these evil things come from inside and make people unclean."

JESUS HELPS A NON-JEWISH WOMAN

²⁴Jesus left that place and went to the area around Tyre.ⁿ When he went into a house, he did not want anyone to know he was there, but he could not stay hidden. ²⁵A woman whose daughter had an evil spirit in her heard that he was there. So she quickly came to Jesus and fell at his feet. ²⁶She was Greek, born in Phoenicia, in Syria. She begged Jesus to force the demon out of her daughter.

²⁷Jesus told the woman, "It is not right to take the children's bread and give it to the dogs. First let the children eat all they want."

²⁸But she answered, "Yes, Lord, but even

the dogs under the table can eat the children's crumbs."

²⁹Then Jesus said, "Because of your answer, you may go. The demon has left your daughter."

³⁰The woman went home and found her daughter lying in bed; the demon was gone.

JESUS HEALS A DEAF MAN

³¹Then Jesus left the area around Tyre and went through Sidon to Lake Galilee, to the area of the Ten Towns.ⁿ ³²While he was there, some people brought a man to him who was deaf and could not talk plainly. The people begged Jesus to put his hand on the man to heal him.

³³Jesus led the man away from the crowd, by himself. He put his fingers in the man's ears and then spit and touched the man's

fight the fight

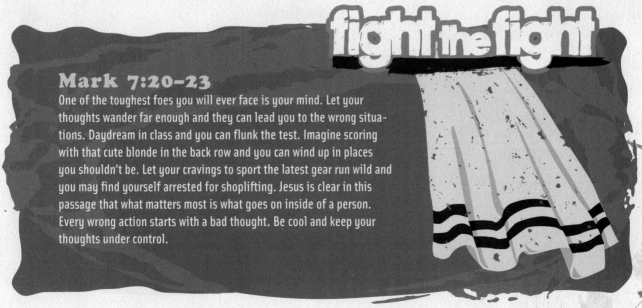

Mark 7:20–23

One of the toughest foes you will ever face is your mind. Let your thoughts wander far enough and they can lead you to the wrong situations. Daydream in class and you can flunk the test. Imagine scoring with that cute blonde in the back row and you can wind up in places you shouldn't be. Let your cravings to sport the latest gear run wild and you may find yourself arrested for shoplifting. Jesus is clear in this passage that what matters most is what goes on inside of a person. Every wrong action starts with a bad thought. Be cool and keep your thoughts under control.

7:16 Let . . . listen. Some Greek copies do not contain the bracketed text.   7:24 Tyre Some Greek copies continue, "and Sidon."   7:31 Ten Towns In Greek, called "Decapolis." It was an area east of Lake Galilee that once had ten main towns.

MARK 7:20-23

WORD: What goes into you will come out of you.

WALK IT: Be careful of what you feed your soul. The next time you go to a movie, be sensitive to what you're seeing, and don't be afraid to walk out if necessary.

tongue. [34]Looking up to heaven, he sighed and said to the man, "Ephphatha!" (This means, "Be opened.") [35]Instantly the man was able to hear and to use his tongue so that he spoke clearly.

[36]Jesus commanded the people not to tell anyone about what happened. But the more he commanded them, the more they told about it. [37]They were completely amazed and said, "Jesus does everything well. He makes the deaf hear! And those who can't talk he makes able to speak."

MORE THAN FOUR THOUSAND PEOPLE FED

8 Another time there was a great crowd with Jesus that had nothing to eat. So Jesus called his followers and said, [2]"I feel sorry for these people, because they have already been with me for three days, and they have nothing to eat. [3]If I send them home hungry, they will faint on the way. Some of them live a long way from here."

[4]Jesus' followers answered, "How can we get enough bread to feed all these people? We are far away from any town."

[5]Jesus asked, "How many loaves of bread do you have?"

They answered, "Seven."

[6]Jesus told the people to sit on the ground. Then he took the seven loaves, gave thanks to God, and divided the bread. He gave the pieces to his followers to give to the people, and they did so. [7]The followers also had a few small fish. After Jesus gave thanks for the fish, he told his followers to give them to the people also. [8]All the people ate and were satisfied. Then his followers filled seven baskets with the leftover pieces of food. [9]There were about four thousand people who ate. After they had eaten, Jesus sent them home. [10]Then right away he got into a boat with his followers and went to the area of Dalmanutha.

THE LEADERS ASK FOR A MIRACLE

[11]The Pharisees came to Jesus and began to ask him questions. Hoping to trap him, they asked Jesus for a miracle from God. [12]Jesus sighed deeply and said, "Why do you people ask for a miracle as a sign? I tell you the truth, no sign will be given to you." [13]Then Jesus left the Pharisees and went in the boat to the other side of the lake.

GUARD AGAINST WRONG TEACHINGS

[14]His followers had only one loaf of bread with them in the boat; they had forgotten to bring more. [15]Jesus warned them, "Be careful! Beware of the yeast of the Pharisees and the yeast of Herod."

[16]His followers discussed the meaning of this, saying, "He said this because we have no bread."

[17]Knowing what they were talking about, Jesus asked them, "Why are you talking about not having bread? Do you still not see or understand? Are your minds closed? [18]You have eyes, but you don't really see. You have ears, but you don't really listen. Remember when [19]I divided five loaves of bread for the five

*REVIEWS MUSIC

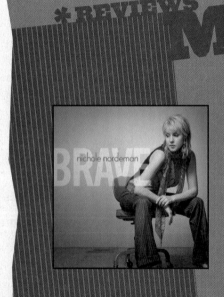

NICHOLE NORDEMAN:
BRAVE

Not every guy likes his music loud, sweaty, and rambunctious. For those of you who appreciate the softer side of artistic expression, Nichole Nordeman's latest is a serious music lover's dream record. The power of Nordeman's lyrical poetry combined with the acoustic, piano-driven production makes *Brave* not only a good record for fans of Jack Johnson and John Mayer, but also a record your girlfriend might enjoy! Though her spiritual exploration gets a little deep in songs such as "Hold On" and "We Build," overall Nordeman's record will make a moving and worshipful addition to your collection.

WHY IT ROCKS:

THE LYRICAL CONTENT IS WITHOUT PEER.

thousand? How many baskets did you fill with leftover pieces of food?"

They answered, "Twelve."

20"And when I divided seven loaves of bread for the four thousand, how many baskets did you fill with leftover pieces of food?"

They answered, "Seven."

21Then Jesus said to them, "Don't you understand yet?"

JESUS HEALS A BLIND MAN

22Jesus and his followers came to Bethsaida. There some people brought a blind man to Jesus and begged him to touch the man. 23So Jesus took the blind man's hand and led him out of the village. Then he spit on the man's eyes and put his hands on the man and asked, "Can you see now?"

24The man looked up and said, "Yes, I see people, but they look like trees walking around."

25Again Jesus put his hands on the man's eyes. Then the man opened his eyes wide and they were healed, and he was able to see everything clearly. 26Jesus told him to go home, saying, "Don't go into the town."[n]

PETER SAYS JESUS IS THE CHRIST

27Jesus and his followers went to the towns around Caesarea Philippi. While they were traveling, Jesus asked them, "Who do people say I am?"

28They answered, "Some say you are John the Baptist. Others say you are Elijah,[n] and others say you are one of the prophets."

29Then Jesus asked, "But who do you say I am?"

Peter answered, "You are the Christ."

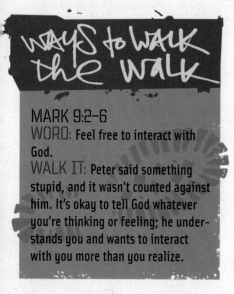

MARK 9:2-6

WORD: Feel free to interact with God.

WALK IT: Peter said something stupid, and it wasn't counted against him. It's okay to tell God whatever you're thinking or feeling; he understands you and wants to interact with you more than you realize.

30Jesus warned his followers not to tell anyone who he was.

31Then Jesus began to teach them that the Son of Man must suffer many things and that he would be rejected by the Jewish elders, the leading priests, and the teachers of the law. He told them that the Son of Man must be killed and then rise from the dead after three days. 32Jesus told them plainly what would happen. Then Peter took Jesus aside and began to tell him not to talk like that. 33But Jesus turned and looked at his followers. Then he told Peter not to talk that way. He said, "Go away from me, Satan![n] You don't care about the things of God, but only about things people think are important."

34Then Jesus called the crowd to him, along with his followers. He said, "If people want to follow me, they must give up the things they want. They must be willing even to give up their lives to follow me. 35Those who want to save their lives will give up true life. But those who give up their lives for me and for the Good News will have true life. 36It is worthless to have the whole world if they lose their souls. 37They could never pay enough to buy back their souls. 38The people who live now are living in a sinful and evil time. If people are ashamed of me and my teaching, the Son of Man will be ashamed of them when he comes with his Father's glory and with the holy angels."

9 Then Jesus said to the people, "I tell you the truth, some people standing here will see the kingdom of God come with power before they die."

JESUS TALKS WITH MOSES AND ELIJAH

2Six days later, Jesus took Peter, James, and John up on a high mountain by themselves. While they watched, Jesus' appearance was changed. 3His clothes became shining white, whiter than any person could make them. 4Then Elijah and Moses[n] appeared to them, talking with Jesus.

5Peter said to Jesus, "Teacher, it is good that we are here. Let us make three tents—one for you, one for Moses, and one for Elijah." 6Peter did not know what to say, because he and the others were so frightened.

7Then a cloud came and covered them, and a voice came from the cloud, saying, "This is my Son, whom I love. Listen to him!"

8Suddenly Peter, James, and John looked around, but they saw only Jesus there alone with them.

9As they were coming down the mountain,

RADICAL FAITH

MARK 8:29-33

Every Bible should come with batteries and blinking red lights to highlight this passage as containing some of the most important words in God's Holy Book. Jesus is quizzing his closest followers, tossing them a couple of pointed questions. First, he asks them who the crowds think he is. The opinions of the masses miss the truth by miles. They imagine that Jesus is John the Baptist or one of God's Old Testament spokesmen come back from the dead. Then Jesus asks his tightest followers who they believe that he is. Peter speaks for the group with an accurate answer: Jesus is the Christ, the Messiah sent by God. While the crowd gawks at Jesus in confusion, Peter's confession reveals stunning awareness of Jesus' true identity. Because the apostles grasped who Jesus was, the Lord started explaining how he would die for the world, then rise from the dead. Yet, that truth was too much for them to process, and Peter objected. But Jesus didn't retract his statement. In fact, he later delivered the goods by dying for all of us.

8:26 town Some Greek copies continue, "Don't even go and tell anyone in the town." **8:28 Elijah** A man who spoke for God and who lived hundreds of years before Christ. See 1 Kings 17. **8:33 Satan** Name for the devil meaning "the enemy." Jesus means that Peter was talking like Satan. **9:4 Elijah and Moses** Two of the most important Jewish leaders in the past. God had given Moses the Law, and Elijah was an important prophet.

55

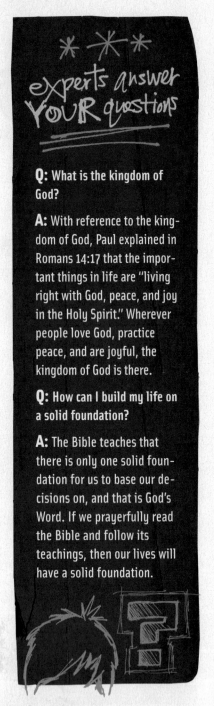

Jesus commanded them not to tell anyone about what they had seen until the Son of Man had risen from the dead.

¹⁰So the followers obeyed Jesus, but they discussed what he meant about rising from the dead.

¹¹Then they asked Jesus, "Why do the teachers of the law say that Elijah must come first?"

¹²Jesus answered, "They are right to say that Elijah must come first and make everything the way it should be. But why does the Scripture say that the Son of Man will suffer much and that people will treat him as if he were nothing? ¹³I tell you that Elijah has already come. And people did to him whatever they wanted to do, just as the Scriptures said it would happen."

JESUS HEALS A SICK BOY

¹⁴When Jesus, Peter, James, and John came back to the other followers, they saw a great crowd around them and the teachers of the law arguing with them. ¹⁵But as soon as the crowd saw Jesus, the people were surprised and ran to welcome him.

¹⁶Jesus asked, "What are you arguing about?"

¹⁷A man answered, "Teacher, I brought my son to you. He has an evil spirit in him that stops him from talking. ¹⁸When the spirit attacks him, it throws him on the ground. Then my son foams at the mouth, grinds his teeth, and becomes very stiff. I asked your followers to force the evil spirit out, but they couldn't."

¹⁹Jesus answered, "You people have no faith. How long must I stay with you? How long must I put up with you? Bring the boy to me."

²⁰So the followers brought him to Jesus. As soon as the evil spirit saw Jesus, it made the boy lose control of himself, and he fell down and rolled on the ground, foaming at the mouth.

²¹Jesus asked the boy's father, "How long has this been happening?"

The father answered, "Since he was very young. ²²The spirit often throws him into a fire or into water to kill him. If you can do anything for him, please have pity on us and help us."

²³Jesus said to the father, "You said, 'If you can!' All things are possible for the one who believes."

²⁴Immediately the father cried out, "I do believe! Help me to believe more!"

²⁵When Jesus saw that a crowd was quickly gathering, he ordered the evil spirit, saying, "You spirit that makes people unable to hear or speak, I command you to come out of this boy and never enter him again!"

²⁶The evil spirit screamed and caused the boy to fall on the ground again. Then the spirit came out. The boy looked as if he were dead, and many people said, "He is dead!" ²⁷But Jesus took hold of the boy's hand and helped him to stand up.

²⁸When Jesus went into the house, his followers began asking him privately, "Why couldn't we force that evil spirit out?"

²⁹Jesus answered, "That kind of spirit can only be forced out by prayer."ⁿ

JESUS TALKS ABOUT HIS DEATH

³⁰Then Jesus and his followers left that place and went through Galilee. He didn't want anyone to know where he was, ³¹because he was teaching his followers. He said to them, "The Son of Man will be handed over to people, and they will kill him. After three days, he will rise from the dead." ³²But the followers did not understand what Jesus meant, and they were afraid to ask him.

WHO IS THE GREATEST?

³³Jesus and his followers went to Capernaum. When they went into a house there, he asked them, "What were you arguing about on the road?" ³⁴But the followers did not answer, because their argument on the road was about which one of them was the greatest.

³⁵Jesus sat down and called the twelve apostles to him. He said, "Whoever wants to be the most important must be last of all and servant of all."

³⁶Then Jesus took a small child and had him stand among them. Taking the child in his arms, he said, ³⁷"Whoever accepts a child like this in my name accepts me. And whoever accepts me accepts the One who sent me."

ANYONE NOT AGAINST US IS FOR US

³⁸Then John said, "Teacher, we saw someone using your name to force demons out of a

9:29 prayer Some Greek copies continue, "and fasting."

person. We told him to stop, because he does not belong to our group."

[39]But Jesus said, "Don't stop him, because anyone who uses my name to do powerful things will not easily say evil things about me. [40]Whoever is not against us is with us. [41]I tell you the truth, whoever gives you a drink of water because you belong to the Christ will truly get his reward.

[42]"If one of these little children believes in me, and someone causes that child to sin, it would be better for that person to have a large stone tied around his neck and be drowned in the sea. [43]If your hand causes you to sin, cut it off. It is better for you to lose part of your body and live forever than to have two hands and go to hell, where the fire never goes out. [[44]In hell the worm does not die; the fire is never put out.][45]If your foot causes you to sin, cut it off. It is better for you to lose part of your body and to live forever than to have two feet and be thrown into hell. [[46]In hell the worm does not die; the fire is never put out.][47]If your eye causes you to sin, take it out. It is better for you to enter the kingdom of God with only one eye than to have two eyes and be thrown into hell. [48]In hell the worm does not die; the fire is never put out. [49]Every person will be salted with fire.

[50]"Salt is good, but if the salt loses its salty taste, you cannot make it salty again. So, be full of salt, and have peace with each other."

JESUS TEACHES ABOUT DIVORCE

10 Then Jesus left that place and went into the area of Judea and across the Jordan River. Again, crowds came to him, and he taught them as he usually did.

[2]Some Pharisees came to Jesus and tried to trick him. They asked, "Is it right for a man to divorce his wife?"

[3]Jesus answered, "What did Moses command you to do?"

[4]They said, "Moses allowed a man to write out divorce papers and send her away."[n]

[5]Jesus said, "Moses wrote that command for you because you were stubborn. [6]But when God made the world, 'he made them male and female.'[n] [7]'So a man will leave his father and mother and be united with his wife,[n] [8]and the two will become one body.'[n] So there are not two, but one. [9]God has joined the two together, so no one should separate them."

[10]Later, in the house, his followers asked Jesus again about the question of divorce. [11]He answered, "Anyone who divorces his wife and marries another woman is guilty of adultery against her. [12]And the woman who divorces her husband and marries another man is also guilty of adultery."

JESUS ACCEPTS CHILDREN

[13]Some people brought their little children to Jesus so he could touch them, but his followers told them to stop. [14]When Jesus saw this, he was upset and said to them, "Let the little children come to me. Don't stop them, because the kingdom of God belongs to people who are like these children. [15]I tell you the truth, you must accept the kingdom of God as if you were a little child, or you will never enter it." [16]Then Jesus took the children in his arms, put his hands on them, and blessed them.

A RICH YOUNG MAN'S QUESTION

[17]As Jesus started to leave, a man ran to him and fell on his knees before Jesus. The man asked, "Good teacher, what must I do to have life forever?"

[18]Jesus answered, "Why do you call me good? Only God is good. [19]You know the commands: 'You must not murder anyone. You must not be guilty of adultery. You must not steal. You must not tell lies about your neighbor. You must not cheat. Honor your father and mother.' "[n]

[20]The man said, "Teacher, I have obeyed all these things since I was a boy."

[21]Jesus, looking at the man, loved him and said, "There is one more thing you need to do. Go and sell everything you have, and give the money to the poor, and you will have treasure in heaven. Then come and follow me."

[22]He was very sad to hear Jesus say this, and he left sorrowfully, because he was rich.

[23]Then Jesus looked at his followers and said, "How hard it will be for the rich to enter the kingdom of God!"

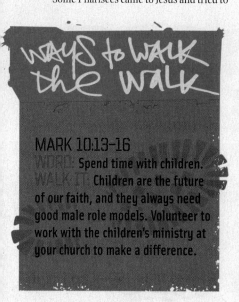

WAYS to WALK the WALK

MARK 10:13–16
WORD: Spend time with children.
WALK IT: Children are the future of our faith, and they always need good male role models. Volunteer to work with the children's ministry at your church to make a difference.

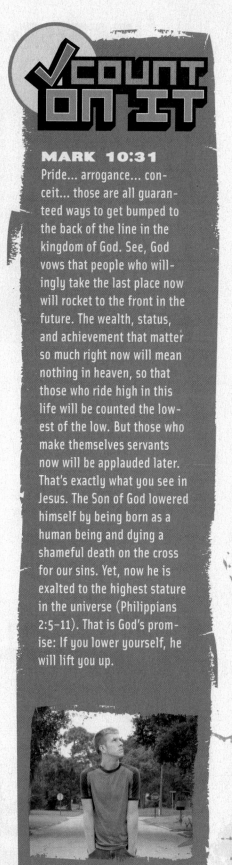

✓ COUNT ON IT

MARK 10:31

Pride... arrogance... conceit... those are all guaranteed ways to get bumped to the back of the line in the kingdom of God. See, God vows that people who willingly take the last place now will rocket to the front in the future. The wealth, status, and achievement that matter so much right now will mean nothing in heaven, so that those who ride high in this life will be counted the lowest of the low. But those who make themselves servants now will be applauded later. That's exactly what you see in Jesus. The Son of God lowered himself by being born as a human being and dying a shameful death on the cross for our sins. Yet, now he is exalted to the highest stature in the universe (Philippians 2:5–11). That is God's promise: If you lower yourself, he will lift you up.

9:44, 46 In . . . out. Some Greek copies do not contain the bracketed text.   10:4 "Moses . . . away." Quotation from Deuteronomy 24:1.   10:6 'he made . . . female' Quotation from Genesis 1:27.   10:7 and . . . wife Some Greek copies do not have this phrase.   10:7–8 'So . . . body.' Quotation from Genesis 2:24.   10:19 'You . . . mother.' Quotation from Exodus 20:12–16; Deuteronomy 5:16–20.

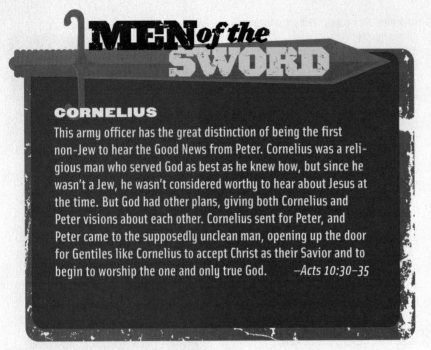

MEN *of the* SWORD

CORNELIUS

This army officer has the great distinction of being the first non-Jew to hear the Good News from Peter. Cornelius was a religious man who served God as best as he knew how, but since he wasn't a Jew, he wasn't considered worthy to hear about Jesus at the time. But God had other plans, giving both Cornelius and Peter visions about each other. Cornelius sent for Peter, and Peter came to the supposedly unclean man, opening up the door for Gentiles like Cornelius to accept Christ as their Savior and to begin to worship the one and only true God.   —Acts 10:30–35

24 The followers were amazed at what Jesus said. But he said again, "My children, it is very hard[n] to enter the kingdom of God! 25 It is easier for a camel to go through the eye of a needle than for a rich person to enter the kingdom of God."

26 The followers were even more surprised and said to each other, "Then who can be saved?"

27 Jesus looked at them and said, "For people this is impossible, but for God all things are possible."

28 Peter said to Jesus, "Look, we have left everything and followed you."

29 Jesus said, "I tell you the truth, all those who have left houses, brothers, sisters, mother, father, children, or farms for me and for the Good News 30 will get more than they left. Here in this world they will have a hundred times more homes, brothers, sisters, mothers, children, and fields. And with those things, they will also suffer for their belief. But in this age they will have life forever. 31 Many who are first now will be last in the future. And many who are last now will be first in the future."

JESUS TALKS ABOUT HIS DEATH

32 As Jesus and the people with him were on the road to Jerusalem, he was leading the way. His followers were amazed, but others in the crowd who followed were afraid. Again Jesus took the twelve apostles aside and began to tell them what was about to happen in Jerusalem. 33 He said, "Look, we are going to Jerusalem. The Son of Man will be turned over to the leading priests and the teachers of the law. They will say that he must die, and they will turn him over to the non-Jewish people, 34 who will laugh at him and spit on him. They will beat him with whips and crucify him. But on the third day, he will rise to life again."

TWO FOLLOWERS ASK JESUS A FAVOR

35 Then James and John, sons of Zebedee, came to Jesus and said, "Teacher, we want to ask you to do something for us."

36 Jesus asked, "What do you want me to do for you?"

37 They answered, "Let one of us sit at your right side and one of us sit at your left side in your glory in your kingdom."

38 Jesus said, "You don't understand what you are asking. Can you drink the cup that I must drink? And can you be baptized with the same kind of baptism that I must go through?"[n]

39 They answered, "Yes, we can."

Jesus said to them, "You will drink the same cup that I will drink, and you will be baptized with the same baptism that I must go through. 40 But I cannot choose who will sit at my right or my left; those places belong to those for whom they have been prepared."

41 When the other ten followers heard this, they began to be angry with James and John.

fight the fight

Mark 11:22–26

This is one of many New Testament passages that talk about faith and prayer. They all make it clear that when you ask God for something, you shouldn't waver in your belief in God's ability to answer. Yet, there is a condition with prayer—God wants us to get rid of any grudges we are holding. These verses are fascinating for the way they start, with Jesus talking about being able to move mountains if you believe. But they wind up with him saying to forgive anyone who has made you angry. If you expect to see God's power in your life, you will need to do what he says.

10:24 hard Some Greek copies continue, "for those who trust in riches." 10:38 Can you . . . through? Jesus was asking if they could suffer the same terrible things that would happen to him.

[42]Jesus called them together and said, "The other nations have rulers. You know that those rulers love to show their power over the people, and their important leaders love to use all their authority. [43]But it should not be that way among you. Whoever wants to become great among you must serve the rest of you like a servant. [44]Whoever wants to become the first among you must serve all of you like a slave. [45]In the same way, the Son of Man did not come to be served. He came to serve others and to give his life as a ransom for many people."

JESUS HEALS A BLIND MAN

[46]Then they came to the town of Jericho. As Jesus was leaving there with his followers and a great many people, a blind beggar named Bartimaeus son of Timaeus was sitting by the road. [47]When he heard that Jesus from Nazareth was walking by, he began to shout, "Jesus, Son of David, have mercy on me!"

[48]Many people warned the blind man to be quiet, but he shouted even more, "Son of David, have mercy on me!"

[49]Jesus stopped and said, "Tell the man to come here."

So they called the blind man, saying, "Cheer up! Get to your feet. Jesus is calling you." [50]The blind man jumped up, left his coat there, and went to Jesus.

[51]Jesus asked him, "What do you want me to do for you?"

The blind man answered, "Teacher, I want to see."

[52]Jesus said, "Go, you are healed because you believed." At once the man could see, and he followed Jesus on the road.

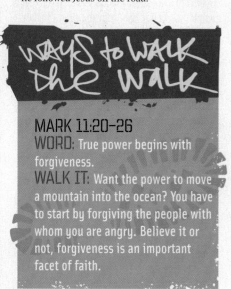

WAYS to WALK the WALK

MARK 11:20–26
WORD: True power begins with forgiveness.
WALK IT: Want the power to move a mountain into the ocean? You have to start by forgiving the people with whom you are angry. Believe it or not, forgiveness is an important facet of faith.

JESUS ENTERS JERUSALEM AS A KING

11 As Jesus and his followers were coming closer to Jerusalem, they came to the towns of Bethphage and Bethany near the Mount of Olives. From there Jesus sent two of his followers [2]and said to them, "Go to the town you can see there. When you enter it, you will quickly find a colt tied, which no one has ever ridden. Untie it and bring it here to me. [3]If anyone asks you why you are doing this, tell him its Master needs the colt, and he will send it at once."

[4]The followers went into the town, found a colt tied in the street near the door of a house, and untied it. [5]Some people were standing there and asked, "What are you doing? Why are you untying that colt?" [6]The followers answered the way Jesus told them to answer, and the people let them take the colt.

[7]They brought the colt to Jesus and put their coats on it, and Jesus sat on it. [8]Many people spread their coats on the road. Others cut branches in the fields and spread them on the road. [9]The people were walking ahead of Jesus and behind him, shouting,

"Praise God!
God bless the One who comes in the name
    of the Lord!   *Psalm 118:26*
[10]God bless the kingdom of our father
    David!
    That kingdom is coming!
Praise[n] to God in heaven!"

[11]Jesus entered Jerusalem and went into the Temple. After he had looked at everything, since it was already late, he went out to Bethany with the twelve apostles.

[12]The next day as Jesus was leaving Bethany, he became hungry. [13]Seeing a fig tree in leaf from far away, he went to see if it had any figs on it. But he found no figs, only leaves, because it was not the right season for figs. [14]So Jesus said to the tree, "May no one ever eat fruit from you again." And Jesus' followers heard him say this.

JESUS GOES TO THE TEMPLE

[15]When Jesus returned to Jerusalem, he went into the Temple and began to throw out those who were buying and selling there. He turned over the tables of those who were exchanging different kinds of money, and he upset the benches of those who were selling doves. [16]Jesus refused to allow anyone to carry goods through the Temple courts. [17]Then he taught the people, saying, "It is written in the Scriptures, 'My Temple will be called a house for prayer for people from all nations.'[n] But you are changing God's house into a 'hideout for robbers.' "[n]

[18]The leading priests and the teachers of the

BIBLE BASICS

DEMON

A demon is an evil spirit from the devil sent to harass people and influence them to sin. Demons are fallen angels led by the devil in rebellion against God, and their ultimate home is hell. Christians have no need to fear demons, as Scripture teaches that believers have been given authority over them in the name of Jesus (Mark 16:17). As disembodied spirits, demons seek full expression through the bodies of people, and, if allowed, may possess someone who does not believe in Jesus Christ. Demons are generally the evil influence behind people committing acts of violence and other dastardly deeds.

law heard all this and began trying to find a way to kill Jesus. They were afraid of him, because all the people were amazed at his teaching. [19]That evening, Jesus and his followers[n] left the city.

THE POWER OF FAITH

[20]The next morning as Jesus was passing by with his followers, they saw the fig tree dry and dead, even to the roots. [21]Peter remembered the tree and said to Jesus, "Teacher, look! The fig tree you cursed is dry and dead!"

[22]Jesus answered, "Have faith in God. [23]I tell you the truth, you can say to this mountain, 'Go, fall into the sea.' And if you have no doubts in your mind and believe that what you

---

11:10 Praise Literally, "Hosanna," a Hebrew word used at first in praying to God for help, but at this time it was probably a shout of joy used in praising God or his Messiah. **11:17** 'My Temple . . . nations.' Quotation from Isaiah 56:7. **11:17** 'hideout for robbers' Quotation from Jeremiah 7:11. **11:19** his followers Some Greek copies mention only Jesus here.

extras:

How to Drive a Standard Transmission Vehicle

Oh, no. The dreaded "stick." Fear not. Driving that standard is simple. To start the vehicle, depress the clutch (the pedal to the far left) and put the gearshift in neutral. Turn the key. With the clutch still depressed, move the gearshift into first gear (to the left and up). This is the tricky part. Gently let out on the clutch while simultaneously pressing down on the accelerator. This should be a smooth transition that ends with the vehicle driving forward. When you reach cruising speed, quickly depress the clutch, shift straight down into second (you'll feel it pop into gear), and let the clutch out. Repeat for third and fourth. To slow down, put the vehicle in neutral and coast to a stop, or downshift in reverse order. It takes practice, but once you get the hang of it, you'll always have the skill. And just like the gears have priority on a standard, your life should be prioritized, too. God should always be first.

say will happen, God will do it for you. [24]So I tell you to believe that you have received the things you ask for in prayer, and God will give them to you. [25]When you are praying, if you are angry with someone, forgive him so that your Father in heaven will also forgive your sins. [[26]But if you don't forgive other people, then your Father in heaven will not forgive your sins.]"[n]

LEADERS DOUBT JESUS' AUTHORITY

[27]Jesus and his followers went again to Jerusalem. As Jesus was walking in the Temple, the leading priests, the teachers of the law, and the elders came to him. [28]They said to him, "What authority do you have to do these things? Who gave you this authority?"

[29]Jesus answered, "I will ask you one question. If you answer me, I will tell you what authority I have to do these things. [30]Tell me: When John baptized people, was that authority from God or just from other people?"

[31]They argued about Jesus' question, saying, "If we answer, 'John's baptism was from God,' Jesus will say, 'Then why didn't you believe him?' [32]But if we say, 'It was from other people,' the crowd will be against us." (These leaders were afraid of the people, because all the people believed that John was a prophet.)

[33]So they answered Jesus, "We don't know."

Jesus said to them, "Then I won't tell you what authority I have to do these things."

A STORY ABOUT GOD'S SON

12 Jesus began to use stories to teach the people. He said, "A man planted a vineyard. He put a wall around it and dug a hole for a winepress and built a tower. Then he leased the land to some farmers and left for a trip. [2]When it was time for the grapes to be picked, he sent a servant to the farmers to get his share of the grapes. [3]But the farmers grabbed the servant and beat him and sent him away empty-handed. [4]Then the man sent another servant. They hit him on the head and showed no respect for him. [5]So the man sent another servant, whom they killed. The man sent many other servants; the farmers beat some of them and killed others.

[6]"The man had one person left to send, his son whom he loved. He sent him last of all, saying, 'They will respect my son.'

[7]"But the farmers said to each other, 'This son will inherit the vineyard. If we kill him, it will be ours.' [8]So they took the son, killed him, and threw him out of the vineyard.

[9]"So what will the owner of the vineyard do? He will come and kill those farmers and will give the vineyard to other farmers. [10]Surely you have read this Scripture:

'The stone that the builders rejected
    became the cornerstone.
[11]The Lord did this,
    and it is wonderful to us.'"

Psalm 118:22–23

[12]The Jewish leaders knew that the story was about them. So they wanted to find a way to arrest Jesus, but they were afraid of the people. So the leaders left him and went away.

IS IT RIGHT TO PAY TAXES OR NOT?

[13]Later, the Jewish leaders sent some Pharisees and Herodians[n] to Jesus to trap him in saying something wrong. [14]They came to him and said, "Teacher, we know that you are an honest man. You are not afraid of what other people think about you, because you pay no attention to who they are. And you teach the truth about God's way. Tell us: Is it right to pay taxes to Caesar or not? [15]Should we pay them, or not?"

But knowing what these men were really trying to do, Jesus said to them, "Why are you trying to trap me? Bring me a coin to look at." [16]They gave Jesus a coin, and he asked, "Whose image and name are on the coin?"

They answered, "Caesar's."

[17]Then Jesus said to them, "Give to Caesar the things that are Caesar's, and give to God the things that are God's." The men were amazed at what Jesus said.

SOME SADDUCEES TRY TO TRICK JESUS

[18]Then some Sadducees came to Jesus and asked him a question. (Sadducees believed that people would not rise from the dead.) [19]They said, "Teacher, Moses wrote that if a man's brother dies, leaving a wife but no children, then that man must marry the widow and have children for his brother. [20]Once there were seven brothers. The first brother married and died, leaving no children. [21]So the second brother married the widow, but he also died and had no children. The same thing happened with the third brother. [22]All seven brothers married her and died, and none of the brothers had any children. Finally the woman died too. [23]Since all seven brothers had married her, when people rise from the dead, whose wife will she be?"

[24]Jesus answered, "Why don't you understand? Don't you know what the Scriptures say, and don't you know about the power of God? [25]When people rise from the dead, they

---

11:26 **But . . . sins.** Some Greek copies do not contain the bracketed text.   12:13 **Herodians** A political group that followed Herod and his family.

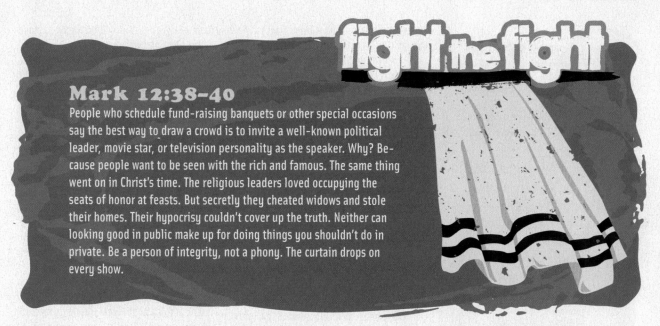

fight the fight

Mark 12:38–40

People who schedule fund-raising banquets or other special occasions say the best way to draw a crowd is to invite a well-known political leader, movie star, or television personality as the speaker. Why? Because people want to be seen with the rich and famous. The same thing went on in Christ's time. The religious leaders loved occupying the seats of honor at feasts. But secretly they cheated widows and stole their homes. Their hypocrisy couldn't cover up the truth. Neither can looking good in public make up for doing things you shouldn't do in private. Be a person of integrity, not a phony. The curtain drops on every show.

will not marry, nor will they be given to someone to marry. They will be like the angels in heaven. [26]Surely you have read what God said about people rising from the dead. In the book in which Moses wrote about the burning bush,[n] it says that God told Moses, 'I am the God of Abraham, the God of Isaac, and the God of Jacob.'[n] [27]God is the God of the living, not the dead. You Sadducees are wrong!"

THE MOST IMPORTANT COMMAND

[28]One of the teachers of the law came and heard Jesus arguing with the Sadducees. Seeing that Jesus gave good answers to their questions, he asked Jesus, "Which of the commands is most important?"

[29]Jesus answered, "The most important command is this: 'Listen, people of Israel! The Lord our God is the only Lord. [30]Love the Lord your God with all your heart, all your soul, all your mind, and all your strength.'[n] [31]The second command is this: 'Love your neighbor as you love yourself.'[n] There are no commands more important than these."

[32]The man answered, "That was a good answer, Teacher. You were right when you said God is the only Lord and there is no other God besides him. [33]One must love God with all his heart, all his mind, and all his strength. And one must love his neighbor as he loves himself. These commands are more important than all the animals and sacrifices we offer to God."

[34]When Jesus saw that the man answered him wisely, Jesus said to him, "You are close to the kingdom of God." And after that, no one was brave enough to ask Jesus any more questions.

[35]As Jesus was teaching in the Temple, he asked, "Why do the teachers of the law say that

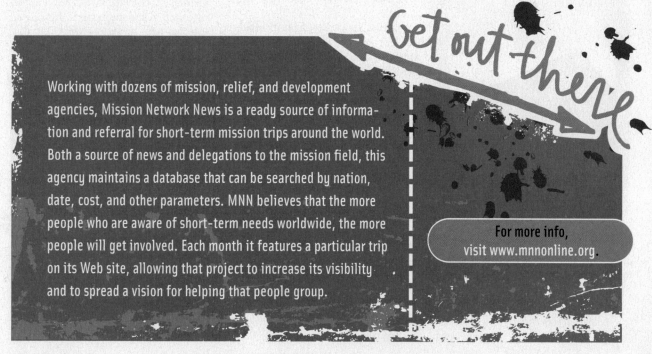

Get out there

Working with dozens of mission, relief, and development agencies, Mission Network News is a ready source of information and referral for short-term mission trips around the world. Both a source of news and delegations to the mission field, this agency maintains a database that can be searched by nation, date, cost, and other parameters. MNN believes that the more people who are aware of short-term needs worldwide, the more people will get involved. Each month it features a particular trip on its Web site, allowing that project to increase its visibility and to spread a vision for helping that people group.

For more info, visit www.mnnonline.org.

12:26 burning bush Read Exodus 3:1–12 in the Old Testament.   **12:26 'I am . . . Jacob.'** Quotation from Exodus 3:6.   **12:29–30 'Listen . . . strength.'** Quotation from Deuteronomy 6:4–5.   **12:31 'Love . . . yourself.'** Quotation from Leviticus 19:18.

MARK 13:31

The lyrics of today's hot song will fade to silence in a few years, if not a few weeks. The year's box office hit will soon transfer to a cheap disc format that no one will be able to read one day. According to Jesus, those aren't the only things that will disappear. At the end of time, even the ground you stand on will shatter. Jesus says there's only one thing you can count on to last forever: the Word of God. The Old Testament declares that the Word of God is everlasting (Psalm 119:89). Unlike changing human opinion polls or trendy schools of thought, the Bible is pure truth that will outlive all of us. Like Isaiah 40:8 says, "The grass dies and the flowers fall, but the word of our God will live forever."

the Christ is the son of David? [36]David himself, speaking by the Holy Spirit, said:

"The Lord said to my Lord,
"Sit by me at my right side,
until I put your enemies under your control." '
                        Psalm 110:1

[37]David himself calls the Christ 'Lord,' so how can the Christ be his son?" The large crowd listened to Jesus with pleasure.

[38]Jesus continued teaching and said, "Beware of the teachers of the law. They like to walk around wearing fancy clothes, and they love for people to greet them with respect in the marketplaces. [39]They love to have the most important seats in the synagogues and at feasts. [40]But they cheat widows and steal their houses and then try to make themselves look good by saying long prayers. They will receive a greater punishment."

TRUE GIVING

[41]Jesus sat near the Temple money box and watched the people put in their money. Many rich people gave large sums of money. [42]Then a poor widow came and put in two small copper coins, which were only worth a few cents. [43]Calling his followers to him, Jesus said, "I tell you the truth, this poor widow gave more than all those rich people. [44]They gave only what they did not need. This woman is very poor, but she gave all she had; she gave all she had to live on."

THE TEMPLE WILL BE DESTROYED

13 As Jesus was leaving the Temple, one of his followers said to him, "Look, Teacher! How beautiful the buildings are! How big the stones are!"

[2]Jesus said, "Do you see all these great buildings? Not one stone will be left on another. Every stone will be thrown down to the ground."

[3]Later, as Jesus was sitting on the Mount of Olives, opposite the Temple, he was alone with Peter, James, John, and Andrew. They asked Jesus, [4]"Tell us, when will these things happen? And what will be the sign that they are going to happen?"

[5]Jesus began to answer them, "Be careful that no one fools you. [6]Many people will come in my name, saying, 'I am the One,' and they will fool many people. [7]When you hear about wars and stories of wars that are coming, don't be afraid. These things must happen before the end comes. [8]Nations will fight against other nations, and kingdoms against other kingdoms. There will be earthquakes in different places, and there will be times when there is no food for people to eat. These things are like the first pains when something new is about to be born.

[9]"You must be careful. People will arrest you and take you to court and beat you in their synagogues. You will be forced to stand before kings and governors, to tell them about me. This will happen to you because you follow me. [10]But before these things happen, the Good News must be told to all people. [11]When you are arrested and judged, don't worry ahead of time about what you should say. Say whatever is given you to say at that time, because it will not really be you speaking; it will be the Holy Spirit.

[12]"Brothers will give their own brothers to be killed, and fathers will give their own children to be killed. Children will fight against their own parents and cause them to be put to death. [13]All people will hate you because you follow me, but those people who keep their faith until the end will be saved.

[14]"You will see 'a blasphemous object that brings destruction'[n] standing where it should not be." (You who read this should understand what it means.) "At that time, the people in Judea should run away to the mountains. [15]If people are on the roofs[n] of their houses, they must not go down or go inside to get anything out of their houses. [16]If people are in the fields, they must not go back to get their coats. [17]At that time, how terrible it will be for women who are pregnant or have nursing babies! [18]Pray that these things will not happen in winter, [19]because those days will be full of trouble. There will be more trouble than there has ever been since the beginning, when God made the world, until now, and nothing as bad will ever happen again. [20]God has decided to make that terrible time short. Otherwise, no one would go on living. But God will make that time short to help the people he has chosen. [21]At that time, someone might say to you,

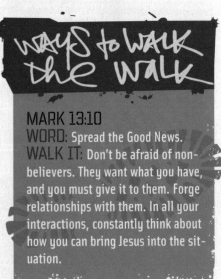

MARK 13:10
WORD: Spread the Good News.
WALK IT: Don't be afraid of nonbelievers. They want what you have, and you must give it to them. Forge relationships with them. In all your interactions, constantly think about how you can bring Jesus into the situation.

'Look, there is the Christ!' Or another person might say, 'There he is!' But don't believe them. ²²False Christs and false prophets will come and perform great wonders and miracles. They will try to fool even the people God has chosen, if that is possible. ²³So be careful. I have warned you about all this before it happens.

²⁴"During the days after this trouble comes,

'the sun will grow dark,
    and the moon will not give its light.
²⁵The stars will fall from the sky.
    And the powers of the heavens will be
        shaken.'   *Isaiah 13:10; 34:4*

²⁶"Then people will see the Son of Man coming in clouds with great power and glory. ²⁷Then he will send his angels all around the earth to gather his chosen people from every part of the earth and from every part of heaven.

²⁸"Learn a lesson from the fig tree: When its branches become green and soft and new leaves appear, you know summer is near. ²⁹In the same way, when you see these things happening, you will know that the time is near, ready to come. ³⁰I tell you the truth, all these things will happen while the people of this time are still living. ³¹Earth and sky will be destroyed, but the words I have said will never be destroyed.

³²"No one knows when that day or time will be, not the angels in heaven, not even the Son. Only the Father knows. ³³Be careful! Always be ready,ⁿ because you don't know when that time will be. ³⁴It is like a man who goes on a trip. He leaves his house and lets his servants take care of it, giving each one a special job to do. The man tells the servant guarding the door always to be watchful. ³⁵So always be ready, because you don't know when the owner of the house will come back. It might be in the evening, or at midnight, or in the morning while it is still dark, or when the sun rises. ³⁶Always be ready. Otherwise he might come back suddenly and find you sleeping. ³⁷I tell you this, and I say this to everyone: 'Be ready!'"

THE PLAN TO KILL JESUS

14 It was now only two days before the Passover and the Feast of Unleavened Bread. The leading priests and teachers of the law were trying to find a trick to arrest Jesus and kill him. ²But they said, "We must not do it during the feast, because the people might cause a riot."

A WOMAN WITH PERFUME FOR JESUS

³Jesus was in Bethany at the house of Simon, who had a skin disease. While Jesus was eating there, a woman approached him with an alabaster jar filled with very expensive perfume, made of pure nard. She opened the jar and poured the perfume on Jesus' head.

⁴Some who were there became upset and said to each other, "Why waste that perfume? ⁵It was worth a full year's work. It could have been sold and the money given to the poor." And they got very angry with the woman.

⁶Jesus said, "Leave her alone. Why are you troubling her? She did an excellent thing for me. ⁷You will always have the poor with you, and you can help them anytime you want. But you will not always have me. ⁸This woman did the only thing she could do for me; she poured perfume on my body to prepare me for burial. ⁹I tell you the truth, wherever the Good News is preached in all the world, what this woman has done will be told, and people will remember her."

JUDAS BECOMES AN ENEMY OF JESUS

¹⁰One of the twelve apostles, Judas Iscariot, went to talk to the leading priests to offer to hand Jesus over to them. ¹¹These priests were pleased about this and promised to pay Judas money. So he watched for the best time to turn Jesus in.

JESUS EATS THE PASSOVER MEAL

¹²It was now the first day of the Feast of Unleavened Bread when the Passover lamb was sacrificed. Jesus' followers said to him, "Where do you want us to go and prepare for you to eat the Passover meal?"

¹³Jesus sent two of his followers and said to them, "Go into the city and a man carrying a jar of water will meet you. Follow him. ¹⁴When he goes into a house, tell the owner of the house, 'The Teacher says: "Where is my guest room in which I can eat the Passover meal with my followers?" ' ¹⁵The owner will show you a large room upstairs that is furnished and ready. Prepare the food for us there."

¹⁶So the followers left and went into the city. Everything happened as Jesus had said, so they prepared the Passover meal.

¹⁷In the evening, Jesus went to that house with the twelve. ¹⁸While they were all eating, Jesus said, "I tell you the truth, one of you will turn against me—one of you eating with me now."

¹⁹The followers were very sad to hear this. Each one began to say to Jesus, "I am not the one, am I?"

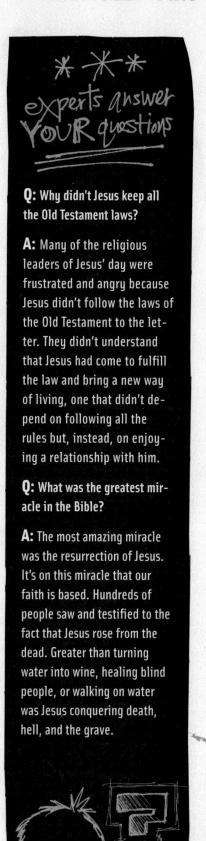

experts answer YOUR questions

Q: Why didn't Jesus keep all the Old Testament laws?

A: Many of the religious leaders of Jesus' day were frustrated and angry because Jesus didn't follow the laws of the Old Testament to the letter. They didn't understand that Jesus had come to fulfill the law and bring a new way of living, one that didn't depend on following all the rules but, instead, on enjoying a relationship with him.

Q: What was the greatest miracle in the Bible?

A: The most amazing miracle was the resurrection of Jesus. It's on this miracle that our faith is based. Hundreds of people saw and testified to the fact that Jesus rose from the dead. Greater than turning water into wine, healing blind people, or walking on water was Jesus conquering death, hell, and the grave.

13:33 ready Some Greek copies continue, "and pray."

Relationships

"But love your enemies, do good to them, and lend to them without hoping to get anything back. Then you will have a great reward" (Luke 6:35a). This has to be one of the wildest, most revolutionary things Jesus ever said, this stuff about loving your enemies. But Jesus loved one of his greatest enemies, and Saul the persecutor later became the apostle Paul as a result. The bottom line is: you never know what will actually happen when you love your enemies, so listen to what Jesus said and put it into action. You may be forming a lifetime relationship.

[20]Jesus answered, "It is one of the twelve—the one who dips his bread into the bowl with me. [21]The Son of Man will die, just as the Scriptures say. But how terrible it will be for the person who hands the Son of Man over to be killed. It would be better for him if he had never been born."

THE LORD'S SUPPER

[22]While they were eating, Jesus took some bread and thanked God for it and broke it. Then he gave it to his followers and said, "Take it; this is my body."

[23]Then Jesus took a cup and thanked God for it and gave it to the followers, and they all drank from the cup.

[24]Then Jesus said, "This is my blood which is the new[n] agreement that God makes with his people. This blood is poured out for many. [25]I tell you the truth, I will not drink of this fruit of the vine[n] again until that day when I drink it new in the kingdom of God."

[26]After singing a hymn, they went out to the Mount of Olives.

JESUS' FOLLOWERS WILL LEAVE HIM

[27]Then Jesus told the followers, "You will all stumble in your faith, because it is written in the Scriptures:

'I will kill the shepherd,
    and the sheep will scatter.'

Zechariah 13:7

[28]But after I rise from the dead, I will go ahead of you into Galilee."

[29]Peter said, "Everyone else may stumble in their faith, but I will not."

[30]Jesus answered, "I tell you the truth, tonight before the rooster crows twice you will say three times you don't know me."

[31]But Peter insisted, "I will never say that I don't know you! I will even die with you!" And all the other followers said the same thing.

JESUS PRAYS ALONE

[32]Jesus and his followers went to a place called Gethsemane. He said to them, "Sit here while I pray." [33]Jesus took Peter, James, and John with him, and he began to be very sad and troubled. [34]He said to them, "My heart is full of sorrow, to the point of death. Stay here and watch."

[35]After walking a little farther away from them, Jesus fell to the ground and prayed that, if possible, he would not have this time of suffering. [36]He prayed, "Abba,[n] Father! You can do all things. Take away this cup[n] of suffering. But do what you want, not what I want."

[37]Then Jesus went back to his followers and found them asleep. He said to Peter, "Simon, are you sleeping? Couldn't you stay awake with me for one hour? [38]Stay awake and pray for strength against temptation. The spirit wants to do what is right, but the body is weak."

[39]Again Jesus went away and prayed the same thing. [40]Then he went back to his followers, and again he found them asleep, because their eyes were very heavy. And they did not know what to say to him.

[41]After Jesus prayed a third time, he went back to his followers and said to them, "Are you still sleeping and resting? That's enough. The time has come for the Son of Man to be handed over to sinful people. [42]Get up, we must go. Look, here comes the man who has turned against me."

JESUS IS ARRESTED

[43]At once, while Jesus was still speaking, Judas, one of the twelve apostles, came up. With him were many people carrying swords and clubs who had been sent from the leading priests, the teachers of the law, and the Jewish elders.

[44]Judas had planned a signal for them, saying, "The man I kiss is Jesus. Arrest him and guard him while you lead him away." [45]So Judas went straight to Jesus and said, "Teacher!" and kissed him. [46]Then the people grabbed Jesus and arrested him. [47]One of his followers standing nearby pulled out his sword and struck the servant of the high priest and cut off his ear.

[48]Then Jesus said, "You came to get me with swords and clubs as if I were a criminal. [49]Every day I was with you teaching in the Temple, and you did not arrest me there. But all these things have happened to make the Scriptures come true." [50]Then all of Jesus' followers left him and ran away.

[51]A young man, wearing only a linen cloth, was following Jesus, and the people also grabbed him. [52]But the cloth he was wearing came off, and he ran away naked.

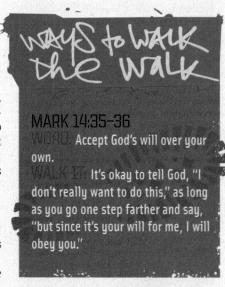

WAYS to WALK the WALK

MARK 14:35-36

WORD Accept God's will over your own.

WALK IT It's okay to tell God, "I don't really want to do this," as long as you go one step farther and say, "but since it's your will for me, I will obey you."

 14:24 new Some Greek copies do not have this word. Compare Luke 22:20.   14:25 fruit of the vine Product of the grapevine; this may also be translated "wine."   14:36 Abba Name that a Jewish child called his father.   14:36 cup Jesus is talking about the terrible things that will happen to him. Accepting these things will be very hard, like drinking a cup of something bitter.

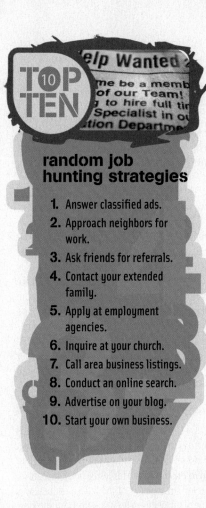

JESUS BEFORE THE LEADERS

[53]The people who arrested Jesus led him to the house of the high priest, where all the leading priests, the elders, and the teachers of the law were gathered. [54]Peter followed far behind and entered the courtyard of the high priest's house. There he sat with the guards, warming himself by the fire.

[55]The leading priests and the whole Jewish council tried to find something that Jesus had done wrong so they could kill him. But the council could find no proof of anything. [56]Many people came and told false things about him, but all said different things—none of them agreed.

[57]Then some people stood up and lied about Jesus, saying, [58]"We heard this man say, 'I will destroy this Temple that people made. And three days later, I will build another Temple not made by people.' " [59]But even the things these people said did not agree.

[60]Then the high priest stood before them and asked Jesus, "Aren't you going to answer? Don't you have something to say about their charges against you?" [61]But Jesus said nothing; he did not answer.

The high priest asked Jesus another question: "Are you the Christ, the Son of the blessed God?"

[62]Jesus answered, "I am. And in the future you will see the Son of Man sitting at the right hand of God, the Powerful One, and coming on clouds in the sky."

[63]When the high priest heard this, he tore his clothes and said, "We don't need any more witnesses! [64]You all heard him say these things against God. What do you think?"

They all said that Jesus was guilty and should die. [65]Some of the people there began to spit at Jesus. They blindfolded him and beat him with their fists and said, "Prove you are a prophet!" Then the guards led Jesus away and beat him.

PETER SAYS HE DOESN'T KNOW JESUS

[66]While Peter was in the courtyard, a servant girl of the high priest came there. [67]She saw Peter warming himself at the fire and looked closely at him.

Then she said, "You also were with Jesus, that man from Nazareth."

[68]But Peter said that he was never with Jesus. He said, "I don't know or understand what you are talking about." Then Peter left and went toward the entrance of the courtyard. And the rooster crowed.[n]

[69]The servant girl saw Peter there, and again she said to the people who were standing nearby, "This man is one of those who followed Jesus." [70]Again Peter said that it was not true.

A short time later, some people were standing near Peter saying, "Surely you are one of those who followed Jesus, because you are from Galilee, too."

[71]Then Peter began to place a curse on himself and swear, "I don't know this man you're talking about!"

[72]At once, the rooster crowed the second time. Then Peter remembered what Jesus had told him: "Before the rooster crows twice, you will say three times that you don't know me." Then Peter lost control of himself and began to cry.

PILATE QUESTIONS JESUS

15 Very early in the morning, the leading priests, the elders, the teachers of the law, and all the Jewish council decided what to do with Jesus. They tied him, led him away, and turned him over to Pilate, the governor.

[2]Pilate asked Jesus, "Are you the king of the Jews?"

Jesus answered, "Those are your words."

[3]The leading priests accused Jesus of many things. [4]So Pilate asked Jesus another question, "You can see that they are accusing you of many things. Aren't you going to answer?"

[5]But Jesus still said nothing, so Pilate was very surprised.

PILATE TRIES TO FREE JESUS

[6]Every year at the time of the Passover the governor would free one prisoner whom the people chose. [7]At that time, there was a man named Barabbas in prison who was a rebel and had committed murder during a riot. [8]The crowd came to Pilate and began to ask him to free a prisoner as he always did.

[9]So Pilate asked them, "Do you want me to free the king of the Jews?" [10]Pilate knew that the leading priests had turned Jesus in to him because they were jealous. [11]But the leading priests had persuaded the people to ask Pilate to free Barabbas, not Jesus.

[12]Then Pilate asked the crowd again, "So what should I do with this man you call the king of the Jews?"

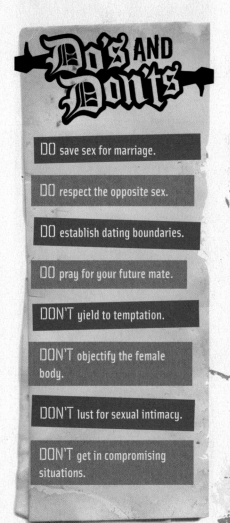

14:68 And the rooster crowed. Some Greek copies do not have this phrase.

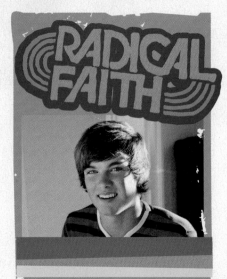

RADICAL FAITH

MARK 15:37

The fact that Jesus died isn't the least bit unusual. Every human being meets that unavoidable fate. Dying on a cross wasn't even all that unique. The Roman Empire crucified tens of thousands of criminals and enemies of the state. But don't mistake Jesus for just another guy from ancient times who happened to be killed on a cross. His death was one-of-a-kind. As the Old Testament predicted hundreds of years before the Cross, "He was crushed for the evil we did" (Isaiah 53:5). Jesus couldn't have been punished for his own wrongdoing, because he had never done anything wrong (Hebrews 4:15), and the people around him recognized that he didn't deserve to die. A thief crucified next to Jesus realized the Lord was innocent of sin, and an army officer who stood at the cross spotted Jesus as the Son of God. Jesus' death is absolutely unique because he perished for your sins and the sins of the world, taking the punishment that human wrongdoing deserves (Romans 6:23). Being a Christian starts with trusting that fact, admitting who Jesus is and what he has done for you.

¹³They shouted, "Crucify him!"

¹⁴Pilate asked, "Why? What wrong has he done?"

But they shouted even louder, "Crucify him!"

¹⁵Pilate wanted to please the crowd, so he freed Barabbas for them. After having Jesus beaten with whips, he handed Jesus over to the soldiers to be crucified.

¹⁶The soldiers took Jesus into the governor's palace (called the Praetorium) and called all the other soldiers together. ¹⁷They put a purple robe on Jesus and used thorny branches to make a crown for his head. ¹⁸They began to call out to him, "Hail, King of the Jews!" ¹⁹The soldiers beat Jesus on the head many times with a stick. They spit on him and made fun of him by bowing on their knees and worshiping him. ²⁰After they finished, the soldiers took off the purple robe and put his own clothes on him again. Then they led him out of the palace to be crucified.

JESUS IS CRUCIFIED

²¹A man named Simon from Cyrene, the father of Alexander and Rufus, was coming from the fields to the city. The soldiers forced Simon to carry the cross for Jesus. ²²They led Jesus to the place called Golgotha, which means the Place of the Skull. ²³The soldiers tried to give Jesus wine mixed with myrrh to drink, but he refused. ²⁴The soldiers crucified Jesus and divided his clothes among themselves, throwing lots to decide what each soldier would get.

²⁵It was nine o'clock in the morning when they crucified Jesus. ²⁶There was a sign with this charge against Jesus written on it: THE KING OF THE JEWS. ²⁷They also put two robbers on crosses beside Jesus, one on the right, and the other on the left. [²⁸And the Scripture came true that says, "They put him with criminals."]ⁿ ²⁹People walked by and insulted Jesus and shook their heads, saying, "You said you could destroy the Temple and build it again in three days. ³⁰So save yourself! Come down from that cross!"

³¹The leading priests and the teachers of the law were also making fun of Jesus. They said to each other, "He saved other people, but he can't save himself. ³²If he is really the Christ, the king of Israel, let him come down now from the cross. When we see this, we will believe in him." The robbers who were being crucified beside Jesus also insulted him.

JESUS DIES

³³At noon the whole country became dark, and the darkness lasted for three hours. ³⁴At three o'clock Jesus cried in a loud voice, "Eloi,

Eloi, lama sabachthani." This means, "My God, my God, why have you abandoned me?"

³⁵When some of the people standing there heard this, they said, "Listen! He is calling Elijah."

³⁶Someone there ran and got a sponge, filled it with vinegar, tied it to a stick, and gave it to Jesus to drink. He said, "We want to see if Elijah will come to take him down from the cross."

³⁷Then Jesus cried in a loud voice and died.

³⁸The curtain in the Templeⁿ was torn into two pieces, from the top to the bottom. ³⁹When the army officer who was standing in front of the cross saw what happened when Jesus died,ⁿ he said, "This man really was the Son of God!"

⁴⁰Some women were standing at a distance from the cross, watching; among them were Mary Magdalene, Salome, and Mary the mother of James and Joseph. (James was her youngest son.) ⁴¹These women had followed Jesus in Galilee and helped him. Many other women were also there who had come with Jesus to Jerusalem.

JESUS IS BURIED

⁴²This was Preparation Day. (That means the day before the Sabbath day.) That evening, ⁴³Joseph from Arimathea was brave enough to go to Pilate and ask for Jesus' body. Joseph, an important member of the Jewish council, was one of the people who was waiting for the kingdom of God to come. ⁴⁴Pilate was amazed that Jesus would have already died, so he called the army officer who had guarded Jesus and asked him if Jesus had already died. ⁴⁵The officer told Pilate that he was dead, so Pilate told Joseph he could have the body. ⁴⁶Joseph bought some linen cloth, took the body down from the

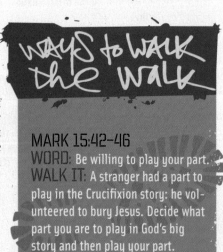

WAYS TO WALK THE WALK

MARK 15:42–46

WORD: Be willing to play your part.
WALK IT: A stranger had a part to play in the Crucifixion story: he volunteered to bury Jesus. Decide what part you are to play in God's big story and then play your part.

 15:28 And . . . criminals." Some Greek copies do not contain the bracketed text, which quotes from Isaiah 53:12.   15:38 curtain in the Temple A curtain divided the Most Holy Place from the other part of the Temple. That was the special building in Jerusalem where God commanded the Jewish people to worship him.   15:39 when Jesus died Some Greek copies read "when Jesus cried out and died."

cross, and wrapped it in the linen. He put the body in a tomb that was cut out of a wall of rock. Then he rolled a very large stone to block the entrance of the tomb. ⁴⁷And Mary Magdalene and Mary the mother of Joseph saw the place where Jesus was laid.

JESUS RISES FROM THE DEAD

16 The day after the Sabbath day, Mary Magdalene, Mary the mother of James, and Salome bought some sweet-smelling spices to put on Jesus' body. ²Very early on that day, the first day of the week, soon after sunrise, the women were on their way to the tomb. ³They said to each other, "Who will roll away for us the stone that covers the entrance of the tomb?"

⁴Then the women looked and saw that the stone had already been rolled away, even though it was very large. ⁵The women entered the tomb and saw a young man wearing a white robe and sitting on the right side, and they were afraid.

⁶But the man said, "Don't be afraid. You are looking for Jesus from Nazareth, who has been crucified. He has risen from the dead; he is not here. Look, here is the place they laid him. ⁷Now go and tell his followers and Peter, 'Jesus is going into Galilee ahead of you, and you will see him there as he told you before.' "

⁸The women were confused and shaking with fear, so they left the tomb and ran away. They did not tell anyone about what happened, because they were afraid.

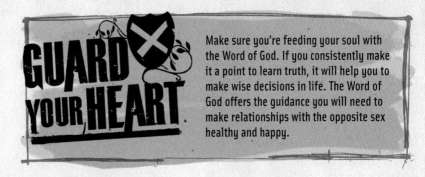

Make sure you're feeding your soul with the Word of God. If you consistently make it a point to learn truth, it will help you to make wise decisions in life. The Word of God offers the guidance you will need to make relationships with the opposite sex healthy and happy.

Verses 9–20 are not included in some of the earliest surviving Greek copies of Mark.

SOME FOLLOWERS SEE JESUS

[⁹After Jesus rose from the dead early on the first day of the week, he showed himself first to Mary Magdalene. One time in the past, he had forced seven demons out of her. ¹⁰After Mary saw Jesus, she went and told his followers, who were very sad and were crying. ¹¹But Mary told them that Jesus was alive. She said that she had seen him, but the followers did not believe her.

¹²Later, Jesus showed himself to two of his followers while they were walking in the country, but he did not look the same as before. ¹³These followers went back to the others and told them what had happened, but again, the followers did not believe them.

JESUS TALKS TO THE APOSTLES

¹⁴Later Jesus showed himself to the eleven apostles while they were eating, and he criticized them because they had no faith. They were stubborn and refused to believe those who had seen him after he had risen from the dead.

¹⁵Jesus said to his followers, "Go everywhere in the world, and tell the Good News to everyone. ¹⁶Anyone who believes and is baptized will be saved, but anyone who does not believe will be punished. ¹⁷And those who believe will be able to do these things as proof: They will use my name to force out demons. They will speak in new languages.ⁿ ¹⁸They will pick up snakes and drink poison without being hurt. They will touch the sick, and the sick will be healed."

¹⁹After the Lord Jesus said these things to his followers, he was carried up into heaven, and he sat at the right side of God. ²⁰The followers went everywhere in the world and told the Good News to people, and the Lord helped them. The Lord proved that the Good News they told was true by giving them power to work miracles.]

16:17 languages This can also be translated "tongues."

LU KE

THE HUMANITY OF JESUS

If the Book of Luke were a reality series, it would outplay, outwit, and outlast any of the competition. This book brims with drama, from Jesus facing down the devil to his escaping mobs trying to kill him. If you've had a view of Jesus as a meek and mild man, then think again. Filled with anger over merchants turning prayer into a method of making money, he chases them out of the courtyard of the holy Temple.

Luke also portrays Christ wrangling with religious leaders of the day. Claiming he blasphemes God, they are infuriated when Jesus heals people on the Sabbath. They claim it breaks the law against working on the day of rest. Yet, Christ boldly calls them hypocrites, pointing out that they make time to water their donkeys on the Sabbath. Even though it later costs him his life, Jesus proves he isn't afraid to speak the truth.

This book is full of familiar stories, such as the parables of the lost son and the Good Samaritan, as well as illustrations of how God cares for the poor and humble. Ultimately, though, this book reminds us that Jesus became a human to die in our place as the only payment for salvation.

LUKE WRITES ABOUT JESUS' LIFE

Many have tried to report on the things that happened among us. [2]They have written the same things that we learned from others—the people who saw those things from the beginning and served God by telling people his message. [3]Since I myself have studied everything carefully from the beginning, most excellent[n] Theophilus, it seemed good for me to write it out for you. I arranged it in order, [4]to help you know that what you have been taught is true.

ZECHARIAH AND ELIZABETH

[5]During the time Herod ruled Judea, there was a priest named Zechariah who belonged to Abijah's group.[n] Zechariah's wife, Elizabeth, came from the family of Aaron. [6]Zechariah and Elizabeth truly did what God said was good. They did everything the Lord commanded and were without fault in keeping his law. [7]But they had no children, because Elizabeth could not have a baby, and both of them were very old.

[8]One day Zechariah was serving as a priest before God, because his group was on duty. [9]According to the custom of the priests, he was chosen by lot to go into the Temple of the Lord and burn incense. [10]There were a great many people outside praying at the time the incense was offered. [11]Then an angel of the Lord appeared to Zechariah, standing on the right side of the incense table. [12]When he saw the angel, Zechariah was startled and frightened. [13]But the angel said to him, "Zechariah, don't be afraid. God has heard your prayer. Your wife, Elizabeth, will give birth to a son, and you will name him John. [14]He will bring you joy and gladness, and many people will be happy because of his birth. [15]John will be a great man for the Lord. He will never drink wine or beer, and even from birth, he will be filled with the Holy Spirit. [16]He will help many people of Israel return to the Lord their God. [17]He will go before the Lord in spirit and power like Elijah. He will make peace between parents and their children and will bring those who are not obeying God back to the right way of thinking, to make a people ready for the coming of the Lord."

[18]Zechariah said to the angel, "How can I know that what you say is true? I am an old man, and my wife is old, too."

[19]The angel answered him, "I am Gabriel. I stand before God, who sent me to talk to you and to tell you this good news. [20]Now, listen! You will not be able to speak until the day these things happen, because you did not believe what I told you. But they will really happen."

[21]Outside, the people were still waiting for Zechariah and were surprised that he was staying so long in the Temple. [22]When Zechariah came outside, he could not speak to them, and they knew he had seen a vision in the Temple. He could only make signs to them and remained unable to speak. [23]When his time of service at the Temple was finished, he went home.

[24]Later, Zechariah's wife, Elizabeth, became pregnant and did not go out of her house for five months. Elizabeth said, [25]"Look what the Lord has done for me! My people were ashamed[n] of me, but now the Lord has taken away that shame."

Eighty-four percent of teens report owning at least one computer, cell phone, or personal digital assistant.

—Pew Internet & American Life Project

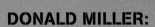

*REVIEWS BOOKS

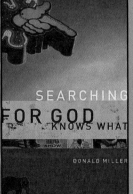

DONALD MILLER:
SEARCHING FOR GOD KNOWS WHAT

In the follow-up to his much-talked-about and much-loved book *Blue Like Jazz*, author Donald Miller shares more stories, experiences, and small truths he's experienced in his life of spiritual ups and downs. In a very conversational, sometimes edgy tone, *Searching for God Knows What* details Miller's chief complaints about modern Christianity. Sometimes his stories are funny and charming. Other times he simply uses his story to make a brilliant point about following God. For anyone who has questions about faith or who simply enjoys an entertaining storyteller, you need to search no further for the right book.

WHY IT ROCKS:

THE STRONG STORYTELLING DELIVERS WITTY WISDOM.

 1:3 excellent This word was used to show respect to an important person like a king or ruler. **1:5 Abijah's group** The Jewish priests were divided into twenty-four groups. See 1 Chronicles 24. **1:25 ashamed** The Jewish people thought it was a disgrace for women not to have children.

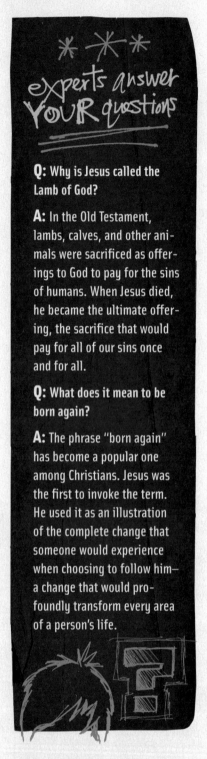

AN ANGEL APPEARS TO MARY

²⁶During Elizabeth's sixth month of pregnancy, God sent the angel Gabriel to Nazareth, a town in Galilee, ²⁷to a virgin. She was engaged to marry a man named Joseph from the family of David. Her name was Mary. ²⁸The angel came to her and said, "Greetings! The Lord has blessed you and is with you."

²⁹But Mary was very startled by what the angel said and wondered what this greeting might mean.

³⁰The angel said to her, "Don't be afraid, Mary; God has shown you his grace. ³¹Listen! You will become pregnant and give birth to a son, and you will name him Jesus. ³²He will be great and will be called the Son of the Most High. The Lord God will give him the throne of King David, his ancestor. ³³He will rule over the people of Jacob forever, and his kingdom will never end."

³⁴Mary said to the angel, "How will this happen since I am a virgin?"

³⁵The angel said to Mary, "The Holy Spirit will come upon you, and the power of the Most High will cover you. For this reason the baby will be holy and will be called the Son of God. ³⁶Now Elizabeth, your relative, is also pregnant with a son though she is very old. Everyone thought she could not have a baby, but she has been pregnant for six months. ³⁷God can do anything!"

³⁸Mary said, "I am the servant of the Lord. Let this happen to me as you say!" Then the angel went away.

MARY VISITS ELIZABETH

³⁹Mary got up and went quickly to a town in the hills of Judea. ⁴⁰She came to Zechariah's house and greeted Elizabeth. ⁴¹When Elizabeth heard Mary's greeting, the unborn baby inside her jumped, and Elizabeth was filled with the Holy Spirit. ⁴²She cried out in a loud voice, "God has blessed you more than any other woman, and he has blessed the baby to which you will give birth. ⁴³Why has this good thing happened to me, that the mother of my Lord comes to me? ⁴⁴When I heard your voice, the baby inside me jumped with joy. ⁴⁵You are blessed because you believed that what the Lord said to you would really happen."

MARY PRAISES GOD

⁴⁶Then Mary said,

"My soul praises the Lord;
⁴⁷   my heart rejoices in God my Savior,
⁴⁸because he has shown his concern for his
        humble servant girl.
    From now on, all people will say that I am
        blessed,
⁴⁹   because the Powerful One has done
        great things for me.
    His name is holy.
⁵⁰God will show his mercy forever and ever
        to those who worship and serve him.
⁵¹He has done mighty deeds by his power.
    He has scattered the people who are
        proud
    and think great things about themselves.
⁵²He has brought down rulers from their
        thrones
    and raised up the humble.
⁵³He has filled the hungry with good things
    and sent the rich away with nothing.
⁵⁴He has helped his servant, the people of
        Israel,
    remembering to show them mercy
⁵⁵as he promised to our ancestors,
    to Abraham and to his children forever."

⁵⁶Mary stayed with Elizabeth for about three months and then returned home.

THE BIRTH OF JOHN

⁵⁷When it was time for Elizabeth to give birth, she had a boy. ⁵⁸Her neighbors and relatives heard how good the Lord was to her, and they rejoiced with her.

⁵⁹When the baby was eight days old, they came to circumcise him. They wanted to name him Zechariah because this was his father's name, ⁶⁰but his mother said, "No! He will be named John."

⁶¹The people said to Elizabeth, "But no one in your family has this name." ⁶²Then they made signs to his father to find out what he would like to name him.

⁶³Zechariah asked for a writing tablet and wrote, "His name is John," and everyone was surprised. ⁶⁴Immediately Zechariah could talk again, and he began praising God. ⁶⁵All their neighbors became alarmed, and in all the mountains of Judea people continued talking about all these things. ⁶⁶The people who heard

ISSUES

SEX

SEX IS AN AWESOME GIFT FROM GOD, BUT IT ISN'T MEANT TO BE OPENED UNTIL MARRIAGE. The mistake many guys make is playing around with the package until it gets broken and they must pick up the pieces. There is no greater present that you can give yourself or your future wife than that of saving yourself sexually for your honeymoon. Besides enjoying the peace that comes with doing it God's way, you'll save yourself and your beloved the heartache that comes with sexual sin. Not only do you risk getting a sexually transmitted disease during premarital sex, but you also put yourself in a position to become a parent prematurely.

RADICAL FAITH

LUKE 2:1–20

If the shepherds who met Jesus at his birth had lived nowadays, they might have sold the scoop to the highest-paying tabloid newspaper. The headline "Baby King Born in Bethlehem!" might have shown up right next to stories about looming alien invasions and pets that spontaneously combust. The shepherds could have hawked trinkets and started a pricey tour business. But they did a simple thing. They went back to herding sheep. That might sound unspiritual. But those shepherds were no longer ordinary guys. For after they heard angels proclaim Christ's arrival, they went looking for God's promised Savior. They confidently informed Jesus' parents of what they had heard (Luke 2:17). And going home, they thanked God for what they had seen. In their own way, they surely kept spreading the news that they had met the world's new King. Today, God wants you to serve him the same way, in the middle of your daily stuff. You can live radically for him right where you are by obeying him in everything and telling everyone within reach that you have spotted the King of kings.

about them wondered, saying, "What will this child be?" because the Lord was with him.

ZECHARIAH PRAISES GOD

⁶⁷Then Zechariah, John's father, was filled with the Holy Spirit and prophesied:

⁶⁸"Let us praise the Lord, the God of Israel,
    because he has come to help his people
        and has given them freedom.
⁶⁹He has given us a powerful Savior
    from the family of God's servant David.
⁷⁰He said that he would do this
    through his holy prophets who lived
        long ago:
⁷¹He promised he would save us from our
        enemies
    and from the power of all those who
        hate us.
⁷²He said he would give mercy to our
        ancestors
    and that he would remember his holy
        promise.
⁷³God promised Abraham, our father,
⁷⁴   that he would save us from the power of
        our enemies
    so we could serve him without fear,
⁷⁵being holy and good before God as long as
    we live.

⁷⁶"Now you, child, will be called a prophet of
        the Most High God.
    You will go before the Lord to prepare
        his way.
⁷⁷You will make his people know that they
        will be saved
    by having their sins forgiven.
⁷⁸With the loving mercy of our God,
    a new day from heaven will dawn upon
        us.
⁷⁹It will shine on those who live in
        darkness,
    in the shadow of death.
    It will guide us into the path of peace."

⁸⁰And so the child grew up and became strong in spirit. John lived in the desert until the time when he came out to preach to Israel.

THE BIRTH OF JESUS

2 At that time, Augustus Caesar sent an order that all people in the countries under Roman rule must list their names in a register. ²This was the first registration;ⁿ it was taken while Quirinius was governor of Syria. ³And all went to their own towns to be registered.

⁴So Joseph left Nazareth, a town in Galilee, and went to the town of Bethlehem in Judea, known as the town of David. Joseph went

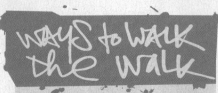

LUKE 2:1-7

WORD: Obey the law of the land.
WALK IT: It can be inconvenient at times, but we are called to obey the laws of the land. Don't break the speed limit. Be honest on your tax returns. Don't become legalistic, but don't be a rebel either.

there because he was from the family of David. ⁵Joseph registered with Mary, to whom he was engagedⁿ and who was now pregnant. ⁶While they were in Bethlehem, the time came for Mary to have the baby, ⁷and she gave birth to her first son. Because there were no rooms left in the inn, she wrapped the baby with pieces of cloth and laid him in a feeding trough.

SHEPHERDS HEAR ABOUT JESUS

⁸That night, some shepherds were in the fields nearby watching their sheep. ⁹Then an angel of the Lord stood before them. The glory of the Lord was shining around them, and they became very frightened. ¹⁰The angel said to them, "Do not be afraid. I am bringing you good news that will be a great joy to all the people. ¹¹Today your Savior was born in the town of David. He is Christ, the Lord. ¹²This is how you will know him: You will find a baby wrapped in pieces of cloth and lying in a feeding box."

¹³Then a very large group of angels from heaven joined the first angel, praising God and saying:

¹⁴"Give glory to God in heaven,
    and on earth let there be peace among
        the people who please God."ⁿ

¹⁵When the angels left them and went back to heaven, the shepherds said to each other, "Let's go to Bethlehem. Let's see this thing that has happened which the Lord has told us about."

¹⁶So the shepherds went quickly and found Mary and Joseph and the baby, who was lying in a feeding trough. ¹⁷When they had seen him, they told what the angels had said about this child. ¹⁸Everyone was amazed at what the shepherds said to them. ¹⁹But Mary

 2:2 registration Census. A counting of all the people and the things they own. **2:5 engaged** For the Jewish people, an engagement was a lasting agreement. It could only be broken by divorce. **2:14 and . . . God** Some Greek copies read "and on earth let there be peace and goodwill among people."

treasured these things and continued to think about them. [20]Then the shepherds went back to their sheep, praising God and thanking him for everything they had seen and heard. It had been just as the angel had told them.

[21]When the baby was eight days old, he was circumcised and was named Jesus, the name given by the angel before the baby began to grow inside Mary.

JESUS IS PRESENTED IN THE TEMPLE

[22]When the time came for Mary and Joseph to do what the law of Moses taught about being made pure,[n] they took Jesus to Jerusalem to present him to the Lord. [23](It is written in the law of the Lord: "Every firstborn male shall be given to the Lord.")[n] [24]Mary and Joseph also went to offer a sacrifice, as the law of the Lord says: "You must sacrifice two doves or two young pigeons."[n]

SIMEON SEES JESUS

[25]In Jerusalem lived a man named Simeon who was a good man and godly. He was waiting for the time when God would take away Israel's sorrow, and the Holy Spirit was in him. [26]Simeon had been told by the Holy Spirit that he would not die before he saw the Christ promised by the Lord. [27]The Spirit led Simeon to the Temple. When Mary and Joseph brought the baby Jesus to the Temple to do what the law said they must do, [28]Simeon took the baby in his arms and thanked God:

[29]"Now, Lord, you can let me, your servant,
    die in peace as you said.
[30]With my own eyes I have seen your
    salvation,
[31] which you prepared before all people.
[32]It is a light for the non-Jewish people to
    see
    and an honor for your people, the
    Israelites."

[33]Jesus' father and mother were amazed at what Simeon had said about him. [34]Then Simeon blessed them and said to Mary, "God has chosen this child to cause the fall and rise of many in Israel. He will be a sign from God that many people will not accept [35]so that the thoughts of many will be made known. And the things that will happen will make your heart sad, too."

ANNA SEES JESUS

[36]There was a prophetess, Anna, from the family of Phanuel in the tribe of Asher. Anna was very old. She had once been married for seven years. [37]Then her husband died, and she was a widow for eighty-four years. Anna never left the Temple but worshiped God, going with-

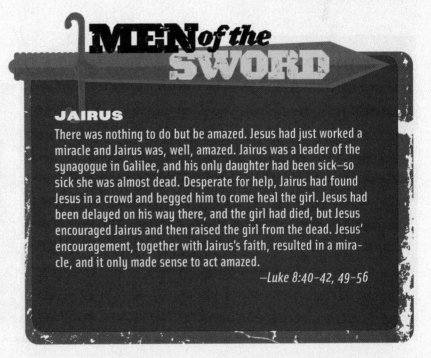

out food and praying day and night. [38]Standing there at that time, she thanked God and spoke about Jesus to all who were waiting for God to free Jerusalem.

JOSEPH AND MARY RETURN HOME

[39]When Joseph and Mary had done everything the law of the Lord commanded, they went home to Nazareth, their own town in Galilee. [40]The little child grew and became strong. He was filled with wisdom, and God's goodness was upon him.

JESUS AS A BOY

[41]Every year Jesus' parents went to Jerusalem for the Passover Feast. [42]When he was twelve years old, they went to the feast as they always did. [43]After the feast days were over, they started home. The boy Jesus stayed behind in Jerusalem, but his parents did not

MEN of the SWORD

JAIRUS

There was nothing to do but be amazed. Jesus had just worked a miracle and Jairus was, well, amazed. Jairus was a leader of the synagogue in Galilee, and his only daughter had been sick—so sick she was almost dead. Desperate for help, Jairus had found Jesus in a crowd and begged him to come heal the girl. Jesus had been delayed on his way there, and the girl had died, but Jesus encouraged Jairus and then raised the girl from the dead. Jesus' encouragement, together with Jairus's faith, resulted in a miracle, and it only made sense to act amazed.

—Luke 8:40–42, 49–56

★ **2:22 pure** The Law of Moses said that forty days after a Jewish woman gave birth to a son, she must be cleansed by a ceremony at the Temple. Read Leviticus 12:2–8. **2:23 "Every . . . Lord."** Quotation from Exodus 13:2. **2:24 "You . . . pigeons."** Quotation from Leviticus 12:8.

73

Do's and Don'ts

DO spend time with your family.

DO respect your parents.

DO help with household chores.

DO pray for your family.

DON'T take your family for granted.

DON'T diss your siblings.

DON'T complain about your family.

DON'T skip family meals.

know it. [44]Thinking that Jesus was with them in the group, they traveled for a whole day. Then they began to look for him among their family and friends. [45]When they did not find him, they went back to Jerusalem to look for him there. [46]After three days they found Jesus sitting in the Temple with the teachers, listening to them and asking them questions. [47]All who heard him were amazed at his understanding and answers. [48]When Jesus' parents saw him, they were astonished. His mother said to him, "Son, why did you do this to us? Your father and I were very worried about you and have been looking for you."

[49]Jesus said to them, "Why were you looking for me? Didn't you know that I must be in my Father's house?" [50]But they did not understand the meaning of what he said.

[51]Jesus went with them to Nazareth and was obedient to them. But his mother kept in her mind all that had happened. [52]Jesus became wiser and grew physically. People liked him, and he pleased God.

THE PREACHING OF JOHN

3 It was the fifteenth year of the rule of Tiberius Caesar. These men were under Caesar: Pontius Pilate, the ruler of Judea; Herod, the ruler of Galilee; Philip, Herod's brother, the ruler of Iturea and Traconitis; and Lysanias, the ruler of Abilene. [2]Annas and Caiaphas were the high priests. At this time, the word of God came to John son of Zechariah in the desert. [3]He went all over the area around the Jordan River preaching a baptism of changed hearts and lives for the forgiveness of sins. [4]As it is written in the book of Isaiah the prophet:

"This is a voice of one
who calls out in the desert:
'Prepare the way for the Lord.
Make the road straight for him.
[5]Every valley should be filled in,
and every mountain and hill should be
made flat.
Roads with turns should be made straight,
and rough roads should be made smooth.
[6]And all people will know about the
salvation of God!'"   *Isaiah 40:3–5*

[7]To the crowds of people who came to be baptized by John, he said, "You are all snakes! Who warned you to run away from God's coming punishment? [8]Do the things that show you really have changed your hearts and lives. Don't begin to say to yourselves, 'Abraham is our father.' I tell you that God could make children for Abraham from these rocks. [9]The ax is now ready to cut down the trees, and every tree that does not produce good fruit will be cut down and thrown into the fire."[n]

[10]The people asked John, "Then what should we do?"

[11]John answered, "If you have two shirts, share with the person who does not have one. If you have food, share that also."

[12]Even tax collectors came to John to be baptized. They said to him, "Teacher, what should we do?"

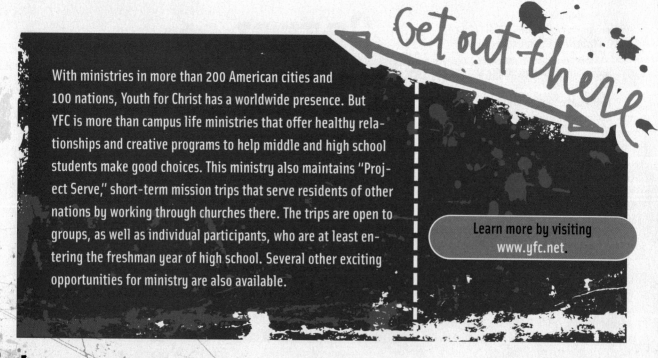

Get out there

With ministries in more than 200 American cities and 100 nations, Youth for Christ has a worldwide presence. But YFC is more than campus life ministries that offer healthy relationships and creative programs to help middle and high school students make good choices. This ministry also maintains "Project Serve," short-term mission trips that serve residents of other nations by working through churches there. The trips are open to groups, as well as individual participants, who are at least entering the freshman year of high school. Several other exciting opportunities for ministry are also available.

Learn more by visiting
www.yfc.net.

3:9 **The ax . . . fire.** This means that God is ready to punish his people who do not obey him.

march

NATIONAL NUTRITION MONTH

"In the end, we will remember not the words of our enemies, but the silence of our friends."
–MARTIN LUTHER KING JR.

1 Make sure you eat your veggies.

2

3 Today is Jessica Biel's big day.

4 It's World Prayer Day, so do it!

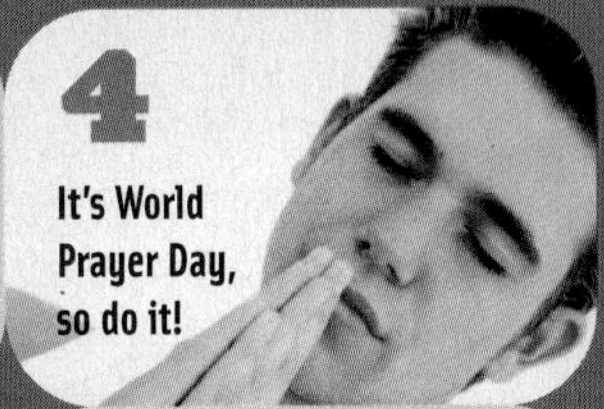

5

6

7 Offer to tutor students needing extra help.

8

9

10 Watch *The Passion of the Christ.*

11 Play basketball with dad today.

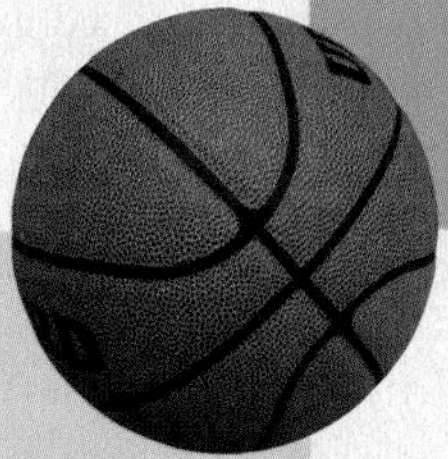

12 It is James Taylor's birthday.

13

14 Thank God for your blessings.

15 Help your mom with spring cleaning.

16

17 Wear green today even if you're not Irish.

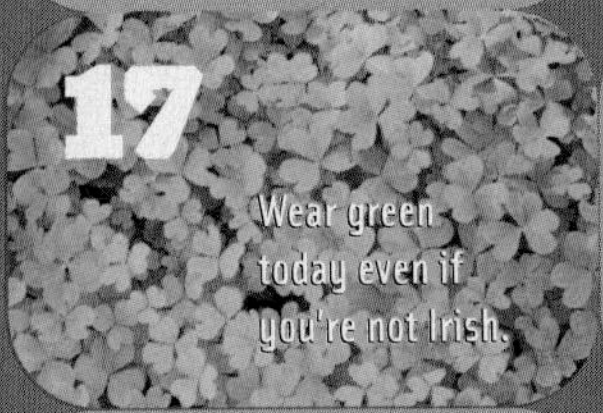

18 It's Brain Awareness Week. Think about it!

19

20

21 It's National Dance Day, so get moving!

22

23 Wear your favorite team's colors in anticipation of March Madness.

24

25 Donate your spare change to a local charity.

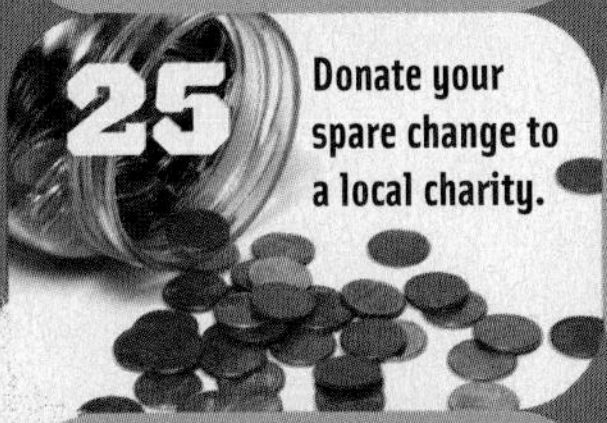

26

27 It is Mariah Carey's birthday.

28

29

30 Ask your best friend how you can pray for him.

31

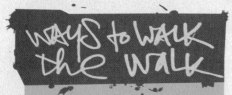

WAYS to WALK the WALK

LUKE 4:1-13

WORD: Study the Word of God.

WALK IT: Jesus overcame temptation by knowing the Scriptures. Write out a different verse each week and attempt to memorize it. That way you'll have ammunition when the devil comes gunning for you.

[13]John said to them, "Don't take more taxes from people than you have been ordered to take."

[14]The soldiers asked John, "What about us? What should we do?"

John said to them, "Don't force people to give you money, and don't lie about them. Be satisfied with the pay you get."

[15]Since the people were hoping for the Christ to come, they wondered if John might be the one.

[16]John answered everyone, "I baptize you with water, but there is one coming who is greater than I am. I am not good enough to untie his sandals. He will baptize you with the Holy Spirit and fire. [17]He will come ready to clean the grain, separating the good grain from the chaff. He will put the good part of the grain into his barn, but he will burn the chaff with a fire that cannot be put out."[n] [18]And John continued to preach the Good News, saying many other things to encourage the people.

[19]But John spoke against Herod, the governor, because of his sin with Herodias, the wife of Herod's brother, and because of the many other evil things Herod did. [20]So Herod did something even worse: He put John in prison.

JESUS IS BAPTIZED BY JOHN

[21]When all the people were being baptized by John, Jesus also was baptized. While Jesus was praying, heaven opened [22]and the Holy Spirit came down on him in the form of a dove. Then a voice came from heaven, saying, "You are my Son, whom I love, and I am very pleased with you."

THE FAMILY HISTORY OF JESUS

[23]When Jesus began his ministry, he was about thirty years old. People thought that Jesus was Joseph's son.

Joseph was the son[n] of Heli.
[24]Heli was the son of Matthat.
Matthat was the son of Levi.
Levi was the son of Melki.
Melki was the son of Jannai.
Jannai was the son of Joseph.
[25]Joseph was the son of Mattathias.
Mattathias was the son of Amos.
Amos was the son of Nahum.
Nahum was the son of Esli.
Esli was the son of Naggai.
[26]Naggai was the son of Maath.
Maath was the son of Mattathias.
Mattathias was the son of Semein.
Semein was the son of Josech.
Josech was the son of Joda.
[27]Joda was the son of Joanan.
Joanan was the son of Rhesa.
Rhesa was the son of Zerubbabel.
Zerubbabel was the grandson of Shealtiel.
Shealtiel was the son of Neri.
[28]Neri was the son of Melki.
Melki was the son of Addi.
Addi was the son of Cosam.
Cosam was the son of Elmadam.
Elmadam was the son of Er.
[29]Er was the son of Joshua.
Joshua was the son of Eliezer.
Eliezer was the son of Jorim.
Jorim was the son of Matthat.

REVIEWS MOVIES

CHRONICLES OF NARNIA: THE LION, THE WITCH AND THE WARDROBE

After the success of *The Lord of the Rings* trilogy, it was only a matter of time before someone turned C. S. Lewis's "Chronicles of Narnia" series into a major motion picture. And a major motion picture it is: the budget for the film was nearly $200 million. But when it comes to a classic, it has to be all about the story. And Disney delivers huge. Everything from the well-developed characterization to the acting detail to the intricate special effects is nearly flawless. Special attention is paid to the initial intent of Lewis's story, with Lewis experts being consulted to ensure authenticity. This one is destined to become a classic.

WHY IT ROCKS:

THIS CLASSIC STORY IS MADE FOR THE BIG SCREEN.

 3:17 **He will . . . out.** This means that Jesus will come to separate good people from bad people, saving the good and punishing the bad.   3:23 **son** "Son" in Jewish lists of ancestors can sometimes mean grandson or more distant relative.

Matthat was the son of Levi.
[30]Levi was the son of Simeon.
Simeon was the son of Judah.
Judah was the son of Joseph.
Joseph was the son of Jonam.
Jonam was the son of Eliakim.
[31]Eliakim was the son of Melea.
Melea was the son of Menna.
Menna was the son of Mattatha.
Mattatha was the son of Nathan.
Nathan was the son of David.
[32]David was the son of Jesse.
Jesse was the son of Obed.
Obed was the son of Boaz.
Boaz was the son of Salmon.[n]
Salmon was the son of Nahshon.
[33]Nahshon was the son of Amminadab.
Amminadab was the son of Admin.
Admin was the son of Arni.
Arni was the son of Hezron.
Hezron was the son of Perez.
Perez was the son of Judah.
[34]Judah was the son of Jacob.
Jacob was the son of Isaac.
Isaac was the son of Abraham.
Abraham was the son of Terah.
Terah was the son of Nahor.
[35]Nahor was the son of Serug.
Serug was the son of Reu.
Reu was the son of Peleg.
Peleg was the son of Eber.
Eber was the son of Shelah.
[36]Shelah was the son of Cainan.
Cainan was the son of Arphaxad.
Arphaxad was the son of Shem.
Shem was the son of Noah.
Noah was the son of Lamech.
[37]Lamech was the son of Methuselah.
Methuselah was the son of Enoch.
Enoch was the son of Jared.
Jared was the son of Mahalalel.
Mahalalel was the son of Kenan.
[38]Kenan was the son of Enosh.
Enosh was the son of Seth.
Seth was the son of Adam.
Adam was the son of God.

JESUS IS TEMPTED BY THE DEVIL

4 Jesus, filled with the Holy Spirit, returned from the Jordan River. The Spirit led Jesus into the desert [2]where the devil tempted Jesus for forty days. Jesus ate nothing during that time, and when those days were ended, he was very hungry.

[3]The devil said to Jesus, "If you are the Son of God, tell this rock to become bread."

[4]Jesus answered, "It is written in the Scriptures: 'A person does not live on bread alone.' "[n]

[5]Then the devil took Jesus and showed him all the kingdoms of the world in an instant. [6]The devil said to Jesus, "I will give you all these kingdoms and all their power and glory. It has all been given to me, and I can give it to anyone I wish. [7]If you worship me, then it will all be yours."

[8]Jesus answered, "It is written in the Scriptures: 'You must worship the Lord your God and serve only him.' "[n]

[9]Then the devil led Jesus to Jerusalem and put him on a high place of the Temple. He said to Jesus, "If you are the Son of God, jump down. [10]It is written in the Scriptures:

'He has put his angels in charge of you
    to watch over you.'   *Psalm 91:11*
[11]It is also written:
'They will catch you in their hands
    so that you will not hit your foot on a
        rock.' "   *Psalm 91:12*

[12]Jesus answered, "But it also says in the Scriptures: 'Do not test the Lord your God.' "[n]

[13]After the devil had tempted Jesus in every way, he left him to wait until a better time.

JESUS TEACHES THE PEOPLE

[14]Jesus returned to Galilee in the power of the Holy Spirit, and stories about him spread all through the area. [15]He began to teach in their synagogues, and everyone praised him.

[16]Jesus traveled to Nazareth, where he had grown up. On the Sabbath day he went to the synagogue, as he always did, and stood up to read. [17]The book of Isaiah the prophet was given to him. He opened the book and found the place where this is written:

[18]"The Lord has put his Spirit in me,
    because he appointed me to tell the
        Good News to the poor.
He has sent me to tell the captives they are
    free
and to tell the blind that they can see
    again.   *Isaiah 61:1*
God sent me to free those who have been
    treated unfairly   *Isaiah 58:6*
[19]   and to announce the time when the
        Lord will show his kindness."
                Isaiah 61:2

[20]Jesus closed the book, gave it back to the assistant, and sat down. Everyone in the synagogue was watching Jesus closely. [21]He began to say to them, "While you heard these words just now, they were coming true!"

[22]All the people spoke well of Jesus and were amazed at the words of grace he spoke. They asked, "Isn't this Joseph's son?"

[23]Jesus said to them, "I know that you will tell me the old saying: 'Doctor, heal yourself.' You want to say, 'We heard about the things

RADICAL FAITH

LUKE 5:27–32

Jesus had extreme guts. When he went scoping for followers he didn't erect a splashy booth at the religious training schools of his day to improve his shot at recruiting the most promising students. He didn't network with the teachers of God's law, religious leaders who knew the dirt on everyone. Instead, he hunted down people ready to meet God, ditch their sin, and follow him. The religious leaders flamed Jesus for befriending sinners, bonding with the lowest of the low by going to their houses and dining with them. He showered compassion on people like prostitutes and tax collectors, sellouts to the occupying Romans who ruthlessly cheated their fellow citizens of Israel. But Jesus had a strategy. The religious people thought they were too good to need him, like healthy people who see no reason to visit a doctor. So he sought out sinful people and showed them how to change their hearts and lives. He even called them as his closest followers. Get the point? No matter where you have been or what you have done, Jesus invites you to be his friend and to follow him.

3:32 **Salmon** Some Greek copies read "Sala." 4:4 '**A person . . . alone.**' Quotation from Deuteronomy 8:3. 4:8 '**You . . . him.**' Quotation from Deuteronomy 6:13. 4:12 '**Do . . . God.**' Quotation from Deuteronomy 6:16.

77

WAYS to WALK the WALK

LUKE 6:27-36
WORD: Like it or not, love your enemies.
WALK IT: It's a tall order, but Jesus tells you to treat others as you would want to be treated. Spend the next week putting yourself in other people's shoes. You'll be surprised at the results.

you did in Capernaum. Do those things here in your own town!' " [24]Then Jesus said, "I tell you the truth, a prophet is not accepted in his hometown. [25]But I tell you the truth, there were many widows in Israel during the time of Elijah. It did not rain in Israel for three and one-half years, and there was no food anywhere in the whole country. [26]But Elijah was sent to none of those widows, only to a widow in Zarephath, a town in Sidon. [27]And there were many with skin diseases living in Israel during the time of the prophet Elisha. But none of them were healed, only Naaman, who was from the country of Syria."

[28]When all the people in the synagogue heard these things, they became very angry. [29]They got up, forced Jesus out of town, and took him to the edge of the cliff on which the town was built. They planned to throw him off the edge, [30]but Jesus walked through the crowd and went on his way.

JESUS FORCES OUT AN EVIL SPIRIT

[31]Jesus went to Capernaum, a city in Galilee, and on the Sabbath day, he taught the people. [32]They were amazed at his teaching, because he spoke with authority. [33]In the synagogue a man who had within him an evil spirit shouted in a loud voice, [34]"Jesus of Nazareth! What do you want with us? Did you come to destroy us? I know who you are—God's Holy One!"

[35]Jesus commanded the evil spirit, "Be quiet! Come out of the man!" The evil spirit threw the man down to the ground before all the people and then left the man without hurting him.

[36]The people were amazed and said to each other, "What does this mean? With authority and power he commands evil spirits, and they come out." [37]And so the news about Jesus spread to every place in the whole area.

JESUS HEALS MANY PEOPLE

[38]Jesus left the synagogue and went to the home of Simon.[n] Simon's mother-in-law was sick with a high fever, and they asked Jesus to help her. [39]He came to her side and commanded the fever to leave. It left her, and immediately she got up and began serving them.

[40]When the sun went down, the people brought those who were sick to Jesus. Putting his hands on each sick person, he healed every one of them. [41]Demons came out of many people, shouting, "You are the Son of God." But Jesus commanded the demons and would not allow them to speak, because they knew Jesus was the Christ.

[42]At daybreak, Jesus went to a lonely place, but the people looked for him. When they found him, they tried to keep him from leaving. [43]But Jesus said to them, "I must preach about God's kingdom to other towns, too. This is why I was sent."

[44]Then he kept on preaching in the synagogues of Judea.[n]

JESUS' FIRST FOLLOWERS

5 One day while Jesus was standing beside Lake Galilee, many people were pressing all around him to hear the word of God. [2]Jesus saw two boats at the shore of the lake. The fishermen had left them and were washing their nets. [3]Jesus got into one of the boats, the one that belonged to Simon,[n] and asked him to push off a little from the land. Then Jesus sat down and continued to teach the people from the boat.

[4]When Jesus had finished speaking, he said to Simon, "Take the boat into deep water, and put your nets in the water to catch some fish."

[5]Simon answered, "Master, we worked hard all night trying to catch fish, and we caught nothing. But you say to put the nets in the water, so I will." [6]When the fishermen did as Jesus told them, they caught so many fish that the nets began to break. [7]They called to their partners in the other boat to come and help them. They came and filled both boats so full that they were almost sinking.

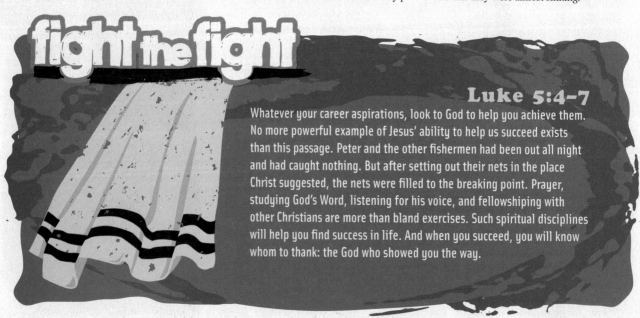

fight the fight

Luke 5:4-7

Whatever your career aspirations, look to God to help you achieve them. No more powerful example of Jesus' ability to help us succeed exists than this passage. Peter and the other fishermen had been out all night and had caught nothing. But after setting out their nets in the place Christ suggested, the nets were filled to the breaking point. Prayer, studying God's Word, listening for his voice, and fellowshiping with other Christians are more than bland exercises. Such spiritual disciplines will help you find success in life. And when you succeed, you will know whom to thank: the God who showed you the way.

4:38; 5:3 Simon Simon's other name was Peter. 4:44 Judea Some Greek copies read "Galilee."

[8]When Simon Peter saw what had happened, he bowed down before Jesus and said, "Go away from me, Lord. I am a sinful man!" [9]He and the other fishermen were amazed at the many fish they caught, as were [10]James and John, the sons of Zebedee, Simon's partners.

Jesus said to Simon, "Don't be afraid. From now on you will fish for people." [11]When the men brought their boats to the shore, they left everything and followed Jesus.

JESUS HEALS A SICK MAN

[12]When Jesus was in one of the towns, there was a man covered with a skin disease. When he saw Jesus, he bowed before him and begged him, "Lord, you can heal me if you will."

[13]Jesus reached out his hand and touched the man and said, "I will. Be healed!" Immediately the disease disappeared. [14]Then Jesus said, "Don't tell anyone about this, but go and show yourself to the priest[n] and offer a gift for your healing, as Moses commanded.[n] This will show the people what I have done."

[15]But the news about Jesus spread even more. Many people came to hear Jesus and to be healed of their sicknesses, [16]but Jesus often slipped away to be alone so he could pray.

JESUS HEALS A PARALYZED MAN

[17]One day as Jesus was teaching the people, the Pharisees and teachers of the law from every town in Galilee and Judea and from Jerusalem were there. The Lord was giving Jesus the power to heal people. [18]Just then, some men were carrying on a mat a man who was paralyzed. They tried to bring him in and put him down before Jesus. [19]But because there were so many people there, they could not find a way in. So they went up on the roof and lowered the man on his mat through the ceiling into the middle of the crowd right before Jesus. [20]Seeing their faith, Jesus said, "Friend, your sins are forgiven."

[21]The Jewish teachers of the law and the Pharisees thought to themselves, "Who is this man who is speaking as if he were God? Only God can forgive sins."

[22]But Jesus knew what they were thinking and said, "Why are you thinking these things? [23]Which is easier: to say, 'Your sins are forgiven,' or to say, 'Stand up and walk'? [24]But I will prove to you that the Son of Man has authority on earth to forgive sins." So Jesus said to the paralyzed man, "I tell you, stand up, take your mat, and go home."

[25]At once the man stood up before them, picked up his mat, and went home, praising God. [26]All the people were fully amazed and began to praise God. They were filled with much respect and said, "Today we have seen amazing things!"

LEVI FOLLOWS JESUS

[27]After this, Jesus went out and saw a tax collector named Levi sitting in the tax collector's booth. Jesus said to him, "Follow me!" [28]So Levi got up, left everything, and followed him.

[29]Then Levi gave a big dinner for Jesus at his house. Many tax collectors and other people were eating there, too. [30]But the Pharisees and the men who taught the law for the Pharisees began to complain to Jesus' followers, "Why do you eat and drink with tax collectors and sinners?"

[31]Jesus answered them, "It is not the healthy people who need a doctor, but the sick. [32]I have not come to invite good people but sinners to change their hearts and lives."

JESUS ANSWERS A QUESTION

[33]They said to Jesus, "John's followers often fast[n] for a certain time and pray, just as the Pharisees do. But your followers eat and drink all the time."

[34]Jesus said to them, "You cannot make the friends of the bridegroom fast while he is still with them. [35]But the time will come when the bridegroom will be taken away from them, and then they will fast."

[36]Jesus told them this story: "No one takes cloth off a new coat to cover a hole in an old coat. Otherwise, he ruins the new coat, and the cloth from the new coat will not be the same as the old cloth. [37]Also, no one ever pours new wine into old leather bags. Otherwise, the new wine will break the bags, the wine will spill out, and the leather bags will be ruined. [38]New wine must be put into new leather bags. [39]No one after drinking old wine wants new wine, because he says, 'The old wine is better.' "

JESUS IS LORD OVER THE SABBATH

[6] One Sabbath day Jesus was walking through some fields of grain. His followers picked the heads of grain, rubbed them in their hands, and ate them. [2]Some Pharisees said, "Why do you do what is not lawful on the Sabbath day?"

[3]Jesus answered, "Have you not read what David did when he and those with him were hungry? [4]He went into God's house and took and ate the holy bread, which is lawful only for priests to eat. And he gave some to the people who were with him." [5]Then Jesus said to the Pharisees, "The Son of Man is Lord of the Sabbath day."

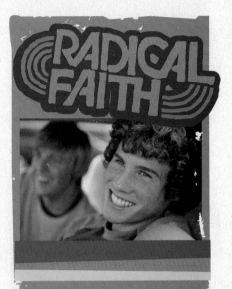

RADICAL FAITH

LUKE 6:27–30

This is the Bible passage that makes some guys think that Christians are doormats, weak people eager to get stomped on by everyone else. On the contrary, Jesus is coaching us on how to be the most powerful people of all. Notice how he asks you to act toward your enemies and people who hate you: love, bless, pray, give. It all adds up to one principle: "Do to others what you would want them to do to you" (Luke 6:31). When you do those things, you are actually imitating God himself, the most powerful Being in the universe, who is kind even to people who are ungrateful and full of sin. God knows that evil breeds evil, and the only way truly to defeat wrong is to respond with love. That doesn't mean governments shouldn't punish criminals or go to war to defend their citizens, because God has given them that role (Romans 13:4). But as you relate to people, dare to put these words into practice. You might turn an enemy into your friend, and God promises you a great reward for doing right.

 5:14 show . . . priest The Law of Moses said a priest must say when a Jewish person with a skin disease was well.   5:14 Moses commanded Read about this in Leviticus 14:1–32.   5:33 fast The people would give up eating for a special time of prayer and worship to God. It was also done to show sadness and disappointment.

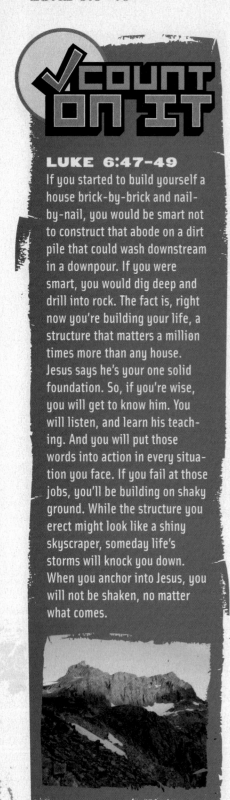

COUNT ON IT

LUKE 6:47-49

If you started to build yourself a house brick-by-brick and nail-by-nail, you would be smart not to construct that abode on a dirt pile that could wash downstream in a downpour. If you were smart, you would dig deep and drill into rock. The fact is, right now you're building your life, a structure that matters a million times more than any house. Jesus says he's your one solid foundation. So, if you're wise, you will get to know him. You will listen, and learn his teaching. And you will put those words into action in every situation you face. If you fail at those jobs, you'll be building on shaky ground. While the structure you erect might look like a shiny skyscraper, someday life's storms will knock you down. When you anchor into Jesus, you will not be shaken, no matter what comes.

JESUS HEALS A MAN'S HAND

⁶On another Sabbath day Jesus went into the synagogue and was teaching, and a man with a crippled right hand was there. ⁷The teachers of the law and the Pharisees were watching closely to see if Jesus would heal on the Sabbath day so they could accuse him. ⁸But he knew what they were thinking, and he said to the man with the crippled hand, "Stand up here in the middle of everyone." The man got up and stood there. ⁹Then Jesus said to them, "I ask you, which is lawful on the Sabbath day: to do good or to do evil, to save a life or to destroy it?" ¹⁰Jesus looked around at all of them and said to the man, "Hold out your hand." The man held out his hand, and it was healed.

¹¹But the Pharisees and the teachers of the law were very angry and discussed with each other what they could do to Jesus.

JESUS CHOOSES HIS APOSTLES

¹²At that time Jesus went off to a mountain to pray, and he spent the night praying to God. ¹³The next morning, Jesus called his followers to him and chose twelve of them, whom he named apostles: ¹⁴Simon (Jesus named him Peter), his brother Andrew, James, John, Philip, Bartholomew, ¹⁵Matthew, Thomas, James son of Alphaeus, Simon (called the Zealot), ¹⁶Judas son of James, and Judas Iscariot, who later turned Jesus over to his enemies.

JESUS TEACHES AND HEALS

¹⁷Jesus and the apostles came down from the mountain, and he stood on level ground. A large group of his followers was there, as well as many people from all around Judea, Jerusalem, and the seacoast cities of Tyre and Sidon. ¹⁸They all came to hear Jesus teach and to be healed of their sicknesses, and he healed those who were troubled by evil spirits. ¹⁹All the people were trying to touch Jesus, because power was coming from him and healing them all.

²⁰Jesus looked at his followers and said,
"You people who are poor are blessed,
  because the kingdom of God belongs to you.
²¹You people who are now hungry are blessed,
  because you will be satisfied.
You people who are now crying are blessed,
  because you will laugh with joy.
²²"People will hate you, shut you out, insult you, and say you are evil because you follow the Son of Man. But when they do, you will be blessed. ²³Be full of joy at that time, because you have a great reward in heaven. Their ancestors did the same things to the prophets.

²⁴"But how terrible it will be for you who are rich,
  because you have had your easy life.
²⁵How terrible it will be for you who are full now,
  because you will be hungry.
How terrible it will be for you who are laughing now,
  because you will be sad and cry.
²⁶"How terrible when everyone says only good things about you, because their ancestors said the same things about the false prophets.

LOVE YOUR ENEMIES

²⁷"But I say to you who are listening, love your enemies. Do good to those who hate you, ²⁸bless those who curse you, pray for those who are cruel to you. ²⁹If anyone slaps you on one cheek, offer him the other cheek, too. If someone takes your coat, do not stop him from taking your shirt. ³⁰Give to everyone who asks you, and when someone takes something that is yours, don't ask for it back. ³¹Do to others what you would want them to do to you. ³²If you love only the people who love you, what praise should you get? Even sinners love the people who love them. ³³If you do good only to those who do good to you, what praise should you get? Even sinners do that! ³⁴If you lend things to people, always hoping to get something back, what praise should you get? Even sinners lend to other sinners so that they can get back the same amount! ³⁵But love your enemies, do good to them, and lend to them without hoping to get anything back. Then you will have a great reward, and you will be children of the Most High God, because he is kind even to people who are ungrateful and full of sin. ³⁶Show mercy, just as your Father shows mercy.

LOOK AT YOURSELVES

³⁷"Don't judge others, and you will not be judged. Don't accuse others of being guilty, and you will not be accused of being guilty. Forgive, and you will be forgiven. ³⁸Give, and you will receive. You will be given much. Pressed down, shaken together, and running over, it will spill into your lap. The way you give to others is the way God will give to you."

³⁹Jesus told them this story: "Can a blind person lead another blind person? No! Both of them will fall into a ditch. ⁴⁰A student is not better than the teacher, but the student who has been fully trained will be like the teacher.

41"Why do you notice the little piece of dust in your friend's eye, but you don't notice the big piece of wood in your own eye? 42How can you say to your friend, 'Friend, let me take that little piece of dust out of your eye' when you cannot see that big piece of wood in your own eye! You hypocrite! First, take the wood out of your own eye. Then you will see clearly to take the dust out of your friend's eye.

TWO KINDS OF FRUIT

43"A good tree does not produce bad fruit, nor does a bad tree produce good fruit. 44Each tree is known by its own fruit. People don't gather figs from thornbushes, and they don't get grapes from bushes. 45Good people bring good things out of the good they stored in their hearts. But evil people bring evil things out of the evil they stored in their hearts. People speak the things that are in their hearts.

TWO KINDS OF PEOPLE

46"Why do you call me, 'Lord, Lord,' but do not do what I say? 47I will show you what everyone is like who comes to me and hears my words and obeys. 48That person is like a man building a house who dug deep and laid the foundation on rock. When the floods came, the water tried to wash the house away, but it could not shake it, because the house was built well. 49But the one who hears my words and does not obey is like a man who built his house on the ground without a foundation. When the floods came, the house quickly fell and was completely destroyed."

JESUS HEALS A SOLDIER'S SERVANT

7 When Jesus finished saying all these things to the people, he went to Capernaum. 2There was an army officer who had a servant who was very important to him. The servant was so sick he was nearly dead. 3When the officer heard about Jesus, he sent some Jewish elders to him to ask Jesus to come and heal his servant. 4The men went to Jesus and begged him, saying, "This officer is worthy of your help. 5He loves our people, and he built us a synagogue."

6So Jesus went with the men. He was getting near the officer's house when the officer sent friends to say, "Lord, don't trouble yourself, because I am not worthy to have you come into my house. 7That is why I did not come to you myself. But you only need to command it, and my servant will be healed. 8I, too, am a man under the authority of others, and I have soldiers under my command. I tell one soldier, 'Go,' and he goes. I tell another soldier, 'Come,' and he comes. I say to my servant, 'Do this,' and my servant does it."

9When Jesus heard this, he was amazed. Turning to the crowd that was following him, he said, "I tell you, this is the greatest faith I have found anywhere, even in Israel."

10Those who had been sent to Jesus went back to the house where they found the servant in good health.

JESUS BRINGS A MAN BACK TO LIFE

11Soon afterwards Jesus went to a town called Nain, and his followers and a large crowd traveled with him. 12When he came near the town gate, he saw a funeral. A mother, who was a widow, had lost her only son. A large crowd from the town was with the mother while her son was being carried out. 13When the Lord saw her, he felt very sorry for her and said, "Don't cry." 14He went up and touched the coffin, and the people who were carrying it stopped. Jesus said, "Young man, I tell you, get up!" 15And the son sat up and began to talk. Then Jesus gave him back to his mother.

16All the people were amazed and began praising God, saying, "A great prophet has come to us! God has come to help his people."

17This news about Jesus spread through all Judea and into all the places around there.

JOHN ASKS A QUESTION

18John's followers told him about all these things. He called for two of his followers 19and sent them to the Lord to ask, "Are you the One who is to come, or should we wait for someone else?"

20When the men came to Jesus, they said, "John the Baptist sent us to you with this question: 'Are you the One who is to come, or should we wait for someone else?'"

21At that time, Jesus healed many people of their sicknesses, diseases, and evil spirits, and he gave sight to many blind people. 22Then Jesus answered John's followers, "Go tell John what you saw and heard here. The blind can see, the crippled can walk, and people with skin diseases are healed. The deaf can hear, the dead are raised to life, and the Good News is preached to the poor. 23Those who do not stumble in their faith because of me are blessed!"

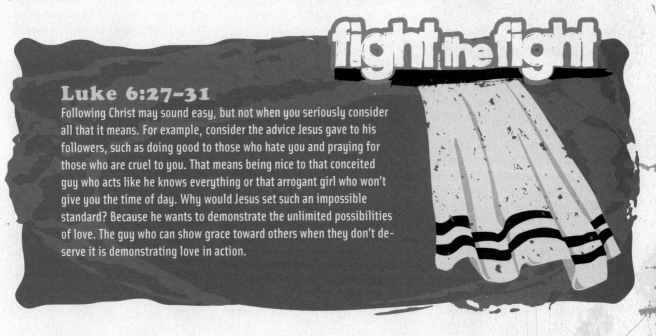

fight the fight

Luke 6:27-31

Following Christ may sound easy, but not when you seriously consider all that it means. For example, consider the advice Jesus gave to his followers, such as doing good to those who hate you and praying for those who are cruel to you. That means being nice to that conceited guy who acts like he knows everything or that arrogant girl who won't give you the time of day. Why would Jesus set such an impossible standard? Because he wants to demonstrate the unlimited possibilities of love. The guy who can show grace toward others when they don't deserve it is demonstrating love in action.

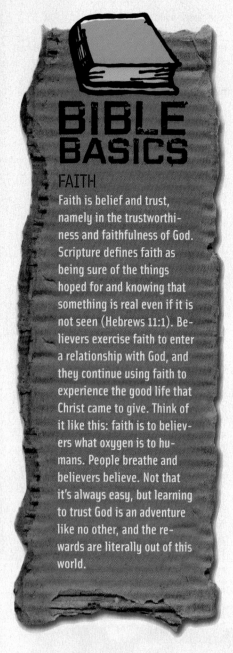

BIBLE BASICS

FAITH

Faith is belief and trust, namely in the trustworthiness and faithfulness of God. Scripture defines faith as being sure of the things hoped for and knowing that something is real even if it is not seen (Hebrews 11:1). Believers exercise faith to enter a relationship with God, and they continue using faith to experience the good life that Christ came to give. Think of it like this: faith is to believers what oxygen is to humans. People breathe and believers believe. Not that it's always easy, but learning to trust God is an adventure like no other, and the rewards are literally out of this world.

[24]When John's followers left, Jesus began talking to the people about John: "What did you go out into the desert to see? A reed[n] blown by the wind? [25]What did you go out to see? A man dressed in fine clothes? No, people who have fine clothes and much wealth live in kings' palaces. [26]But what did you go out to see? A prophet? Yes, and I tell you, John is more than a prophet. [27]This was written about him:

'I will send my messenger ahead of you,
    who will prepare the way for you.'

Malachi 3:1

[28]I tell you, John is greater than any other person ever born, but even the least important person in the kingdom of God is greater than John."

[29](When the people, including the tax collectors, heard this, they all agreed that God's teaching was good, because they had been baptized by John. [30]But the Pharisees and experts on the law refused to accept God's plan for themselves; they did not let John baptize them.)

[31]Then Jesus said, "What shall I say about the people of this time? What are they like? [32]They are like children sitting in the marketplace, calling to one another and saying,

'We played music for you, but you did not
    dance;
    we sang a sad song, but you did not cry.'

[33]John the Baptist came and did not eat bread or drink wine, and you say, 'He has a demon in him.' [34]The Son of Man came eating and drinking, and you say, 'Look at him! He eats too much and drinks too much wine, and he is a friend of tax collectors and sinners!' [35]But wisdom is proved to be right by what it does."

A WOMAN WASHES JESUS' FEET

[36]One of the Pharisees asked Jesus to eat with him, so Jesus went into the Pharisee's house and sat at the table. [37]A sinful woman in the town learned that Jesus was eating at the Pharisee's house. So she brought an alabaster jar of perfume [38]and stood behind Jesus at his feet, crying. She began to wash his feet with her tears, and she dried them with her hair, kissing them many times and rubbing them with the perfume. [39]When the Pharisee who asked Jesus to come to his house saw this, he thought to himself, "If Jesus were a prophet, he would know that the woman touching him is a sinner!"

[40]Jesus said to the Pharisee, "Simon, I have something to say to you."

Simon said, "Teacher, tell me."

[41]Jesus said, "Two people owed money to the same banker. One owed five hundred coins[n] and the other owed fifty. [42]They had no money to pay what they owed, but the banker told both of them they did not have to pay him. Which person will love the banker more?"

[43]Simon, the Pharisee, answered, "I think it would be the one who owed him the most money."

Jesus said to Simon, "You are right." [44]Then Jesus turned toward the woman and said to Simon, "Do you see this woman? When I came into your house, you gave me no water for my feet, but she washed my feet with her tears and dried them with her hair. [45]You gave me no kiss of greeting, but she has been kissing my feet since I came in. [46]You did not put oil on my head, but she poured perfume on my feet. [47]I tell you that her many sins are forgiven, so she showed great love. But the person who is forgiven only a little will love only a little."

[48]Then Jesus said to her, "Your sins are forgiven."

[49]The people sitting at the table began to say among themselves, "Who is this who even forgives sins?"

[50]Jesus said to the woman, "Because you believed, you are saved from your sins. Go in peace."

THE GROUP WITH JESUS

8 After this, while Jesus was traveling through some cities and small towns, he preached and told the Good News about God's kingdom. The twelve apostles were with him, 2and also some women who had been healed of sicknesses and evil spirits: Mary, called Magdalene, from whom seven demons had gone out; 3Joanna, the wife of Cuza (the manager of Herod's house); Susanna; and many others. These women used their own money to help Jesus and his apostles.

A STORY ABOUT PLANTING SEED

[4]When a great crowd was gathered, and people were coming to Jesus from every town, he told them this story:

[5]"A farmer went out to plant his seed. While he was planting, some seed fell by the road. People walked on the seed, and the birds ate it up. [6]Some seed fell on rock, and when it began to grow, it died because it had no water. [7]Some seed fell among thorny weeds, but the weeds grew up with it and choked the good plants. [8]And some seed fell on good ground and grew and made a hundred times more."

WAYS to WALK the WALK

LUKE 8:38-39

WORD: Chronicle the good things God has done for you.

WALK IT: There's nothing more personal than your own story of what God has done in your life. The next time he does something good, write it down and go tell someone.

 7:24 reed It means that John was not ordinary or weak like grass blown by the wind. **7:41 coins** Roman denarii. One coin was the average pay for one day's work.

As Jesus finished the story, he called out, "Let those with ears use them and listen!"

[9]Jesus' followers asked him what this story meant.

[10]Jesus said, "You have been chosen to know the secrets about the kingdom of God. But I use stories to speak to other people so that:

'They will look, but they may not see.
They will listen, but they may not
    understand.'   Isaiah 6:9

[11]"This is what the story means: The seed is God's message. [12]The seed that fell beside the road is like the people who hear God's teaching, but the devil comes and takes it away from them so they cannot believe it and be saved. [13]The seed that fell on rock is like those who hear God's teaching and accept it gladly, but they don't allow the teaching to go deep into their lives. They believe for a while, but when trouble comes, they give up. [14]The seed that fell among the thorny weeds is like those who hear God's teaching, but they let the worries, riches, and pleasures of this life keep them from growing and producing good fruit. [15]And the seed that fell on the good ground is like those who hear God's teaching with good, honest hearts and obey it and patiently produce good fruit.

USE WHAT YOU HAVE

[16]"No one after lighting a lamp covers it with a bowl or hides it under a bed. Instead, the person puts it on a lampstand so those who come in will see the light. [17]Everything that is hidden will become clear, and every secret thing will be made known. [18]So be careful how you listen. Those who have understanding will be given more. But those who do not have understanding, even what they think they have will be taken away from them."

JESUS' TRUE FAMILY

[19]Jesus' mother and brothers came to see him, but there was such a crowd they could not get to him. [20]Someone said to Jesus, "Your mother and your brothers are standing outside, wanting to see you."

[21]Jesus answered them, "My mother and my brothers are those who listen to God's teaching and obey it!"

JESUS CALMS A STORM

[22]One day Jesus and his followers got into a boat, and he said to them, "Let's go across the lake." And so they started across. [23]While they were sailing, Jesus fell asleep. A very strong wind blew up on the lake, causing the boat to fill with water, and they were in danger.

[24]The followers went to Jesus and woke him, saying, "Master! Master! We will drown!"

Jesus got up and gave a command to the wind and the waves. They stopped, and it became calm. [25]Jesus said to his followers, "Where is your faith?"

The followers were afraid and amazed and said to each other, "Who is this that commands even the wind and the water, and they obey him?"

A MAN WITH DEMONS INSIDE HIM

[26]Jesus and his followers sailed across the lake from Galilee to the area of the Gerasene[n] people. [27]When Jesus got out on the land, a man from the town who had demons inside him came to Jesus. For a long time he had worn no clothes and had lived in the burial caves, not in a house. [28]When he saw Jesus, he cried out and fell down before him. He said with a loud voice, "What do you want with me, Jesus, Son of the Most High God? I beg you, don't torture me!" [29]He said this because Jesus was commanding the evil spirit to come out of the man. Many times it had taken hold of him. Though he had been kept under guard and chained hand and foot, he had broken his chains and had been forced by the demon out into a lonely place.

[30]Jesus asked him, "What is your name?"

He answered, "Legion,"[n] because many demons were in him. [31]The demons begged Jesus not to send them into eternal darkness.[n] [32]A large herd of pigs was feeding on a hill, and the demons begged Jesus to allow them to go into the pigs. So Jesus allowed them to do this. [33]When the demons came out of the man, they went into the pigs, and the herd ran down the hill into the lake and was drowned.

[34]When the herdsmen saw what had happened, they ran away and told about this in the town and the countryside. [35]And people went to see what had happened. When they came to Jesus, they found the man sitting at Jesus' feet, clothed and in his right mind, because the demons were gone. But the people were frightened. [36]The people who saw this happen told the others how Jesus had made the man well. [37]All the people of the Gerasene country asked Jesus to leave, because they were all very afraid. So Jesus got into the boat and went back to Galilee.

[38]The man whom Jesus had healed begged to go with him, but Jesus sent him away, saying, [39]"Go back home and tell people how much God has done for you." So the man went all over town telling how much Jesus had done for him.

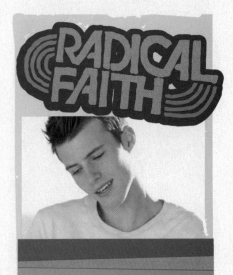

LUKE 8:15

Jesus says that a faithful guy's heart is like good dirt. It safely envelops the seeds scattered on it, then soaks up the rain and sun that makes plants sprout. Jesus isn't talking about actual plants sprouting inside your soul, but he's explaining the way people respond to God's Word. Some guys are like seed thrown on the side of a road—they hear the Bible's truths, but Satan keeps them from believing. Others resemble seed landing on rock—the truth starts to grow but doesn't penetrate their lives. Still others are like seeds sown among weeds—the truth gets choked by worry and temptation. If you're good dirt, you listen to God's Word and put its teaching into practice. You don't just stay awake during sermons or youth group. You take charge of your time and create opportunities to investigate the Bible, focusing your whole attention on figuring out how it applies to your life and willingly obeying what you learn. If you do that, Jesus says you will steadily produce a huge crop of spiritual growth. You will know God well and live tight with him.

8:26 **Gerasene** From Gerasa, an area southeast of Lake Galilee. The exact location is uncertain and some Greek copies read "Gadarene"; others read "Gergesene."   8:30 **Legion** Means very many. A legion was about five thousand men in the Roman army.
8:31 **eternal darkness** Literally, "the abyss," something like a pit or a hole that has no end.

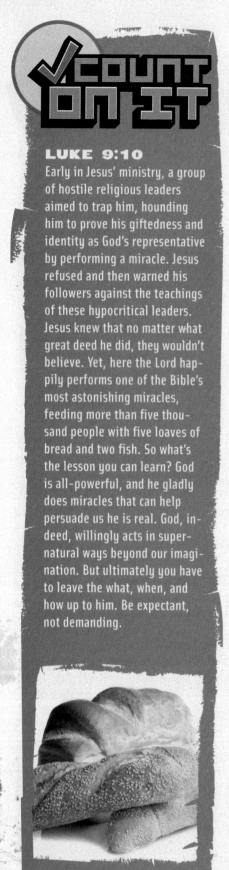

COUNT ON IT

LUKE 9:10

Early in Jesus' ministry, a group of hostile religious leaders aimed to trap him, hounding him to prove his giftedness and identity as God's representative by performing a miracle. Jesus refused and then warned his followers against the teachings of these hypocritical leaders. Jesus knew that no matter what great deed he did, they wouldn't believe. Yet, here the Lord happily performs one of the Bible's most astonishing miracles, feeding more than five thousand people with five loaves of bread and two fish. So what's the lesson you can learn? God is all-powerful, and he gladly does miracles that can help persuade us he is real. God, indeed, willingly acts in supernatural ways beyond our imagination. But ultimately you have to leave the what, when, and how up to him. Be expectant, not demanding.

JESUS GIVES LIFE TO A DEAD GIRL AND HEALS A SICK WOMAN

[40]When Jesus got back to Galilee, a crowd welcomed him, because everyone was waiting for him. [41]A man named Jairus, a leader of the synagogue, came to Jesus and fell at his feet, begging him to come to his house. [42]Jairus' only daughter, about twelve years old, was dying.

While Jesus was on his way to Jairus' house, the people were crowding all around him. [43]A woman was in the crowd who had been bleeding for twelve years,[n] but no one was able to heal her. [44]She came up behind Jesus and touched the edge of his coat, and instantly her bleeding stopped. [45]Then Jesus said, "Who touched me?"

When all the people said they had not touched him, Peter said, "Master, the people are all around you and are pushing against you."

[46]But Jesus said, "Someone did touch me, because I felt power go out from me." [47]When the woman saw she could not hide, she came forward, shaking, and fell down before Jesus. While all the people listened, she told why she had touched him and how she had been instantly healed. [48]Jesus said to her, "Dear woman, you are made well because you believed. Go in peace."

[49]While Jesus was still speaking, someone came from the house of the synagogue leader and said to him, "Your daughter is dead. Don't bother the teacher anymore."

[50]When Jesus heard this, he said to Jairus, "Don't be afraid. Just believe, and your daughter will be well."

[51]When Jesus went to the house, he let only Peter, John, James, and the girl's father and mother go inside with him. [52]All the people were crying and feeling sad because the girl was dead, but Jesus said, "Stop crying. She is not dead, only asleep."

[53]The people laughed at Jesus because they knew the girl was dead. [54]But Jesus took hold of her hand and called to her, "My child, stand up!" [55]Her spirit came back into her, and she stood up at once. Then Jesus ordered that she be given something to eat. [56]The girl's parents were amazed, but Jesus told them not to tell anyone what had happened.

JESUS SENDS OUT THE APOSTLES

9 Jesus called the twelve apostles together and gave them power and authority over all demons and the ability to heal sicknesses. [2]He sent the apostles out to tell about God's kingdom and to heal the sick. [3]He said to them, "Take nothing for your trip, neither a walking stick, bag, bread, money, or extra clothes. [4]When you enter a house, stay there until it is time to leave. [5]If people do not welcome you, shake the dust off of your feet[n] as you leave the town, as a warning to them."

[6]So the apostles went out and traveled through all the towns, preaching the Good News and healing people everywhere.

HEROD IS CONFUSED ABOUT JESUS

[7]Herod, the governor, heard about all the things that were happening and was confused, because some people said, "John the Baptist has risen from the dead." [8]Others said, "Elijah has come to us." And still others said, "One of the prophets who lived long ago has risen from the dead." [9]Herod said, "I cut off John's head, so who is this man I hear such things about?" And Herod kept trying to see Jesus.

MORE THAN FIVE THOUSAND FED

[10]When the apostles returned, they told Jesus everything they had done. Then Jesus took them with him to a town called Bethsaida where they could be alone together. [11]But the people learned where Jesus went and followed him. He welcomed them and talked with them about God's kingdom and healed those who needed to be healed.

[12]Late in the afternoon, the twelve apostles came to Jesus and said, "Send the people away. They need to go to the towns and countryside around here and find places to sleep and something to eat, because no one lives in this place."

[13]But Jesus said to them, "You give them something to eat."

They said, "We have only five loaves of bread and two fish, unless we go buy food for all these people." [14](There were about five thousand men there.)

Jesus said to his followers, "Tell the people to sit in groups of about fifty people."

[15]So the followers did this, and all the people sat down. [16]Then Jesus took the five loaves of bread and two fish, and looking up to heaven, he thanked God for the food. Then he divided the food and gave it to the followers to give to the people. [17]They all ate and were satisfied, and what was left over was gathered up, filling twelve baskets.

JESUS IS THE CHRIST

[18]One time when Jesus was praying alone, his followers were with him, and he asked them, "Who do the people say I am?"

[19]They answered, "Some say you are John the Baptist. Others say you are Elijah.[n] And others say you are one of the prophets from long ago who has come back to life."

8:43 years Some Greek copies continue, "and she had spent all the money she had on doctors." **9:5 shake . . . feet** A warning. It showed that they had rejected these people. **9:19 Elijah** A man who spoke for God and who lived hundreds of years before Christ. See 1 Kings 17.

²⁰Then Jesus asked, "But who do you say I am?"

Peter answered, "You are the Christ from God."

²¹Jesus warned them not to tell anyone, saying, ²²"The Son of Man must suffer many things. He will be rejected by the Jewish elders, the leading priests, and the teachers of the law. He will be killed and after three days will be raised from the dead."

²³Jesus said to all of them, "If people want to follow me, they must give up the things they want. They must be willing to give up their lives daily to follow me. ²⁴Those who want to save their lives will give up true life. But those who give up their lives for me will have true life. ²⁵It is worthless to have the whole world if they themselves are destroyed or lost. ²⁶If people are ashamed of me and my teaching, then the Son of Man will be ashamed of them when he comes in his glory and with the glory of the Father and the holy angels. ²⁷I tell you the truth, some people standing here will see the kingdom of God before they die."

JESUS TALKS WITH MOSES AND ELIJAH

²⁸About eight days after Jesus said these things, he took Peter, John, and James and went up on a mountain to pray. ²⁹While Jesus was praying, the appearance of his face changed, and his clothes became shining white. ³⁰Then two men, Moses and Elijah,ⁿ were talking with Jesus. ³¹They appeared in heavenly glory, talking about his departure which he would soon bring about in Jerusalem. ³²Peter and the others were very sleepy, but when they awoke fully, they saw the glory of Jesus and the two men standing with him. ³³When Moses and Elijah were about to leave, Peter said to Jesus, "Master, it is good that we are here. Let us make three tents—one for you, one for Moses, and one for Elijah." (Peter did not know what he was talking about.)

³⁴While he was saying these things, a cloud came and covered them, and they became afraid as the cloud covered them. ³⁵A voice came from the cloud, saying, "This is my Son, whom I have chosen. Listen to him!"

³⁶When the voice finished speaking, only Jesus was there. Peter, John, and James said nothing and told no one at that time what they had seen.

JESUS HEALS A SICK BOY

³⁷The next day, when they came down from the mountain, a large crowd met Jesus. ³⁸A man in the crowd shouted to him, "Teacher, please come and look at my son, because he is my only child. ³⁹An evil spirit seizes my son, and suddenly he screams. It causes him to lose control of himself and foam at the mouth. The evil spirit keeps on hurting him and almost never leaves him. ⁴⁰I begged your followers to force the evil spirit out, but they could not do it."

⁴¹Jesus answered, "You people have no faith, and your lives are all wrong. How long must I stay with you and put up with you? Bring your son here."

⁴²While the boy was coming, the demon threw him on the ground and made him lose control of himself. But Jesus gave a strong command to the evil spirit and healed the boy and gave him back to his father. ⁴³All the people were amazed at the great power of God.

JESUS TALKS ABOUT HIS DEATH

While everyone was wondering about all that Jesus did, he said to his followers, ⁴⁴"Don't forget what I tell you now: The Son of Man will be handed over to people." ⁴⁵But the followers did not understand what this meant; the meaning was hidden from them so they could not understand. But they were afraid to ask Jesus about it.

WHO IS THE GREATEST?

⁴⁶Jesus' followers began to have an argument about which one of them was the greatest. ⁴⁷Jesus knew what they were thinking, so he took a little child and stood the child beside him. ⁴⁸Then Jesus said, "Whoever accepts this little child in my name accepts me. And whoever accepts me accepts the One who sent me, because whoever is least among you all is really the greatest."

Relationships

"I give you a new command: Love each other. You must love each other as I have loved you. All people will know that you are my followers if you love each other" (John 13:34–35). That's a pretty big statement: people will know if you follow Jesus by how much you love other people. You don't have to be best friends with the entire school, but you should be open to forming relationships, however minor, with others. And that doesn't just mean girls. As a Christian, you're part of the family of God, so you need to love like a family member.

GUARD YOUR HEART

Spend time hanging out with happily married couples in your church. You might even consider asking one of them to mentor you by sharing his or her personal advice about relationships. Because married folks have spent years making their relationship work, they can often give you some valuable insight about growing together gracefully.

9:30 **Moses and Elijah** Two of the most important Jewish leaders in the past. God had given Moses the Law, and Elijah was an important prophet.

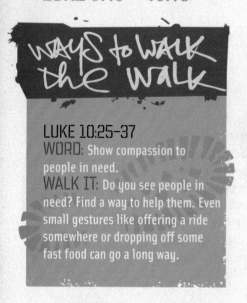

ways to WALK the WALK

LUKE 10:25-37

WORD: Show compassion to people in need.

WALK IT: Do you see people in need? Find a way to help them. Even small gestures like offering a ride somewhere or dropping off some fast food can go a long way.

ANYONE NOT AGAINST US IS FOR US

⁴⁹John answered, "Master, we saw someone using your name to force demons out of people. We told him to stop, because he does not belong to our group."

⁵⁰But Jesus said to him, "Don't stop him, because whoever is not against you is for you."

A TOWN REJECTS JESUS

⁵¹When the time was coming near for Jesus to depart, he was determined to go to Jerusalem. ⁵²He sent some messengers ahead of him, who went into a town in Samaria to make everything ready for him. ⁵³But the people there would not welcome him, because he was set on going to Jerusalem. ⁵⁴When James and John, followers of Jesus, saw this, they said, "Lord, do you want us to call fire down from heaven and destroy those people?"[n]

⁵⁵But Jesus turned and scolded them. [And Jesus said, "You don't know what kind of spirit you belong to. ⁵⁶The Son of Man did not come to destroy the souls of people but to save them."][n] Then they went to another town.

FOLLOWING JESUS

⁵⁷As they were going along the road, someone said to Jesus, "I will follow you any place you go."

⁵⁸Jesus said to them, "The foxes have holes to live in, and the birds have nests, but the Son of Man has no place to rest his head."

⁵⁹Jesus said to another man, "Follow me!"

But he said, "Lord, first let me go and bury my father."

⁶⁰But Jesus said to him, "Let the people who are dead bury their own dead. You must go and tell about the kingdom of God."

⁶¹Another man said, "I will follow you, Lord, but first let me go and say good-bye to my family."

⁶²Jesus said, "Anyone who begins to plow a field but keeps looking back is of no use in the kingdom of God."

JESUS SENDS OUT THE SEVENTY-TWO

10 After this, the Lord chose seventy-two[n] others and sent them out in pairs ahead of him into every town and place where he planned to go. ²He said to them, "There are a great many people to harvest, but there are only a few workers. So pray to God, who owns the harvest, that he will send more workers to help gather his harvest. ³Go now, but listen! I am sending you out like sheep among wolves. ⁴Don't carry a purse, a bag, or sandals, and don't waste time talking with people on the road. ⁵Before you go into a house, say, 'Peace be with this house.' ⁶If peace-loving people live there, your blessing of peace will stay with them, but if not, then your blessing will come back to you. ⁷Stay in the same house, eating and drinking what the people there give you. A worker should be given his pay. Don't move from house to house. ⁸If you go into a town and the people welcome you, eat what they give you. ⁹Heal the sick who live there, and tell them, 'The kingdom of God is near you.' ¹⁰But if you go into a town, and the people don't welcome you, then go into the streets and say, ¹¹'Even the dirt from your town that sticks to our feet we wipe off against you.[n] But remember that the kingdom of God is near.' ¹²I tell you, on the Judgment Day it will be better for the people of Sodom[n] than for the people of that town.

JESUS WARNS UNBELIEVERS

¹³"How terrible for you, Korazin! How terrible for you, Bethsaida! If the miracles I did in you had happened in Tyre and Sidon,[n] those people would have changed their lives long ago. They would have worn rough cloth and put ashes on themselves to show they had changed. ¹⁴But on the Judgment Day it will be better for Tyre and Sidon than for you. ¹⁵And you, Capernaum,[n] will you be lifted up to heaven? No! You will be thrown down to the depths!

¹⁶"Whoever listens to you listens to me, and whoever refuses to accept you refuses to accept me. And whoever refuses to accept me refuses to accept the One who sent me."

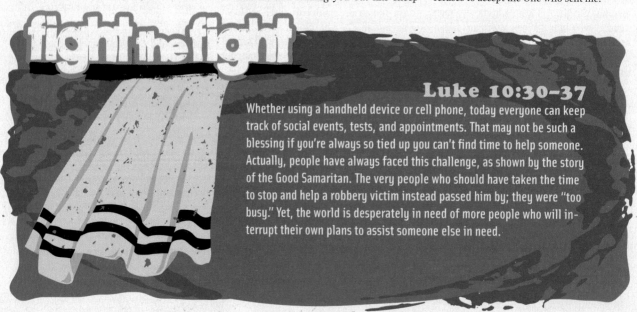

fight the fight

Luke 10:30-37

Whether using a handheld device or cell phone, today everyone can keep track of social events, tests, and appointments. That may not be such a blessing if you're always so tied up you can't find time to help someone. Actually, people have always faced this challenge, as shown by the story of the Good Samaritan. The very people who should have taken the time to stop and help a robbery victim instead passed him by; they were "too busy." Yet, the world is desperately in need of more people who will interrupt their own plans to assist someone else in need.

9:54 people Some Greek copies continue "as Elijah did." **9:55-56 And . . . them.** Some Greek copies do not contain the bracketed text. **10:1 seventy-two** Some Greek copies read "seventy." **10:11 dirt . . . you** A warning. It showed that they had rejected these people. **10:12 Sodom** City that God destroyed because the people were so evil. **10:13 Tyre and Sidon** Towns where wicked people lived. **10:13, 15 Korazin . . . Bethsaida . . . Capernaum** Towns by Lake Galilee where Jesus preached to the people.

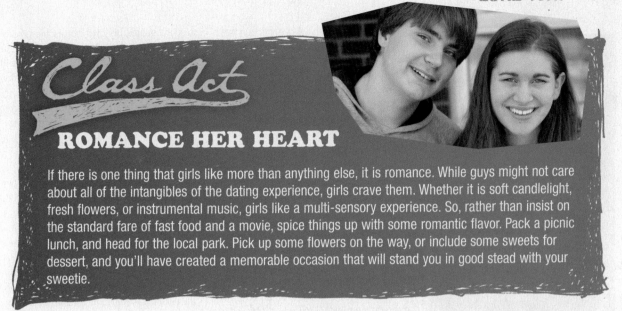

Class Act

ROMANCE HER HEART

If there is one thing that girls like more than anything else, it is romance. While guys might not care about all of the intangibles of the dating experience, girls crave them. Whether it is soft candlelight, fresh flowers, or instrumental music, girls like a multi-sensory experience. So, rather than insist on the standard fare of fast food and a movie, spice things up with some romantic flavor. Pack a picnic lunch, and head for the local park. Pick up some flowers on the way, or include some sweets for dessert, and you'll have created a memorable occasion that will stand you in good stead with your sweetie.

SATAN FALLS

[17]When the seventy-two[n] came back, they were very happy and said, "Lord, even the demons obeyed us when we used your name!" [18]Jesus said, "I saw Satan fall like lightning from heaven. [19]Listen, I have given you power to walk on snakes and scorpions, power that is greater than the enemy has. So nothing will hurt you. [20]But you should not be happy because the spirits obey you but because your names are written in heaven."

JESUS PRAYS TO THE FATHER

[21]Then Jesus rejoiced in the Holy Spirit and said, "I praise you, Father, Lord of heaven and earth, because you have hidden these things from the people who are wise and smart. But you have shown them to those who are like little children. Yes, Father, this is what you really wanted.

[22]"My Father has given me all things. No one knows who the Son is, except the Father. And no one knows who the Father is, except the Son and those whom the Son chooses to tell."

[23]Then Jesus turned to his followers and said privately, "You are blessed to see what you now see. [24]I tell you, many prophets and kings wanted to see what you now see, but they did not, and they wanted to hear what you now hear, but they did not."

THE GOOD SAMARITAN

[25]Then an expert on the law stood up to test Jesus, saying, "Teacher, what must I do to get life forever?"

[26]Jesus said, "What is written in the law? What do you read there?"

[27]The man answered, "Love the Lord your God with all your heart, all your soul, all your strength, and all your mind."[n] Also, "Love your neighbor as you love yourself."[n]

[28]Jesus said to him, "Your answer is right. Do this and you will live."

[29]But the man, wanting to show the importance of his question, said to Jesus, "And who is my neighbor?"

[30]Jesus answered, "As a man was going down from Jerusalem to Jericho, some robbers attacked him. They tore off his clothes, beat him, and left him lying there, almost dead. [31]It happened that a priest was going down that road. When he saw the man, he walked by on the other side. [32]Next, a Levite[n] came there, and after he went over and looked at the man, he walked by on the other side of the road. [33]Then a Samaritan[n] traveling down the road came to where the hurt man was. When he saw the man, he felt very sorry for him. [34]The Samaritan went to him, poured olive oil and wine[n] on his wounds, and bandaged them. Then he put the hurt man on his own donkey and took him to an inn where he cared for him. [35]The next day, the Samaritan brought out two coins,[n] gave them to the innkeeper, and said, 'Take care of this man. If you spend more money on him, I will pay it back to you when I come again.'"

[36]Then Jesus said, "Which one of these three men do you think was a neighbor to the man who was attacked by the robbers?"

[37]The expert on the law answered, "The one who showed him mercy."

Jesus said to him, "Then go and do what he did."

MARY AND MARTHA

[38]While Jesus and his followers were traveling, Jesus went into a town. A woman named Martha let Jesus stay at her house. [39]Martha had a sister named Mary, who was sitting at Jesus' feet and listening to him teach. [40]But Martha was busy with all the work to be done. She went in and said, "Lord, don't you care that my sister has left me alone to do all the work? Tell her to help me."

[41]But the Lord answered her, "Martha, Martha, you are worried and upset about many things. [42]Only one thing is important. Mary has chosen the better thing, and it will never be taken away from her."

JESUS TEACHES ABOUT PRAYER

One time Jesus was praying in a certain place. When he finished, one of his followers said to him, "Lord, teach us to pray as John taught his followers."

 10:17 seventy-two Some Greek copies read "seventy." 10:27 "Love . . . mind." Quotation from Deuteronomy 6:5. 10:27 "Love . . . yourself." Quotation from Leviticus 19:18. 10:32 Levite Levites were members of the tribe of Levi who helped the Jewish priests with their work in the Temple. Read 1 Chronicles 23:24–32. 10:33 Samaritan Samaritans were people from Samaria. These people were part Jewish, but the Jews did not accept them as true Jews. Samaritans and Jews disliked each other. 10:34 olive oil and wine Oil and wine were used like medicine to soften and clean wounds. 10:35 coins Roman denarii. One coin was the average pay for one day's work.

experts answer YOUR questions

Q: What should I do to obey God?

A: There are many things that God asks of us: to love him, serve people, love others, help our neighbors. But the most important work of God, Jesus tells us, is simply to believe in him. The first step is not to do anything but make a decision—the decision to believe and place our trust in Jesus as our Lord.

Q: How can I respond when people question what I believe?

A: It can be difficult when others question your faith. While it's good to know the logical reasons to defend your faith, you don't have to know a lot of specific arguments. No one can argue against your experience. Just share your journey of faith: why you believe in Jesus and what he has meant to you.

[2]Jesus said to them, "When you pray, say:
'Father, may your name always be kept holy.
May your kingdom come.
[3]Give us the food we need for each day.
[4]Forgive us for our sins,
because we forgive everyone who has done wrong to us.
And do not cause us to be tempted.' "[n]

CONTINUE TO ASK

[5]Then Jesus said to them, "Suppose one of you went to your friend's house at midnight and said to him, 'Friend, loan me three loaves of bread. [6]A friend of mine has come into town to visit me, but I have nothing for him to eat.' [7]Your friend inside the house answers, 'Don't bother me! The door is already locked, and my children and I are in bed. I cannot get up and give you anything.' [8]I tell you, if friendship is not enough to make him get up to give you the bread, your boldness will make him get up and give you whatever you need. [9]So I tell you, ask, and God will give to you. Search, and you will find. Knock, and the door will open for you. [10]Yes, everyone who asks will receive. The one who searches will find. And everyone who knocks will have the door opened. [11]If your children ask for[n] a fish, which of you would give them a snake instead? [12]Or, if your children ask for an egg, would you give them a scorpion? [13]Even though you are bad, you know how to give good things to your children. How much more your heavenly Father will give the Holy Spirit to those who ask him!"

JESUS' POWER IS FROM GOD

[14]One time Jesus was sending out a demon who could not talk. When the demon came out, the man who had been unable to speak, then spoke. The people were amazed. [15]But some of them said, "Jesus uses the power of Beelzebul, the ruler of demons, to force demons out of people."

[16]Other people, wanting to test Jesus, asked him to give them a sign from heaven. [17]But knowing their thoughts, he said to them, "Every kingdom that is divided against itself will be destroyed. And a family that is divided against itself will not continue. [18]So if Satan is divided against himself, his kingdom will not continue. You say that I use the power of Beelzebul to force out demons. [19]But if I use the power of Beelzebul to force out demons, what power do your people use to force demons out? So they will be your judges. [20]But if I use the power of God to force out demons, then the kingdom of God has come to you.

[21]"When a strong person with many weapons guards his own house, his possessions are safe. [22]But when someone stronger comes and defeats him, the stronger one will take away the weapons the first man trusted and will give away the possessions.

[23]"Anyone who is not with me is against me, and anyone who does not work with me is working against me.

THE EMPTY PERSON

[24]"When an evil spirit comes out of a person, it travels through dry places, looking for a place to rest. But when it finds no place, it says, 'I will go back to the house I left.' [25]And when it comes back, it finds that house swept clean and made neat. [26]Then the evil spirit goes out and brings seven other spirits more evil than it is, and they go in and live there. So the person has even more trouble than before."

PEOPLE WHO ARE TRULY BLESSED

[27]As Jesus was saying these things, a woman in the crowd called out to Jesus, "Blessed is the mother who gave birth to you and nursed you."

[28]But Jesus said, "No, blessed are those who hear the teaching of God and obey it."

THE PEOPLE WANT A MIRACLE

[29]As the crowd grew larger, Jesus said, "The people who live today are evil. They want to see a miracle for a sign, but no sign will be given them, except the sign of Jonah.[n] [30]As Jonah was a sign for those people who lived in Nineveh, the Son of Man will be a sign for the people of this time. [31]On the Judgment Day the Queen of the South[n] will stand up with the people who live now. She will show they are guilty, because she came from far away to listen to Solomon's wise teaching. And I tell you that someone greater than Solomon is here. [32]On the Judgment Day the people of Nineveh will stand up with the people who live now, and they will show that you are guilty. When Jonah preached to them, they were sorry and changed their lives. And I tell you that someone greater than Jonah is here.

BE A LIGHT FOR THE WORLD

[33]"No one lights a lamp and puts it in a secret place or under a bowl, but on a lampstand so the people who come in can see. [34]Your eye is a light for the body. When your eyes are good, your whole body will be full of light. But when your eyes are evil, your whole body will be full of darkness. [35]So be careful not to let the light in you become darkness. [36]If your whole body is full of

11:2–4 'Father . . . tempted.' Some Greek copies include phrases from Matthew's version of this prayer (Matthew 6:9–13). 11:11 for Some Greek copies include the phrase "for bread, which of you would give them a stone, or if they ask for . . ." 11:29 sign of Jonah Jonah's three days in the fish are like Jesus' three days in the tomb. See Matthew 12:40. 11:31 Queen of the South The Queen of Sheba. She traveled a thousand miles to learn God's wisdom from Solomon. Read 1 Kings 10:1–3.

light, and none of it is dark, then you will shine bright, as when a lamp shines on you."

JESUS ACCUSES THE PHARISEES

[37]After Jesus had finished speaking, a Pharisee asked Jesus to eat with him. So Jesus went in and sat at the table. [38]But the Pharisee was surprised when he saw that Jesus did not wash his hands[n] before the meal. [39]The Lord said to him, "You Pharisees clean the outside of the cup and the dish, but inside you are full of greed and evil. [40]You foolish people! The same one who made what is outside also made what is inside. [41]So give what is in your dishes to the poor, and then you will be fully clean. [42]How terrible for you Pharisees! You give God one-tenth of even your mint, your rue, and every other plant in your garden. But you fail to be fair to others and to love God. These are the things you should do while continuing to do those other things. [43]How terrible for you Pharisees, because you love to have the most important seats in the synagogues, and you love to be greeted with respect in the marketplaces. [44]How terrible for you, because you are like hidden graves, which people walk on without knowing."

JESUS TALKS TO EXPERTS ON THE LAW

[45]One of the experts on the law said to Jesus, "Teacher, when you say these things, you are insulting us, too."

[46]Jesus answered, "How terrible for you, you experts on the law! You make strict rules that are very hard for people to obey, but you yourselves don't even try to follow those rules. [47]How terrible for you, because you build tombs for the prophets whom your ancestors

killed! [48]And now you show that you approve of what your ancestors did. They killed the prophets, and you build tombs for them! [49]This is why in his wisdom God said, 'I will send prophets and apostles to them. They will kill some, and they will treat others cruelly.' [50]So you who live now will be punished for the deaths of all the prophets who were killed since the beginning of the world— [51]from the killing of Abel to the killing of Zechariah,[n] who died between the altar and the Temple. Yes, I tell you that you who are alive now will be punished for them all.

[52]"How terrible for you, you experts on the law. You have taken away the key to learning about God. You yourselves would not learn, and you stopped others from learning, too."

[53]When Jesus left, the teachers of the law and the Pharisees began to give him trouble, asking him questions about many things, [54]trying to catch him saying something wrong.

DON'T BE LIKE THE PHARISEES

12 So many thousands of people had gathered that they were stepping on each other. Jesus spoke first to his followers, saying, "Beware of the yeast of the Pharisees, because they are hypocrites. [2]Everything that is hidden will be shown, and everything that is secret will be made known. [3]What you have said in the dark will be heard in the light, and what you have whispered in an inner room will be shouted from the housetops.

[4]"I tell you, my friends, don't be afraid of people who can kill the body but after that can do nothing more to hurt you. [5]I will show you the one to fear. Fear the one who has the power to kill you and also to throw you into hell. Yes, this is the one you should fear.

[6]"Five sparrows are sold for only two pennies, and God does not forget any of them. [7]But God even knows how many hairs you have on your head. Don't be afraid. You are worth much more than many sparrows.

DON'T BE ASHAMED OF JESUS

[8]"I tell you, all those who stand before others and say they believe in me, I, the Son of Man, will say before the angels of God that they belong to me. [9]But all who stand before others and say they do not believe in me, I will say before the angels of God that they do not belong to me.

[10]"Anyone who speaks against the Son of Man can be forgiven, but anyone who speaks against the Holy Spirit will not be forgiven.

[11]"When you are brought into the synagogues before the leaders and other powerful

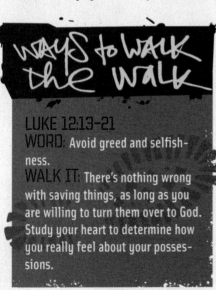

ways to WALK the WALK

LUKE 12:13–21
WORD: Avoid greed and selfishness.
WALK IT: There's nothing wrong with saving things, as long as you are willing to turn them over to God. Study your heart to determine how you really feel about your possessions.

LUKE 12:34
Want to know what's highest on the list of things most important to you? Just keep track of all the places you spend your money for a month or so. You might discover that you drop all of your hard-earned dough on roses for your mother or biscuits for your dog, but chances are you get rid of much of your moolah on snacks, sports, music, or other consumables. You might have a girlfriend who drains your wallet as fast as you fill it. Or maybe the movie theatre or nearby electronics superstore is where your cash goes. Like Jesus says here, "Your heart will be where your treasure is." In the words leading up to that verse, the Lord points out that the stuff at the top of most shopping lists doesn't last very long. Thieves steal it, moths eat it, or time ruins it. Wise people use their money for what matters most, sharing what they have and focusing on stuff that lasts—knowing God better and helping others find an eternal home in heaven. If those are your most important possessions, you get to hang on to them forever.

11:38 **wash his hands** This was a Jewish religious custom that the Pharisees thought was very important.   11:51 **Abel . . . Zechariah** In the Hebrew Old Testament, the first and last men to be murdered.

TOP TEN

random aerobic exercise ideas

1. Walk around the neighborhood.
2. Bicycle to and from school.
3. Swim at the local pool.
4. Use stairs instead of elevators.
5. Jog in one place.
6. Jump rope to music.
7. Ride a stationary bicycle.
8. Exercise on a treadmill.
9. Go running with a friend.
10. Do jumping jacks.

people, don't worry about how to defend yourself or what to say. [12]At that time the Holy Spirit will teach you what you must say."

JESUS WARNS AGAINST SELFISHNESS

[13]Someone in the crowd said to Jesus, "Teacher, tell my brother to divide with me the property our father left us."

[14]But Jesus said to him, "Who said I should judge or decide between you?" [15]Then Jesus said to them, "Be careful and guard against all kinds of greed. Life is not measured by how much one owns."

[16]Then Jesus told this story: "There was a rich man who had some land, which grew a good crop. [17]He thought to himself, 'What will I do? I have no place to keep all my crops.' [18]Then he said, 'This is what I will do: I will tear down my barns and build bigger ones, and there I will store all my grain and other goods. [19]Then I can say to myself, "I have enough good things stored to last for many years. Rest, eat, drink, and enjoy life!" '

[20]"But God said to him, 'Foolish man! Tonight your life will be taken from you. So who will get those things you have prepared for yourself?'

[21]"This is how it will be for those who store up things for themselves and are not rich toward God."

DON'T WORRY

[22]Jesus said to his followers, "So I tell you, don't worry about the food you need to live, or about the clothes you need for your body. [23]Life is more than food, and the body is more than clothes. [24]Look at the birds. They don't plant or harvest, they don't have storerooms or barns, but God feeds them. And you are worth much more than birds. [25]You cannot add any time to your life by worrying about it. [26]If you cannot do even the little things, then why worry about the big things? [27]Consider how the lilies grow; they don't work or make clothes for themselves. But I tell you that even Solomon with his riches was not dressed as beautifully as one of these flowers. [28]God clothes the grass in the field, which is alive today but tomorrow is thrown into the fire. So how much more will God clothe you? Don't have so little faith! [29]Don't always think about what you will eat or what you will drink, and don't keep worrying. [30]All the people in the world are trying to get these things, and your Father knows you need them. [31]But seek God's kingdom, and all your other needs will be met as well.

DON'T TRUST IN MONEY

[32]"Don't fear, little flock, because your Father wants to give you the kingdom. [33]Sell your possessions and give to the poor. Get for

*REVIEWS MUSIC

UNDEROATH:
THEY'RE ONLY CHASING SAFETY

Underoath, a band of guys barely in their twenties, combines infectiously loud guitar riffs with surprisingly melodic sing-scream vocals for a record that might have been the best of its genre last year. Highlights include the punk-influenced "A Boy Brushed Red . . . Living in Black and White" and the hardcore "I Don't Feel Very Receptive Today." Though the spiritual content of this record is sometimes hard to hear over the loud music and raspy, grungelike vocals, the album does add some interesting insights to Christian truth. Underoath's strongest trait is definitely its live show. As up-and-coming rockers, the group offers an intense punch to the musical gut.

WHY IT ROCKS:

LISTENING IS MADE A MUSICAL ADVENTURE.

yourselves purses that will not wear out, the treasure in heaven that never runs out, where thieves can't steal and moths can't destroy. ³⁴Your heart will be where your treasure is.

ALWAYS BE READY

³⁵"Be dressed, ready for service, and have your lamps shining. ³⁶Be like servants who are waiting for their master to come home from a wedding party. When he comes and knocks, the servants immediately open the door for him. ³⁷They will be blessed when their master comes home, because he sees that they were watching for him. I tell you the truth, the master will dress himself to serve and tell the servants to sit at the table, and he will serve them. ³⁸Those servants will be blessed when he comes in and finds them still waiting, even if it is midnight or later. ³⁹"Remember this: If the owner of the house knew what time a thief was coming, he would not allow the thief to enter his house. ⁴⁰So you also must be ready, because the Son of Man will come at a time when you don't expect him!"

WHO IS THE TRUSTED SERVANT?

⁴¹Peter said, "Lord, did you tell this story to us or to all people?"

⁴²The Lord said, "Who is the wise and trusted servant that the master trusts to give the other servants their food at the right time? ⁴³When the master comes and finds the servant doing his work, the servant will be blessed. ⁴⁴I tell you the truth, the master will choose that servant to take care of everything he owns. ⁴⁵But suppose the servant thinks to himself, 'My master will not come back soon,' and he begins to beat the other servants, men and women, and to eat and drink and get drunk. ⁴⁶The master will come when that servant is not ready and is not expecting him. Then the master will cut him in pieces and send him away to be with the others who don't obey.

⁴⁷"The servant who knows what his master wants but is not ready, or who does not do what the master wants, will be beaten with many blows! ⁴⁸But the servant who does not know what his master wants and does things that should be punished will be beaten with few blows. From everyone who has been given much, much will be demanded. And from the one trusted with much, much more will be expected.

JESUS CAUSES DIVISION

⁴⁹"I came to set fire to the world, and I wish it were already burning! ⁵⁰I have a baptismⁿ to suffer through, and I feel very troubled until it is over. ⁵¹Do you think I came to give peace to the earth? No, I tell you, I came to divide it. ⁵²From now on, a family with five people will be divided, three against two, and two against three. ⁵³They will be divided: father against son and son against father, mother against daughter and daughter against mother, mother-in-law against daughter-in-law and daughter-in-law against mother-in-law."

UNDERSTANDING THE TIMES

⁵⁴Then Jesus said to the people, "When you see clouds coming up in the west, you say, 'It's going to rain,' and it happens. ⁵⁵When you feel the wind begin to blow from the south, you say, 'It will be a hot day,' and it happens. ⁵⁶Hypocrites! You know how to understand the appearance of the earth and sky. Why don't you understand what is happening now?

SETTLE YOUR PROBLEMS

⁵⁷"Why can't you decide for yourselves what is right? ⁵⁸If your enemy is taking you to court, try hard to settle it on the way. If you don't, your enemy might take you to the judge, and the judge might turn you over to the officer, and the officer might throw you into jail. ⁵⁹I tell you, you will not get out of there until you have paid everything you owe."

CHANGE YOUR HEARTS

13 At that time some people were there who told Jesus that Pilateⁿ had killed some people from Galilee while they were worshiping. He mixed their blood with the blood of the animals they were sacrificing to God. ²Jesus answered, "Do you think this happened to them because they were more sinful than all others from Galilee? ³No, I tell you. But unless you change your hearts and lives, you will be destroyed as they were!

Extras: How to Impress on the First Date

You finally gathered the courage to ask her out, and she said, "Yes." Now what? If you have enough lead-time, call the girl a couple of days before and let her know you're excited about taking her out. You don't have to say any more than that. When date time arrives, make sure you are on time. And when you're out with the girl, the best advice is simply to be on your best behavior, but be yourself. Really, be the best version of yourself. Be honest and open with her from the beginning. Treat her like a lady and respect her opinions (and her space). To make an extra impression, call her a couple of days afterward and let her know how much you enjoyed going out with her. The best way to impress a girl is to have a firm relationship with the Lord. Not only is it attractive, but it also attracts the right types of girls.

GUARD YOUR HEART

If the girl you're interested in doesn't know what she wants in a relationship, be leery of dating her. People with no life direction tend to be flaky, and the people who date them usually wind up being hurt in the end. If a girl doesn't know what she's looking for, you don't need to waste your time pursuing her.

12:50 I . . . baptism Jesus was talking about the suffering he would soon go through.   13:1 Pilate Pontius Pilate was the Roman governor of Judea from A.D. 26 to A.D. 36.

91

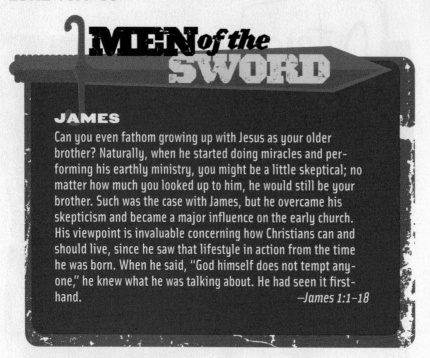

MEN of the SWORD

JAMES

Can you even fathom growing up with Jesus as your older brother? Naturally, when he started doing miracles and performing his earthly ministry, you might be a little skeptical; no matter how much you looked up to him, he would still be your brother. Such was the case with James, but he overcame his skepticism and became a major influence on the early church. His viewpoint is invaluable concerning how Christians can and should live, since he saw that lifestyle in action from the time he was born. When he said, "God himself does not tempt anyone," he knew what he was talking about. He had seen it first-hand.

—James 1:1–18

STORIES OF MUSTARD SEED AND YEAST

[18]Then Jesus said, "What is God's kingdom like? What can I compare it with? [19]It is like a mustard seed that a man plants in his garden. The seed grows and becomes a tree, and the wild birds build nests in its branches."

[20]Jesus said again, "What can I compare God's kingdom with? [21]It is like yeast that a woman took and hid in a large tub of flour until it made all the dough rise."

THE NARROW DOOR

[22]Jesus was teaching in every town and village as he traveled toward Jerusalem. [23]Someone said to Jesus, "Lord, will only a few people be saved?"

Jesus said, [24]"Try hard to enter through the narrow door, because many people will try to enter there, but they will not be able. [25]When the owner of the house gets up and closes the door, you can stand outside and knock on the door and say, 'Sir, open the door for us.' But he will answer, 'I don't know you or where you come from.' [26]Then you will say, 'We ate and drank with you, and you taught in the streets of our town.' [27]But he will say to you, 'I don't know you or where you come from. Go away from me, all you who do evil!' [28]You will cry and grind your teeth with pain when you see Abraham, Isaac, Jacob, and all the prophets in God's kingdom, but you yourselves thrown outside. [29]People will come from the east, west, north, and south and will sit down at the table in the kingdom of God. [30]There are those who are last now who will be first in the future. And there are those who are first now who will be last in the future."

JESUS WILL DIE IN JERUSALEM

[31]At that time some Pharisees came to Jesus and said, "Go away from here! Herod wants to kill you!"

[32]Jesus said to them, "Go tell that fox Herod, 'Today and tomorrow I am forcing demons out and healing people. Then, on the third day, I will reach my goal.' [33]Yet I must be on my way today and tomorrow and the next day. Surely it cannot be right for a prophet to be killed anywhere except in Jerusalem.

[34]"Jerusalem, Jerusalem! You kill the prophets and stone to death those who are sent to you. Many times I wanted to gather your people as a hen gathers her chicks under her wings, but you would not let me. [35]Now your house is left completely empty. I tell you, you will not see me until that time when you will say, 'God bless the One who comes in the name of the Lord.' "[n]

[4]What about those eighteen people who died when the tower of Siloam fell on them? Do you think they were more sinful than all the others who live in Jerusalem? [5]No, I tell you. But unless you change your hearts and lives, you will all be destroyed too!"

THE USELESS TREE

[6]Jesus told this story: "A man had a fig tree planted in his vineyard. He came looking for some fruit on the tree, but he found none. [7]So the man said to his gardener, 'I have been looking for fruit on this tree for three years, but I never find any. Cut it down. Why should it waste the ground?' [8]But the servant answered, 'Master, let the tree have one more year to produce fruit. Let me dig up the dirt around it and put on some fertilizer. [9]If the tree produces

there who, for eighteen years, had an evil spirit in her that made her crippled. Her back was always bent; she could not stand up straight. [12]When Jesus saw her, he called her over and said, "Woman, you are free from your sickness." [13]Jesus put his hands on her, and immediately she was able to stand up straight and began praising God.

[14]The synagogue leader was angry because Jesus healed on the Sabbath day. He said to the people, "There are six days when one has to work. So come to be healed on one of those days, and not on the Sabbath day."

[15]The Lord answered, "You hypocrites! Doesn't each of you untie your work animals and lead them to drink water every day—even on the Sabbath day? [16]This woman that I healed, a daughter of Abraham, has been held

Thirty percent of those who have graduated from college volunteer their time compared with 20 percent of those who have not attended college.

—Barna.org

fruit next year, good. But if not, you can cut it down.' "

JESUS HEALS ON THE SABBATH

[10]Jesus was teaching in one of the synagogues on the Sabbath day. [11]A woman was

by Satan for eighteen years. Surely it is not wrong for her to be freed from her sickness on a Sabbath day!" [17]When Jesus said this, all of those who were criticizing him were ashamed, but the entire crowd rejoiced at all the wonderful things Jesus was doing.

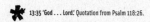 13:35 'God . . . Lord.' Quotation from Psalm 118:26.

HEALING ON THE SABBATH

14 On a Sabbath day, when Jesus went to eat at the home of a leading Pharisee, the people were watching Jesus very closely. ²And in front of him was a man with dropsy.ⁿ ³Jesus said to the Pharisees and experts on the law, "Is it right or wrong to heal on the Sabbath day?" ⁴But they would not answer his question. So Jesus took the man, healed him, and sent him away. ⁵Jesus said to the Pharisees and teachers of the law, "If your childⁿ or ox falls into a well on the Sabbath day, will you not pull him out quickly?" ⁶And they could not answer him.

DON'T MAKE YOURSELF IMPORTANT

⁷When Jesus noticed that some of the guests were choosing the best places to sit, he told this story: ⁸"When someone invites you to a wedding feast, don't take the most important seat, because someone more important than you may have been invited. ⁹The host, who invited both of you, will come to you and say, 'Give this person your seat.' Then you will be embarrassed and will have to move to the last place. ¹⁰So when you are invited, go sit in a seat that is not important. When the host comes to you, he may say, 'Friend, move up here to a more important place.' Then all the other guests will respect you. ¹¹All who make themselves great will be made humble, but those who make themselves humble will be made great."

YOU WILL BE REWARDED

¹²Then Jesus said to the man who had invited him, "When you give a lunch or a dinner, don't invite only your friends, your family, your other relatives, and your rich neighbors. At another time they will invite you to eat with them, and you will be repaid. ¹³Instead, when you give a feast, invite the poor, the crippled, the lame, and the blind. ¹⁴Then you will be blessed, because they have nothing and cannot pay you back. But you will be repaid when the good people rise from the dead."

A STORY ABOUT A BIG BANQUET

¹⁵One of those at the table with Jesus heard these things and said to him, "Blessed are the people who will share in the meal in God's kingdom."

¹⁶Jesus said to him, "A man gave a big banquet and invited many people. ¹⁷When it was time to eat, the man sent his servant to tell the guests, 'Come. Everything is ready.'

¹⁸"But all the guests made excuses. The first one said, 'I have just bought a field, and I must go look at it. Please excuse me.' ¹⁹Another said, 'I have just bought five pairs of oxen; I must go and try them. Please excuse me.' ²⁰A third person said, 'I just got married; I can't come.' ²¹So the servant returned and told his master what had happened. Then the master became angry and said, 'Go at once into the streets and alleys of the town, and bring in the poor, the crippled, the blind, and the lame.' ²²Later the servant said to him, 'Master, I did what you commanded, but we still have room.' ²³The master said to the servant, 'Go out to the roads and country lanes, and urge the people there to come so my house will be full. ²⁴I tell you, none of those whom I invited first will eat with me.'"

THE COST OF BEING JESUS' FOLLOWER

²⁵Large crowds were traveling with Jesus, and he turned and said to them, ²⁶"If anyone comes to me but loves his father, mother, wife, children, brothers, or sisters—or even life—more than me, he cannot be my follower. ²⁷Whoever is not willing to carry his cross and follow me cannot be my follower. ²⁸If you want to build a tower, you first sit down and decide how much it will cost, to see if you have enough money to finish the job. ²⁹If you don't, you might lay the foundation, but you would not be able to finish. Then all who would see it would make fun of you, ³⁰saying, 'This person began to build but was not able to finish.' ³¹If a king is going to fight another king, first he will sit down and plan. He will decide if he and his ten thousand soldiers can defeat the other king who has twenty thousand soldiers. ³²If he can't, then while the other king is still far away, he will send some people to speak to him and ask for peace. ³³In the same way, you must give up everything you have to be my follower.

DON'T LOSE YOUR INFLUENCE

³⁴"Salt is good, but if it loses its salty taste, you cannot make it salty again. ³⁵It is no good

RADICAL FAITH

LUKE 14:7-11

When you spend top dollar on a ticket to your favorite sports game, you don't aim for a seat in the nosebleed section. When you escort your prom date to dinner, you don't settle for sitting six tables away. Or if you get elected president of your class, you don't expect to preside from the far corner of your school auditorium. Get it? No matter what your situation in life is, you try to score the best seat you can. It's normal to want to sit in the place that looks important, near the center of the action, at the seat with the best view. But Jesus mocked people who stroll in and take the seat of honor at a party, then get bumped down to their proper place. He said it's better to take a lowly seat and get called upward. The Lord isn't just talking about shrewd party behavior. He means that your highest goal shouldn't be to seek a place of honor among the prettiest and most popular people in the grand party of life. If you humble yourself, he will make you great.

WAYS to WALK the WALK

LUKE 14:34-35

Don't lose your influence. Your influence and integrity are what make you savory to the world. Fight to protect them both by avoiding temptation and trusting in Jesus to uphold your reputation.

experts answer YOUR questions

Q: Why should I serve others?

A: John 13:15 says that Jesus tells us to follow his example by serving each other. So, if there's a task that needs to be done and no one wants to do it, you should take the initiative and do it yourself as an act of service to other people.

Q: Is Jesus the only way to know God?

A: Although it's hard to understand in a culture that talks a lot about different faiths, Jesus made it clear that he is the way, the truth, and the life. By his life and death, he demonstrated what God is like and how much God loves us. That's good news for all.

for the soil or for manure; it is thrown away. "Let those with ears use them and listen."

A LOST SHEEP, A LOST COIN

15 The tax collectors and sinners all came to listen to Jesus. ²But the Pharisees and the teachers of the law began to complain: "Look, this man welcomes sinners and even eats with them."

³Then Jesus told them this story: ⁴"Sup- pose one of you has a hundred sheep but loses one of them. Then he will leave the other ninety-nine sheep in the open field and go out and look for the lost sheep until he finds it. ⁵And when he finds it, he happily puts it on his shoulders ⁶and goes home. He calls to his friends and neighbors and says, 'Be happy with me because I found my lost sheep.' ⁷In the same way, I tell you there is more joy in heaven over one sinner who changes his heart and life, than over ninety-nine good people who don't need to change.

⁸"Suppose a woman has ten silver coins,ⁿ but loses one. She will light a lamp, sweep the house, and look carefully for the coin until she finds it. ⁹And when she finds it, she will call her friends and neighbors and say, 'Be happy with me because I have found the coin that I lost.' ¹⁰In the same way, there is joy in the pres- ence of the angels of God when one sinner changes his heart and life."

THE SON WHO LEFT HOME

¹¹Then Jesus said, "A man had two sons. ¹²The younger son said to his father, 'Give me my share of the property.' So the father divided the property between his two sons. ¹³Then the younger son gathered up all that was his and traveled far away to another country. There he wasted his money in foolish living. ¹⁴After he had spent everything, a time came when there was no food anywhere in the country, and the son was poor and hungry. ¹⁵So he got a job with one of the citizens there who sent the son into the fields to feed pigs. ¹⁶The son was so hungry that he wanted to eat the pods the pigs were eating, but no one gave him anything. ¹⁷When he realized what he was doing, he thought, 'All of my father's servants have plenty of food. But I am here, almost dying with hunger. ¹⁸I will leave and return to my fa- ther and say to him, "Father, I have sinned against God and against you. ¹⁹I am no longer worthy to be called your son, but let me be like one of your servants." ' ²⁰So the son left and went to his father.

"While the son was still a long way off, his father saw him and felt sorry for his son. So the father ran to him and hugged and kissed him. ²¹The son said, 'Father, I have sinned against God and against you. I am no longer worthy to be called your son.'ⁿ ²²But the father said to his servants, 'Hurry! Bring the best clothes and put them on him. Also, put a ring on his finger and sandals on his feet. ²³And get our fat calf and kill it so we can have a feast and celebrate. ²⁴My son was dead, but now he is alive again! He was lost, but now he is found!' So they began to celebrate.

²⁵"The older son was in the field, and as he came closer to the house, he heard the sound of music and dancing. ²⁶So he called to one of the servants and asked what all this meant. ²⁷The servant said, 'Your brother has come back, and your father killed the fat calf, be- cause your brother came home safely.' ²⁸The older son was angry and would not go in to the feast. So his father went out and begged him to come in. ²⁹But the older son said to his father, 'I have served you like a slave for many years and have always obeyed your commands. But you never gave me even a young goat to have at a feast with my friends. ³⁰But your other son, who wasted all your money on prosti- tutes, comes home, and you kill the fat calf for him!' ³¹The father said to him, 'Son, you are al- ways with me, and all that I have is yours. ³²We had to celebrate and be happy because your brother was dead, but now he is alive. He was lost, but now he is found.' "

TRUE WEALTH

16 Jesus also said to his followers, "Once there was a rich man who had a manager to take care of his business. This manager was accused of cheating him. ²So he called the manager in and said to him, 'What is this I hear about you? Give me a report of what you have done with my money, because you can't be my manager any longer.' ³The man- ager thought to himself, 'What will I do since my master is taking my job away from me? I am not strong enough to dig ditches, and I am ashamed to beg. ⁴I know what I'll do so that when I lose my job people will welcome me into their homes.'

⁵"So the manager called in everyone who owed the master any money. He asked the first one, 'How much do you owe?' ⁶He answered, 'Eight hundred gallons of olive oil.' The man- ager said to him, 'Take your bill, sit down quickly, and write four hundred gallons.' ⁷Then the manager asked another one, 'How much do you owe?' He answered, 'One thousand bushels of wheat.' Then the manager said to him, 'Take your bill and write eight hundred bushels.' ⁸So, the master praised the dishonest manager for being clever. Yes, worldly people are more clever with their own kind than spir- itual people are.

⁹"I tell you, make friends for yourselves using worldly riches so that when those riches are gone, you will be welcomed in those homes that continue forever. ¹⁰Whoever can be trusted with a little can also be trusted with a lot, and whoever is dishonest with a little is dishonest with a lot. ¹¹If you cannot be trusted with worldly riches, then who will trust you

 15:8 *silver coins* Roman denarii. One coin was the average pay for one day's work. **15:21** *son* Some Greek copies continue, "but let me be like one of your servants" (see verse 19).

with true riches? [12]And if you cannot be trusted with things that belong to someone else, who will give you things of your own?

[13]"No servant can serve two masters. The servant will hate one master and love the other, or will follow one master and refuse to follow the other. You cannot serve both God and worldly riches."

GOD'S LAW CANNOT BE CHANGED

[14]The Pharisees, who loved money, were listening to all these things and made fun of Jesus. [15]He said to them, "You make yourselves look good in front of people, but God knows what is really in your hearts. What is important to people is hateful in God's sight.

[16]"The law of Moses and the writings of the prophets were preached until John[n] came. Since then the Good News about the kingdom of God is being told, and everyone tries to enter it by force. [17]It would be easier for heaven and earth to pass away than for the smallest part of a letter in the law to be changed.

DIVORCE AND REMARRIAGE

[18]"If a man divorces his wife and marries another woman, he is guilty of adultery, and the man who marries a divorced woman is also guilty of adultery."

THE RICH MAN AND LAZARUS

[19]Jesus said, "There was a rich man who always dressed in the finest clothes and lived in luxury every day. [20]And a very poor man named Lazarus, whose body was covered with sores, was laid at the rich man's gate. [21]He wanted to eat only the small pieces of food that fell from the rich man's table. And the dogs would come and lick his sores. [22]Later, Lazarus died, and the angels carried him to the arms of Abraham. The rich man died, too, and was buried. [23]In the place of the dead, he was in much pain. The rich man saw Abraham far away with Lazarus at his side. [24]He called, 'Father Abraham, have mercy on me! Send Lazarus to dip his finger in water and cool my tongue, because I am suffering in this fire!' [25]But Abraham said, 'Child, remember when you were alive you had the good things in life, but bad things happened to Lazarus. Now he is comforted here, and you are suffering. [26]Besides, there is a big pit between you and us, so no one can cross over to you, and no one can leave there and come here.' [27]The rich man said, 'Father, then please send Lazarus to my father's house. [28]I have five brothers, and Lazarus could warn them so that they will not come to this place of pain.' [29]But Abraham said, 'They have the law of Moses and the writings of the prophets; let them learn from them.' [30]The rich man said, 'No, father Abraham! If someone goes to them from the dead, they would believe and change their hearts and lives.' [31]But Abraham said to him, 'If they will not listen to Moses and the prophets, they will not listen to someone who comes back from the dead.' "

SIN AND FORGIVENESS

17 Jesus said to his followers, "Things that cause people to sin will happen, but how terrible for the person who causes them to happen! [2]It would be better for

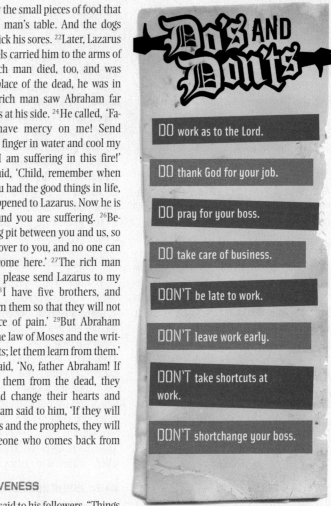

DO's AND Don'ts

DO work as to the Lord.

DO thank God for your job.

DO pray for your boss.

DO take care of business.

DON'T be late to work.

DON'T leave work early.

DON'T take shortcuts at work.

DON'T shortchange your boss.

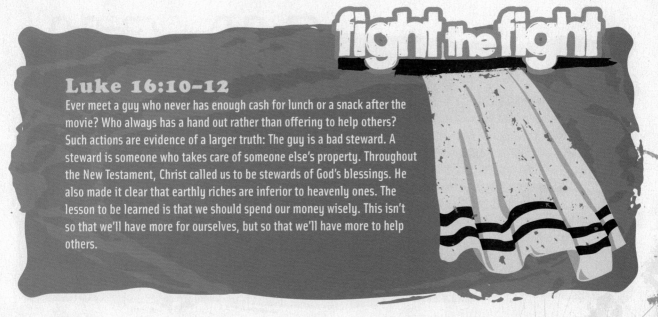

fight the fight

Luke 16:10–12

Ever meet a guy who never has enough cash for lunch or a snack after the movie? Who always has a hand out rather than offering to help others? Such actions are evidence of a larger truth: The guy is a bad steward. A steward is someone who takes care of someone else's property. Throughout the New Testament, Christ called us to be stewards of God's blessings. He also made it clear that earthly riches are inferior to heavenly ones. The lesson to be learned is that we should spend our money wisely. This isn't so that we'll have more for ourselves, but so that we'll have more to help others.

16:16 John John the Baptist, who preached to people about Christ's coming (Matthew 3, Luke 3).

you to be thrown into the sea with a large stone around your neck than to cause one of these little ones to sin. [3]So be careful!

"If another follower sins, warn him, and if he is sorry and stops sinning, forgive him. [4]If he sins against you seven times in one day and says that he is sorry each time, forgive him."

HOW BIG IS YOUR FAITH?

[5]The apostles said to the Lord, "Give us more faith!"

[6]The Lord said, "If your faith were the size of a mustard seed, you could say to this mulberry tree, 'Dig yourself up and plant yourself in the sea,' and it would obey you.

BE GOOD SERVANTS

[7]"Suppose one of you has a servant who has been plowing the ground or caring for the sheep. When the servant comes in from working in the field, would you say, 'Come in and sit down to eat'? [8]No, you would say to him, 'Prepare something for me to eat. Then get yourself ready and serve me. After I finish eating and drinking, you can eat.' [9]The servant does not get any special thanks for doing what his master commanded. [10]It is the same with you. When you have done everything you are told to do, you should say, 'We are unworthy servants; we have only done the work we should do.' "

BE THANKFUL

[11]While Jesus was on his way to Jerusalem, he was going through the area between Samaria and Galilee. [12]As he came into a small town, ten men who had a skin disease met him there. They did not come close to Jesus [13]but called to him, "Jesus! Master! Have mercy on us!"

[14]When Jesus saw the men, he said, "Go and show yourselves to the priests."[n]

As the ten men were going, they were healed. [15]When one of them saw that he was healed, he went back to Jesus, praising God in a loud voice. [16]Then he bowed down at Jesus' feet and thanked him. (And this man was a Samaritan.) [17]Jesus said, "Weren't ten men healed? Where are the other nine? [18]Is this Samaritan the only one who came back to thank God?" [19]Then Jesus said to him, "Stand up and go on your way. You were healed because you believed."

GOD'S KINGDOM IS WITHIN YOU

[20]Some of the Pharisees asked Jesus, "When will the kingdom of God come?"

Jesus answered, "God's kingdom is coming, but not in a way that you will be able to see with your eyes. [21]People will not say, 'Look, here it is!' or, 'There it is!' because God's kingdom is within[n] you."

[22]Then Jesus said to his followers, "The time will come when you will want very much to see one of the days of the Son of Man. But you will not see it. [23]People will say to you, 'Look, there he is!' or, 'Look, here he is!' Stay where you are; don't go away and search.

WHEN JESUS COMES AGAIN

[24]"When the Son of Man comes again, he will shine like lightning, which flashes across the sky and lights it up from one side to the other. [25]But first he must suffer many things and be rejected by the people of this time. [26]When the Son of Man comes again, it will be as it was when Noah lived. [27]People were eating, drinking, marrying, and giving their children to be married until the day Noah entered the boat. Then the flood came and killed them all. [28]It will be the same as during the time of Lot. People were eating, drinking, buying, selling, planting, and building. [29]But the day Lot left Sodom,[n] fire and sulfur rained down from the sky and killed them all. [30]This is how it will be when the Son of Man comes again.

[31]"On that day, a person who is on the roof and whose belongings are in the house should not go inside to get them. A person who is in the field should not go back home. [32]Remember Lot's wife.[n] [33]Those who try to keep their lives will lose them. But those who give up their lives will save them. [34]I tell you, on that night two people will be sleeping in one bed; one will be taken and the other will be left. [35]There will be two women grinding grain together; one will be taken, and the other will be left. [[36]Two people will be in the field. One will be taken, and the other will be left.][n]

[37]The followers asked Jesus, "Where will this be, Lord?"

Jesus answered, "Where there is a dead body, there the vultures will gather."

GOD WILL ANSWER HIS PEOPLE

18 Then Jesus used this story to teach his followers that they should always pray and never lose hope. [2]"In a certain town there was a judge who did not respect God or care about people. [3]In that same town there was a widow who kept coming to this

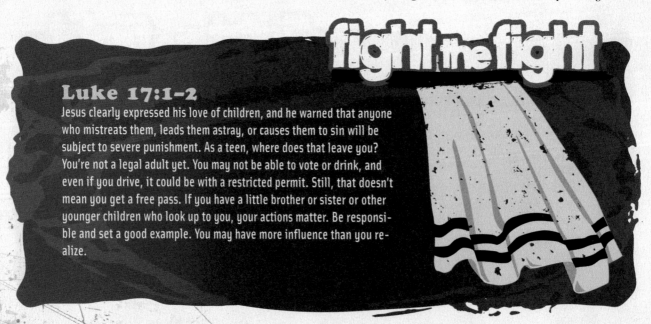

fight the fight

Luke 17:1-2

Jesus clearly expressed his love of children, and he warned that anyone who mistreats them, leads them astray, or causes them to sin will be subject to severe punishment. As a teen, where does that leave you? You're not a legal adult yet. You may not be able to vote or drink, and even if you drive, it could be with a restricted permit. Still, that doesn't mean you get a free pass. If you have a little brother or sister or other younger children who look up to you, your actions matter. Be responsible and set a good example. You may have more influence than you realize.

17:14 **show . . . priests** The Law of Moses said a priest must say when a person with a skin disease became well.   17:21 **within** Or "among."   17:29 **Sodom** City that God destroyed because the people were so evil.   17:32 **Lot's wife** A story about what happened to Lot's wife is found in Genesis 19:15–17, 26.   17:36 **Two . . . left.** Some Greek copies do not contain the bracketed text.

judge, saying, 'Give me my rights against my enemy.' [4]For a while the judge refused to help her. But afterwards, he thought to himself, 'Even though I don't respect God or care about people, [5]I will see that she gets her rights. Otherwise she will continue to bother me until I am worn out.' "

[6]The Lord said, "Listen to what the unfair judge said. [7]God will always give what is right to his people who cry to him night and day, and he will not be slow to answer them. [8]I tell you, God will help his people quickly. But when the Son of Man comes again, will he find those on earth who believe in him?"

BEING RIGHT WITH GOD

[9]Jesus told this story to some people who thought they were very good and looked down on everyone else: [10]"A Pharisee and a tax collector both went to the Temple to pray. [11]The Pharisee stood alone and prayed, 'God, I thank you that I am not like other people who steal, cheat, or take part in adultery, or even like this tax collector. [12]I fast[n] twice a week, and I give one-tenth of everything I get!'

[13]"The tax collector, standing at a distance, would not even look up to heaven. But he beat on his chest because he was so sad. He said, 'God, have mercy on me, a sinner.' [14]I tell you, when this man went home, he was right with God, but the Pharisee was not. All who make themselves great will be made humble, but all who make themselves humble will be made great."

WHO WILL ENTER GOD'S KINGDOM?

[15]Some people brought even their babies to Jesus so he could touch them. When the followers saw this, they told them to stop. [16]But Jesus called for the children, saying, "Let the little children come to me. Don't stop them, because the kingdom of God belongs to people who are like these children. [17]I tell you the truth, you must accept the kingdom of God as if you were a child, or you will never enter it."

A RICH MAN'S QUESTION

[18]A certain leader asked Jesus, "Good Teacher, what must I do to have life forever?"

[19]Jesus said to him, "Why do you call me good? Only God is good. [20]You know the commands: 'You must not be guilty of adultery. You must not murder anyone. You must not steal. You must not tell lies about your neighbor. Honor your father and mother.' "[n]

[21]But the leader said, "I have obeyed all these commands since I was a boy."

[22]When Jesus heard this, he said to him, "There is still one more thing you need to do.

Sell everything you have and give it to the poor, and you will have treasure in heaven. Then come and follow me." [23]But when the man heard this, he became very sad, because he was very rich.

[24]Jesus looked at him and said, "It is very hard for rich people to enter the kingdom of God. [25]It is easier for a camel to go through the eye of a needle than for a rich person to enter the kingdom of God."

WHO CAN BE SAVED?

[26]When the people heard this, they asked, "Then who can be saved?"

[27]Jesus answered, "The things impossible for people are possible for God."

[28]Peter said, "Look, we have left everything and followed you."

[29]Jesus said, "I tell you the truth, all those who have left houses, wives, brothers, parents, or children for the kingdom of God [30]will get much more in this life. And in the age that is coming, they will have life forever."

JESUS WILL RISE FROM THE DEAD

[31]Then Jesus took the twelve apostles aside and said to them, "We are going to Jerusalem. Everything the prophets wrote about the Son of Man will happen. [32]He will be turned over to those who are evil. They will laugh at him, insult him, spit on him, [33]beat him with whips, and kill him. But on the third day, he will rise to life again." [34]The apostles did not understand this; the meaning was hidden from them, and they did not realize what was said.

Relationships

"The greatest love a person can show is to die for his friends" (John 15:13). Whoa, this is heavy stuff. Think about your friends for a moment, the people you have close relationships with, both girls and guys. How much do these friends contribute to your life? Are your friends the types of people you'd *die* for? Or to put it another way, are they the types of people who would die for *you*? If so, congratulations. If not, maybe you should seek some new relationships. And don't forget to make it a point to *live* for your friends, also.

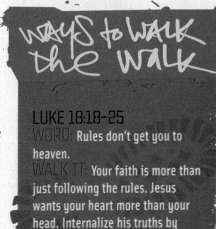

JESUS HEALS A BLIND MAN

[35]As Jesus came near the city of Jericho, a blind man was sitting beside the road, begging. [36]When he heard the people coming down the road, he asked, "What is happening?"

[37]They told him, "Jesus, from Nazareth, is going by."

[38]The blind man cried out, "Jesus, Son of David, have mercy on me!"

ways to WALK the WALK

LUKE 18:18–25
WORD: Rules don't get you to heaven.
WALK IT: Your faith is more than just following the rules. Jesus wants your heart more than your head. Internalize his truths by reading the Bible aloud to yourself.

18:12 **fast** The people would give up eating for a special time of prayer and worship to God. It was also done to show sadness and disappointment.   18:20 **'You . . . mother.'** Quotation from Exodus 20:12–16; Deuteronomy 5:16–20.

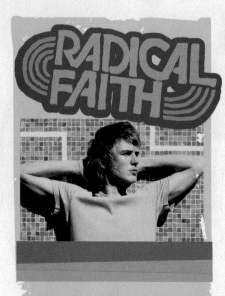

RADICAL FAITH

LUKE 19:38

People swarm whenever a major celebrity like a president or pope shows up, and that's exactly what happened as Jesus entered the city of Jerusalem. A mob of fans covered the road with their coats and palm branches as a sign of honor, cushioning his ride. The crowd applauded Jesus as a prophet and miracle worker sent by God and praised him as the rightful heir to the throne of David, ancient king of Israel. The city exploded with awe, yet the rock-star welcome didn't last. Less than a week after this triumphant entry, the crowd's excitement had fizzled. Jesus' enemies put him on trial and then killed him on a cross. Even his closest followers fled. Each year Christians commemorate this royal entry as Palm Sunday, a week before Easter. But you can reenact this royal party every day, welcoming Jesus with an electric loyalty that doesn't go away. You can welcome Jesus as King of your life, following him totally, even when the mobs don't shout his praises. Worshiping Christ isn't always popular, but it is always proper, so do your part.

[39] The people leading the group warned the blind man to be quiet. But the blind man shouted even more, "Son of David, have mercy on me!"

[40] Jesus stopped and ordered the blind man to be brought to him. When he came near, Jesus asked him, [41] "What do you want me to do for you?"

He said, "Lord, I want to see."

[42] Jesus said to him, "Then see. You are healed because you believed."

[43] At once the man was able to see, and he followed Jesus, thanking God. All the people who saw this praised God.

ZACCHAEUS MEETS JESUS

19 Jesus was going through the city of Jericho. [2] A man was there named Zacchaeus, who was a very important tax collector, and he was wealthy. [3] He wanted to see who Jesus was, but he was not able because he was too short to see above the crowd. [4] He ran ahead to a place where Jesus would come, and he climbed a sycamore tree so he could see him. [5] When Jesus came to that place, he looked up and said to him, "Zacchaeus, hurry and come down! I must stay at your house today."

[6] Zacchaeus came down quickly and welcomed him gladly. [7] All the people saw this and began to complain, "Jesus is staying with a sinner!"

[8] But Zacchaeus stood and said to the Lord, "I will give half of my possessions to the poor. And if I have cheated anyone, I will pay back four times more."

[9] Jesus said to him, "Salvation has come to this house today, because this man also belongs to the family of Abraham. [10] The Son of Man came to find lost people and save them."

A STORY ABOUT THREE SERVANTS

[11] As the people were listening to this, Jesus told them a story because he was near Jerusalem and they thought God's kingdom would appear immediately. [12] He said: "A very important man went to a country far away to be made a king and then to return home. [13] So he called ten of his servants and gave a coin[n] to each servant. He said, 'Do business with this money until I get back.' [14] But the people in the kingdom hated the man. So they sent a group to follow him and say, 'We don't want this man to be our king.'

[15] "But the man became king. When he returned home, he said, 'Call those servants who have my money so I can know how much they earned with it.'

[16] "The first servant came and said, 'Sir, I earned ten coins with the one you gave me.' [17] The king said to the servant, 'Excellent! You are a good servant. Since I can trust you with small things, I will let you rule over ten of my cities.'

[18] "The second servant said, 'Sir, I earned five coins with your one.' [19] The king said to this servant, 'You can rule over five cities.'

[20] "Then another servant came in and said to the king, 'Sir, here is your coin which I wrapped in a piece of cloth and hid. [21] I was afraid of you, because you are a hard man. You even take money that you didn't earn and gather food that you didn't plant.' [22] Then the king said to the servant, 'I will condemn you by your own words, you evil servant. You knew that I am a hard man, taking money that I didn't earn and gathering food that I didn't plant. [23] Why then didn't you put my money in the bank? Then when I came back, my money would have earned some interest.'

[24] "The king said to the men who were standing by, 'Take the coin away from this servant and give it to the servant who earned ten coins.' [25] They said, 'But sir, that servant already has ten coins.' [26] The king said, 'Those who have will be given more, but those who do not have anything will have everything taken away from them. [27] Now where are my enemies who didn't want me to be king? Bring them here and kill them before me.' "

JESUS ENTERS JERUSALEM AS A KING

[28] After Jesus said this, he went on toward Jerusalem. [29] As Jesus came near Bethphage and Bethany, towns near the hill called the Mount of Olives, he sent out two of his followers. [30] He said, "Go to the town you can see there. When you enter it, you will find a colt tied there, which no one has ever ridden. Untie it and bring it here to me. [31] If anyone asks you why you are untying it, say that the Master needs it."

[32] The two followers went into town and found the colt just as Jesus had told them. [33] As they were untying it, its owners came out and asked the followers, "Why are you untying our colt?"

[34] The followers answered, "The Master needs it." [35] So they brought it to Jesus, threw their coats on the colt's back, and put Jesus on it. [36] As Jesus rode toward Jerusalem, others spread their coats on the road before him.

[37] As he was coming close to Jerusalem, on the way down the Mount of Olives, the whole crowd of followers began joyfully shouting praise to God for all the miracles they had seen. [38] They said,

"God bless the king who comes in the
name of the Lord!   *Psalm 118:26*

 19:13 **coin** A Greek "mina." One mina was enough money to pay a person for working three months.

There is peace in heaven and glory to God!"

[39]Some of the Pharisees in the crowd said to Jesus, "Teacher, tell your followers not to say these things."

[40]But Jesus answered, "I tell you, if my followers didn't say these things, then the stones would cry out."

JESUS CRIES FOR JERUSALEM

[41]As Jesus came near Jerusalem, he saw the city and cried for it, [42]saying, "I wish you knew today what would bring you peace. But now it is hidden from you. [43]The time is coming when your enemies will build a wall around you and will hold you in on all sides. [44]They will destroy you and all your people, and not one stone will be left on another. All this will happen because you did not recognize the time when God came to save you."

JESUS GOES TO THE TEMPLE

[45]Jesus went into the Temple and began to throw out the people who were selling things there. [46]He said, "It is written in the Scriptures, 'My Temple will be a house for prayer.'[n] But you have changed it into a 'hideout for robbers'!"[n]

[47]Jesus taught in the Temple every day. The leading priests, the experts on the law, and some of the leaders of the people wanted to kill Jesus. [48]But they did not know how they could do it, because all the people were listening closely to him.

JEWISH LEADERS QUESTION JESUS

20 One day Jesus was in the Temple, teaching the people and telling them the Good News. The leading priests, teachers of the law, and elders came up to talk with him, [2]saying, "Tell us what authority you have to do these things? Who gave you this authority?"

[3]Jesus answered, "I will also ask you a question. Tell me: [4]When John baptized people, was that authority from God or just from other people?"

[5]They argued about this, saying, "If we answer, 'John's baptism was from God,' Jesus will say, 'Then why did you not believe him?' [6]But if we say, 'It was from other people,' all the people will stone us to death, because they believe John was a prophet." [7]So they answered that they didn't know where it came from.

[8]Jesus said to them, "Then I won't tell you what authority I have to do these things."

A STORY ABOUT GOD'S SON

[9]Then Jesus told the people this story: "A man planted a vineyard and leased it to some farmers. Then he went away for a long time. [10]When it was time for the grapes to be picked, he sent a servant to the farmers to get some of the grapes. But they beat the servant and sent him away empty-handed. [11]Then he sent another servant. They beat this servant also, and showed no respect for him, and sent him away empty-handed. [12]So the man sent a third servant. The farmers wounded him and threw him out. [13]The owner of the vineyard said, 'What will I do now? I will send my son whom I love. Maybe they will respect him.' [14]But when the farmers saw the son, they said to each other, 'This son will inherit the vineyard. If we kill him, it will be ours.' [15]So the farmers threw the son out of the vineyard and killed him.

"What will the owner of this vineyard do to them? [16]He will come and kill those farmers and will give the vineyard to other farmers."

When the people heard this story, they said, "Let this never happen!"

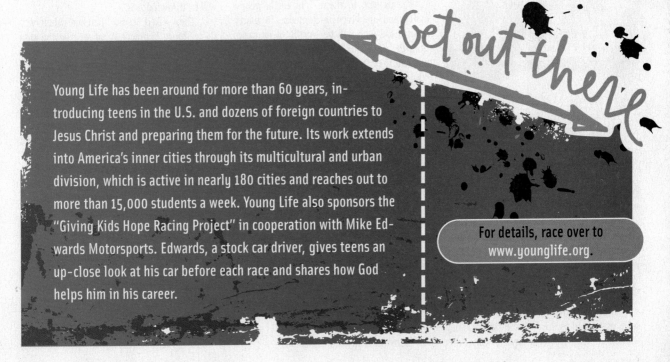

Get out there

Young Life has been around for more than 60 years, introducing teens in the U.S. and dozens of foreign countries to Jesus Christ and preparing them for the future. Its work extends into America's inner cities through its multicultural and urban division, which is active in nearly 180 cities and reaches out to more than 15,000 students a week. Young Life also sponsors the "Giving Kids Hope Racing Project" in cooperation with Mike Edwards Motorsports. Edwards, a stock car driver, gives teens an up-close look at his car before each race and shares how God helps him in his career.

For details, race over to www.younglife.org.

19:46 'My Temple . . . prayer.' Quotation from Isaiah 56:7.   19:46 'hideout for robbers' Quotation from Jeremiah 7:11.

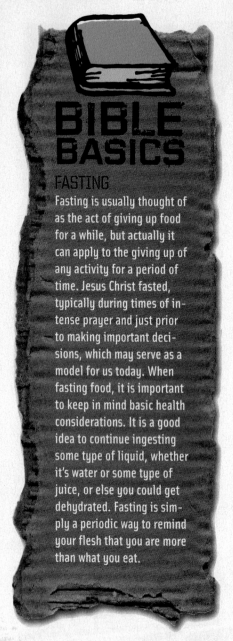

BIBLE BASICS

FASTING

Fasting is usually thought of as the act of giving up food for a while, but actually it can apply to the giving up of any activity for a period of time. Jesus Christ fasted, typically during times of intense prayer and just prior to making important decisions, which may serve as a model for us today. When fasting food, it is important to keep in mind basic health considerations. It is a good idea to continue ingesting some type of liquid, whether it's water or some type of juice, or else you could get dehydrated. Fasting is simply a periodic way to remind your flesh that you are more than what you eat.

[17]But Jesus looked at them and said, "Then what does this verse mean:

'The stone that the builders rejected
  became the cornerstone'? *Psalm 118:22*

[18]Everyone who falls on that stone will be broken, and the person on whom it falls, that person will be crushed!"

[19]The teachers of the law and the leading priests wanted to arrest Jesus at once, because they knew the story was about them. But they were afraid of what the people would do.

IS IT RIGHT TO PAY TAXES OR NOT?

[20]So they watched Jesus and sent some spies who acted as if they were sincere. They wanted to trap Jesus in saying something wrong so they could hand him over to the authority and power of the governor. [21]So the spies asked Jesus, "Teacher, we know that what you say and teach is true. You pay no attention to who people are, and you always teach the truth about God's way. [22]Tell us, is it right for us to pay taxes to Caesar or not?"

[23]But Jesus, knowing they were trying to trick him, said, [24]"Show me a coin. Whose image and name are on it?"

They said, "Caesar's."

[25]Jesus said to them, "Then give to Caesar the things that are Caesar's, and give to God the things that are God's."

[26]So they were not able to trap Jesus in anything he said in the presence of the people. And being amazed at his answer, they became silent.

SOME SADDUCEES TRY TO TRICK JESUS

[27]Some Sadducees, who believed people would not rise from the dead, came to Jesus. [28]They asked, "Teacher, Moses wrote that if a man's brother dies and leaves a wife but no children, then that man must marry the widow and have children for his brother. [29]Once there were seven brothers. The first brother married and died, but had no children. [30]Then the second brother married the widow, and he died. [31]And the third brother married the widow, and he died. The same thing happened with all seven brothers; they died and had no children. [32]Finally, the woman died also. [33]Since all seven brothers had married her, whose wife will she be when people rise from the dead?"

[34]Jesus said to them, "On earth, people marry and are given to someone to marry. [35]But those who will be worthy to be raised from the dead and live again will not marry, nor will they be given to someone to marry. [36]In that life they are like angels and cannot die. They are children of God, because they have been raised from the dead. [37]Even Moses clearly showed that the dead are raised to life. When he wrote about the burning bush,[n] he said that the Lord is 'the God of Abraham, the God of Isaac, and the God of Jacob.'[n] [38]God is the God of the living, not the dead, because all people are alive to him."

[39]Some of the teachers of the law said, "Teacher, your answer was good." [40]No one was brave enough to ask him another question.

IS THE CHRIST THE SON OF DAVID?

[41]Then Jesus said, "Why do people say that the Christ is the Son of David? [42]In the book of Psalms, David himself says:

'The Lord said to my Lord,
 "Sit by me at my right side,
[43] until I put your enemies under your
    control." '[n]   *Psalm 110:1*

[44]David calls the Christ 'Lord,' so how can the Christ be his son?"

JESUS ACCUSES SOME LEADERS

[45]While all the people were listening, Jesus said to his followers, [46]"Beware of the teachers of the law. They like to walk around wearing fancy clothes, and they love for people to greet them with respect in the marketplaces. They love to have the most important seats in the synagogues and at feasts. [47]But they cheat widows and steal their houses and then try to make themselves look good by saying long prayers. They will receive a greater punishment."

TRUE GIVING

21 As Jesus looked up, he saw some rich people putting their gifts into the Temple money box.[n] [2]Then he saw a poor widow putting two small copper coins into the box. [3]He said, "I tell you the truth, this poor widow gave more than all those rich people. [4]They gave only what they did not need. This woman is very poor, but she gave all she had to live on."

THE TEMPLE WILL BE DESTROYED

[5]Some people were talking about the Temple and how it was decorated with beautiful stones and gifts offered to God.

But Jesus said, [6]"As for these things you are looking at, the time will come when not one stone will be left on another. Every stone will be thrown down."

[7]They asked Jesus, "Teacher, when will these things happen? What will be the sign that they are about to take place?"

[8]Jesus said, "Be careful so you are not fooled. Many people will come in my name, saying, 'I am the One' and, 'The time has come!' But don't follow them. [9]When you hear about wars and riots, don't be afraid, because these things must happen first, but the end will come later."

[10]Then he said to them, "Nations will fight against other nations, and kingdoms against other kingdoms. [11]In various places there will be great earthquakes, sicknesses, and a lack of food. Fearful events and great signs will come from heaven.

[12]"But before all these things happen, people will arrest you and treat you cruelly. They will judge you in their synagogues and put you in jail and force you to stand before kings and governors, because you follow me. [13]But this will give you an opportunity to tell about me. [14]Make up your minds not to worry ahead of

 20:37 burning bush Read Exodus 3:1–12 in the Old Testament.   **20:37 'the God of . . . Jacob'** These words are taken from Exodus 3:6.   **20:43 until . . . control** Literally, "until I make your enemies a footstool for your feet."   **21:1 money box** A special box in the Jewish place of worship where people put their gifts to God.

time about what you will say. [15]I will give you the wisdom to say things that none of your enemies will be able to stand against or prove wrong. [16]Even your parents, brothers, relatives, and friends will turn against you, and they will kill some of you. [17]All people will hate you because you follow me. [18]But none of these things can really harm you. [19]By continuing to have faith you will save your lives.

JERUSALEM WILL BE DESTROYED

[20]"When you see armies all around Jerusalem, you will know it will soon be destroyed. [21]At that time, the people in Judea should run away to the mountains. The people in Jerusalem must get out, and those who are near the city should not go in. [22]These are the days of punishment to bring about all that is written in the Scriptures. [23]How terrible it will be for women who are pregnant or have nursing babies! Great trouble will come upon this land, and God will be angry with these people. [24]They will be killed by the sword and taken as prisoners to all nations. Jerusalem will be crushed by non-Jewish people until their time is over.

DON'T FEAR

[25]"There will be signs in the sun, moon, and stars. On earth, nations will be afraid and confused because of the roar and fury of the sea. [26]People will be so afraid they will faint, wondering what is happening to the world, because the powers of the heavens will be shaken. [27]Then people will see the Son of Man coming in a cloud with power and great glory. [28]When these things begin to happen, look up and hold your heads high, because the time when God will free you is near!"

JESUS' WORDS WILL LIVE FOREVER

[29]Then Jesus told this story: "Look at the fig tree and all the other trees. [30]When their leaves appear, you know that summer is near. [31]In the same way, when you see these things happening, you will know that God's kingdom is near.

[32]"I tell you the truth, all these things will happen while the people of this time are still living. [33]Earth and sky will be destroyed, but the words I have spoken will never be destroyed.

BE READY ALL THE TIME

[34]"Be careful not to spend your time feasting, drinking, or worrying about worldly things. If you do, that day might come on you suddenly, [35]like a trap on all people on earth. [36]So be ready all the time. Pray that you will be strong enough to escape all these things that will happen and that you will be able to stand before the Son of Man."

[37]During the day, Jesus taught the people in the Temple, and at night he went out of the city and stayed on the Mount of Olives. [38]Every morning all the people got up early to go to the Temple to listen to him.

JUDAS BECOMES AN ENEMY OF JESUS

22 It was almost time for the Feast of Unleavened Bread, called the Passover Feast. [2]The leading priests and teachers of the law were trying to find a way to kill Jesus, because they were afraid of the people.

[3]Satan entered Judas Iscariot, one of Jesus' twelve apostles. [4]Judas went to the leading priests and some of the soldiers who guarded the Temple and talked to them about a way to hand Jesus over to them. [5]They were pleased and agreed to give Judas money. [6]He agreed and watched for the best time to hand Jesus over to them when he was away from the crowd.

JESUS EATS THE PASSOVER MEAL

[7]The Day of Unleavened Bread came when the Passover lambs had to be sacrificed. [8]Jesus said to Peter and John, "Go and prepare the Passover meal for us to eat."

[9]They asked, "Where do you want us to prepare it?" [10]Jesus said to them, "After you go into the city, a man carrying a jar of water will meet you. Follow him into the house that he

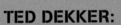

BOOKS

TED DEKKER:
THE SLUMBER OF CHRISTIANITY

Ted Dekker is best known for his exciting and suspenseful fiction titles such as *Black* and *Obsessed*. But this time around, he engages his audience with a theory he has about modern Christianity: Christians think too much about the things of this world. Using compelling language and scriptural truth, Dekker encourages readers to set their minds on heaven, eternity, and the hope to come. This book might not interest every teenager, but mature teens who are looking to go a little deeper in their faith will no doubt find *The Slumber of Christianity* to be a wake-up call worth reading.

WHY IT ROCKS:

READING IT GIVES YOU AN ETERNAL PERSPECTIVE.

experts answer YOUR questions

Q: What does the Holy Spirit do?

A: Jesus knew that his followers would need a way to hear his voice and understand what he wanted after he returned to heaven. That's why he sent the Holy Spirit—to help us to know the truth. Although Jesus isn't physically on the earth to teach us, he is present through his Spirit, who helps us understand what God is saying.

Q: What does Jesus want for the church?

A: Just before Jesus died, he prayed for the church. His prayer was that we would be one. Today, division is often a problem in the church, from differences among denominations to splits within congregations. As Christians, we should make it our priority to fulfill Jesus' prayer by building unity among all believers.

enters, [11]and tell the owner of the house, 'The Teacher says: "Where is the guest room in which I may eat the Passover meal with my followers?" ' [12]Then he will show you a large, furnished room upstairs. Prepare the Passover meal there."

[13]So Peter and John left and found everything as Jesus had said. And they prepared the Passover meal.

THE LORD'S SUPPER

[14]When the time came, Jesus and the apostles were sitting at the table. [15]He said to them, "I wanted very much to eat this Passover meal with you before I suffer. [16]I will not eat another Passover meal until it is given its true meaning in the kingdom of God."

[17]Then Jesus took a cup, gave thanks, and said, "Take this cup and share it among yourselves. [18]I will not drink again from the fruit of the vine[n] until God's kingdom comes."

[19]Then Jesus took some bread, gave thanks, broke it, and gave it to the apostles, saying, "This is my body,[n] which I am giving for you. Do this to remember me." [20]In the same way, after supper, Jesus took the cup and said, "This cup is the new agreement that God makes with his people. This new agreement begins with my blood which is poured out for you.

WHO WILL TURN AGAINST JESUS?

[21]"But one of you will turn against me, and his hand is with mine on the table. [22]What God has planned for the Son of Man will happen, but how terrible it will be for that one who turns against the Son of Man."

[23]Then the apostles asked each other which one of them would do that.

BE LIKE A SERVANT

[24]The apostles also began to argue about which one of them was the most important. [25]But Jesus said to them, "The kings of the non-Jewish people rule over them, and those who have authority over others like to be called 'friends of the people.' [26]But you must not be like that. Instead, the greatest among you should be like the youngest, and the leader should be like the servant. [27]Who is more important: the one sitting at the table or the one serving? You think the one at the table is more important, but I am like a servant among you. [28]"You have stayed with me through my struggles. [29]Just as my Father has given me a kingdom, I also give you a kingdom [30]so you may eat and drink at my table in my kingdom. And you will sit on thrones, judging the twelve tribes of Israel.

DON'T LOSE YOUR FAITH!

[31]"Simon, Simon, Satan has asked to test all of you as a farmer sifts his wheat. [32]I have prayed that you will not lose your faith! Help your brothers be stronger when you come back to me."

[33]But Peter said to Jesus, "Lord, I am ready to go with you to prison and even to die with you!"

[34]But Jesus said, "Peter, before the rooster crows this day, you will say three times that you don't know me."

BE READY FOR TROUBLE

[35]Then Jesus said to the apostles, "When I sent you out without a purse, a bag, or sandals, did you need anything?"

They said, "No."

[36]He said to them, "But now if you have a purse or a bag, carry that with you. If you don't have a sword, sell your coat and buy one. [37]The Scripture says, 'He was treated like a criminal,'[n] and I tell you this scripture must have its full meaning. It was written about me, and it is happening now."

[38]His followers said, "Look, Lord, here are two swords."

He said to them, "That is enough."

JESUS PRAYS ALONE

[39]Jesus left the city and went to the Mount of Olives, as he often did, and his followers went with him. [40]When he reached the place, he said to them, "Pray for strength against temptation."

[41]Then Jesus went about a stone's throw away from them. He kneeled down and prayed, [42]"Father, if you are willing, take away this cup[n] of suffering. But do what you want, not what I want." [43]Then an angel from heaven appeared to him to strengthen him. [44]Being full of pain, Jesus prayed even harder. His sweat was like drops of blood falling to the ground. [45]When he finished praying, he went to his followers and found them asleep because of their sadness. [46]Jesus said to them, "Why are you sleeping? Get up and pray for strength against temptation."

JESUS IS ARRESTED

[47]While Jesus was speaking, a crowd came up, and Judas, one of the twelve apostles, was leading them. He came close to Jesus so he could kiss him.

[48]But Jesus said to him, "Judas, are you using the kiss to give the Son of Man to his enemies?"

[49]When those who were standing around

 22:18 fruit of the vine Product of the grapevine; this may also be translated "wine." **22:19b–20** body Some Greek copies do not have the rest of verse 19 or verse 20. **22:37** 'He . . . criminal.' Quotation from Isaiah 53:12. **22:42** cup Jesus is talking about the painful things that will happen to him. Accepting these things will be hard, like drinking a cup of something bitter.

him saw what was happening, they said, "Lord, should we strike them with our swords?" ⁵⁰And one of them struck the servant of the high priest and cut off his right ear.

⁵¹Jesus said, "Stop! No more of this." Then he touched the servant's ear and healed him.

⁵²Those who came to arrest Jesus were the leading priests, the soldiers who guarded the Temple, and the elders. Jesus said to them, "You came out here with swords and clubs as though I were a criminal. ⁵³I was with you every day in the Temple, and you didn't arrest me there. But this is your time—the time when darkness rules."

PETER SAYS HE DOESN'T KNOW JESUS

⁵⁴They arrested Jesus, and led him away, and brought him into the house of the high priest. Peter followed far behind them. ⁵⁵After the soldiers started a fire in the middle of the courtyard and sat together, Peter sat with them. ⁵⁶A servant girl saw Peter sitting there in the firelight, and looking closely at him, she said, "This man was also with him."

⁵⁷But Peter said this was not true; he said, "Woman, I don't know him."

⁵⁸A short time later, another person saw Peter and said, "You are also one of them."

But Peter said, "Man, I am not!"

⁵⁹About an hour later, another man insisted, "Certainly this man was with him, because he is from Galilee, too."

⁶⁰But Peter said, "Man, I don't know what you are talking about!"

At once, while Peter was still speaking, a rooster crowed. ⁶¹Then the Lord turned and looked straight at Peter. And Peter remembered what the Lord had said: "Before the rooster crows this day, you will say three times that

you don't know me." ⁶²Then Peter went outside and cried painfully.

THE PEOPLE MAKE FUN OF JESUS

⁶³The men who were guarding Jesus began making fun of him and beating him.

⁶⁴They blindfolded him and said, "Prove that you are a prophet, and tell us who hit you." ⁶⁵They said many cruel things to Jesus.

JESUS BEFORE THE LEADERS

⁶⁶When day came, the council of the elders of the people, both the leading priests and the teachers of the law, came together and led Jesus to their highest court. ⁶⁷They said, "If you are the Christ, tell us."

Jesus said to them, "If I tell you, you will not believe me. ⁶⁸And if I ask you, you will not answer. ⁶⁹But from now on, the Son of Man will sit at the right hand of the powerful God."

⁷⁰They all said, "Then are you the Son of God?"

Jesus said to them, "You say that I am."

⁷¹They said, "Why do we need witnesses now? We ourselves heard him say this."

PILATE QUESTIONS JESUS

23 Then the whole group stood up and led Jesus to Pilate.ⁿ ²They began to accuse Jesus, saying, "We caught this man telling things that mislead our people. He says that we should not pay taxes to Caesar, and he calls himself the Christ, a king."

³Pilate asked Jesus, "Are you the king of the Jews?"

Jesus answered, "Those are your words."

⁴Pilate said to the leading priests and the people, "I find nothing against this man."

⁵They were insisting, saying, "But Jesus makes trouble with the people, teaching all around Judea. He began in Galilee, and now he is here."

PILATE SENDS JESUS TO HEROD

⁶Pilate heard this and asked if Jesus was from Galilee. ⁷Since Jesus was under Herod's authority, Pilate sent Jesus to Herod, who was in Jerusalem at that time. ⁸When Herod saw Jesus, he was very glad, because he had heard about Jesus and had wanted to meet him for a long time. He was hoping to see Jesus work a miracle. ⁹Herod asked Jesus many questions, but Jesus said nothing. ¹⁰The leading priests and teachers of the law were standing there, strongly accusing Jesus. ¹¹After Herod and his soldiers had made fun of Jesus, they dressed him in a kingly robe and sent him back to Pilate. ¹²In the past, Pilate and Herod had always been enemies, but on that day they became friends.

JESUS MUST DIE

¹³Pilate called the people together with the leading priests and the rulers. ¹⁴He said to them, "You brought this man to me, saying he makes trouble among the people. But I have questioned him before you all, and I have not found him guilty of what you say. ¹⁵Also, Herod found nothing wrong with him; he sent him back to us. Look, he has done nothing for which he should die. ¹⁶So, after I punish him, I will let him go free." [¹⁷Every year at the Passover Feast, Pilate had to release one prisoner to the people.]ⁿ

¹⁸But the people shouted together, "Take this man away! Let Barabbas go free!" ¹⁹(Barabbas was a man who was in prison for his part in a riot in the city and for murder.)

²⁰Pilate wanted to let Jesus go free and told this to the crowd. ²¹But they shouted again, "Crucify him! Crucify him!"

²²A third time Pilate said to them, "Why? What wrong has he done? I can find no reason to kill him. So I will have him punished and set him free."

²³But they continued to shout, demanding that Jesus be crucified. Their yelling became so loud that ²⁴Pilate decided to give them what they wanted. ²⁵He set free the man who was in jail for rioting and murder, and he handed Jesus over to them to do with him as they wished.

23:1 Pilate Pontius Pilate was the Roman governor of Judea from A.D. 26 to A.D. 36.   23:17 Every . . . people. Some Greek copies do not contain the bracketed text.

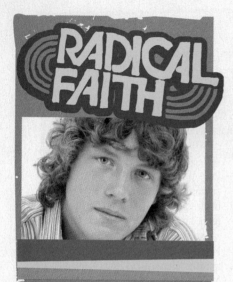

RADICAL FAITH

LUKE 24:6-7

The resurrection of Jesus is either the world's biggest fraud or the most astonishing truth you can ever wrap your noodle around. And you can be tough-minded about the facts surrounding the Lord's real-life rising from the dead. For starters, no one can claim that Jesus wasn't actually dead. He died by crucifixion, an exceedingly cruel and extreme form of execution. As if that wasn't enough to certify his deadness, a soldier drove a spear into his side (John 19:34). It's also farfetched to assert that his followers stole his body from the tomb. Those terrified men were in no shape to slip past the contingent of brutal, heavily armed Roman soldiers guarding the place, then silently heave away the enormous stone that locked the Lord's body in the grave. The most straightforward explanation of the empty tomb is that Jesus rose from the dead by the power of God. Trusting this as truth is the core of what it means to be a Christian, because Jesus' resurrection makes believers right with God (Romans 4:25). Since Jesus rose from the dead, you, too, can live a new life, now and forever.

JESUS IS CRUCIFIED

[26]As they led Jesus away, Simon, a man from Cyrene, was coming in from the fields. They forced him to carry Jesus' cross and to walk behind him.

[27]A large crowd of people was following Jesus, including some women who were sad and crying for him. [28]But Jesus turned and said to them, "Women of Jerusalem, don't cry for me. Cry for yourselves and for your children. [29]The time is coming when people will say, 'Blessed are the women who cannot have children and who have no babies to nurse.' [30]Then people will say to the mountains, 'Fall on us!' And they will say to the hills, 'Cover us!' [31]If they act like this now when life is good, what will happen when bad times come?"[n]

[32]There were also two criminals led out with Jesus to be put to death. [33]When they came to a place called the Skull, the soldiers crucified Jesus and the criminals—one on his right and the other on his left. [34]Jesus said, "Father, forgive them, because they don't know what they are doing."[n]

The soldiers threw lots to decide who would get his clothes. [35]The people stood there watching. And the leaders made fun of Jesus, saying, "He saved others. Let him save himself if he is God's Chosen One, the Christ."

[36]The soldiers also made fun of him, coming to Jesus and offering him some vinegar. [37]They said, "If you are the king of the Jews, save yourself!" [38]At the top of the cross these words were written: THIS IS THE KING OF THE JEWS.

[39]One of the criminals on a cross began to shout insults at Jesus: "Aren't you the Christ? Then save yourself and us."

[40]But the other criminal stopped him and said, "You should fear God! You are getting the same punishment he is. [41]We are punished justly, getting what we deserve for what we did. But this man has done nothing wrong." [42]Then he said, "Jesus, remember me when you come into your kingdom."

[43]Jesus said to him, "I tell you the truth, today you will be with me in paradise."[n]

JESUS DIES

[44]It was about noon, and the whole land became dark until three o'clock in the afternoon, [45]because the sun did not shine. The curtain in the Temple[n] was torn in two. [46]Jesus cried out in a loud voice, "Father, I give you my life." After Jesus said this, he died.

[47]When the army officer there saw what happened, he praised God, saying, "Surely this was a good man!"

[48]When all the people who had gathered there to watch saw what happened, they returned home, beating their chests because they were so sad. [49]But those who were close friends of Jesus, including the women who had followed him from Galilee, stood at a distance and watched.

JOSEPH TAKES JESUS' BODY

[50]There was a good and religious man named Joseph who was a member of the council. [51]But he had not agreed to the other leaders' plans and actions against Jesus. He was from the town of Arimathea and was waiting for the kingdom of God to come. [52]Joseph went to Pilate to ask for the body of Jesus. [53]He took the body down from the cross, wrapped it in cloth, and put it in a tomb that was cut out of a wall of rock. This tomb had never been used before. [54]This was late on Preparation Day, and when the sun went down, the Sabbath day would begin.

[55]The women who had come from Galilee with Jesus followed Joseph and saw the tomb and how Jesus' body was laid. [56]Then the women left to prepare spices and perfumes.

On the Sabbath day they rested, as the law of Moses commanded.

JESUS RISES FROM THE DEAD

24 Very early on the first day of the week, at dawn, the women came to the tomb, bringing the spices they had prepared. [2]They found the stone rolled away from the entrance of the tomb, [3]but when they went in, they did not find the body of the Lord Jesus. [4]While they were wondering about this, two men in shining clothes suddenly stood beside them. [5]The women were very afraid and bowed their heads to the ground. The men said to them, "Why are you looking for a living person in this place for the dead? [6]He is not here; he has risen from the dead. Do you remember what he told you in Galilee? [7]He said the Son of Man must be handed over to sinful people, be crucified, and rise from the dead on the third day." [8]Then the women remembered what Jesus had said.

[9]The women left the tomb and told all these things to the eleven apostles and the other followers. [10]It was Mary Magdalene, Joanna, Mary the mother of James, and some other women who told the apostles everything that had happened at the tomb. [11]But they did not believe the women, because it sounded like nonsense. [12]But Peter got up and ran to the tomb. Bending down and looking in, he saw only the cloth that Jesus' body had been wrapped in. Peter went away to his home, wondering about what had happened.

 23:31 If . . . come? Literally, "If they do these things in the green tree, what will happen in the dry?" **23:34** Jesus . . . doing." Some Greek copies do not have this first part of verse 34. **23:43** paradise Another word for heaven. **23:45** curtain in the Temple A curtain divided the Most Holy Place from the other part of the Temple, the special building in Jerusalem where God commanded the Jewish people to worship him.

JESUS ON THE ROAD TO EMMAUS

¹³That same day two of Jesus' followers were going to a town named Emmaus, about seven miles from Jerusalem. ¹⁴They were talking about everything that had happened. ¹⁵While they were talking and discussing, Jesus himself came near and began walking with them, ¹⁶but they were kept from recognizing him. ¹⁷Then he said, "What are these things you are talking about while you walk?"

The two followers stopped, looking very sad. ¹⁸The one named Cleopas answered, "Are you the only visitor in Jerusalem who does not know what just happened there?"

¹⁹Jesus said to them, "What are you talking about?"

They said, "About Jesus of Nazareth. He was a prophet who said and did many powerful things before God and all the people. ²⁰Our leaders and the leading priests handed him over to be sentenced to death, and they crucified him. ²¹But we were hoping that he would free Israel. Besides this, it is now the third day since this happened. ²²And today some women among us amazed us. Early this morning they went to the tomb, ²³but they did not find his body there. They came and told us that they had seen a vision of angels who said that Jesus was alive! ²⁴So some of our group went to the tomb, too. They found it just as the women said, but they did not see Jesus."

²⁵Then Jesus said to them, "You are foolish and slow to believe everything the prophets said. ²⁶They said that the Christ must suffer these things before he enters his glory." ²⁷Then starting with what Moses and all the prophets had said about him, Jesus began to explain everything that had been written about himself in the Scriptures.

²⁸They came near the town of Emmaus, and Jesus acted as if he were going farther.

²⁹But they begged him, "Stay with us, because it is late; it is almost night." So he went in to stay with them.

³⁰When Jesus was at the table with them, he took some bread, gave thanks, divided it, and gave it to them. ³¹And then, they were allowed to recognize Jesus. But when they saw who he was, he disappeared. ³²They said to each other, "It felt like a fire burning in us when Jesus talked to us on the road and explained the Scriptures to us."

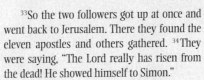

³³So the two followers got up at once and went back to Jerusalem. There they found the eleven apostles and others gathered. ³⁴They were saying, "The Lord really has risen from the dead! He showed himself to Simon."

³⁵Then the two followers told what had happened on the road and how they recognized Jesus when he divided the bread.

JESUS APPEARS TO HIS FOLLOWERS

³⁶While the two followers were telling this, Jesus himself stood right in the middle of them and said, "Peace be with you."

³⁷They were fearful and terrified and thought they were seeing a ghost. ³⁸But Jesus said, "Why are you troubled? Why do you doubt what you see? ³⁹Look at my hands and my feet. It is I myself! Touch me and see, because a ghost does not have a living body as you see I have."

⁴⁰After Jesus said this, he showed them his hands and feet. ⁴¹While they still could not believe it because they were amazed and happy, Jesus said to them, "Do you have any food here?" ⁴²They gave him a piece of broiled fish. ⁴³While the followers watched, Jesus took the fish and ate it.

⁴⁴He said to them, "Remember when I was with you before? I said that everything written about me must happen—everything in the law of Moses, the books of the prophets, and the Psalms."

⁴⁵Then Jesus opened their minds so they could understand the Scriptures. ⁴⁶He said to them, "It is written that the Christ would suffer and rise from the dead on the third day ⁴⁷and that a change of hearts and lives and forgiveness of sins would be preached in his name to all nations, starting at Jerusalem. ⁴⁸You are witnesses of these things. ⁴⁹I will send you what my Father has promised, but you must stay in Jerusalem until you have received that power from heaven."

JESUS GOES BACK TO HEAVEN

⁵⁰Jesus led his followers as far as Bethany, and he raised his hands and blessed them. ⁵¹While he was blessing them, he was separated from them and carried into heaven. ⁵²They worshiped him and returned to Jerusalem very happy. ⁵³They stayed in the Temple all the time, praising God.

JOHN

THE LOVE OF CHRIST

Searching for happiness, fulfillment, and a better way to live? John promises that Jesus is the answer. As proof, the last of the four gospel accounts opens with several bold declarations. Jesus is called the Light of the world. He is named the Word, who is full of truth and shows humanity what God is like. He is referred to as the Lamb of God, the one who removes the sin of the world. Later, Jesus also is revealed as the miracle worker who changed water into wine at a wedding feast.

In a key encounter, Jesus confronts a religious leader of the day, Nicodemus, who wants to know how to be saved. During their talk, Jesus tells him the only way to enter heaven is by being born again. He explains to him that this is a spiritual act and happens by believing in Christ for salvation from sin.

More than anything, we see the Lord as a man of love in the Book of John. Whether through simple acts such as talking with a woman at a well or through mighty miracles such as raising his good friend Lazarus from the dead, Jesus proves he loves people. Finally, he promises that those who believe in him will do even greater works than he did.

CHRIST COMES TO THE WORLD

1 In the beginning there was the Word.[n] The Word was with God, and the Word was God. [2]He was with God in the beginning. [3]All things were made by him, and nothing was made without him. [4]In him there was life, and that life was the light of all people. [5]The Light shines in the darkness, and the darkness has not overpowered[n] it.

[6]There was a man named John[n] who was sent by God. [7]He came to tell people the truth about the Light so that through him all people could hear about the Light and believe. [8]John was not the Light, but he came to tell people the truth about the Light. [9]The true Light that gives light to all was coming into the world!

[10]The Word was in the world, and the world was made by him, but the world did not know him. [11]He came to the world that was his own, but his own people did not accept him. [12]But to all who did accept him and believe in him he gave the right to become children of God. [13]They did not become his children in any human way—by any human parents or human desire. They were born of God.

[14]The Word became a human and lived among us. We saw his glory—the glory that belongs to the only Son of the Father—and he was full of grace and truth. [15]John tells the truth about him and cries out, saying, "This is the One I told you about: 'The One who comes after me is greater than I am, because he was living before me.'"

[16]Because he was full of grace and truth, from him we all received one gift after another. [17]The law was given through Moses, but grace and truth came through Jesus Christ. [18]No one has ever seen God. But God the only Son is very close to the Father,[n] and he has shown us what God is like.

JOHN TELLS PEOPLE ABOUT JESUS

[19]Here is the truth John[n] told when the leaders in Jerusalem sent priests and Levites to ask him, "Who are you?"

[20]John spoke freely and did not refuse to answer. He said, "I am not the Christ."

[21]So they asked him, "Then who are you? Are you Elijah?"[n]

He answered, "No, I am not."

"Are you the Prophet?"[n] they asked.

He answered, "No."

[22]Then they said, "Who are you? Give us an answer to tell those who sent us. What do you say about yourself?"

[23]John told them in the words of the prophet Isaiah:

"I am the voice of one
    calling out in the desert:
'Make the road straight for the Lord.'"

Isaiah 40:3

[24]Some Pharisees who had been sent asked John: [25]"If you are not the Christ or Elijah or the Prophet, why do you baptize people?"

[26]John answered, "I baptize with water, but there is one here with you that you don't know about. [27]He is the One who comes after me. I am not good enough to untie the strings of his sandals."

[28]This all happened at Bethany on the other side of the Jordan River, where John was baptizing people.

[29]The next day John saw Jesus coming toward him. John said, "Look, the Lamb of God,[n] who takes away the sin of the world! [30]This is the One I was talking about when I said, 'A man will come after me, but he is greater than I am, because he was living before me.' [31]Even I did not know who he was, although I came baptizing with water so that the people of Israel would know who he is."

[32-33]Then John said, "I saw the Spirit come down from heaven in the form of a dove and rest on him. Until then I did not know who the Christ was. But the God who sent me to baptize with water told me, 'You will see the Spirit come down and rest on a man; he is the One who will baptize with the Holy Spirit.' [34]I have seen this happen, and I tell you the truth: This man is the Son of God."[n]

THE FIRST FOLLOWERS OF JESUS

[35]The next day John[n] was there again with two of his followers. [36]When he saw Jesus walking by, he said, "Look, the Lamb of God!"[n]

[37]The two followers heard John say this, so they followed Jesus. [38]When Jesus turned and

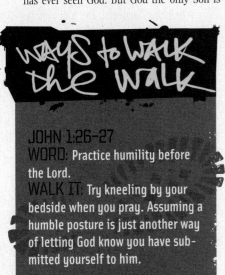

ways to WALK the WALK

JOHN 1:26-27
WORD: Practice humility before the Lord.
WALK IT: Try kneeling by your bedside when you pray. Assuming a humble posture is just another way of letting God know you have submitted yourself to him.

RADICAL FAITH

JOHN 1:1
When you read a few verses past John 1:1, you figure out that the person whom the apostle John is writing about is his good friend Jesus. But at the start of his book John calls Jesus by a different nickname, "the Word." In a few tight phrases, the apostle John sums up key points you need to know about Jesus. John launches in at "the beginning," the moment of creation, and says, "Jesus already existed." He notes that Jesus was "with God," that Jesus and God the Father are distinct. Yet, Jesus also "was God," identical with him. Along with the Father, Jesus cocreated the universe. John goes on to relate more mind-bending facts: Jesus is the true Light for the world (John 1:9); Jesus became God-in-a-body, being born as a man on the planet he created (John 1:10); yet, some people rejected him (John 1:11). Those who believe in him, however, become God's children. John sums it all up by saying that Jesus is full of "glory," God's own bright and shining power. When you follow Jesus, you're chasing infinitely more than a mere man. You're hanging tight with God himself.

 1:1 **Word** The Greek word is "logos," meaning any kind of communication; it could be translated "message." Here, it means Christ, because Christ was the way God told people about himself. 1:5 **overpowered** This can also be translated, "understood." 1:6, 19, 35 **John** John the Baptist, who preached to people about Christ's coming (Matthew 3, Luke 3). 1:18 **But ... Father** This could be translated, "But the only God is very close to the Father." Also, some Greek copies read "But the only Son is very close to the Father." 1:21 **Elijah** A prophet who spoke for God. He lived hundreds of years before Christ and was expected to return before Christ (Malachi 4:5-6). 1:21 **Prophet** They probably meant the prophet that God told Moses he would send (Deuteronomy 18:15-19). 1:29, 36 **Lamb of God** Name for Jesus. Jesus is like the lambs that were offered for a sacrifice to God. 1:34 **the Son of God** Some Greek copies read "God's Chosen One."

JOHN 1:12

The Bible's promises don't get any bigger than this. At the start of this Bible book, the apostle John launches into an account of the life, death, and resurrection of Jesus by summing up the truth about Jesus. He wants you to make no mistake: Jesus is totally God (John 1:1). Not everyone, however, admits that. The whole world belongs to Jesus, yet despite the fact that he revealed himself to the world as a human being, many rejected him. But here's the astonishing promise: Everyone who believes in Jesus becomes God's child. That doesn't mean holding a fuzzy belief that Jesus was just a good guy and a religious teacher, but trusting that he is the Son of God and Savior of the world (John 20:31). If you truly believe in Jesus, then you will be adopted as God's own son.

saw them following him, he asked, "What are you looking for?"

They said, "Rabbi, where are you staying?" ("Rabbi" means "Teacher.")

[39]He answered, "Come and see." So the two men went with Jesus and saw where he was staying and stayed there with him that day. It was about four o'clock in the afternoon.

[40]One of the two men who followed Jesus after they heard John speak about him was Andrew, Simon Peter's brother. [41]The first thing Andrew did was to find his brother Simon and say to him, "We have found the Messiah." ("Messiah" means "Christ.")

[42]Then Andrew took Simon to Jesus. Jesus looked at him and said, "You are Simon son of John. You will be called Cephas." ("Cephas" means "Peter."[n])

[43]The next day Jesus decided to go to Galilee. He found Philip and said to him, "Follow me."

[44]Philip was from the town of Bethsaida, where Andrew and Peter lived. [45]Philip found Nathanael and told him, "We have found the man that Moses wrote about in the law, and the prophets also wrote about him. He is Jesus, the son of Joseph, from Nazareth."

[46]But Nathanael said to Philip, "Can anything good come from Nazareth?"

Philip answered, "Come and see."

[47]As Jesus saw Nathanael coming toward him, he said, "Here is truly an Israelite. There is nothing false in him."

[48]Nathanael asked, "How do you know me?"

Jesus answered, "I saw you when you were under the fig tree, before Philip told you about me."

[49]Then Nathanael said to Jesus, "Teacher, you are the Son of God; you are the King of Israel."

[50]Jesus said to Nathanael, "Do you believe simply because I told you I saw you under the fig tree? You will see greater things than that." [51]And Jesus said to them, "I tell you the truth, you will all see heaven open and 'angels of God going up and coming down'[n] on the Son of Man."

THE WEDDING AT CANA

2 Two days later there was a wedding in the town of Cana in Galilee. Jesus' mother was there, [2]and Jesus and his followers were also invited to the wedding. [3]When all the wine was gone, Jesus' mother said to him, "They have no more wine."

[4]Jesus answered, "Dear woman, why come to me? My time has not yet come."

[5]His mother said to the servants, "Do whatever he tells you to do."

[6]In that place there were six stone water jars that the Jews used in their washing ceremony.[n] Each jar held about twenty or thirty gallons.

[7]Jesus said to the servants, "Fill the jars with water." So they filled the jars to the top.

[8]Then he said to them, "Now take some out and give it to the master of the feast."

So they took the water to the master. [9]When he tasted it, the water had become wine. He did not know where the wine came from, but the servants who had brought the water knew. The master of the wedding called the bridegroom [10]and said to him, "People always serve the best wine first. Later, after the guests have been drinking awhile, they serve the cheaper wine. But you have saved the best wine till now."

[11]So in Cana of Galilee Jesus did his first miracle. There he showed his glory, and his followers believed in him.

JESUS IN THE TEMPLE

[12]After this, Jesus went to the town of Capernaum with his mother, brothers, and followers. They stayed there for just a few days. [13]When it was almost time for the Jewish Passover Feast, Jesus went to Jerusalem. [14]In the Temple he found people selling cattle, sheep, and doves. He saw others sitting at tables, exchanging different kinds of money. [15]Jesus made a whip out of cords and forced all of them, both the sheep and cattle, to leave the Temple. He turned over the tables and scattered the money of those who were exchanging it. [16]Then he said to those who were selling pigeons, "Take these things out of here! Don't make my Father's house a place for buying and selling!"

[17]When this happened, the followers remembered what was written in the Scriptures: "My strong love for your Temple completely controls me."[n]

[18]Some of his people said to Jesus, "Show us a miracle to prove you have the right to do these things."

[19]Jesus answered them, "Destroy this temple, and I will build it again in three days."

[20]They answered, "It took forty-six years to build this Temple! Do you really believe you can build it again in three days?"

[21](But the temple Jesus meant was his own body. [22]After Jesus was raised from the dead, his followers remembered that Jesus had said this. Then they believed the Scripture and the words Jesus had said.)

[23]When Jesus was in Jerusalem for the Passover Feast, many people believed in him

 1:42 Peter The Greek name "Peter," like the Aramaic name "Cephas," means "rock." **1:51 'angels . . . down'** These words are from Genesis 28:12. **2:6 washing ceremony** The Jewish people washed themselves in special ways before eating, before worshiping in the Temple, and at other special times. **2:17 "My . . . me."** Quotation from Psalm 69:9.

april

NATIONAL HUMOR MONTH

"Meaning is more important than money in life. You can have plenty to live on and still have nothing to live for" -RICK WARREN

1 It's April Fool's Day, but don't be foolish.	**2** It's Golden Rule Week. Put it into practice.	**3**	**4** Heath Ledger turns another year older.
5	**6** Call your favorite aunt and tell her you love her.	**7** Tell your friends a clean joke.	**8**
9 Pray for the president today.	**10** Today is Mandy Moore's birthday.	**11**	**12** Take your youth pastor out for lunch.
13	**14**	**15** Learn how to do sign language.	**16**
17 It's National Ex-Girlfriend Day. Pray for yours.	**18** Hang out with an unpopular kid today.	**19** It's Maria Sharapova's birthday.	**20**
21 Volunteer to wash the family car.	**22** Give your parents a break by offering to baby-sit your siblings for free.	**23**	**24** Kelly Clarkson is celebrating her birthday today.
25	**26**	**27** Mop the kitchen floor for your mom.	**28**
29	**30** Go plant a tree.		

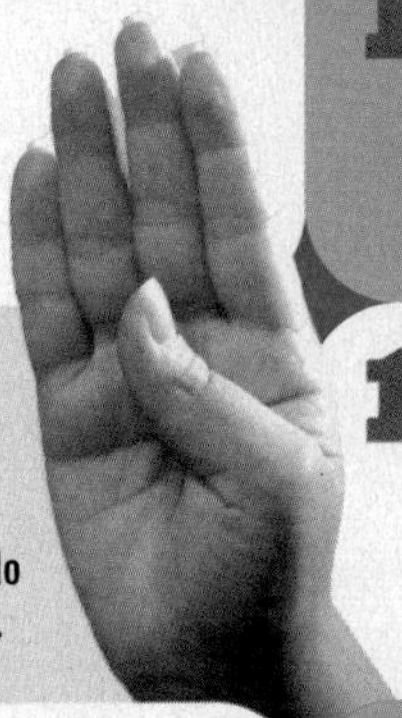

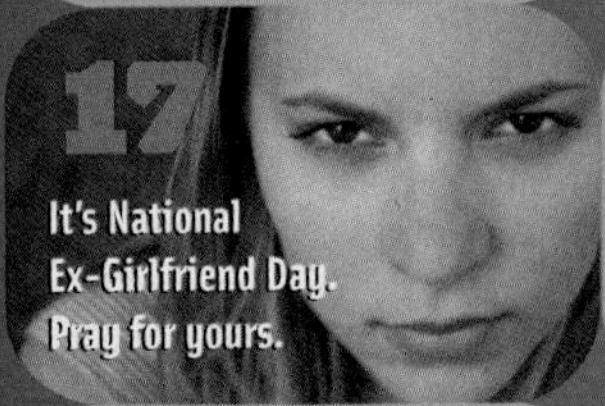

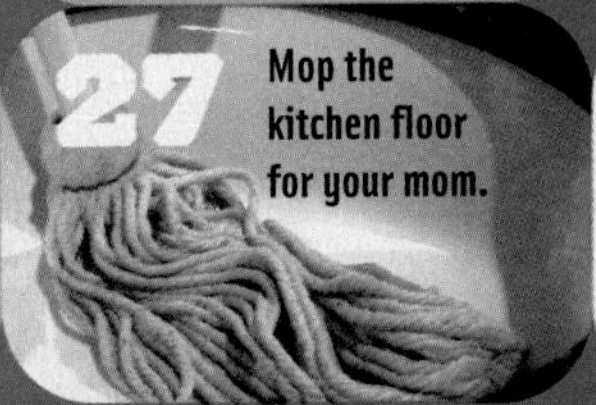

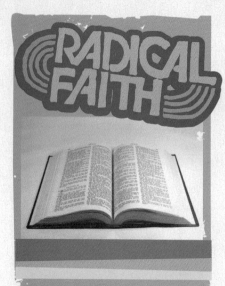

JOHN 3:16

If you had to choose one verse that packs together the whole message of the Bible, John 3:16 might be your top choice. It relates the colossal truth that God loves the world. It explains that love caused God to send his only Son to earth, so that no human being has to be lost. Wrapped inside that truth is the point that humanity has a problem. It's disconnected from God, dying because of its sin. Yet, because Jesus came to save us, everyone who believes can have eternal life in heaven with him. Whether that's news to you or a fact you have known your whole life, John 3:16 is information too good to keep to yourself. It's a capsule of spiritual wisdom than can spare the people around you from an eternity of being separated from God in hell. Even if you have never spoken up about Jesus, this is a power-packed fact you can pass on to people who don't know God. It's the truth that saves you. It's the truth that can save everyone who accepts it (Acts 4:12). Dare to believe it. Be bold and share it.

because they saw the miracles he did. ²⁴But Jesus did not believe in them because he knew them all. ²⁵He did not need anyone to tell him about people, because he knew what was in people's minds.

NICODEMUS COMES TO JESUS

3 There was a man named Nicodemus who was one of the Pharisees and an important Jewish leader. ²One night Nicodemus came to Jesus and said, "Teacher, we know you are a teacher sent from God, because no one can do the miracles you do unless God is with him."

³Jesus answered, "I tell you the truth, unless you are born again, you cannot be in God's kingdom."

⁴Nicodemus said, "But if a person is already old, how can he be born again? He cannot enter his mother's womb again. So how can a person be born a second time?"

⁵But Jesus answered, "I tell you the truth, unless you are born from water and the Spirit, you cannot enter God's kingdom. ⁶Human life comes from human parents, but spiritual life comes from the Spirit. ⁷Don't be surprised when I tell you, 'You must all be born again.' ⁸The wind blows where it wants to and you hear the sound of it, but you don't know where the wind comes from or where it is going. It is the same with every person who is born from the Spirit."

⁹Nicodemus asked, "How can this happen?"

¹⁰Jesus said, "You are an important teacher in Israel, and you don't understand these things? ¹¹I tell you the truth, we talk about what we know, and we tell about what we have seen, but you don't accept what we tell you. ¹²I have told you about things here on earth, and you do not believe me. So you will not believe me if I tell you about things of heaven. ¹³The only one who has ever gone up to heaven is the One who came down from heaven—the Son of Man.ⁿ

¹⁴"Just as Moses lifted up the snake in the desert,ⁿ the Son of Man must also be lifted up.

¹⁵So that everyone who believes can have eternal life in him.

¹⁶"God loved the world so much that he gave his one and only Son so that whoever believes in him may not be lost, but have eternal life. ¹⁷God did not send his Son into the world to judge the world guilty, but to save the world through him. ¹⁸People who believe in God's Son are not judged guilty. Those who do not believe have already been judged guilty, because they have not believed in God's one and only Son. ¹⁹They are judged by this fact: The Light has come into the world, but they did not want light. They wanted darkness, because they were doing evil things. ²⁰All who do evil hate the light and will not come to the light, because it will show all the evil things they do. ²¹But those who follow the true way come to the light, and it shows that the things they do were done through God."

JESUS AND JOHN THE BAPTIST

²²After this, Jesus and his followers went into the area of Judea, where he stayed with his followers and baptized people. ²³John was also baptizing in Aenon, near Salim, because there was plenty of water there. People were going there to be baptized. ²⁴(This was before John was put into prison.)

²⁵Some of John's followers had an argument with a Jew about religious washing.ⁿ ²⁶So they came to John and said, "Teacher, remember the man who was with you on the other side of the Jordan River, the one you spoke about so much? He is baptizing, and everyone is going to him."

²⁷John answered, "A man can get only what God gives him. ²⁸You yourselves heard me say, 'I am not the Christ, but I am the one sent to prepare the way for him.' ²⁹The bride belongs only to the bridegroom. But the friend who helps the bridegroom stands by and listens to him. He is thrilled that he gets to hear the bridegroom's voice. In the same way, I am really happy. ³⁰He must become greater, and I must become less important.

Get an accountability partner. If you're actively in a relationship, then make sure you have a good guy friend to discuss things with. Make sure it's a guy you trust. Meet a couple of times a month to discuss your relationships. You both can help each other keep life in perspective and your relationships with girls healthy.

 3:13 the Son of Man Some Greek copies continue, "who is in heaven." 3:14 Moses . . . desert When the Israelites were dying from snakebites, God told Moses to put a bronze snake on a pole. The people who looked at the snake were healed (Numbers 21:4–9). 3:25 religious washing The Jewish people washed themselves in special ways before eating, before worshiping in the Temple, and at other special times.

ISSUES

DEPRESSION

LIFE ISN'T EASY AND SOMETIMES IT CAN GET YOU DOWN. If you have ever struggled with feelings of depression, you are not alone. The teenage experience leaves many feeling left out of the loop, if not alienated from life altogether. But that doesn't mean you need to be dominated by such emotions. It is only natural occasionally to feel like the odds are stacked against you. But with Christ on your side, you are more than capable of getting through whatever trials you face with flying colors. One way to break through depression is to do a good deed for someone less fortunate than you. By helping others you help yourself, also.

How to Thwart an Alien Invasion

Those pesky aliens keep showing up every few years to invade our planet, and every time some random guy (you, perhaps?) rises to the occasion of sending them packing. The army may try to do something about it, but traditional weapons will be powerless against them, so don't worry about packing a gun in your survival kit. If at all possible, find a way to get aboard their mother ship and cause it to explode. This is usually difficult, though, so the best advice is to lay low and protect yourself, using the skills you have. It's actually best to let God take care of the invaders—they always have some sort of flaw in their plan that betrays a weakness, and they end up either dying here or jetting home in a hurry, never to return. Your spiritual enemy will try to invade your space, too, so you must protect yourself by praying and quoting God's Word.

THE ONE WHO COMES FROM HEAVEN

[31]"The One who comes from above is greater than all. The one who is from the earth belongs to the earth and talks about things on the earth. But the One who comes from heaven is greater than all. [32]He tells what he has seen and heard, but no one accepts what he says. [33]Whoever accepts what he says has proven that God is true. [34]The One whom God sent speaks the words of God, because God gives him the Spirit fully. [35]The Father loves the Son and has given him power over everything. [36]Those who believe in the Son have eternal life, but those who do not obey the Son will never have life. God's anger stays on them."

JESUS AND A SAMARITAN WOMAN

4 The Pharisees heard that Jesus was making and baptizing more followers than John, [2]although Jesus himself did not baptize people, but his followers did. [3]Jesus knew that the Pharisees had heard about him, so he left Judea and went back to Galilee. [4]But on the way he had to go through the country of Samaria.

[5]In Samaria Jesus came to the town called Sychar, which is near the field Jacob gave to his son Joseph. [6]Jacob's well was there. Jesus was tired from his long trip, so he sat down beside the well. It was about twelve o'clock noon. [7]When a Samaritan woman came to the well to get some water, Jesus said to her, "Please give me a drink." [8](This happened while Jesus' followers were in town buying some food.)

[9]The woman said, "I am surprised that you ask me for a drink, since you are a Jewish man and I am a Samaritan woman." (Jewish people are not friends with Samaritans.[n])

[10]Jesus said, "If you only knew the free gift of God and who it is that is asking you for water, you would have asked him, and he would have given you living water."

[11]The woman said, "Sir, where will you get this living water? The well is very deep, and you have nothing to get water with. [12]Are you greater than Jacob, our father, who gave us this well and drank from it himself along with his sons and flocks?"

[13]Jesus answered, "Everyone who drinks this water will be thirsty again, [14]but whoever drinks the water I give will never be thirsty. The water I give will become a spring of water gushing up inside that person, giving eternal life."

[15]The woman said to him, "Sir, give me this water so I will never be thirsty again and will not have to come back here to get more water."

[16]Jesus told her, "Go get your husband and come back here."

fight the fight

John 3:5–8

Your grandparents, parents, and close friends may all believe in Christ and be faithful church members. But their beliefs won't help you enter heaven. Ultimately, each person will stand before God on the basis of whether he or she has believed that Jesus is the Son of God and, consequently, has entered into a personal relationship with him. In this passage, Christ spelled out the way to eternal life: You must be born again. Being born again is a matter of the heart. Don't treat this decision lightly, since it has eternal consequences. And no one else can make the decision for you.

4:9 Jewish people . . . Samaritans. This can also be translated "Jewish people don't use things that Samaritans have used."

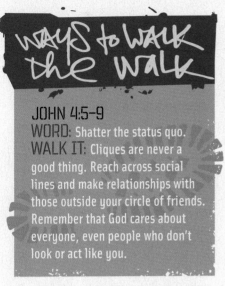

WAYS to WALK the WALK

JOHN 4:5-9

WORD: Shatter the status quo.
WALK IT: Cliques are never a good thing. Reach across social lines and make relationships with those outside your circle of friends. Remember that God cares about everyone, even people who don't look or act like you.

[17]The woman answered, "I have no husband."

Jesus said to her, "You are right to say you have no husband. [18]Really you have had five husbands, and the man you live with now is not your husband. You told the truth."

[19]The woman said, "Sir, I can see that you are a prophet. [20]Our ancestors worshiped on this mountain, but you say that Jerusalem is the place where people must worship."

[21]Jesus said, "Believe me, woman. The time is coming when neither in Jerusalem nor on this mountain will you actually worship the Father. [22]You Samaritans worship something you don't understand. We understand what we worship, because salvation comes from the Jews. [23]The time is coming when the true worshipers will worship the Father in spirit and truth, and that time is here already. You see, the Father too is actively seeking such people to worship him. [24]God is spirit, and those who worship him must worship in spirit and truth."

[25]The woman said, "I know that the Messiah is coming." (Messiah is the One called Christ.) "When the Messiah comes, he will explain everything to us."

[26]Then Jesus said, "I am he—I, the one talking to you."

[27]Just then his followers came back from town and were surprised to see him talking with a woman. But none of them asked, "What do you want?" or "Why are you talking with her?"

[28]Then the woman left her water jar and went back to town. She said to the people, [29]"Come and see a man who told me everything I ever did. Do you think he might be the Christ?" [30]So the people left the town and went to see Jesus.

[31]Meanwhile, his followers were begging him, "Teacher, eat something."

[32]But Jesus answered, "I have food to eat that you know nothing about."

[33]So the followers asked themselves, "Did somebody already bring him food?"

[34]Jesus said, "My food is to do what the One who sent me wants me to do and to finish his work. [35]You have a saying, 'Four more months till harvest.' But I tell you, open your eyes and look at the fields ready for harvest now. [36]Already, the one who harvests is being paid and is gathering crops for eternal life. So the one who plants and the one who harvests celebrate at the same time. [37]Here the saying is true, 'One person plants, and another harvests.' [38]I sent you to harvest a crop that you did not work on. Others did the work, and you get to finish up their work."[n]

[39]Many of the Samaritans in that town believed in Jesus because of what the woman said: "He told me everything I ever did." [40]When the Samaritans came to Jesus, they begged him to stay with them, so he stayed there two more days. [41]And many more believed because of the things he said.

[42]They said to the woman, "First we believed in Jesus because of what you said, but now we believe because we heard him ourselves. We know that this man really is the Savior of the world."

JESUS HEALS AN OFFICER'S SON

[43]Two days later, Jesus left and went to Galilee. [44](Jesus had said before that a prophet is not respected in his own country.) [45]When Jesus arrived in Galilee, the people there welcomed him. They had seen all the things he did at the Passover Feast in Jerusalem, because they had been there, too.

[46]Jesus went again to visit Cana in Galilee where he had changed the water into wine. One of the king's important officers lived in the city of Capernaum, and his son was sick. [47]When he heard that Jesus had come from Judea to Galilee, he went to Jesus and begged him to come to Capernaum and heal his son, because his son was almost dead. [48]Jesus said to him, "You people must see signs and miracles before you will believe in me."

[49]The officer said, "Sir, come before my child dies."

[50]Jesus answered, "Go. Your son will live."

The man believed what Jesus told him and went home. [51]On the way the man's servants came and met him and told him, "Your son is alive."

[52]The man asked, "What time did my son begin to get well?"

They answered, "Yesterday at one o'clock the fever left him."

[53]The father knew that one o'clock was the exact time that Jesus had said, "Your son will live." So the man and all the people who lived in his house believed in Jesus.

[54]That was the second miracle Jesus did after coming from Judea to Galilee.

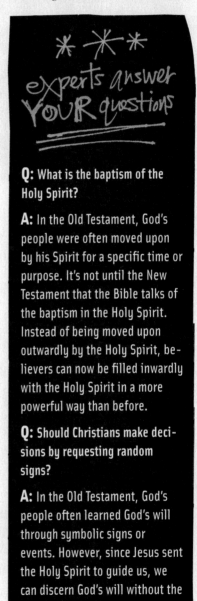

experts answer YOUR questions

Q: What is the baptism of the Holy Spirit?

A: In the Old Testament, God's people were often moved upon by his Spirit for a specific time or purpose. It's not until the New Testament that the Bible talks of the baptism in the Holy Spirit. Instead of being moved upon outwardly by the Holy Spirit, believers can now be filled inwardly with the Holy Spirit in a more powerful way than before.

Q: Should Christians make decisions by requesting random signs?

A: In the Old Testament, God's people often learned God's will through symbolic signs or events. However, since Jesus sent the Holy Spirit to guide us, we can discern God's will without the use of symbols or signs.

4:38 I . . . their work. As a farmer sends workers to harvest grain, Jesus sends his followers out to bring people to God.

113

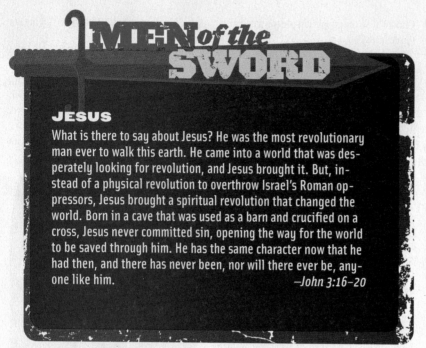

MEN of the SWORD

JESUS

What is there to say about Jesus? He was the most revolutionary man ever to walk this earth. He came into a world that was desperately looking for revolution, and Jesus brought it. But, instead of a physical revolution to overthrow Israel's Roman oppressors, Jesus brought a spiritual revolution that changed the world. Born in a cave that was used as a barn and crucified on a cross, Jesus never committed sin, opening the way for the world to be saved through him. He has the same character now that he had then, and there has never been, nor will there ever be, anyone like him.

—John 3:16–20

JESUS HEALS A MAN AT A POOL

5 Later Jesus went to Jerusalem for a special feast. [2] In Jerusalem there is a pool with five covered porches, which is called Bethesda[n] in the Hebrew language.[n] This pool is near the Sheep Gate. [3] Many sick people were lying on the porches beside the pool. Some were blind, some were crippled, and some were paralyzed [, and they waited for the water to move. [4] Sometimes an angel of the Lord came down to the pool and stirred up the water. After the angel did this, the first person to go into the pool was healed from any sickness he had].[n] [5] A man was lying there who had been sick for thirty-eight years. [6] When Jesus saw the man and knew that he had been sick for such a long time, Jesus asked him, "Do you want to be well?"

was well; he picked up his mat and began to walk.

The day this happened was a Sabbath day. [10] So the Jews said to the man who had been healed, "Today is the Sabbath. It is against our law for you to carry your mat on the Sabbath day."

[11] But he answered, "The man who made me well told me, 'Pick up your mat and walk.'"

[12] Then they asked him, "Who is the man who told you to pick up your mat and walk?"

[13] But the man who had been healed did not know who it was, because there were many people in that place, and Jesus had left.

[14] Later, Jesus found the man at the Temple and said to him, "See, you are well now. Stop sinning so that something worse does not happen to you."

[7] The sick man answered, "Sir, there is no one to help me get into the pool when the water starts moving. While I am coming to the water, someone else always gets in before me."

[8] Then Jesus said, "Stand up. Pick up your mat and walk." [9] And immediately the man

[15] Then the man left and told his people that Jesus was the one who had made him well.

[16] Because Jesus was doing this on the Sabbath day, some evil people began to persecute him. [17] But Jesus said to them, "My Father never stops working, and so I keep working, too."

[18] This made them try still harder to kill him. They said, "First Jesus was breaking the law about the Sabbath day. Now he says that God is his own Father, making himself equal with God!"

JESUS HAS GOD'S AUTHORITY

[19] But Jesus said, "I tell you the truth, the Son can do nothing alone. The Son does only what he sees the Father doing, because the Son does whatever the Father does. [20] The Father loves the Son and shows the Son all the things he himself does. But the Father will show the Son even greater things than this so that you can all be amazed. [21] Just as the Father raises the dead and gives them life, so also the Son gives life to those he wants to. [22] In fact, the Father judges no one, but he has given the Son power to do all the judging [23] so that all people will honor the Son as much as they honor the Father. Anyone who does not honor the Son does not honor the Father who sent him.

[24] "I tell you the truth, whoever hears what I say and believes in the One who sent me has eternal life. That person will not be judged guilty but has already left death and entered life. [25] I tell you the truth, the time is coming and is already here when the dead will hear the voice of the Son of God, and those who hear will have life. [26] Life comes from the Father himself, and he has allowed the Son to have life in himself as well. [27] And the Father has given the Son the approval to judge, because he is the Son of Man. [28] Don't be surprised at this: A time is coming when all who are dead and in their graves will hear his voice. [29] Then they will come out of their graves. Those who did good will rise and have life forever, but those who did evil will rise to be judged guilty.

JESUS IS GOD'S SON

[30] "I can do nothing alone. I judge only the way I am told, so my judgment is fair. I don't try to please myself, but I try to please the One who sent me.

[31] "If only I tell people about myself, what I say is not true. [32] But there is another who tells about me, and I know that the things he says about me are true.

[33] "You have sent people to John, and he has told you the truth. [34] It is not that I need what humans say; I tell you this so you can be saved. [35] John was like a burning and shining lamp, and you were happy to enjoy his light for a while.

[36] "But I have a proof about myself that is greater than that of John. The things I do, which are the things my Father gave me to do, prove that the Father sent me. [37] And the Father

 5:2 Bethesda Some Greek copies read "Bethzatha" or "Bethsaida," different names for the pool of Bethesda. **5:2 Hebrew language** Or Aramaic, the languages of many people in this region in the first century. **5:3–4 and . . . had** Some Greek copies do not contain all or most of the bracketed text.

114

himself who sent me has given proof about me. You have never heard his voice or seen what he looks like. [38]His teaching does not live in you, because you don't believe in the One the Father sent. [39]You carefully study the Scriptures because you think they give you eternal life. They do in fact tell about me, [40]but you refuse to come to me to have that life.

[41]"I don't need praise from people. [42]But I know you—I know that you don't have God's love in you. [43]I have come from my Father and speak for him, but you don't accept me. But when another person comes, speaking only for himself, you will accept him. [44]You try to get praise from each other, but you do not try to get the praise that comes from the only God. So how can you believe? [45]Don't think that I will stand before the Father and say you are wrong. The one who says you are wrong is Moses, the one you hoped would save you. [46]If you really believed Moses, you would believe me, because Moses wrote about me. [47]But if you don't believe what Moses wrote, how can you believe what I say?"

MORE THAN FIVE THOUSAND FED

6 After this, Jesus went across Lake Galilee (or, Lake Tiberias). [2]Many people followed him because they saw the miracles he did to heal the sick. [3]Jesus went up on a hill and sat down there with his followers. [4]It was almost the time for the Jewish Passover Feast.

[5]When Jesus looked up and saw a large crowd coming toward him, he said to Philip, "Where can we buy enough bread for all these people to eat?" [6](Jesus asked Philip this question to test him, because Jesus already knew what he planned to do.)

[7]Philip answered, "Someone would have to work almost a year to buy enough bread for each person to have only a little piece."

[8]Another one of his followers, Andrew, Simon Peter's brother, said, [9]"Here is a boy with five loaves of barley bread and two little fish, but that is not enough for so many people."

[10]Jesus said, "Tell the people to sit down." There was plenty of grass there, and about five thousand men sat down there. [11]Then Jesus took the loaves of bread, thanked God for them, and gave them to the people who were sitting there. He did the same with the fish, giving as much as the people wanted.

[12]When they had all had enough to eat, Jesus said to his followers, "Gather the leftover pieces of fish and bread so that nothing is wasted." [13]So they gathered up the pieces and filled twelve baskets with the pieces left from the five barley loaves.

[14]When the people saw this miracle that Jesus did, they said, "He must truly be the Prophet[n] who is coming into the world."

[15]Jesus knew that the people planned to come and take him by force and make him their king, so he left and went into the hills alone.

JESUS WALKS ON THE WATER

[16]That evening Jesus' followers went down to Lake Galilee. [17]It was dark now, and Jesus had not yet come to them. The followers got into a boat and started across the lake to Capernaum. [18]By now a strong wind was blowing, and the waves on the lake were getting bigger. [19]When they had rowed the boat about three or four miles, they saw Jesus walking on the water, coming toward the boat. The followers were afraid, [20]but Jesus said to them, "It is I. Do not be afraid." [21]Then they were glad to take him into the boat. At once the boat came to land at the place where they wanted to go.

THE PEOPLE SEEK JESUS

[22]The next day the people who had stayed on the other side of the lake knew that Jesus had not gone in the boat with his followers but that they had left without him. And they knew that only one boat had been there. [23]But then some boats came from Tiberias and landed near the place where the people had eaten the bread after the Lord had given thanks. [24]When the people saw that Jesus and his followers were not there now, they got into boats and went to Capernaum to find Jesus.

JESUS, THE BREAD OF LIFE

[25]When the people found Jesus on the other side of the lake, they asked him, "Teacher, when did you come here?"

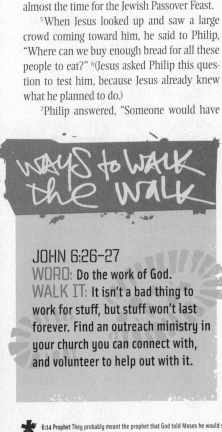

WAYS to WALK the WALK

JOHN 6:26-27

WORD: Do the work of God.

WALK IT: It isn't a bad thing to work for stuff, but stuff won't last forever. Find an outreach ministry in your church you can connect with, and volunteer to help out with it.

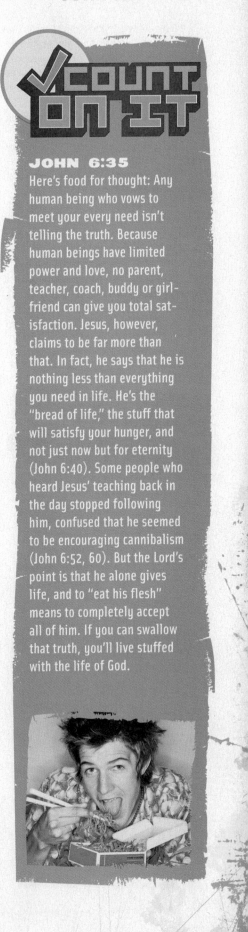

COUNT ON IT

JOHN 6:35

Here's food for thought: Any human being who vows to meet your every need isn't telling the truth. Because human beings have limited power and love, no parent, teacher, coach, buddy or girlfriend can give you total satisfaction. Jesus, however, claims to be far more than that. In fact, he says that he is nothing less than everything you need in life. He's the "bread of life," the stuff that will satisfy your hunger, and not just now but for eternity (John 6:40). Some people who heard Jesus' teaching back in the day stopped following him, confused that he seemed to be encouraging cannibalism (John 6:52, 60). But the Lord's point is that he alone gives life, and to "eat his flesh" means to completely accept all of him. If you can swallow that truth, you'll live stuffed with the life of God.

6:14 Prophet They probably meant the prophet that God told Moses he would send (Deuteronomy 18:15–19).

115

26Jesus answered, "I tell you the truth, you aren't looking for me because you saw me do miracles. You are looking for me because you ate the bread and were satisfied. 27Don't work for the food that spoils. Work for the food that stays good always and gives eternal life. The Son of Man will give you this food, because on him God the Father has put his power."

28The people asked Jesus, "What are the things God wants us to do?"

29Jesus answered, "The work God wants you to do is this: Believe the One he sent."

30So the people asked, "What miracle will you do? If we see a miracle, we will believe you. What will you do? 31Our ancestors ate the manna in the desert. This is written in the Scriptures: 'He gave them bread from heaven to eat.'"[n]

32Jesus said, "I tell you the truth, it was not Moses who gave you bread from heaven; it is my Father who is giving you the true bread from heaven. 33God's bread is the One who comes down from heaven and gives life to the world."

34The people said, "Sir, give us this bread always."

Relationships

"In the same way, men stopped having natural sex and began wanting each other. Men did shameful things with other men, and in their bodies they received the punishment for those wrongs" (Romans 1:27). Homosexuality is becoming a hot-button issue nowadays, especially as it becomes more and more accepted in the mainstream culture. But God doesn't call it an alternative lifestyle; he calls it a sin. Some guys your age may be trying to determine whether or not they're gay. You can be an instrument of God's love to them by accepting them as a person while leading them away from sin.

Do's and Don'ts

DO listen to wholesome music.

DO learn how to play an instrument.

DO appreciate different types of music.

DO tune out raunchy song lyrics.

DON'T listen to rebellious tunes.

DON'T download music illegally.

DON'T wear headphones while driving.

DON'T listen to extremely loud music.

35Then Jesus said, "I am the bread that gives life. Whoever comes to me will never be hungry, and whoever believes in me will never be thirsty. 36But as I told you before, you have seen me and still don't believe. 37The Father gives me the people who are mine. Every one of them will come to me, and I will always accept them. 38I came down from heaven to do what God wants me to do, not what I want to do. 39Here is what the One who sent me wants me to do: I must not lose even one whom God gave me, but I must raise them all on the last day. 40Those who see the Son and believe in him have eternal life, and I will raise them on the last day. This is what my Father wants."

41Some people began to complain about Jesus because he said, "I am the bread that comes down from heaven." 42They said, "This is Jesus, the son of Joseph. We know his father and mother. How can he say, 'I came down from heaven'?"

43But Jesus answered, "Stop complaining to each other. 44The Father is the One who sent me. No one can come to me unless the Father draws him to me, and I will raise that person up on the last day. 45It is written in the prophets, 'They will all be taught by God.'[n] Everyone who listens to the Father and learns from him comes to me. 46No one has seen the Father except the One who is from God; only he has seen the Father. 47I tell you the truth, whoever believes has eternal life. 48I am the bread that gives life. 49Your ancestors ate the manna in the desert, but still they died. 50Here is the bread that comes down from heaven. Anyone who eats this bread will never die. 51I am the living bread that came down from heaven. Anyone who eats this bread will live forever. This bread is my flesh, which I will give up so that the world may have life."

52Then the evil people began to argue among themselves, saying, "How can this man give us his flesh to eat?"

53Jesus said, "I tell you the truth, you must eat the flesh of the Son of Man and drink his blood. Otherwise, you won't have real life in you. 54Those who eat my flesh and drink my blood have eternal life, and I will raise them up on the last day. 55My flesh is true food, and my blood is true drink. 56Those who eat my flesh and drink my blood live in me, and I live in them. 57The living Father sent me, and I live because of the Father. So whoever eats me will live because of me. 58I am not like the bread your ancestors ate. They ate that bread and still died. I am the bread that came down from heaven, and whoever eats this bread will live forever." 59Jesus said all these things while he was teaching in the synagogue in Capernaum.

THE WORDS OF ETERNAL LIFE

60When the followers of Jesus heard this, many of them said, "This teaching is hard. Who can accept it?"

6:31 'He gave . . . eat.' Quotation from Psalm 78:24.   6:45 'They . . . God.' Quotation from Isaiah 54:13.

[61]Knowing that his followers were complaining about this, Jesus said, "Does this teaching bother you? [62]Then will it also bother you to see the Son of Man going back to the place where he came from? [63]It is the Spirit that gives life. The flesh doesn't give life. The words I told you are spirit, and they give life. [64]But some of you don't believe." (Jesus knew from the beginning who did not believe and who would turn against him.) [65]Jesus said, "That is the reason I said, 'If the Father does not bring a person to me, that one cannot come.'"

[66]After Jesus said this, many of his followers left him and stopped following him.

[67]Jesus asked the twelve followers, "Do you want to leave, too?"

[68]Simon Peter answered him, "Lord, who would we go to? You have the words that give eternal life. [69]We believe and know that you are the Holy One from God."

[70]Then Jesus answered, "I chose all twelve of you, but one of you is a devil."

[71]Jesus was talking about Judas, the son of Simon Iscariot. Judas was one of the twelve, but later he was going to turn against Jesus.

JESUS' BROTHERS DON'T BELIEVE

7 After this, Jesus traveled around Galilee. He did not want to travel in Judea, because some evil people there wanted to kill him. [2]It was time for the Feast of Shelters. [3]So Jesus' brothers said to him, "You should leave here and go to Judea so your followers there can see the miracles you do. [4]Anyone who wants to be well known does not hide what he does. If you are doing these things, show yourself to the world." [5](Even Jesus' brothers did not believe in him.)

[6]Jesus said to his brothers, "The right time for me has not yet come, but any time is right for you. [7]The world cannot hate you, but it hates me, because I tell it the evil things it does. [8]So you go to the feast. I will not go yet[n] to this feast, because the right time for me has not yet come." [9]After saying this, Jesus stayed in Galilee.

[10]But after Jesus' brothers had gone to the feast, Jesus went also. But he did not let people see him. [11]At the feast some people were looking for him and saying, "Where is that man?"

[12]Within the large crowd there, many people were whispering to each other about Jesus. Some said, "He is a good man."

Others said, "No, he fools the people." [13]But no one was brave enough to talk about Jesus openly, because they were afraid of the elders.

JESUS TEACHES AT THE FEAST

[14]When the feast was about half over, Jesus went to the Temple and began to teach. [15]The people were amazed and said, "This man has never studied in school. How did he learn so much?"

[16]Jesus answered, "The things I teach are not my own, but they come from him who sent me. [17]If people choose to do what God wants, they will know that my teaching comes from God and not from me. [18]Those who teach their own ideas are trying to get honor for themselves. But those who try to bring honor to the one who sent them speak the truth, and there is nothing false in them. [19]Moses gave you the law,[n] but none of you obeys that law. Why are you trying to kill me?"

[20]The people answered, "A demon has come into you. We are not trying to kill you."

[21]Jesus said to them, "I did one miracle, and you are all amazed. [22]Moses gave you the law about circumcision. (But really Moses did not give you circumcision; it came from our ancestors.) And yet you circumcise a baby boy on a Sabbath day. [23]If a baby boy can be circumcised on a Sabbath day to obey the law of Moses, why are you angry at me for healing a person's whole body on the Sabbath day? [24]Stop judging by the way things look, but judge by what is really right."

 7:8 yet Some Greek copies do not have this word. **7:19 law** Moses gave God's people the Law that God gave him on Mount Sinai (Exodus 34:29–32).

IS JESUS THE CHRIST?

[25]Then some of the people who lived in Jerusalem said, "This is the man they are trying to kill. [26]But he is teaching where everyone can see and hear him, and no one is trying

Don't pursue girls using the Internet. When you're older, the Internet might be a place to meet people, but it's not at your age. As with all things cyber, you never know what you're getting involved with, and it's always better simply not to get involved than to chance the consequences of decisions gone wrong.

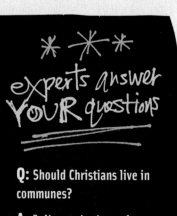

experts answer YOUR questions

Q: Should Christians live in communes?

A: Believers in the early church shared all their possessions with each other, meeting jointly and enjoying fellowship every day. Although we don't have to take this example as a rule for how we have to live, we should certainly always be ready to share our money, our food, and our homes with Christian brothers and sisters.

Q: What if I'm afraid to share my faith?

A: It can be intimidating to share your faith. Early Christians drew the courage to talk about what they believed from the time that they had spent with Jesus. We also can become bolder in sharing our testimony as we daily spend time with Jesus and get to know him better.

to stop him. Maybe the leaders have decided he really is the Christ. [27]But we know where this man is from. Yet when the real Christ comes, no one will know where he comes from."

[28]Jesus, teaching in the Temple, cried out, "Yes, you know me, and you know where I am from. But I have not come by my own authority. I was sent by the One who is true, whom you don't know. [29]But I know him, because I am from him, and he sent me."

[30]When Jesus said this, they tried to seize him. But no one was able to touch him, because it was not yet the right time. [31]But many of the people believed in Jesus. They said, "When the Christ comes, will he do more miracles than this man has done?"

THE LEADERS TRY TO ARREST JESUS

[32]The Pharisees heard the crowd whispering these things about Jesus. So the leading priests and the Pharisees sent some Temple guards to arrest him. [33]Jesus said, "I will be with you a little while longer. Then I will go back to the One who sent me. [34]You will look for me, but you will not find me. And you cannot come where I am."

[35]Some people said to each other, "Where will this man go so we cannot find him? Will he go to the Greek cities where our people live and teach the Greek people there? [36]What did he mean when he said, 'You will look for me, but you will not find me,' and 'You cannot come where I am'?"

JESUS TALKS ABOUT THE SPIRIT

[37]On the last and most important day of the feast Jesus stood up and said in a loud voice, "Let anyone who is thirsty come to me and drink. [38]If anyone believes in me, rivers of living water will flow out from that person's heart, as the Scripture says." [39]Jesus was talking about the Holy Spirit. The Spirit had not yet been given, because Jesus had not yet been raised to glory. But later, those who believed in Jesus would receive the Spirit.

THE PEOPLE ARGUE ABOUT JESUS

[40]When the people heard Jesus' words, some of them said, "This man really is the Prophet."[n]

[41]Others said, "He is the Christ."

Still others said, "The Christ will not come from Galilee. [42]The Scripture says that the Christ will come from David's family and from Bethlehem, the town where David lived." [43]So the people did not agree with each other about Jesus. [44]Some of them wanted to arrest him, but no one was able to touch him.

SOME LEADERS WON'T BELIEVE

[45]The Temple guards went back to the leading priests and the Pharisees, who asked, "Why didn't you bring Jesus?"

[46]The guards answered, "The words he says are greater than the words of any other person who has ever spoken!"

[47]The Pharisees answered, "So Jesus has fooled you also! [48]Have any of the leaders or the Pharisees believed in him? No! [49]But these people, who know nothing about the law, are under God's curse."

[50]Nicodemus, who had gone to see Jesus before, was in that group.[n] He said, [51]"Our law does not judge a person without hearing him and knowing what he has done."

[52]They answered, "Are you from Galilee, too? Study the Scriptures, and you will learn that no prophet comes from Galilee."

―――――

Some of the earliest surviving Greek copies do not contain 7:53—8:11.

[[53]And everyone left and went home.

THE WOMAN CAUGHT IN ADULTERY

8 Jesus went to the Mount of Olives. [2]But early in the morning he went back to the Temple, and all the people came to him, and he sat and taught them. [3]The teachers of the law and the Pharisees brought a woman who had been caught in adultery. They forced her to stand before the people. [4]They said to Jesus, "Teacher, this woman was caught having

7:40 **Prophet** They probably meant the prophet God told Moses he would send (Deuteronomy 18:15–19).   7:50 **Nicodemus . . . group.** The story about Nicodemus going and talking to Jesus is in John 3:1–21.

sexual relations with a man who is not her husband. [5]The law of Moses commands that we stone to death every woman who does this. What do you say we should do?" [6]They were asking this to trick Jesus so that they could have some charge against him.

But Jesus bent over and started writing on the ground with his finger. [7]When they continued to ask Jesus their question, he raised up and said, "Anyone here who has never sinned can throw the first stone at her." [8]Then Jesus bent over again and wrote on the ground.

[9]Those who heard Jesus began to leave one by one, first the older men and then the others. Jesus was left there alone with the woman standing before him. [10]Jesus raised up again and asked her, "Woman, where are they? Has no one judged you guilty?"

[11]She answered, "No one, sir."

Then Jesus said, "I also don't judge you guilty. You may go now, but don't sin anymore."]

JESUS IS THE LIGHT OF THE WORLD

[12]Later, Jesus talked to the people again, saying, "I am the light of the world. The person who follows me will never live in darkness but will have the light that gives life."

[13]The Pharisees said to Jesus, "When you talk about yourself, you are the only one to say these things are true. We cannot accept what you say."

[14]Jesus answered, "Yes, I am saying these things about myself, but they are true. I know where I came from and where I am going. But you don't know where I came from or where I am going. [15]You judge by human standards. I am not judging anyone. [16]But when I do judge, I judge truthfully, because I am not alone. The Father who sent me is with me. [17]Your own law says that when two witnesses say the same thing, you must accept what they say. [18]I am one of the witnesses who speaks about myself, and the Father who sent me is the other witness."

[19]They asked, "Where is your father?"

Jesus answered, "You don't know me or my Father. If you knew me, you would know my Fa-

ther, too." [20]Jesus said these things while he was teaching in the Temple, near where the money is kept. But no one arrested him, because the right time for him had not yet come.

THE PEOPLE MISUNDERSTAND JESUS

[21]Again, Jesus said to the people, "I will leave you, and you will look for me, but you will die in your sins. You cannot come where I am going."

[22]So the Jews asked, "Will he kill himself? Is that why he said, 'You cannot come where I am going'?"

[23]Jesus said, "You people are from here below, but I am from above. You belong to this world, but I don't belong to this world. [24]So I told you that you would die in your sins. Yes, you will die in your sins if you don't believe that I am he."

[25]They asked, "Then who are you?"

Jesus answered, "I am what I have told you from the beginning. [26]I have many things to say and decide about you. But I tell people only the things I have heard from the One who sent me, and he speaks the truth."

[27]The people did not understand that he was talking to them about the Father. [28]So Jesus said to them, "When you lift up the Son of Man, you will know that I am he. You will know that these things I do are not by my own authority but that I say only what the Father has taught me. [29]The One who sent me is with me. I always do what is pleasing to him, so he

has not left me alone." [30]While Jesus was saying these things, many people believed in him.

FREEDOM FROM SIN

[31]So Jesus said to the Jews who believed in him, "If you continue to obey my teaching, you are truly my followers. [32]Then you will know the truth, and the truth will make you free."

[33]They answered, "We are Abraham's children, and we have never been anyone's slaves. So why do you say we will be free?"

[34]Jesus answered, "I tell you the truth, everyone who lives in sin is a slave to sin. [35]A slave does not stay with a family forever, but a

son belongs to the family forever. [36]So if the Son makes you free, you will be truly free. [37]I know you are Abraham's children, but you want to kill me because you don't accept my teaching. [38]I am telling you what my Father has shown me, but you do what your father has told you."

[39]They answered, "Our father is Abraham."

Jesus said, "If you were really Abraham's children, you would do[n] the things Abraham did. [40]I am a man who has told you the truth which I heard from God, but you are trying to kill me. Abraham did nothing like that. [41]So you are doing the things your own father did."

But they said, "We are not like children who never knew who their father was. God is our Father; he is the only Father we have."

[42]Jesus said to them, "If God were really your Father, you would love me, because I came from God and now I am here. I did not come by my own authority; God sent me. [43]You don't understand what I say, because you cannot accept my teaching. [44]You belong to your father the devil, and you want to do what he wants. He was a murderer from the beginning and was against the truth, because there is no truth in him. When he tells a lie, he shows what he is really like, because he is a liar and the father of lies. [45]But because I speak the truth, you don't believe me. [46]Can any of you prove that I am guilty of sin? If I am telling the truth, why don't you believe me? [47]The person who belongs to God accepts what God says. But you don't accept what God says, because you don't belong to God."

JESUS IS GREATER THAN ABRAHAM

[48]They answered, "We say you are a Samaritan and have a demon in you. Are we not right?"

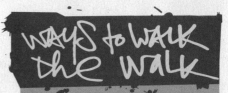

✱ 8:39 **If . . . do** Some Greek copies read "If you are really Abraham's children, you will do."

JOHN 10:10

You wouldn't sign up to follow Jesus if you felt he threatened to take away all the fun from your life. Yet, deep down inside, you might harbor fear that God plans to lead you into a life of misery and pain. Many are duped into believing that he's a joy-killer, a fun-robber, and a party-stopper. But the truth is, he has promised you not only life, but "life in all its fullness." When you follow Jesus, you're united with the wisest being in the universe. Not only that, but he also is the type of guy who wants to share all those smarts with you. A full life comes from studying what God says in the Bible and applying it. Lots of people claim to point you in the right direction, but Jesus himself is the way, the truth, and the life (John 14:6).

⁴⁹Jesus answered, "I have no demon in me. I give honor to my Father, but you dishonor me. ⁵⁰I am not trying to get honor for myself. There is One who wants this honor for me, and he is the judge. ⁵¹I tell you the truth, whoever obeys my teaching will never die."

⁵²They said to Jesus, "Now we know that you have a demon in you! Even Abraham and the prophets died. But you say, 'Whoever obeys my teaching will never die.' ⁵³Do you think you are greater than our father Abraham, who died? And the prophets died, too. Who do you think you are?"

⁵⁴Jesus answered, "If I give honor to myself, that honor is worth nothing. The One who gives me honor is my Father, and you say he is your God. ⁵⁵You don't really know him, but I know him. If I said I did not know him, I would be a liar like you. But I do know him, and I obey what he says. ⁵⁶Your father Abraham was very happy that he would see my day. He saw that day and was glad."

⁵⁷They said to him, "You have never seen Abraham! You are not even fifty years old."

⁵⁸Jesus answered, "I tell you the truth, before Abraham was even born, I am!" ⁵⁹When Jesus said this, the people picked up stones to throw at him. But Jesus hid himself, and then he left the Temple.

JESUS HEALS A MAN BORN BLIND

9 As Jesus was walking along, he saw a man who had been born blind. ²His followers asked him, "Teacher, whose sin caused this man to be born blind—his own sin or his parents' sin?"

³Jesus answered, "It is not this man's sin or his parents' sin that made him blind. This man was born blind so that God's power could be shown in him. ⁴While it is daytime, we must continue doing the work of the One who sent me. Night is coming, when no one can work. ⁵While I am in the world, I am the light of the world."

⁶After Jesus said this, he spit on the ground and made some mud with it and put the mud on the man's eyes. ⁷Then he told the man, "Go and wash in the Pool of Siloam." (Siloam means Sent.) So the man went, washed, and came back seeing.

⁸The neighbors and some people who had earlier seen this man begging said, "Isn't this the same man who used to sit and beg?"

⁹Some said, "He is the one," but others said, "No, he only looks like him."

The man himself said, "I am the man."

¹⁰They asked, "How did you get your sight?"

¹¹He answered, "The man named Jesus made some mud and put it on my eyes. Then he told me to go to Siloam and wash. So I went and washed, and then I could see."

¹²They asked him, "Where is this man?"

"I don't know," he answered.

PHARISEES QUESTION THE HEALING

¹³Then the people took to the Pharisees the man who had been blind. ¹⁴The day Jesus had made mud and healed his eyes was a Sabbath day. ¹⁵So now the Pharisees asked the man, "How did you get your sight?"

He answered, "He put mud on my eyes, I washed, and now I see."

¹⁶So some of the Pharisees were saying, "This man does not keep the Sabbath day, so he is not from God."

But others said, "A man who is a sinner can't do miracles like these." So they could not agree with each other.

¹⁷They asked the man again, "What do you say about him since it was your eyes he opened?"

The man answered, "He is a prophet."

¹⁸These leaders did not believe that he had been blind and could now see again. So they sent for the man's parents ¹⁹and asked them, "Is this your son who you say was born blind? Then how does he now see?"

²⁰His parents answered, "We know that this is our son and that he was born blind. ²¹But we don't know how he can now see. We don't know who opened his eyes. Ask him. He is old enough to speak for himself." ²²His parents said this because they were afraid of the elders, who had already decided that anyone who said Jesus was the Christ would be avoided. ²³That is why his parents said, "He is old enough. Ask him."

²⁴So for the second time, they called the man who had been blind. They said, "You should give God the glory by telling the truth. We know that this man is a sinner."

²⁵He answered, "I don't know if he is a sinner. One thing I do know: I was blind, and now I see."

²⁶They asked, "What did he do to you? How did he make you see again?"

²⁷He answered, "I already told you, and you didn't listen. Why do you want to hear it again? Do you want to become his followers, too?"

²⁸Then they insulted him and said, "You are his follower, but we are followers of Moses. ²⁹We know that God spoke to Moses, but we don't even know where this man comes from."

³⁰The man answered, "This is a very strange thing. You don't know where he comes from, and yet he opened my eyes. ³¹We all know that God does not listen to sinners, but he listens to anyone who worships and obeys him. ³²Nobody has ever heard of anyone giving sight to a man born blind. ³³If this

man were not from God, he could do nothing."

[34]They answered, "You were born full of sin! Are you trying to teach us?" And they threw him out.

SPIRITUAL BLINDNESS

[35]When Jesus heard that they had thrown him out, Jesus found him and said, "Do you believe in the Son of Man?"

[36]He asked, "Who is the Son of Man, sir, so that I can believe in him?"

[37]Jesus said to him, "You have seen him. The Son of Man is the one talking with you."

[38]He said, "Lord, I believe!" Then the man worshiped Jesus.

[39]Jesus said, "I came into this world so that the world could be judged. I came so that the blind[n] would see and so that those who see will become blind."

[40]Some of the Pharisees who were nearby heard Jesus say this and asked, "Are you saying we are blind, too?"

[41]Jesus said, "If you were blind, you would not be guilty of sin. But since you keep saying you see, your guilt remains."

THE SHEPHERD AND HIS SHEEP

10 Jesus said, "I tell you the truth, the person who does not enter the sheepfold by the door, but climbs in some other way, is a thief and a robber. [2]The one who enters by the door is the shepherd of the sheep. [3]The one who guards the door opens it for him. And the sheep listen to the voice of the shepherd. He calls his own sheep by name and leads them out. [4]When he brings all his sheep out, he goes ahead of them, and they follow him because they know his voice. [5]But they will never follow a stranger. They will run away from him because they don't know his voice." [6]Jesus told the people this story, but they did not understand what it meant.

JESUS IS THE GOOD SHEPHERD

[7]So Jesus said again, "I tell you the truth, I am the door for the sheep. [8]All the people who came before me were thieves and robbers. The sheep did not listen to them. [9]I am the door, and the person who enters through me will be saved and will be able to come in and go out and find pasture. [10]A thief comes to steal and kill and destroy, but I came to give life—life in all its fullness.

[11]"I am the good shepherd. The good shepherd gives his life for the sheep. [12]The worker who is paid to keep the sheep is different from the shepherd who owns them. When the worker sees a wolf coming, he runs away and leaves the sheep alone. Then the wolf attacks the sheep and scatters them. [13]The man runs away because he is only a paid worker and does not really care about the sheep.

[14]"I am the good shepherd. I know my sheep, and my sheep know me, [15]just as the Father knows me, and I know the Father. I give my life for the sheep. [16]I have other sheep that are not in this flock, and I must bring them also. They will listen to my voice, and there will be one flock and one shepherd. [17]The Father loves me because I give my life so that I can take it back again. [18]No one takes it away from me; I give my own life freely. I have the right to give my life, and I have the right to take it back. This is what my Father commanded me to do."

[19]Again the leaders did not agree with each other because of these words of Jesus. [20]Many of them said, "A demon has come into him and made him crazy. Why listen to him?"

[21]But others said, "A man who is crazy with a demon does not say things like this. Can a demon open the eyes of the blind?"

JESUS IS REJECTED

[22]The time came for the Feast of Dedication at Jerusalem. It was winter, [23]and Jesus was walking in the Temple in Solomon's Porch. [24]Some people gathered around him and said, "How long will you make us wonder about you? If you are the Christ, tell us plainly."

[25]Jesus answered, "I told you already, but you did not believe. The miracles I do in my Father's name show who I am. [26]But you don't believe, because you are not my sheep. [27]My sheep listen to my voice; I know them, and they follow me. [28]I give them eternal life, and they will never die, and no one can steal them out of my hand. [29]My Father gave my sheep to me. He is greater than all, and no person can steal my sheep out of my Father's hand. [30]The Father and I are one."

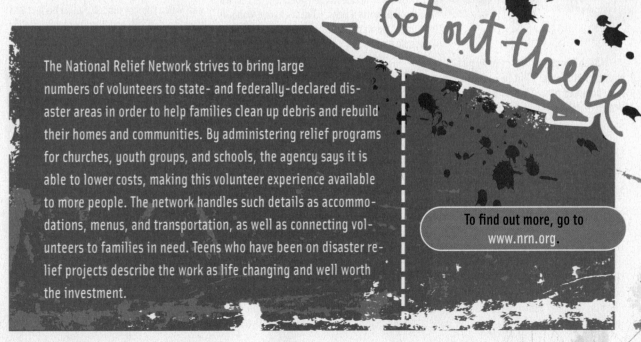

The National Relief Network strives to bring large numbers of volunteers to state- and federally-declared disaster areas in order to help families clean up debris and rebuild their homes and communities. By administering relief programs for churches, youth groups, and schools, the agency says it is able to lower costs, making this volunteer experience available to more people. The network handles such details as accommodations, menus, and transportation, as well as connecting volunteers to families in need. Teens who have been on disaster relief projects describe the work as life changing and well worth the investment.

To find out more, go to www.nrn.org.

9:39 **blind** Jesus is talking about people who are spiritually blind, not physically blind.

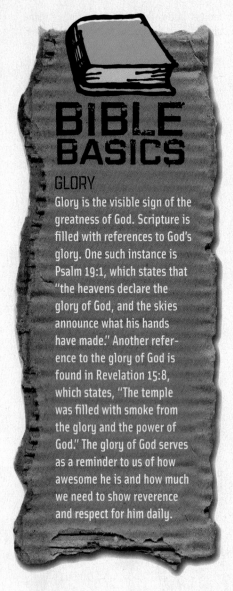

BIBLE BASICS

GLORY

Glory is the visible sign of the greatness of God. Scripture is filled with references to God's glory. One such instance is Psalm 19:1, which states that "the heavens declare the glory of God, and the skies announce what his hands have made." Another reference to the glory of God is found in Revelation 15:8, which states, "The temple was filled with smoke from the glory and the power of God." The glory of God serves as a reminder to us of how awesome he is and how much we need to show reverence and respect for him daily.

[31]Again some of the people picked up stones to kill Jesus. [32]But he said to them, "I have done many good works from the Father. Which of these good works are you killing me for?"

[33]They answered, "We are not killing you because of any good work you did, but because you speak against God. You are only a human, but you say you are the same as God!"

[34]Jesus answered, "It is written in your law that God said, 'I said, you are gods.'[n] [35]This Scripture called those people gods who received God's message, and Scripture is always true. [36]So why do you say that I speak against God because I said, 'I am God's Son'? I am the one God chose and sent into the world. [37]If I don't do what my Father does, then don't believe me. [38]But if I do what my Father does, even though you don't believe in me, believe what I do. Then you will know and understand that the Father is in me and I am in the Father."

[39]They tried to take Jesus again, but he escaped from them.

[40]Then he went back across the Jordan River to the place where John had first baptized. Jesus stayed there, [41]and many people came to him and said, "John never did a miracle, but everything John said about this man is true." [42]And in that place many believed in Jesus.

THE DEATH OF LAZARUS

11 A man named Lazarus was sick. He lived in the town of Bethany, where Mary and her sister Martha lived. [2]Mary was the woman who later put perfume on the Lord and wiped his feet with her hair. Mary's brother was Lazarus, the man who was now sick. [3]So Mary and Martha sent someone to tell Jesus, "Lord, the one you love is sick."

[4]When Jesus heard this, he said, "This sickness will not end in death. It is for the glory of God, to bring glory to the Son of God." [5]Jesus loved Martha and her sister and Lazarus. [6]But when he heard that Lazarus was sick, he stayed where he was for two more days. [7]Then Jesus said to his followers, "Let's go back to Judea."

[8]The followers said, "But Teacher, some people there tried to stone you to death only a short time ago. Now you want to go back there?"

[9]Jesus answered, "Are there not twelve hours in the day? If anyone walks in the daylight, he will not stumble, because he can see by this world's light. [10]But if anyone walks at night, he stumbles because there is no light to help him see."

[11]After Jesus said this, he added, "Our friend Lazarus has fallen asleep, but I am going there to wake him."

[12]The followers said, "But Lord, if he is only asleep, he will be all right."

[13]Jesus meant that Lazarus was dead, but his followers thought he meant Lazarus was really sleeping. [14]So then Jesus said plainly, "Lazarus is dead. [15]And I am glad for your sakes I was not there so that you may believe. But let's go to him now."

[16]Then Thomas (the one called Didymus) said to the other followers, "Let us also go so that we can die with him."

JESUS IN BETHANY

[17]When Jesus arrived, he learned that Lazarus had already been dead and in the tomb for four days. [18]Bethany was about two miles from Jerusalem. [19]Many of the Jews had come there to comfort Martha and Mary about their brother.

[20]When Martha heard that Jesus was coming, she went out to meet him, but Mary stayed home. [21]Martha said to Jesus, "Lord, if you had been here, my brother would not have died. [22]But I know that even now God will give you anything you ask."

[23]Jesus said, "Your brother will rise and live again."

[24]Martha answered, "I know that he will rise and live again in the resurrection[n] on the last day."

[25]Jesus said to her, "I am the resurrection and the life. Those who believe in me will have life even if they die. [26]And everyone who lives and believes in me will never die. Martha, do you believe this?"

[27]Martha answered, "Yes, Lord. I believe that you are the Christ, the Son of God, the One coming to the world."

JESUS CRIES

[28]After Martha said this, she went back and talked to her sister Mary alone. Martha said, "The Teacher is here and he is asking for you." [29]When Mary heard this, she got up quickly and went to Jesus. [30]Jesus had not yet come into the town but was still at the place where Martha had met him. [31]The Jews were with Mary in the house, comforting her. When they saw her stand and leave quickly, they followed her, thinking she was going to the tomb to cry there.

[32]But Mary went to the place where Jesus was. When she saw him, she fell at his feet and said, "Lord, if you had been here, my brother would not have died."

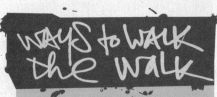

WAYS to WALK the WALK

JOHN 11:11–15

WORD: Pay attention to God's word for you.

WALK IT: It's easy to try to make the Bible or teachings from it conform to preconceived notions. As you read and listen to messages from it, ask God to speak to your heart and to give you the ability to hear and understand.

 10:34 'I . . . gods.' Quotation from Psalm 82:6. **11:24 resurrection** Being raised from the dead to live again.

[33]When Jesus saw Mary crying and the Jews who came with her also crying, he was upset and was deeply troubled. [34]He asked, "Where did you bury him?"

"Come and see, Lord," they said.

[35]Jesus cried.

[36]So the Jews said, "See how much he loved him."

[37]But some of them said, "If Jesus opened the eyes of the blind man, why couldn't he keep Lazarus from dying?"

JESUS RAISES LAZARUS

[38]Again feeling very upset, Jesus came to the tomb. It was a cave with a large stone covering the entrance. [39]Jesus said, "Move the stone away."

Martha, the sister of the dead man, said, "But, Lord, it has been four days since he died. There will be a bad smell."

[40]Then Jesus said to her, "Didn't I tell you that if you believed you would see the glory of God?"

[41]So they moved the stone away from the entrance. Then Jesus looked up and said, "Father, I thank you that you heard me. [42]I know that you always hear me, but I said these things because of the people here around me. I want them to believe that you sent me." [43]After Jesus said this, he cried out in a loud voice, "Lazarus, come out!" [44]The dead man came out, his hands and feet wrapped with pieces of cloth, and a cloth around his face.

Jesus said to them, "Take the cloth off of him and let him go."

THE PLAN TO KILL JESUS

[45]Many of the people, who had come to visit Mary and saw what Jesus did, believed in him. [46]But some of them went to the Pharisees and told them what Jesus had done. [47]Then the leading priests and Pharisees called a meeting of the council. They asked, "What should we do? This man is doing many miracles. [48]If we let him continue doing these things, everyone will believe in him. Then the Romans will come and take away our Temple and our nation."

[49]One of the men there was Caiaphas, the high priest that year. He said, "You people know nothing! [50]You don't realize that it is better for one man to die for the people than for the whole nation to be destroyed."

[51]Caiaphas did not think of this himself. As high priest that year, he was really prophesying that Jesus would die for their nation [52]and for God's scattered children to bring them all together and make them one.

[53]That day they started planning to kill Jesus. [54]So Jesus no longer traveled openly

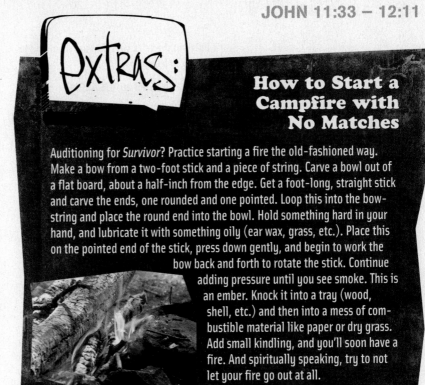

among the people. He left there and went to a place near the desert, to a town called Ephraim and stayed there with his followers.

[55]It was almost time for the Passover Feast. Many from the country went up to Jerusalem before the Passover to do the special things to make themselves pure. [56]The people looked for Jesus and stood in the Temple asking each other, "Is he coming to the Feast? What do you think?" [57]But the leading priests and the Pharisees had given orders that if anyone knew where Jesus was, he must tell them. Then they could arrest him.

her hair. And the sweet smell from the perfume filled the whole house.

[4]Judas Iscariot, one of Jesus' followers who would later turn against him, was there. Judas said, [5]"This perfume was worth an entire year's wages. Why wasn't it sold and the money given to the poor?" [6]But Judas did not really care about the poor; he said this because he was a thief. He was the one who kept the money box, and he often stole from it.

[7]Jesus answered, "Leave her alone. It was right for her to save this perfume for today, the

JESUS WITH FRIENDS IN BETHANY

12 Six days before the Passover Feast, Jesus went to Bethany, where Lazarus lived. (Lazarus is the man Jesus raised from the dead.) [2]There they had a dinner for Jesus. Martha served the food, and Lazarus was one of the people eating with Jesus. [3]Mary brought in a pint of very expensive perfume made from pure nard. She poured the perfume on Jesus' feet, and then she wiped his feet with

day for me to be prepared for burial. [8]You will always have the poor with you, but you will not always have me."

THE PLOT AGAINST LAZARUS

[9]A large crowd of people heard that Jesus was in Bethany. So they went there to see not only Jesus but Lazarus, whom Jesus raised from the dead. [10]So the leading priests made plans to kill Lazarus, too. [11]Because of Lazarus

JOHN 13:4–5

Jesus tackled a job no bigheaded guy would sign up for. In fact, he volunteered for a task that normally fell to the lowest of household servants. The Lord and his closest followers had been trudging along Israel's dry roads. When they arrived in the hidden room where they would eat a Passover feast with Jesus, there was dirty work to do. Someone had to wash off the dust that was caked to the stinking feet of these sweaty guys. No apostle stepped up to this foul task, but Jesus stripped off his outer tunic and wrapped himself in a towel, taking the pose of a slave. Then he turned his act of servanthood into a teachable moment, telling his followers that his humble deed was an example they should all follow (John 13:15). It was his last chance to pound home a lesson he had been teaching them from the start. If they tried to grab greatness, they would be denied. If they lowered themselves to serve each other and their world, they would be raised up. The same goes for you. If you want to be great, start by being a servant to all.

many of the Jews were leaving them and believing in Jesus.

JESUS ENTERS JERUSALEM

[12] The next day a great crowd who had come to Jerusalem for the Passover Feast heard that Jesus was coming there. [13] So they took branches of palm trees and went out to meet Jesus, shouting,

"Praise[n] God!
God bless the One who comes in the name
of the Lord!
God bless the King of Israel!"

Psalm 118:25–26

[14] Jesus found a colt and sat on it. This was as the Scripture says,

[15] "Don't be afraid, people of Jerusalem!
Your king is coming,
sitting on the colt of a donkey."

Zechariah 9:9

[16] The followers of Jesus did not understand this at first. But after Jesus was raised to glory, they remembered that this had been written about him and that they had done these things to him.

PEOPLE TELL ABOUT JESUS

[17] There had been many people with Jesus when he raised Lazarus from the dead and told him to come out of the tomb. Now they were telling others about what Jesus did. [18] Many people went out to meet Jesus, because they had heard about this miracle. [19] So the Pharisees said to each other, "You can see that nothing is going right for us. Look! The whole world is following him."

JESUS TALKS ABOUT HIS DEATH

[20] There were some Greek people, too, who came to Jerusalem to worship at the Passover Feast. [21] They went to Philip, who was from Bethsaida in Galilee, and said, "Sir, we would like to see Jesus." [22] Philip told Andrew, and then Andrew and Philip told Jesus.

[23] Jesus said to them, "The time has come for the Son of Man to receive his glory. [24] I tell you the truth, a grain of wheat must fall to the ground and die to make many seeds. But if it never dies, it remains only a single seed. [25] Those who love their lives will lose them, but those who hate their lives in this world will keep true life forever. [26] Whoever serves me must follow me. Then my servant will be with me everywhere I am. My Father will honor anyone who serves me.

[27] "Now I am very troubled. Should I say, 'Father, save me from this time'? No, I came to this time so I could suffer. [28] Father, bring glory to your name!"

Then a voice came from heaven, "I have brought glory to it, and I will do it again."

[29] The crowd standing there, who heard the voice, said it was thunder.

But others said, "An angel has spoken to him."

[30] Jesus said, "That voice was for your sake, not mine. [31] Now is the time for the world to be judged; now the ruler of this world will be thrown down. [32] If I am lifted up from the earth, I will draw all people toward me." [33] Jesus said this to show how he would die.

[34] The crowd said, "We have heard from the law that the Christ will live forever. So why do you say, 'The Son of Man must be lifted up'? Who is this 'Son of Man'?"

[35] Then Jesus said, "The light will be with you for a little longer, so walk while you have the light. Then the darkness will not catch you. If you walk in the darkness, you will not know where you are going. [36] Believe in the light while you still have it so that you will become children of light." When Jesus had said this, he left and hid himself from them.

SOME PEOPLE WON'T BELIEVE IN JESUS

[37] Though Jesus had done many miracles in front of the people, they still did not believe in him. [38] This was to bring about what Isaiah the prophet had said:

"Lord, who believed what we told them?
Who saw the Lord's power in this?"

Isaiah 53:1

[39] This is why the people could not believe: Isaiah also had said,

[40] "He has blinded their eyes,
and he has closed their minds.
Otherwise they would see with their eyes
and understand in their minds
and come back to me and be healed."

Isaiah 6:10

[41] Isaiah said this because he saw Jesus' glory and spoke about him.

[42] But many believed in Jesus, even many of the leaders. But because of the Pharisees, they did not say they believed in him for fear they would be put out of the synagogue. [43] They loved praise from people more than praise from God.

[44] Then Jesus cried out, "Whoever believes in me is really believing in the One who sent me. [45] Whoever sees me sees the One who sent me. [46] I have come as light into the world so that whoever believes in me would not stay in darkness.

[47] "Anyone who hears my words and does not obey them, I do not judge, because I did

12:13 Praise Literally, "Hosanna," a Hebrew word used at first in praying to God for help, but at this time it was probably a shout of joy used in praising God or his Messiah.

124

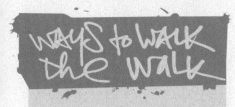

ways to walk the walk

JOHN 13:36-38
WORD: Jesus honors an honest heart.
WALK IT: Be honest with Jesus, just as Peter tried to be. He didn't always think everything through, but he had an earnest heart.

not come to judge the world, but to save the world. ⁴⁸There is a judge for those who refuse to believe in me and do not accept my words. The word I have taught will be their judge on the last day. ⁴⁹The things I taught were not from myself. The Father who sent me told me what to say and what to teach. ⁵⁰And I know that eternal life comes from what the Father commands. So whatever I say is what the Father told me to say."

JESUS WASHES HIS FOLLOWERS' FEET

13 It was almost time for the Passover Feast. Jesus knew that it was time for him to leave this world and go back to the Father. He had always loved those who were his own in the world, and he loved them all the way to the end.

²Jesus and his followers were at the evening meal. The devil had already persuaded Judas Iscariot, the son of Simon, to turn against Jesus. ³Jesus knew that the Father had given him power over everything and that he had come from God and was going back to God. ⁴So during the meal Jesus stood up and took off his outer clothing. Taking a towel, he wrapped it around his waist. ⁵Then he poured water into a bowl and began to wash the followers' feet, drying them with the towel that was wrapped around him.

⁶Jesus came to Simon Peter, who said to him, "Lord, are you going to wash my feet?"

⁷Jesus answered, "You don't understand now what I am doing, but you will understand later."

⁸Peter said, "No, you will never wash my feet."

Jesus answered, "If I don't wash your feet, you are not one of my people."

⁹Simon Peter answered, "Lord, then wash not only my feet, but wash my hands and my head, too!"

¹⁰Jesus said, "After a person has had a bath, his whole body is clean. He needs only to wash his feet. And you men are clean, but not all of you." ¹¹Jesus knew who would turn against him, and that is why he said, "Not all of you are clean."

¹²When he had finished washing their feet, he put on his clothes and sat down again. He asked, "Do you understand what I have just done for you? ¹³You call me 'Teacher' and 'Lord,' and you are right, because that is what I am. ¹⁴If I, your Lord and Teacher, have washed your feet, you also should wash each other's feet. ¹⁵I did this as an example so that you should do as I have done for you. ¹⁶I tell you the truth, a servant is not greater than his master. A messenger is not greater than the one who sent him. ¹⁷If you know these things, you will be blessed if you do them.

¹⁸"I am not talking about all of you. I know those I have chosen. But this is to bring about what the Scripture said: 'The man who ate at my table has turned against me.'ⁿ ¹⁹I am telling you this now before it happens so that when it happens, you will believe that I am he. ²⁰I tell you the truth, whoever accepts anyone I send also accepts me. And whoever accepts me also accepts the One who sent me."

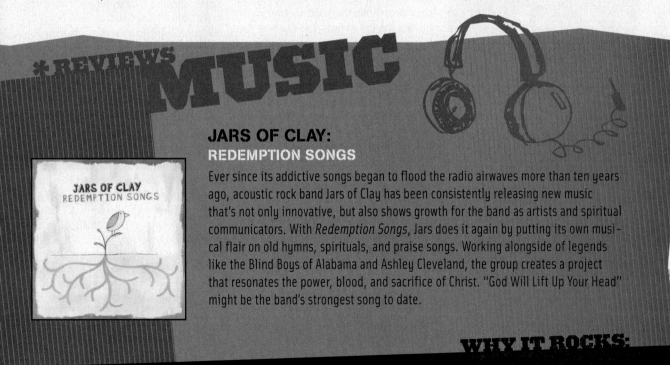

*REVIEWS MUSIC

JARS OF CLAY:
REDEMPTION SONGS

Ever since its addictive songs began to flood the radio airwaves more than ten years ago, acoustic rock band Jars of Clay has been consistently releasing new music that's not only innovative, but also shows growth for the band as artists and spiritual communicators. With *Redemption Songs*, Jars does it again by putting its own musical flair on old hymns, spirituals, and praise songs. Working alongside of legends like the Blind Boys of Alabama and Ashley Cleveland, the group creates a project that resonates the power, blood, and sacrifice of Christ. "God Will Lift Up Your Head" might be the band's strongest song to date.

WHY IT ROCKS:

THE ACOUSTIC VIBE CREATES SWEET WORSHIP MUSIC.

13:18 'The man . . . me.' Quotation from Psalm 41:9.

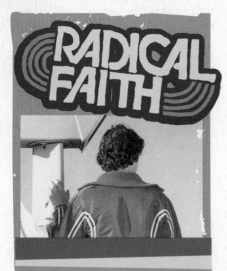

RADICAL FAITH

JOHN 14:1-6

You might have heard that "all roads lead to heaven," that every religion is equally good at helping people meet God and find their way to an eternal home in heaven. You might even wonder if Jesus would go along with that open-minded opinion. But the Lord couldn't disagree more profoundly. Right after he warned his followers that he would soon die (John 13:33), he reassured them that he was going to prepare a place where they could again join him. He would come back and show them the way to heaven, his Father's home. When his bewildered followers wailed that they couldn't understand where he was going or how to get there, Jesus said that he, himself, was "the way, and the truth, and the life." Not only that, but he added that "the only way to the Father is through me." So Jesus didn't claim to be one of many ways to heaven, but the *one* way. He not only knows the path, but he *is* the path. He carved the road to heaven through his own body (Colossians 1:22). If you want to get to heaven, he's your one and only way.

JESUS TALKS ABOUT HIS DEATH

[21]After Jesus said this, he was very troubled. He said openly, "I tell you the truth, one of you will turn against me."

[22]The followers all looked at each other, because they did not know whom Jesus was talking about. [23]One of the followers sitting[n] next to Jesus was the follower Jesus loved. [24]Simon Peter motioned to him to ask Jesus whom he was talking about.

[25]That follower leaned closer to Jesus and asked, "Lord, who is it?"

[26]Jesus answered, "I will dip this bread into the dish. The man I give it to is the man who will turn against me." So Jesus took a piece of bread, dipped it, and gave it to Judas Iscariot, the son of Simon. [27]As soon as Judas took the bread, Satan entered him. Jesus said to him, "The thing that you will do—do it quickly." [28]No one at the table understood why Jesus said this to Judas. [29]Since he was the one who kept the money box, some of the followers thought Jesus was telling him to buy what was needed for the feast or to give something to the poor.

[30]Judas took the bread Jesus gave him and immediately went out. It was night.

[31]When Judas was gone, Jesus said, "Now the Son of Man receives his glory, and God receives glory through him. [32]If God receives glory through him,[n] then God will give glory to the Son through himself. And God will give him glory quickly."

[33]Jesus said, "My children, I will be with you only a little longer. You will look for me, and what I told the Jews, I tell you now: Where I am going you cannot come.

[34]"I give you a new command: Love each other. You must love each other as I have loved you. [35]All people will know that you are my followers if you love each other."

PETER WILL SAY HE DOESN'T KNOW JESUS

[36]Simon Peter asked Jesus, "Lord, where are you going?"

Jesus answered, "Where I am going you cannot follow now, but you will follow later."

[37]Peter asked, "Lord, why can't I follow you now? I am ready to die for you!"

[38]Jesus answered, "Are you ready to die for me? I tell you the truth, before the rooster crows, you will say three times that you don't know me."

JESUS COMFORTS HIS FOLLOWERS

14 Jesus said, "Don't let your hearts be troubled. Trust in God, and trust in me. [2]There are many rooms in my Father's house; I would not tell you this if it were not true. I am going there to prepare a place for you. [3]After I go and prepare a place for you, I will come back and take you to be with me so that you may be where I am. [4]You know the way to the place where I am going."[n]

[5]Thomas said to Jesus, "Lord, we don't know where you are going. So how can we know the way?"

[6]Jesus answered, "I am the way, and the truth, and the life. The only way to the Father is through me. [7]If you really knew me, you would know my Father, too. But now you do know him, and you have seen him."

[8]Philip said to him, "Lord, show us the Father. That is all we need."

[9]Jesus answered, "I have been with you a long time now. Do you still not know me, Philip? Whoever has seen me has seen the Father. So why do you say, 'Show us the Father'? [10]Don't you believe that I am in the Father and the Father is in me? The words I say to you don't come from me, but the Father lives in me and does his own work. [11]Believe me when I say that I am in the Father and the Father is in me. Or believe because of the miracles I have done. [12]I tell you the truth, whoever believes in me will do the same things that I do. Those who believe will do even greater things than these, because I am going to the Father. [13]And if you ask for anything in my name, I will do it for you so that the Father's glory will be shown through the Son. [14]If you ask me for anything in my name, I will do it.

THE PROMISE OF THE HOLY SPIRIT

[15]"If you love me, you will obey my commands. [16]I will ask the Father, and he will give you another Helper[n] to be with you forever— [17]the Spirit of truth. The world cannot accept him, because it does not see him or know him. But you know him, because he lives with you and he will be in you.

[18]"I will not leave you all alone like orphans; I will come back to you. [19]In a little while the world will not see me anymore, but you will see me. Because I live, you will live, too. [20]On that day you will know that I am in my Father, and that you are in me and I am in you. [21]Those who know my commands and obey them are the ones who love me, and my Father will love those who love me. I will love them and will show myself to them."

[22]Then Judas (not Judas Iscariot) said, "But, Lord, why do you plan to show yourself to us and not to the rest of the world?"

23Jesus answered, "If people love me, they will obey my teaching. My Father will love them, and we will come to them and make our home with them. 24Those who do not love me do not obey my teaching. This teaching that you hear is not really mine; it is from my Father, who sent me.

25"I have told you all these things while I am with you. 26But the Helper will teach you everything and will cause you to remember all that I told you. This Helper is the Holy Spirit whom the Father will send in my name.

27"I leave you peace; my peace I give you. I do not give it to you as the world does. So don't let your hearts be troubled or afraid. 28You heard me say to you, 'I am going, but I am coming back to you.' If you loved me, you should be happy that I am going back to the Father, because he is greater than I am. 29I have told you this now, before it happens, so that when it happens, you will believe. 30I will not talk with you much longer, because the ruler of this world is coming. He has no power over me, 31but the world must know that I love the Father, so I do exactly what the Father told me to do.

"Come now, let us go.

JESUS IS LIKE A VINE

15 "I am the true vine; my Father is the gardener. 2He cuts off every branch of mine that does not produce fruit. And he trims and cleans every branch that produces fruit so that it will produce even more fruit. 3You are already clean because of the words I have spoken to you. 4Remain in me, and I will remain in you. A branch cannot produce fruit alone but must remain in the vine. In the same way, you cannot produce fruit alone but must remain in me.

5"I am the vine, and you are the branches. If any remain in me and I remain in them, they produce much fruit. But without me they can do nothing. 6If any do not remain in me, they are like a branch that is thrown away and then dies. People pick up dead branches, throw them into the fire, and burn them. 7If you remain in me and follow my teachings, you can ask anything you want, and it will be given to you. 8You should produce much fruit and show that you are my followers, which brings glory to my Father. 9I loved you as the Father loved me. Now remain in my love. 10I have obeyed my Father's commands, and I remain in his love. In the same way, if you obey my commands, you will remain in my love. 11I have told you these things so that you can have the same joy I have and so that your joy will be the fullest possible joy.

12"This is my command: Love each other as I have loved you. 13The greatest love a person can show is to die for his friends. 14You are my friends if you do what I command you. 15I no longer call you servants, because a servant does not know what his master is doing. But I

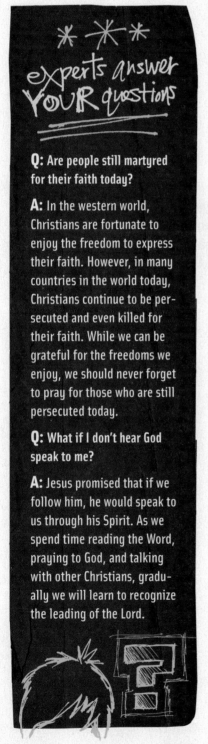

experts answer YOUR questions

Q: Are people still martyred for their faith today?

A: In the western world, Christians are fortunate to enjoy the freedom to express their faith. However, in many countries in the world today, Christians continue to be persecuted and even killed for their faith. While we can be grateful for the freedoms we enjoy, we should never forget to pray for those who are still persecuted today.

Q: What if I don't hear God speak to me?

A: Jesus promised that if we follow him, he would speak to us through his Spirit. As we spend time reading the Word, praying to God, and talking with other Christians, gradually we will learn to recognize the leading of the Lord.

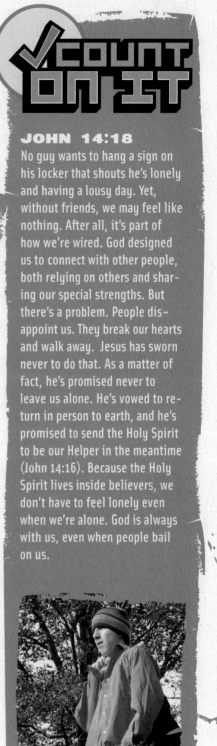

COUNT ON IT

JOHN 14:18

No guy wants to hang a sign on his locker that shouts he's lonely and having a lousy day. Yet, without friends, we may feel like nothing. After all, it's part of how we're wired. God designed us to connect with other people, both relying on others and sharing our special strengths. But there's a problem. People disappoint us. They break our hearts and walk away. Jesus has sworn never to do that. As a matter of fact, he's promised never to leave us alone. He's vowed to return in person to earth, and he's promised to send the Holy Spirit to be our Helper in the meantime (John 14:16). Because the Holy Spirit lives inside believers, we don't have to feel lonely even when we're alone. God is always with us, even when people bail on us.

call you friends, because I have made known to you everything I heard from my Father. 16You did not choose me; I chose you. And I gave you this work: to go and produce fruit, fruit that will last. Then the Father will give

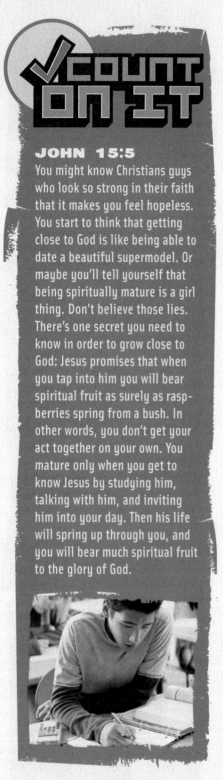

✓ COUNT ON IT

JOHN 15:5

You might know Christians guys who look so strong in their faith that it makes you feel hopeless. You start to think that getting close to God is like being able to date a beautiful supermodel. Or maybe you'll tell yourself that being spiritually mature is a girl thing. Don't believe those lies. There's one secret you need to know in order to grow close to God: Jesus promises that when you tap into him you will bear spiritual fruit as surely as raspberries spring from a bush. In other words, you don't get your act together on your own. You mature only when you get to know Jesus by studying him, talking with him, and inviting him into your day. Then his life will spring up through you, and you will bear much spiritual fruit to the glory of God.

you anything you ask for in my name. [17]This is my command: Love each other.

JESUS WARNS HIS FOLLOWERS

[18]"If the world hates you, remember that it hated me first. [19]If you belonged to the world, it would love you as it loves its own. But I have chosen you out of the world, so you don't belong to it. That is why the world hates you. [20]Remember what I told you: A servant is not greater than his master. If people did wrong to me, they will do wrong to you, too. And if they obeyed my teaching, they will obey yours, too. [21]They will do all this to you on account of me, because they do not know the One who sent me. [22]If I had not come and spoken to them, they would not be guilty of sin, but now they have no excuse for their sin. [23]Whoever hates me also hates my Father. [24]I did works among them that no one else has ever done. If I had not done these works, they would not be guilty of sin. But now they have seen what I have done, and yet they have hated both me and my Father. [25]But this happened so that what is written in their law would be true: 'They hated me for no reason.'[n]

people of the world the truth about sin, about being right with God, and about judgment. [9]He will prove to them that sin is not believing in me. [10]He will prove to them that being right with God comes from my going to the Father and not being seen anymore. [11]And the Helper will prove to them that judgment happened when the ruler of this world was judged.

[12]"I have many more things to say to you, but they are too much for you now. [13]But when the Spirit of truth comes, he will lead you into all truth. He will not speak his own words, but he will speak only what he hears, and he will tell you what is to come. [14]The Spirit of truth will bring glory to me, because he will take what I have to say and tell it to you. [15]All that the Father has is mine. That is why I said that the Spirit will take what I have to say and tell it to you.

[26]"I will send you the Helper[n] from the Father; he is the Spirit of truth who comes from the Father. When he comes, he will tell about me, [27]and you also must tell people about me, because you have been with me from the beginning.

16

"I have told you these things to keep you from giving up. [2]People will put you out of their synagogues. Yes, the time is coming when those who kill you will think they are offering service to God. [3]They will do this because they have not known the Father and they have not known me. [4]I have told you these things now so that when the time comes you will remember that I warned you.

THE WORK OF THE HOLY SPIRIT

"I did not tell you these things at the beginning, because I was with you then. [5]Now I am going back to the One who sent me. But none of you asks me, 'Where are you going?' [6]Your hearts are filled with sadness because I have told you these things. [7]But I tell you the truth, it is better for you that I go away. When I go away, I will send the Helper[n] to you. If I do not go away, the Helper will not come. [8]When the Helper comes, he will prove to the

SADNESS WILL BECOME HAPPINESS

[16]"After a little while you will not see me, and then after a little while you will see me again."

[17]Some of the followers said to each other, "What does Jesus mean when he says, 'After a little while you will not see me, and then after a little while you will see me again'? And what does he mean when he says, 'Because I am going to the Father'?" [18]They also asked, "What does he mean by 'a little while'? We don't understand what he is saying."

[19]Jesus saw that the followers wanted to ask him about this, so he said to them, "Are you asking each other what I meant when I said, 'After a little while you will not see me, and then after a little while you will see me again'? [20]I tell you the truth, you will cry and be sad, but the world will be happy. You will be sad, but your sadness will become joy. [21]When a woman gives birth to a baby, she has pain, because her time has come. But when her baby is born, she forgets the pain, because she is so happy that a child has been born into the world. [22]It is the same with you. Now you are sad, but I will see you again and you will be happy, and no one will take away your joy. [23]In that day you will not ask me for anything. I tell

★ 15:25 'They ... reason.' These words could be from Psalm 35:19 or Psalm 69:4. 15:26; 16:7 Helper "Counselor" or "Comforter." Jesus is talking about the Holy Spirit.

 128

you the truth, my Father will give you anything you ask for in my name. ²⁴Until now you have not asked for anything in my name. Ask and you will receive, so that your joy will be the fullest possible joy.

VICTORY OVER THE WORLD

²⁵"I have told you these things indirectly in stories. But the time will come when I will not use stories like that to tell you things; I will speak to you in plain words about the Father. ²⁶In that day you will ask the Father for things in my name. I mean, I will not need to ask the Father for you. ²⁷The Father himself loves you. He loves you because you loved me and believed that I came from God. ²⁸I came from the Father into the world. Now I am leaving the world and going back to the Father."

²⁹Then the followers of Jesus said, "You are speaking clearly to us now and are not using stories that are hard to understand. ³⁰We can see now that you know all things. You can answer a person's question even before it is asked. This makes us believe you came from God."

³¹Jesus answered, "So now you believe? ³²Listen to me; a time is coming when you will be scattered, each to your own home. That time is now here. You will leave me alone, but I am never really alone, because the Father is with me.

³³"I told you these things so that you can have peace in me. In this world you will have trouble, but be brave! I have defeated the world."

Relationships

"Do not offer the parts of your body to serve sin, as things to be used in doing evil. Instead, offer yourselves to God as people who have died and now live. Offer the parts of your body to God to be used in doing good" (Romans 6:13). As a Christian teenager, you probably get tired of being hammered with the whole "don't have sex" message. You know you shouldn't, but sometimes it's difficult. So, instead of thinking about what you *can't* have, think of what you *can*. Pray and ask God how you can use your body for his purposes instead of your own.

JESUS PRAYS FOR HIS FOLLOWERS

17 After Jesus said these things, he looked toward heaven and prayed, "Father, the time has come. Give glory to your Son so that the Son can give glory to you. ²You gave the Son power over all people so that the Son could give eternal life to all those you gave him. ³And this is eternal life: that people know you, the only true God, and that they know Jesus Christ, the One you sent. ⁴Having finished the work you gave me to do, I brought you glory on earth. ⁵And now, Father, give me glory with you; give me the glory I had with you before the world was made.

⁶"I showed what you are like to those you gave me from the world. They belonged to you, and you gave them to me, and they have

fight the fight

John 15:1-5

Just as you wouldn't dream of trying to bench-press your weight unless you had worked to develop your muscles, neither should you try making it through life without exercising your faith in Christ. In this passage, Jesus compares himself to a vine, his followers to branches, and his Father to a gardener. You will always grapple with complex choices, decisions, and dilemmas. But when you know what the Bible says about various topics, when you enjoy a consistent prayer life, and when you seek advice from spiritual leaders, you will be hooked to the vine. Your life will bear the fruits of peace and security instead of the rotten consequences of bad judgments.

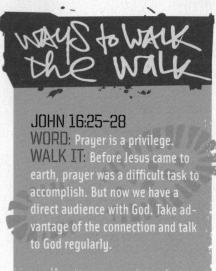

JOHN 16:13

Picture having a personal tutor for the most brain straining class you have ever had at school. Not just any tutor, but the genius who invented the subject and wrote the textbook. Then imagine that tutor installing broadband straight to your brain so that you can download maximum understanding. That's a bit like what the Holy Spirit does for you. Jesus promised that after his departure from earth, the Holy Spirit would arrive in a fresh way to guide and teach believers. He's not just with you. He lives inside everyone who trusts in Jesus (1 Corinthians 3:16). Among his top jobs is to teach you the truth about Jesus, making sure you get the total truth about your Savior. He doesn't invent new thoughts, but he, instead, opens your eyes to Scripture, helping you understand, believe, and obey God's Holy Word. Of course, you can pull the plug on the download by ignoring his instructions. But that would be as insane as skipping study sessions with a tutor who can guarantee you good grades as long as you listen up.

obeyed your teaching. [7]Now they know that everything you gave me comes from you. [8]I gave them the teachings you gave me, and they accepted them. They knew that I truly came from you, and they believed that you sent me. [9]I am praying for them. I am not praying for people in the world but for those you gave me, because they are yours. [10]All I have is yours, and all you have is mine. And my glory is shown through them. [11]I am coming to you; I will not stay in the world any longer. But they are still in the world. Holy Father, keep them safe by the power of your name, the name you gave me, so that they will be one, just as you and I are one. [12]While I was with them, I kept them safe by the power of your name, the name you gave me. I protected them, and only one of them, the one worthy of destruction, was lost so that the Scripture would come true.

[13]"I am coming to you now. But I pray these things while I am still in the world so that these followers can have all of my joy in them. [14]I have given them your teaching. And the world has hated them, because they don't belong to the world, just as I don't belong to the world. [15]I am not asking you to take them out of the world but to keep them safe from the Evil One. [16]They don't belong to the world, just as I don't belong to the world. [17]Make them ready for your service through your truth; your teaching is truth. [18]I have sent them into the world, just as you sent me into the world. [19]For their sake, I am making myself ready to serve so that they can be ready for their service of the truth.

[20]"I pray for these followers, but I am also praying for all those who will believe in me because of their teaching. [21]Father, I pray that they can be one. As you are in me and I am in you, I pray that they can also be one in us. Then the world will believe that you sent me. [22]I have given these people the glory that you gave me so that they can be one, just as you and I are one. [23]I will be in them and you will be in me so that they will be completely one. Then the world will know that you sent me and that you loved them just as much as you loved me.

[24]"Father, I want these people that you gave me to be with me where I am. I want them to see my glory, which you gave me because you loved me before the world was made. [25]Father, you are the One who is good. The world does not know you, but I know you, and these people know you sent me. [26]I showed them what you are like, and I will show them again. Then they will have the

same love that you have for me, and I will live in them."

JESUS IS ARRESTED

18 When Jesus finished praying, he went with his followers across the Kidron Valley. On the other side there was a garden, and Jesus and his followers went into it.

[2]Judas knew where this place was, because Jesus met there often with his followers. Judas was the one who turned against Jesus. [3]So Judas came there with a group of soldiers and some guards from the leading priests and the Pharisees. They were carrying torches, lanterns, and weapons.

[4]Knowing everything that would happen to him, Jesus went out and asked, "Who is it you are looking for?"

[5]They answered, "Jesus from Nazareth."

"I am he," Jesus said. (Judas, the one who turned against Jesus, was standing there with them.) [6]When Jesus said, "I am he," they moved back and fell to the ground.

[7]Jesus asked them again, "Who is it you are looking for?"

They said, "Jesus of Nazareth."

[8]"I told you that I am he," Jesus said. "So if you are looking for me, let the others go." [9]This happened so that the words Jesus said before would come true: "I have not lost any of the ones you gave me."

[10]Simon Peter, who had a sword, pulled it out and struck the servant of the high priest, cutting off his right ear. (The servant's name was Malchus.) [11]Jesus said to Peter, "Put your sword back. Shouldn't I drink the cup[n] the Father gave me?"

18:11 cup Jesus is talking about the painful things that will happen to him. Accepting these things will be very hard, like drinking a cup of something bitter.

JESUS IS BROUGHT BEFORE ANNAS

¹²Then the soldiers with their commander and the guards arrested Jesus. They tied him ¹³and led him first to Annas, the father-in-law of Caiaphas, the high priest that year. ¹⁴Caiaphas was the one who told the Jews that it would be better if one man died for all the people.

PETER SAYS HE DOESN'T KNOW JESUS

¹⁵Simon Peter and another one of Jesus' followers went along after Jesus. This follower knew the high priest, so he went with Jesus into the high priest's courtyard. ¹⁶But Peter waited outside near the door. The follower who knew the high priest came back outside, spoke to the girl at the door, and brought Peter inside. ¹⁷The girl at the door said to Peter, "Aren't you also one of that man's followers?"

Peter answered, "No, I am not!"

¹⁸It was cold, so the servants and guards had built a fire and were standing around it, warming themselves. Peter also was standing with them, warming himself.

THE HIGH PRIEST QUESTIONS JESUS

¹⁹The high priest asked Jesus questions about his followers and his teaching. ²⁰Jesus answered, "I have spoken openly to everyone. I have always taught in synagogues and in the Temple, where all the Jews come together. I never said anything in secret. ²¹So why do you question me? Ask the people who heard my teaching. They know what I said."

²²When Jesus said this, one of the guards standing there hit him. The guard said, "Is that the way you answer the high priest?"

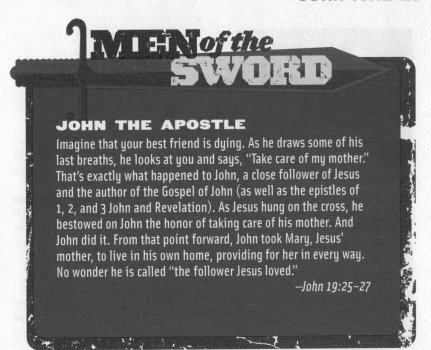

JOHN THE APOSTLE

Imagine that your best friend is dying. As he draws some of his last breaths, he looks at you and says, "Take care of my mother." That's exactly what happened to John, a close follower of Jesus and the author of the Gospel of John (as well as the epistles of 1, 2, and 3 John and Revelation). As Jesus hung on the cross, he bestowed on John the honor of taking care of his mother. And John did it. From that point forward, John took Mary, Jesus' mother, to live in his own home, providing for her in every way. No wonder he is called "the follower Jesus loved."

—John 19:25–27

²³Jesus answered him, "If I said something wrong, then show what it was. But if what I said is true, why do you hit me?"

²⁴Then Annas sent Jesus, who was still tied, to Caiaphas the high priest.

PETER SAYS AGAIN HE DOESN'T KNOW JESUS

²⁵As Simon Peter was standing and warming himself, they said to him, "Aren't you one of that man's followers?"

Peter said it was not true; he said, "No, I am not."

²⁶One of the servants of the high priest was there. This servant was a relative of the man whose ear Peter had cut off. The servant said, "Didn't I see you with him in the garden?"

²⁷Again Peter said it wasn't true. At once a rooster crowed.

JESUS IS BROUGHT BEFORE PILATE

²⁸Early in the morning they led Jesus from Caiaphas's house to the Roman governor's palace. They would not go inside the palace, because they did not want to make themselves unclean;ⁿ they wanted to eat the Passover

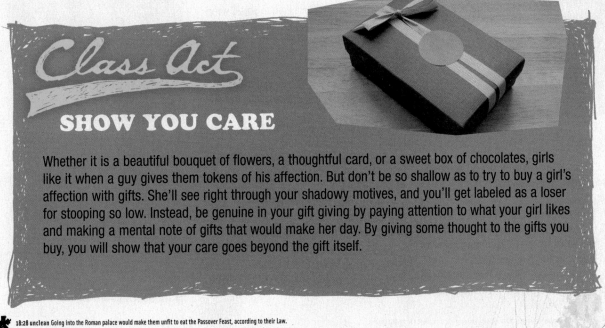

SHOW YOU CARE

Whether it is a beautiful bouquet of flowers, a thoughtful card, or a sweet box of chocolates, girls like it when a guy gives them tokens of his affection. But don't be so shallow as to try to buy a girl's affection with gifts. She'll see right through your shadowy motives, and you'll get labeled as a loser for stooping so low. Instead, be genuine in your gift giving by paying attention to what your girl likes and making a mental note of gifts that would make her day. By giving some thought to the gifts you buy, you will show that your care goes beyond the gift itself.

18:28 unclean Going into the Roman palace would make them unfit to eat the Passover Feast, according to their Law.

experts answer YOUR questions

Q: Does God want me to have only Christian friends?

A: The first Christians believed that only Jews could become Christians. However, God made it clear to the apostle Paul that he wanted his message to be shared with all people. God also wants us to reach out to those who are unlike us and to share his truth with people in need around us.

Q: How can I share my faith with others in a way that won't offend them?

A: Paul gave us a great example in Acts 17:22-31 of how we should share our faith by drawing from the culture around us, not criticizing it. By preaching about the "unknown god" of the Athenians, Paul used their beliefs and culture to share the truth about Jesus.

meal. ²⁹So Pilate went outside to them and asked, "What charges do you bring against this man?"

³⁰They answered, "If he were not a criminal, we wouldn't have brought him to you."

³¹Pilate said to them, "Take him yourselves and judge him by your own law."

"But we are not allowed to put anyone to death," the Jews answered. ³²(This happened so that what Jesus said about how he would die would come true.)

³³Then Pilate went back inside the palace and called Jesus to him and asked, "Are you the king of the Jews?"

³⁴Jesus said, "Is that your own question, or did others tell you about me?"

³⁵Pilate answered, "I am not one of you. It was your own people and their leading priests who handed you over to me. What have you done wrong?"

³⁶Jesus answered, "My kingdom does not belong to this world. If it belonged to this world, my servants would have fought to keep me from being given over to the Jewish leaders. But my kingdom is from another place."

³⁷Pilate said, "So you are a king!"

Jesus answered, "You are the one saying I am a king. This is why I was born and came into the world: to tell people the truth. And everyone who belongs to the truth listens to me."

³⁸Pilate said, "What is truth?" After he said this, he went out to the crowd again and said to them, "I find nothing against this man. ³⁹But it is your custom that I free one prisoner to you at Passover time. Do you want me to free the 'king of the Jews'?"

⁴⁰They shouted back, "No, not him! Let Barabbas go free!" (Barabbas was a robber.)

19 Then Pilate ordered that Jesus be taken away and whipped. ²The soldiers made a crown from some thorny branches and put it on Jesus' head and put a purple robe around him. ³Then they came to him many times and said, "Hail, King of the Jews!" and hit him in the face.

⁴Again Pilate came out and said to them, "Look, I am bringing Jesus out to you. I want you to know that I find nothing against him." ⁵So Jesus came out, wearing the crown of thorns and the purple robe. Pilate said to them, "Here is the man!"

⁶When the leading priests and the guards saw Jesus, they shouted, "Crucify him! Crucify him!"

But Pilate answered, "Crucify him yourselves, because I find nothing against him."

⁷The leaders answered, "We have a law that says he should die, because he said he is the Son of God."

⁸When Pilate heard this, he was even more afraid. ⁹He went back inside the palace and asked Jesus, "Where do you come from?" But Jesus did not answer him. ¹⁰Pilate said, "You refuse to speak to me? Don't you know I have power to set you free and power to have you crucified?"

¹¹Jesus answered, "The only power you have over me is the power given to you by God. The man who turned me in to you is guilty of a greater sin."

¹²After this, Pilate tried to let Jesus go. But some in the crowd cried out, "Anyone who makes himself king is against Caesar. If you let this man go, you are no friend of Caesar."

¹³When Pilate heard what they were saying, he brought Jesus out and sat down on the judge's seat at the place called The Stone Pavement. (In the Hebrew language^n the name is Gabbatha.) ¹⁴It was about noon on Preparation Day of Passover week. Pilate said to the crowd, "Here is your king!"

¹⁵They shouted, "Take him away! Take him away! Crucify him!"

Pilate asked them, "Do you want me to crucify your king?"

The leading priests answered, "The only king we have is Caesar."

¹⁶So Pilate handed Jesus over to them to be crucified.

Do's AND Don'ts

DO make good friends.

DO pray for your friends.

DO respect your friends.

DO give your friends space.

DON'T let friends weigh you down.

DON'T make fun of your friends.

DON'T ignore a friend in need.

DON'T be a phony friend.

19:13 Hebrew language Or Aramaic, the languages of many people in this region in the first century.

JESUS IS CRUCIFIED

The soldiers took charge of Jesus. [17]Carrying his own cross, Jesus went out to a place called The Place of the Skull, which in the Hebrew language[n] is called Golgotha. [18]There they crucified Jesus. They also crucified two other men, one on each side, with Jesus in the middle. [19]Pilate wrote a sign and put it on the cross. It read: JESUS OF NAZARETH, THE KING OF THE JEWS. [20]The sign was written in Hebrew, in Latin, and in Greek. Many of the people read the sign, because the place where Jesus was crucified was near the city. [21]The leading priests said to Pilate, "Don't write, 'The King of the Jews.' But write, 'This man said, "I am the King of the Jews." ' "

[22]Pilate answered, "What I have written, I have written."

[23]After the soldiers crucified Jesus, they took his clothes and divided them into four parts, with each soldier getting one part. They also took his long shirt, which was all one piece of cloth, woven from top to bottom. [24]So the soldiers said to each other, "We should not tear this into parts. Let's throw lots to see who will get it." This happened so that this Scripture would come true:

"They divided my clothes among them,
and they threw lots for my clothing."
Psalm 22:18

So the soldiers did this.

[25]Standing near his cross were Jesus' mother, his mother's sister, Mary the wife of Clopas, and Mary Magdalene. [26]When Jesus saw his mother and the follower he loved standing nearby, he said to his mother, "Dear woman, here is your son." [27]Then he said to the follower, "Here is your mother." From that time on, the follower took her to live in his home.

JESUS DIES

[28]After this, Jesus knew that everything had been done. So that the Scripture would come true, he said, "I am thirsty."[n] [29]There was a jar full of vinegar there, so the soldiers soaked a sponge in it, put the sponge on a branch of a hyssop plant, and lifted it to Jesus' mouth. [30]When Jesus tasted the vinegar, he said, "It is finished." Then he bowed his head and died.

[31]This day was Preparation Day, and the next day was a special Sabbath day. Since the religious leaders did not want the bodies to stay on the cross on the Sabbath day, they asked Pilate to order that the legs of the men be broken[n] and the bodies be taken away. [32]So the soldiers came and broke the legs of the first man on the cross beside Jesus. Then they broke the legs of the man on the other cross beside Jesus. [33]But when the soldiers came to Jesus and saw that he was already dead, they did not break his legs. [34]But one of the soldiers stuck his spear into Jesus' side, and at once blood and water came out. [35](The one who saw this happen is the one who told us this, and whatever he says is true. And he knows that he tells the truth, and he tells it so that you might believe.) [36]These things happened to make the Scripture come true: "Not one of his bones will be broken."[n] [37]And another Scripture says, "They will look at the one they stabbed."[n]

JESUS IS BURIED

[38]Later, Joseph from Arimathea asked Pilate if he could take the body of Jesus. (Joseph was a secret follower of Jesus, because he was afraid of some of the leaders.) Pilate gave his permission, so Joseph came and took Jesus' body away. [39]Nicodemus, who earlier had come to

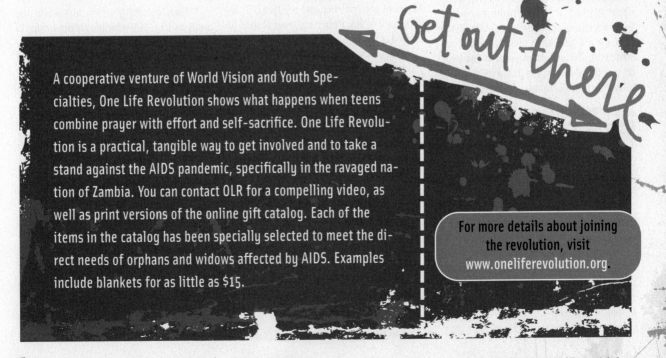

Get out there

A cooperative venture of World Vision and Youth Specialties, One Life Revolution shows what happens when teens combine prayer with effort and self-sacrifice. One Life Revolution is a practical, tangible way to get involved and to take a stand against the AIDS pandemic, specifically in the ravaged nation of Zambia. You can contact OLR for a compelling video, as well as print versions of the online gift catalog. Each of the items in the catalog has been specially selected to meet the direct needs of orphans and widows affected by AIDS. Examples include blankets for as little as $15.

For more details about joining the revolution, visit www.oneliferevolution.org.

19:17 Hebrew language Or Aramaic, the languages of many people in this region in the first century. 19:28 "I am thirsty." Read Psalms 22:15; 69:21. 19:31 broken The breaking of their bones would make them die sooner. 19:36 "Not one . . . broken." Quotation from Psalm 34:20. The idea is from Exodus 12:46; Numbers 9:12. 19:37 "They . . . stabbed." Quotation from Zechariah 12:10.

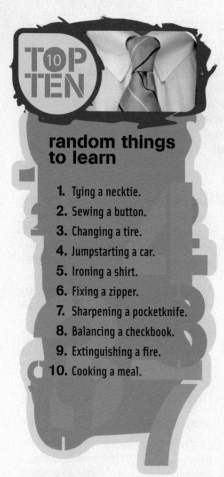

random things to learn

1. Tying a necktie.
2. Sewing a button.
3. Changing a tire.
4. Jumpstarting a car.
5. Ironing a shirt.
6. Fixing a zipper.
7. Sharpening a pocketknife.
8. Balancing a checkbook.
9. Extinguishing a fire.
10. Cooking a meal.

Jesus at night, went with Joseph. He brought about seventy-five pounds of myrrh and aloes. [40]These two men took Jesus' body and wrapped it with the spices in pieces of linen cloth, which is how they bury the dead. [41]In the place where Jesus was crucified, there was a garden. In the garden was a new tomb that had never been used before. [42]The men laid Jesus in that tomb because it was nearby, and they were preparing to start their Sabbath day.

JESUS' TOMB IS EMPTY

20 Early on the first day of the week, Mary Magdalene went to the tomb while it was still dark. When she saw that the large stone had been moved away from the tomb, [2]she ran to Simon Peter and the follower whom Jesus loved. Mary said, "They have taken the Lord out of the tomb, and we don't know where they have put him."

[3]So Peter and the other follower started for the tomb. [4]They were both running, but the other follower ran faster than Peter and reached the tomb first. [5]He bent down and looked in and saw the strips of linen cloth lying there, but he did not go in. [6]Then follow-

ing him, Simon Peter arrived and went into the tomb and saw the strips of linen lying there. [7]He also saw the cloth that had been around Jesus' head, which was folded up and laid in a different place from the strips of linen. [8]Then the other follower, who had reached the tomb first, also went in. He saw and believed. [9](They did not yet understand from the Scriptures that Jesus must rise from the dead.)

JESUS APPEARS TO MARY MAGDALENE

[10]Then the followers went back home. [11]But Mary stood outside the tomb, crying. As she was crying, she bent down and looked inside the tomb. [12]She saw two angels dressed in white, sitting where Jesus' body had been, one at the head and one at the feet.

[13]They asked her, "Woman, why are you crying?"

She answered, "They have taken away my Lord, and I don't know where they have put him." [14]When Mary said this, she turned around and saw Jesus standing there, but she did not know it was Jesus.

[15]Jesus asked her, "Woman, why are you crying? Whom are you looking for?"

Thinking he was the gardener, she said to him, "Did you take him away, sir? Tell me where you put him, and I will get him."

[16]Jesus said to her, "Mary."

Mary turned toward Jesus and said in the Hebrew language,[n] "Rabboni." (This means "Teacher.")

[17]Jesus said to her, "Don't hold on to me, because I have not yet gone up to the Father. But go to my brothers and tell them, 'I am going back to my Father and your Father, to my God and your God.' "

[18]Mary Magdalene went and said to the followers, "I saw the Lord!" And she told them what Jesus had said to her.

JESUS APPEARS TO HIS FOLLOWERS

[19]When it was evening on the first day of the week, Jesus' followers were together. The doors were locked, because they were afraid of

the elders. Then Jesus came and stood right in the middle of them and said, "Peace be with you." [20]After he said this, he showed them his hands and his side. His followers were thrilled when they saw the Lord.

[21]Then Jesus said again, "Peace be with you. As the Father sent me, I now send you." [22]After he said this, he breathed on them and said, "Receive the Holy Spirit. [23]If you forgive anyone his sins, they are forgiven. If you don't forgive them, they are not forgiven."

JESUS APPEARS TO THOMAS

[24]Thomas (called Didymus), who was one of the twelve, was not with them when Jesus came. [25]The other followers kept telling Thomas, "We saw the Lord."

But Thomas said, "I will not believe it until I see the nail marks in his hands and put my finger where the nails were and put my hand into his side."

[26]A week later the followers were in the house again, and Thomas was with them. The doors were locked, but Jesus came in and stood right in the middle of them. He said, "Peace be with you." [27]Then he said to Thomas, "Put your finger here, and look at my hands. Put your hand here in my side. Stop being an unbeliever and believe."

[28]Thomas said to him, "My Lord and my God!"

[29]Then Jesus told him, "You believe because you see me. Those who believe without seeing me will be truly blessed."

WHY JOHN WROTE THIS BOOK

[30]Jesus did many other miracles in the presence of his followers that are not written in this book. [31]But these are written so that you may believe that Jesus is the Christ, the Son of God. Then, by believing, you may have life through his name.

JESUS APPEARS TO SEVEN FOLLOWERS

21 Later, Jesus showed himself to his followers again—this time at Lake

Don't date a girl who you know doesn't follow Jesus. Having a relationship with someone who does not believe as you do will not strengthen your faith. In fact, it will usually bring you down. It is cool to hang out with your non-Christian friends. Just don't fall in love with them.

20:16 Hebrew language Or Aramaic, the languages of many people in this region in the first century.

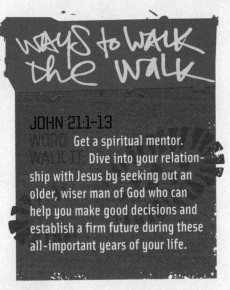

JOHN 21:1-13

WORD
WALK IT Get a spiritual mentor. Dive into your relationship with Jesus by seeking out an older, wiser man of God who can help you make good decisions and establish a firm future during these all-important years of your life.

Galilee.[n] This is how he showed himself: [2]Some of the followers were together: Simon Peter, Thomas (called Didymus), Nathanael from Cana in Galilee, the two sons of Zebedee, and two other followers. [3]Simon Peter said, "I am going out to fish."

The others said, "We will go with you." So they went out and got into the boat. They fished that night but caught nothing.

[4]Early the next morning Jesus stood on the shore, but the followers did not know it was Jesus. [5]Then he said to them, "Friends, did you catch any fish?"

They answered, "No."

[6]He said, "Throw your net on the right side of the boat, and you will find some." So they did, and they caught so many fish they could not pull the net back into the boat.

[7]The follower whom Jesus loved said to Peter, "It is the Lord!" When Peter heard him say this, he wrapped his coat around himself. (Peter had taken his clothes off.) Then he jumped into the water. [8]The other followers went to shore in the boat, dragging the net full of fish. They were not very far from shore, only about a hundred yards. [9]When the followers stepped out of the boat and onto the shore, they saw a fire of hot coals. There were fish on the fire, and there was bread.

[10]Then Jesus said, "Bring some of the fish you just caught."

[11]Simon Peter went into the boat and pulled the net to the shore. It was full of big fish, one hundred fifty-three in all, but even though there were so many, the net did not tear. [12]Jesus said to them, "Come and eat." None of the followers dared ask him, "Who are you?" because they knew it was the Lord.

[13]Jesus came and took the bread and gave it to them, along with the fish.

[14]This was now the third time Jesus showed himself to his followers after he was raised from the dead.

JESUS TALKS TO PETER

[15]When they finished eating, Jesus said to Simon Peter, "Simon son of John, do you love me more than these?"

He answered, "Yes, Lord, you know that I love you."

Jesus said, "Feed my lambs."

[16]Again Jesus said, "Simon son of John, do you love me?"

He answered, "Yes, Lord, you know that I love you."

Jesus said, "Take care of my sheep."

[17]A third time he said, "Simon son of John, do you love me?"

Peter was hurt because Jesus asked him the third time, "Do you love me?" Peter said, "Lord, you know everything; you know that I love you!"

He said to him, "Feed my sheep. [18]I tell you the truth, when you were younger, you tied your own belt and went where you wanted. But when you are old, you will put out your hands and someone else will tie you and take you where you don't want to go." [19](Jesus said this to show how Peter would die to give glory to God.) Then Jesus said to Peter, "Follow me!"

[20]Peter turned and saw that the follower Jesus loved was walking behind them. (This was the follower who had leaned against Jesus at the supper and had said, "Lord, who will turn against you?") [21]When Peter saw him behind them, he asked Jesus, "Lord, what about him?"

[22]Jesus answered, "If I want him to live until I come back, that is not your business. You follow me."

[23]So a story spread among the followers that this one would not die. But Jesus did not say he would not die. He only said, "If I want him to live until I come back, that is not your business."

[24]That follower is the one who is telling these things and who has now written them down. We know that what he says is true.

[25]There are many other things Jesus did. If every one of them were written down, I suppose the whole world would not be big enough for all the books that would be written.

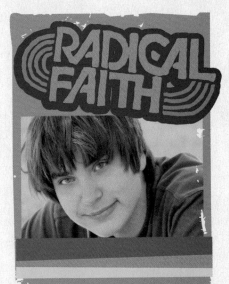

RADICAL FAITH

JOHN 21:15

The apostle Peter gives every guy hope, because he was a flawed man whom Jesus rebuilt into one of the strongest believers ever. Along with James and John, Peter belonged to Jesus' inner circle of friends. When Jesus foretold that he soon would be seized and nailed to a cross, Peter insisted he was ready to suffer and even die for his Lord. But Jesus said that Peter would deny ever knowing him. True to that prediction, this burly fisherman swore three times that he had never hung close to Jesus. He even cowered before the accusations of a young servant girl. Yet, Peter showed instant regret, crying huge tears. After the Resurrection, Jesus gently poked at Peter. The Lord prodded his forlorn friend to repeat three times that he truly loved the Lord. Jesus not only pulled Peter back into tight friendship, but he gave him a lead part in telling the world about him. That's a bright picture for every believer. When you fail Jesus, he can pull you close again. And he can make you stronger than you have ever imagined.

ACTS

THE CHURCH COMES TO LIFE

Coffee bars, praise bands, video clips during the sermon—many churches have left behind the images of stained-glass sanctuaries rumbling with organ notes. Yet, Acts demonstrates how the time-tested methods of love and friendship are the best church growth models ever conceived. This book describes Christ's followers meeting daily for meals, spiritual teaching, and fellowship. They give willingly to help those in need and act so generously toward each other that the world takes notice.

Acts also illustrates a church filled with the Holy Spirit's power. Apostles heal a lame beggar, perform great miracles and wonders, and proclaim Christ as Savior despite intense opposition. One of the most courageous, Stephen, receives great power from God before being stoned to death by an angry mob. The alarming event touches off a wave of persecution; but, instead of ruining the church, it inspires believers and makes them even bolder.

Acts also includes the story of one of history's most powerful conversions. Saul, the persecutor of Christians, becomes Paul, the apostle who writes nearly half of the New Testament. This goes to show that when God gets hold of your life, there is no telling what great things he can do with it.

LUKE WRITES ANOTHER BOOK

1 To Theophilus.

The first book I wrote was about everything Jesus began to do and teach [2]until the day he was taken up into heaven. Before this, with the help of the Holy Spirit, Jesus told the apostles he had chosen what they should do. [3]After his death, he showed himself to them and proved in many ways that he was alive. The apostles saw Jesus during the forty days after he was raised from the dead, and he spoke to them about the kingdom of God. [4]Once when he was eating with them, he told them not to leave Jerusalem. He said, "Wait here to receive the promise from the Father which I told you about. [5]John baptized people with water, but in a few days you will be baptized with the Holy Spirit."

JESUS IS TAKEN UP INTO HEAVEN

[6]When the apostles were all together, they asked Jesus, "Lord, are you now going to give the kingdom back to Israel?"

[7]Jesus said to them, "The Father is the only One who has the authority to decide dates and times. These things are not for you to know. [8]But when the Holy Spirit comes to you, you will receive power. You will be my witnesses—in Jerusalem, in all of Judea, in Samaria, and in every part of the world."

[9]After he said this, as they were watching, he was lifted up, and a cloud hid him from their sight. [10]As he was going, they were looking into the sky. Suddenly, two men wearing white clothes stood beside them. [11]They said, "Men of Galilee, why are you standing here looking into the sky? Jesus, whom you saw taken up from you into heaven, will come back in the same way you saw him go."

A NEW APOSTLE IS CHOSEN

[12]Then they went back to Jerusalem from the Mount of Olives. (This mountain is about half a mile from Jerusalem.) [13]When they entered the city, they went to the upstairs room where they were staying. Peter, John, James, Andrew, Philip, Thomas, Bartholomew, Matthew, James son of Alphaeus, Simon (known as the Zealot), and Judas son of James were there. [14]They all continued praying together with some women, including Mary the mother of Jesus, and Jesus' brothers.

[15]During this time there was a meeting of the believers (about one hundred twenty of them). Peter stood up and said, [16-17]"Brothers and sisters, in the Scriptures the Holy Spirit said through David something that must happen involving Judas. He was one of our own group and served together with us. He led those who arrested Jesus." [18](Judas bought a field with the money he got for his evil act. But he fell to his death, his body burst open, and all his intestines poured out. [19]Everyone in Jerusalem learned about this so they named this place Akeldama. In their language Akeldama means "Field of Blood.") [20]"In the Book of Psalms," Peter said, "this is written:

'May his place be empty;
leave no one to live in it.'   *Psalm 69:25*

And it is also written:

'Let another man replace him as leader.'
                                          Psalm 109:8

[21-22]"So now a man must become a witness with us of Jesus' being raised from the dead. He must be one of the men who were part of our group during all the time the Lord Jesus was among us—from the time John was baptizing people until the day Jesus was taken up from us to heaven."

[23]They put the names of two men before the group. One was Joseph Barsabbas, who was also called Justus. The other was Matthias. [24-25]The apostles prayed, "Lord, you know the thoughts of everyone. Show us which one of these two you have chosen to do this work. Show us who should be an apostle in place of Judas, who turned away and went where he belongs." [26]Then they used lots to choose between them, and the lots showed that Matthias was the one. So he became an apostle with the other eleven.

THE COMING OF THE HOLY SPIRIT

2 When the day of Pentecost came, they were all together in one place. [2]Suddenly a noise like a strong, blowing wind came from heaven and filled the whole house where they were sitting. [3]They saw something like flames of fire that were separated and stood over each person there. [4]They were all filled with the Holy Spirit, and they began to speak different languages[n] by the power the Holy Spirit was giving them.

[5]There were some religious Jews staying in Jerusalem who were from every country in the world. [6]When they heard this noise, a crowd came together. They were all surprised, because each one heard them speaking in his own language. [7]They were completely amazed at this. They said, "Look! Aren't all these people that we hear speaking from Galilee? [8]Then how is it possible that we each hear them in our own languages? We are from different places: [9]Parthia, Media, Elam, Mesopotamia, Judea, Cappadocia, Pontus, Asia, [10]Phrygia, Pamphylia, Egypt, the areas of Libya near Cyrene, Rome [11](both Jews and those who had become Jews), Crete, and Arabia. But we hear them telling in our own languages about the great things God has done!" [12]They were all

✓ COUNT ON IT

ACTS 1:8

After Jesus' closest followers fled during his arrest (Matthew 26:56), they needed a major turnaround to boldly take the Good News about the Resurrection to the world. So Jesus told them to hang out until the power of the Holy Spirit hit them. He predicted they would spread the word first to their hometown of Jerusalem, then to outlying areas, then to the rest of the earth. With the Holy Spirit empowering them, those cowards turned fearless in a hurry. Their preaching added three thousand believers to the church in one day (Acts 2:41). They spoke fearlessly to religious leaders who imprisoned them, and they continued to speak up even when some of their number began to be killed for the faith (Acts 7:60). And here's the amazing part: God will give you the same power to speak up for him if you'll just ask.

How to Get People to See Your Short Film

It's easier to make a short film these days than it's ever been—getting people to watch it is a different story. Start by submitting your film to festivals in your city or state. If you know of someone who teaches film or drama, offer to send him a copy for feedback. If he likes it, he can pass it on to someone, or at least talk it up. Networking is an important part of the movie business. It's all about making connections, so the more people you can meet, the better. Even if your film doesn't get accepted to a fest, go anyway and bring a battery-powered DVD player to show your film at a moment's notice. Your life is also a film (of sorts) about God—one that people are watching. Live it in such a way that you accurately reflect God's character, and you'll get rave reviews.

amazed and confused, asking each other, "What does this mean?"

[13]But others were making fun of them, saying, "They have had too much wine."

PETER SPEAKS TO THE PEOPLE

[14]But Peter stood up with the eleven apostles, and in a loud voice he spoke to the crowd: "My fellow Jews, and all of you who are in Jerusalem, listen to me. Pay attention to what I have to say. [15]These people are not drunk, as you think; it is only nine o'clock in the morning! [16]But Joel the prophet wrote about what is happening here today:

[17]'God says: In the last days
   I will pour out my Spirit on all kinds of
      people.
   Your sons and daughters will prophesy.
   Your young men will see visions,
      and your old men will dream
         dreams.
[18]At that time I will pour out my Spirit

   also on my male slaves and female
      slaves,
   and they will prophesy.
[19]I will show miracles
   in the sky and on the earth:
      blood, fire, and thick smoke.
[20]The sun will become dark,
   the moon red as blood,
   before the overwhelming and glorious
      day of the Lord will come.
[21]Then anyone who calls on the Lord will be
   saved.'   Joel 2:28–32

[22]"People of Israel, listen to these words: Jesus from Nazareth was a very special man. God clearly showed this to you by the miracles, wonders, and signs he did through Jesus. You all know this, because it happened right here among you. [23]Jesus was given to you, and with the help of those who don't know the law, you put him to death by nailing him to a cross. But this was God's plan which he had made long ago; he knew all this would happen. [24]God raised Jesus from the dead and set him free from the pain of death, because death could not hold him. [25]For David said this about him:

'I keep the Lord before me always.
   Because he is close by my side,
      I will not be hurt.
[26]So I am glad, and I rejoice.
   Even my body has hope,
[27]because you will not leave me in the grave.
   You will not let your Holy One rot.
[28]You will teach me how to live a holy life.
   Being with you will fill me with joy.'
                     Psalm 16:8–11

[29]"Brothers and sisters, I can tell you truly that David, our ancestor, died and was buried. His

fight the fight

Some cite this verse to explain the necessity of sending missionaries to all parts of the world. While missionaries are certainly needed, Jesus was saying here that we need to be his witnesses in our city, state, nation, and then overseas, in that order. He also promised we would receive power from the Holy Spirit for this task. However, this doesn't mean that everyone will be a minister. Nor is everyone a public speaker. Nevertheless, each person has some way he can tell others about Jesus. We can be witnesses by showing love toward others in tangible ways, whether by doing chores, giving gifts, or offering a listening ear.

grave is still here with us today. ³⁰He was a prophet and knew God had promised him that he would make a person from David's family a king just as he was.ⁿ ³¹Knowing this before it happened, David talked about the Christ rising from the dead. He said:

'He was not left in the grave.

His body did not rot.'

³²So Jesus is the One whom God raised from the dead. And we are all witnesses to this. ³³Jesus was lifted up to heaven and is now at God's right side. The Father has given the Holy Spirit to Jesus as he promised. So Jesus has poured out that Spirit, and this is what you now see and hear. ³⁴David was not the one who was lifted up to heaven, but he said:

'The Lord said to my Lord,

"Sit by me at my right side,

³⁵ until I put your enemies under your control." 'ⁿ   *Psalm 110:1*

³⁶"So, all the people of Israel should know this truly: God has made Jesus—the man you nailed to the cross—both Lord and Christ."

³⁷When the people heard this, they felt guilty and asked Peter and the other apostles, "What shall we do?"

³⁸Peter said to them, "Change your hearts and lives and be baptized, each one of you, in the name of Jesus Christ for the forgiveness of your sins. And you will receive the gift of the Holy Spirit. ³⁹This promise is for you, for your children, and for all who are far away. It is for everyone the Lord our God calls to himself."

⁴⁰Peter warned them with many other words. He begged them, "Save yourselves from the evil of today's people!" ⁴¹Then those people who accepted what Peter said were baptized. About three thousand people were added to the number of believers that day.

Relationships

"Do your best to live in peace with everyone" (Romans 12:18). This sounds like a tall order, but there's some comfort to be found here. After all, this passage doesn't tell you to absolutely live in total peace with everyone. It just says to "do your best." Isn't that refreshing? Relationships are tough, and you aren't going to get along with everyone, but if you do your best to do just that, you're living up to God's word. Think of someone you're having trouble relating to. If you are doing your best to live at peace with him or her, you are doing all God asks of you.

⁴²They spent their time learning the apostles' teaching, sharing, breaking bread,ⁿ and praying together.

THE BELIEVERS SHARE

⁴³The apostles were doing many miracles and signs, and everyone felt great respect for God. ⁴⁴All the believers were together and shared everything. ⁴⁵They would sell their land and the things they owned and then divide the money and give it to anyone who needed it. ⁴⁶The believers met together in the Temple every day. They ate together in their homes, happy to share their food with joyful hearts. ⁴⁷They praised God and were liked by all the people. Every day the Lord added those who were being saved to the group of believers.

PETER HEALS A CRIPPLED MAN

3 One day Peter and John went to the Temple at three o'clock, the time set each day for the afternoon prayer service. ²There, at the Temple gate called Beautiful Gate, was a man who had been crippled all his life. Every day he was carried to this gate to beg for money from the people going into the Temple. ³The man saw Peter and John going into the Temple and asked them for money. ⁴Peter and John looked straight at him and said, "Look at us!" ⁵The man looked at them, thinking they were going to give him some money. ⁶But Peter said, "I don't have any silver or gold, but I do have something else I can give you. By the power of Jesus Christ from Nazareth, stand up and walk!" ⁷Then Peter took the man's right hand and lifted him up. Immediately the man's feet and ankles became strong. ⁸He jumped up, stood on his feet, and began to walk. He went into the Temple with them, walking and jumping and praising God. ⁹⁻¹⁰All the people recognized him as the crippled man who always sat by the Beautiful Gate begging for money. Now they saw this same man walking and praising God, and they were amazed. They wondered how this could happen.

PETER SPEAKS TO THE PEOPLE

¹¹While the man was holding on to Peter and John, all the people were amazed and ran to them at Solomon's Porch. ¹²When Peter saw this, he said to them, "People of Israel, why are you surprised? You are looking at us as if it were our own power or goodness that made this man walk. ¹³The God of Abraham, Isaac, and Jacob, the God of our ancestors, gave glory to Jesus, his servant. But you handed him over to be killed. Pilate decided to let him go free, but you told Pilate you did not want Jesus. ¹⁴You did not want the One who is holy and good but asked Pilate to give you a murdererⁿ instead. ¹⁵And so you killed the One who gives life, but God raised him from the dead. We are

WAYS to WALK the WALK

ACTS 2:43-47

WORD: Share your stuff with others.

WALK IT: It's practically impossible to share everything in common as Jesus' followers did, but there are things in your life you can share with others. Determine what you'd like to share and watch God bless you.

2:30 God . . . was See 2 Samuel 7:13; Psalm 132:11.   **2:35 until . . . control** Literally, "until I make your enemies a footstool for your feet."   **2:42 breaking bread** This may mean a meal as in verse 46, or the Lord's Supper, the special meal Jesus told his followers to eat to remember him (Luke 22:14–20).   **3:14 murderer** Barabbas, the man the crowd asked Pilate to set free instead of Jesus (Luke 23:18).

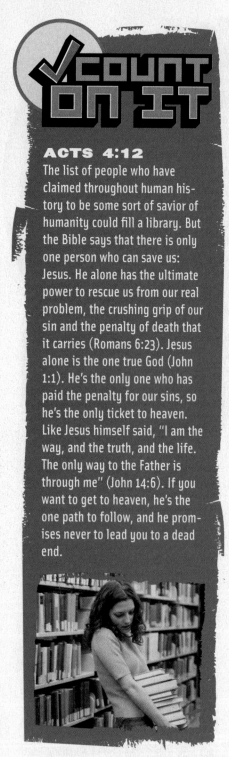

COUNT ON IT

ACTS 4:12

The list of people who have claimed throughout human history to be some sort of savior of humanity could fill a library. But the Bible says that there is only one person who can save us: Jesus. He alone has the ultimate power to rescue us from our real problem, the crushing grip of our sin and the penalty of death that it carries (Romans 6:23). Jesus alone is the one true God (John 1:1). He's the only one who has paid the penalty for our sins, so he's the only ticket to heaven. Like Jesus himself said, "I am the way, and the truth, and the life. The only way to the Father is through me" (John 14:6). If you want to get to heaven, he's the one path to follow, and he promises never to lead you to a dead end.

witnesses to this. [16]It was faith in Jesus that made this crippled man well. You can see this man, and you know him. He was made completely well because of trust in Jesus, and you all saw it happen!

[17]"Brothers and sisters, I know you did those things to Jesus because neither you nor your leaders understood what you were doing. [18]God said through the prophets that his Christ would suffer and die. And now God has made these things come true in this way. [19]So you must change your hearts and lives! Come back to God, and he will forgive your sins. Then the Lord will send the time of rest. [20]And he will send Jesus, the One he chose to be the Christ. [21]But Jesus must stay in heaven until the time comes when all things will be made right again. God told about this time long ago when he spoke through his holy prophets. [22]Moses said, 'The Lord your God will give you a prophet like me, who is one of your own people. You must listen to everything he tells you. [23]Anyone who does not listen to that prophet will die, cut off from God's people.'[n] [24]Samuel, and all the other prophets who spoke for God after Samuel, told about this time now. [25]You are descendants of the prophets. You have received the agreement God made with your ancestors. He said to your father Abraham, 'Through your descendants all the nations on the earth will be blessed.'[n] [26]God has raised up his servant Jesus and sent him to you first to bless you by turning each of you away from doing evil."

PETER AND JOHN AT THE COUNCIL

4 While Peter and John were speaking to the people, priests, the captain of the soldiers that guarded the Temple, and Sadducees came up to them. [2]They were upset because the two apostles were teaching the people and were preaching that people will rise from the dead through the power of Jesus. [3]The older leaders grabbed Peter and John and put them in jail. Since it was already night, they kept them in jail until the next day. [4]But many of those who had heard Peter and John preach believed the things they said. There were now about five thousand in the group of believers.

[5]The next day the rulers, the elders, and the teachers of the law met in Jerusalem. [6]Annas the high priest, Caiaphas, John, and Alexander were there, as well as everyone from the high priest's family. [7]They made Peter and John stand before them and then asked them, "By what power or authority did you do this?"

[8]Then Peter, filled with the Holy Spirit, said to them, "Rulers of the people and you elders, [9]are you questioning us about a good thing that was done to a crippled man? Are you asking us who made him well? [10]We want all of you and all the people to know that this man was made well by the power of Jesus Christ from Nazareth. You crucified him, but God raised him from the dead. This man was crippled, but he is now well and able to stand here before you because of the power of Jesus. [11]Jesus is

'the stone[n] that you builders rejected,
which has become the cornerstone.'
Psalm 118:22

[12]Jesus is the only One who can save people. No one else in the world is able to save us."

[13]The leaders saw that Peter and John were not afraid to speak, and they understood that these men had no special training or education. So they were amazed. Then they realized that Peter and John had been with Jesus. [14]Because they saw the healed man standing there beside the two apostles, they could say nothing against them. [15]After the leaders ordered them to leave the meeting, they began to talk to each other. [16]They said, "What shall we do with these men? Everyone in Jerusalem knows they have done a great miracle, and we cannot say it is not true. [17]But to keep it from spreading among the people, we must warn them not to talk to people anymore using that name."

[18]So they called Peter and John in again and told them not to speak or to teach at all in the name of Jesus. [19]But Peter and John answered them, "You decide what God would want. Should we obey you or God? [20]We cannot keep quiet. We must speak about what we have seen and heard." [21]The leaders warned the apostles again and let them go free. They could not find a way to punish them, because all the people were praising God for what had been done. [22]The man who received the miracle of healing was more than forty years old.

THE BELIEVERS PRAY

[23]After Peter and John left the meeting of leaders, they went to their own group and told them everything the leading priests and the elders had said to them. [24]When the believers heard this, they prayed to God together, "Lord, you are the One who made the sky, the earth, the sea, and everything in them. [25]By the Holy Spirit, through our father David your servant, you said:

'Why are the nations so angry?
Why are the people making useless plans?
[26]The kings of the earth prepare to fight,
and their leaders make plans together against the Lord
and his Christ.'
Psalm 2:1–2

[27]These things really happened when Herod, Pontius Pilate, and some Jews and non-Jews all came together against Jesus here in Jerusalem. Jesus is your holy servant, the One you made to be the Christ. [28]These people made your

3:22–23 'The Lord . . . people.' Quotation from Deuteronomy 18:15, 19.   3:25 'Through . . . blessed.' Quotation from Genesis 22:18; 26:4.   4:11 stone A symbol meaning Jesus.

SCHOOL

SCHOOL MAY SEEM LIKE TORTURE SOMETIMES, BUT IT IS ACTUALLY YOUR TICKET TO A BETTER LIFE. Education helps prepare you for the working world, and if you're smart, high school is just the start. Whether or not you go to college later, the skills you learn in high school will lay the foundation for a lifetime of learning. Playing around now will cost you in the end, but hitting the books pays you rewards for life. Even subjects that you think are useless will help you develop the discipline you will need for living. Do yourself a favor and prepare for your future by studying today. And don't forget to ask God to help you learn.

ACTS 4:19–20

The first time the apostle Peter stood up to preach about Jesus, three thousand people became believers (Acts 2:41). The religious leaders who had opposed and crucified the Lord wanted to stomp out those new followers, the church being born before their eyes. The leaders burned when they heard that Peter and John were claiming that people would rise from the dead through the power of Jesus, so they had the soldiers who guarded the Jewish Temple toss Peter and John in jail (Acts 4:3). When the two apostles got the chance to defend themselves the next day, they told the rulers that they preached Jesus, who alone can save people (Acts 4:12). And when the leaders said they must stop talking about the Lord, Peter and John had just one response: "You decide what God would want. Should we obey you or God?" They wouldn't put human rules before obedience to God, and they couldn't help but talk about their Savior. No matter what some people say, you have a right and a reason to talk about Jesus. Don't ever let your fear of people stop you from sharing Jesus.

plan happen because of your power and your will. ²⁹And now, Lord, listen to their threats. Lord, help us, your servants, to speak your word without fear. ³⁰Show us your power to heal. Give proofs and make miracles happen by the power of Jesus, your holy servant."

³¹After they had prayed, the place where they were meeting was shaken. They were all filled with the Holy Spirit, and they spoke God's word without fear.

THE BELIEVERS SHARE

³²The group of believers were united in their hearts and spirit. All those in the group acted as though their private property belonged to everyone in the group. In fact, they shared everything. ³³With great power the apostles were telling people that the Lord Jesus was truly raised from the dead. And God blessed all the believers very much. ³⁴There were no needy people among them. From time to time those who owned fields or houses sold them, brought the money, ³⁵and gave it to the apostles. Then the money was given to anyone who needed it.

³⁶One of the believers was named Joseph, a Levite born in Cyprus. The apostles called him Barnabas (which means "one who encourages"). ³⁷Joseph owned a field, sold it, brought the money, and gave it to the apostles.

ANANIAS AND SAPPHIRA DIE

5 But a man named Ananias and his wife Sapphira sold some land. ²He kept back part of the money for himself; his wife knew about this and agreed to it. But he brought the rest of the money and gave it to the apostles. ³Peter said, "Ananias, why did you let Satan rule your thoughts to lie to the Holy Spirit and to keep for yourself part of the money you received for the land? ⁴Before you sold the land, it belonged to you. And even after you sold it, you could have used the money any way you wanted. Why did you think of doing this? You lied to God, not to us!" ⁵⁻⁶When Ananias heard this, he fell down and died. Some young men came in, wrapped up his body, carried it out, and buried it. And everyone who heard about this was filled with fear.

⁷About three hours later his wife came in, but she did not know what had happened. ⁸Peter said to her, "Tell me, was the money you got for your field this much?"

Sapphira answered, "Yes, that was the price."

⁹Peter said to her, "Why did you and your husband agree to test the Spirit of the Lord? Look! The men who buried your husband are

at the door, and they will carry you out." ¹⁰At that moment Sapphira fell down by his feet and died. When the young men came in and saw that she was dead, they carried her out and buried her beside her husband. ¹¹The whole church and all the others who heard about these things were filled with fear.

THE APOSTLES HEAL MANY

¹²The apostles did many signs and miracles among the people. And they would all meet together on Solomon's Porch. ¹³None of the others dared to join them, but all the people respected them. ¹⁴More and more men and women believed in the Lord and were added to the group of believers. ¹⁵The people placed their sick on beds and mats in the streets, hoping that when Peter passed by at least his shadow might fall on them. ¹⁶Crowds came from all the towns around Jerusalem, bringing their sick and those who were bothered by evil spirits, and all of them were healed.

LEADERS TRY TO STOP THE APOSTLES

¹⁷The high priest and all his friends (a group called the Sadducees) became very jealous. ¹⁸They took the apostles and put them in jail. ¹⁹But during the night, an angel of the Lord opened the doors of the jail and led the apostles outside. The angel said, ²⁰"Go stand in the Temple and tell the people everything about this new life." ²¹When the apostles heard this, they obeyed and went into the Temple early in the morning and continued teaching.

When the high priest and his friends arrived, they called a meeting of the leaders and all the important elders. They sent some men to the jail to bring the apostles to them. ²²But,

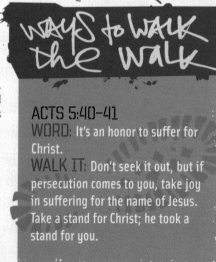

ACTS 5:40–41

WORD: It's an honor to suffer for Christ.
WALK IT: Don't seek it out, but if persecution comes to you, take joy in suffering for the name of Jesus. Take a stand for Christ; he took a stand for you.

may

NATIONAL OLDER AMERICAN MONTH

"God doesn't require us to succeed; he only requires that you try." -MOTHER THERESA

1 It's National Family Week. Spend time with yours.	**2** David Beckham celebrates another birthday.	**3**	**4** 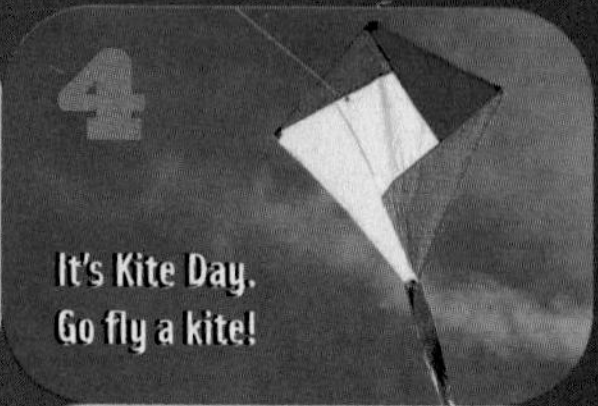 It's Kite Day. Go fly a kite!
5	**6** Volunteer at your local nursing home.	**7** Mother's Day is coming. Do NOT forget.	**8** Collect a family offering to send mom on a retreat.
9	**10** Pray for your boss.	**11** 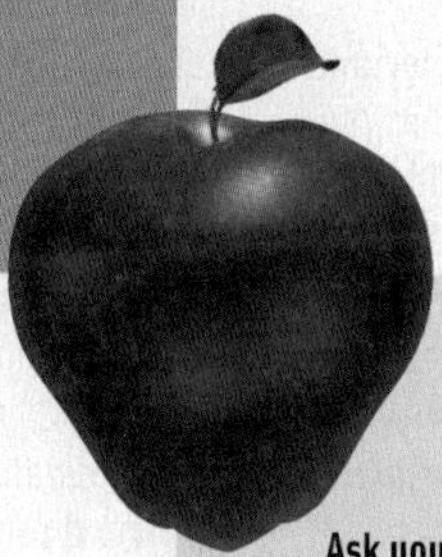	**12** Today is Stephen Baldwin's birthday. Pray for his ministry.
13	**14**	**15** Ask your favorite teacher how you can pray for him.	**16**
17	**18** Today is Michael Tait's birthday. Listen to *Jesus Freak*!	**19**	**20**
21 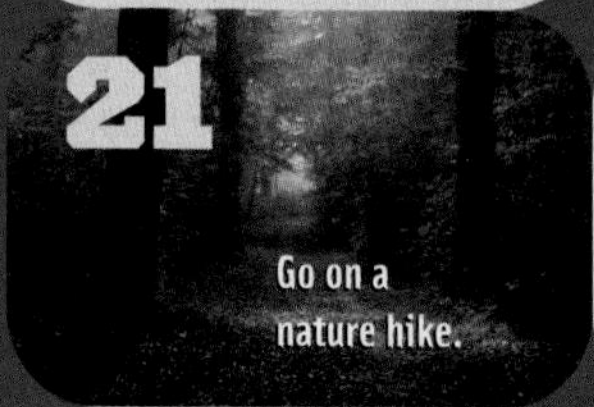 Go on a nature hike.	**22**	**23** Today is Ken Jennings's birthday. Watch "Jeopardy" tonight!	**24**
25 Plan a trip with your friends to the beach.	**26**	**27** Do something nice for a veteran.	**28**
29 Bebo Norman is one year older today.	**30**	**31** 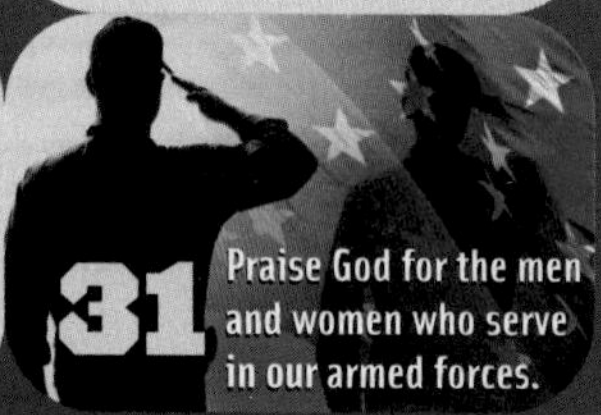 Praise God for the men and women who serve in our armed forces.	

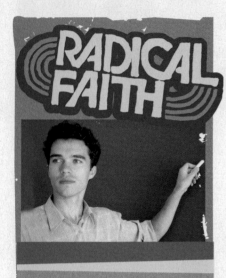

RADICAL FAITH

ACTS 6:1–8

You likely shiver with cold sweats imagining yourself grabbing a pulpit to preach Jesus. Or you might feel guilty when you hear other Christians easily insert smooth ad-libs about Jesus into everyday conversations with nonbelievers. Honestly, those feelings might be rooted in fear of talking boldly about Jesus. That's not so good. But, then again, your queasiness might be a sign that God hasn't given you the gift of talking publicly about him. He might have wired you with another set of skills and filled you with his Holy Spirit to help you accomplish other spiritual tasks. For example, check out this passage for a pattern: the ministers were being distracted with tending to practical needs in the church, such as making sure poor widows had enough to eat. So they appointed other guys with different gifts to oversee these matters. God treats you the same way. He wants you to put your best gifts into action for him. But no matter what you do, be prepared for promotion. Stephen, the leader of the food distribution crew, became a bold preacher and the first believer to die for his faith in Jesus.

upon arriving, the officers could not find the apostles. So they went back and reported to the leaders. 23They said, "The jail was closed and locked, and the guards were standing at the doors. But when we opened the doors, the jail was empty!" 24Hearing this, the captain of the Temple guards and the leading priests were confused and wondered what was happening.

25Then someone came and told them, "Listen! The men you put in jail are standing in the Temple teaching the people." 26Then the captain and his men went out and brought the apostles back. But the soldiers did not use force, because they were afraid the people would stone them to death.

27The soldiers brought the apostles to the meeting and made them stand before the leaders. The high priest questioned them, 28saying, "We gave you strict orders not to continue teaching in that name. But look, you have filled Jerusalem with your teaching and are trying to make us responsible for this man's death."

29Peter and the other apostles answered, "We must obey God, not human authority! 30You killed Jesus by hanging him on a cross. But God, the God of our ancestors, raised Jesus up from the dead! 31Jesus is the One whom God raised to be on his right side, as Leader and Savior. Through him, all people could change their hearts and lives and have their sins forgiven. 32We saw all these things happen. The Holy Spirit, whom God has given to all who obey him, also proves these things are true."

33When the leaders heard this, they became angry and wanted to kill them. 34But a Pharisee named Gamaliel stood up in the meeting. He was a teacher of the law, and all the people respected him. He ordered the apostles to leave the meeting for a little while. 35Then he said, "People of Israel, be careful what you are planning to do to these men. 36Remember when Theudas appeared? He said he was a great man, and about four hundred men joined him. But he was killed, and all his followers were scattered; they were able to do nothing. 37Later, a man named Judas came from Galilee at the time of the registration.ⁿ He also led a group of followers and was killed, and all his followers were scattered. 38And so now I tell you: Stay away from these men, and leave them alone. If their plan comes from human authority, it will fail. 39But if it is from God, you will not be able to stop them. You might even be fighting against God himself!"

The leaders agreed with what Gamaliel said. 40They called the apostles in, beat them, and told them not to speak in the name of Jesus again. Then they let them go free. 41The apostles left the meeting full of joy because they were given the honor of suffering disgrace for Jesus. 42Every day in the Temple and in people's homes they continued teaching the people and telling the Good News—that Jesus is the Christ.

SEVEN LEADERS ARE CHOSEN

6 The number of followers was growing. But during this same time, the Greek-speaking followers had an argument with the other followers. The Greek-speaking widows were not getting their share of the food that was given out every day. 2The twelve apostles called the whole group of followers together and said, "It is not right for us to stop our work of teaching God's word in order to serve tables. 3So, brothers and sisters, choose seven of your own men who are good, full of the Spirit and full of wisdom. We will put them in charge of this work. 4Then we can continue to pray and to teach the word of God."

5The whole group liked the idea, so they chose these seven men: Stephen (a man with great faith and full of the Holy Spirit), Philip,ⁿ Procorus, Nicanor, Timon, Parmenas, and Nicolas (a man from Antioch who had become a follower of the Jewish religion). 6Then they put these men before the apostles, who prayed and laid their handsⁿ on them.

7The word of God was continuing to spread. The group of followers in Jerusalem increased, and a great number of the Jewish priests believed and obeyed.

STEPHEN IS ACCUSED

8Stephen was richly blessed by God who gave him the power to do great miracles and signs among the people. 9But some people were against him. They belonged to the synagogue of Free Menⁿ (as it was called), which included people from Cyrene, Alexandria, Cilicia, and Asia. They all came and argued with Stephen.

10But the Spirit was helping him to speak with wisdom, and his words were so strong that they could not argue with him. 11So they secretly urged some men to say, "We heard Stephen speak against Moses and against God."

12This upset the people, the elders, and the teachers of the law. They came and grabbed Stephen and brought him to a meeting of the leaders. 13They brought in some people to tell lies about Stephen, saying, "This man is always speaking against this holy place and the law of Moses. 14We heard him say that Jesus from Nazareth will destroy this place and that

---

5:37 registration Census. A counting of all the people and the things they own. **6:5 Philip** Not the apostle named Philip. **6:6 laid their hands** The laying on of hands had many purposes, including the giving of a blessing, power, or authority. **6:9 Free Men** Jewish people who had been slaves or whose fathers had been slaves, but were now free.

Jesus will change the customs Moses gave us." [15]All the people in the meeting were watching Stephen closely and saw that his face looked like the face of an angel.

STEPHEN'S SPEECH

7 The high priest said to Stephen, "Are these things true?"

[2]Stephen answered, "Brothers and fathers, listen to me. Our glorious God appeared to Abraham, our ancestor, in Mesopotamia before he lived in Haran. [3]God said to Abraham, 'Leave your country and your relatives, and go to the land I will show you.'[n] [4]So Abraham left the country of Chaldea and went to live in Haran. After Abraham's father died, God sent him to this place where you now live. [5]God did not give Abraham any of this land, not even a foot of it. But God promised that he would give this land to him and his descendants, even before Abraham had a child. [6]This is what God said to him: 'Your descendants will be strangers in a land they don't own. The people there will make them slaves and will mistreat them for four hundred years. [7]But I will punish the nation where they are slaves. Then your descendants will leave that land and will worship me in this place.'[n] [8]God made an agreement with Abraham, the sign of which was circumcision. And so when Abraham had his son

Inactivity can lead to boredom and that often leads to troublemaking. So make sure that if you're going to be alone with your girlfriend, there's a plan to stay out of trouble. Go to the mall together or play video games at a mutual friend's house. Do whatever is necessary to avoid compromising situations.

Isaac, Abraham circumcised him when he was eight days old. Isaac also circumcised his son Jacob, and Jacob did the same for his sons, the twelve ancestors[n] of our people.

[9]"Jacob's sons became jealous of Joseph and sold him to be a slave in Egypt. But God was with him [10]and saved him from all his troubles. The king of Egypt liked Joseph and respected him because of the wisdom God gave him. The king made him governor of Egypt and put him in charge of all the people in his palace.

[11]"Then all the land of Egypt and Canaan became so dry that nothing would grow, and the people suffered very much. Jacob's sons, our ancestors, could not find anything to eat. [12]But when Jacob heard there was grain in Egypt, he sent his sons there. This was their first trip to Egypt. [13]When they went there a second time, Joseph told his brothers who he was, and the king learned about Joseph's family. [14]Then Joseph sent messengers to invite Jacob, his father, to come to Egypt along with all his relatives (seventy-five persons altogether). [15]So Jacob went down to Egypt, where he and his sons died. [16]Later their bodies were moved to Shechem and put in a grave there. (It was the same grave Abraham had bought for a sum of money from the sons of Hamor in Shechem.)

[17]"The promise God made to Abraham was soon to come true, and the number of people in Egypt grew large. [18]Then a new king, who did not know who Joseph was, began to rule Egypt. [19]This king tricked our people and was cruel to our ancestors, forcing them to leave their babies outside to die. [20]At this time Moses was born, and he was very beautiful.

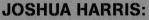

*REVIEWS BOOKS

JOSHUA HARRIS:
STOP DATING THE CHURCH

Joshua Harris wrote a couple of best-selling books about dating titled *I Kissed Dating Goodbye* and *Boy Meets Girl*. But in his latest work, he turns away from talking about dating relationships and instead tackles the subject of commitment to the local church. In *Stop Dating the Church*, Harris challenges Christians to begin taking seriously the relationship they have with the ministries, pastors, and happenings of the church. With so many disillusioned churchgoers in society today, this is a book that truly speaks to a prevalent need of our time. Although some of his answers are simplistic, Harris makes a great case for local church involvement.

WHY IT ROCKS:

THE TRUTH SOMETIMES HURTS BEFORE IT HELPS.

 7:3 'Leave . . . you.' Quotation from Genesis 12:1.   7:6–7 'Your descendants . . . place.' Quotation from Genesis 15:13–14 and Exodus 3:12.   7:8 twelve ancestors Important ancestors of the people of Israel; the leaders of the twelve tribes of Israel.

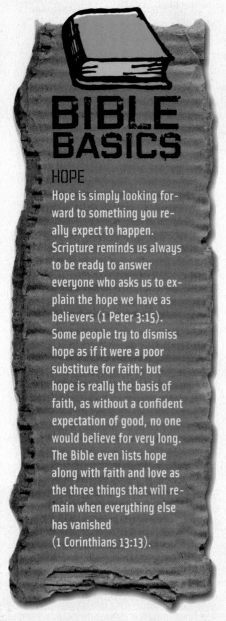

BIBLE BASICS

HOPE

Hope is simply looking forward to something you really expect to happen. Scripture reminds us always to be ready to answer everyone who asks us to explain the hope we have as believers (1 Peter 3:15). Some people try to dismiss hope as if it were a poor substitute for faith; but hope is really the basis of faith, as without a confident expectation of good, no one would believe for very long. The Bible even lists hope along with faith and love as the three things that will remain when everything else has vanished (1 Corinthians 13:13).

For three months Moses was cared for in his father's house. [21]When they put Moses outside, the king's daughter adopted him and raised him as if he were her own son. [22]The Egyptians taught Moses everything they knew, and he was a powerful man in what he said and did.

[23]"When Moses was about forty years old, he thought it would be good to visit his own people, the people of Israel. [24]Moses saw an Egyptian mistreating one of his people, so he defended the Israelite and punished the Egyptian by killing him. [25]Moses thought his own people would understand that God was using him to save them, but they did not. [26]The next day when Moses saw two men of Israel fighting, he tried to make peace between them. He said, 'Men, you are brothers. Why are you hurting each other?' [27]The man who was hurting the other pushed Moses away and said, 'Who made you our ruler and judge? [28]Are you going to kill me as you killed the Egyptian yesterday?'[n] [29]When Moses heard him say this, he left Egypt and went to live in the land of Midian where he was a stranger. While Moses lived in Midian, he had two sons.

[30]"Forty years later an angel appeared to Moses in the flames of a burning bush as he was in the desert near Mount Sinai. [31]When Moses saw this, he was amazed and went near to look closer. Moses heard the Lord's voice say, [32]'I am the God of your ancestors, the God of Abraham, Isaac, and Jacob.'[n] Moses began to shake with fear and was afraid to look. [33]The Lord said to him, 'Take off your sandals, because you are standing on holy ground. [34]I have seen the troubles my people have suffered in Egypt. I have heard their cries and have come down to save them. And now, Moses, I am sending you back to Egypt.'[n]

[35]"This Moses was the same man the two men of Israel rejected, saying, 'Who made you a ruler and judge?'[n] Moses is the same man God sent to be a ruler and savior, with the help of the angel that Moses saw in the burning bush. [36]So Moses led the people out of Egypt. He worked miracles and signs in Egypt, at the Red Sea, and then in the desert for forty years. [37]This is the same Moses that said to the people of Israel, 'God will give you a prophet like me, who is one of your own people.'[n] [38]This is the Moses who was with the gathering of the Israelites in the desert. He was with the angel that spoke to him at Mount Sinai, and he was with our ancestors. He received commands from God that give life, and he gave those commands to us.

[39]"But our ancestors did not want to obey Moses. They rejected him and wanted to go back to Egypt. [40]They said to Aaron, 'Make us gods who will lead us. Moses led us out of Egypt, but we don't know what has happened to him.'[n] [41]So the people made an idol that looked like a calf. Then they brought sacrifices to it and were proud of what they had made with their own hands. [42]But God turned against them and did not try to stop them from worshiping the sun, moon, and stars. This is what is written in the book of the prophets: God says,

'People of Israel, you did not bring me
sacrifices and offerings
while you traveled in the desert for forty
years.
[43]You have carried with you
the tent to worship Molech
and the idols of the star god Rephan that
you made to worship.
So I will send you away beyond Babylon.'

Amos 5:25–27

[44]"The Holy Tent where God spoke to our ancestors was with them in the desert. God told Moses how to make this Tent, and he made it like the plan God showed him. [45]Later, Joshua led our ancestors to capture the lands of the other nations. Our people went in, and God forced the other people out. When our people went into this new land, they took with them this same Tent they had received from their ancestors. They kept it until the time of David, [46]who pleased God and asked God to let him build a house for him, the God of Jacob.[n] [47]But Solomon was the one who built the Temple.

[48]"But the Most High does not live in houses that people build with their hands. As the prophet says:

[49]'Heaven is my throne,
and the earth is my footstool.

Do's AND Don'ts

DO drive defensively.

DO wear your seatbelt.

DO drive the speed limit.

DO pay attention while driving.

DON'T drive recklessly.

DON'T drive the wrong way.

DON'T drive without a license.

DON'T drive while on your cell phone.

So do you think you can build a house for
me? says the Lord.
Do I need a place to rest?
[50]Remember, my hand made all these
things!' " *Isaiah 66:1–2*
[51]Stephen continued speaking: "You stubborn people! You have not given your hearts to God, nor will you listen to him! You are always against what the Holy Spirit is trying to tell you, just as your ancestors were. [52]Your ancestors tried to hurt every prophet who ever lived. Those prophets said long ago that the One who is good would come, but your ancestors killed them. And now you have turned against and killed the One who is good. [53]You received the law of Moses, which God gave you through his angels, but you haven't obeyed it."

STEPHEN IS KILLED

[54]When the leaders heard this, they became furious. They were so mad they were grinding their teeth at Stephen. [55]But Stephen was full of the Holy Spirit. He looked up to heaven and saw the glory of God and Jesus standing at God's right side. [56]He said, "Look! I see heaven open and the Son of Man standing at God's right side."

[57]Then they shouted loudly and covered their ears and all ran at Stephen. [58]They took him out of the city and began to throw stones at him to kill him. And those who told lies against Stephen left their coats with a young man named Saul. [59]While they were throwing stones, Stephen prayed, "Lord Jesus, receive my spirit." [60]He fell on his knees and cried in a loud voice, "Lord, do not hold this sin against them." After Stephen said this, he died.

 Saul agreed that the killing of Stephen was good.

TROUBLES FOR THE BELIEVERS

On that day the church of Jerusalem began to be persecuted, and all the believers, except the apostles, were scattered throughout Judea and Samaria.

[2]And some religious people buried Stephen and cried loudly for him. [3]Saul was also trying to destroy the church, going from house to house, dragging out men and women and putting them in jail. [4]And wherever they were scattered, they told people the Good News.

PHILIP PREACHES IN SAMARIA

[5]Philip went to the city of Samaria and preached about the Christ. [6]When the people there heard Philip and saw the miracles he was doing, they all listened carefully to what he said. [7]Many of these people had evil spirits in them, but Philip made the evil spirits leave. The spirits made a loud noise when they came out. Philip also healed many weak and crippled people there. [8]So the people in that city were very happy.

[9]But there was a man named Simon in that city. Before Philip came there, Simon had practiced magic and amazed all the people of Samaria. He bragged and called himself a great man. [10]All the people—the least important and the most important—paid attention to Simon, saying, "This man has the power of God, called 'the Great Power'!" [11]Simon had amazed them with his magic so long that the people became his followers. [12]But when Philip told them the Good News about the kingdom of God and the power of Jesus Christ, men and women believed Philip and were baptized. [13]Simon himself believed, and after he was baptized, he stayed very close to Philip. When he saw the miracles and the powerful things Philip did, Simon was amazed.

[14]When the apostles who were still in Jerusalem heard that the people of Samaria had accepted the word of God, they sent Peter and John to them. [15]When Peter and John arrived, they prayed that the Samaritan believers might receive the Holy Spirit. [16]These people had been baptized in the name of the Lord Jesus, but the Holy Spirit had not yet come upon any of them. [17]Then, when the two apostles began laying their hands on the people, they received the Holy Spirit.

[18]Simon saw that the Spirit was given to people when the apostles laid their hands on them. So he offered the apostles money, [19]saying, "Give me also this power so that anyone on whom I lay my hands will receive the Holy Spirit."

[20]Peter said to him, "You and your money should both be destroyed, because you thought you could buy God's gift with money. [21]You cannot share with us in this work since your heart is not right before God. [22]Change your heart! Turn away from this evil thing you have done, and pray to the Lord. Maybe he will forgive you for thinking this. [23]I see that you are full of bitter jealousy and ruled by sin."

[24]Simon answered, "Both of you pray for me to the Lord so the things you have said will not happen to me."

[25]After Peter and John told the people what they had seen Jesus do and after they had spoken the message of the Lord, they went back to Jerusalem. On the way, they went through many Samaritan towns and preached the Good News to the people.

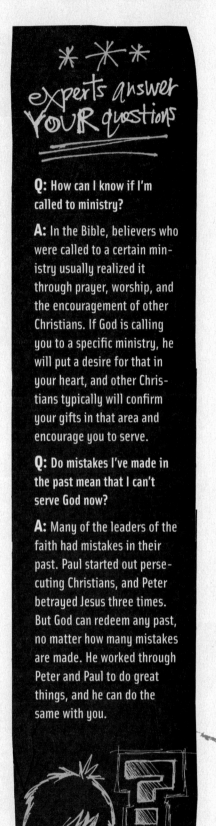

experts answer YOUR questions

Q: How can I know if I'm called to ministry?

A: In the Bible, believers who were called to a certain ministry usually realized it through prayer, worship, and the encouragement of other Christians. If God is calling you to a specific ministry, he will put a desire for that in your heart, and other Christians typically will confirm your gifts in that area and encourage you to serve.

Q: Do mistakes I've made in the past mean that I can't serve God now?

A: Many of the leaders of the faith had mistakes in their past. Paul started out persecuting Christians, and Peter betrayed Jesus three times. But God can redeem any past, no matter how many mistakes are made. He worked through Peter and Paul to do great things, and he can do the same with you.

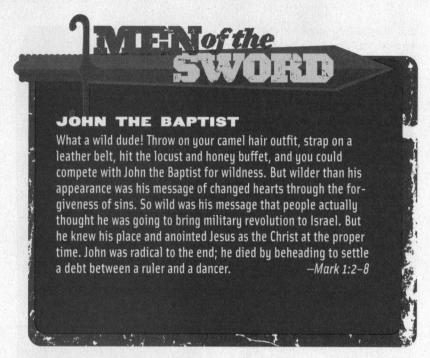

MEN of the SWORD

JOHN THE BAPTIST

What a wild dude! Throw on your camel hair outfit, strap on a leather belt, hit the locust and honey buffet, and you could compete with John the Baptist for wildness. But wilder than his appearance was his message of changed hearts through the forgiveness of sins. So wild was his message that people actually thought he was going to bring military revolution to Israel. But he knew his place and anointed Jesus as the Christ at the proper time. John was radical to the end; he died by beheading to settle a debt between a ruler and a dancer.   —Mark 1:2–8

PHILIP TEACHES AN ETHIOPIAN

26An angel of the Lord said to Philip, "Get ready and go south to the road that leads down to Gaza from Jerusalem—the desert road." 27So Philip got ready and went. On the road he saw a man from Ethiopia, a eunuch. He was an important officer in the service of Candace, the queen of the Ethiopians; he was responsible for taking care of all her money. He had gone to Jerusalem to worship. 28Now, as he was on his way home, he was sitting in his chariot reading from the Book of Isaiah, the prophet. 29The Spirit said to Philip, "Go to that chariot and stay near it."

30So when Philip ran toward the chariot, he heard the man reading from Isaiah the prophet. Philip asked, "Do you understand what you are reading?"

31He answered, "How can I understand unless someone explains it to me?" Then he invited Philip to climb in and sit with him. 32The portion of Scripture he was reading was this:

"He was like a sheep being led to be killed.
   He was quiet, as a lamb is quiet while its
      wool is being cut;
he never opened his mouth.
33   He was shamed and was treated unfairly.
   He died without children to continue his
      family.
   His life on earth has ended."

Isaiah 53:7–8

34The officer said to Philip, "Please tell me, who is the prophet talking about—himself or someone else?" 35Philip began to speak, and starting with this same Scripture, he told the man the Good News about Jesus.

36While they were traveling down the road, they came to some water. The officer said, "Look, here is water. What is stopping me from being baptized?" [37Philip answered, "If you believe with all your heart, you can." The officer said, "I believe that Jesus Christ is the Son of God."]*n* 38Then the officer commanded the chariot to stop. Both Philip and the officer went down into the water, and Philip baptized him. 39When they came up out of the water, the Spirit of the Lord took Philip away; the officer never saw him again. And the officer continued on his way home, full of joy. 40But Philip appeared in a city called Azotus and preached the Good News in all the towns on the way from Azotus to Caesarea.

SAUL IS CONVERTED

9 In Jerusalem Saul was still threatening the followers of the Lord by saying he would kill them. So he went to the high priest 2and asked him to write letters to the synagogues in the city of Damascus. Then if Saul found any followers of Christ's Way, men or women, he would arrest them and bring them back to Jerusalem.

3So Saul headed toward Damascus. As he came near the city, a bright light from heaven suddenly flashed around him. 4Saul fell to the ground and heard a voice saying to him, "Saul, Saul! Why are you persecuting me?"

5Saul said, "Who are you, Lord?"

The voice answered, "I am Jesus, whom you are persecuting. 6Get up now and go into the city. Someone there will tell you what you must do."

7The people traveling with Saul stood there but said nothing. They heard the voice, but they saw no one. 8Saul got up from the ground and opened his eyes, but he could not see. So those with Saul took his hand and led him into Damascus. 9For three days Saul could not see and did not eat or drink.

10There was a follower of Jesus in Damascus named Ananias. The Lord spoke to Ananias in a vision, "Ananias!"

Ananias answered, "Here I am, Lord."

11The Lord said to him, "Get up and go to Straight Street. Find the house of Judas,*n* and ask for a man named Saul from the city of Tarsus. He is there now, praying. 12Saul has seen a vision in which a man named Ananias comes to him and lays his hands on him. Then he is able to see again."

13But Ananias answered, "Lord, many people have told me about this man and the terrible things he did to your holy people in Jerusalem. 14Now he has come here to Damascus, and the leading priests have given him the power to arrest everyone who worships you."

15But the Lord said to Ananias, "Go! I have chosen Saul for an important work. He must tell about me to those who are not Jews, to kings, and to the people of Israel. 16I will show him how much he must suffer for my name."

17So Ananias went to the house of Judas. He laid his hands on Saul and said, "Brother Saul, the Lord Jesus sent me. He is the one you saw on the road on your way here. He sent me so that you can see again and be filled with the Holy Spirit." 18Immediately, something that looked like fish scales fell from Saul's eyes, and

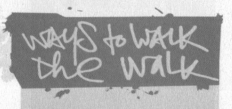

wAYS to WALK the WALK

ACTS 8:26–38

WORD: Change your plans for God.
WALK IT: Be attentive to what the Holy Spirit is telling you. Sometimes you have to put your own plans and tasks on hold to do something for the Lord. Listen for direction, and follow through.

8:37 **Philip . . . God."** Some Greek copies do not contain the bracketed text.   9:11 **Judas** This is not either of the apostles named Judas.

he was able to see again! Then Saul got up and was baptized. ¹⁹After he ate some food, his strength returned.

SAUL PREACHES IN DAMASCUS

Saul stayed with the followers of Jesus in Damascus for a few days. ²⁰Soon he began to preach about Jesus in the synagogues, saying, "Jesus is the Son of God."

²¹All the people who heard him were amazed. They said, "This is the man who was in Jerusalem trying to destroy those who trust in this name! He came here to arrest the followers of Jesus and take them back to the leading priests."

²²But Saul grew more powerful. His proofs that Jesus is the Christ were so strong that his own people in Damascus could not argue with him.

²³After many days, they made plans to kill Saul. ²⁴They were watching the city gates day and night, but Saul learned about their plan. ²⁵One night some followers of Saul helped him leave the city by lowering him in a basket through an opening in the city wall.

SAUL PREACHES IN JERUSALEM

²⁶When Saul went to Jerusalem, he tried to join the group of followers, but they were all afraid of him. They did not believe he was really a follower. ²⁷But Barnabas accepted Saul and took him to the apostles. Barnabas explained to them that Saul had seen the Lord on the road and the Lord had spoken to Saul. Then he told them how boldly Saul had preached in the name of Jesus in Damascus.

²⁸And so Saul stayed with the followers, going everywhere in Jerusalem, preaching boldly in the name of the Lord. ²⁹He would often talk and argue with the Jewish people who spoke Greek, but they were trying to kill him. ³⁰When the followers learned about this, they took Saul to Caesarea and from there sent him to Tarsus.

³¹The church everywhere in Judea, Galilee, and Samaria had a time of peace and became stronger. Respecting the Lord by the way they lived, and being encouraged by the Holy Spirit, the group of believers continued to grow.

PETER HEALS AENEAS

³²As Peter was traveling through all the area, he visited God's people who lived in Lydda. ³³There he met a man named Aeneas, who was paralyzed and had not been able to leave his bed for the past eight years. ³⁴Peter said to him, "Aeneas, Jesus Christ heals you. Stand up and make your bed." Aeneas stood up immediately. ³⁵All the people living in Lydda and on the Plain of Sharon saw him and turned to the Lord.

PETER HEALS TABITHA

³⁶In the city of Joppa there was a follower named Tabitha (whose Greek name was Dorcas). She was always doing good deeds and kind acts. ³⁷While Peter was in Lydda, Tabitha became sick and died. Her body was washed and put in a room upstairs. ³⁸Since Lydda is near Joppa and the followers in Joppa heard that Peter was in Lydda, they sent two messengers to Peter. They begged him, "Hurry, please come to us!" ³⁹So Peter got ready and went with them. When he arrived, they took him to the upstairs room where all the widows stood around Peter, crying. They showed him the shirts and coats Tabitha had made when she was still alive. ⁴⁰Peter sent everyone out of the room and kneeled and prayed. Then he turned to the body and said, "Tabitha, stand up." She opened her eyes, and when she saw Peter, she sat up. ⁴¹He gave her his hand and helped her up. Then he called the saints and the widows into the room and showed them that Tabitha was alive. ⁴²People everywhere in Joppa learned about this, and many believed in the Lord. ⁴³Peter stayed in Joppa for many days with a man named Simon who was a tanner.

PETER TEACHES CORNELIUS

10 At Caesarea there was a man named Cornelius, an officer in the Italian group of the Roman army. ²Cornelius was a religious man. He and all the other people who lived in his house worshiped the true God. He gave much of his money to the poor and prayed to God often. ³One afternoon about three o'clock, Cornelius clearly saw a vision. An angel of God came to him and said, "Cornelius!"

⁴Cornelius stared at the angel. He became afraid and said, "What do you want, Lord?"

The angel said, "God has heard your

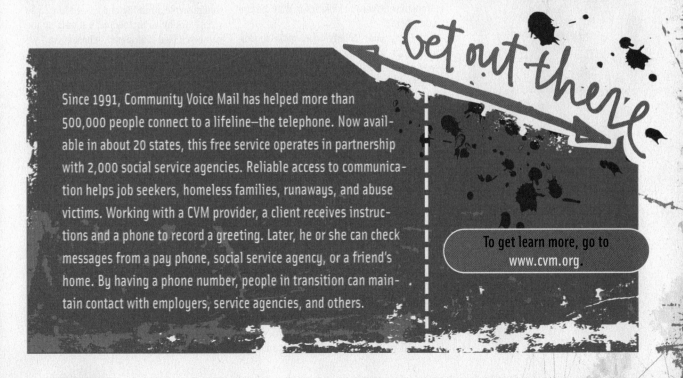

GUARD YOUR HEART

Do yourself a favor and read 1 Corinthians 13 in which Paul spends an entire chapter describing what true love looks like. It'll help you not to treat love lightly. Love is a deep commitment that requires hard work and dedication. It's not simply a feeling; it's an act of surrender that's forever.

prayers. He has seen that you give to the poor, and he remembers you. 5Send some men now to Joppa to bring back a man named Simon who is also called Peter. 6He is staying with a man, also named Simon, who is a tanner and has a house beside the sea." 7When the angel who spoke to Cornelius left, Cornelius called two of his servants and a soldier, a religious man who worked for him. 8Cornelius explained everything to them and sent them to Joppa.

9About noon the next day as they came near Joppa, Peter was going up to the roof[n] to pray. 10He was hungry and wanted to eat, but while the food was being prepared, he had a vision. 11He saw heaven opened and something coming down that looked like a big sheet being lowered to earth by its four corners. 12In it were all kinds of animals, reptiles, and birds. 13Then a voice said to Peter, "Get up, Peter; kill and eat."

14But Peter said, "No, Lord! I have never eaten food that is unholy or unclean."

15But the voice said to him again, "God has made these things clean, so don't call them 'unholy'!" 16This happened three times, and at once the sheet was taken back to heaven.

17While Peter was wondering what this vision meant, the men Cornelius sent had found Simon's house and were standing at the gate. 18They asked, "Is Simon Peter staying here?"

19While Peter was still thinking about the vision, the Spirit said to him, "Listen, three men are looking for you. 20Get up and go downstairs. Go with them without doubting, because I have sent them to you."

21So Peter went down to the men and said, "I am the one you are looking for. Why did you come here?"

22They said, "A holy angel spoke to Cornelius, an army officer and a good man; he worships God. All the people respect him. The angel told Cornelius to ask you to come to his house so that he can hear what you have to say." 23So Peter asked the men to come in and spend the night.

The next day Peter got ready and went with them, and some of the followers from Joppa joined him. 24On the following day they came to Caesarea. Cornelius was waiting for them and had called together his relatives and close friends. 25When Peter entered, Cornelius met him, fell at his feet, and worshiped him. 26But Peter helped him up, saying, "Stand up. I too am only a human." 27As he talked with Cornelius, Peter went inside where he saw many people gathered. 28He said, "You people understand that it is against our law for Jewish people to associate with or visit anyone who is not Jewish. But God has shown me that I should not call any person 'unholy' or 'unclean.'

29That is why I did not argue when I was asked to come here. Now, please tell me why you sent for me."

30Cornelius said, "Four days ago, I was praying in my house at this same time—three o'clock in the afternoon. Suddenly, there was a man standing before me wearing shining clothes. 31He said, 'Cornelius, God has heard your prayer and has seen that you give to the poor and remembers you. 32So send some men to Joppa and ask Simon Peter to come. Peter is staying in the house of a man, also named Simon, who is a tanner and has a house beside the sea.' 33So I sent for you immediately, and it was very good of you to come. Now we are all here before God to hear everything the Lord has commanded you to tell us."

34Peter began to speak: "I really understand now that to God every person is the same. 35In every country God accepts anyone who worships him and does what is right. 36You know the message that God has sent to the people of Israel is the Good News that peace has come through Jesus Christ. Jesus is the Lord of all people! 37You know what has happened all over Judea, beginning in Galilee after John[n] preached to the people about baptism. 38You know about Jesus from Nazareth, that God gave him the Holy Spirit and power. You know how Jesus went everywhere doing good and healing those who were ruled by the devil, because God was with him. 39We saw what Jesus did in Judea and in Jerusalem, but the Jews in Jerusalem killed him by hanging him on a cross. 40Yet, on the third day, God raised Jesus to life and caused him to be seen, 41not by all the people, but only by the witnesses God had already chosen. And we are those witnesses who ate and drank with him after he was raised from the dead. 42He told us to preach to the people and to tell them that he is the one whom God chose to be the judge of the living and the dead. 43All the prophets say it is true that all who believe in Jesus will be forgiven of their sins through Jesus' name."

44While Peter was still saying this, the Holy Spirit came down on all those who were listening. 45The Jewish believers who came with Peter were amazed that the gift of the Holy Spirit had been given even to the nations. 46These believers heard them speaking in different languages[n] and praising God. Then Peter said, 47"Can anyone keep these people from being baptized with water? They have received the Holy Spirit just as we did!" 48So Peter ordered that they be baptized in the name of Jesus Christ. Then they asked Peter to stay with them for a few days.

TOP TEN

random summer vacation plans

1. Lounge by the pool.
2. Work an extra job.
3. Head to the beach.
4. Read a good book.
5. Play games with friends.
6. Start a garage band.
7. Volunteer at a shelter.
8. Hang out with family.
9. Learn a new language.
10. Take a mission trip.

 10:9 roof In Bible times houses were built with flat roofs. The roof was used for drying things such as flax and fruit. And it was used as an extra room, as a place for worship, and as a cool place to sleep in the summer.   **10:37 John** John the Baptist, who preached to people about Christ's coming (Luke 3).   **10:46 languages** This can also be translated "tongues."

ways to WALK the WALK

ACTS 11:23-24

WORD: Encourage others with your words.

WALK IT: Set aside time daily for encouragement. Tell three different people each day something encouraging, whether it's about their appearance, their performance, or their behavior. Encourage people and make their day.

PETER RETURNS TO JERUSALEM

11 The apostles and the believers in Judea heard that some who were not Jewish had accepted God's teaching too. ²But when Peter came to Jerusalem, some people argued with him. ³They said, "You went into the homes of people who are not circumcised and ate with them!"

⁴So Peter explained the whole story to them. ⁵He said, "I was in the city of Joppa, and while I was praying, I had a vision. I saw something that looked like a big sheet being lowered from heaven by its four corners. It came very close to me. ⁶I looked inside it and saw animals, wild beasts, reptiles, and birds. ⁷I heard a voice say to me, 'Get up, Peter. Kill and eat.' ⁸But I said, 'No, Lord! I have never eaten anything that is unholy or unclean.' ⁹But the voice from heaven spoke again, 'God has made these things clean, so don't call them unholy.' ¹⁰This happened three times. Then the whole thing was taken back to heaven. ¹¹Right then three men who were sent to me from Caesarea came to the house where I was staying. ¹²The Spirit told me to go with them without doubting. These six believers here also went with me, and we entered the house of Cornelius. ¹³He told us about the angel he saw standing in his house. The angel said to him, 'Send some men to Joppa and invite Simon Peter to come. ¹⁴By the words he will say to you, you and all your family will be saved.' ¹⁵When I began my speech, the Holy Spirit came on them just as he came on us at the beginning. ¹⁶Then I remembered the words of the Lord. He said, 'John baptized with water, but you will be baptized with the Holy Spirit.' ¹⁷Since God gave them the same gift he gave us who believed in the Lord Jesus Christ, how could I stop the work of God?"

¹⁸When the believers heard this, they stopped arguing. They praised God and said, "So God is allowing even other nations to turn to him and live."

THE GOOD NEWS COMES TO ANTIOCH

¹⁹Many of the believers were scattered when they were persecuted after Stephen was killed. Some of them went as far as Phoenicia, Cyprus, and Antioch telling the message to others, but only to Jews. ²⁰Some of these believers were people from Cyprus and Cyrene. When they came to Antioch, they spoke also to Greeks,ⁿ telling them the Good News about the Lord Jesus. ²¹The Lord was helping the believers, and a large group of people believed and turned to the Lord.

²²The church in Jerusalem heard about all of this, so they sent Barnabas to Antioch. ²³⁻²⁴Barnabas was a good man, full of the Holy Spirit and full of faith. When he reached Antioch and saw how God had blessed the people, he was glad. He encouraged all the believers in Antioch always to obey the Lord with all their hearts, and many people became followers of the Lord.

²⁵Then Barnabas went to the city of Tarsus to look for Saul, ²⁶and when he found Saul, he brought him to Antioch. For a whole year Saul and Barnabas met with the church and taught many people there. In Antioch the followers were called Christians for the first time.

²⁷About that time some prophets came from Jerusalem to Antioch. ²⁸One of them, named Agabus, stood up and spoke with the help of the Holy Spirit. He said, "A very hard time is coming to the whole world. There will be no food to eat." (This happened when Claudius ruled.) ²⁹The followers all decided to help the believers who lived in Judea, as much as each one could. ³⁰They gathered the money and gave it to Barnabas and Saul, who brought it to the elders in Judea.

HEROD AGRIPPA HURTS THE CHURCH

12 During that same time King Herod began to mistreat some who belonged to the church. ²He ordered James, the brother of John, to be killed by the sword. ³Herod saw that some of the people liked this, so he decided to arrest Peter, too. (This happened during the time of the Feast of Unleavened Bread.)

⁴After Herod arrested Peter, he put him in jail and handed him over to be guarded by sixteen soldiers. Herod planned to bring Peter before the people for trial after the Passover Feast. ⁵So Peter was kept in jail, but the church prayed earnestly to God for him.

RADICAL FAITH

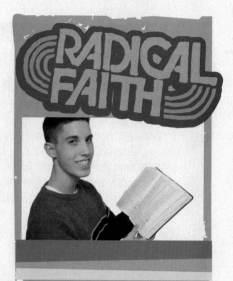

ACTS 11:26

At first, the rapidly expanding group of believers that sprung up after Jesus died and rose from the dead was called "the Way" (Acts 19:9). But soon the believers were being called "Christians" because they worshiped Christ, the Messiah. Though the name was likely first used to mock believers, Jesus' followers took the name gladly. Not many years after Jesus died, the famous Jewish historian Josephus called believers "that tribe of Christians." Roman historian Tacitus referred to them as "Christians, a name derived from Christ." When you call yourself a Christian, you're saying that you have dedicated yourself to Jesus. Your inner attitude and outer behavior should reflect the One whose name you wear. Just like your parents might prod you to live up to your family name, being known to others as a Christian is a hefty responsibility. You share an identity with Christian brothers and sisters who have lived throughout the ages, including many killed for their faith. Most of all, you're called to live up to the royal name of Jesus, who reigns as the ruler over all.

11:20 Greeks Some Greek copies read "Hellenists," non-Greeks who spoke Greek.

Extras:

How to Build Your Own Web Site

Seems like almost everyone has a Web site these days—why not you? Building a Web site can be a fun, rewarding task, but it takes some effort to learn. Start by obtaining a domain name and a hosting company. Find a good one by asking tech-savvy friends whom you trust will give you good information. There are several Web site construction programs and accompanying books that will help you build your site. As for design, surf the Internet with a critical eye, finding sites you like and determining what you like about them. Incorporate those things into your site as you build it, and you'll have a Web site to be proud of. Just keep your eyes open for ideas and consistently practice to get better at your site-building skills. Consistency pays off in your spiritual disciplines, too. Stay consistent with prayer, and keep alert for ways God can use you to build up others.

PETER LEAVES THE JAIL

⁶The night before Herod was to bring him to trial, Peter was sleeping between two soldiers, bound with two chains. Other soldiers were guarding the door of the jail. ⁷Suddenly, an angel of the Lord stood there, and a light shined in the cell. The angel struck Peter on the side and woke him up. "Hurry! Get up!" the angel said. And the chains fell off Peter's hands. ⁸Then the angel told him, "Get dressed and put on your sandals." And Peter did. Then the angel said, "Put on your coat and follow me." ⁹So Peter followed him out, but he did not know if what the angel was doing was real; he thought he might be seeing a vision. ¹⁰They went past the first and second guards and came to the iron gate that separated them from the city. The gate opened by itself for them, and they went through it. When they had walked down one street, the angel suddenly left him.

¹¹Then Peter realized what had happened. He thought, "Now I know that the Lord really sent his angel to me. He rescued me from Herod and from all the things the people thought would happen."

¹²When he considered this, he went to the home of Mary, the mother of John Mark. Many people were gathered there, praying. ¹³Peter knocked on the outside door, and a servant girl named Rhoda came to answer it. ¹⁴When she recognized Peter's voice, she was so happy she forgot to open the door. Instead, she ran inside and told the group, "Peter is at the door!"

¹⁵They said to her, "You are crazy!" But she kept on saying it was true, so they said, "It must be Peter's angel."

¹⁶Peter continued to knock, and when they opened the door, they saw him and were

amazed. [17]Peter made a sign with his hand to tell them to be quiet. He explained how the Lord led him out of the jail, and he said, "Tell James and the other believers what happened." Then he left to go to another place.

[18]The next day the soldiers were very upset and wondered what had happened to Peter. [19]Herod looked everywhere for him but could not find him. So he questioned the guards and ordered that they be killed.

THE DEATH OF HEROD AGRIPPA

Later Herod moved from Judea and went to the city of Caesarea, where he stayed. [20]Herod was very angry with the people of Tyre and Sidon, but the people of those cities all came in a group to him. After convincing Blastus, the king's personal servant, to be on their side, they asked Herod for peace, because their country got its food from his country.

[21]On a chosen day Herod put on his royal robes, sat on his throne, and made a speech to the people. [22]They shouted, "This is the voice of a god, not a human!" [23]Because Herod did not give the glory to God, an angel of the Lord immediately caused him to become sick, and he was eaten by worms and died.

[24]God's message continued to spread and reach people.

[25]After Barnabas and Saul finished their task in Jerusalem, they returned to Antioch, taking John Mark with them.

BARNABAS AND SAUL ARE CHOSEN

13 In the church at Antioch there were these prophets and teachers: Barnabas, Simeon (also called Niger), Lucius (from the city of Cyrene), Manaen (who had grown up with Herod, the ruler), and Saul. [2]They were all worshiping the Lord and fasting[n] for a certain time. During this time the Holy Spirit said to them, "Set apart for me Barnabas and Saul to do a special work for which I have chosen them."

[3]So after they fasted and prayed, they laid their hands on[n] Barnabas and Saul and sent them out.

BARNABAS AND SAUL IN CYPRUS

[4]Barnabas and Saul, sent out by the Holy Spirit, went to the city of Seleucia. From there they sailed to the island of Cyprus. [5]When they came to Salamis, they preached the Good News of God in the synagogues. John Mark was with them to help.

[6]They went across the whole island to Paphos where they met a magician named Bar-Jesus. He was a false prophet [7]who always stayed close to Sergius Paulus, the governor and a smart man. He asked Barnabas and Saul to come to him, because he wanted to hear the message of God. [8]But Elymas, the magician, was against them. (Elymas is the name for Bar-Jesus in the Greek language.) He tried to stop the governor from believing in Jesus. [9]But Saul, who was also called Paul, was filled with the Holy Spirit. He looked straight at Elymas [10]and said, "You son of the devil! You are an enemy of everything that is right! You are full of evil tricks and lies, always trying to change the Lord's truths into lies. [11]Now the Lord will touch you, and you will be blind. For a time you will not be able to see anything—not even the light from the sun."

Then everything became dark for Elymas, and he walked around, trying to find someone to lead him by the hand. [12]When the governor saw this, he believed because he was amazed at the teaching about the Lord.

PAUL AND BARNABAS LEAVE CYPRUS

[13]Paul and those with him sailed from Paphos and came to Perga, in Pamphylia. There John Mark left them to return to Jerusalem. [14]They continued their trip from Perga and went to Antioch, a city in Pisidia. On the Sabbath day they went into the synagogue and sat down. [15]After the law of Moses and the writings of the prophets were read, the leaders of the synagogue sent a message to Paul and Barnabas: "Brothers, if you have any message that will encourage the people, please speak."

[16]Paul stood up, raised his hand, and said, "You Israelites and you who worship God, please listen! [17]The God of the Israelites chose our ancestors. He made the people great during the time they lived in Egypt, and he brought them out of that country with great power. [18]And he was patient with them[n] for forty years in the desert. [19]God destroyed seven nations in the land of Canaan and gave the land to his people. [20]All this happened in about four hundred fifty years.

"After this, God gave them judges until the time of Samuel the prophet. [21]Then the people asked for a king, so God gave them Saul son of Kish. Saul was from the tribe of Benjamin and was king for forty years. [22]After God took him away, God made David their king. God said about him: 'I have found in David son of Jesse the kind of man I want. He will do all I want him to do.' [23]So God has brought Jesus, one of David's descendants, to Israel to be its Savior, as he promised. [24]Before Jesus came, John[n] preached to all the people of Israel about a baptism of changed hearts and lives. [25]When he was finishing his work, he said, 'Who do you

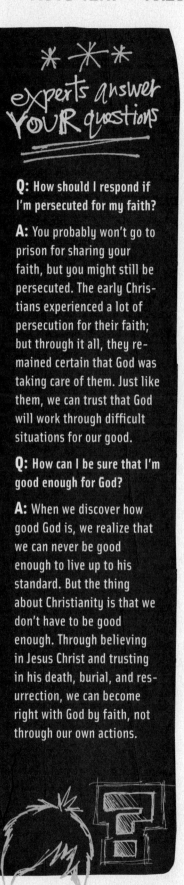

✳ ✳ ✳
experts answer YOUR questions

Q: How should I respond if I'm persecuted for my faith?

A: You probably won't go to prison for sharing your faith, but you might still be persecuted. The early Christians experienced a lot of persecution for their faith; but through it all, they remained certain that God was taking care of them. Just like them, we can trust that God will work through difficult situations for our good.

Q: How can I be sure that I'm good enough for God?

A: When we discover how good God is, we realize that we can never be good enough to live up to his standard. But the thing about Christianity is that we don't have to be good enough. Through believing in Jesus Christ and trusting in his death, burial, and resurrection, we can become right with God by faith, not through our own actions.

 13:2 fasting The people would give up eating for a special time of prayer and worship to God. It was also done sometimes to show sadness and disappointment. **13:3 laid their hands on** The laying on of hands had many purposes, including the giving of a blessing, power, or authority. **13:18 And . . . them** Some Greek copies read "And he cared for them." **13:24 John** John the Baptist, who preached to people about Christ's coming (Luke 3).

Relationships

"So run away from sexual sin. Every other sin people do is outside their bodies, but those who sin sexually sin against their own bodies" (1 Corinthians 6:18). It's a spiritual fact: mess around with sexual sin and you're only messing up yourself. When you commit sin sexually, you're going against God's plan and taking it out on your own body. And think about this: what will your future wife think of your current level of sexual involvement? Take care of her by taking care of yourself sexually. It's one of the best investments you can ever make, and its dividends are more than worth it.

think I am? I am not the Christ. He is coming later, and I am not worthy to untie his sandals.'

[26]"Brothers, sons of the family of Abraham, and others who worship God, listen! The news about this salvation has been sent to us. [27]Those who live in Jerusalem and their leaders did not realize that Jesus was the Savior. They did not understand the words that the prophets wrote, which are read every Sabbath day. But they made them come true when they said Jesus was guilty. [28]They could not find any real reason for Jesus to be put to death, but they asked Pilate to have him killed. [29]When they had done to him all that the Scriptures had said, they took him down from the cross and laid him in a tomb. [30]But God raised him up from the dead! [31]After this, for many days, those who had gone with Jesus from Galilee to Jerusalem saw him. They are now his witnesses to the people. [32]We tell you the Good News about the promise God made to our ancestors. [33]God has made this promise come true for us, his children, by raising Jesus from the dead. We read about this also in Psalm 2:

'You are my Son.
Today I have become your Father.'
Psalm 2:7

[34]God raised Jesus from the dead, and he will never go back to the grave and become dust. So God said:

'I will give you the holy and sure blessings that I promised to David.' *Isaiah 55:3*

[35]But in another place God says:

'You will not let your Holy One rot.'
Psalm 16:10

[36]David did God's will during his lifetime. Then he died and was buried beside his ancestors, and his body did rot in the grave. [37]But the One God raised from the dead did not rot in the grave. [38-39]Brothers, understand what we are telling you: You can have forgiveness of your sins through Jesus. The law of Moses could not free you from your sins. But through Jesus everyone who believes is free from all sins. [40]Be careful! Don't let what the prophets said happen to you:

[41]'Listen, you people who doubt!
You can wonder, and then die.
I will do something in your lifetime
that you won't believe even when
you are told about it!' "
Habakkuk 1:5

[42]While Paul and Barnabas were leaving the synagogue, the people asked them to tell them more about these things on the next Sabbath. [43]When the meeting was over, many people with those who had changed to worship God followed Paul and Barnabas from that place. Paul and Barnabas were persuading them to continue trusting in God's grace.

[44]On the next Sabbath day, almost everyone in the city came to hear the word of the Lord. [45]Seeing the crowd, the Jewish people became very jealous and said insulting things and argued against what Paul said. [46]But Paul and Barnabas spoke very boldly, saying, "We must speak the message of God to you first. But you refuse to listen. You are judging yourselves not worthy of having eternal life! So we will now go to the people of other nations. [47]This is what the Lord told us to do, saying:

'I have made you a light for the nations;
you will show people all over the world
the way to be saved.' "
Isaiah 49:6

[48]When those who were not Jewish heard Paul say this, they were happy and gave honor to the message of the Lord. And the people who were chosen to have life forever believed the message.

[49]So the message of the Lord was spreading through the whole country. [50]But the Jewish people stirred up some of the important religious women and the leaders of the city. They started trouble against Paul and Barnabas and forced them out of their area. [51]So Paul and Barnabas shook the dust off their feet[n] and went to Iconium. [52]But the followers were filled with joy and the Holy Spirit.

PAUL AND BARNABAS IN ICONIUM

14 In Iconium, Paul and Barnabas went as usual to the synagogue. They spoke so well that a great many Jews and Greeks believed. [2]But some people who did not believe excited the others and turned them against the believers. [3]Paul and Barnabas stayed in Iconium a long time and spoke bravely for the Lord. He showed that their message about his grace was true by giving them the power to work miracles and signs. [4]But the city was divided. Some of the people agreed with the Jews, and others believed the apostles.

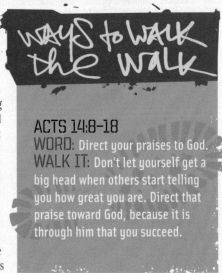

ways to WALK the WALK

ACTS 14:8-18
WORD: Direct your praises to God.
WALK IT: Don't let yourself get a big head when others start telling you how great you are. Direct that praise toward God, because it is through him that you succeed.

13:51 shook . . . feet A warning. It showed that they had rejected these people.

[5]Some who were not Jews, some Jews, and some of their rulers wanted to mistreat Paul and Barnabas and to stone them to death. [6]When Paul and Barnabas learned about this, they ran away to Lystra and Derbe, cities in Lycaonia, and to the areas around those cities. [7]They announced the Good News there, too.

PAUL IN LYSTRA AND DERBE

[8]In Lystra there sat a man who had been born crippled; he had never walked. [9]As this man was listening to Paul speak, Paul looked straight at him and saw that he believed God could heal him. [10]So he cried out, "Stand up on your feet!" The man jumped up and began walking around. [11]When the crowds saw what Paul did, they shouted in the Lycaonian language, "The gods have become like humans and have come down to us!" [12]Then the people began to call Barnabas "Zeus,"[n] and Paul "Hermes,"[n] because he was the main speaker. [13]The priest in the temple of Zeus, which was near the city, brought some bulls and flowers to the city gates. He and the people wanted to offer a sacrifice to Paul and Barnabas. [14]But when the apostles, Barnabas and Paul, heard about it, they tore their clothes. They ran in among the people, shouting, [15]"Friends, why are you doing these things? We are only human beings like you. We are bringing you the Good News and are telling you to turn away from these worthless things and turn to the living God. He is the One who made the sky, the earth, the sea, and everything in them. [16]In the past, God let all the nations do what they wanted. [17]Yet he proved he is real by showing kindness, by giving you rain from heaven and crops at the right times, by giving you food and filling your hearts with joy." [18]Even with these words, they were barely able to keep the crowd from offering sacrifices to them.

[19]Then some evil people came from Antioch and Iconium and persuaded the people to turn against Paul. So they threw stones at him and dragged him out of town, thinking they had killed him. [20]But the followers gathered around him, and he got up and went back into the town. The next day he and Barnabas left and went to the city of Derbe.

THE RETURN TO ANTIOCH IN SYRIA

[21]Paul and Barnabas told the Good News in Derbe, and many became followers. Paul and Barnabas returned to Lystra, Iconium, and Antioch, [22]making the followers of Jesus stronger and helping them stay in the faith. They said, "We must suffer many things to enter God's kingdom." [23]They chose elders for each church, by praying and fasting[n] for a certain time. These elders had trusted the Lord, so Paul and Barnabas put them in the Lord's care.

[24]Then they went through Pisidia and came to Pamphylia. [25]When they had preached the message in Perga, they went down to Attalia. [26]And from there they sailed away to Antioch where the believers had put them into God's care and had sent them out to do this work. Now they had finished.

[27]When they arrived in Antioch, Paul and Barnabas gathered the church together. They told the church all about what God had done with them and how God had made it possible for those who were not Jewish to believe. [28]And they stayed there a long time with the followers.

THE MEETING AT JERUSALEM

15 Then some people came to Antioch from Judea and began teaching the non-Jewish believers: "You cannot be saved if you are not circumcised as Moses taught us." [2]Paul and Barnabas were against this teaching and argued with them about it. So the church decided to send Paul, Barnabas, and some others to Jerusalem where they could talk more about this with the apostles and elders.

[3]The church helped them leave on the trip, and they went through the countries of Phoenicia and Samaria, telling all about how the other nations had turned to God. This made all the believers very happy. [4]When they arrived in Jerusalem, they were welcomed by the apostles, the elders, and the church. Paul,

Barnabas, and the others told about everything God had done with them. [5]But some of the believers who belonged to the Pharisee group came forward and said, "The non-Jewish believers must be circumcised. They must be told to obey the law of Moses."

[6]The apostles and the elders gathered to consider this problem. [7]After a long debate, Peter stood up and said to them, "Brothers, you know that in the early days God chose me from among you to preach the Good News to the nations. They heard the Good News from me, and they believed. [8]God, who knows the thoughts of everyone, accepted them. He showed this to us by giving them the Holy Spirit, just as he did to us. [9]To God, those people are not different from us. When they believed, he made their hearts pure. [10]So now why are you testing God by putting a heavy load around the necks of the non-Jewish believers? It is a load that neither we nor our ancestors were able to carry. [11]But we believe that we and they too will be saved by the grace of the Lord Jesus."

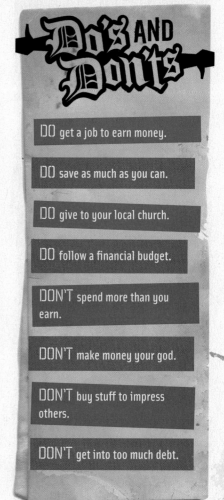

DO get a job to earn money.

DO save as much as you can.

DO give to your local church.

DO follow a financial budget.

DON'T spend more than you earn.

DON'T make money your god.

DON'T buy stuff to impress others.

DON'T get into too much debt.

14:12 "Zeus" The Greeks believed in many false gods, of whom Zeus was most important. **14:12 "Hermes"** The Greeks believed he was a messenger for the other gods. **14:23 fasting** The people would give up eating for a special time of prayer and worship to God. It was also done sometimes to show sadness and disappointment.

ACTS 16:30-31

Here is a guy who asked a straightforward question: "What must I do to be saved?" The jail keeper craved the real route to get right with God, the way to spend eternity in heaven. In direct response, Paul and Silas gave him a straightforward answer: "Believe in the Lord Jesus, and you will be saved." Nothing more was needed than simple trust in God's mighty saving power. The jailer and his entire family immediately trusted Jesus, and they then demonstrated their faith by being baptized. The result of the family believing in God was instant happiness (Acts 16:34). You might not feel that same rush of raging ecstasy when you first trust in God, but you can experience the same assurance of salvation. Believe in Jesus, and you will be saved. It is as simple, and yet as profound, as that.

¹²Then the whole group became quiet. They listened to Paul and Barnabas tell about all the miracles and signs that God did through them among the people. ¹³After they finished speaking, James said, "Brothers, listen to me.

¹⁴Simon has told us how God showed his love for those people. For the first time he is accepting from among them a people to be his own. ¹⁵The words of the prophets agree with this too:

¹⁶'After these things I will return.
    The kingdom of David is like a fallen tent.
But I will rebuild its ruins,
    and I will set it up.
¹⁷Then those people who are left alive may ask the Lord for help,
    and the other nations that belong to me, says the Lord,
    who will make it happen.
¹⁸And these things have been known for a long time.'   *Amos 9:11–12*

¹⁹"So I think we should not bother the other people who are turning to God. ²⁰Instead, we should write a letter to them telling them these things: Stay away from food that has been offered to idols (which makes it unclean), any kind of sexual sin, eating animals that have been strangled, and blood. ²¹They should do these things, because for a long time in every city the law of Moses has been taught. And it is still read in the synagogue every Sabbath day."

LETTER TO NON-JEWISH BELIEVERS

²²The apostles, the elders, and the whole church decided to send some of their men with Paul and Barnabas to Antioch. They chose Judas Barsabbas and Silas, who were respected by the believers. ²³They sent the following letter with them:

From the apostles and elders, your brothers.
To all the non-Jewish believers in Antioch, Syria, and Cilicia:
Greetings!
²⁴We have heard that some of our group have come to you and said things that trouble and upset you. But we did not tell them to do this. ²⁵We have all agreed to choose some messengers and send them to you with our dear friends Barnabas and Paul— ²⁶people who have given their lives to serve our Lord Jesus Christ. ²⁷So we are sending Judas and Silas, who will tell you the same things. ²⁸It has pleased the Holy Spirit that you should not have a heavy load to carry, and we agree. You need to do only these things: ²⁹Stay away from any food that has been offered to idols, eating any animals that have been strangled, and blood, and any kind of sexual sin. If you

stay away from these things, you will do well.
Good-bye.

³⁰So they left Jerusalem and went to Antioch where they gathered the church and gave them the letter. ³¹When they read it, they were very happy because of the encouraging message. ³²Judas and Silas, who were also prophets, said many things to encourage the believers and make them stronger. ³³After some time Judas and Silas were sent off in peace by the believers, and they went back to those who had sent them [, ³⁴but Silas decided to remain there].ⁿ

³⁵But Paul and Barnabas stayed in Antioch and, along with many others, preached the Good News and taught the people the message of the Lord.

PAUL AND BARNABAS SEPARATE

³⁶After some time, Paul said to Barnabas, "We should go back to all those towns where we preached the message of the Lord. Let's visit the believers and see how they are doing." ³⁷Barnabas wanted to take John Mark with them, ³⁸but he had left them at Pamphylia; he did not continue with them in the work. So Paul did not think it was a good idea to take him. ³⁹Paul and Barnabas had such a serious argument about this that they separated and went different ways. Barnabas took Mark and sailed to Cyprus, ⁴⁰but Paul chose Silas and left. The believers in Antioch put Paul into the Lord's care, ⁴¹and he went through Syria and Cilicia, giving strength to the churches.

TIMOTHY GOES WITH PAUL

16 Paul came to Derbe and Lystra, where a follower named Timothy lived. Timothy's mother was Jewish and a believer, but his father was a Greek. ²The believers in Lystra and Iconium respected Timothy and said good things about him. ³Paul wanted Timothy to travel with him, but all the people living in that area knew that Timothy's father was Greek. So Paul circumcised Timothy to please his mother's people. ⁴Paul and those with him traveled from town to town and gave the decisions made by the apostles and elders in Jerusalem for the people to obey. ⁵So the churches became stronger in the faith and grew larger every day.

PAUL IS CALLED OUT OF ASIA

⁶Paul and those with him went through the areas of Phrygia and Galatia since the Holy Spirit did not let them preach the Good News in Asia. ⁷When they came near the

country of Mysia, they tried to go into Bithynia, but the Spirit of Jesus did not let them. [8]So they passed by Mysia and went to Troas. [9]That night Paul saw in a vision a man from Macedonia. The man stood and begged, "Come over to Macedonia and help us." [10]After Paul had seen the vision, we immediately prepared to leave for Macedonia, understanding that God had called us to tell the Good News to those people.

LYDIA BECOMES A CHRISTIAN

[11]We left Troas and sailed straight to the island of Samothrace. The next day we sailed to Neapolis.[n] [12]Then we went by land to Philippi, a Roman colony[n] and the leading city in that part of Macedonia. We stayed there for several days.

> ## Alcohol is linked to two-thirds of all sexual assaults and date rapes of teens, and it greatly increases the likelihood of contracting HIV or sexually transmitted diseases.
> —U.S. Department of Health and Human Services

[13]On the Sabbath day we went outside the city gate to the river where we thought we would find a special place for prayer. Some women had gathered there, so we sat down and talked with them. [14]One of the listeners was a woman named Lydia from the city of Thyatira whose job was selling purple cloth. She worshiped God, and he opened her mind to pay attention to what Paul was saying. [15]She and all the people in her house were baptized. Then she invited us to her home, saying, "If you think I am truly a believer in the Lord, then come stay in my house." And she persuaded us to stay with her.

PAUL AND SILAS IN JAIL

[16]Once, while we were going to the place for prayer, a servant girl met us. She had a special spirit[n] in her, and she earned a lot of money for her owners by telling fortunes. [17]This girl followed Paul and us, shouting, "These men are servants of the Most High God. They are telling you how you can be saved."

[18]She kept this up for many days. This bothered Paul, so he turned and said to the spirit, "By the power of Jesus Christ, I command you to come out of her!" Immediately, the spirit came out.

[19]When the owners of the servant girl saw this, they knew that now they could not use her to make money. So they grabbed Paul and

Silas and dragged them before the city rulers in the marketplace. [20]They brought Paul and Silas to the Roman rulers and said, "These men are Jews and are making trouble in our city. [21]They are teaching things that are not right for us as Romans to do."

[22]The crowd joined the attack against them. The Roman officers tore the clothes of Paul and Silas and had them beaten with rods. [23]Then Paul and Silas were thrown into jail, and the jailer was ordered to guard them carefully. [24]When he heard this order, he put them far inside the jail and pinned their feet down between large blocks of wood.

[25]About midnight Paul and Silas were praying and singing songs to God as the other prisoners listened. [26]Suddenly, there was a strong earthquake that shook the foundation of the jail. Then all the doors of the jail broke open, and all the prisoners were freed from their chains. [27]The jailer woke up and saw that the jail doors were open. Thinking that the prisoners had already escaped, he got his sword and was about to kill himself.[n] [28]But Paul shouted, "Don't hurt yourself! We are all here."

[29]The jailer told someone to bring a light. Then he ran inside and, shaking with fear, fell down before Paul and Silas. [30]He brought them outside and said, "Men, what must I do to be saved?"

[31]They said to him, "Believe in the Lord Jesus and you will be saved—you and all the people in your house." [32]So Paul and Silas told the message of the Lord to the jailer and all the people in his house. [33]At that hour of the night the jailer took Paul and Silas and washed their wounds. Then he and all his people were baptized immediately. [34]After this the jailer took Paul and Silas home and gave them food. He and his family were very happy because they now believed in God.

[35]The next morning, the Roman officers sent the police to tell the jailer, "Let these men go free."

[36]The jailer said to Paul, "The officers have sent an order to let you go free. You can leave now. Go in peace."

[37]But Paul said to the police, "They beat us

Q: Why are Christians called "the sons of Abraham"?

A: Abraham, the ancestor of the Jewish people, is called the father of faith. Although Christians are not physically the descendants of Abraham, we are the heirs of Abraham's faith. Just like Abraham, when we put our faith in God, we receive the gift of God's righteousness, or right standing with God.

Q: What is the Good News?

A: The Good News of the New Testament is that God gave his Son as a sacrifice for our sins. We don't have to make ourselves good enough for God; God chose to love us while we were still sinners. That is incredibly good news!

in public without a trial, even though we are Roman citizens.[n] And they threw us in jail. Now they want to make us go away quietly. No! Let them come themselves and bring us out."

[38]The police told the Roman officers what Paul said. When the officers heard that Paul and Silas were Roman citizens, they were afraid. [39]So they came and told Paul and Silas they were sorry and took them out of jail and asked them to leave the city. [40]So when they came out of the jail, they went to Lydia's house where they saw some of the believers and encouraged them. Then they left.

 16:11 Neapolis City in Macedonia. It was the first city Paul visited on the continent of Europe. **16:12 Roman colony** A town begun by Romans with Roman laws, customs, and privileges. **16:16 spirit** This was a spirit from the devil, which caused her to say she had special knowledge. **16:27 kill himself** He thought the leaders would kill him for letting the prisoners escape. **16:37 Roman citizens** Roman law said that Roman citizens must not be beaten before they had a trial.

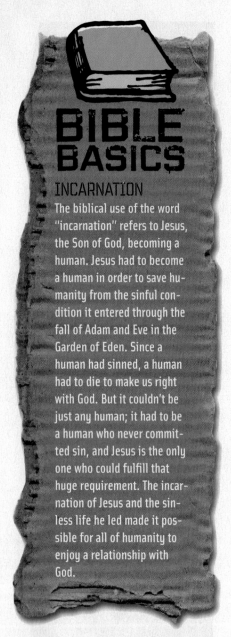

BIBLE BASICS

INCARNATION

The biblical use of the word "incarnation" refers to Jesus, the Son of God, becoming a human. Jesus had to become a human in order to save humanity from the sinful condition it entered through the fall of Adam and Eve in the Garden of Eden. Since a human had sinned, a human had to die to make us right with God. But it couldn't be just any human; it had to be a human who never committed sin, and Jesus is the only one who could fulfill that huge requirement. The incarnation of Jesus and the sinless life he led made it possible for all of humanity to enjoy a relationship with God.

PAUL AND SILAS IN THESSALONICA

17 Paul and Silas traveled through Amphipolis and Apollonia and came to Thessalonica where there was a synagogue. [2]Paul went into the synagogue as he always did, and on each Sabbath day for three weeks, he talked with his fellow Jews about the Scriptures. [3]He explained and proved that the Christ must die and then rise from the dead. He said, "This Jesus I am telling you about is the Christ." [4]Some of them were convinced and joined Paul and Silas, along with many of the Greeks who worshiped God and many of the important women.

[5]But some others became jealous. So they got some evil men from the marketplace, formed a mob, and started a riot. They ran to Jason's house, looking for Paul and Silas, wanting to bring them out to the people. [6]But when they did not find them, they dragged Jason and some other believers to the leaders of the city. The people were yelling, "These people have made trouble everywhere in the world, and now they have come here too! [7]Jason is keeping them in his house. All of them do things against the laws of Caesar, saying there is another king, called Jesus."

[8]When the people and the leaders of the city heard these things, they became very upset. [9]They made Jason and the others put up a sum of money. Then they let the believers go free.

PAUL AND SILAS GO TO BEREA

[10]That same night the believers sent Paul and Silas to Berea where they went to the synagogue. [11]These people were more willing to listen than the people in Thessalonica. The Bereans were eager to hear what Paul and Silas said and studied the Scriptures every day to find out if these things were true. [12]So, many of them believed, as well as many important Greek women and men. [13]But the people in Thessalonica learned that Paul was preaching the word of God in Berea, too. So they came there, upsetting the people and making trouble. [14]The believers quickly sent Paul away to the coast, but Silas and Timothy stayed in Berea. [15]The people leading Paul went with him to Athens. Then they carried a message from Paul back to Silas and Timothy for them to come to him as soon as they could.

PAUL PREACHES IN ATHENS

[16]While Paul was waiting for Silas and Timothy in Athens, he was troubled because he saw that the city was full of idols. [17]In the synagogue, he talked with the Jews and the Greeks who worshiped God. He also talked every day with people in the marketplace. [18]Some of the Epicurean and Stoic philosophers[n] argued with him, saying, "This man doesn't know what he is talking about. What is he trying to say?" Others said, "He seems to be telling us about some other gods," because Paul was telling them about Jesus and his rising from the dead. [19]They got Paul and took him to a meeting of the Areopagus,[n] where they said, "Please explain to us this new idea you have been teaching. [20]The things you are saying are new to us, and we want to know what this teaching means." [21](All the people of Athens and those from other countries who lived there always used their time to talk about the newest ideas.)

[22]Then Paul stood before the meeting of the Areopagus and said, "People of Athens, I can see you are very religious in all things. [23]As I was going through your city, I saw the objects you worship. I found an altar that had these words written on it: TO A GOD WHO IS NOT KNOWN. You worship a god that you don't know, and this is the God I am telling you about! [24]The God who made the whole world and everything in it is the Lord of the land and the sky. He does not live in temples built by human hands. [25]This God is the One who gives life, breath, and everything else to people. He does not need any help from them; he has everything he needs. [26]God began by making one person, and from him came all the different people who live everywhere in the world. God decided exactly when and where they must live. [27]God wanted them to look for him and perhaps search all around for him and find him, though he is not far from any of us: [28]'By his power we live and move and exist.' Some of your own poets have said: 'For we are his children.' [29]Since we are God's children, you must not think that God is like something that people imagine or make from gold, silver, or rock. [30]In the past, people did not understand God, and he ignored this. But now, God tells all people in the world to change their hearts and lives. [31]God has set a day that he will judge all the world with fairness, by the man he chose long ago. And God has proved this to everyone by raising that man from the dead!"

[32]When the people heard about Jesus being raised from the dead, some of them laughed. But others said, "We will hear more about this from you later." [33]So Paul went away from them. [34]But some of the people believed Paul and joined him. Among those who believed

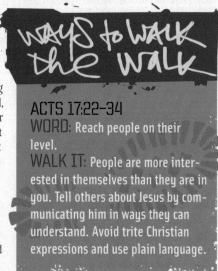

ways to WALK the WALK

ACTS 17:22–34

WORD: Reach people on their level.

WALK IT: People are more interested in themselves than they are in you. Tell others about Jesus by communicating him in ways they can understand. Avoid trite Christian expressions and use plain language.

17:18 **Epicurean and Stoic philosophers** Philosophers were those who searched for truth. Epicureans believed that pleasures, especially pleasures of the mind, were the goal of life. Stoics believed that life should be without feelings of joy or grief.
17:19 **Areopagus** A council or group of important leaders in Athens. They were like judges.

was Dionysius, a member of the Areopagus, a woman named Damaris, and some others.

PAUL IN CORINTH

18 Later Paul left Athens and went to Corinth. [2]Here he met a Jew named Aquila who had been born in the country of Pontus. But Aquila and his wife, Priscilla, had recently moved to Corinth from Italy, because Claudius[n] commanded that all Jews must leave Rome. Paul went to visit Aquila and Priscilla. [3]Because they were tentmakers, just as he was, he stayed with them and worked with them. [4]Every Sabbath day he talked with the Jews and Greeks in the synagogue, trying to persuade them to believe in Jesus.

[5]Silas and Timothy came from Macedonia and joined Paul in Corinth. After this, Paul spent all his time telling people the Good News, showing them that Jesus is the Christ. [6]But they would not accept Paul's teaching and said some evil things. So he shook off the dust from his clothes[n] and said to them, "If you are not saved, it will be your own fault! I have done all I can do! After this, I will go to other nations." [7]Paul left the synagogue and moved into the home of Titius Justus, next to the synagogue. This man worshiped God. [8]Crispus was the leader of that synagogue, and he and all the people living in his house believed in the Lord. Many others in Corinth also listened to Paul and believed and were baptized.

[9]During the night, the Lord told Paul in a vision: "Don't be afraid. Continue talking to people and don't be quiet. [10]I am with you, and no one will hurt you because many of my people are in this city." [11]Paul stayed there for a year and a half, teaching God's word to the people.

PAUL IS BROUGHT BEFORE GALLIO

[12]When Gallio was the governor of the country of Southern Greece, some people came together against Paul and took him to the court. [13]They said, "This man is teaching people to worship God in a way that is against our law."

[14]Paul was about to say something, but Gallio spoke, saying, "I would listen to you if you were complaining about a crime or some wrong. [15]But the things you are saying are only questions about words and names—arguments about your own law. So you must solve this problem yourselves. I don't want to be a judge of these things." [16]And Gallio made them leave the court.

[17]Then they all grabbed Sosthenes, the

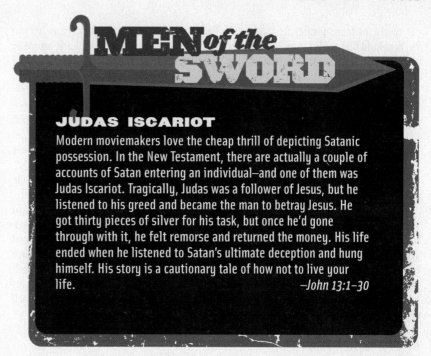

MEN of the SWORD

JUDAS ISCARIOT

Modern moviemakers love the cheap thrill of depicting Satanic possession. In the New Testament, there are actually a couple of accounts of Satan entering an individual—and one of them was Judas Iscariot. Tragically, Judas was a follower of Jesus, but he listened to his greed and became the man to betray Jesus. He got thirty pieces of silver for his task, but once he'd gone through with it, he felt remorse and returned the money. His life ended when he listened to Satan's ultimate deception and hung himself. His story is a cautionary tale of how not to live your life.

—John 13:1–30

leader of the synagogue, and beat him there before the court. But this did not bother Gallio.

PAUL RETURNS TO ANTIOCH

[18]Paul stayed with the believers for many more days. Then he left and sailed for Syria, with Priscilla and Aquila. At Cenchrea Paul cut off his hair,[n] because he had made a promise to God. [19]Then they went to Ephesus, where Paul left Priscilla and Aquila. While Paul was there, he went into the synagogue and talked with the people. [20]When they asked him to stay with them longer, he refused. [21]But as he left, he said, "I will come back to you again if God wants me to." And so he sailed away from Ephesus.

[22]When Paul landed at Caesarea, he went and gave greetings to the church in Jerusalem. After that, Paul went to Antioch. [23]He stayed there for a while and then left and went through the regions of Galatia and Phrygia. He traveled from town to town in these regions, giving strength to all the followers.

APOLLOS IN EPHESUS AND CORINTH

[24]A Jew named Apollos came to Ephesus. He was born in the city of Alexandria and was a good speaker who knew the Scriptures well. [25]He had been taught about the way of the Lord and was always very excited when he spoke and taught the truth about Jesus. But the only baptism Apollos knew about was the baptism that John[n] taught. [26]Apollos began to speak very boldly in the synagogue, and when Priscilla and Aquila heard him, they took him

to their home and helped him better understand the way of God. [27]Now Apollos wanted to go to the country of Southern Greece. So the believers helped him and wrote a letter to the followers there, asking them to accept him. These followers had believed in Jesus because of God's grace, and when Apollos arrived, he helped them very much. [28]He argued very strongly with the Jews before all the people, clearly proving with the Scriptures that Jesus is the Christ.

PAUL IN EPHESUS

19 While Apollos was in Corinth, Paul was visiting some places on the way to Ephesus. There he found some followers [2]and asked them, "Did you receive the Holy Spirit when you believed?"

They said, "We have never even heard of a Holy Spirit."

[3]So he asked, "What kind of baptism did you have?"

They said, "It was the baptism that John taught."

[4]Paul said, "John's baptism was a baptism of changed hearts and lives. He told people to believe in the one who would come after him, and that one is Jesus."

[5]When they heard this, they were baptized in the name of the Lord Jesus. [6]Then Paul laid his hands on them,[n] and the Holy Spirit came upon them. They began speaking different languages[n] and prophesying. [7]There were about twelve people in this group.

[8]Paul went into the synagogue and spoke

 18:2 Claudius The emperor (ruler) of Rome, A.D. 41–54.   18:6 shook . . . clothes This was a warning to show that Paul was finished talking to the people in that city.   18:18 cut . . . hair Jews did this to show that the time of a special promise to God was finished.   18:25 John John the Baptist, who preached to people about Christ's coming (Luke 3).   19:6 laid his hands on them The laying on of hands had many purposes, including the giving of a blessing, power, or authority.   19:6 languages This can also be translated "tongues."

out boldly for three months. He talked with the people and persuaded them to accept the things he said about the kingdom of God. [9]But some of them became stubborn. They refused to believe and said evil things about the Way of Jesus before all the people. So Paul left them, and taking the followers with him, he went to the school of a man named Tyrannus. There Paul talked with people every day [10]for two years. Because of his work, every Jew and Greek in Asia heard the word of the Lord.

THE SONS OF SCEVA

[11]God used Paul to do some very special miracles. [12]Some people took handkerchiefs and clothes that Paul had used and put them on the sick. When they did this, the sick were healed and evil spirits left them.

[13]But some people also were traveling around and making evil spirits go out of people. They tried to use the name of the Lord Jesus to force the evil spirits out. They would say, "By the same Jesus that Paul talks about, I order you to come out!" [14]Seven sons of Sceva, a leading priest, were doing this.

[15]But one time an evil spirit said to them, "I know Jesus, and I know about Paul, but who are you?"

[16]Then the man who had the evil spirit jumped on them. Because he was so much stronger than all of them, they ran away from the house naked and hurt. [17]All the people in Ephesus—Jews and Greeks—learned about this and were filled with fear and gave great honor to the Lord Jesus. [18]Many of the believers began to confess openly and tell all the evil things they had done. [19]Some of them who had used magic brought their magic books and burned them before everyone. Those books were worth about fifty thousand silver coins."

[20]So in a powerful way the word of the Lord kept spreading and growing.

[21]After these things, Paul decided to go to Jerusalem, planning to go through the countries of Macedonia and Southern Greece and then on to Jerusalem. He said, "After I have been to Jerusalem, I must also visit Rome." [22]Paul sent Timothy and Erastus, two of his helpers, ahead to Macedonia, but he himself stayed in Asia for a while.

TROUBLE IN EPHESUS

[23]And during that time, there was some serious trouble in Ephesus about the Way of Jesus. [24]A man named Demetrius, who worked with silver, made little silver models that looked like the temple of the goddess Artemis." Those who did this work made much money. [25]Demetrius had a meeting with them and some others who did the same kind of work.

He told them, "Men, you know that we make a lot of money from our business. [26]But look at what this man Paul is doing. He has convinced and turned away many people in Ephesus and in almost all of Asia! He says the gods made by human hands are not real. [27]There is a danger that our business will lose its good name, but there is also another danger: People will begin to think that the temple of the great goddess Artemis is not important. Her greatness will be destroyed, and Artemis is the goddess that everyone in Asia and the whole world worships."

[28]When the others heard this, they became very angry and shouted, "Artemis, the goddess of Ephesus, is great!" [29]The whole city became confused. The people grabbed Gaius and Aristarchus, who were from Macedonia and were traveling with Paul, and ran to the theater. [30]Paul wanted to go in and talk to the crowd, but the followers did not let him. [31]Also, some leaders of Asia who were friends of Paul sent him a message, begging him not to go into the theater. [32]Some people were shouting one thing, and some were shouting another. The meeting was completely confused; most of them did not know why they had come together. [33]They put a man named Alexander in front of the people, and some of them told him what to do. Alexander waved his

*REVIEWS MUSIC

SANCTUS REAL:
FIGHT THE TIDE

With savvy pop hooks, cleanly produced vocals, and creative melodies, Sanctus Real's *Fight the Tide* takes the band to new rock heights—both artistically and spiritually. The album is an achingly honest offering; within the lyrics of its songs the band opens up about topics like pride, sin, and passion. But it's not all seriousness; you can hear Sanctus Real having fun on tracks such as, "The Fight Song" and "Message." Not a band to shy away from upfront songs about Jesus, those who crave a lot of gospel in their grooves will love the lead-off song, "Everything About You."

sanctus real
FIGHT THE TIDE

WHY IT ROCKS:

THIS IS CREATIVE CHRISTIAN ROCK FOR DEEP THINKERS.

19:19 **fifty thousand silver coins** Probably drachmas. One coin was enough to pay a worker for one day's labor.   19:24 **Artemis** A Greek goddess that the people of Asia Minor worshiped.

GUARD YOUR HEART

So you're scared to ask the girl of your dreams out on a date. Maybe you're afraid she'll say, "No." Well, she might do that, but that's usually the worst that can come from it. And if she were to say something meaner than "no," you don't really want to hang out with her anyway.

hand so he could explain things to the people. [34]But when they saw that Alexander was a Jew, they all shouted the same thing for two hours: "Great is Artemis of Ephesus!"

[35]Then the city clerk made the crowd be quiet. He said, "People of Ephesus, everyone knows that Ephesus is the city that keeps the temple of the great goddess Artemis and her holy stone[n] that fell from heaven. [36]Since no one can say this is not true, you should be quiet. Stop and think before you do anything. [37]You brought these men here, but they have not said anything evil against our goddess or stolen anything from her temple. [38]If Demetrius and those who work with him have a charge against anyone they should go to the courts and judges where they can argue with each other. [39]If there is something else you want to talk about, it can be decided at the regular town meeting of the people. [40]I say this because some people might see this trouble today and say that we are rioting. We could not explain this, because there is no real reason for this meeting." [41]After the city clerk said these things, he told the people to go home.

PAUL IN MACEDONIA AND GREECE

20 When the trouble stopped, Paul sent for the followers to come to him. After he encouraged them and then told them good-bye, he left and went to the country of Macedonia. [2]He said many things to strengthen the followers in the different places on his way through Macedonia. Then he went to Greece, [3]where he stayed for three months. He was ready to sail for Syria, but some evil people were planning something against him. So Paul decided to go back through Macedonia to Syria. [4]The men who went with him were Sopater son of Pyrrhus, from the city of Berea; Aristarchus and Secundus, from the city of Thessalonica; Gaius, from Derbe; Timothy; and Tychicus and Trophimus, two men from Asia. [5]These men went on ahead and waited for us at Troas. [6]We sailed from Philippi after the Feast of Unleavened Bread. Five days later we met them in Troas, where we stayed for seven days.

PAUL'S LAST VISIT TO TROAS

[7]On the first day of the week,[n] we all met together to break bread,[n] and Paul spoke to the group. Because he was planning to leave the next day, he kept on talking until midnight. [8]We were all together in a room upstairs, and there were many lamps in the room. [9]A young man named Eutychus was sitting in the window. As Paul continued talking, Eutychus was falling into a deep sleep. Finally, he went sound asleep and fell to the ground from the third floor. When they picked him up, he was dead. [10]Paul went down to Eutychus, knelt down, and put his arms around him. He said, "Don't worry. He is alive now." [11]Then Paul went upstairs again, broke bread, and ate. He spoke to them a long time, until it was early morning, and then he left. [12]They took the young man home alive and were greatly comforted.

THE TRIP FROM TROAS TO MILETUS

[13]We went on ahead of Paul and sailed for the city of Assos, where he wanted to join us on the ship. Paul planned it this way because he wanted to go to Assos by land. [14]When he met us there, we took him aboard and went to Mitylene. [15]We sailed from Mitylene and the next day came to a place near Kios. The following day we sailed to Samos, and the next day we reached Miletus. [16]Paul had already decided not to stop at Ephesus, because he did not want to stay too long in Asia. He was hurrying to be in Jerusalem on the day of Pentecost, if that were possible.

THE ELDERS FROM EPHESUS

[17]Now from Miletus Paul sent to Ephesus and called for the elders of the church. [18]When they came to him, he said, "You know about my life from the first day I came to Asia. You know the way I lived all the time I was with you. [19]The evil people made plans against me, which troubled me very much. But you know I always served the Lord unselfishly, and I often cried. [20]You know I preached to you and did not hold back anything that would help you. You know that I taught you in public and in your homes. [21]I warned both Jews and Greeks to change their lives and turn to God and believe in our Lord Jesus. [22]But now I must obey the Holy Spirit and go to Jerusalem. I don't know what will happen to me there. [23]I know only that in every city the Holy Spirit tells me that troubles and even jail wait for me. [24]I don't care about my own life. The most important thing is that I complete my mission, the work that the Lord Jesus gave me—to tell people the Good News about God's grace.

[25]"And now, I know that none of you among whom I was preaching the kingdom of God will ever see me again. [26]So today I tell you that if any of you should be lost, I am not responsible, [27]because I have told you everything God wants you to know. [28]Be careful for yourselves and for all the people the Holy Spirit has given to you to oversee. You must be like shepherds to the church of God,[n] which he bought with the death of his own son. [29]I know that after I leave, some people will come like wild wolves and try to destroy the flock. [30]Also, some from your own group will rise up and twist the truth and will lead away followers after them. [31]So be careful! Always remember that for three years, day and night, I never stopped warning each of you, and I often cried over you.

[32]"Now I am putting you in the care of God and the message about his grace. It is able to give you strength, and it will give you the blessings God has for all his holy people. [33]When I was with you, I never wanted anyone's money or fine clothes. [34]You know I

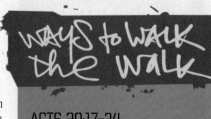

WAYS to WALK the WALK

ACTS 20:17–24
WORD: Obey the call of God.
WALK IT: Paul set an example of obedience that's good to follow. Stay tuned to what the Holy Spirit would say to you, and follow his voice, no matter what. He has your best interests at heart.

19:35 **holy stone** Probably a meteorite or stone that the people thought looked like Artemis. 20:7 **first day of the week** Sunday, which for Jews began at sunset on our Saturday. But if in this part of Asia a different system of time was used, then the meeting was on our Sunday night. 20:7 **break bread** Probably the Lord's Supper, the special meal that Jesus told his followers to eat to remember him (Luke 22:14–20). 20:28 **of God** Some Greek copies read "of the Lord."

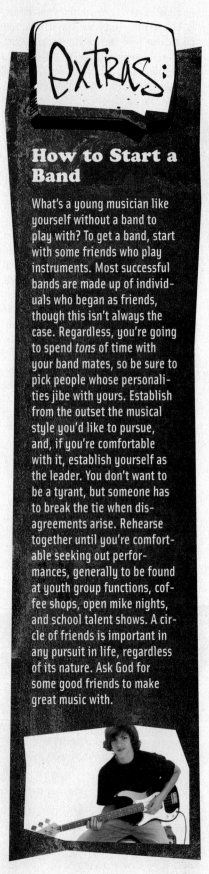

Extras:

How to Start a Band

What's a young musician like yourself without a band to play with? To get a band, start with some friends who play instruments. Most successful bands are made up of individuals who began as friends, though this isn't always the case. Regardless, you're going to spend *tons* of time with your band mates, so be sure to pick people whose personalities jibe with yours. Establish from the outset the musical style you'd like to pursue, and, if you're comfortable with it, establish yourself as the leader. You don't want to be a tyrant, but someone has to break the tie when disagreements arise. Rehearse together until you're comfortable seeking out performances, generally to be found at youth group functions, coffee shops, open mike nights, and school talent shows. A circle of friends is important in any pursuit in life, regardless of its nature. Ask God for some good friends to make great music with.

always worked to take care of my own needs and the needs of those who were with me. [35] I showed you in all things that you should work as I did and help the weak. I taught you to remember the words Jesus said: 'It is more blessed to give than to receive.' "

[36] When Paul had said this, he knelt down with all of them and prayed. [37-38] And they all cried because Paul had said they would never see him again. They put their arms around him and kissed him. Then they went with him to the ship.

PAUL GOES TO JERUSALEM

21 After we all said good-bye to them, we sailed straight to the island of Cos. The next day we reached Rhodes, and from there we went to Patara. [2] There we found a ship going to Phoenicia, so we went aboard and sailed away. [3] We sailed near the island of Cyprus, seeing it to the north, but we sailed on to Syria. We stopped at Tyre because the ship needed to unload its cargo there. [4] We found some followers in Tyre and stayed with them for seven days. Through the Holy Spirit they warned Paul not to go to Jerusalem. [5] When we finished our visit, we left and continued our trip. All the followers, even the women and children, came outside the city with us. After we all knelt on the beach and prayed, [6] we said good-bye and got on the ship, and the followers went back home.

[7] We continued our trip from Tyre and arrived at Ptolemais, where we greeted the believers and stayed with them for a day. [8] The next day we left Ptolemais and went to the city of Caesarea. There we went into the home of Philip the preacher, one of the seven helpers,[n] and stayed with him. [9] He had four unmarried daughters who had the gift of prophesying. [10] After we had been there for some time, a prophet named Agabus arrived from Judea. [11] He came to us and borrowed Paul's belt and used it to tie his own hands and feet. He said, "The Holy Spirit says, 'This is how evil people in Jerusalem will tie up the man who wears this belt. Then they will give him to the older leaders.' "

[12] When we all heard this, we and the people there begged Paul not to go to Jerusalem. [13] But he said, "Why are you crying and making me so sad? I am not only ready to be tied up in Jerusalem, I am ready to die for the Lord Jesus!"

[14] We could not persuade him to stay away from Jerusalem. So we stopped begging him and said, "We pray that what the Lord wants will be done."

[15] After this, we got ready and started on

our way to Jerusalem. [16] Some of the followers from Caesarea went with us and took us to the home of Mnason, where we would stay. He was from Cyprus and was one of the first followers.

PAUL VISITS JAMES

[17] In Jerusalem the believers were glad to see us. [18] The next day Paul went with us to visit James, and all the elders were there. [19] Paul greeted them and told them everything God had done among the other nations through him. [20] When they heard this, they praised God. Then they said to Paul, "Brother, you can see that many thousands of our people have become believers. And they think it is very important to obey the law of Moses. [21] They have heard about your teaching, that you tell our people who live among the nations to leave the law of Moses. They have heard that you tell them not to circumcise their children and not to obey customs. [22] What should we do? They will learn that you have come. [23] So we will tell you what to do: Four of our men have made a promise to God. [24] Take these men with you and share in their cleansing ceremony.[n] Pay their expenses so they can shave their heads.[n] Then it will prove to everyone that what they have heard about you is not true and that you follow the law of Moses in your own life. [25] We have already sent a letter to the non-Jewish believers. The letter said: 'Do not eat food that has been offered to idols, or blood, or animals that have been strangled. Do not take part in sexual sin.' "

[26] The next day Paul took the four men and shared in the cleansing ceremony with them. Then he went to the Temple and announced the time when the days of the cleansing ceremony would be finished. On the last day an offering would be given for each of the men.

[27] When the seven days were almost over, some of his people from Asia saw Paul at the Temple. They caused all the people to be upset and grabbed Paul. [28] They shouted, "People of Israel, help us! This is the man who goes everywhere teaching against the law of Moses, against our people, and against this Temple. Now he has brought some Greeks into the Temple and has made this holy place unclean!" [29] (They said this because they had seen Trophimus, a man from Ephesus, with Paul in Jerusalem. They thought that Paul had brought him into the Temple.)

[30] All the people in Jerusalem became upset. Together they ran, took Paul, and dragged him out of the Temple. The Temple doors were closed immediately. [31] While they were trying to kill Paul, the commander of the

---

21:8 helpers The seven men chosen for a special work described in Acts 6:1–6. Sometimes they are called "deacons." **21:24 cleansing ceremony** The special things Jews did to end the Nazirite promise. **21:24 shave their heads** Jews did this to show that their promise was finished.

Roman army in Jerusalem learned that there was trouble in the whole city. [32]Immediately he took some officers and soldiers and ran to the place where the crowd was gathered. When the people saw them, they stopped beating Paul. [33]The commander went to Paul and arrested him. He told his soldiers to tie Paul with two chains. Then he asked who he was and what he had done wrong. [34]Some in the crowd were yelling one thing, and some were yelling another. Because of all this confusion and shouting, the commander could not learn what had happened. So he ordered the soldiers to take Paul to the army building. [35]When Paul came to the steps, the soldiers had to carry him because the people were ready to hurt him. [36]The whole mob was following them, shouting, "Kill him!"

[37]As the soldiers were about to take Paul into the army building, he spoke to the commander, "May I say something to you?"

The commander said, "Do you speak Greek? [38]I thought you were the Egyptian who started some trouble against the government not long ago and led four thousand killers out to the desert."

[39]Paul said, "No, I am a Jew from Tarsus in the country of Cilicia. I am a citizen of that important city. Please, let me speak to the people."

[40]The commander gave permission, so Paul stood on the steps and waved his hand to quiet the people. When there was silence, he spoke to them in the Hebrew language.

PAUL SPEAKS TO THE PEOPLE

22 Paul said, "Brothers and fathers, listen to my defense to you." [2]When they heard him speaking the Hebrew language,[n] they became very quiet. Paul said, [3]"I am a Jew, born in Tarsus in the country of Cilicia, but I grew up in this city. I was a student of Gamaliel,[n] who carefully taught me everything about the law of our ancestors. I was very serious about serving God, just as are all of you here today. [4]I persecuted the people who followed the Way of Jesus, and some of them were even killed. I arrested men and women and put them in jail. [5]The high priest and the whole council of elders can tell you this is true. They gave me letters to the brothers in Damascus. So I was going there to arrest these people and bring them back to Jerusalem to be punished.

[6]"About noon when I came near Damascus, a bright light from heaven suddenly flashed all around me. [7]I fell to the ground and heard a voice saying, 'Saul, Saul, why are you persecuting me?' [8]I asked, 'Who are you, Lord?' The voice said, 'I am Jesus from Nazareth whom you are persecuting.' [9]Those who were with me did not understand the voice, but they saw the light. [10]I said, 'What shall I do, Lord?' The Lord answered, 'Get up and go to Damascus. There you will be told about all the things I have planned for you to do.' [11]I could not see, because the bright light had made me blind. So my companions led me into Damascus.

[12]"There a man named Ananias came to me. He was a religious man; he obeyed the law of Moses, and all the Jews who lived there respected him. [13]He stood by me and said, 'Brother Saul, see again!' Immediately I was able to see him. [14]He said, 'The God of our ancestors chose you long ago to know his plan, to see the Righteous One, and to hear words from him. [15]You will be his witness to all people, telling them about what you have seen and heard. [16]Now, why wait any longer? Get up, be baptized, and wash your sins away, trusting in him to save you.'

[17]"Later, when I returned to Jerusalem, I was praying in the Temple, and I saw a vision. [18]I saw the Lord saying to me, 'Hurry! Leave Jerusalem now! The people here will not accept the truth about me.' [19]But I said, 'Lord, they know that in every synagogue I put the believers in jail and beat them. [20]They also know I was there when Stephen, your witness, was killed. I stood there agreeing and holding the coats of those who were killing him!' [21]But the Lord said to me, 'Leave now. I will send you far away to the other nations.' "

[22]The crowd listened to Paul until he said this. Then they began shouting, "Get rid of him! He doesn't deserve to live!" [23]They shouted, threw off their coats,[n] and threw dust into the air.[n]

[24]Then the commander ordered the soldiers to take Paul into the army building and beat him. He wanted to make Paul tell why the people were shouting against him like this. [25]But as the soldiers were tying him up, preparing to beat him, Paul said to an officer nearby, "Do you have the right to beat a Roman citizen[n] who has not been proven guilty?"

[26]When the officer heard this, he went to the commander and reported it. The officer said, "Do you know what you are doing? This man is a Roman citizen."

[27]The commander came to Paul and said, "Tell me, are you really a Roman citizen?"

He answered, "Yes."

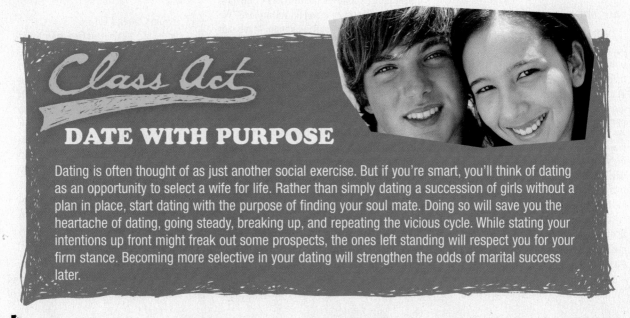

Class Act

DATE WITH PURPOSE

Dating is often thought of as just another social exercise. But if you're smart, you'll think of dating as an opportunity to select a wife for life. Rather than simply dating a succession of girls without a plan in place, start dating with the purpose of finding your soul mate. Doing so will save you the heartache of dating, going steady, breaking up, and repeating the vicious cycle. While stating your intentions up front might freak out some prospects, the ones left standing will respect you for your firm stance. Becoming more selective in your dating will strengthen the odds of marital success later.

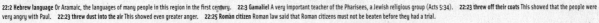

22:2 **Hebrew language** Or Aramaic, the languages of many people in this region in the first century. 22:3 **Gamaliel** A very important teacher of the Pharisees, a Jewish religious group (Acts 5:34). 22:23 **threw off their coats** This showed that the people were very angry with Paul. 22:23 **threw dust into the air** This showed even greater anger. 22:25 **Roman citizen** Roman law said that Roman citizens must not be beaten before they had a trial.

Relationships

"The wife does not have full rights over her own body; her husband shares them. And the husband does not have full rights over his own body; his wife shares them" (1 Corinthians 7:4). Some guys think sex is a free-for-all in marriage. However, they couldn't be more wrong. Marriage isn't about gratifying selfish desires; it's all about shared experiences between a husband and wife. God invented sex, but he reserved it for married couples to enjoy. Get your thinking straight about it now, and you will be better prepared for the experience. Your future wife will thank you, too.

28 The commander said, "I paid a lot of money to become a Roman citizen."

But Paul said, "I was born a citizen."

29 The men who were preparing to question Paul moved away from him immediately. The commander was frightened because he had already tied Paul, and Paul was a Roman citizen.

PAUL SPEAKS TO LEADERS

30 The next day the commander decided to learn why the Jews were accusing Paul. So he ordered the leading priests and the council to meet. The commander took Paul's chains off. Then he brought Paul out and stood him before their meeting.

23 Paul looked at the council and said, "Brothers, I have lived my life without guilt feelings before God up to this day." 2 Ananias,[n] the high priest, heard this and told the men who were standing near Paul to hit him on the mouth. 3 Paul said to Ananias, "God will hit you, too! You are like a wall that has been painted white. You sit there and judge me, using the law of Moses, but you are telling them to hit me, and that is against the law."

4 The men standing near Paul said to him, "You cannot insult God's high priest like that!"

5 Paul said, "Brothers, I did not know this man was the high priest. It is written in the Scriptures, 'You must not curse a leader of your people.' "[n]

6 Some of the men in the meeting were Sadducees, and others were Pharisees. Knowing this, Paul shouted to them, "My brothers, I am a Pharisee, and my father was a Pharisee. I am on trial here because I believe that people will rise from the dead."

7 When Paul said this, there was an argument between the Pharisees and the Sadducees, and the group was divided. 8 (The Sadducees do not believe in angels or spirits or that people will rise from the dead. But the Pharisees believe in them all.) 9 So there was a great uproar. Some of the teachers of the law, who were Pharisees, stood up and argued, "We find nothing wrong with this man. Maybe an angel or a spirit did speak to him."

10 The argument was beginning to turn into such a fight that the commander was afraid some evil people would tear Paul to pieces. So he told the soldiers to go down and take Paul away and put him in the army building.

11 The next night the Lord came and stood by Paul. He said, "Be brave! You have told people in Jerusalem about me. You must do the same in Rome."

12 In the morning some evil people made a plan to kill Paul, and they took an oath not to eat or drink anything until they had killed him. 13 There were more than forty men who made this plan. 14 They went to the leading priests and the elders and said, "We have taken an oath not to eat or drink until we have killed Paul. 15 So this is what we want you to do: Send

a message to the commander to bring Paul out to you as though you want to ask him more questions. We will be waiting to kill him while he is on the way here."

16 But Paul's nephew heard about this plan and went to the army building and told Paul. 17 Then Paul called one of the officers and said, "Take this young man to the commander. He has a message for him."

18 So the officer brought Paul's nephew to the commander and said, "The prisoner, Paul, asked me to bring this young man to you. He wants to tell you something."

19 The commander took the young man's hand and led him to a place where they could be alone. He asked, "What do you want to tell me?"

20 The young man said, "The Jews have decided to ask you to bring Paul down to their council meeting tomorrow. They want you to think they are going to ask him more questions. 21 But don't believe them! More than forty men are hiding and waiting to kill Paul. They have all taken an oath not to eat or drink until they have killed him. Now they are waiting for you to agree."

22 The commander sent the young man away, ordering him, "Don't tell anyone that you have told me about their plan."

PAUL IS SENT TO CAESAREA

23 Then the commander called two officers and said, "I need some men to go to Caesarea. Get two hundred soldiers, seventy horsemen, and two hundred men with spears ready to leave at nine o'clock tonight. 24 Get some horses for Paul to ride so he can be taken to Governor Felix safely." 25 And he wrote a letter that said:

26 From Claudius Lysias.
To the Most Excellent Governor Felix: Greetings.

27 Some of the Jews had taken this man and planned to kill him. But I learned that he is a Roman citizen, so I went with my soldiers and saved him. 28 I wanted to know why they were accusing him, so I brought him before their council meeting. 29 I learned that these people said Paul did some things that were wrong by their own laws, but no charge was worthy of jail or death. 30 When I was told that some of them were planning to kill Paul, I sent him to you at once. I also told them to tell you what they have against him.

31 So the soldiers did what they were told and took Paul and brought him to the city of

 23:2 *Ananias* This is not the same man named Ananias in ACTS 22:12. 23:5 *'You . . . people.'* Quotation from Exodus 22:28.

Antipatris that night. [32]The next day the horsemen went with Paul to Caesarea, but the other soldiers went back to the army building in Jerusalem. [33]When the horsemen came to Caesarea and gave the letter to the governor, they turned Paul over to him. [34]The governor read the letter and asked Paul, "What area are you from?" When he learned that Paul was from Cilicia, [35]he said, "I will hear your case when those who are against you come here, too." Then the governor gave orders for Paul to be kept under guard in Herod's palace.

PAUL IS ACCUSED

24 Five days later Ananias, the high priest, went to the city of Caesarea with some of the elders and a lawyer named Tertullus. They had come to make charges against Paul before the governor. [2]Paul was called into the meeting, and Tertullus began to accuse him, saying, "Most Excellent Felix! Our people enjoy much peace because of you, and many wrong things in our country are being made right through your wise help. [3]We accept these things always and in every place, and we are thankful for them. [4]But not wanting to take any more of your time, I beg you to be kind and listen to our few words. [5]We have found this man to be a troublemaker, stirring up his people everywhere in the world. He is a leader of the Nazarene group. [6]Also, he was trying to make the Temple unclean, but we stopped him. [And we wanted to judge him by our own law. [7]But the officer Lysias came and used much force to take him from us. [8]And Lysias commanded those who wanted to accuse Paul to come to you.]* By asking him questions yourself, you can decide if all these things are true. [9]The others agreed and said that all of this was true.

[10]When the governor made a sign for Paul to speak, Paul said, "Governor Felix, I know you have been a judge over this nation for a long time. So I am happy to defend myself before you. [11]You can learn for yourself that I went to worship in Jerusalem only twelve days ago. [12]Those who are accusing me did not find me arguing with anyone in the Temple or stirring up the people in the synagogues or in the city. [13]They cannot prove the things they are saying against me now. [14]But I will tell you this: I worship the God of our ancestors as a follower of the Way of Jesus. The others say that the Way of Jesus is not the right way. But I believe everything that is taught in the law of Moses and that is written in the books of the Prophets. [15]I have the same hope in God that they have—the hope that all people, good and bad, will surely be raised from the dead. [16]This is why I always try to do what I believe is right before God and people.

[17]"After being away from Jerusalem for several years, I went back to bring money to my people and to offer sacrifices. [18]I was doing this when they found me in the Temple. I had finished the cleansing ceremony and had not made any trouble; no people were gathering around me. [19]But there were some people from Asia who should be here, standing before you. If I have really done anything wrong, they are the ones who should accuse me. [20]Or ask these people here if they found any wrong in me when I stood before the council in Jerusalem. [21]But I did shout one thing when I stood before them: 'You are judging me today because I believe that people will rise from the dead!'"

[22]Felix already understood much about the Way of Jesus. He stopped the trial and said, "When commander Lysias comes here, I will decide your case." [23]Felix told the officer to keep Paul guarded but to give him some

Get out there

Statistics on hunger aren't pretty: An estimated 1 billion people in the world suffer from hunger and malnutrition. That includes children in this country, where 13 million live in households where people have to skip meals or eat less to make ends meet. Bread for the World Institute attacks the problem by pressing for legislation affecting hungry people in the U.S. and other nations. An interdenominational organization, Bread for the World involves dozens of churches and community organizations. Personal action can include such steps as writing to congressional representatives, getting your church involved in the fight against hunger, or activating your school campus.

For more information, check www.bread.org.

24:6–8 **And . . . you.** Some Greek copies do not contain the bracketed text.

freedom and to let his friends bring what he needed.

PAUL SPEAKS TO FELIX AND HIS WIFE

24After some days Felix came with his wife, Drusilla, who was Jewish, and asked for Paul to be brought to him. He listened to Paul talk about believing in Christ Jesus. 25But Felix became afraid when Paul spoke about living right, self-control, and the time when God will judge the world. He said, "Go away now. When I have more time, I will call for you." 26At the same time Felix hoped that Paul would give him some money, so he often sent for Paul and talked with him.

27But after two years, Felix was replaced by Porcius Festus as governor. But Felix had left Paul in prison to please the Jews.

PAUL ASKS TO SEE CAESAR

25 Three days after Festus became governor, he went from Caesarea to Jerusalem. 2There the leading priests and the important leaders made charges against Paul before Festus. 3They asked Festus to do them a favor. They wanted him to send Paul back to Jerusalem, because they had a plan to kill him on the way. 4But Festus answered that Paul would be kept in Caesarea and that he himself was returning there soon. 5He said, "Some of your leaders should go with me. They can accuse the man there in Caesarea, if he has really done something wrong."

6Festus stayed in Jerusalem another eight or ten days and then went back to Caesarea. The next day he told the soldiers to bring Paul before him. Festus was seated on the judge's seat 7when Paul came into the room. The people who had come from Jerusalem stood around him, making serious charges against him, which they could not prove. 8This is what Paul said to defend himself: "I have done nothing wrong against the law, against the Temple, or against Caesar."

9But Festus wanted to please the people. So he asked Paul, "Do you want to go to Jerusalem for me to judge you there on these charges?"

10Paul said, "I am standing at Caesar's judgment seat now, where I should be judged. I have done nothing wrong to them; you know this is true. 11If I have done something wrong and the law says I must die, I do not ask to be saved from death. But if these charges are not true, then no one can give me to them. I want Caesar to hear my case!"

12Festus talked about this with his advisers. Then he said, "You have asked to see Caesar, so you will go to Caesar!"

PAUL BEFORE KING AGRIPPA

13A few days later King Agrippa and Bernice came to Caesarea to visit Festus. 14They stayed there for some time, and Festus told the king about Paul's case. Festus said, "There is a man that Felix left in prison. 15When I went to Jerusalem, the leading priests and the elders there made charges against him, asking me to sentence him to death. 16But I answered, 'When a man is accused of a crime, Romans do not hand him over until he has been allowed to face his accusers and defend himself against their charges.' 17So when these people came here to Caesarea for the trial, I did not waste time. The next day I sat on the judge's seat and commanded that the man be brought in. 18They stood up and accused him, but not of any serious crime as I thought they would. 19The things they said were about their own religion and about a man named Jesus who died. But Paul said that he is still alive. 20Not knowing how to find out about these questions, I asked Paul, 'Do you want to go to Jerusalem and be judged there?' 21But he asked to be kept in Caesarea. He wants a decision from the emperor.* So I ordered that he be held until I could send him to Caesar."

22Agrippa said to Festus, "I would also like to hear this man myself."

Festus said, "Tomorrow you will hear him."

23The next day Agrippa and Bernice appeared with great show, acting like very important people. They went into the judgment room with the army leaders and the important men of Caesarea. Then Festus ordered the soldiers to bring Paul in. 24Festus said, "King Agrippa and all who are gathered here with us, you see this man. All the people, here and in Jerusalem, have complained to me about him, shouting that he should not live any longer. 25When I judged him, I found no reason to order his death. But since he asked to be judged by Caesar, I decided to send him. 26But I have nothing definite to write the emperor about him. So I have brought him before all of you—especially you, King Agrippa. I hope you can question him and give me something to write. 27I think it is foolish to send a prisoner to Caesar without telling what charges are against him."

PAUL DEFENDS HIMSELF

26 Agrippa said to Paul, "You may now speak to defend yourself."

Then Paul raised his hand and began to speak. 2He said, "King Agrippa, I am very blessed to stand before you and will answer all the charges the evil people make against me. 3You know so much about all the customs and the things they argue about, so please listen to me patiently.

4"All my people know about my whole life, how I lived from the beginning in my own

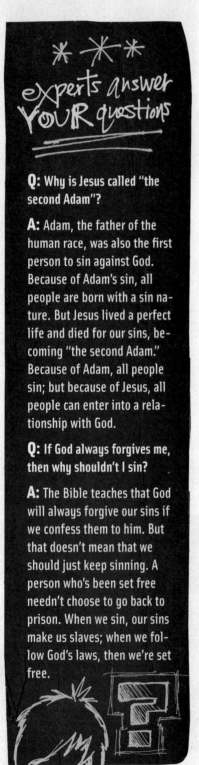

Q: Why is Jesus called "the second Adam"?

A: Adam, the father of the human race, was also the first person to sin against God. Because of Adam's sin, all people are born with a sin nature. But Jesus lived a perfect life and died for our sins, becoming "the second Adam." Because of Adam, all people sin; but because of Jesus, all people can enter into a relationship with God.

Q: If God always forgives me, then why shouldn't I sin?

A: The Bible teaches that God will always forgive our sins if we confess them to him. But that doesn't mean that we should just keep sinning. A person who's been set free needn't choose to go back to prison. When we sin, our sins make us slaves; when we follow God's laws, then we're set free.

 25:21 emperor The ruler of the Roman Empire, which was almost all the known world.

166

country and later in Jerusalem. [5]They have known me for a long time. If they want to, they can tell you that I was a good Pharisee. And the Pharisees obey the laws of my tradition more carefully than any other group. [6]Now I am on trial because I hope for the promise that God made to our ancestors. [7]This is the promise that the twelve tribes of our people hope to receive as they serve God day and night. My king, they have accused me because I hope for this same promise! [8]Why do any of you people think it is impossible for God to raise people from the dead?

[9]"I, too, thought I ought to do many things against Jesus from Nazareth. [10]And that is what I did in Jerusalem. The leading priests gave me the power to put many of God's people in jail, and when they were being killed, I agreed it was a good thing. [11]In every synagogue, I often punished them and tried to make them speak against Jesus. I was so angry against them I even went to other cities to find them and punish them.

[12]"One time the leading priests gave me permission and the power to go to Damascus. [13]On the way there, at noon, I saw a light from heaven. It was brighter than the sun and flashed all around me and those who were traveling with me. [14]We all fell to the ground. Then I heard a voice speaking to me in the Hebrew language,[n] saying, 'Saul, Saul, why are you persecuting me? You are only hurting yourself by fighting me.' [15]I said, 'Who are you, Lord?' The Lord said, 'I am Jesus, the one you are persecuting. [16]Stand up! I have chosen you to be my servant and my witness—you will tell people the things that you have seen and the things that I will show you. This is why I have come to you today. [17]I will keep you safe from your own people and also from the others. I am sending you to them [18]to open their eyes so that they may turn away from darkness to the light, away from the power of Satan and to God. Then their sins can be forgiven, and they can have a place with those people who have been made holy by believing in me.'

[19]"King Agrippa, after I had this vision from heaven, I obeyed it. [20]I began telling people that they should change their hearts and lives and turn to God and do things to show they really had changed. I told this first to those in Damascus, then in Jerusalem, and in every part of Judea, and also to the other people. [21]This is why the Jews took me and were trying to kill me in the Temple. [22]But God has helped me, and so I stand here today, telling all people, small and great, what I have seen. But I am saying only what Moses and the prophets said would happen— [23]that the Christ would

die, and as the first to rise from the dead, he would bring light to all people."

PAUL TRIES TO PERSUADE AGRIPPA

[24]While Paul was saying these things to defend himself, Festus said loudly, "Paul, you are out of your mind! Too much study has driven you crazy!"

[25]Paul said, "Most excellent Festus, I am not crazy. My words are true and sensible. [26]King Agrippa knows about these things, and I can speak freely to him. I know he has heard about all of these things, because they did not happen off in a corner. [27]King Agrippa, do you believe what the prophets wrote? I know you believe."

[28]King Agrippa said to Paul, "Do you think you can persuade me to become a Christian in such a short time?"

[29]Paul said, "Whether it is a short or a long time, I pray to God that not only you but every person listening to me today would be saved and be like me—except for these chains I have."

[30]Then King Agrippa, Governor Festus, Bernice, and all the people sitting with them stood up [31]and left the room. Talking to each other, they said, "There is no reason why this man should die or be put in jail." [32]And Agrippa said to Festus, "We could let this man go free, but he has asked Caesar to hear his case."

PAUL SAILS FOR ROME

27 It was decided that we would sail for Italy. An officer named Julius, who served in the emperor's[n] army, guarded Paul and some other prisoners. [2]We got on a ship that was from the city of Adramyttium and was about to sail to different ports in Asia. Aristarchus, a man from the city of Thessalonica in Macedonia, went with us. [3]The next day we came to Sidon. Julius was very good to Paul and gave him freedom to go visit his friends, who took care of his needs. [4]We left Sidon and sailed close to the island of Cyprus, because the wind was blowing against us. [5]We went across the sea by Cilicia and Pamphylia and landed at the city of Myra, in Lycia. [6]There the officer found a ship from Alexandria that was going to Italy, so he put us on it.

[7]We sailed slowly for many days. We had a hard time reaching Cnidus because the wind was blowing against us, and we could not go any farther. So we sailed by the south side of the island of Crete near Salmone. [8]Sailing past it was hard. Then we came to a place called Fair Havens, near the city of Lasea.

DO'S AND DON'TS

DO wash your car periodically.

DO keep the tires properly inflated.

DO change the engine oil regularly.

DO carpool with others to save gas.

DON'T forget to rotate the tires.

DON'T leave your car unlocked.

DON'T ignore the engine warning light.

DON'T pump gas while using a cell phone.

[9]We had lost much time, and it was now dangerous to sail, because it was already after the Day of Cleansing.[n] So Paul warned them, [10]"Men, I can see there will be a lot of trouble on this trip. The ship, the cargo, and even our lives may be lost." [11]But the captain and the owner of the ship did not agree with Paul, and the officer believed what the captain and owner of the ship said. [12]Since that harbor was not a good place for the ship to stay for the winter, most of the men decided that the ship should leave. They hoped we could go to Phoenix and stay there for the winter. Phoenix, a city on the island of Crete, had a harbor which faced southwest and northwest.

THE STORM

[13]When a good wind began to blow from the south, the men on the ship thought, "This is the wind we wanted, and now we have it." So they pulled up the anchor, and we sailed very close to the island of Crete. [14]But then a very strong wind named the "northeaster" came

26:14 Hebrew language Or Aramaic, the languages of many people in this region in the first century. **27:1 emperor** The ruler of the Roman Empire, which was almost all the known world. **27:9 Day of Cleansing** An important Jewish holy day in the fall of the year. This was the time of year that bad storms arose on the sea.

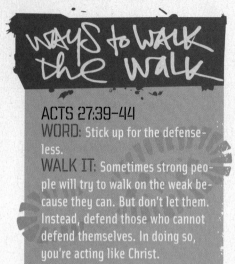

ways to walk the walk

ACTS 27:39–44

WORD: Stick up for the defenseless.

WALK IT: Sometimes strong people will try to walk on the weak because they can. But don't let them. Instead, defend those who cannot defend themselves. In doing so, you're acting like Christ.

from the island. [15]The ship was caught in it and could not sail against it. So we stopped trying and let the wind carry us. [16]When we went below a small island named Cauda, we were barely able to bring in the lifeboat. [17]After the men took the lifeboat in, they tied ropes around the ship to hold it together. The men were afraid that the ship would hit the sandbanks of Syrtis,[n] so they lowered the sail and let the wind carry the ship. [18]The next day the storm was blowing us so hard that the men threw out some of the cargo. [19]A day later with their own hands they threw out the ship's equipment. [20]When we could not see the sun or the stars for many days, and the storm was very bad, we lost all hope of being saved.

[21]After the men had gone without food for a long time, Paul stood up before them and said, "Men, you should have listened to me. You should not have sailed from Crete. Then you would not have all this trouble and loss. [22]But now I tell you to cheer up because none of you will die. Only the ship will be lost. [23]Last night an angel came to me from the God I belong to and worship. [24]The angel said, 'Paul, do not be afraid. You must stand before Caesar. And God has promised you that he will save the lives of everyone sailing with you.' [25]So men, have courage. I trust in God that everything will happen as his angel told me. [26]But we will crash on an island."

[27]On the fourteenth night we were still being carried around in the Adriatic Sea.[n] About midnight the sailors thought we were close to land, [28]so they lowered a rope with a weight on the end of it into the water. They found that the water was one hundred twenty feet deep. They went a little farther and lowered the rope again. It was ninety feet deep. [29]The sailors were afraid that we would hit the rocks, so they threw four anchors into the water and prayed for daylight to come. [30]Some of the sailors wanted to leave the ship, and they lowered the lifeboat, pretending they were throwing more anchors from the front of the ship. [31]But Paul told the officer and the other soldiers, "If these men do not stay in the ship, your lives cannot be saved." [32]So the soldiers cut the ropes and let the lifeboat fall into the water.

[33]Just before dawn Paul began persuading all the people to eat something. He said, "For the past fourteen days you have been waiting and watching and not eating. [34]Now I beg you to eat something. You need it to stay alive. None of you will lose even one hair off your heads." [35]After he said this, Paul took some bread and thanked God for it before all of them. He broke off a piece and began eating. [36]They all felt better and started eating, too. [37]There were two hundred seventy-six people on the ship. [38]When they had eaten all they wanted, they began making the ship lighter by throwing the grain into the sea.

THE SHIP IS DESTROYED

[39]When daylight came, the sailors saw land. They did not know what land it was, but they saw a bay with a beach and wanted to sail the ship to the beach if they could. [40]So they cut the ropes to the anchors and left the anchors in the sea. At the same time, they untied the ropes that were holding the rudders. Then they raised the front sail into the wind and

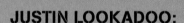

JUSTIN LOOKADOO:
THE DIRT ON SEX

Justin Lookadoo has written several books about teenagers and the lives some of them lead. In *The Dirt on Sex*, Lookadoo expounds bluntly on everything from masturbation to oral sex and from abstinence to wet dreams. He even tackles homosexuality. Most of the time, he gives sound scriptural references to back up what he says. Although sometimes he uses language that comes across like he is trying too hard to be cool, *The Dirt on Sex* is a great book to read as you grapple with the onslaught of puberty. As sex becomes more of an issue to you, this book will help give you valuable answers to your questions.

WHY IT ROCKS:

IT TACKLES THE TOUGH ISSUE OF SEX WITH STRENGTH.

 27:17 **Syrtis** Shallow area in the sea near the Libyan coast.   27:27 **Adriatic Sea** The sea between Greece and Italy, including the central Mediterranean.

sailed toward the beach. [41]But the ship hit a sandbank. The front of the ship stuck there and could not move, but the back of the ship began to break up from the big waves.

[42]The soldiers decided to kill the prisoners so none of them could swim away and escape. [43]But Julius, the officer, wanted to let Paul live and did not allow the soldiers to kill the prisoners. Instead he ordered everyone who could swim to jump into the water first and swim to land. [44]The rest were to follow using wooden boards or pieces of the ship. And this is how all the people made it safely to land.

PAUL ON THE ISLAND OF MALTA

28 When we were safe on land, we learned that the island was called Malta. [2]The people who lived there were very good to us. Because it was raining and very cold, they made a fire and welcomed all of us. [3]Paul gathered a pile of sticks and was putting them on the fire when a poisonous snake came out because of the heat and bit him on the hand. [4]The people living on the island saw the snake hanging from Paul's hand and said to each other, "This man must be a murderer! He did not die in the sea, but Justice[n] does not want him to live." [5]But Paul shook the snake off into the fire and was not hurt. [6]The people thought that Paul would swell up or fall down dead. They waited and watched him for a long time, but nothing bad happened to him. So they changed their minds and said, "He is a god!"

[7]There were some fields around there owned by Publius, an important man on the island. He welcomed us into his home and was very good to us for three days. [8]Publius' father was sick with a fever and dysentery.[n] Paul went to him, prayed, and put his hands on the man and healed him. [9]After this, all the other sick people on the island came to Paul, and he healed them, too. [10-11]The people on the island gave us many honors. When we were ready to leave, three months later, they gave us the things we needed.

PAUL GOES TO ROME

We got on a ship from Alexandria that had stayed on the island during the winter. On the front of the ship was the sign of the twin gods.[n] [12]We stopped at Syracuse for three days. [13]From there we sailed to Rhegium. The next day a wind began to blow from the south, and a day later we came to Puteoli. [14]We found some believers there who asked us to stay with them for a week. Finally, we came to Rome. [15]The believers in Rome heard that we were

there and came out as far as the Market of Appius[n] and the Three Inns[n] to meet us. When Paul saw them, he was encouraged and thanked God.

PAUL IN ROME

[16]When we arrived at Rome, Paul was allowed to live alone, with the soldier who guarded him.

[17]Three days later Paul sent for the leaders there. When they came together, he said, "Brothers, I have done nothing against our people or the customs of our ancestors. But I was arrested in Jerusalem and given to the Romans. [18]After they asked me many questions, they could find no reason why I should be killed. They wanted to let me go free, [19]but the evil people there argued against that. So I had to ask to come to Rome to have my trial before Caesar. But I have no charge to bring against my own people. [20]That is why I wanted to see you and talk with you. I am bound with this chain because I believe in the hope of Israel."

[21]They answered Paul, "We have received no letters from Judea about you. None of our Jewish brothers who have come from there brought news or told us anything bad about you. [22]But we want to hear your ideas, because we know that people everywhere are speaking against this religious group."

[23]Paul and the people chose a day for a meeting and on that day many more of the Jews met with Paul at the place he was staying. He spoke to them all day long. Using the law of Moses and the prophets' writings, he explained the kingdom of God, and he tried to persuade them to believe these things about Jesus. [24]Some believed what Paul said, but others did not. [25]So they argued and began leaving after Paul said one more thing to them: "The Holy Spirit spoke the truth to your ancestors through Isaiah the prophet, saying,
[26]'Go to this people and say:
You will listen and listen, but you will not understand.
You will look and look, but you will not learn,
[27]because these people have become stubborn.
They don't hear with their ears,
and they have closed their eyes.
Otherwise, they might really understand what they see with their eyes
and hear with their ears.
They might really understand in their minds
and come back to me and be healed.'
Isaiah 6:9–10
[28]"I want you to know that God has also

sent his salvation to all nations, and they will listen!" [[29]After Paul said this, the Jews left. They were arguing very much with each other.][n]

[30]Paul stayed two full years in his own rented house and welcomed all people who came to visit him. [31]He boldly preached about the kingdom of God and taught about the Lord Jesus Christ, and no one stopped him.

 28:4 Justice The people thought there was a god named Justice who would punish bad people. **28:8 dysentery** A sickness like diarrhea. **28:10–11 twin gods** Statues of Castor and Pollux, gods in old Greek tales. **28:15 Market of Appius** A town about twenty-seven miles from Rome. **28:15 Three Inns** A town about thirty miles from Rome. **28:29 After . . . other.** Some Greek copies do not contain the bracketed text.

ROMANS

DELIVERING GUIDELINES AND GOOD NEWS

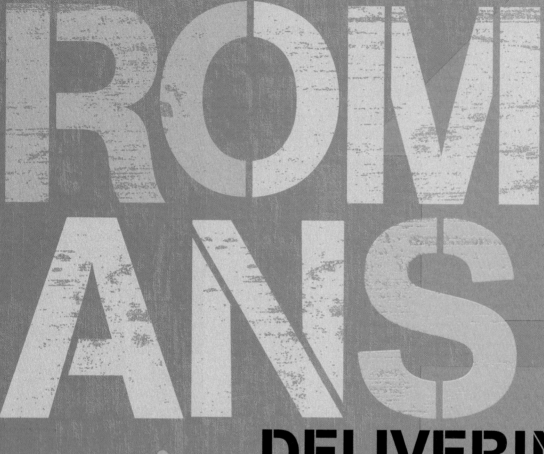

Many argue today that there is no right and wrong, only personal truth. But that idea falls flat when examining current examples of sinful actions, like teachers having sex with students, executives ripping off millions from businesses, and fathers abandoning their families. The writer of Romans, the apostle Paul, doesn't agree with excusing away such behavior. In this letter, he argues in favor of taking responsibility for one's actions.

Paul explains that God has revealed the truth about himself to people, so there is no excuse for doing wrong. He also warns of the price of turning away from God—a life full of evil, selfishness, hatred, and jealousy. People cannot do anything they choose and rationalize that it's okay because it's easier to get God's forgiveness than his permission.

Despite what may seem like a lecture, Romans contains plenty of encouragement. Revealing that he struggles with doing wrong, too, Paul thanks God for his grace. He rejoices that through Jesus Christ we are saved from our mistakes. Thanks to Paul's honesty, Romans becomes a blueprint for telling others about Christ. By its measure we see that everyone falls short, but God sent Jesus to die for us. By believing in him we can have eternal life. That is good news!

1 From Paul, a servant of Christ Jesus. God called me to be an apostle and chose me to tell the Good News.

[2]God promised this Good News long ago through his prophets, as it is written in the Holy Scriptures. [3-4]The Good News is about God's Son, Jesus Christ our Lord. As a man, he was born from the family of David. But through the Spirit of holiness he was declared to be God's Son with great power by rising from the dead. [5]Through Christ, God gave me the special work of an apostle, which was to lead people of all nations to believe and obey. I do this work for him. [6]And you who are in Rome are also called to belong to Jesus Christ.

[7]To all of you in Rome whom God loves and has called to be his holy people:

Grace and peace to you from God our Father and the Lord Jesus Christ.

A PRAYER OF THANKS

[8]First I want to say that I thank my God through Jesus Christ for all of you, because people everywhere in the world are talking about your faith. [9]God, whom I serve with my whole heart by telling the Good News about his Son, knows that I always mention you [10]every time I pray. I pray that I will be allowed to come to you, and this will happen if God wants it. [11]I want very much to see you, to give you some spiritual gift to make you strong. [12]I mean that I want us to help each other with the faith we have. Your faith will help me, and my faith will help you. [13]Brothers and sisters, I want you to know that I planned many times to come to you, but this has not been possible. I wanted to come so that I could help you grow spiritually as I have helped the other non-Jewish people.

[14]I have a duty to all people—Greeks and those who are not Greeks, the wise and the foolish. [15]That is why I want so much to preach the Good News to you in Rome.

[16]I am not ashamed of the Good News, because it is the power God uses to save everyone who believes—to save the Jews first, and then to save non-Jews. [17]The Good News shows how God makes people right with himself—that it begins and ends with faith. As the Scripture says, "But those who are right with God will live by faith."[n]

ALL PEOPLE HAVE DONE WRONG

[18]God's anger is shown from heaven against all the evil and wrong things people do. By their own evil lives they hide the truth. [19]God shows his anger because some knowledge of him has been made clear to them. Yes, God has shown himself to them. [20]There are things about him that people cannot see—his eternal power and all the things that make him God. But since the beginning of the world those things have been easy to understand by what God has made. So people have no excuse for the bad things they do. [21]They knew God, but they did not give glory to God or thank him. Their thinking became useless. Their foolish minds were filled with darkness. [22]They said they were wise, but they became fools. [23]They traded the glory of God who lives forever for the worship of idols made to look like earthly people, birds, animals, and snakes.

[24]Because they did these things, God left them and let them go their sinful way, wanting only to do evil. As a result, they became full of sexual sin, using their bodies wrongly with each other. [25]They traded the truth of God for a lie. They worshiped and served what had been created instead of the God who created those things, who should be praised forever. Amen.

[26]Because people did those things, God left them and let them do the shameful things they wanted to do. Women stopped having natural sex and started having sex with other women. [27]In the same way, men stopped having natural sex and began wanting each other. Men did shameful things with other men, and in their bodies they received the punishment for those wrongs.

[28]People did not think it was important to have a true knowledge of God. So God left them and allowed them to have their own worthless thinking and to do things they should not do. [29]They are filled with every kind of sin, evil, selfishness, and hatred. They are full of jealousy, murder, fighting, lying, and thinking the worst about each other. They gossip [30]and say evil things about each other. They hate God. They are rude and conceited and brag about themselves. They invent ways of doing evil. They do not obey their parents. [31]They are foolish, they do not keep their promises, and they show no kindness or mercy to others. [32]They know God's law says that those who live like this should die. But they themselves not only continue to do these evil things, they applaud others who do them.

YOU PEOPLE ALSO ARE SINFUL

2 If you think you can judge others, you are wrong. When you judge them, you are really judging yourself guilty, because you do the same things they do. [2]God judges those who do wrong things, and we know that his judging is right. [3]You judge those who do wrong, but you do wrong yourselves. Do you think you will be able to escape the judgment of God? [4]He has been very kind and patient, waiting for you to change, but you think nothing of his kindness. Perhaps you do not understand that God is kind to you so you will

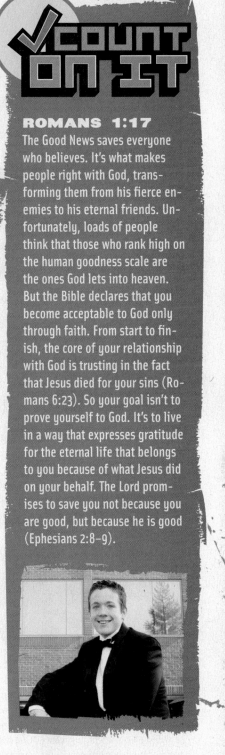

ROMANS 1:17

The Good News saves everyone who believes. It's what makes people right with God, transforming them from his fierce enemies to his eternal friends. Unfortunately, loads of people think that those who rank high on the human goodness scale are the ones God lets into heaven. But the Bible declares that you become acceptable to God only through faith. From start to finish, the core of your relationship with God is trusting in the fact that Jesus died for your sins (Romans 6:23). So your goal isn't to prove yourself to God. It's to live in a way that expresses gratitude for the eternal life that belongs to you because of what Jesus did on your behalf. The Lord promises to save you not because you are good, but because he is good (Ephesians 2:8–9).

1:17 "But those . . . faith." Quotation from Habakkuk 2:4.

171

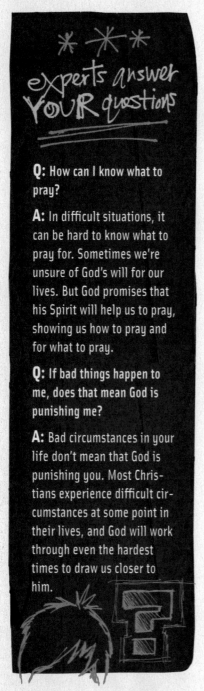

Q: How can I know what to pray?

A: In difficult situations, it can be hard to know what to pray for. Sometimes we're unsure of God's will for our lives. But God promises that his Spirit will help us to pray, showing us how to pray and for what to pray.

Q: If bad things happen to me, does that mean God is punishing me?

A: Bad circumstances in your life don't mean that God is punishing you. Most Christians experience difficult circumstances at some point in their lives, and God will work through even the hardest times to draw us closer to him.

change your hearts and lives. ⁵But you are stubborn and refuse to change, so you are making your own punishment even greater on the day he shows his anger. On that day everyone will see God's right judgments. ⁶God will reward or punish every person for what that person has done. ⁷Some people, by always continuing to do good, live for God's glory, for honor, and for life that has no end. God will give them life forever. ⁸But other people are selfish. They refuse to follow truth and, instead, follow evil. God will give them his pun-ishment and anger. ⁹He will give trouble and suffering to everyone who does evil—to the Jews first and also to those who are not Jews. ¹⁰But he will give glory, honor, and peace to everyone who does good—to the Jews first and also to those who are not Jews. ¹¹For God judges all people in the same way.

¹²People who do not have the law and who are sinners will be lost, although they do not have the law. And, in the same way, those who have the law and are sinners will be judged by the law. ¹³Hearing the law does not make people right with God. It is those who obey the law who will be right with him. ¹⁴(Those who are not Jews do not have the law, but when they freely do what the law commands, they are the law for themselves. This is true even though they do not have the law. ¹⁵They show that in their hearts they know what is right and wrong, just as the law commands. And they show this by their consciences. Sometimes their thoughts tell them they did wrong, and sometimes their thoughts tell them they did right.) ¹⁶All these things will happen on the day when God, through Christ Jesus, will judge people's secret thoughts. The Good News that I preach says this.

THE JEWS AND THE LAW

¹⁷What about you? You call yourself a Jew. You trust in the law of Moses and brag that you are close to God. ¹⁸You know what he wants you to do and what is important, because you have learned the law. ¹⁹You think you are a guide for the blind and a light for those who are in darkness. ²⁰You think you can show foolish people what is right and teach those who know nothing. You have the law; so you think you know everything and have all truth. ²¹You teach others, so why don't you teach yourself? You tell others not to steal, but you steal. ²²You say that others must not take part in adultery, but you are guilty of that sin. You hate idols, but you steal from temples. ²³You brag about having God's law, but you bring shame to God by breaking his law, ²⁴just as the Scriptures say: "Those who are not Jews speak against God's name because of you."[n]

²⁵If you follow the law, your circumcision has meaning. But if you break the law, it is as if you were never circumcised. ²⁶People who are not Jews are not circumcised, but if they do what the law says, it is as if they were circumcised. ²⁷You Jews have the written law and circumcision, but you break the law. So those who are not circumcised in their bodies, but still obey the law, will show that you are guilty. ²⁸They can do this because a person is not a true Jew if he is only a Jew in his physical body; true circumcision is not only on the outside of the body. ²⁹A person is a Jew only if he is a Jew inside; true circumcision is done in the heart by the Spirit, not by the written law. Such a person gets praise from God rather than from people.

3 So, do Jews have anything that other people do not have? Is there anything special about being circumcised? ²Yes, of course, there is in every way. The most important thing is this: God trusted the Jews with his teachings. ³If some Jews were not faithful to him, will that stop God from doing what he promised? ⁴No! God will continue to be true even when every person is false. As the Scriptures say:

"So you will be shown to be right when you speak,
and you will win your case." *Psalm 51:4*

⁵When we do wrong, that shows more clearly that God is right. So can we say that God is wrong to punish us? (I am talking as people might talk.) ⁶No! If God could not punish us, he could not judge the world.

⁷A person might say, "When I lie, it really gives him glory, because my lie shows God's truth. So why am I judged a sinner?" ⁸It would be the same to say, "We should do evil so that good will come." Some people find fault with us and say we teach this, but they are wrong and deserve the punishment they will receive.

ALL PEOPLE ARE GUILTY

⁹So are we Jews better than others? No! We have already said that Jews and those who are not Jews are all guilty of sin. ¹⁰As the Scriptures say:

"There is no one who always does what is right,
not even one.

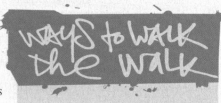

ways to WALK the WALK

ROMANS 2:1

WORD: Don't judge other people.
WALK IT: It's tempting to look at other people and criticize their flaws. Next time you feel like doing that, remember that you're flawed, too. Better leave the judging up to God.

 2:24 "Those . . . you." Quotation from Isaiah 52:5; Ezekiel 36:20.

[11]There is no one who understands.
There is no one who looks to God for
help.
[12]All have turned away.
Together, everyone has become useless.
There is no one who does anything good;
there is not even one."   *Psalm 14:1–3*
[13]"Their throats are like open graves;
they use their tongues for telling lies."
Psalm 5:9
"Their words are like snake poison."
Psalm 140:3
[14]   "Their mouths are full of cursing and
hate."   *Psalm 10:7*
[15]"They are always ready to kill people.
[16]   Everywhere they go they cause ruin and
misery.
[17]They don't know how to live in peace."
Isaiah 59:7–8
[18]   "They have no fear of God."   *Psalm 36:1*
[19]We know that the law's commands are
for those who have the law. This stops all excuses and brings the whole world under God's
judgment, [20]because no one can be made right
with God by following the law. The law only
shows us our sin.

HOW GOD MAKES PEOPLE RIGHT

[21]But God has a way to make people right
with him without the law, and he has now
shown us that way which the law and the
prophets told us about. [22]God makes people
right with himself through their faith in Jesus
Christ. This is true for all who believe in
Christ, because all people are the same:
[23]Everyone has sinned and fallen short of
God's glorious standard, [24]and all need to be
made right with God by his grace, which is a
free gift. They need to be made free from sin
through Jesus Christ. [25]God sent him to die in
our place to take away our sins. We receive forgiveness through faith in the blood of Jesus'
death. This showed that God always does what
is right and fair, as in the past when he was patient and did not punish people for their sins.
[26]And God gave Jesus to show today that he
does what is right. God did this so he could
judge rightly and so he could make right any
person who has faith in Jesus.

[27]So do we have a reason to brag about ourselves? No! And why not? It is the way of faith
that stops all bragging, not the way of trying to
obey the law. [28]A person is made right with
God through faith, not through obeying the
law. [29]Is God only the God of the Jews? Is he
not also the God of those who are not Jews?
[30]Of course he is, because there is only one
God. He will make Jews right with him by their
faith, and he will also make those who are not
Jews right with him through their faith. [31]So do
we destroy the law by following the way of
faith? No! Faith causes us to be what the law
truly wants.

MEN *of the* SWORD

JUDE

Have you ever been in a position where you really wanted to do
or say something that you thought would be right, but felt like
God was telling you to do or say something else? That was the
case with Jude, an early Christian leader (and younger brother
of Jesus) who wrote a short, open letter to Christians. He wanted
to talk about salvation, but instead wrote an impassioned plea
to avoid false teachings about grace as an excuse to sin. His letter, while brief, is a frank look at the devil's schemes to get
Christians to go astray. The Book of Jude may be small, but it is
vital.   —Jude 1

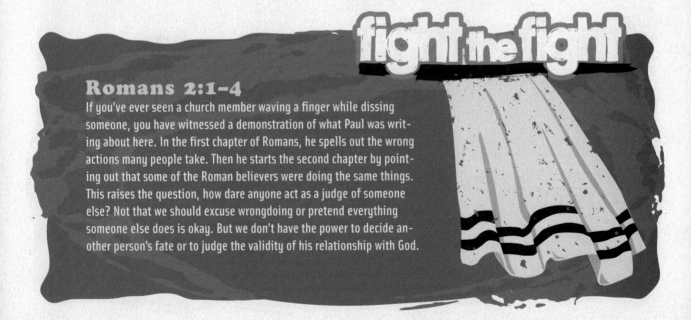

fight the fight

Romans 2:1–4

If you've ever seen a church member waving a finger while dissing
someone, you have witnessed a demonstration of what Paul was writing about here. In the first chapter of Romans, he spells out the wrong
actions many people take. Then he starts the second chapter by pointing out that some of the Roman believers were doing the same things.
This raises the question, how dare anyone act as a judge of someone
else? Not that we should excuse wrongdoing or pretend everything
someone else does is okay. But we don't have the power to decide another person's fate or to judge the validity of his relationship with God.

THE EXAMPLE OF ABRAHAM

4 So what can we say that Abraham,[n] the father of our people, learned about faith? [2]If Abraham was made right by the things he did, he had a reason to brag. But this is not God's view, [3]because the Scripture says, "Abraham believed God, and God accepted Abraham's faith, and that faith made him right with God."[n]

[4]When people work, their pay is not given as a gift, but as something earned. [5]But people cannot do any work that will make them right with God. So they must trust in him, who makes even evil people right in his sight. Then God accepts their faith, and that makes them right with him. [6]David said the same thing. He said that people are truly blessed when God, without paying attention to their deeds, makes people right with himself.

[7]"Blessed are they
    whose sins are forgiven,
    whose wrongs are pardoned.
[8]Blessed is the person
    whom the Lord does not consider
      guilty."   *Psalm 32:1–2*

[9]Is this blessing only for those who are circumcised or also for those who are not circumcised? We have already said that God accepted Abraham's faith and that faith made him right with God. [10]So how did this happen? Did God accept Abraham before or after he was circumcised? It was before his circumcision. [11]Abraham was circumcised to show that he was right with God through faith before he was circumcised. So Abraham is the father of all those who believe but are not circumcised; he is the father of all believers who are accepted as being right with God. [12]And Abraham is also the father of those who have been circumcised and who live following the faith that our father Abraham had before he was circumcised.

GOD KEEPS HIS PROMISE

[13]Abraham[n] and his descendants received the promise that they would get the whole world. He did not receive that promise through the law, but through being right with God by his faith. [14]If people could receive what God promised by following the law, then faith is worthless. And God's promise to Abraham is worthless, [15]because the law can only bring God's anger. But if there is no law, there is nothing to disobey.

[16]So people receive God's promise by having faith. This happens so the promise can be a free gift. Then all of Abraham's children can have that promise. It is not only for those who live under the law of Moses but for anyone who lives with faith like that of Abraham, who is the father of us all. [17]As it is written in the Scriptures: "I am making you a father of many nations."[n] This is true before God, the God Abraham believed, the God who gives life to the dead and who creates something out of nothing.

[18]There was no hope that Abraham would have children. But Abraham believed God and continued hoping, and so he became the father of many nations. As God told him, "Your descendants also will be too many to count."[n]

[19]Abraham was almost a hundred years old, much past the age for having children, and Sarah could not have children. Abraham thought about all this, but his faith in God did not become weak. [20]He never doubted that God would keep his promise, and he never stopped believing. He grew stronger in his faith and gave praise to God. [21]Abraham felt sure that God was able to do what he had promised. [22]So, "God accepted Abraham's faith, and that faith made him right with God."[n] [23]Those words ("God accepted Abraham's faith") were written not only for Abraham [24]but also for us. God will accept us also because we believe in the One who raised Jesus our Lord from the dead. [25]Jesus was given to die for our sins, and he was raised from the dead to make us right with God.

RIGHT WITH GOD

5 Since we have been made right with God by our faith, we have[n] peace with God. This happened through our Lord Jesus Christ, [2]who through our faith[n] has brought us

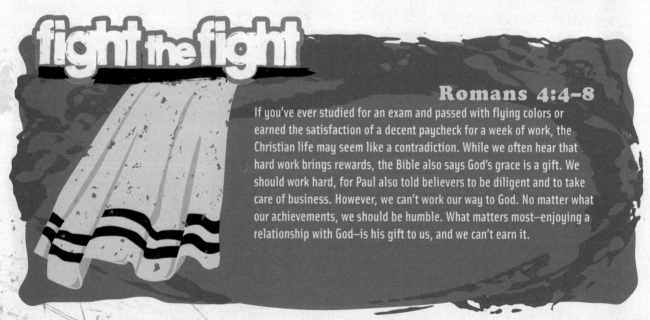

Romans 4:4-8

If you've ever studied for an exam and passed with flying colors or earned the satisfaction of a decent paycheck for a week of work, the Christian life may seem like a contradiction. While we often hear that hard work brings rewards, the Bible also says God's grace is a gift. We should work hard, for Paul also told believers to be diligent and to take care of business. However, we can't work our way to God. No matter what our achievements, we should be humble. What matters most—enjoying a relationship with God—is his gift to us, and we can't earn it.

✴ **4:1, 13 Abraham** Most respected ancestor of the Jews. Every Jew hoped to see Abraham.   **4:3 "Abraham . . . God."** Quotation from Genesis 15:6.   **4:17 "I . . . nations."** Quotation from Genesis 17:5.   **4:18 "Your . . . count."** Quotation from Genesis 15:5.   **4:22 "God . . . God."** Quotation from Genesis 15:6.   **5:1 we have** Some Greek copies read "let us have."   **5:2 through our faith** Some Greek copies do not have this phrase.

174

june

NATIONAL DAIRY MONTH

"God has given us two hands, one to receive with and the other to give with."
-BILLY GRAHAM

1 Pat Boone turns another year younger today.	2 Drink plenty of milk.	3 It's Donut Day. Sweet treats for everyone!	4
5 Brian McKnight is another year older today.	6 Ask God to show you how to spend your summer vacation.	7 Start learning to play a musical instrument.	8
9	10	11 It's Chris Rice's birthday.	12
13	14 Fly the American flag for Flag Day.	15	16
17 Ride bikes around the neighborhood with your dad.	18 Pray for your summer mission project.	19	20
21 Plan a trip to the lake.	22	23	24 Start to read a good book today.
25 Volunteer to help at a homeless shelter.	26	27 Tobey Maguire celebrates another birthday.	28 Check out a Christian music festival.
29	30 Pray for the members of the Supreme Court today.		

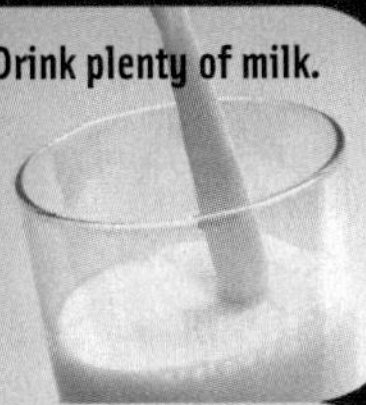

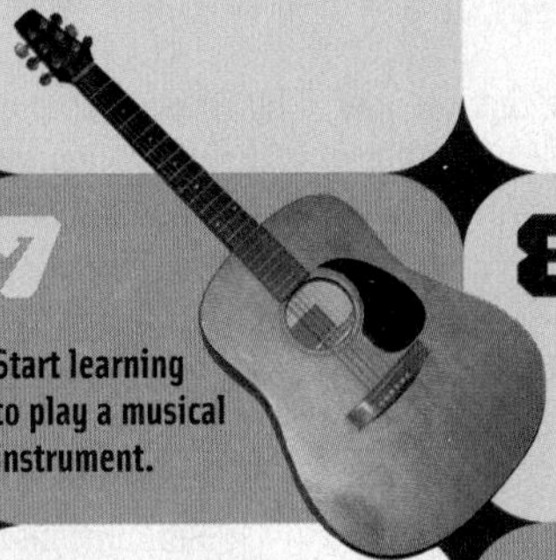

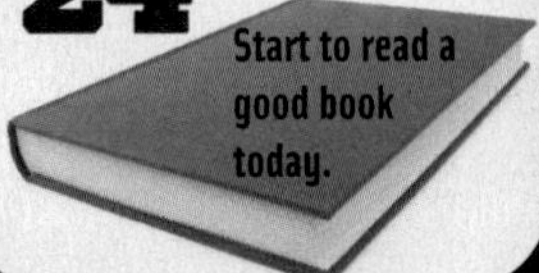

GUARD YOUR HEART

Some guys, even Christian guys, find themselves attracted to others of the same sex. If this includes you, don't be afraid to seek the care you need. Start by asking God to help you deal with the issue of homosexuality and to give you someone wise and compassionate to share your struggles with.

into that blessing of God's grace that we now enjoy. And we are happy because of the hope we have of sharing God's glory. ³We also have joy with our troubles, because we know that these troubles produce patience. ⁴And patience produces character, and character produces hope. ⁵And this hope will never disappoint us, because God has poured out his love to fill our hearts. He gave us his love through the Holy Spirit, whom God has given to us.

⁶When we were unable to help ourselves, at the right time, Christ died for us, although we were living against God. ⁷Very few people will die to save the life of someone else. Although perhaps for a good person someone might possibly die. ⁸But God shows his great love for us in this way: Christ died for us while we were still sinners.

⁹So through Christ we will surely be saved from God's anger, because we have been made right with God by the blood of Christ's death. ¹⁰While we were God's enemies, he made us his friends through the death of his Son. Surely, now that we are his friends, he will save us through his Son's life. ¹¹And not only that, but now we are also very happy in God through our Lord Jesus Christ. Through him we are now God's friends again.

ADAM AND CHRIST COMPARED

¹²Sin came into the world because of what one man did, and with sin came death. This is why everyone must die—because everyone sinned. ¹³Sin was in the world before the law of Moses, but sin is not counted against us as breaking a command when there is no law. ¹⁴But from the time of Adam to the time of Moses, everyone had to die, even those who had not sinned by breaking a command, as Adam had.

Adam was like the One who was coming in the future. ¹⁵But God's free gift is not like Adam's sin. Many people died because of the sin of that one man. But the grace from God was much greater; many people received God's gift of life by the grace of the one man, Jesus Christ. ¹⁶After Adam sinned once, he was judged guilty. But the gift of God is different. God's free gift came after many sins, and it makes people right with God. ¹⁷One man sinned, and so death ruled all people because of that one man. But now those people who accept God's full grace and the great gift of being made right with him will surely have true life and rule through the one man, Jesus Christ.

¹⁸So as one sin of Adam brought the punishment of death to all people, one good act that Christ did makes all people right with God. And that brings true life for all. ¹⁹One man disobeyed God, and many became sinners. In the same way, one man obeyed God, and many will be made right. ²⁰The law came to make sin worse. But when sin grew worse, God's grace increased. ²¹Sin once used death to rule us, but God gave people more of his grace so that grace could rule by making people right with him. And this brings life forever through Jesus Christ our Lord.

DEAD TO SIN BUT ALIVE IN CHRIST

6 So do you think we should continue sinning so that God will give us even more grace? ²No! We died to our old sinful lives, so how can we continue living with sin? ³Did you forget that all of us became part of Christ when we were baptized? We shared his death in our baptism. ⁴When we were baptized, we were buried with Christ and shared his death. So, just as Christ was raised from the dead by the wonderful power of the Father, we also can live a new life.

⁵Christ died, and we have been joined with him by dying too. So we will also be joined with him by rising from the dead as he did. ⁶We know that our old life died with Christ on the cross so that our sinful selves would have no power over us and we would not be slaves to sin. ⁷Anyone who has died is made free from sin's control.

⁸If we died with Christ, we know we will also live with him. ⁹Christ was raised from the dead, and we know that he cannot die again. Death has no power over him now. ¹⁰Yes, when Christ died, he died to defeat the power of sin one time— enough for all time. He now has a new life, and his new life is with God. ¹¹In the same way, you should see yourselves as being dead to the power of sin and alive with God through Christ Jesus.

¹²So, do not let sin control your life here on earth so that you do what your sinful self wants to do. ¹³Do not offer the parts of your body to serve sin, as things to be used in doing

Extras:

How to Handle Rejection

It's a rough world out there, and you're eventually going to get rejected. Whether it's a lost job or a particularly difficult breakup, there are some practical things you can do to take it in stride. For starters, be honest with yourself and the way you are feeling. Allow yourself to grieve, and don't push yourself to get over it quickly. Take your time and nurture yourself; don't use the rejection as an excuse to sin. Spend time with friends you trust, and talk through your feelings with them, seeking their input and godly wisdom. Consider writing down your thoughts in a journal; this can be a very therapeutic way to work through emotions you may never have known you had. And, most importantly, lean on God through the experience. He has been there and done that, so you know you can rely on him to get you through the pain of rejection.

ISSUES

DRIVING

MOTOR VEHICLE ACCIDENTS ARE THE PRIMARY CAUSE OF DEATH AMONG TEENS, KILLING ABOUT 5,000 EACH YEAR. What makes this tragedy even worse is the fact that many of the accidents are caused by underage drivers who recklessly endanger themselves and their passengers by illegally driving without a license and the training that goes with it. If you are ever tempted to drive before your time, or ride with someone who is driving illegally, wise up before it's too late. No matter how convenient or thrilling it may seem at the time, it'll never outweigh the devastation and heartache that so often follow such tragic decisions.

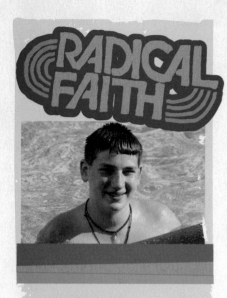

RADICAL FAITH

ROMANS 6:4

Becoming a Christian means you are destined for something way better than spending your life swamped by sin. God doesn't intend for you to be dragged under in a dirty marsh of evildoing like a guy caught in quicksand. Actually, God puts you under a whole different kind of water. If you're a believer, he wants you to be baptized (Matthew 28:19). Whatever baptism looks like at your church, that powerful act portrays your deep relationship with Jesus. You go under the water to show that your sinful self is dead in the grave with him. You come up from the water as a picture of your rising to new life. In baptism you not only become part of Jesus' death, but you also share in his resurrection. When you rise, you have a promise that God will work in you with the same astounding power that propelled Jesus from the grave. As you stick close to God, he will bust you loose from the power of sin so that it no longer drags you under its power (Romans 6:12).

evil. Instead, offer yourselves to God as people who have died and now live. Offer the parts of your body to God to be used in doing good. [14]Sin will not be your master, because you are not under law but under God's grace.

BE SLAVES OF RIGHTEOUSNESS

[15]So what should we do? Should we sin because we are under grace and not under law? No! [16]Surely you know that when you give yourselves like slaves to obey someone, then you are really slaves of that person. The person you obey is your master. You can follow sin, which brings spiritual death, or you can obey God, which makes you right with him. [17]In the past you were slaves to sin—sin controlled you. But thank God, you fully obeyed the things that you were taught. [18]You were made free from sin, and now you are slaves to goodness. [19]I use this example because this is hard for you to understand. In the past you offered the parts of your body to be slaves to sin and evil; you lived only for evil. In the same way now you must give yourselves to be slaves of goodness. Then you will live only for God.

[20]In the past you were slaves to sin, and goodness did not control you. [21]You did evil things, and now you are ashamed of them. Those things only bring death. [22]But now you are free from sin and have become slaves of God. This brings you a life that is only for God, and this gives you life forever. [23]The payment for sin is death. But God gives us the free gift of life forever in Christ Jesus our Lord.

AN EXAMPLE FROM MARRIAGE

7 Brothers and sisters, all of you understand the law of Moses. So surely you know that the law rules over people only while they are alive. [2]For example, a woman must stay married to her husband as long as he is alive. But if her husband dies, she is free from the law of marriage. [3]But if she marries another man while her husband is still alive, the law says she is guilty of adultery. But if her husband dies, she is free from the law of marriage. Then if she marries another man, she is not guilty of adultery.

[4]In the same way, my brothers and sisters, your old selves died, and you became free from the law through the body of Christ. This happened so that you might belong to someone else—the One who was raised from the dead—and so that we might be used in service to God. [5]In the past, we were ruled by our sinful selves. The law made us want to do sinful things that controlled our bodies, so the things

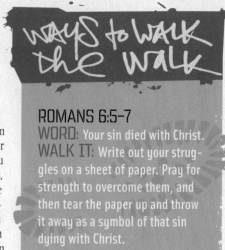
we did were bringing us death. [6]In the past, the law held us like prisoners, but our old selves died, and we were made free from the law. So now we serve God in a new way with the Spirit, and not in the old way with written rules.

OUR FIGHT AGAINST SIN

[7]You might think I am saying that sin and the law are the same thing. That is not true. But the law was the only way I could learn what sin meant. I would never have known what it means to want to take something belonging to someone else if the law had not said, "You must not want to take your neighbor's things."[n] [8]And sin found a way to use that command and cause me to want all kinds of things I should not want. But without the law, sin has no power. [9]I was alive before I knew the law. But when the law's command came to me, then sin began to live, [10]and I died. The command was meant to bring life, but for me it brought death. [11]Sin found a way to fool me by using the command to make me die.

[12]So the law is holy, and the command is holy and right and good. [13]Does this mean that something that is good brought death to me? No! Sin used something that is good to bring death to me. This happened so that I could see what sin is really like; the command was used to show that sin is very evil.

THE WAR WITHIN US

[14]We know that the law is spiritual, but I am not spiritual since sin rules me as if I were its slave. [15]I do not understand the things I do. I do not do what I want to do, and I do the things I hate. [16]And if I do not want to do the hated things I do, that means I agree that the law is

 7:7 "You . . . things." Quotation from Exodus 20:17.

good. [17]But I am not really the one who is doing these hated things; it is sin living in me that does them. [18]Yes, I know that nothing good lives in me—I mean nothing good lives in the part of me that is earthly and sinful. I want to do the things that are good, but I do not do them. [19]I do not do the good things I want to do, but I do the bad things I do not want to do. [20]So if I do things I do not want to do, then I am not the one doing them. It is sin living in me that does those things.

[21]So I have learned this rule: When I want to do good, evil is there with me. [22]In my mind, I am happy with God's law. [23]But I see another law working in my body, which makes war against the law that my mind accepts. That other law working in my body is the law of sin, and it makes me its prisoner. [24]What a miserable man I am! Who will save me from this body that brings me death? [25]I thank God for saving me through Jesus Christ our Lord!

So in my mind I am a slave to God's law, but in my sinful self I am a slave to the law of sin.

BE RULED BY THE SPIRIT

8 So now, those who are in Christ Jesus are not judged guilty.[n] [2]Through Christ Jesus the law of the Spirit that brings life made you[n] free from the law that brings sin and death. [3]The law was without power, because the law was made weak by our sinful selves. But God did what the law could not do. He sent his own Son to earth with the same human life that others use for sin. By sending his Son to be an offering for sin, God used a human life to destroy sin. [4]He did this so that we could be the kind of people the law correctly wants us to be. Now we do not live following our sinful selves, but we live following the Spirit.

[5]Those who live following their sinful selves think only about things that their sinful selves want. But those who live following the Spirit are thinking about the things the Spirit wants them to do. [6]If people's thinking is controlled by the sinful self, there is death. But if their thinking is controlled by the Spirit, there is life and peace. [7]When people's thinking is controlled by the sinful self, they are against God, because they refuse to obey God's law and really are not even able to obey God's law. [8]Those people who are ruled by their sinful selves cannot please God.

[9]But you are not ruled by your sinful selves. You are ruled by the Spirit, if that Spirit of God really lives in you. But the person who does not have the Spirit of Christ does not

Relationships

"But in the Lord women are not independent of men, and men are not independent of women" (1 Corinthians 11:11). Hear that, guys? Girls need you . . . just as you need girls. And this verse is not talking about "need" in some sort of lustful, possessive way. Girls are not something for you to obtain; and you aren't around for them to manipulate. Instead, you are to learn from each other and to depend on each other. If a girl starts trying to manipulate you, let her go, and if you find yourself objectifying a girl, cut it out. See girls for what they really are: sacred gifts from God.

fight the fight

Romans 6:1-4

What would you think of a guy who talked on Sunday of how much he loved Jesus, but who liked to smoke dope on Saturday? You would probably call him a hypocrite! So think about what standards you are applying to yourself. Just as Paul wrote of those who liked to use God's grace as an excuse to sin, the same thing goes on today. By all accounts, the practice is rampant among youth today. But once you pledge to follow Christ, your actions should change. Instead of fitting in with the crowd, show that you are different. Christ stayed on the cross so we could stay away from sin.

8:1 guilty Some Greek copies continue, "those who do not live in the power of their sinful selves, but in the power of the Spirit." 8:2 you Some Greek copies read "me."

RADICAL FAITH

ROMANS 8:11

You know how it goes. You think you have kicked the habit, made a fresh start, busted loose from a sin that keeps driving a wedge between you and God. Just when you think you're free, you blow it again. If you want to get up and move on, you need to know two facts. The first fact is that every believer sins, yet your mighty God always makes forgiveness available to you. He simply wants you to own up to your sin and confess it to him (1 John 1:8–9). The second fact is that God won't settle for anything less than setting you free from your slavery to wrongdoing. He doesn't just keep on barking rules over and over. Instead, he puts a radical new power inside of you, the spiritual brawn of his Holy Spirit that enables you to live for him. It's the same power that sprung Jesus from the tomb. Your key to breaking free is to keep listening to the Holy Spirit as he coaches you. Continually set your thinking on what God wants, and you will start to experience fresh life and ample peace (Romans 8:6).

belong to Christ. [10]Your body will always be dead because of sin. But if Christ is in you, then the Spirit gives you life, because Christ made you right with God. [11]God raised Jesus from the dead, and if God's Spirit is living in you, he will also give life to your bodies that die. God is the One who raised Christ from the dead, and he will give life through[n] his Spirit that lives in you.

[12]So, my brothers and sisters, we must not be ruled by our sinful selves or live the way our sinful selves want. [13]If you use your lives to do the wrong things your sinful selves want, you will die spiritually. But if you use the Spirit's help to stop doing the wrong things you do with your body, you will have true life.

[14]The true children of God are those who let God's Spirit lead them. [15]The Spirit we received does not make us slaves again to fear; it makes us children of God. With that Spirit we cry out, "Father."[n] [16]And the Spirit himself joins with our spirits to say we are God's children. [17]If we are God's children, we will receive blessings from God together with Christ. But we must suffer as Christ suffered so that we will have glory as Christ has glory.

OUR FUTURE GLORY

[18]The sufferings we have now are nothing compared to the great glory that will be shown to us. [19]Everything God made is waiting with excitement for God to show his children's glory completely. [20]Everything God made was changed to become useless, not by its own wish but because God wanted it and because all along there was this hope: [21]that everything God made would be set free from ruin to have the freedom and glory that belong to God's children.

[22]We know that everything God made has been waiting until now in pain, like a woman ready to give birth. [23]Not only the world, but we also have been waiting with pain inside us. We have the Spirit as the first part of God's promise. So we are waiting for God to finish making us his own children, which means our bodies will be made free. [24]We were saved, and we have this hope. If we see what we are waiting for, that is not really hope. People do not hope for something they already have. [25]But we are hoping for something we do not have yet, and we are waiting for it patiently.

[26]Also, the Spirit helps us with our weakness. We do not know how to pray as we should. But the Spirit himself speaks to God for us, even begs God for us with deep feelings that words cannot explain. [27]God can see what

* * *

experts answer YOUR questions

Q: How does God help me through hard times?

A: God never promises that our lives will always be easy even if we follow him. However, he does promise that he will always be with us to strengthen and encourage us. No matter how difficult the trials we face, we can always be certain that God still loves us and is still with us through them.

Q: How can I be saved?

A: Being saved doesn't require that you do all the right things, go to the right church, or know all the right people. All that God asks of us is one simple thing: to believe. The Bible promises us that if we acknowledge Jesus as the Lord of our lives and believe in his death, burial, and resurrection, then we will be saved.

is in people's hearts. And he knows what is in the mind of the Spirit, because the Spirit speaks to God for his people in the way God wants.

[28]We know that in everything God works for the good of those who love him.[n] They are the people he called, because that was his plan.

 8:11 through Some Greek copies read "because of." **8:15 "Father"** Literally, "Abba, Father." Jewish children called their fathers "Abba." **8:28 We . . . him.** Some Greek copies read "We know that everything works together for good for those who love God."

²⁹God knew them before he made the world, and he chose them to be like his Son so that Jesus would be the firstborn[n] of many brothers and sisters. ³⁰God planned for them to be like his Son; and those he planned to be like his Son, he also called; and those he called, he also made right with him; and those he made right, he also glorified.

GOD'S LOVE IN CHRIST JESUS

³¹So what should we say about this? If God is for us, no one can defeat us. ³²He did not spare his own Son but gave him for us all. So with Jesus, God will surely give us all things. ³³Who can accuse the people God has chosen? No one, because God is the One who makes them right. ³⁴Who can say God's people are guilty? No one, because Christ Jesus died, but he was also raised from the dead, and now he is on God's right side, appealing to God for us. ³⁵Can anything separate us from the love Christ has for us? Can troubles or problems or sufferings or hunger or nakedness or danger or violent death? ³⁶As it is written in the Scriptures:

"For you we are in danger of death all the time.
People think we are worth no more than sheep to be killed."   *Psalm 44:22*

³⁷But in all these things we are completely victorious through God who showed his love for us. ³⁸Yes, I am sure that neither death, nor life, nor angels, nor ruling spirits, nothing now, nothing in the future, no powers, ³⁹nothing above us, nothing below us, nor anything else in the whole world will ever be able to separate us from the love of God that is in Christ Jesus our Lord.

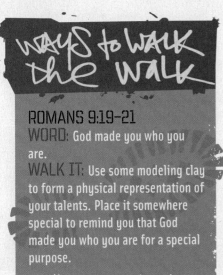

ROMANS 9:19-21
WORD: God made you who you are.
WALK IT: Use some modeling clay to form a physical representation of your talents. Place it somewhere special to remind you that God made you who you are for a special purpose.

GOD AND THE JEWISH PEOPLE

9 I am in Christ, and I am telling you the truth; I do not lie. My conscience is ruled by the Holy Spirit, and it tells me I am not lying. ²I have great sorrow and always feel much sadness. ³I wish I could help my Jewish brothers and sisters, my people. I would even wish that I were cursed and cut off from Christ if that would help them. ⁴They are the people of Israel, God's chosen children. They have seen the glory of God, and they have the agreements that God made between himself and his people. God gave them the law of Moses and the right way of worship and his promises. ⁵They are the descendants of our great ancestors, and they are the earthly family into which Christ was born, who is God over all. Praise him forever![n] Amen.

⁶It is not that God failed to keep his promise to them. But only some of the people of Israel are truly God's people,[n] ⁷and only some of Abraham's[n] descendants are true children of Abraham. But God said to Abraham: "The descendants I promised you will be from Isaac."[n] ⁸This means that not all of Abraham's descendants are God's true children. Abraham's true children are those who become God's children because of the promise God made to Abraham. ⁹God's promise to Abraham was this: "At the right time I will return, and Sarah will have a son."[n] ¹⁰And that is not all. Rebekah's sons had the same father, our father Isaac. ¹¹⁻¹²But before the two boys were born, God told Rebekah, "The older will serve the younger."[n] This was before the boys had done anything good or bad. God said this so that the one chosen would be chosen because of God's own plan. He was chosen because he was the one God wanted to call, not because of anything he did. ¹³As the Scripture says, "I loved Jacob, but I hated Esau."[n]

¹⁴So what should we say about this? Is God unfair? In no way. ¹⁵God said to Moses, "I will show kindness to anyone to whom I want to show kindness, and I will show mercy to anyone to whom I want to show mercy."[n] ¹⁶So God will choose the one to whom he decides to show mercy; his choice does not depend on what people want or try to do. ¹⁷The Scripture says to the king of Egypt: "I made you king for this reason: to show my power in you so that my name will be talked about in all the earth."[n] ¹⁸So God shows mercy where he wants to show mercy, and he makes stubborn the people he wants to make stubborn.

¹⁹So one of you will ask me: "Then why does God blame us for our sins? Who can fight his will?" ²⁰You are only human, and human

✓ COUNT ON IT

ROMANS 8:28
Life can resemble a game of extreme elimination, but there is a way you can finish the game triumphant no matter what you face. Just keep in mind that nowhere does the Bible say Jesus' followers are destined for wall-to-wall fun. In fact, Jesus said, "In this world you will have trouble, but be brave! I have defeated the world" (John 16:33). This means that while God won't make every miserable situation disappear into sweet nothingness, he will stand with you and make good come out of bad. God's hand on your life might not always be apparent, but he promises to work things out for your benefit. God is for you, and he always works for your good. Remembering the goodness of God during a trial will help you to come out the other side of it.

beings have no right to question God. An object should not ask the person who made it, "Why did you make me like this?" ²¹The potter can make anything he wants to make. He can use the same clay to make one thing for special use and another thing for daily use.

 8:29 firstborn Here this probably means that Christ was the first in God's family to share God's glory.   **9:5 born . . . forever!** This can also mean "born. May God, who rules over all things, be praised forever!"   **9:6 God's people** Literally, "Israel," the people God chose to bring his blessings to the world.   **9:7 Abraham** Most respected ancestor of the Jews. Every Jew hoped to see Abraham.   **9:7 "The descendants . . . Isaac."** Quotation from Genesis 21:12.   **9:9 "At . . . son."** Quotation from Genesis 18:10, 14.   **9:11–12 "The older . . . younger."** Quotation from Genesis 25:23.   **9:13 "I . . . Esau."** Quotation from Malachi 1:2–3.   **9:15 "I . . . mercy."** Quotation from Exodus 33:19.   **9:17 "I . . . earth."** Quotation from Exodus 9:16.

GUARD YOUR HEART

Get to know your girlfriend's parents. It's always to your advantage to have a good relationship with them. Parents can offer some good advice, and you'll get insight into your girlfriend from spending time with her parents. You'll be wiser for it, and they will respect you for your maturity.

[22]It is the same way with God. He wanted to show his anger and to let people see his power. But he patiently stayed with those people he was angry with—people who were made ready to be destroyed. [23]He waited with patience so that he could make known his rich glory to the people who receive his mercy. He has prepared these people to have his glory, [24]and we are those people whom God called. He called us not from the Jews only but also from those who are not Jews. [25]As the Scripture says in Hosea:

"I will say, 'You are my people'
    to those I had called 'not my people.'
And I will show my love
    to those people I did not love."
                              Hosea 2:1, 23

[26]"They were called,
    'You are not my people,'
but later they will be called
    'children of the living God.' "
                              Hosea 1:10

[27]And Isaiah cries out about Israel:
"The people of Israel are many,
    like the grains of sand by the sea.
But only a few of them will be saved,
[28]   because the Lord will quickly and
        completely punish the people on
        the earth."   *Isaiah 10:22–23*

[29]It is as Isaiah said:
"The Lord All-Powerful
    allowed a few of our descendants to live.
Otherwise we would have been completely
        destroyed
    like the cities of Sodom and
        Gomorrah."[n]   *Isaiah 1:9*

[30]So what does all this mean? Those who are not Jews were not trying to make them-

selves right with God, but they were made right with God because of their faith. [31]The people of Israel tried to follow a law to make themselves right with God. But they did not succeed, [32]because they tried to make themselves right by the things they did instead of trusting in God to make them right. They stumbled over the stone that causes people to stumble. [33]As it is written in the Scripture:

"I will put in Jerusalem a stone that causes
        people to stumble,
    a rock that makes them fall.
Anyone who trusts in him will never be
    disappointed."   *Isaiah 8:14; 28:16*

10 Brothers and sisters, the thing I want most is for all the Jews to be saved. That is my prayer to God. [2]I can say this about them: They really try to follow God, but they do not know the right way. [3]Because they did not know the way that God makes people right with him, they tried to make themselves right in their own way. So they did not accept God's way of making people right. [4]Christ ended the law so that everyone who believes in him may be right with God.

[5]Moses writes about being made right by following the law. He says, "A person who obeys these things will live because of them."[n] [6]But this is what the Scripture says about

REVIEWS MOVIES

BATMAN BEGINS

The Batman franchise returns once again to the big screen with a prequel to the other four movies. In *Batman Begins*, we get to see the real Bruce Wayne, including his troubled past, his desperate attempt at making life better, and what finally drove him to don a cape and catch bad guys. As one of the best films of 2005, this *Batman* movie is in no way a trite comic strip flick. It features superb storytelling about a legendary hero, and Christian Bale is phenomenal as the caped crusader. This is one movie you'll want to see again and again.

WHY IT ROCKS:

THIS IS THE BATMAN YOU ALWAYS WANTED TO SEE.

 9:29 Sodom and Gomorrah Two cities that God destroyed because the people were so evil. **10:5 "A person . . . them."** Quotation from Leviticus 18:5.

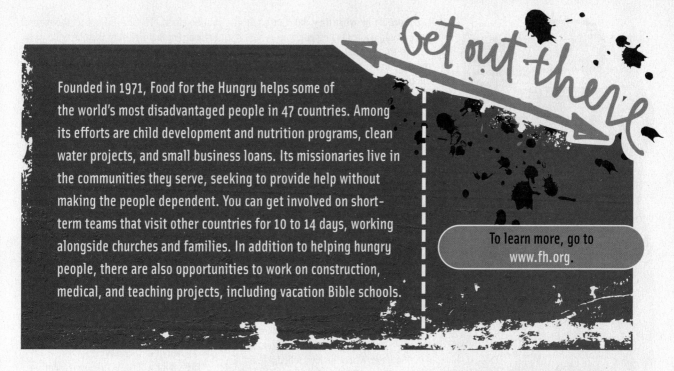

Get out there

Founded in 1971, Food for the Hungry helps some of the world's most disadvantaged people in 47 countries. Among its efforts are child development and nutrition programs, clean water projects, and small business loans. Its missionaries live in the communities they serve, seeking to provide help without making the people dependent. You can get involved on short-term teams that visit other countries for 10 to 14 days, working alongside churches and families. In addition to helping hungry people, there are also opportunities to work on construction, medical, and teaching projects, including vacation Bible schools.

To learn more, go to www.fh.org.

being made right through faith: "Don't say to yourself, 'Who will go up into heaven?'" (That means, "Who will go up to heaven and bring Christ down to earth?") [7]"And do not say, 'Who will go down into the world below?'" (That means, "Who will go down and bring Christ up from the dead?") [8]This is what the Scripture says: "The word is near you; it is in your mouth and in your heart."[n] That is the teaching of faith that we are telling. [9]If you declare with your mouth, "Jesus is Lord," and if you believe in your heart that God raised Jesus from the dead, you will be saved. [10]We believe with our hearts, and so we are made right with God. And we declare with our mouths that we believe, and so we are saved. [11]As the Scripture says, "Anyone who trusts in him will never be disappointed."[n] [12]That Scripture says "anyone" because there is no difference between those who are Jews and those who are not. The same Lord is the Lord of all and gives many blessings to all who trust in him, [13]as the Scripture says, "Anyone who calls on the Lord will be saved."[n]

[14]But before people can ask the Lord for help, they must believe in him; and before they can believe in him, they must hear about him; and for them to hear about the Lord, someone must tell them; [15]and before someone can go and tell them, that person must be sent. It is written, "How beautiful is the person who comes to bring good news."[n] [16]But not all the Jews accepted the good news. Isaiah said, "Lord, who believed what we told them?"[n] [17]So

faith comes from hearing the Good News, and people hear the Good News when someone tells them about Christ.

[18]But I ask: Didn't people hear the Good News? Yes, they heard—as the Scripture says:
"Their message went out through all the
world;
their words go everywhere on earth."
Psalm 19:4
[19]Again I ask: Didn't the people of Israel understand? Yes, they did understand. First, Moses says:
"I will use those who are not a nation to
make you jealous.
I will use a nation that does not
understand to make you angry."
Deuteronomy 32:21
[20]Then Isaiah is bold enough to say:
"I was found by those who were not asking
me for help.
I made myself known to people who
were not looking for me."
Isaiah 65:1
[21]But about Israel God says,
"All day long I stood ready to accept
people who disobey and are stubborn."
Isaiah 65:2

GOD SHOWS MERCY TO ALL PEOPLE

11 So I ask: Did God throw out his people? No! I myself am an Israelite from the family of Abraham, from the tribe of Benjamin. [2]God chose the Israelites to be his people before they were born, and he has not

Do's AND Don'ts

DO attend church regularly.

DO pray for your pastor.

DO invite friends to church.

DO volunteer at your church.

DON'T talk during church.

DON'T get to church late.

DON'T fight going to church.

DON'T forget your Bible.

10:6–8 But . . . heart." Quotations from Deuteronomy 9:4; 30:12–14; Psalm 107:26. **10:11 "Anyone . . . disappointed."** Quotation from Isaiah 28:16. **10:13 "Anyone . . . saved."** Quotation from Joel 2:32. **10:15 "How . . . news."** Quotation from Isaiah 52:7. **10:16 "Lord, . . . them?"** Quotation from Isaiah 53:1.

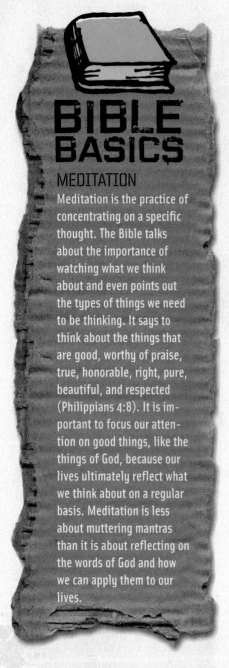

BIBLE BASICS

MEDITATION

Meditation is the practice of concentrating on a specific thought. The Bible talks about the importance of watching what we think about and even points out the types of things we need to be thinking. It says to think about the things that are good, worthy of praise, true, honorable, right, pure, beautiful, and respected (Philippians 4:8). It is important to focus our attention on good things, like the things of God, because our lives ultimately reflect what we think about on a regular basis. Meditation is less about muttering mantras than it is about reflecting on the words of God and how we can apply them to our lives.

thrown his people out. Surely you know what the Scripture says about Elijah, how he prayed to God against the people of Israel. ³"Lord," he said, "they have killed your prophets, and they have destroyed your altars. I am the only prophet left, and now they are trying to kill me, too."ⁿ ⁴But what answer did God give Elijah? He said, "But I have left seven thousand people in Israel who have never bowed down before Baal."ⁿ ⁵It is the same now. There are a few people that God has chosen by his grace. ⁶And if he chose them by grace, it is not for the things they have done. If they could be made

God's people by what they did, God's gift of grace would not really be a gift.

⁷So this is what has happened: Although the Israelites tried to be right with God, they did not succeed, but the ones God chose did become right with him. The others were made stubborn and refused to listen to God. ⁸As it is written in the Scriptures:

"God gave the people a dull mind so they
could not understand."

Isaiah 29:10

"He closed their eyes so they could not see
and their ears so they could not hear.
This continues until today."

Deuteronomy 29:4

⁹And David says:

"Let their own feasts trap them and cause
their ruin;
let their feasts cause them to stumble
and be paid back.
¹⁰Let their eyes be closed so they cannot see
and their backs be forever weak from
troubles." *Psalm 69:22–23*

¹¹So I ask: When the Jews fell, did that fall destroy them? No! But their failure brought salvation to those who are not Jews, in order to make the Jews jealous. ¹²The Jews' failure brought rich blessings for the world, and the Jews' loss brought rich blessings for the non-Jewish people. So surely the world will receive much richer blessings when enough Jews become the kind of people God wants.

¹³Now I am speaking to you who are not Jews. I am an apostle to those who are not Jews, and since I have that work, I will make the most of it. ¹⁴I hope I can make my own people jealous and, in that way, help some of them to be saved. ¹⁵When God turned away from the Jews, he became friends with other people in the world. So when God accepts the Jews, surely that will bring them life after death.

¹⁶If the first piece of bread is offered to God, then the whole loaf is made holy. If the roots of a tree are holy, then the tree's branches are holy too.

¹⁷It is as if some of the branches from an olive tree have been broken off. You non-Jewish people are like the branch of a wild olive tree that has been joined to that first tree. You now share the strength and life of the first tree, the Jews. ¹⁸So do not brag about those branches that were broken off. If you brag, remember that you do not support the root, but the root supports you. ¹⁹You will say, "Branches were broken off so that I could be joined to their tree." ²⁰That is true. But those branches were broken off because they did not believe, and you continue to be part of the tree only because you believe. Do not be proud,

but be afraid. ²¹If God did not let the natural branches of that tree stay, then he will not let you stay if you don't believe.

²²So you see that God is kind and also very strict. He punishes those who stop following him. But God is kind to you, if you continue following in his kindness. If you do not, you will be cut off from the tree. ²³And if the Jews will believe in God again, he will accept them back. God is able to put them back where they were. ²⁴It is not natural for a wild branch to be part of a good tree. And you who are not Jews are like a branch cut from a wild olive tree and joined to a good olive tree. But since those Jews are like a branch that grew from the good tree, surely they can be joined to their own tree again.

²⁵I want you to understand this secret, brothers and sisters, so you will understand that you do not know everything: Part of Israel has been made stubborn, but that will change when many who are not Jews have come to God. ²⁶And that is how all Israel will be saved. It is written in the Scriptures:

"The Savior will come from Jerusalem;
he will take away all evil from the
family of Jacob."ⁿ

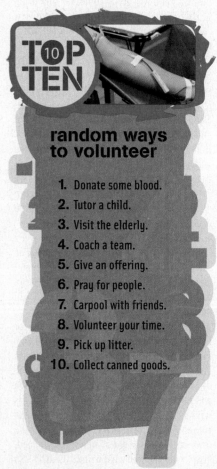

TOP 10 TEN

random ways to volunteer

1. Donate some blood.
2. Tutor a child.
3. Visit the elderly.
4. Coach a team.
5. Give an offering.
6. Pray for people.
7. Carpool with friends.
8. Volunteer your time.
9. Pick up litter.
10. Collect canned goods.

11:3 "they . . . too" Quotation from 1 Kings 19:10, 14.   11:4 "But . . . Baal." Quotation from 1 Kings 19:18.   11:26 Jacob Father of the twelve family groups of Israel, the people God chose to be his people.

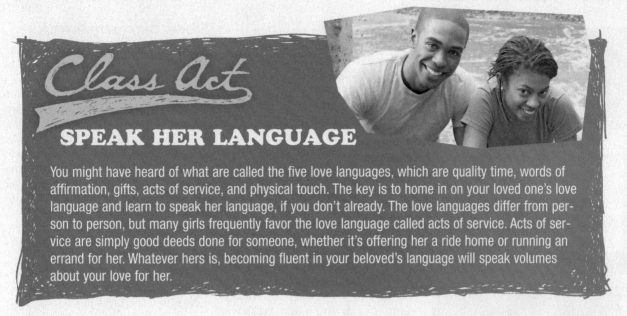

Class Act

SPEAK HER LANGUAGE

You might have heard of what are called the five love languages, which are quality time, words of affirmation, gifts, acts of service, and physical touch. The key is to home in on your loved one's love language and learn to speak her language, if you don't already. The love languages differ from person to person, but many girls frequently favor the love language called acts of service. Acts of service are simply good deeds done for someone, whether it's offering her a ride home or running an errand for her. Whatever hers is, becoming fluent in your beloved's language will speak volumes about your love for her.

27And I will make this agreement
   with those people
when I take away their sins."
Isaiah 59:20–21; 27:9

28The Jews refuse to accept the Good News, so they are God's enemies. This has happened to help you who are not Jews. But the Jews are still God's chosen people, and he loves them very much because of the promises he made to their ancestors. 29God never changes his mind about the people he calls and the things he gives them. 30At one time you refused to obey God. But now you have received mercy, because those people refused to obey. 31And now the Jews refuse to obey, because God showed mercy to you. But this happened so that they also can[n] receive mercy from him. 32God has given all people over to their stubborn ways so that he can show mercy to all.

PRAISE TO GOD

33Yes, God's riches are very great, and his wisdom and knowledge have no end! No one can explain the things God decides or understand his ways. 34As the Scripture says,

"Who has known the mind of the Lord,
   or who has been able to give him
      advice?"   *Isaiah 40:13*
35"No one has ever given God anything
   that he must pay back."   *Job 41:11*
36Yes, God made all things, and everything continues through him and for him. To him be the glory forever! Amen.

GIVE YOUR LIVES TO GOD

12 So brothers and sisters, since God has shown us great mercy, I beg you to offer your lives as a living sacrifice to him. Your offering must be only for God and pleasing to him, which is the spiritual way for you to worship. 2Do not be shaped by this world; instead be changed within by a new way of thinking. Then you will be able to decide what God wants for you; you will know what is good and pleasing to him and what is perfect. 3Because God has given me a special gift, I have something to say to everyone among you. Do not think you are better than you are. You must decide what you really are by the amount of faith God has given you. 4Each one of us has a body with many parts, and these parts all have different uses. 5In the same way, we are many, but in Christ we are all one body. Each one is a part of that body, and each part belongs to all the other parts. 6We all have different gifts, each of which came because of the grace God gave us. The person who has the gift of prophecy should use that gift in agreement with the faith. 7Anyone who has the gift of serving should serve. Anyone who has the gift of teaching should teach. 8Whoever has the gift of encouraging others should encourage. Whoever has the gift of giving to others should give freely. Anyone who has the gift of being a leader should try hard when he leads. Whoever has the gift of showing mercy to others should do so with joy.

9Your love must be real. Hate what is evil, and hold on to what is good. 10Love each other like brothers and sisters. Give each other more honor than you want for yourselves. 11Do not be lazy but work hard, serving the Lord with all your heart. 12Be joyful because you have hope. Be patient when trouble comes, and pray at all times. 13Share with God's people who need help. Bring strangers in need into your homes.

14Wish good for those who harm you; wish them well and do not curse them. 15Be happy with those who are happy, and be sad with those who are sad. 16Live in peace with each other. Do not be proud, but make friends with those who seem unimportant. Do not think how smart you are.

17If someone does wrong to you, do not pay him back by doing wrong to him. Try to do what everyone thinks is right. 18Do your best to live in peace with everyone. 19My friends, do not try to punish others when they wrong you, but wait for God to punish them with his anger. It is written: "I will punish those who do wrong; I will repay them,"[n] says the Lord. 20But you should do this:

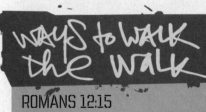

ways to WALK the WALK

ROMANS 12:15
WORD: Meet others where they are.
WALK IT: Throw a party for a friend who has just had a major achievement. Gather some other friends to encourage someone who has just experienced a major disappointment. Meet all of them where they are.

11:31 can Some Greek copies read "can now." 12:19 "I . . . them." Quotation from Deuteronomy 32:35.

185

ROMANS 13:1–4

You might have concluded that the authorities in charge of your life are the last people on the planet who deserve your obedience. Even if you're correct about their being evil and undeserving, God still says you owe them your respect. You can't blunt the point of the Bible's words: "All of you must yield to the government rulers." That's true even when authorities are as bad as Nero (A.D. 54–68), the emperor of Rome who was in power when the apostle Paul wrote these words. Nero cruelly persecuted Christians by tossing them to lions or savage dogs and by crucifying them, yet Paul urged believers to submit to Nero's rule. Don't take that to mean you can't protest the actions of people over you. You can appeal to your elders with the same respect you use when you need to negotiate with your parents (1 Timothy 5:1–2). You should stand up for justice, and you should never let anyone compel you to disobey God. But in the end, all authority is established by God. Yielding to authority is God's plan to do you good.

"If your enemy is hungry, feed him;
if he is thirsty, give him a drink.
Doing this will be like pouring burning
coals on his head."

Proverbs 25:21–22

²¹Do not let evil defeat you, but defeat evil by doing good.

CHRISTIANS SHOULD OBEY THE LAW

13 All of you must yield to the government rulers. No one rules unless God has given him the power to rule, and no one rules now without that power from God. ²So those who are against the government are really against what God has commanded. And they will bring punishment on themselves. ³Those who do right do not have to fear the rulers; only those who do wrong fear them. Do you want to be unafraid of the rulers? Then do what is right, and they will praise you. ⁴The ruler is God's servant to help you. But if you do wrong, then be afraid. He has the power to punish; he is God's servant to punish those who do wrong. ⁵So you must yield to the government, not only because you might be punished, but because you know it is right.

⁶This is also why you pay taxes. Rulers are working for God and give their time to their work. ⁷Pay everyone, then, what you owe. If you owe any kind of tax, pay it. Show respect and honor to them all.

LOVING OTHERS

⁸Do not owe people anything, except always owe love to each other, because the person who loves others has obeyed all the law. ⁹The law says, "You must not be guilty of adultery. You must not murder anyone. You must not steal. You must not want to take your neighbor's things."ⁿ All these commands and all others are really only one rule: "Love your neighbor as you love yourself."ⁿ ¹⁰Love never hurts a neighbor, so loving is obeying all the law.

¹¹Do this because we live in an important time. It is now time for you to wake up from your sleep, because our salvation is nearer now than when we first believed. ¹²The "night"ⁿ is almost finished, and the "day"ⁿ is almost here. So we should stop doing things that belong to darkness and take up the weapons used for fighting in the light. ¹³Let us live in a right way, like people who belong to the day. We should not have wild parties or get drunk. There should be no sexual sins of any kind, no fighting or jealousy. ¹⁴But clothe yourselves with the Lord Jesus Christ and forget about satisfying your sinful self.

DO NOT CRITICIZE OTHER PEOPLE

14 Accept into your group someone who is weak in faith, and do not argue about opinions. ²One person believes it is right to eat all kinds of food.ⁿ But another, who is weak, believes it is right to eat only vegetables. ³The one who knows that it is right to eat any kind of food must not reject the one who eats only vegetables. And the person who eats only vegetables must not think that the one who eats all foods is wrong, because God has accepted that person. ⁴You cannot judge another person's servant. The master decides if the servant is doing well or not. And the Lord's servant will do well because the Lord helps him do well.

⁵Some think that one day is more important than another, and others think that every day is the same. Let all be sure in their own mind. ⁶Those who think one day is more important than other days are doing that for the Lord. And those who eat all kinds of food are doing that for the Lord, and they give thanks to God. Others who refuse to eat some foods do that for the Lord, and they give thanks to God. ⁷We do not live or die for ourselves. ⁸If we live, we are living for the Lord, and if we die, we are dying for the Lord. So living or dying, we belong to the Lord.

⁹The reason Christ died and rose from the dead to live again was so he would be Lord over both the dead and the living. ¹⁰So why do you judge your brothers or sisters in Christ? And why do you think you are better than they are? We will all stand before God to be judged, ¹¹because it is written in the Scriptures:

" 'As surely as I live,' says the Lord,
'Everyone will bow before me;
everyone will say that I am God.' "

Isaiah 45:23

¹²So each of us will have to answer to God.

DO NOT CAUSE OTHERS TO SIN

¹³For that reason we should stop judging each other. We must make up our minds not to do anything that will make another Christian sin. ¹⁴I am in the Lord Jesus, and I know that there is no food that is wrong to eat. But if a person believes something is wrong, that thing is wrong for him. ¹⁵If you hurt your brother's or sister's faith because of something you eat, you are not really following the way of love. Do not destroy someone's faith by eating food he thinks is wrong, because Christ died for him. ¹⁶Do not allow what you think is good to become what others say is evil. ¹⁷In the kingdom of God, eating and drinking are not important. The important things are living right

 13:9 "You . . . things." Quotation from Exodus 20:13–15, 17.   13:9 "Love . . . yourself." Quotation from Leviticus 19:18.   13:12 "night" This is used as a symbol of the sinful world we live in. This world will soon end.   13:12 "day" This is used as a symbol of the good time that is coming, when we will be with God.   14:2 all . . . food The Jewish law said there were some foods Jews should not eat. When Jews became Christians, some of them did not understand they could now eat all foods.

186

with God, peace, and joy in the Holy Spirit. ¹⁸Anyone who serves Christ by living this way is pleasing God and will be accepted by other people.

¹⁹So let us try to do what makes peace and helps one another. ²⁰Do not let the eating of food destroy the work of God. All foods are all right to eat, but it is wrong to eat food that causes someone else to sin. ²¹It is better not to eat meat or drink wine or do anything that will cause your brother or sister to sin.

²²Your beliefs about these things should be kept secret between you and God. People are happy if they can do what they think is right without feeling guilty. ²³But those who eat something without being sure it is right are wrong because they did not believe it was right. Anything that is done without believing it is right is a sin.

15 We who are strong in faith should help the weak with their weaknesses, and not please only ourselves. ²Let each of us please our neighbors for their good, to help them be stronger in faith. ³Even Christ did not live to please himself. It was as the Scriptures said: "When people insult you, it hurts me."ⁿ ⁴Everything that was written in the past was written to teach us. The Scriptures give us patience and encouragement so that we can have hope. ⁵May the patience and encour-

agement that come from God allow you to live in harmony with each other the way Christ Jesus wants. ⁶Then you will all be joined together, and you will give glory to God the Father of our Lord Jesus Christ. ⁷Christ accepted you, so you should accept each other, which will bring glory to God. ⁸I tell you that Christ

Relationships

"Love patiently accepts all things. It always trusts, always hopes, and always endures" (1 Corinthians 13:7). Let's face it: guys don't always know the best way to treat girls. But right here's a prescription in the Bible for how to treat that special someone in your life. Verses 4–6 teach you to be patient and kind with her. Steer clear of jealousy, and don't brag about her like she's your possession. Don't be rude or selfish, and don't keep a checklist of her flaws and faults. Instead, trust, hope, and endure. Rejoice in this truth, and you'll be one blessed guy.

*REVIEWS MUSIC

PAUL COLMAN:
LET IT GO

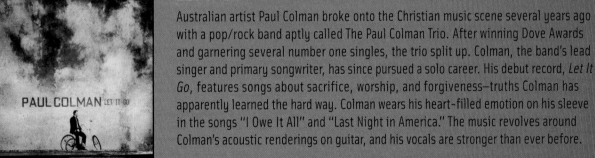

Australian artist Paul Colman broke onto the Christian music scene several years ago with a pop/rock band aptly called The Paul Colman Trio. After winning Dove Awards and garnering several number one singles, the trio split up. Colman, the band's lead singer and primary songwriter, has since pursued a solo career. His debut record, *Let It Go*, features songs about sacrifice, worship, and forgiveness—truths Colman has apparently learned the hard way. Colman wears his heart-filled emotion on his sleeve in the songs "I Owe It All" and "Last Night in America." The music revolves around Colman's acoustic renderings on guitar, and his vocals are stronger than ever before.

WHY IT ROCKS:

HUMILITY HAS REMADE THIS MAN OF GOD.

 15:3 "When . . . me." Quotation from Psalm 69:9.

187

became a servant of the Jews to show that God's promises to the Jewish ancestors are true. [9]And he also did this so that those who are not Jews could give glory to God for the mercy he gives to them. It is written in the Scriptures:

"So I will praise you among the non-Jewish
people.

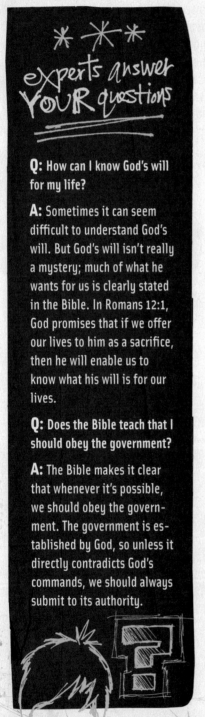

experts answer YOUR questions

Q: How can I know God's will for my life?

A: Sometimes it can seem difficult to understand God's will. But God's will isn't really a mystery; much of what he wants for us is clearly stated in the Bible. In Romans 12:1, God promises that if we offer our lives to him as a sacrifice, then he will enable us to know what his will is for our lives.

Q: Does the Bible teach that I should obey the government?

A: The Bible makes it clear that whenever it's possible, we should obey the government. The government is established by God, so unless it directly contradicts God's commands, we should always submit to its authority.

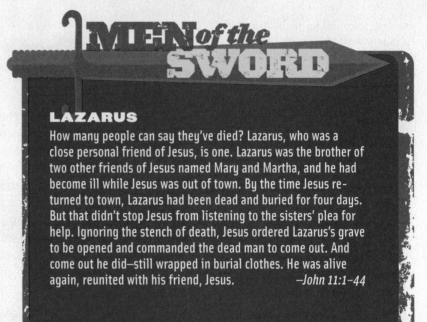

MEN of the SWORD

LAZARUS

How many people can say they've died? Lazarus, who was a close personal friend of Jesus, is one. Lazarus was the brother of two other friends of Jesus named Mary and Martha, and he had become ill while Jesus was out of town. By the time Jesus returned to town, Lazarus had been dead and buried for four days. But that didn't stop Jesus from listening to the sisters' plea for help. Ignoring the stench of death, Jesus ordered Lazarus's grave to be opened and commanded the dead man to come out. And come out he did—still wrapped in burial clothes. He was alive again, reunited with his friend, Jesus. —*John 11:1-44*

I will sing praises to your name."
Psalm 18:49

[10]The Scripture also says,
"Be happy, you who are not Jews, together
with his people."
Deuteronomy 32:43

[11]Again the Scripture says,
"All you who are not Jews, praise the
Lord.
All you people, sing praises to him."
Psalm 117:1

[12]And Isaiah says,
"A new king will come from the family of
Jesse.[n]
He will come to rule over the
non-Jewish people,
and they will have hope because of him."
Isaiah 11:10

[13]I pray that the God who gives hope will fill you with much joy and peace while you trust in him. Then your hope will overflow by the power of the Holy Spirit.

PAUL TALKS ABOUT HIS WORK

[14]My brothers and sisters, I am sure that you are full of goodness. I know that you have all the knowledge you need and that you are able to teach each other. [15]But I have written to you very openly about some things I wanted you to remember. I did this because God gave me this special gift: [16]to be a minister of Christ Jesus to those who are not Jews. I served God by teaching his Good News, so that the non-Jewish people could be an offering that God

would accept—an offering made holy by the Holy Spirit.

[17]So I am proud of what I have done for God in Christ Jesus. [18]I will not talk about anything except what Christ has done through me in leading those who are not Jews to obey God. They have obeyed God because of what I have said and done, [19]because of the power of miracles and the great things they saw, and because of the power of the Holy Spirit. I preached the Good News from Jerusalem all the way around to Illyricum, and so I have finished that part of my work. [20]I always want to preach the Good News in places where people have never heard of Christ, because I do not want to build on the work someone else has already started. [21]But it is written in the Scriptures:

"Those who were not told about him will
see,
and those who have not heard about
him will understand." *Isaiah 52:15*

PAUL'S PLAN TO VISIT ROME

[22]This is the reason I was stopped many times from coming to you. [23]Now I have finished my work here. Since for many years I have wanted to come to you, [24]I hope to visit you on my way to Spain. After I enjoy being with you for a while, I hope you can help me on my trip. [25]Now I am going to Jerusalem to help God's people. [26]The believers in Macedonia and Southern Greece were happy to give their money to help the poor among God's people at Jerusalem. [27]They were

15:12 Jesse Jesse was the father of David, king of Israel. Jesus was from their family.

188

happy to do this, and really they owe it to them. These who are not Jews have shared in the Jews' spiritual blessings, so they should use their material possessions to help the Jews. [28]After I am sure the poor in Jerusalem get the money that has been given for them, I will leave for Spain and stop and visit you. [29]I know that when I come to you I will bring Christ's full blessing.

[30]Brothers and sisters, I beg you to help me in my work by praying to God for me. Do this because of our Lord Jesus and the love that the Holy Spirit gives us. [31]Pray that I will be saved from the nonbelievers in Judea and that this help I bring to Jerusalem will please God's people there. [32]Then, if God wants me to, I will come to you with joy, and together you and I will have a time of rest. [33]The God who gives peace be with you all. Amen.

GREETINGS TO THE CHRISTIANS

16 I recommend to you our sister Phoebe, who is a helper[n] in the church in Cenchrea. [2]I ask you to accept her in the Lord in the way God's people should. Help her with anything she needs, because she has helped me and many other people also.

[3]Give my greetings to Priscilla and Aquila, who work together with me in Christ Jesus [4]and who risked their own lives to save my life. I am thankful to them, and all the non-Jewish churches

Treat your girlfriend with the respect she deserves. Open the car door for her on dates. Hold the umbrella for her when it's raining. Show your affection toward her through simple acts of kindness. For some this might seem elementary, but male chivalry has become a lost art among today's guys, and it never goes out of style.

are thankful as well. [5]Also, greet for me the church that meets at their house.

Greetings to my dear friend Epenetus, who was the first person in Asia to follow Christ. [6]Greetings to Mary, who worked very hard for you. [7]Greetings to Andronicus and Junia, my relatives, who were in prison with me. They are very important apostles. They were believers in Christ before I was. [8]Greetings to Ampliatus, my dear friend in the Lord. [9]Greetings to Urbanus, a worker together with me for Christ. And greetings to my dear friend Stachys. [10]Greetings to Apelles, who was tested and proved that he truly loves Christ. Greetings to all those who are in the family of Aristobulus. [11]Greetings to Herodion, my fellow citizen. Greetings to all those in the family of Narcissus who belong to the Lord. [12]Greetings to Tryphena and Tryphosa, women who work very hard for the Lord. Greetings to my dear friend Persis, who also has worked very hard for the Lord. [13]Greetings

to Rufus, who is a special person in the Lord, and to his mother, who has been like a mother to me also. [14]Greetings to Asyncritus, Phlegon, Hermes, Patrobas, Hermas, and all the brothers and sisters who are with them. [15]Greetings to Philologus and Julia, Nereus and his sister, and Olympas, and to all God's people with them. [16]Greet each other with a holy kiss. All of Christ's churches send greetings to you.

[17]Brothers and sisters, I ask you to look out for those who cause people to be against each other and who upset other people's faith. They are against the true teaching you learned, so stay away from them. [18]Such people are not serving our Lord Christ but are only doing what pleases themselves. They use fancy talk and fine words to fool the minds of those who do not know about evil. [19]All the believers have heard that you obey, so I am very happy because of you. But I want you to be wise in what is good and innocent in what is evil.

[20]The God who brings peace will soon defeat Satan and give you power over him.

The grace of our Lord Jesus be with you.

[21]Timothy, a worker together with me, sends greetings, as well as Lucius, Jason, and Sosipater, my relatives.

[22]I am Tertius, and I am writing this letter from Paul. I send greetings to you in the Lord.

[23]Gaius is letting me and the whole church here use his home. He also sends greetings to you, as do Erastus, the city treasurer, and our brother Quartus. [[24]The grace of our Lord Jesus Christ be with all of you. Amen.][n]

[25]Glory to God who can make you strong in faith by the Good News that I tell people and by the message about Jesus Christ. The message about Christ is the secret that was hidden for long ages past but is now made known. [26]It has been made clear through the writings of the prophets. And by the command of the eternal God it is made known to all nations that they might believe and obey.

[27]To the only wise God be glory forever through Jesus Christ! Amen.

How to Find Your Secret Admirer

So someone's playing hard-to-get. Not a problem; you're a detective mastermind. Did you receive a note from your secret admirer? Analyze the handwriting to see if you recognize it. Compare it to samples of people you know. Did you receive a gift? Check with the store it came from and ask for a description of the sender. You might even be able to get her name if she paid with a credit card or check. Maybe you got an anonymous e-mail or instant message. If so, check with the server database and look for familiar names. And don't go it alone—get your friends to help you think of people who've been paying more attention to you lately. Usually, secret admirers want to be found out, so look for clues they might leave. One thing that shouldn't be secret is your admiration for God— live boldly for him, and you'll be all the more attractive to others.

16:1 **helper** Literally, "deaconess." This might mean the same as one of the special women helpers in 1 Timothy 3:11.   16:24 **The . . . Amen.** Some Greek copies do not contain the bracketed text.

1 CORINTHIANS

A LETTER OF CORRECTION

A close look at 1 Corinthians reveals all the makings of a soap opera: people getting drunk, winking at incest, suing each other, following misguided leaders, and boasting endlessly. And all this was happening in the church! As in our day, the influence of the surrounding city's pagan idols and cults had crept into God's house. So Paul has to write a loving letter of correction to remind the people of certain basic principles.

Among the crucial truths the apostle reviews is the fact that believers are God's temple, a living home of the Holy Spirit. Not only should they avoid promiscuity, drunkenness, and idol worship, they shouldn't even associate with others who do such things. Paul isn't trying to spoil their fun. He just wants them to be aware that actions have consequences. He wants them to realize that adulterers, liars, thieves, and other wrongdoers won't enter God's kingdom.

This letter also provides valuable instructions on other topics, such as marital relations, unity of the church, and the necessity of love. Paul's classic description of love in 1 Corinthians 13 is a helpful reminder of its characteristics even today. When all is said and done, it is love that we need.

1 From Paul. God called me to be an apostle of Christ Jesus because that is what God wanted. Also from Sosthenes, our brother in Christ.

2 To the church of God in Corinth, to you who have been made holy in Christ Jesus. You were called to be God's holy people with all people everywhere who pray in the name of the Lord Jesus Christ—their Lord and ours:

3 Grace and peace to you from God our Father and the Lord Jesus Christ.

PAUL GIVES THANKS TO GOD

4 I always thank my God for you because of the grace God has given you in Christ Jesus. 5 I thank God because in Christ you have been made rich in every way, in all your speaking and in all your knowledge. 6 Just as our witness about Christ has been guaranteed to you, 7 so you have every gift from God while you wait for our Lord Jesus Christ to come again. 8 Jesus will keep you strong until the end so that there will be no wrong in you on the day our Lord Jesus Christ comes again. 9 God, who has called you into fellowship with his Son, Jesus Christ our Lord, is faithful.

PROBLEMS IN THE CHURCH

10 I beg you, brothers and sisters, by the name of our Lord Jesus Christ that all of you agree with each other and not be split into groups. I beg that you be completely joined together by having the same kind of thinking and the same purpose. 11 My brothers and sisters, some people from Chloe's family have told me quite plainly that there are quarrels among you. 12 This is what I mean: One of you says, "I follow Paul"; another says, "I follow Apollos"; another says, "I follow Peter"; and another says, "I follow Christ." 13 Christ has been divided up into different groups! Did Paul die on the cross for you? No! Were you baptized in the name of Paul? No! 14 I thank God I did not baptize any of you except Crispus and Gaius 15 so that now no one can say you were baptized in my name. 16 (I also baptized the family of Stephanas, but I do not remember that I baptized anyone else.) 17 Christ did not send me to baptize people but to preach the Good News. And he sent me to preach the Good News without using words of human wisdom so that the cross[n] of Christ would not lose its power.

CHRIST IS GOD'S POWER AND WISDOM

18 The teaching about the cross is foolishness to those who are being lost, but to us who are being saved it is the power of God. 19 It is written in the Scriptures:

"I will cause the wise to lose their wisdom;
I will make the wise unable to
  understand."   *Isaiah 29:14*

20 Where is the wise person? Where is the educated person? Where is the skilled talker of this world? God has made the wisdom of the world foolish. 21 In the wisdom of God the world did not know God through its own wisdom. So God chose to use the message that sounds foolish to save those who believe. 22 The Jews ask for miracles, and the Greeks want wisdom. 23 But we preach a crucified Christ. This causes the Jews to stumble and is foolishness to non-Jews. 24 But Christ is the power of God and the wisdom of God to those people God has called—Jews and Greeks. 25 Even the foolishness of God is wiser than human wisdom, and the weakness of God is stronger than human strength.

26 Brothers and sisters, look at what you were when God called you. Not many of you were wise in the way the world judges

1:17 cross Paul uses the cross as a picture of the Good News, the story of Christ's death and rising from the dead for people's sins. The cross, or Christ's death, was God's way to save people.

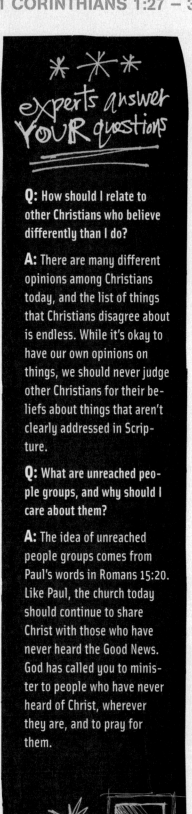

Q: How should I relate to other Christians who believe differently than I do?

A: There are many different opinions among Christians today, and the list of things that Christians disagree about is endless. While it's okay to have our own opinions on things, we should never judge other Christians for their beliefs about things that aren't clearly addressed in Scripture.

Q: What are unreached people groups, and why should I care about them?

A: The idea of unreached people groups comes from Paul's words in Romans 15:20. Like Paul, the church today should continue to share Christ with those who have never heard the Good News. God has called you to minister to people who have never heard of Christ, wherever they are, and to pray for them.

wisdom. Not many of you had great influence. Not many of you came from important families. [27]But God chose the foolish things of the world to shame the wise, and he chose the weak things of the world to shame the strong. [28]He chose what the world thinks is unimportant and what the world looks down on and thinks is nothing in order to destroy what the world thinks is important. [29]God did this so that no one can brag in his presence. [30]Because of God you are in Christ Jesus, who has become for us wisdom from God. In Christ we are put right with God, and have been made holy, and have been set free from sin. [31]So, as the Scripture says, "If people want to brag, they should brag only about the Lord."[n]

THE MESSAGE OF CHRIST'S DEATH

2 Dear brothers and sisters, when I came to you, I did not come preaching God's secret[n] with fancy words or a show of human wisdom. [2]I decided that while I was with you I would forget about everything except Jesus Christ and his death on the cross. [3]So when I came to you, I was weak and fearful and trembling. [4]My teaching and preaching were not with words of human wisdom that persuade people but with proof of the power that the Spirit gives. [5]This was so that your faith would be in God's power and not in human wisdom.

GOD'S WISDOM

[6]However, I speak a wisdom to those who are mature. But this wisdom is not from this world or from the rulers of this world, who are losing their power. [7]I speak God's secret wisdom, which he has kept hidden. Before the world began, God planned this wisdom for our glory. [8]None of the rulers of this world understood it. If they had, they would not have crucified the Lord of glory. [9]But as it is written in the Scriptures:

"No one has ever seen this,
    and no one has ever heard about it.
No one has ever imagined
    what God has prepared for those who
        love him."   *Isaiah 64:4*

[10]But God has shown us these things through the Spirit.

The Spirit searches out all things, even the deep secrets of God. [11]Who knows the thoughts that another person has? Only a person's spirit that lives within him knows his thoughts. It is the same with God. No one knows the thoughts of God except the Spirit of God. [12]Now we did not receive the spirit of the world, but we received the Spirit that is from God so that we can know all that God has given

us. [13]And we speak about these things, not with words taught us by human wisdom but with words taught us by the Spirit. And so we explain spiritual truths to spiritual people. [14]A person who does not have the Spirit does not accept the truths that come from the Spirit of God. That person thinks they are foolish and cannot understand them, because they can only be judged to be true by the Spirit. [15]The spiritual person is able to judge all things, but no one can judge him. The Scripture says:

[16]"Who has known the mind of the Lord?
    Who has been able to teach him?"
                          Isaiah 40:13

But we have the mind of Christ.

FOLLOWING PEOPLE IS WRONG

3 Brothers and sisters, in the past I could not talk to you as I talk to spiritual people. I had to talk to you as I would to people without the Spirit—babies in Christ. [2]The teaching I gave you was like milk, not solid food, because you were not able to take

Do's AND Don'ts

DO learn to appreciate art.

DO develop your creativity.

DO use your imagination.

DO color outside the lines.

DON'T make fun of artists.

DON'T take art for granted.

DON'T ignore the artist in you.

DON'T dismiss the power of art.

1:31 "If . . . Lord." Quotation from Jeremiah 9:24.   2:1 God's secret Some Greek copies read "God's message."

192

solid food. And even now you are not ready. ³You are still not spiritual, because there is jealousy and quarreling among you, and this shows that you are not spiritual. You are acting like people of the world. ⁴One of you says, "I belong to Paul," and another says, "I belong to Apollos." When you say things like this, you are acting like people of the world.

⁵Is Apollos important? No! Is Paul important? No! We are only servants of God who helped you believe. Each one of us did the work God gave us to do. ⁶I planted the seed, and Apollos watered it. But God is the One who made it grow. ⁷So the one who plants is not important, and the one who waters is not important. Only God, who makes things grow, is important. ⁸The one who plants and the one who waters have the same purpose, and each will be rewarded for his own work. ⁹We are God's workers, working together; you are like God's farm, God's house.

¹⁰Using the gift God gave me, I laid the foundation of that house like an expert builder. Others are building on that foundation, but all people should be careful how they build on it. ¹¹The foundation that has already been laid is Jesus Christ, and no one can lay down any other foundation. ¹²But if people build on that foundation, using gold, silver, jewels, wood, grass, or straw, ¹³their work will be clearly seen, because the Day of Judgment[n] will make it visible. That Day will appear with fire, and the fire will test everyone's work to show what sort of work it was. ¹⁴If the building that has been put on the foundation still stands, the builder will get a reward. ¹⁵But if the building is burned up, the builder will suffer loss. The builder will be saved, but it will be as one who escaped from a fire.

¹⁶Don't you know that you are God's temple and that God's Spirit lives in you? ¹⁷If anyone destroys God's temple, God will destroy that person, because God's temple is holy and you are that temple.

¹⁸Do not fool yourselves. If you think you are wise in this world, you should become a fool so that you can become truly wise, ¹⁹because the wisdom of this world is foolishness with God. It is written in the Scriptures, "He catches those who are wise in their own clever traps."[n] ²⁰It is also written in the Scriptures, "The Lord knows what wise people think. He knows their thoughts are just a puff of wind."[n] ²¹So you should not brag about human leaders. All things belong to you: ²²Paul, Apollos, and Peter; the world, life, death, the present, and the future—all these belong to you. ²³And you belong to Christ, and Christ belongs to God.

APOSTLES ARE SERVANTS OF CHRIST

4 People should think of us as servants of Christ, the ones God has trusted with his secrets. ²Now in this way those who are trusted with something valuable must show they are worthy of that trust. ³As for myself, I do not care if I am judged by you or by any human court. I do not even judge myself. ⁴I know of no wrong I have done, but this does not make me right before the Lord. The Lord is the One who judges me. ⁵So do not judge before the right time; wait until the Lord comes. He will bring to light things that are now hidden in darkness, and will make known the secret purposes of people's hearts. Then God will praise each one of them.

⁶Brothers and sisters, I have used Apollos and myself as examples so you could learn through us the meaning of the saying, "Follow only what is written in the Scriptures." Then you will not be more proud of one person than another. ⁷Who says you are better than others? What do you have that was not given to you? And if it was given to you, why do you brag as if you did not receive it as a gift?

⁸You think you already have everything you need. You think you are rich. You think you have become kings without us. I wish you really were kings so we could be kings together with you. ⁹But it seems to me that God has put us apostles in last place, like those sentenced to die. We are like a show for the whole world to see—angels and people. ¹⁰We are fools for Christ's sake, but you are very wise in Christ. We are weak, but you are strong. You receive honor, but we are shamed. ¹¹Even to this very hour we do not have enough to eat or drink or to wear. We are often beaten, and we have no homes in which to live. ¹²We work hard with our own hands for our food. When people curse us, we bless them. When they hurt us, we put up with it. ¹³When they tell evil lies about us, we speak nice words about them. Even today, we are treated as though we were the garbage of the world—the filth of the earth.

¹⁴I am not trying to make you feel ashamed. I am writing this to give you a warning as my own dear children. ¹⁵For though you may have ten thousand teachers in Christ, you do not have many fathers. Through the Good News I became your father in Christ Jesus, ¹⁶so I beg you, please follow my example. ¹⁷That is why I am sending to you Timothy, my son in the Lord. I love Timothy, and he is faithful. He will help you remember my way of life in Christ Jesus, just as I teach it in all the churches everywhere.

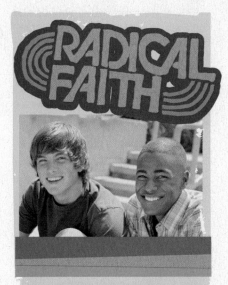

RADICAL FAITH

1 CORINTHIANS 4:7

Some guys feel a screaming need to push others down in order to pull themselves up. But the words of the apostle Paul hit like a clothesline to the neck of anyone who raises himself above others: "Who says you are better than others?" Back in the Old Testament, God gave bragging a different twist. He declared, "The wise must not brag about their wisdom. The strong must not brag about their strength. The rich must not brag about their money" (Jeremiah 9:23). So what do real men talk big about? Check these words straight from the mouth of God: "'But if people want to brag, let them brag that they understand and know me. Let them brag that I am the Lord, and that I am kind and fair, and that I do things that are right on earth. This kind of bragging pleases me,' says the Lord" (Jeremiah 9:24). The truth is, you are packed with talents you can be proud of. The trick is to admit that everything great about you comes from God. As Paul says, "What do you have that was not given to you?" If you're going to brag, talk up the One who put those gifts in you.

3:13 **Day of Judgment** The day Christ will come to judge all people and take his people home to live with him. 3:19 **"He . . . traps."** Quotation from Job 5:13. 3:20 **"The Lord . . . wind."** Quotation from Psalm 94:11.

[18]Some of you have become proud, thinking that I will not come to you again. [19]But I will come to you very soon if the Lord wishes. Then I will know what the proud ones do, not what they say, [20]because the kingdom of God is present not in talk but in power. [21]Which do you want: that I come to you with punishment or with love and gentleness?

WICKEDNESS IN THE CHURCH

5 It is actually being said that there is sexual sin among you. And it is a kind that does not happen even among people who do not know God. A man there has his father's

GUARD YOUR HEART

How you treat the other women in your life—your sister, mom, aunt, grandmother—will likely be how you will end up treating your girlfriend. Practice good manners with the women you know now, and when you're with a girlfriend, you'll know what a girl really wants and needs from you.

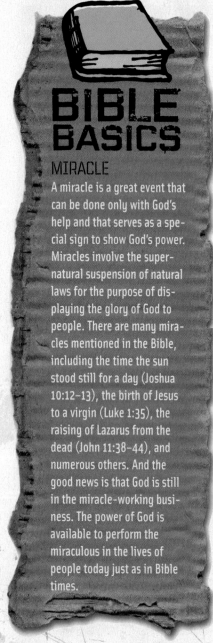

BIBLE BASICS

MIRACLE

A miracle is a great event that can be done only with God's help and that serves as a special sign to show God's power. Miracles involve the supernatural suspension of natural laws for the purpose of displaying the glory of God to people. There are many miracles mentioned in the Bible, including the time the sun stood still for a day (Joshua 10:12–13), the birth of Jesus to a virgin (Luke 1:35), the raising of Lazarus from the dead (John 11:38–44), and numerous others. And the good news is that God is still in the miracle-working business. The power of God is available to perform the miraculous in the lives of people today just as in Bible times.

wife. [2]And you are proud! You should have been filled with sadness so that the man who did this should be put out of your group. [3]I am not there with you in person, but I am with you in spirit. And I have already judged the man who did that sin as if I were really there. [4]When you meet together in the name of our Lord Jesus, and I meet with you in spirit with the power of our Lord Jesus, [5]then hand this man over to Satan. So his sinful self[n] will be destroyed, and his spirit will be saved on the day of the Lord.

[6]Your bragging is not good. You know the saying, "Just a little yeast makes the whole batch of dough rise." [7]Take out all the old yeast so that you will be a new batch of dough without yeast, which you really are. For Christ, our Passover lamb, has been sacrificed. [8]So let us celebrate this feast, but not with the bread that has the old yeast—the yeast of sin and wickedness. Let us celebrate this feast with the bread that has no yeast—the bread of goodness and truth.

[9]I wrote you in my earlier letter not to associate with those who sin sexually. [10]But I did not mean you should not associate with those of this world who sin sexually, or with the greedy, or robbers, or those who worship idols. To get away from them you would have to leave this world. [11]I am writing to tell you that you must not associate with those who call themselves believers in Christ but who sin sexually, or are greedy, or worship idols, or abuse others with words, or get drunk, or cheat people. Do not even eat with people like that.

[12-13]It is not my business to judge those who are not part of the church. God will judge them. But you must judge the people who are part of the church. The Scripture says, "You must get rid of the evil person among you."[n]

JUDGING PROBLEMS AMONG CHRISTIANS

6 When you have something against another Christian, how can you bring yourself to go before judges who are not right with God? Why do you not let God's people decide who is right? [2]Surely you know that God's people will judge the world. So if you are to judge the world, are you not able to judge small cases as well? [3]You know that in the future we will judge angels, so surely we can judge the ordinary things of this life. [4]If you have ordinary cases that must be judged, are you going to appoint people as judges who mean nothing to the church? [5]I say this to shame you. Surely there is someone among you wise enough to judge a complaint between believers? [6]But now one believer goes to court against another believer—and you do this in front of unbelievers!

[7]The fact that you have lawsuits against each other shows that you are already defeated. Why not let yourselves be wronged? Why not let yourselves be cheated? [8]But you yourselves do wrong and cheat, and you do this to other believers!

[9-10]Surely you know that the people who do wrong will not inherit God's kingdom. Do not be fooled. Those who sin sexually, worship idols, take part in adultery, those who are male prostitutes, or men who have sexual relations with other men, those who steal, are greedy, get drunk, lie about others, or rob—these people will not inherit God's kingdom. [11]In the past, some of you were like that, but you were washed clean. You were made holy, and you were made right with God in the name of the Lord Jesus Christ and in the Spirit of our God.

USE YOUR BODIES FOR GOD'S GLORY

[12]"I am allowed to do all things," but not all things are good for me to do. "I am allowed to do all things," but I will not let anything make me its slave. [13]"Food is for the stomach, and the stomach for food," but God will destroy them both. The body is not for sexual sin but for the Lord, and the Lord is for the body. [14]By his power God has raised the Lord from the dead and will also raise us from the dead. [15]Surely you know that your bodies are parts of Christ himself. So I must never take the

---

5:5 **sinful self** Literally, "flesh." This could also mean his body. 5:12–13 **"You . . . you."** Quotation from Deuteronomy 17:7; 19:19; 22:21, 24; 24:7.

parts of Christ and join them to a prostitute! [16]It is written in the Scriptures, "The two will become one body."[n] So you should know that anyone who joins with a prostitute becomes one body with the prostitute. [17]But the one who joins with the Lord is one spirit with the Lord.

[18]So run away from sexual sin. Every other sin people do is outside their bodies, but those who sin sexually sin against their own bodies. [19]You should know that your body is a temple for the Holy Spirit who is in you. You have received the Holy Spirit from God. So you do not belong to yourselves, [20]because you were bought by God for a price. So honor God with your bodies.

ABOUT MARRIAGE

7 Now I will discuss the things you wrote me about. It is good for a man not to have sexual relations with a woman. [2]But because sexual sin is a danger, each man should have his own wife, and each woman should have her own husband. [3]The husband should give his wife all that he owes her as his wife. And the wife should give her husband all that she owes him as her husband. [4]The wife does not have full rights over her own body; her husband shares them. And the husband does not have full rights over his own body; his wife shares them. [5]Do not refuse to give your bodies to each other, unless you both agree to stay away from sexual relations for a time so you can give your time to prayer. Then come together again so Satan cannot tempt you because of a lack of self-control. [6]I say this to give you permission to stay away from sexual relations for a time. It is not a command to do so. [7]I wish that everyone were like me, but each

person has his own gift from God. One has one gift, another has another gift.

[8]Now for those who are not married and for the widows I say this: It is good for them to stay unmarried as I am. [9]But if they cannot control themselves, they should marry. It is better to marry than to burn with sexual desire.

[10]Now I give this command for the married people. (The command is not from me; it is from the Lord.) A wife should not leave her husband. [11]But if she does leave, she must not marry again, or she should make up with her husband. Also the husband should not divorce his wife.

[12]For all the others I say this (I am saying this, not the Lord): If a Christian man has a wife who is not a believer, and she is happy to live with him, he must not divorce her. [13]And if a Christian woman has a husband who is not a believer, and he is happy to live with her, she must not divorce him. [14]The husband who is not a believer is made holy through his believing wife. And the wife who is not a believer is made holy through her believing husband. If this were not true, your children would not be clean, but now your children are holy.

[15]But if those who are not believers decide to leave, let them leave. When this happens, the Christian man or woman is free. But God called us[n] to live in peace. [16]Wife, you don't know; maybe you will save your husband. And husband, you don't know; maybe you will save your wife.

LIVE AS GOD CALLED YOU

[17]But in any case each one of you should continue to live the way God has given you to live—the way you were when God called you. This is a rule I make in all the churches. [18]If a man was already circumcised when he was called, he should not undo his circumcision. If a man was without circumcision when he was called, he should not be circumcised. [19]It is not important if a man is circumcised or not. The important thing is obeying God's commands. [20]Each one of you should stay the way you were when God called you. [21]If you were a slave when God called you, do not let that bother you. But if you can be free, then make good use of your freedom. [22]Those who were slaves when the Lord called them are free persons who belong to the Lord. In the same way, those who were free when they were called are now Christ's slaves. [23]You all were bought at a great price, so do not become slaves of people. [24]Brothers and sisters, each of you should stay as you were when you were called, and stay there with God.

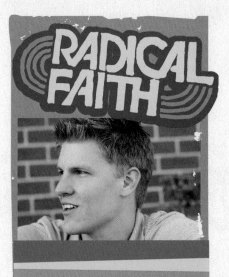

6:16 "The two . . . body." Quotation from Genesis 2:24.   7:15 us Some Greek copies read "you."

QUESTIONS ABOUT GETTING MARRIED

25Now I write about people who are not married. I have no command from the Lord about this; I give my opinion. But I can be trusted, because the Lord has shown me mercy. 26The present time is a time of trouble, so I think it is good for you to stay the way you

they own nothing. 31Those who use the things of the world should live as if they were not using them, because this world in its present form will soon be gone.

32I want you to be free from worry. A man who is not married is busy with the Lord's work, trying to please the Lord. 33But a man

most past the best age to marry and he feels he should marry her, he should do what he wants. They should get married. It is no sin. 37But if a man is sure in his mind that there is no need for marriage, and has his own desires under control, and has decided not to marry the one to whom he is engaged, he is doing the right thing. 38So the man who marries his girl does right, but the man who does not marry will do better.

39A woman must stay with her husband as long as he lives. But if her husband dies, she is free to marry any man she wants, but she must marry another believer. 40The woman is happier if she does not marry again. This is my opinion, but I believe I also have God's Spirit.

are. 27If you have a wife, do not try to become free from her. If you are not married, do not try to find a wife. 28But if you decide to marry, you have not sinned. And if a girl who has never married decides to marry, she has not sinned. But those who marry will have trouble in this life, and I want you to be free from trouble.

29Brothers and sisters, this is what I mean: We do not have much time left. So starting now, those who have wives should live as if they had no wives. 30Those who are crying should live as if they were not crying. Those who are happy should live as if they were not happy. Those who buy things should live as if

who is married is busy with things of the world, trying to please his wife. 34He must think about two things—pleasing his wife and pleasing the Lord. A woman who is not married or a girl who has never married is busy with the Lord's work. She wants to be holy in body and spirit. But a married woman is busy with things of the world, as to how she can please her husband. 35I am saying this to help you, not to limit you. But I want you to live in the right way, to give yourselves fully to the Lord without concern for other things.

36If a man thinks he is not doing the right thing with the girl he is engaged to, if she is al-

ABOUT FOOD OFFERED TO IDOLS

8 Now I will write about meat that is sacrificed to idols. We know that "we all have knowledge." Knowledge puffs you up with pride, but love builds up. 2If you think you know something, you do not yet know anything as you should. 3But if any person loves God, that person is known by God.

4So this is what I say about eating meat sacrificed to idols: We know that an idol is really nothing in the world, and we know there is only one God. 5Even though there are things called gods, in heaven or on earth (and there

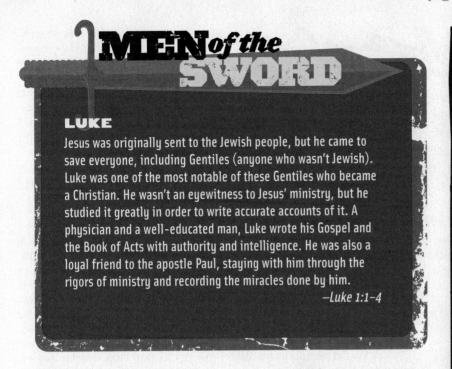

MEN of the SWORD

LUKE

Jesus was originally sent to the Jewish people, but he came to save everyone, including Gentiles (anyone who wasn't Jewish). Luke was one of the most notable of these Gentiles who became a Christian. He wasn't an eyewitness to Jesus' ministry, but he studied it greatly in order to write accurate accounts of it. A physician and a well-educated man, Luke wrote his Gospel and the Book of Acts with authority and intelligence. He was also a loyal friend to the apostle Paul, staying with him through the rigors of ministry and recording the miracles done by him.

—Luke 1:1–4

are many "gods" and "lords"), 6for us there is only one God—our Father. All things came from him, and we live for him. And there is only one Lord—Jesus Christ. All things were made through him, and we also were made through him.

7But not all people know this. Some people are still so used to idols that when they eat meat, they still think of it as being sacrificed to an idol. Because their conscience is weak, when they eat it, they feel guilty. 8But food will not bring us closer to God. Refusing to eat does not make us less pleasing to God, and eating does not make us better in God's sight.

9But be careful that your freedom does not cause those who are weak in faith to fall into sin. 10Suppose one of you who has knowledge eats in an idol's temple.ⁿ Someone who is weak in faith might see you eating there and be encouraged to eat meat sacrificed to idols while thinking it is wrong to do so. 11This weak believer for whom Christ died is ruined because of your "knowledge." 12When you sin against your brothers and sisters in Christ like this and cause them to do what they feel is wrong, you are also sinning against Christ. 13So if the food I eat causes them to fall into sin, I will never eat meat again so that I will not cause any of them to sin.

PAUL IS LIKE THE OTHER APOSTLES

9 I am a free man. I am an apostle. I have seen Jesus our Lord. You people are all an example of my work in the Lord. 2If others do not accept me as an apostle, surely you do, because you are proof that I am an apostle in the Lord.

3This is the answer I give people who want to judge me: 4Do we not have the right to eat and drink? 5Do we not have the right to bring a believing wife with us when we travel as do the other apostles and the Lord's brothers and Peter? 6Are Barnabas and I the only ones who must work to earn our living? 7No soldier ever serves in the army and pays his own salary. No one ever plants a vineyard without eating some of the grapes. No person takes care of a flock without drinking some of the milk.

8I do not say this by human authority; God's law also says the same thing. 9It is written in the law of Moses: "When an ox is working in the grain, do not cover its mouth to keep it from eating."ⁿ When God said this, was he thinking only about oxen? No. 10He was really talking about us. Yes, that Scripture was written for us, because it goes on to say: "The one who plows and the one who works in the grain should hope to get some of the grain for their work." 11Since we planted spiritual seed among you, is it too much if we should harvest material things? 12If others have the right to get something from you, surely we have this right, too. But we do not use it. No, we put up with everything ourselves so that we will not keep anyone from believing the Good News of Christ. 13Surely you know that those who work at the Temple get their food from the Temple, and those who serve at the altar get part of what is offered at the altar. 14In the same way, the Lord has commanded that those

experts answer YOUR questions

Q: What can I do if my church is divided or splitting?

A: It can be difficult and painful to watch people who used to be like family fighting over something that may seem unimportant. We need to remind each other of the most important truth: the message of Jesus. When we focus on truth, often we find that our differences aren't so important after all.

Q: How can I understand the Bible?

A: Some things in the Bible are difficult to understand, but God promises to send his Spirit to help us. If you put your faith in Jesus, then he promises that the Holy Spirit will give you the wisdom to understand the Bible.

who tell the Good News should get their living from this work.

15But I have not used any of these rights. And I am not writing this now to get anything from you. I would rather die than to have my reason for bragging taken away. 16Telling the Good News does not give me any reason for bragging. Telling the Good News is my duty—something I must do. And how terrible it will

Relationships

"God . . . comforts us every time we have trouble, so when others have trouble, we can comfort them with the same comfort God gives us" (2 Corinthians 1:3–4). God doesn't ask us to do something that he doesn't do himself. As a matter of fact, he not only comforts us when we need it, but he even gives us the comfort to share with other people. Remember that the next time you get to feeling like no one cares. God cares about you so much that he wants to comfort you and the people you come in contact with. So share the comfort that he gives you with others in need.

be for me if I do not tell the Good News. [17]If I preach because it is my own choice, I have a reward. But if I preach and it is not my choice to do so, I am only doing the duty that was given to me. [18]So what reward do I get? This is my reward: that when I tell the Good News I can offer it freely. I do not use my full rights in my work of preaching the Good News.

[19]I am free and belong to no one. But I make myself a slave to all people to win as many as I can. [20]To the Jews I became like a Jew to win the Jews. I myself am not ruled by the law. But to those who are ruled by the law I became like a person who is ruled by the law. I did this to win those who are ruled by the law. [21]To those who are without the law I became like a person who is without the law. I did this to win those people who are without the law. (But really, I am not without God's law—I am ruled by Christ's law.) [22]To those who are weak, I became weak so I could win the weak. I have become all things to all people so I could save some of them in any way possible. [23]I do all this because of the

Good News and so I can share in its blessings.

[24]You know that in a race all the runners run, but only one gets the prize. So run to win! [25]All those who compete in the games use self-control so they can win a crown. That crown is an earthly thing that lasts only a short time, but our crown will never be destroyed. [26]So I do not run without a goal. I fight like a boxer who is hitting something—not just the air. [27]I treat my body hard and make it my slave so that I myself will not be disqualified after I have preached to others.

WARNINGS FROM ISRAEL'S PAST

10 Brothers and sisters, I want you to know what happened to our ancestors who followed Moses. They were all under the cloud and all went through the sea. [2]They were all baptized as followers of Moses in the cloud and in the sea. [3]They all ate the same spiritual food, [4]and all drank the same spiritual drink. They drank from that spiritual rock that followed them, and that rock was Christ. [5]But God was not pleased with most of them, so they died in the desert.

[6]And these things happened as examples for us, to stop us from wanting evil things as those people did. [7]Do not worship idols, as some of them did. Just as it is written in the Scriptures: "They sat down to eat and drink, and then they got up and sinned sexually."[n] [8]We must not take part in sexual sins, as some of them did. In one day twenty-three thousand of them died because of their sins. [9]We must not test Christ as some of them did; they were killed by snakes. [10]Do not complain as some of them did; they were killed by the angel that destroys.

[11]The things that happened to those peo-

fight the fight

1 Corinthians 9:24-27

Sports have been popular throughout history, which is why Paul refers to boxing, running, and other athletics here. Yet, he is making a larger point. Just as athletes need self-discipline to win a race, building a spiritual life takes effort. Are you spending hours a day in front of a television but only a few minutes in prayer? Are you hanging out at the mall but rarely spending time with other believers? It isn't easy to read the Bible when you could be playing games. But seeking insight from God's Word more than the world will make all the difference.

10:7 "They . . . sexually." Quotation from Exodus 32:6.

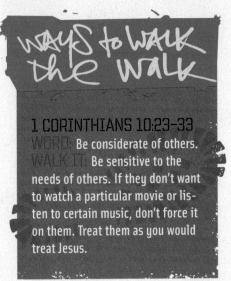

ways to walk the walk

1 CORINTHIANS 10:23-33
WORD Be considerate of others.
WALK IT Be sensitive to the needs of others. If they don't want to watch a particular movie or listen to certain music, don't force it on them. Treat them as you would treat Jesus.

ple are examples. They were written down to teach us, because we live in a time when all these things of the past have reached their goal. ¹²If you think you are strong, you should be careful not to fall. ¹³The only temptation that has come to you is that which everyone has. But you can trust God, who will not permit you to be tempted more than you can stand. But when you are tempted, he will also give you a way to escape so that you will be able to stand it.

¹⁴So, my dear friends, run away from the worship of idols. ¹⁵I am speaking to you as to reasonable people; judge for yourselves what I say. ¹⁶We give thanks for the cup of blessing,ⁿ which is a sharing in the blood of Christ. And the bread that we break is a sharing in the body of Christ. ¹⁷Because there is one loaf of bread, we who are many are one body, because we all share that one loaf.

¹⁸Think about the Israelites: Do not those who eat the sacrifices share in the altar? ¹⁹I do not mean that the food sacrificed to an idol is important. I do not mean that an idol is anything at all. ²⁰But I say that what is sacrificed to idols is offered to demons, not to God. And I do not want you to share anything with demons. ²¹You cannot drink the cup of the Lord and the cup of demons also. You cannot share in the Lord's table and the table of demons. ²²Are we trying to make the Lord jealous? We are not stronger than he is, are we?

HOW TO USE CHRISTIAN FREEDOM

²³"We are allowed to do all things," but not all things are good for us to do. "We are allowed to do all things," but not all things help others grow stronger. ²⁴Do not look out only for yourselves. Look out for the good of others also.

²⁵Eat any meat that is sold in the meat market. Do not ask questions about it. ²⁶You may eat it, "because the earth belongs to the Lord, and everything in it."ⁿ

²⁷Those who are not believers may invite you to eat with them. If you want to go, eat anything that is put before you. Do not ask questions about it. ²⁸But if anyone says to you, "That food was offered to idols," do not eat it. Do not eat it because of that person who told you and because eating it might be thought to be wrong. ²⁹I don't mean you think it is wrong, but the other person might. But why, you ask, should my freedom be judged by someone else's conscience? ³⁰If I eat the meal with thankfulness, why am I criticized because of something for which I thank God?

³¹The answer is, if you eat or drink, or if you do anything, do it all for the glory of God. ³²Never do anything that might hurt others— Jews, Greeks, or God's church— ³³just as I, also, try to please everybody in every way. I am not trying to do what is good for me but what is good for most people so they can be saved.

11 Follow my example, as I follow the example of Christ.

BEING UNDER AUTHORITY

²I praise you because you remember me in everything, and you follow closely the teachings just as I gave them to you. ³But I want you to understand this: The head of every man is Christ, the head of a woman is the man,ⁿ and the head of Christ is God. ⁴Every man who prays or prophesies with his head covered brings shame to his head. ⁵But every woman who prays or prophesies with her head uncovered brings shame to her head. She is the same as a woman who has her head shaved. ⁶If a woman does not cover her head, she should have her hair cut off. But since it is shameful for a woman to cut off her hair or to shave her head, she should cover her head. ⁷But a man should not cover his head, because he is the likeness and glory of God. But woman is man's glory. ⁸Man did not come from woman, but woman came from man. ⁹And man was not made for woman, but woman was made for man. ¹⁰So that is why a woman should have a symbol of authority on her head, because of the angels.

¹¹But in the Lord women are not independent of men, and men are not independent of women. ¹²This is true because woman came from man, but also man is born from woman. But everything comes from God. ¹³Decide this for yourselves: Is it right for a woman to pray to God with her head uncovered? ¹⁴Even nature

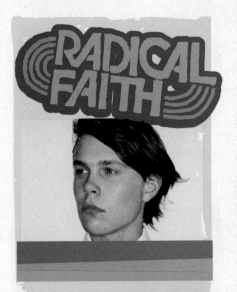

RADICAL FAITH

1 CORINTHIANS 10:6
You might assume that if you witnessed God doing a mound of miracles, then obeying him would be automatically easy. That isn't what you see happening in the stories of the Old Testament. The Lord rescued those old-school believers from slavery in Egypt by a series of miraculous plagues. He led them through the desert with a cloud and a flaming pillar (Exodus 13:21). He filled their stomachs with bread dropped from heaven (Exodus 16:13-15). But they still bowed to fake gods. They partied and sinned sexually. They grumbled and refused to trust God, so he let them die in the desert for their disobedience. There's only one bit of good news in that list of evil: Their pain can be your gain. The Bible informs you of all the misdeeds of God's ancient people so you can learn from their ghastly example of wanting evil things. Not only that, but God has shown you an even greater miracle than those Old Testament people ever saw: raising Jesus from the dead. Don't ignore what you know. A memory is a terrible thing to waste.

10:16 cup of blessing The cup of the fruit of the vine that Christians thank God for and drink at the Lord's Supper. **10:26 "because . . . it"** Quotation from Psalms 24:1; 50:12; 89:11. **11:3 the man** This could also mean "her husband."

199

1 CORINTHIANS 10:13

Temptation to do wrong might feel like a bullet you can't dodge, a pressure to sin that you can't resist. But God promises that the tug to do evil is an enemy you can outrun. As this verse points out, every person on earth feels drawn to sin: "The only temptation that has come to you is that which everyone has." Even Jesus was tempted to sin in every way that we are, but he never yielded (Hebrews 4:15). God guarantees that a temptation will never enter your life that is bigger than you can handle. He always creates a way out, so that every chance to do evil presents you with a choice to do right. So when you feel tempted, look for God's way out. Rather than trying to fight temptation, your escape route is usually to run from it instead.

itself teaches you that wearing long hair is shameful for a man. [15]But long hair is a woman's glory. Long hair is given to her as a covering. [16]Some people may still want to argue about this, but I would add that neither we nor the churches of God have any other practice.

THE LORD'S SUPPER

[17]In the things I tell you now I do not praise you, because when you come together you do more harm than good. [18]First, I hear that when you meet together as a church you are divided, and I believe some of this. [19](It is necessary to have differences among you so that it may be clear which of you really have God's approval.) [20]When you come together, you are not really eating the Lord's Supper.[n] [21]This is because when you eat, each person eats without waiting for the others. Some people do not get enough to eat, while others have too much to drink. [22]You can eat and drink in your own homes! You seem to think God's church is not important, and you embarrass those who are poor. What should I tell you? Should I praise you? I do not praise you for doing this.

[23]The teaching I gave you is the same teaching I received from the Lord: On the night when the Lord Jesus was handed over to be killed, he took bread [24]and gave thanks for it. Then he broke the bread and said, "This is my body; it is[n] for you. Do this to remember me." [25]In the same way, after they ate, Jesus took the cup. He said, "This cup is the new agreement that is sealed with the blood of my death. When you drink this, do it to remember me." [26]Every time you eat this bread and drink this cup you are telling others about the Lord's death until he comes.

[27]So a person who eats the bread or drinks the cup of the Lord in a way that is not worthy of it will be guilty of sinning against the body and the blood of the Lord. [28]Look into your own hearts before you eat the bread and drink the cup, [29]because all who eat the bread and drink the cup without recognizing the body eat and drink judgment against themselves. [30]That is why many in your group are sick and weak, and some of you have died. [31]But if we judged ourselves in the right way, God would not judge us. [32]But when the Lord judges us, he disciplines us so that we will not be destroyed along with the world.

[33]So my brothers and sisters, when you come together to eat, wait for each other. [34]Anyone who is too hungry should eat at home so that in meeting together you will not bring God's judgment on yourselves. I will tell you what to do about the other things when I come.

GIFTS FROM THE HOLY SPIRIT

12 Now, brothers and sisters, I want you to understand about spiritual gifts. [2]You know the way you lived before you were believers. You let yourselves be influenced and led away to worship idols—things that could not speak. [3]So I want you to understand that no one who is speaking with the help of God's Spirit says, "Jesus be cursed." And no one can say, "Jesus is Lord," without the help of the Holy Spirit.

[4]There are different kinds of gifts, but they are all from the same Spirit. [5]There are different ways to serve but the same Lord to serve. [6]And there are different ways that God works through people but the same God. God works in all of us in everything we do. [7]Something from the Spirit can be seen in each person, for the common good. [8]The Spirit gives one person the ability to speak with wisdom, and the same Spirit gives another the ability to speak with knowledge. [9]The same Spirit gives faith to one person. And, to another, that one Spirit gives gifts of healing. [10]The Spirit gives to another person the power to do miracles, to another the ability to prophesy. And he gives to another the ability to know the difference between good and evil spirits. The Spirit gives

Do's and Don'ts

DO use computers responsibly.

DO research projects online.

DO protect your online identity.

DO limit your computer time.

DON'T surf objectionable sites.

DON'T hog the family computer.

DON'T share your personal passwords.

DON'T enter questionable chat rooms.

11:20 Lord's Supper The meal Jesus told his followers to eat to remember him (Luke 22:14–20). 11:24 it is Some Greek copies read "it is broken."

july

NATIONAL CELL PHONE COURTESY MONTH

"One of the greatest discoveries a man makes, one of his great surprises, is to find he can do what he was afraid he couldn't do." -HENRY FORD

1 If you have a girlfriend, do something special for her today.

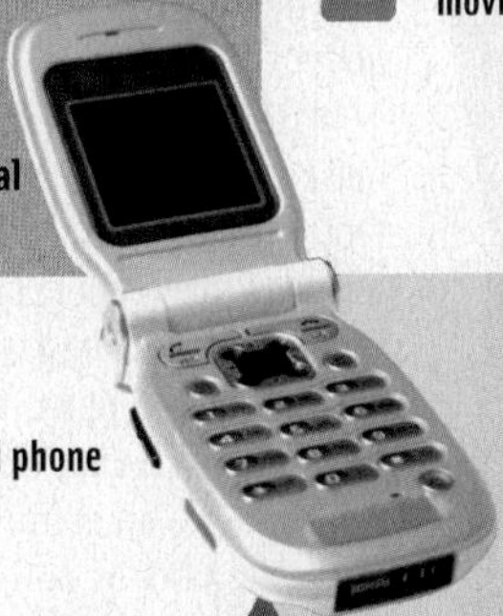

2 Plan a trip to the movie theatre.

3

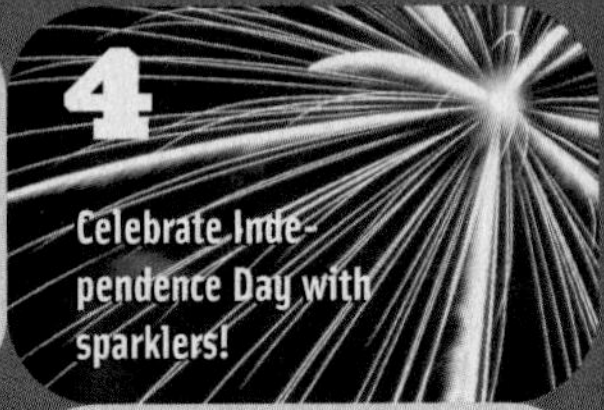

4 Celebrate Independence Day with sparklers!

5 Turn off your cell phone in public.

6

7

8 Jars of Clay's Steve Mason is celebrating a birthday today.

9

10

11 Ask your mom if you can help her with her flower garden.

12

13 Harrison Ford turns another year older.

14

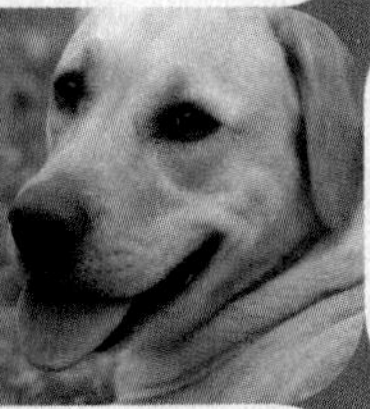

15 Walk your dog around the block.

16

17 Take a day off from your summer job and go to an amusement park.

18

19 Organize your sports card collection.

20 !t's Special Olympics Day. Pray for someone you know with special needs.

21

22 Play video games with friends.

23

24

25

26 Rebecca St. James is one year older today.

27

28 Pray for overseas missionaries today.

29

30 Today is Hilary Swank's birthday.

31 Start your own blog.

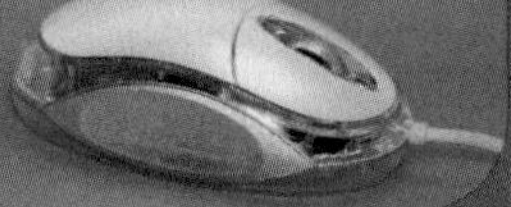

How to Juggle Three of Anything

To avoid confusion, let's just assume you're juggling balls. Start with one ball, tossing it in an arcing motion from one hand to another. You want it to peak right around the level of your eyes. Once you can do this easily, start with two balls: one in each hand. Toss a ball into the air, and when it reaches the peak, toss the other one. Catch both balls and repeat until you have it down. Then add the third ball in the same way, starting just like you've been doing. But this time, when the second ball is at the peak, toss the third one and keep going. It's hectic, but a little practice will see you juggling in no time. Life is hectic, too, but just like juggling, it can be managed by taking one thing at a time. Ask God for wisdom to know which balls you need to keep in the air.

one person the ability to speak in different kinds of languages[n] and to another the ability to interpret those languages. [11]One Spirit, the same Spirit, does all these things, and the Spirit decides what to give each person.

THE BODY OF CHRIST WORKS TOGETHER

[12]A person's body is one thing, but it has many parts. Though there are many parts to a body, all those parts make only one body.

Christ is like that also. [13]Some of us are Jews, and some are Greeks. Some of us are slaves, and some are free. But we were all baptized into one body through one Spirit. And we were all made to share in the one Spirit.

[14]The human body has many parts. [15]The foot might say, "Because I am not a hand, I am not part of the body." But saying this would not stop the foot from being a part of the body. [16]The ear might say, "Because I am not an eye, I am not part of the body." But saying this would not stop the ear from being a part of the body. [17]If the whole body were an eye, it would not be able to hear. If the whole body were an ear, it would not be able to smell. [18-19]If each part of the body were the same part, there would be no body. But truly God put all the parts, each one of them, in the body as he wanted them. [20]So then there are many parts, but only one body.

[21]The eye cannot say to the hand, "I don't need you!" And the head cannot say to the foot, "I don't need you!" [22]No! Those parts of the body that seem to be the weaker are really necessary. [23]And the parts of the body we think are less deserving are the parts to which we give the most honor. We give special respect to the parts we want to hide. [24]The more respectable parts of our body need no special care. But God put the body together and gave more honor to the parts that need it [25]so our body would not be divided. God wanted the different parts to care the same for each other. [26]If one part of the body suffers, all the other parts suffer with it. Or if one part of our body is honored, all the other parts share its honor.

[27]Together you are the body of Christ, and each one of you is a part of that body. [28]In the church God has given a place first to apostles, second to prophets, and third to teachers. Then God has given a place to those who do miracles, those who have gifts of healing, those who can help others, those who are able to govern, and those who can speak in different languages.[n] [29]Not all are apostles. Not all are prophets. Not all are teachers. Not all do miracles. [30]Not all have gifts of healing. Not all

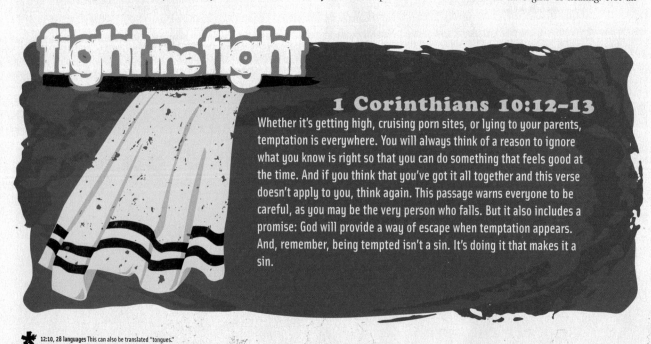

fight the fight

1 Corinthians 10:12–13

Whether it's getting high, cruising porn sites, or lying to your parents, temptation is everywhere. You will always think of a reason to ignore what you know is right so that you can do something that feels good at the time. And if you think that you've got it all together and this verse doesn't apply to you, think again. This passage warns everyone to be careful, as you may be the very person who falls. But it also includes a promise: God will provide a way of escape when temptation appears. And, remember, being tempted isn't a sin. It's doing it that makes it a sin.

12:10, 28 languages This can also be translated "tongues."

ISSUES

MONEY

YOU CAN'T LIVE WITHOUT MONEY, BUT YOU DON'T WANT IT CONTROLLING YOU LIFE EITHER. So what's a guy to do? The answer lies in what is known as being a good steward. A steward is a manager or overseer of another's goods. When it comes to money, God considers you a steward of what he entrusts you with, whether large or small. The key to becoming a good steward is being able to possess money without allowing it to possess you. God doesn't mind that you have fun with your funds as long as you aren't frivolous with the finances he gives you.

RADICAL FAITH

1 CORINTHIANS 12:4–7

Helping people get tight with God isn't just a job of pastors and parents. God has given each Christian one or more gifts from the Holy Spirit, special abilities meant for the good of everyone, inside and outside of the church. These "spiritual gifts" take you above and beyond the natural talents God also has built into you. Spiritual gifts include up-front abilities like teaching, behind-the-scene acts like giving and serving, and a few spectacular skills like healing, prophesying, and speaking in tongues. If you flip through the Bible, you find these gifts mentioned in several spots, including Romans 12:4–8, Ephesians 4:11–13, and 1 Corinthians 12:1–31, as well as 14:1–30. The apostle Paul wrote at length to the church in Corinth about spiritual gifts because they were clobbering each other with their spiritual ignorance. Some people thought their flashy gifts were better than all others, while some believers felt their gifts were hidden and worthless. Actually, the church can't function well without all the gifts in operation, any more than a body works well without all its parts. Ask God to show you your spiritual gift. Then exercise whatever it is.

speak in different languages. Not all interpret those languages. [31]But you should truly want to have the greater gifts.

LOVE IS THE GREATEST GIFT

And now I will show you the best way of all.

13 I may speak in different languages[n] of people or even angels. But if I do not have love, I am only a noisy bell or a crashing cymbal. [2]I may have the gift of prophecy. I may understand all the secret things of God and have all knowledge, and I may have faith so great I can move mountains. But even with all these things, if I do not have love, then I am nothing. [3]I may give away everything I have, and I may even give my body as an offering to be burned.[n] But I gain nothing if I do not have love.

[4]Love is patient and kind. Love is not jealous, it does not brag, and it is not proud. [5]Love is not rude, is not selfish, and does not get upset with others. Love does not count up wrongs that have been done. [6]Love takes no pleasure in evil but rejoices over the truth. [7]Love patiently accepts all things. It always trusts, always hopes, and always endures.

[8]Love never ends. There are gifts of prophecy, but they will be ended. There are gifts of speaking in different languages, but those gifts will stop. There is the gift of knowledge, but it will come to an end. [9]The reason is that our knowledge and our ability to prophesy are not perfect. [10]But when perfection comes, the things that are not perfect will end. [11]When I was a child, I talked like a child, I thought like a child, I reasoned like a child. When I became a man, I stopped those childish ways. [12]It is the same with us. Now we see a dim reflection, as if we were looking into a mirror, but then we shall see clearly. Now I know only a part, but then I will know fully, as God has known me. [13]So these three things continue forever: faith, hope, and love. And the greatest of these is love.

DESIRE SPIRITUAL GIFTS

14 You should seek after love, and you should truly want to have the spiritual gifts, especially the gift of prophecy. [2]I will explain why. Those who have the gift of speaking in different languages[n] are not speaking to people; they are speaking to God. No one understands them; they are speaking secret things through the Spirit. [3]But those who prophesy are speaking to people to give them strength, encouragement, and comfort. [4]The ones who speak in different languages are helping only themselves, but those who prophesy are helping the whole church. [5]I wish all of you had the gift of speaking in different kinds of languages, but more, I wish you would prophesy. Those who prophesy are greater than those who can only speak in different languages—unless someone is there who can explain what is said so that the whole church can be helped.

[6]Brothers and sisters, will it help you if I come to you speaking in different languages? No! It will help you only if I bring you a new truth or some new knowledge, or prophecy, or teaching. [7]It is the same as with lifeless things that make sounds—like a flute or a harp. If they do not make clear musical notes, you will not know what is being played. [8]And in a war, if the trumpet does not give a clear sound, who will prepare for battle? [9]It is the same with you. Unless you speak clearly with your tongue, no one can understand what you are saying. You will be talking into the air! [10]It may be true that there are all kinds of sounds in the world, and none is without meaning. [11]But unless I understand the meaning of what someone says to me, we will be like foreigners to each other. [12]It is the same with you. Since you want spiritual gifts very much, seek most of all to have the gifts that help the church grow stronger.

[13]The one who has the gift of speaking in a different language should pray for the gift to interpret what is spoken. [14]If I pray in a different language, my spirit is praying, but my mind does nothing. [15]So what should I do? I will pray with my spirit, but I will also pray with my mind. I will sing with my spirit, but I will also sing with my mind. [16]If you praise God with your spirit, those persons there without understanding cannot say amen[n] to your prayer of thanks, because they do not know what you are saying. [17]You may be thanking God in a good way, but the other person is not helped.

[18]I thank God that I speak in different kinds of languages more than all of you. [19]But in the church meetings I would rather speak five words I understand in order to teach others than thousands of words in a different language.

[20]Brothers and sisters, do not think like children. In evil things be like babies, but in your thinking you should be like adults. [21]It is written in the Scriptures:

"With people who use strange words and
    foreign languages
I will speak to these people.
But even then they will not listen to me,"
               Isaiah 28:11–12

says the Lord.

 13:1; 14:2 **languages** This can also be translated "tongues." 13:3 **give . . . burned** Other Greek copies read "hand over my body in order that I may brag." 14:16 **amen** To say amen means to agree with the things that were said.

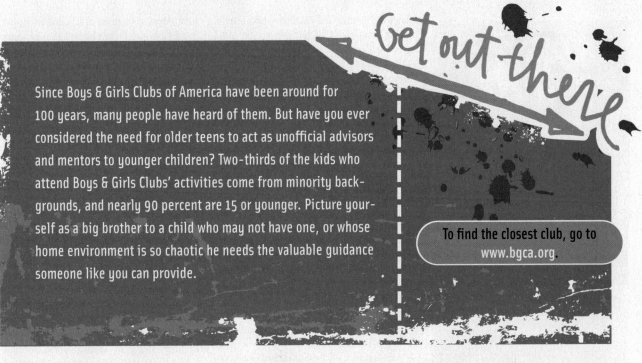

Since Boys & Girls Clubs of America have been around for 100 years, many people have heard of them. But have you ever considered the need for older teens to act as unofficial advisors and mentors to younger children? Two-thirds of the kids who attend Boys & Girls Clubs' activities come from minority backgrounds, and nearly 90 percent are 15 or younger. Picture yourself as a big brother to a child who may not have one, or whose home environment is so chaotic he needs the valuable guidance someone like you can provide.

To find the closest club, go to www.bgca.org.

²²So the gift of speaking in different kinds of languages is a sign for those who do not believe, not for those who do believe. And prophecy is for people who believe, not for those who do not believe. ²³Suppose the whole church meets together and everyone speaks in different languages. If some people come in who do not understand or do not believe, they will say you are crazy. ²⁴But suppose everyone is prophesying and some people come in who do not believe or do not understand. If everyone is prophesying, their sin will be shown to them, and they will be judged by all that they hear. ²⁵The secret things in their hearts will be made known. So they will bow down and worship God saying, "Truly, God is with you."

MEETINGS SHOULD HELP THE CHURCH

²⁶So, brothers and sisters, what should you do? When you meet together, one person has a song, and another has a teaching. Another has

*REVIEWS MOVIES

KINGDOM OF HEAVEN

Director Ridley Scott's epic tale is set during the Crusades of the Dark Ages when Christianity and Islam were in the midst of fighting their 200-year war. The movie follows the story of Balian, played by Orlando Bloom, as he grows from an uninterested bystander to a reluctant leader who protects his people against incredible odds. Although the movie certainly has its spots of action and excitement, it tends to be somewhat biased in its depiction of Christianity and historic events. Great cinematic visuals, huge stage sets, and superb acting make *Kingdom of Heaven* an enjoyable, if not entirely accurate, movie to watch.

WHY IT ROCKS:

THE STORY AND ACTING MAKE IT A MOVING PICTURE.

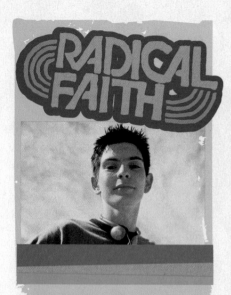

RADICAL FAITH

1 CORINTHIANS 15:1–8

If an alien from another star system landed a spaceship in your backyard and quizzed you about the key teachings of Christianity, would you know what to say? Or how about if a totally nonchurchgoing classmate asked you what it means to believe in Jesus? Or could you help clarify the big points for a friend who has wildly mixed-up ideas about what the Bible says? At the start of his letter to the Corinthians, the apostle Paul wants the Christians in Corinth to remember the core details of the Good News about Jesus, so they can keep believing the truth and stay strong in faith. Here's the scoop: Jesus died for the sins of the world. He was buried. But three days later he rose from the dead. Note that he wasn't spotted by a couple of drunk guys in some remote backwoods. He was seen by hundreds of people willing to die for the truth of what they had seen, most of whom were still around when Paul wrote, in case anyone wanted to double-check the facts. That's the short version of God's Good News. Those are the facts that save people who believe them.

a new truth from God. Another speaks in a different language,[n] and another person interprets that language. The purpose of all these things should be to help the church grow strong. [27]When you meet together, if anyone speaks in a different language, it should be only two, or not more than three, who speak. They should speak one after the other, and someone should interpret. [28]But if there is no interpreter, then those who speak in a different language should be quiet in the church meeting. They should speak only to themselves and to God.

[29]Only two or three prophets should speak, and the others should judge what they say. [30]If a message from God comes to another person who is sitting, the first speaker should stop. [31]You can all prophesy one after the other. In this way all the people can be taught and encouraged. [32]The spirits of prophets are under the control of the prophets themselves. [33]God is not a God of confusion but a God of peace.

As is true in all the churches of God's people, [34]women should keep quiet in the church meetings. They are not allowed to speak, but they must yield to this rule as the law says. [35]If they want to learn something, they should ask their own husbands at home. It is shameful for a woman to speak in the church meeting. [36]Did God's teaching come from you? Or are you the only ones to whom it has come?

[37]Those who think they are prophets or spiritual persons should understand that what I am writing to you is the Lord's command. [38]Those who ignore this will be ignored by God.[n]

[39]So my brothers and sisters, you should truly want to prophesy. But do not stop people from using the gift of speaking in different kinds of languages. [40]But let everything be done in a right and orderly way.

THE GOOD NEWS ABOUT CHRIST

15 Now, brothers and sisters, I want you to remember the Good News I brought to you. You received this Good News and continue strong in it. [2]And you are being saved by it if you continue believing what I told you. If you do not, then you believed for nothing.

[3]I passed on to you what I received, of which this was most important: that Christ died for our sins, as the Scriptures say; [4]that he was buried and was raised to life on the third day as the Scriptures say; [5]and that he was seen by Peter and then by the twelve apostles. [6]After that, Jesus was seen by more than five hundred of the believers at the same time. Most of them are still living today, but some have died. [7]Then he was seen by James and later by all the apostles. [8]Last of all he was seen by me—as by a person not born at the normal time. [9]All the other apostles are greater than I am. I am not even good enough to be called an apostle, because I persecuted the church of God. [10]But God's grace has made me what I am, and his grace to me was not wasted. I worked harder than all the other apostles. (But it was not I really; it was God's grace that was with me.) [11]So if I preached to you or the other apostles preached to you, we all preach the same thing, and this is what you believed.

WE WILL BE RAISED FROM THE DEAD

[12]Now since we preached that Christ was raised from the dead, why do some of you say that people will not be raised from the dead? [13]If no one is ever raised from the dead, then Christ has not been raised. [14]And if Christ has not been raised, then our preaching is worth nothing, and your faith is worth nothing. [15]And also, we are guilty of lying about God, because we testified of him that he raised Christ from the dead. But if people are not raised from the dead, then God never raised Christ. [16]If the dead are not raised, Christ has not been raised either. [17]And if Christ has not been raised, then your faith has nothing to it; you are still guilty of your sins. [18]And those in Christ who have already died are lost. [19]If our hope in Christ is for this life only, we should be pitied more than anyone else in the world.

[20]But Christ has truly been raised from the dead—the first one and proof that those who sleep in death will also be raised. [21]Death has come because of what one man did, but the rising from death also comes because of one man.

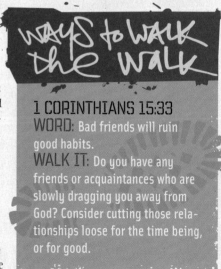

WAYS to WALK the WALK

1 CORINTHIANS 15:33
WORD: Bad friends will ruin good habits.
WALK IT: Do you have any friends or acquaintances who are slowly dragging you away from God? Consider cutting those relationships loose for the time being, or for good.

✱ **14:26 language** This can also be translated "tongue." **14:38 Those . . . God.** Some Greek copies read "Those who are ignorant of this will stay ignorant."

TOP TEN

random family household chores

1. Take out the garbage.
2. Straighten your room.
3. Wash the car.
4. Mow the lawn.
5. Clean the garage.
6. Fold your laundry.
7. Set the dinner table.
8. Unload the dishwasher.
9. Hang up your clothes.
10. Make your bed.

That is true, brothers and sisters, just as it is true that I brag about you in Christ Jesus our Lord. ³²If I fought wild animals in Ephesus only with human hopes, I have gained nothing. If the dead are not raised, "Let us eat and drink, because tomorrow we will die."ⁿ

³³Do not be fooled: "Bad friends will ruin good habits." ³⁴Come back to your right way of thinking and stop sinning. Some of you do not know God—I say this to shame you.

WHAT KIND OF BODY WILL WE HAVE?

³⁵But someone may ask, "How are the dead raised? What kind of body will they have?" ³⁶Foolish person! When you sow a seed, it must die in the ground before it can live and grow. ³⁷And when you sow it, it does not have the same "body" it will have later. What you sow is only a bare seed, maybe wheat or something else. ³⁸But God gives it a body that he has planned for it, and God gives each kind of seed its own body. ³⁹All things made of flesh are not the same: People have one kind of flesh, animals have another, birds have another, and fish have another. ⁴⁰Also there are heavenly bodies and earthly bodies. But the beauty of the heavenly bodies is one kind, and the beauty of the earthly bodies is another. ⁴¹The sun has one kind of beauty, the moon has another beauty, and the stars have another. And each star is different in its beauty.

⁴²It is the same with the dead who are raised to life. The body that is "planted" will ruin and decay, but it is raised to a life that cannot be destroyed. ⁴³When the body is "planted," it is without honor, but it is raised in glory. When the body is "planted," it is weak, but when it is raised, it is powerful. ⁴⁴The body that is "planted" is a physical body. When it is raised, it is a spiritual body.

There is a physical body, and there is also a spiritual body. ⁴⁵It is written in the Scriptures: "The first man, Adam, became a living person."ⁿ But the last Adam became a spirit that gives life. ⁴⁶The spiritual did not come first, but the physical and then the spiritual. ⁴⁷The first man came from the dust of the earth. The second man came from heaven. ⁴⁸People who belong to the earth are like the first man of earth. But those people who belong to heaven are like the man of heaven. ⁴⁹Just as we were made like the man of earth, so we willⁿ also be made like the man of heaven.

⁵⁰I tell you this, brothers and sisters: Flesh and blood cannot have a part in the kingdom of God. Something that will ruin cannot have a part in something that never ruins. ⁵¹But look! I tell you this secret: We will not all sleep in death, but we will all be

²²In Adam all of us die. In the same way, in Christ all of us will be made alive again. ²³But everyone will be raised to life in the right order. Christ was first to be raised. When Christ comes again, those who belong to him will be raised to life, ²⁴and then the end will come. At that time Christ will destroy all rulers, authorities, and powers, and he will hand over the kingdom to God the Father. ²⁵Christ must rule until he puts all enemies under his control. ²⁶The last enemy to be destroyed will be death. ²⁷The Scripture says that God put all things under his control.ⁿ When it says "all things" are under him, it is clear this does not include God himself. God is the One who put everything under his control. ²⁸After everything has been put under the Son, then he will put himself under God, who had put all things under him. Then God will be the complete ruler over everything.

²⁹If the dead are never raised, what will people do who are being baptized for the dead? If the dead are not raised at all, why are people being baptized for them?

³⁰And what about us? Why do we put ourselves in danger every hour? ³¹I die every day.

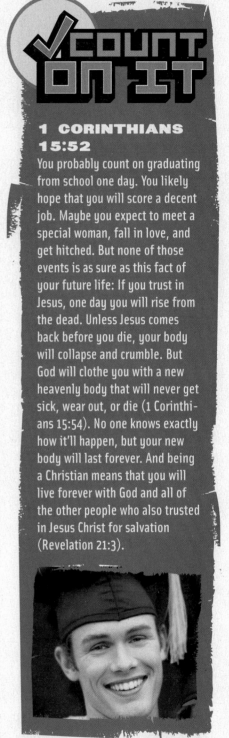

changed. ⁵²It will take only a second—as quickly as an eye blinks—when the last trumpet sounds. The trumpet will sound, and those who have died will be raised to live forever, and we will all be changed. ⁵³This body that can be destroyed must clothe itself with

15:27 God put . . . control. From Psalm 8:6.　15:32 "Let us . . . die." Quotation from Isaiah 22:13; 56:12.　15:45 "The first . . . person." Quotation from Genesis 2:7.　15:49 so we will Some Greek copies read "so let us."

207

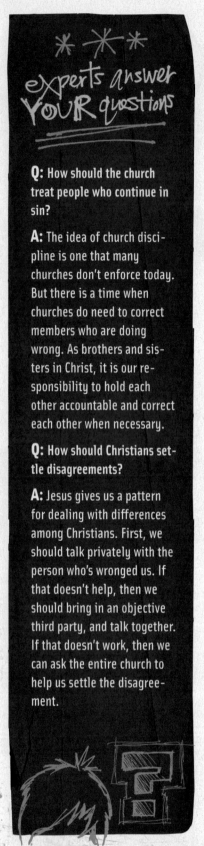

Q: How should the church treat people who continue in sin?

A: The idea of church discipline is one that many churches don't enforce today. But there is a time when churches do need to correct members who are doing wrong. As brothers and sisters in Christ, it is our responsibility to hold each other accountable and correct each other when necessary.

Q: How should Christians settle disagreements?

A: Jesus gives us a pattern for dealing with differences among Christians. First, we should talk privately with the person who's wronged us. If that doesn't help, then we should bring in an objective third party, and talk together. If that doesn't work, then we can ask the entire church to help us settle the disagreement.

GUARD YOUR HEART

If you tell your girlfriend you're going to call her at certain time, then call her at that time. If you're late with that very important "good night" phone call for no apparent reason, you're telling your girl a lot more about your feelings for her than anything you will ever say over the phone.

something that can never be destroyed. And this body that dies must clothe itself with something that can never die. ⁵⁴So this body that can be destroyed will clothe itself with that which can never be destroyed, and this body that dies will clothe itself with that which can never die. When this happens, this Scripture will be made true:

"Death is destroyed forever in victory."

Isaiah 25:8

⁵⁵"Death, where is your victory?

Death, where is your pain?" *Hosea 13:14*
⁵⁶Death's power to hurt is sin, and the power of sin is the law. ⁵⁷But we thank God! He gives us the victory through our Lord Jesus Christ.

⁵⁸So my dear brothers and sisters, stand strong. Do not let anything move you. Always give yourselves fully to the work of the Lord, because you know that your work in the Lord is never wasted.

THE GIFT FOR OTHER BELIEVERS

16 Now I will write about the collection of money for God's people. Do the same thing I told the Galatian churches to do: ²On the first day of every week, each one of you should put aside money as you have been blessed. Save it up so you will not have to collect money after I come. ³When I arrive, I will send whomever you approve to take your gift to Jerusalem. I will send them with letters of introduction, ⁴and if it seems good for me to go also, they will go along with me.

PAUL'S PLANS

⁵I plan to go through Macedonia, so I will come to you after I go through there. ⁶Perhaps I will stay with you for a time or even all winter. Then you can help me on my trip, wherever I go. ⁷I do not want to see you now just in passing. I hope to stay a longer time with you if the Lord allows it. ⁸But I will stay at Ephesus until Pentecost, ⁹because a good opportunity for a great and growing work has been given to

me now. And there are many people working against me.

¹⁰If Timothy comes to you, see to it that he has nothing to fear with you, because he is working for the Lord just as I am. ¹¹So none of you should treat Timothy as unimportant, but help him on his trip in peace so that he can come back to me. I am expecting him to come with the brothers.

¹²Now about our brother Apollos: I strongly encouraged him to visit you with the other brothers. He did not at all want to come now; he will come when he has the opportunity.

PAUL ENDS HIS LETTER

¹³Be alert. Continue strong in the faith. Have courage, and be strong. ¹⁴Do everything in love.

¹⁵You know that the family of Stephanas were the first believers in Southern Greece and that they have given themselves to the service of God's people. I ask you, brothers and sisters, ¹⁶to follow the leading of people like these and anyone else who works and serves with them.

¹⁷I am happy that Stephanas, Fortunatus, and Achaicus have come. You are not here, but they have filled your place. ¹⁸They have refreshed my spirit and yours. You should recognize the value of people like these.

¹⁹The churches in Asia send greetings to you. Aquila and Priscilla greet you in the Lord, as does the church that meets in their house. ²⁰All the brothers and sisters here send greetings. Give each other a holy kiss when you meet.

²¹I, Paul, am writing this greeting with my own hand.

²²If anyone does not love the Lord, let him be separated from God—lost forever!

Come, O Lord!

²³The grace of the Lord Jesus be with you.

²⁴My love be with all of you in Christ Jesus.ᵃ

ᵃ **16:24 My . . . Jesus.** Some Greek copies add "Amen."

* *** notes

2 CORINTHIANS

SENDING A REMINDER NOTICE

SERVICE
COR
13
POST

If one of your parents has ever gotten angry with you and shouted, "Someday I hope you have a kid just like you," you can sense some of the frustration Paul must have felt after he wrote to the church at Corinth. Despite giving them sound advice, several months after his first letter to them he had to write another one. Moreover, false teachers challenged his authority and integrity, forcing him to defend himself.

You can sense Paul's emotions erupt in these pages. He painfully reviews the suffering he has endured for God's sake. Among other things, he has been beaten and thrown into prison by rioting mobs.

Some have called him and his fellow ministers liars and evildoers. Such mean-spirited indignities would trouble even the most mild-mannered person.

Yet, through it all, Paul is steadfast. He encourages the church to serve Christ faithfully. Just as Jesus suffered, so they also must suffer yet persevere no matter how others act, he reminds them. Paul's concern for the church at large also comes through in this letter. In the middle of it, he urges believers to be generous givers, since showing compassion for others is the essence of love and the duty of all believers.

1 From Paul, an apostle of Christ Jesus. I am an apostle because that is what God wanted. Also from Timothy our brother in Christ.

To the church of God in Corinth, and to all of God's people everywhere in Southern Greece:

2 Grace and peace to you from God our Father and the Lord Jesus Christ.

PAUL GIVES THANKS TO GOD

3 Praise be to the God and Father of our Lord Jesus Christ. God is the Father who is full of mercy and all comfort. 4 He comforts us every time we have trouble, so when others have trouble, we can comfort them with the same comfort God gives us. 5 We share in the

write to you only what you can read and understand. And I hope that as you have understood some things about us, you may come to know everything about us. Then you can be proud of us, as we will be proud of you on the day our Lord Jesus Christ comes again.

15 I was so sure of all this that I made plans to visit you first so you could be blessed twice. 16 I planned to visit you on my way to Macedonia and again on my way back. I wanted to get help from you for my trip to Judea. 17 Do you think that I made these plans without really meaning it? Or maybe you think I make plans as the world does, so that I say yes, yes and at the same time no, no.

18 But since you can believe God, you can believe that what we tell you is never both yes

RADICAL FAITH

many sufferings of Christ. In the same way, much comfort comes to us through Christ. 6 If we have troubles, it is for your comfort and salvation, and if we have comfort, you also have comfort. This helps you to accept patiently the same sufferings we have. 7 Our hope for you is strong, knowing that you share in our sufferings and also in the comfort we receive.

8 Brothers and sisters, we want you to know about the trouble we suffered in Asia. We had great burdens there that were beyond our own strength. We even gave up hope of living. 9 Truly, in our own hearts we believed we would die. But this happened so we would not trust in ourselves but in God, who raises people from the dead. 10 God saved us from these great dangers of death, and he will continue to save us. We have put our hope in him, and he will save us again. 11 And you can help us with your prayers. Then many people will give thanks for us—that God blessed us because of their many prayers.

THE CHANGE IN PAUL'S PLANS

12 This is what we are proud of, and I can say it with a clear conscience: In everything we have done in the world, and especially with you, we have had an honest[a] and sincere heart from God. We did this by God's grace, not by the kind of wisdom the world has. 13-14 We

and no. 19 The Son of God, Jesus Christ, that Silas and Timothy and I preached to you, was not yes and no. In Christ it has always been yes. 20 The yes to all of God's promises is in Christ, and through Christ we say yes to the glory of God. 21 Remember, God is the One who makes you and us strong in Christ. God made us his chosen people. 22 He put his mark on us to show that we are his, and he put his Spirit in our hearts to be a guarantee for all he has promised.

23 I tell you this, and I ask God to be my witness that this is true: The reason I did not come back to Corinth was to keep you from being punished or hurt. 24 We are not trying to control your faith. You are strong in faith. But we are workers with you for your own joy.

2 So I decided that my next visit to you would not be another one to make you sad. 2 If I make you sad, who will make me glad? Only you can make me glad—particularly the person whom I made sad. 3 I wrote you a letter for this reason: that when I came to you I would not be made sad by the people who should make me happy. I felt sure of all of you, that you would share my joy. 4 When I wrote to you before, I was very troubled and unhappy in my heart, and I wrote with many tears. I did not write to make you sad, but to let you know how much I love you.

2 CORINTHIANS 2:14–16

You have a distinct aroma about you. Not because you rolled in decomposing leftovers and then skipped showering for a week. To some people, you reek simply because you believe in Jesus. Actually, to people who are getting to know your Savior, you smell even better than the costliest cologne at the mall. As you trek through life demonstrating what it means to know God, you let loose a fragrance that wafts through your surroundings smelling even nicer than linens on laundry day. But to people who don't know Christ, you smell like death. You are a reminder that they're headed for judgment, and there's nothing fragrant about that. While this metaphor sounds strange to us, the apostle Paul was using an image familiar to his readers, a street scene of triumphant Roman soldiers parading through a town waving incense. To the conquerors, the smoke was the smell of victory. To the captives, it meant death was ahead. You don't have to feel bad if people think you stink, because that response is really about Jesus. But tell others the Good News. Help people smell the sweetness of your Savior.

 1:12 honest Some Greek copies read "holy."

FORGIVE THE SINNER

[5]Someone there among you has caused sadness, not to me, but to all of you. I mean he caused sadness to all in some way. (I do not want to make it sound worse than it really is.) [6]The punishment that most of you gave him is enough for him. [7]But now you should forgive him and comfort him to keep him from having too much sadness and giving up completely. [8]So I beg you to show that you love him. [9]I wrote you to test you and to see if you obey in everything. [10]If you forgive someone, I also forgive him. And what I have forgiven—if I had anything to forgive—I forgave it for you, as if Christ were with me. [11]I did this so that Satan would not win anything from us, because we know very well what Satan's plans are.

PAUL'S CONCERN IN TROAS

[12]When I came to Troas to preach the Good News of Christ, the Lord gave me a good opportunity there. [13]But I had no peace, because I did not find my brother Titus. So I said good-bye to them at Troas and went to Macedonia.

VICTORY THROUGH CHRIST

[14]But thanks be to God, who always leads us as captives in Christ's victory parade. God uses us to spread his knowledge everywhere like a sweet-smelling perfume. [15]Our offering to God is this: We are the sweet smell of Christ among those who are being saved and among those who are being lost. [16]To those who are lost, we are the smell of death that brings death, but to those who are being saved, we are the smell of life that brings life. So who is able to do this work? [17]We do not sell the word of God for a profit as many other people do. But in Christ we speak the truth before God, as messengers of God.

SERVANTS OF THE NEW AGREEMENT

3 Are we starting to brag about ourselves again? Do we need letters of introduction to you or from you, like some other people? [2]You yourselves are our letter, written on our hearts, known and read by everyone. [3]You show that you are a letter from Christ sent through us. This letter is not written with ink but with the Spirit of the living God. It is not written on stone tablets[n] but on human hearts.

[4]We can say this, because through Christ we feel certain before God. [5]We are not saying that we can do this work ourselves. It is God who makes us able to do all that we do. [6]He made us able to be servants of a new agreement from himself to his people. This new agreement is not a written law, but it is of the Spirit. The written law brings death, but the Spirit gives life.

[7]The law that brought death was written in words on stone. It came with God's glory, which made Moses' face so bright that the Israelites could not continue to look at it. But that glory later disappeared. [8]So surely the new way that brings the Spirit has even more glory. [9]If the law that judged people guilty of sin had glory, surely the new way that makes

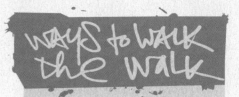
people right with God has much greater glory. [10]That old law had glory, but it really loses its glory when it is compared to the much greater glory of this new way. [11]If that law which disappeared came with glory, then this new way which continues forever has much greater glory.

[12]We have this hope, so we are very bold. [13]We are not like Moses, who put a covering over his face so the Israelites would not see it. The glory was disappearing, and Moses did not want them to see it end. [14]But their minds were closed, and even today that same covering hides the meaning when they read the old agreement. That covering is taken away only through Christ. [15]Even today, when they read the law of Moses, there is a covering over their minds. [16]But when a person changes and follows the Lord, that covering is taken away. [17]The Lord is the Spirit, and where the Spirit of the Lord is, there is freedom. [18]Our faces, then, are not covered. We all show the Lord's glory, and we are being changed to be like him. This change in us brings ever greater glory, which comes from the Lord, who is the Spirit.

PREACHING THE GOOD NEWS

4 God, with his mercy, gave us this work to do, so we don't give up. [2]But we have turned away from secret and shameful ways. We use no trickery, and we do not change the teaching of God. We teach the truth plainly, showing everyone who we are. Then they can know in their hearts what kind of people we are in God's sight. [3]If the Good News that we preach is hidden, it is hidden only to those who are lost. [4]The devil who rules this world has blinded the minds of those who do not believe. They cannot see the light of the

BIBLE BASICS

PEACE

Peace is more than simply the absence of war. It is a sense that things will turn out okay, even when circumstances indicate otherwise. The New Testament is full of references to peace, including the passage in John 14:27, where Jesus Christ, who is the Prince of Peace, reminded all believers: "I leave you peace; my peace I give you." And later in Philippians 4:7, Paul reminds readers: "And God's peace, which is so great we cannot understand it, will keep your hearts and minds in Christ Jesus." The ultimate peace comes from experiencing a relationship with God through Jesus. By accepting Christ as Lord, we are made right with God, and peace is ours.

✳ 3:3 **stone tablets** Meaning the Law of Moses that was written on stone tablets (Exodus 24:12; 25:16).

Good News—the Good News about the glory of Christ, who is exactly like God. ⁵We do not preach about ourselves, but we preach that Jesus Christ is Lord and that we are your servants for Jesus. ⁶God once said, "Let the light shine out of the darkness!" This is the same God who made his light shine in our hearts by letting us know the glory of God that is in the face of Christ.

SPIRITUAL TREASURE IN CLAY JARS

⁷We have this treasure from God, but we are like clay jars that hold the treasure. This shows that the great power is from God, not from us. ⁸We have troubles all around us, but we are not defeated. We do not know what to do, but we do not give up the hope of living. ⁹We are persecuted, but God does not leave us. We are hurt sometimes, but we are not destroyed. ¹⁰We carry the death of Jesus in our own bodies so that the life of Jesus can also be seen in our bodies. ¹¹We are alive, but for Jesus we are always in danger of death so that the life of Jesus can be seen in our bodies that die. ¹²So death is working in us, but life is working in you.

¹³It is written in the Scriptures, "I believed, so I spoke."ª Our faith is like this, too. We believe, and so we speak. ¹⁴God raised the Lord Jesus from the dead, and we know that God will also raise us with Jesus. God will bring us together with you, and we will stand before him. ¹⁵All these things are for you. And so the grace of God that is being given to more and more people will bring increasing thanks to God for his glory.

Relationships

"In Christ, there is no difference between Jew and Greek, slave and free person, male and female. You are all the same in Christ Jesus" (Galatians 3:28). So one passage of Scripture says that God made girls and guys different, but now this one says we're all the same. What's the deal? Well, we are different in lots of ways, but girls and guys are the same on the level of respect they're due. Don't look down on girls as objects, and don't raise them up on pedestals. The point to keep in mind is that they are people just like you.

LIVING BY FAITH

¹⁶So we do not give up. Our physical body is becoming older and weaker, but our spirit inside us is made new every day. ¹⁷We have small troubles for a while now, but they are helping us gain an eternal glory that is much greater than the troubles. ¹⁸We set our eyes not on what we see but on what we cannot see. What we see will last only a short time, but what we cannot see will last forever.

5 We know that our body—the tent we live in here on earth—will be destroyed. But when that happens, God will have a house for us. It will not be a house made by human hands; instead, it will be a home in heaven that will last forever. ²But now we groan in this tent. We want God to give us our heavenly home, ³because it will clothe us so we will not be naked. ⁴While we live in this body, we have burdens, and we groan. We do not want to be naked, but we want to be

fight the fight

2 Corinthians 4:8-10

No matter what obstacles you're now facing, whatever worries you have about the future or whatever pains are buried in your past, you are not alone. Among the many messages Paul gave to the church was to persevere in spite of its problems. Yes, there is trouble all around us, but that doesn't mean we should give up hope or that God has left us alone. Because Christ lives in us, we have the power to offer hope to others. Not through our perfection, but through our love, service, and compassion. The world will always tell you to give up and look out for yourself. Instead, remember that God is looking out for you.

4:13 "I . . . spoke." Quotation from Psalm 116:10.

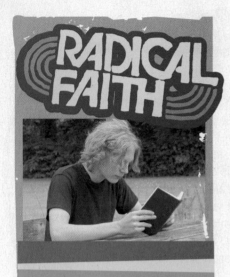

2 CORINTHIANS 5:14–15

So you've trusted Jesus and become a Christian. You're persuaded that he died for your sins and you now realize that through faith in Jesus and what he has accomplished, God has forgiven you. You've told God that you want to ditch sin and accept his gift of forgiveness. You might feel like coasting. Not because you really think you should, but because you don't know any better. Believing in Jesus gives you fire insurance against hell and life insurance that heads you to heaven. So what more is there? Well, Jesus wants you to think hard until you spot the connection between his death and your life. The apostle Paul says it straight: Jesus died for you so that you wouldn't continue to live for yourself. He died and rose so you would live for him. When you realize the heft of what Jesus has done for you, you are grateful to God. Love from him and for him powers your existence. So, instead of coasting, crack open your Bible and start reading. Figure out how to spend the rest of your life tight with God. Jesus died for you, so now live for him.

clothed with our heavenly home. Then this body that dies will be fully covered with life. [5] This is what God made us for, and he has given us the Spirit to be a guarantee for this new life.

[6] So we always have courage. We know that while we live in this body, we are away from the Lord. [7] We live by what we believe, not by what we can see. [8] So I say that we have courage. We really want to be away from this body and be at home with the Lord. [9] Our only goal is to please God whether we live here or there, [10] because we must all stand before Christ to be judged. Each of us will receive what we should get—good or bad—for the things we did in the earthly body.

BECOMING FRIENDS WITH GOD

[11] Since we know what it means to fear the Lord, we try to help people accept the truth about us. God knows what we really are, and I hope that in your hearts you know, too. [12] We are not trying to prove ourselves to you again, but we are telling you about ourselves so you will be proud of us. Then you will have an answer for those who are proud about things that can be seen rather than what is in the heart. [13] If we are out of our minds, it is for God. If we have our right minds, it is for you. [14] The love of Christ controls us, because we know that One died for all, so all have died. [15] Christ died for all so that those who live would not continue to live for themselves. He died for them and was raised from the dead so that they would live for him.

[16] From this time on we do not think of anyone as the world does. In the past we thought of Christ as the world thinks, but we no longer think of him in that way. [17] If anyone belongs to Christ, there is a new creation. The old things have gone; everything is made new! [18] All this is from God. Through Christ, God made peace between us and himself, and God gave us the work of telling everyone about the peace we can have with him. [19] God was in Christ, making peace between the world and himself. In Christ, God did not hold the world guilty of its sins. And he gave us this message of peace. [20] So we have been sent to speak for Christ. It is as if God is calling to you through us. We speak for Christ when we beg you to be at peace with God. [21] Christ had no sin, but God made him become sin so that in Christ we could become right with God.

6 We are workers together with God, so we beg you: Do not let the grace that you received from God be for nothing. [2] God says,

"At the right time I heard your prayers.
On the day of salvation I helped you."

Isaiah 49:8

I tell you that the "right time" is now, and the "day of salvation" is now.

[3] We do not want anyone to find fault with our work, so nothing we do will be a problem for anyone. [4] But in every way we show we are servants of God: in accepting many hard things, in troubles, in difficulties, and in great problems. [5] We are beaten and thrown into

MARK

Even the most committed believer in Christ can run afoul of his fellow man. Such was the case with Mark, author of the Gospel of Mark. Mark wasn't actually one of the twelve original followers of Christ, but he was a valued helper in the early church, assisting both Paul and Peter with various needs. He helped Paul and Barnabas on their first missionary journey, but had a lapse of judgment and deserted them, an action that Paul took personally. Their relationship was severed for a time, but through hard work and diligence, Mark atoned for his error and again became a valued, requested helper to Paul.   —2 Timothy 4:11

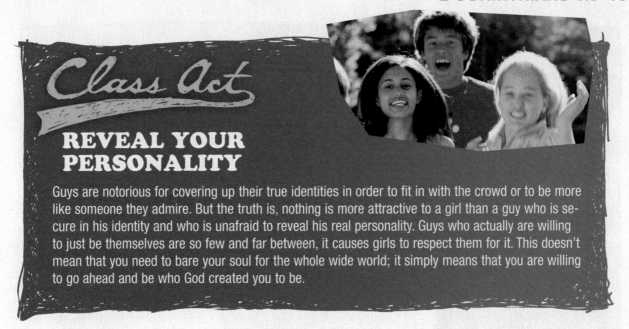

Class Act

REVEAL YOUR PERSONALITY

Guys are notorious for covering up their true identities in order to fit in with the crowd or to be more like someone they admire. But the truth is, nothing is more attractive to a girl than a guy who is secure in his identity and who is unafraid to reveal his real personality. Guys who actually are willing to just be themselves are so few and far between, it causes girls to respect them for it. This doesn't mean that you need to bare your soul for the whole wide world; it simply means that you are willing to go ahead and be who God created you to be.

prison. We meet those who become upset with us and start riots. We work hard, and sometimes we get no sleep or food. [6] We show we are servants of God by our pure lives, our understanding, patience, and kindness, by the Holy Spirit, by true love, [7] by speaking the truth, and by God's power. We use our right living to defend ourselves against everything. [8] Some people honor us, but others blame us. Some people say evil things about us, but others say good things. Some people say we are liars, but we speak the truth. [9] We are not known, but we are well known. We seem to be dying, but we continue to live. We are punished, but we are not killed. [10] We have much sadness, but we are always rejoicing. We are poor, but we are making many people rich in faith. We have nothing, but really we have everything.

[11] We have spoken freely to you in Corinth and have opened our hearts to you. [12] Our feelings of love for you have not stopped, but you have stopped your feelings of love for us. [13] I speak to you as if you were my children. Do to us as we have done—open your hearts to us.

*REVIEWS MUSIC

COPELAND:
IN MOTION

Innovative rock band Copeland weaves in a bit of electronica with its cool guitar sounds and bouncy melodies to create a sound that is impressively unique. But it is the vocals that make this band and record such a favorite among fans and critics alike. The group's lead singer has a falsetto so distinct and whimsical that it seems to dance over the loud, whirling guitars. Perhaps a bit reminiscent of Coldplay, Copeland doesn't preach or rally around some big spiritual cause, but *In Motion* is hot music that's sure to make your head spin into a rally all its own.

COPELAND
In Motion

WHY IT ROCKS:

THIS IS LAID-BACK ROCK FOR MATURE MUSIC LOVERS.

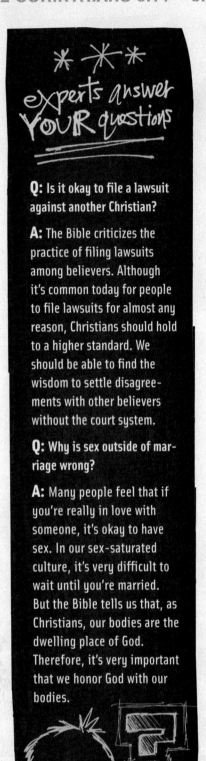

experts answer YOUR questions

Q: Is it okay to file a lawsuit against another Christian?

A: The Bible criticizes the practice of filing lawsuits among believers. Although it's common today for people to file lawsuits for almost any reason, Christians should hold to a higher standard. We should be able to find the wisdom to settle disagreements with other believers without the court system.

Q: Why is sex outside of marriage wrong?

A: Many people feel that if you're really in love with someone, it's okay to have sex. In our sex-saturated culture, it's very difficult to wait until you're married. But the Bible tells us that, as Christians, our bodies are the dwelling place of God. Therefore, it's very important that we honor God with our bodies.

WARNING ABOUT NON-CHRISTIANS

[14]You are not the same as those who do not believe. So do not join yourselves to them. Good and bad do not belong together. Light and darkness cannot share together. [15]How can Christ and Belial, the devil, have any agreement? What can a believer have together with a nonbeliever? [16]The temple of God cannot have any agreement with idols, and we are the temple of the living God. As God said: "I will live with them and walk with them. And I will be their God, and they will be my people."[n]

[17]"Leave those people,
   and be separate, says the Lord.
Touch nothing that is unclean,
   and I will accept you."
   Isaiah 52:11; Ezekiel 20:34, 41

[18]"I will be your father,
   and you will be my sons and daughters,
   says the Lord Almighty."   *2 Samuel 7:14*

7 Dear friends, we have these promises from God, so we should make ourselves pure—free from anything that makes body or soul unclean. We should try to become holy in the way we live, because we respect God.

PAUL'S JOY

[2]Open your hearts to us. We have not done wrong to anyone, we have not ruined the faith of anyone, and we have not cheated anyone. [3]I do not say this to blame you. I told you before that we love you so much we would live or die with you. [4]I feel very sure of you and am very proud of you. You give me much comfort, and in all of our troubles I have great joy.

[5]When we came into Macedonia, we had no rest. We found trouble all around us. We had fighting on the outside and fear on the inside. [6]But God, who comforts those who are troubled, comforted us when Titus came. [7]We were comforted, not only by his coming but also by the comfort you gave him. Titus told us about your wish to see me and that you are very sorry for what you did. He also told me about your great care for me, and when I heard this, I was much happier.

[8]Even if my letter made you sad, I am not sorry I wrote it. At first I was sorry, because it made you sad, but you were sad only for a

GUARD YOUR HEART

Okay, so you acted the fool and made your girlfriend angry. You could send her flowers, but humility will get you a lot further. Simply admit you were wrong. Say you are sorry and mean it. Humility doesn't always guarantee she'll take you back, so that's where flowers will come in handy.

short time. [9]Now I am happy, not because you were made sad, but because your sorrow made you change your lives. You became sad in the way God wanted you to, so you were not hurt by us in any way. [10]The kind of sorrow God wants makes people change their hearts and lives. This leads to salvation, and you cannot be sorry for that. But the kind of sorrow the world has brings death. [11]See what this sorrow—the sorrow God wanted you to have—has done to you: It has made you very serious. It made you want to restore yourselves. It made you angry and afraid. It made you want to see me. It made you care. It made you want to do the right thing. In every way you have regained your innocence. [12]I wrote that letter, not because of the one who did the wrong or because of the person who was hurt. I wrote the letter so you could see, before God, the great care you have for us. [13]That is why we were comforted.

Not only were we very comforted, we were even happier to see that Titus was so happy. All of you made him feel much better. [14]I bragged to Titus about you, and you showed that I was right. Everything we said to you was true, and you have proved that what we bragged about to Titus is true. [15]And his love for you is stronger when he remembers that you were all ready to obey. You welcomed him with respect and fear. [16]I am very happy that I can trust you fully.

CHRISTIAN GIVING

8 And now, brothers and sisters, we want you to know about the grace God gave the churches in Macedonia. [2]They have been tested by great troubles, and they are very poor. But they gave much because of their great joy. [3]I can tell you that they gave as much as they were able and even more than they could afford. No one told them to do it. [4]But they begged and pleaded with us to let them share in this service for God's people. [5]And they gave in a way we did not expect: They first gave themselves to the Lord and to us. This is what God wants. [6]So we asked Titus to help you finish this special work of grace

---

6:16 "I . . . people." Quotation from Leviticus 26:11-12; Jeremiah 32:38; Ezekiel 37:27.

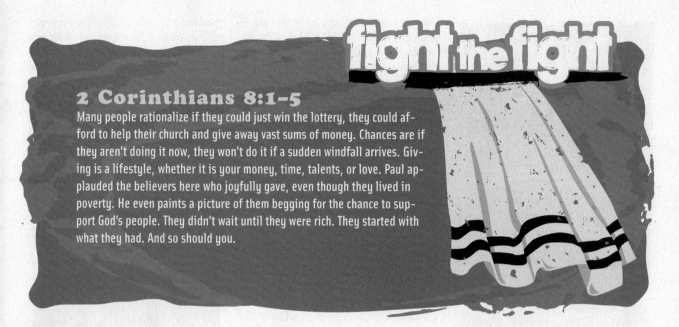

fight the fight

2 Corinthians 8:1–5

Many people rationalize if they could just win the lottery, they could afford to help their church and give away vast sums of money. Chances are if they aren't doing it now, they won't do it if a sudden windfall arrives. Giving is a lifestyle, whether it is your money, time, talents, or love. Paul applauded the believers here who joyfully gave, even though they lived in poverty. He even paints a picture of them begging for the chance to support God's people. They didn't wait until they were rich. They started with what they had. And so should you.

since he is the one who started it. [7]You are rich in everything—in faith, in speaking, in knowledge, in truly wanting to help, and in the love you learned from us.[n] In the same way, be strong also in the grace of giving.

[8]I am not commanding you to give. But I want to see if your love is true by comparing you with others that really want to help. [9]You know the grace of our Lord Jesus Christ. You know that Christ was rich, but for you he became poor so that by his becoming poor you might become rich.

[10]This is what I think you should do: Last year you were the first to want to give, and you were the first who gave. [11]So now finish the work you started. Then your "doing" will be equal to your "wanting to do." Give from what you have. [12]If you want to give, your gift will be accepted. It will be judged by what you have, not by what you do not have. [13]We do not want you to have troubles while other people are at ease, but we want everything to be equal. [14]At this time you have plenty. What you have can help others who are in need.

Then later, when they have plenty, they can help you when you are in need, and all will be equal. [15]As it is written in the Scriptures, "The person who gathered more did not have too much, nor did the person who gathered less have too little."[n]

TITUS AND HIS COMPANIONS HELP

[16]I thank God because he gave Titus the same love for you that I have. [17]Titus accepted what we asked him to do. He wanted very much to go to you, and this was his own idea.

Get out there

Since 1980, the Make-A-Wish Foundation has helped brighten the lives of more than 144,000 children across the world. The agency's mission is to grant the wishes of children with life-threatening medical conditions to enrich their lives and give them hope, strength, and joy. Not all problems are life threatening; many children who qualify go on to lead healthy lives. Nor is money the only need. Some 25,000 volunteers enable the foundation to carry out its work. Its 74 chapters and 28 international affiliates need volunteers in such areas as Web site design, public relations, special events, and administration.

To see if you can help, check www.wish.org.

8:7 in . . . us Some Greek copies read "in your love for us." 8:15 "The person . . . little." Quotation from Exodus 16:18.

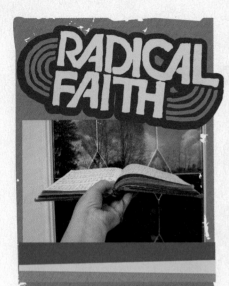

RADICAL FAITH

2 CORINTHIANS 9:7

God doesn't mistreat you like an older brother who cranks your arm around your back to shake you down for spare change. God's Word sums up his rules for sharing: Give what you have made up your own mind to give. Giving shouldn't be grudging. Other people can't make you give. And God smiles when you give with a smile. Now you can read all that in two ways. The first way is to think that if you don't feel like giving, then you don't have to. The second is to think that if you don't feel like giving, maybe you need his help learning how to give happily. That second attitude makes a lot more sense. God has given you everything you need for life, from food and clothing to spiritual blessings and good health. He doesn't want you to horde his gifts, yet he hates prying them from greedy hands. So, if you don't have a good habit of giving, ask God to show you why sharing the riches he has given you is such a great idea. Then look for ways to spread the wealth.

[18] We are sending with him the brother who is praised by all the churches because of his service in preaching the Good News. [19] Also, this brother was chosen by the churches to go with us when we deliver this gift of money. We are doing this service to bring glory to the Lord and to show that we really want to help.

[20] We are being careful so that no one will criticize us for the way we are handling this large gift. [21] We are trying hard to do what the Lord accepts as right and also what people think is right.

[22] Also, we are sending with them our brother, who is always ready to help. He has proved this to us in many ways, and he wants to help even more now, because he has much faith in you.

[23] Now about Titus—he is my partner who is working with me to help you. And about the other brothers—they are sent from the churches, and they bring glory to Christ. [24] So show these men the proof of your love and the reason we are proud of you. Then all the churches can see it.

HELP FOR FELLOW CHRISTIANS

9 I really do not need to write you about this help for God's people. [2] I know you want to help. I have been bragging about this to the people in Macedonia, telling them that you in Southern Greece have been ready to give since last year. And your desire to give has made most of them ready to give also. [3] But I am sending the brothers to you so that our bragging about you in this will not be empty words. I want you to be ready, as I said you would be. [4] If any of the people from Macedonia come with me and find that you are not ready, we will be ashamed that we were so sure of you. (And you will be ashamed, too!) [5] So I thought I should ask these brothers to go to you before we do. They will finish getting in order the generous gift you promised so it will be ready when we come. And it will be a generous gift—not one that you did not want to give.

[6] Remember this: The person who plants a little will have a small harvest, but the person who plants a lot will have a big harvest. [7] Each of you should give as you have decided in your heart to give. You should not be sad when you give, and you should not give because you feel forced to give. God loves the person who gives happily. [8] And God can give you more blessings than you need. Then you will always have plenty of everything—enough to give to every good work. [9] It is written in the Scriptures:

"He gives freely to the poor.
The things he does are right and will
continue forever." *Psalm 112:9*

[10] God is the One who gives seed to the farmer and bread for food. He will give you all the seed you need and make it grow so there will be a great harvest from your goodness. [11] He will make you rich in every way so that you can always give freely. And your giving through us will cause many to give thanks to God. [12] This service you do not only helps the needs of God's people, it also brings many more thanks to God. [13] It is a proof of your faith. Many people will praise God because you obey the Good News of Christ—the gospel you say you believe—and because you freely share with them and with all others. [14] And when they pray, they will wish they could be with you because of the great grace that God has given

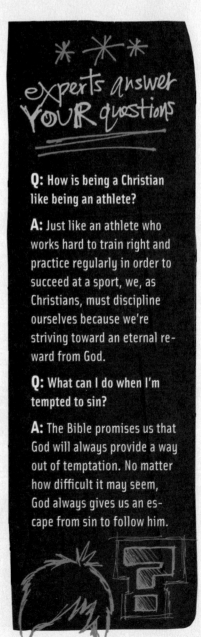

experts answer YOUR questions

Q: How is being a Christian like being an athlete?

A: Just like an athlete who works hard to train right and practice regularly in order to succeed at a sport, we, as Christians, must discipline ourselves because we're striving toward an eternal reward from God.

Q: What can I do when I'm tempted to sin?

A: The Bible promises us that God will always provide a way out of temptation. No matter how difficult it may seem, God always gives us an escape from sin to follow him.

Do's AND Don'ts

DO read for pleasure.

DO get a library card.

DO visit local bookstores.

DO return books that are due.

DON'T read in poor light.

DON'T believe all that you read.

DON'T read only schoolbooks.

DON'T take reading for granted.

you. [15]Thanks be to God for his gift that is too wonderful for words.

PAUL DEFENDS HIS MINISTRY

10 I, Paul, am begging you with the gentleness and the kindness of Christ. Some people say that I am easy on you when I am with you and bold when I am away. [2]They think we live in a worldly way, and I plan to be very bold with them when I come. I beg you that when I come I will not need to use that same boldness with you. [3]We do live in the world, but we do not fight in the same way the world fights. [4]We fight with weapons that are different from those the world uses. Our weapons have power from God that can destroy the enemy's strong places. We destroy people's arguments [5]and every proud thing that raises itself against the knowledge of God. We capture every thought and make it give up and obey Christ. [6]We are ready to punish anyone there who does not obey, but first we want you to obey fully.

[7]You must look at the facts before you. If you feel sure that you belong to Christ, you must remember that we belong to Christ just as you do. [8]It is true that we brag freely about the authority the Lord gave us. But this authority is to build you up, not to tear you down. So I will not be ashamed. [9]I do not want you to think I am trying to scare you with my letters. [10]Some people say, "Paul's letters are powerful and sound important, but when he is with us, he is weak. And his speaking is nothing." [11]They should know this: We are not there with you now, so we say these things in letters. But when we are there with you, we will show the same authority that we show in our letters.

[12]We do not dare to compare ourselves with those who think they are very important. They use themselves to measure themselves, and they judge themselves by what they themselves are. This shows that they know nothing. [13]But we will not brag about things outside the work that was given us to do. We will limit our bragging to the work that God gave us, and this includes our work with you. [14]We are not bragging too much, as we would be if we had not already come to you. But we have come to you with the Good News of Christ. [15]We limit our bragging to the work that is ours, not what others have done. We hope that as your faith continues to grow, you will help our work to grow much larger. [16]We want to tell the Good News in the areas beyond your city. We do not want to brag about work that has already been done in another person's area. [17]But, "If people want to brag, they should brag only about the Lord."[n] [18]It is not those who say they are good who are accepted but those the Lord thinks are good.

PAUL AND THE FALSE APOSTLES

11 I wish you would be patient with me even when I am a little foolish, but you are already doing that. [2]I am jealous over you with a jealousy that comes from God. I promised to give you to Christ, as your only husband. I want to give you as his pure bride. [3]But I am afraid that your minds will be led away from your true and pure following of Christ just as Eve was tricked by the snake with his evil ways. [4]You are very patient with anyone who comes to you and preaches a different Jesus from the one we preached. You are very willing to accept a spirit or gospel that is different from the Spirit and Good News you received from us.

[5]I do not think that those "great apostles" are any better than I am. [6]I may not be a trained speaker, but I do have knowledge. We have shown this to you clearly in every way.

RADICAL FAITH

2 CORINTHIANS 10:3–5

When the apostle Paul wrote these words, he no doubt had in mind a hilltop fortress that overlooked the ancient city of Corinth. A prominent sight, the jagged towers rose above the city. It dramatically illustrated a huge spiritual point. And, spiritually speaking, Paul suggests here that believers ravage the strongholds, taking every enemy captive. No, this isn't a command to wage war using military might. It's a call to do battle against every thought, argument, plan, and proud smirk that claims to be smarter than God. Paul reminds readers not to lie back and wait to be attacked. He urges believers to use the Word of God and to go on the offensive, making every idea yield in obedience to Jesus. This is the ferocious battle you should wage within your brain whenever you think you know better than your Lord. You fight Satan's lies with God's words of truth from the Bible. You demolish doubts about God's care for you by clinging to God's clear promises. In the battle for your mind, you need to capture every thought that rebels against Jesus.

 10:17 "If . . . Lord." Quotation from Jeremiah 9:24.

219

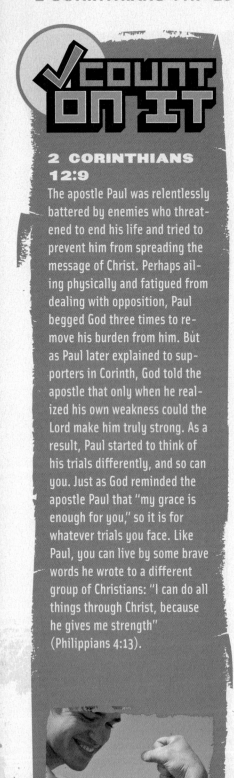

✓ COUNT ON IT

2 CORINTHIANS 12:9

The apostle Paul was relentlessly battered by enemies who threatened to end his life and tried to prevent him from spreading the message of Christ. Perhaps ailing physically and fatigued from dealing with opposition, Paul begged God three times to remove his burden from him. But as Paul later explained to supporters in Corinth, God told the apostle that only when he realized his own weakness could the Lord make him truly strong. As a result, Paul started to think of his trials differently, and so can you. Just as God reminded the apostle Paul that "my grace is enough for you," so it is for whatever trials you face. Like Paul, you can live by some brave words he wrote to a different group of Christians: "I can do all things through Christ, because he gives me strength" (Philippians 4:13).

[7] I preached God's Good News to you without pay. I made myself unimportant to make you important. Do you think that was wrong? [8] I accepted pay from other churches, taking their money so I could serve you. [9] If I needed something when I was with you, I did not trouble any of you. The brothers who came from Macedonia gave me all that I needed. I did not allow myself to depend on you in any way, and I will never depend on you. [10] No one in Southern Greece will stop me from bragging about that. I say this with the truth of Christ in me. [11] And why do I not depend on you? Do you think it is because I do not love you? God knows that I love you.

[12] And I will continue doing what I am doing now, because I want to stop those people from having a reason to brag. They would like to say that the work they brag about is the same as ours. [13] Such men are not true apostles but are workers who lie. They change themselves to look like apostles of Christ. [14] This does not surprise us. Even Satan changes himself to look like an angel of light.[n] [15] So it does not surprise us if Satan's servants also make themselves look like servants who work for what is right. But in the end they will be punished for what they do.

PAUL TELLS ABOUT HIS SUFFERINGS

[16] I tell you again: No one should think I am a fool. But if you think so, accept me as you would accept a fool. Then I can brag a little, too. [17] When I brag because I feel sure of myself, I am not talking as the Lord would talk but as a fool. [18] Many people are bragging about their lives in the world. So I will brag too. [19] You are wise, so you will gladly be patient with fools! [20] You are even patient with those who order you around, or use you, or trick you, or think they are better than you, or hit you in the face. [21] It is shameful to me to say this, but we were too "weak" to do those things to you!

But if anyone else is brave enough to brag, then I also will be brave and brag. (I am talking as a fool.) [22] Are they Hebrews?[n] So am I. Are

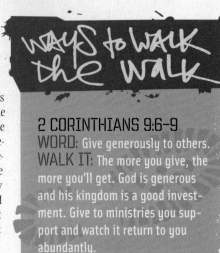

WAYS to WALK the WALK

2 CORINTHIANS 9:6–9
WORD: Give generously to others.
WALK IT: The more you give, the more you'll get. God is generous and his kingdom is a good investment. Give to ministries you support and watch it return to you abundantly.

they Israelites? So am I. Are they from Abraham's family? So am I. [23] Are they serving Christ? I am serving him more. (I am crazy to talk like this.) I have worked much harder than they. I have been in prison more often. I have been hurt more in beatings. I have been near death many times. [24] Five times the Jews have given me their punishment of thirty-nine lashes with a whip. [25] Three different times I was beaten with rods. One time I was almost stoned to death. Three times I was in ships that wrecked, and one of those times I spent a night and a day in the sea. [26] I have gone on many travels and have been in danger from rivers, thieves, my own people, the Jews, and those who are not Jews. I have been in danger in cities, in places where no one lives, and on the sea. And I have been in danger with false Christians. [27] I have done hard and tiring work, and many times I did not sleep. I have been hungry and thirsty, and many times I have been without food. I have been cold and without clothes. [28] Besides all this, there is on me every day the load of my concern for all the churches. [29] I feel weak every time someone is weak, and I feel upset every time someone is led into sin.

GUARD YOUR HEART

Everyone dislikes the guy who is cocky and self-centered. You know who you are. You might very well be as terrific as you think, but no one wants to hear you talk about it, especially not your girlfriend. Your mama might put up with your antics, but that's only because she lives with you.

✱ **11:14 angel of light** Messenger from God. The devil fools people so that they think he is from God.   **11:22 Hebrews** A name for the Jews that some Jews were very proud of.

30 If I must brag, I will brag about the things that show I am weak. 31 God knows I am not lying. He is the God and Father of the Lord Jesus Christ, and he is to be praised forever. 32 When I was in Damascus, the governor under King Aretas wanted to arrest me, so he put guards around the city. 33 But my friends lowered me in a basket through a hole in the city wall. So I escaped from the governor.

A SPECIAL BLESSING IN PAUL'S LIFE

12 I must continue to brag. It will do no good, but I will talk now about visions and revelations[n] from the Lord. 2 I know a man in Christ who was taken up to the third heaven fourteen years ago. I do not know whether the man was in his body or out of his body, but God knows. 3-4 And I know that this man was taken up to paradise.[n] I don't know if he was in his body or away from his body, but God knows. He heard things he is not able to explain, things that no human is allowed to tell. 5 I will brag about a man like that, but I will not brag about myself, except about my weaknesses. 6 But if I wanted to brag about myself, I would not be a fool, because I would be telling the truth. But I will not brag about myself. I do not want people to think more of me than what they see me do or hear me say.

7 So that I would not become too proud of the wonderful things that were shown to me, a painful physical problem[n] was given to me. This problem was a messenger from Satan, sent to beat me and keep me from being too proud. 8 I begged the Lord three times to take this problem away from me. 9 But he said to me, "My grace is enough for you. When you are weak, my power is made perfect in you." So I am very happy to brag about my weaknesses. Then Christ's power can live in me. 10 For this reason I am happy when I have weaknesses, insults, hard times, sufferings, and all kinds of troubles for Christ. Because when I am weak, then I am truly strong.

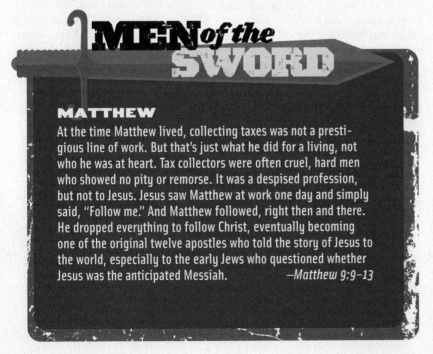

Extras:

How to Open a Stuck Jar Lid

What do you do when you're called upon to open a jar that no one else can crack? If the jar is new, you might need to break the vacuum seal by placing a bottle opener or butter knife under the tip of the lid and pulling away from the jar. Or you might need to loosen dried food from the threads of the jar by tapping the lid with a spoon. To gain a better grip, wrap the lid in a dishtowel, or stretch a rubber band around it. And if that doesn't work, run it under hot water for a minute or two—the heat will cause the metal lid to expand slightly and make your job easy.

Brute strength isn't always the best solution, and the same holds true with spiritual battles. In the midst of temptation, don't rely on your own fortitude; ask God for wisdom to see a way out. It'll always be there.

PAUL'S LOVE FOR THE CHRISTIANS

11 I have been talking like a fool, but you made me do it. You are the ones who should say good things about me. I am worth nothing, but those "great apostles" are not worth any more than I am! 12 When I was with you, I patiently did the things that prove I am an apostle—signs, wonders, and miracles. 13 So you received everything that the other churches have received. Only one thing was different: I was not a burden to you. Forgive me for this!

14 I am now ready to visit you the third time, and I will not be a burden to you. I want nothing from you, except you. Children should not have to save up to give to their parents. Parents should save to give to their children. 15 So I am happy to give everything I have for you, even myself. If I love you more, will you love me less?

16 It is clear I was not a burden to you, but you think I was tricky and lied to catch you. 17 Did I cheat you by using any of the messengers I sent to you? No, you know I did not. 18 I asked Titus to go to you, and I sent our brother with him. Titus did not cheat you, did he? No, you know that Titus and I did the same thing and with the same spirit.

19 Do you think we have been defending ourselves to you all this time? We have been speaking in Christ and before God. You are our dear friends, and everything we do is to make

MEN of the SWORD

MATTHEW

At the time Matthew lived, collecting taxes was not a prestigious line of work. But that's just what he did for a living, not who he was at heart. Tax collectors were often cruel, hard men who showed no pity or remorse. It was a despised profession, but not to Jesus. Jesus saw Matthew at work one day and simply said, "Follow me." And Matthew followed, right then and there. He dropped everything to follow Christ, eventually becoming one of the original twelve apostles who told the story of Jesus to the world, especially to the early Jews who questioned whether Jesus was the anticipated Messiah.
                                              —Matthew 9:9–13

12:1 revelations Revelation is making known a truth that was hidden.   **12:3–4 paradise** Another word for heaven.   **12:7 painful physical problem** Literally, "thorn in the flesh."

221

Relationships

"My brothers and sisters, God called you to be free, but do not use your freedom as an excuse to do what pleases your sinful self. Serve each other with love" (Galatians 5:13). In our sex-crazed culture, too many people are looking for ways to please themselves. Even Christians can look at the grace of Christ and use it as an excuse to sin. But the Bible warns us against that type of behavior and plainly calls it sin, not love. You need to lovingly serve the girls in your life, not try to take advantage of them for a few minutes of selfish pleasure.

experts answer YOUR questions

Q: What are spiritual gifts?

A: The Bible teaches that all believers have spiritual gifts, or special abilities and talents that God gives us through his Spirit so that we can serve each other and the church.

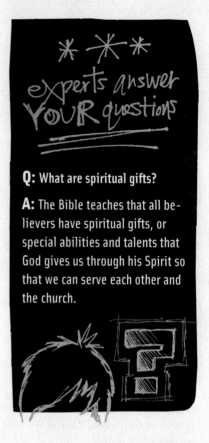

you stronger. [20] I am afraid that when I come, you will not be what I want you to be, and I will not be what you want me to be. I am afraid that among you there may be arguing, jealousy, anger, selfish fighting, evil talk, gossip, pride, and confusion. [21] I am afraid that when I come to you again, my God will make me ashamed before you. I may be saddened by many of those who have sinned because they have not changed their hearts or turned from their sexual sins and the shameful things they have done.

FINAL WARNINGS AND GREETINGS

13 I will come to you for the third time. "Every case must be proved by two or three witnesses."[n] [2] When I was with you the second time, I gave a warning to those who had sinned. Now I am away from you, and I give a warning to all the others. When I come to you again, I will not be easy with them. [3] You want proof that Christ is speaking through me. My proof is that he is not weak among you, but he is powerful. [4] It is true that he was weak when he was killed on the cross, but he lives now by God's power. It is true that we are weak in Christ, but for you we will be alive in Christ by God's power.

[5] Look closely at yourselves. Test yourselves to see if you are living in the faith. You know that Jesus Christ is in you—unless you fail the test. [6] But I hope you will see that we ourselves have not failed the test. [7] We pray to God that you will not do anything wrong. It is not important to see that we have passed the test, but it is important that you do what is right, even if it seems we have failed. [8] We cannot do anything against the truth, but only for the truth. [9] We are happy to be weak, if you are strong, and we pray that you will become complete. [10] I am writing this while I am away from you so that when I come I will not have to be harsh in my use of authority. The Lord gave me this authority to build you up, not to tear you down.

[11] Now, brothers and sisters, I say good-bye. Live in harmony. Do what I have asked you to do. Agree with each other, and live in peace. Then the God of love and peace will be with you.

[12] Greet each other with a holy kiss. [13] All of God's holy people send greetings to you.

[14] The grace of the Lord Jesus Christ, the love of God, and the fellowship of the Holy Spirit be with you all.

13:1 "Every . . . witnesses." Quotation from Deuteronomy 19:15.

222

notes

GALATIANS

IT'S ABOUT RELATION-SHIP, NOT RULES

You have probably heard some kind of lecture about the need to "obey the rules." On the one hand, there are good reasons for rules. Think of them as guidelines for a better life. But, on the other hand, nobody can follow every rule perfectly. So keeping the rules isn't the prime example of our faith.

This is the problem Paul confronts in his letter to a group of churches in the region called Galatia. Some teachers stressed the need to follow traditional customs and laws in order to be right with God. Paul reminds them that a person is not made right with God by following laws, but by trusting in Jesus in order to enter a relationship with God.

The apostle tells the Galatians who have bought into the lie that they must revert to old ways that they have been tricked. If they began their life in Christ, he asks why they are trying to perfect it through their own strength. You can sense Paul's anger at false teachers and his concern for the followers of Christ they are leading astray. He wants them to know the freedom that Christ offers to those who accept his grace. So, in the midst of a message delivered with strong words, Paul's love comes shining through.

From Paul, an apostle. I was not chosen to be an apostle by human beings, nor was I sent from human beings. I was made an apostle through Jesus Christ and God the Father who raised Jesus from the dead. [2]This letter is also from all those of God's family[n] who are with me.

To the churches in Galatia:[n]

[3]Grace and peace to you from God our Father and the Lord Jesus Christ. [4]Jesus gave himself for our sins to free us from this evil world we live in, as God the Father planned. [5]The glory belongs to God forever and ever. Amen.

THE ONLY GOOD NEWS

[6]God, by his grace through Christ, called you to become his people. So I am amazed that you are turning away so quickly and believing something different than the Good News. [7]Really, there is no other Good News. But some people are confusing you; they want to change the Good News of Christ. [8]We preached to you the Good News. So if we ourselves, or even an angel from heaven, should preach to you something different, we should be judged guilty! [9]I said this before, and now I say it again: You have already accepted the Good News. If anyone is preaching something different to you, let that person be judged guilty!

[10]Do you think I am trying to make people accept me? No, God is the One I am trying to please. Am I trying to please people? If I still wanted to please people, I would not be a servant of Christ.

PAUL'S AUTHORITY IS FROM GOD

[11]Brothers and sisters, I want you to know that the Good News I preached to you was not made up by human beings. [12]I did not get it from humans, nor did anyone teach it to me, but Jesus Christ showed it to me.

[13]You have heard about my past life in the Jewish religion. I attacked the church of God and tried to destroy it. [14]I was becoming a leader in the Jewish religion, doing better than most other Jews of my age. I tried harder than anyone else to follow the teachings handed down by our ancestors.

[15]But God had special plans for me and set me apart for his work even before I was born. He called me through his grace [16]and showed his son to me so that I might tell the Good News about him to those who are not Jewish. When God called me, I did not get advice or help from any person. [17]I did not go to Jerusalem to see those who were apostles before I was. But, without waiting, I went away to Arabia and later went back to Damascus.

[18]After three years I went to Jerusalem to meet Peter and stayed with him for fifteen days. [19]I met no other apostles, except James, the brother of the Lord. [20]God knows that these things I write are not lies. [21]Later, I went to the areas of Syria and Cilicia.

[22]In Judea the churches in Christ had never met me. [23]They had only heard it said, "This man who was attacking us is now preaching the same faith that he once tried to destroy." [24]And these believers praised God because of me.

OTHER APOSTLES ACCEPTED PAUL

After fourteen years I went to Jerusalem again, this time with Barnabas. I also took Titus with me. [2]I went because God showed me I should go. I met with the believers there, and in private I told their leaders the Good News that I preach to the non-Jewish people. I did not want my past work and the work I am now doing to be wasted. [3]Titus was with me, but he was not forced to be circumcised, even though he was a Greek. [4]We talked about this problem because some false believers had come into our group secretly. They came in like spies to overturn the freedom we have in Christ Jesus. They wanted to make us slaves. [5]But we did not give in to those false believers for a minute. We wanted the truth of the Good News to continue for you.

[6]Those leaders who seemed to be important did not change the Good News that I preach. (It doesn't matter to me if they were "important" or not. To God everyone is the same.) [7]But these leaders saw that I had been given the work of telling the Good News to those who are not Jewish, just as Peter had the work of telling the Jews. [8]God gave Peter the

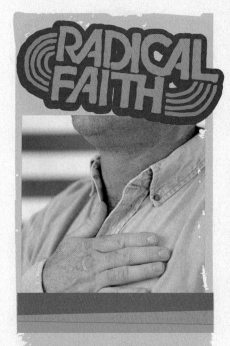

RADICAL FAITH

GALATIANS 2:20

The fact that God lives in you isn't the easiest idea in the Bible to process. When you become a Christian, you are united with Christ. That bond is so tight that the Bible says he comes to live in you, "indwelling" you through the Holy Spirit. That's not a physical experience or an emotional sensation, but a spiritual reality. Through the Spirit, Jesus invades your heart, the core of your being, the place where you think, feel, and decide (Romans 8:9). Having God working on you from your insides out has mighty results. Like the apostle Paul prayed, "I ask the Father in his great glory to give you the power to be strong inwardly through his Spirit. I pray that Christ will live in your hearts by faith and that your life will be strong in love and be built on love" (Ephesians 3:16–17). Live for the one who loves you with all the strength he himself provides you.

WAYS to WALK the WALK

GALATIANS 1:10

WORD: Please God with your life.
WALK IT: You'll never be able to please people all the time, so focus instead on pleasing God. When faced with a difficult decision, choose the option that would please God.

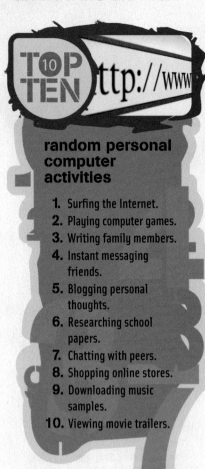

TOP TEN http://www

random personal computer activities

1. Surfing the Internet.
2. Playing computer games.
3. Writing family members.
4. Instant messaging friends.
5. Blogging personal thoughts.
6. Researching school papers.
7. Chatting with peers.
8. Shopping online stores.
9. Downloading music samples.
10. Viewing movie trailers.

power to work as an apostle for the Jewish people. But he also gave me the power to work as an apostle for those who are not Jews. [9]James, Peter, and John, who seemed to be the leaders, understood that God had given me this special grace, so they accepted Barnabas and me. They agreed that they would go to the Jewish people and that we should go to those who are not Jewish. [10]The only thing they asked us was to remember to help the poor—something I really wanted to do.

PAUL SHOWS THAT PETER WAS WRONG

[11]When Peter came to Antioch, I challenged him to his face, because he was wrong. [12]Peter ate with the non-Jewish people until some Jewish people sent from James came to Antioch. When they arrived, Peter stopped eating with those who weren't Jewish, and he separated himself from them. He was afraid of the Jews. [13]So Peter was a hypocrite, as were the other Jewish believers who joined with him. Even Barnabas was influenced by what these Jewish believers did. [14]When I saw they were not following the truth of the Good News, I spoke to Peter in front of them all. I said, "Peter, you are a Jew, but you are not living like a Jew. You are living like those who are not Jewish. So why do you now try to force those who are not Jewish to live like Jews?"

[15]We were not born as non-Jewish "sinners," but as Jews. [16]Yet we know that a person is made right with God not by following the law, but by trusting in Jesus Christ. So we, too, have put our faith in Christ Jesus, that we might be made right with God because we trusted in Christ. It is not because we followed the law, because no one can be made right with God by following the law.

[17]We Jews came to Christ, trying to be made right with God, and it became clear that we are sinners, too. Does this mean that Christ encourages sin? No! [18]But I would really be wrong to begin teaching again those things that I gave up. [19]It was the law that put me to death, and I died to the law so that I can now live for God. [20]I was put to death on the cross with Christ, and I do not live anymore—it is Christ who lives in me. I still live in my body, but I live by faith in the Son of God who loved me and gave himself to save me. [21]By saying these things I am not going against God's grace. Just the opposite, if the law could make us right with God, then Christ's death would be useless.

BLESSING COMES THROUGH FAITH

3 You people in Galatia were told very clearly about the death of Jesus Christ on the cross. But you were foolish; you let

*REVIEWS BOOKS

STEPHEN ARTERBURN:
EVERY YOUNG MAN'S BATTLE

Stephen Arterburn and his "Every Man" series have helped millions of men come to grips with their sexual being. Whether it's pornography, divorce, adultery, homosexuality, or masturbation, *Every Man's Battle* has helped bring into light the secret lives of men. In *Every Young Man's Battle*, Arterburn and his team of professionals dive into the sexual lives of male teenagers, college students, and twenty-somethings. The result is a compelling and convicting book that gets to the heart of what makes young men tick sexually and how God has designed them for health and holiness, not for the sin and sickness so many experience.

WHY IT ROCKS: IT GIVES A BIBLICAL PERSPECTIVE OF MALE SEXUALITY.

ISSUES

ALCOHOL

DRINKING ALCOHOL MAY SEEM COOL AND HIP, BUT DON'T FORGET THAT YOU'RE NOT EVEN OLD ENOUGH TO DRINK LEGALLY. And can you really afford to lose any more brain cells? While alcohol can give you a temporary high, the hangover the next day is never worth it. What is really scary is how many people get hooked on the hooch at an early age and pay for it the rest of their lives. The dangers of alcohol are many, but one of the stupidest things you could ever do is to drink and drive or ride with someone who is intoxicated. Remember, God loves you and wants you to take care of the body he's given you.

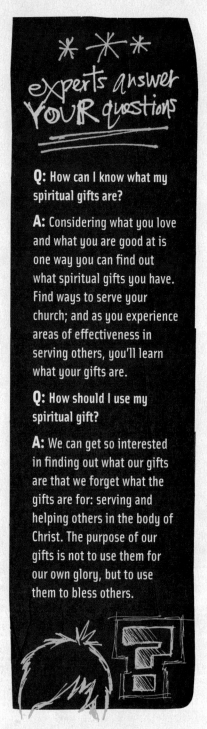

experts answer YOUR questions

Q: How can I know what my spiritual gifts are?

A: Considering what you love and what you are good at is one way you can find out what spiritual gifts you have. Find ways to serve your church; and as you experience areas of effectiveness in serving others, you'll learn what your gifts are.

Q: How should I use my spiritual gift?

A: We can get so interested in finding out what our gifts are that we forget what the gifts are for: serving and helping others in the body of Christ. The purpose of our gifts is not to use them for our own glory, but to use them to bless others.

GUARD YOUR HEART

As a Christian guy in a dating relationship, it's important you learn early what it means to be a spiritual leader. Spend time talking with respected peers, your youth pastor, or your father about what it means to be a godly influence in a relationship. Leaders are made, not born.

someone trick you. [2]Tell me this one thing: How did you receive the Holy Spirit? Did you receive the Spirit by following the law? No, you received the Spirit because you heard the Good News and believed it. [3]You began your life in Christ by the Spirit. Now are you trying to make it complete by your own power? That is foolish. [4]Were all your experiences wasted? I hope not! [5]Does God give you the Spirit and work miracles among you because you follow the law? No, he does these things because you heard the Good News and believed it.

[6]The Scriptures say the same thing about Abraham: "Abraham believed God, and God accepted Abraham's faith, and that faith made him right with God."[n] [7]So you should know that the true children of Abraham are those who have faith. [8]The Scriptures, telling what would happen in the future, said that God would make the non-Jewish people right through their faith. This Good News was told to Abraham beforehand, as the Scripture says: "All nations will be blessed through you."[n] [9]So all who believe as Abraham believed are blessed just as Abraham was. [10]But those who depend on following the law to make them right are under a curse, because the Scriptures say, "Anyone will be cursed who does not always obey what is written in the Book of the Law."[n] [11]Now it is clear that no one can be made right with God by the law, because the Scriptures say, "Those who are right with God will live by faith."[n] [12]The law is not based on faith. It says, "A person who obeys these things will live because of them."[n] [13]Christ took away the curse the law put on us. He changed places with us and put himself under that curse. It is written in the Scriptures, "Anyone whose body is displayed on a tree[n] is cursed." [14]Christ did this so that God's blessing promised to Abraham might come through Jesus Christ to those who are not Jews. Jesus died so that by our believing we could receive the Spirit that God promised.

THE LAW AND THE PROMISE

[15]Brothers and sisters, let us think in human terms: Even an agreement made between two persons is firm. After that agreement is accepted by both people, no one can stop it or add anything to it. [16]God made promises both to Abraham and to his descendant. God did not say, "and to your descendants." That would mean many people. But God said, "and to your descendant." That means only one person; that person is Christ. [17]This is what I mean: God had an agreement with Abraham and promised to keep it. The law, which came four hundred thirty years later, cannot change that agreement and so destroy God's promise to Abraham. [18]If the law could give us Abraham's blessing, then the promise would not be necessary. But that is not possible, because God freely gave his blessings to Abraham through the promise he had made.

[19]So what was the law for? It was given to show that the wrong things people do are against God's will. And it continued until the special descendant, who had been promised, came. The law was given through angels who used Moses for a mediator[n] to give the law to people. [20]But a mediator is not needed when there is only one side, and God is only one.

THE PURPOSE OF THE LAW OF MOSES

[21]Does this mean that the law is against God's promises? Never! That would be true only if the law could make us right with God. But God did not give a law that can bring life. [22]Instead, the Scriptures showed that the whole world is bound by sin. This was so the promise would be given through faith to people who believe in Jesus Christ.

[23]Before this faith came, we were all held prisoners by the law. We had no freedom until God showed us the way of faith that was coming. [24]In other words, the law was our guardian leading us to Christ so that we could be made right with God through faith. [25]Now the way of faith has come, and we no longer live under a guardian.

[26-27]You were all baptized into Christ, and so you were all clothed with Christ. This means that you are all children of God through faith in Christ Jesus. [28]In Christ, there is no difference between Jew and Greek, slave and free person, male and female. You are all the same in Christ Jesus. [29]You belong to Christ, so you are Abraham's descendants. You will inherit all of God's blessings because of the promise God made to Abraham.

4 I want to tell you this: While those who will inherit their fathers' property are still children, they are no different

 3:6 "Abraham . . . God." Quotation from Genesis 15:6. **3:8** "All . . . you." Quotation from Genesis 12:3 and 18:18. **3:10** "Anyone . . . Law." Quotation from Deuteronomy 27:26. **3:11** "Those . . . faith." Quotation from Habakkuk 2:4. **3:12** "A person . . . them." Quotation from Leviticus 18:5. **3:13 displayed on a tree** Deuteronomy 21:22–23 says that when a person was killed for doing wrong, the body was hung on a tree to show shame. Paul means that the cross of Jesus was like that. **3:19 mediator** A person who helps one person talk to or give something to another person.

august

NATIONAL INVENTORS MONTH

1  It's Girlfriend Day. Treat yours like a queen.

2

3 Tom Brady is celebrating a birthday today.

4 Look for a volunteer opportunity at a local hospice.

5

6 Enjoy one more day at the pool before summer ends.

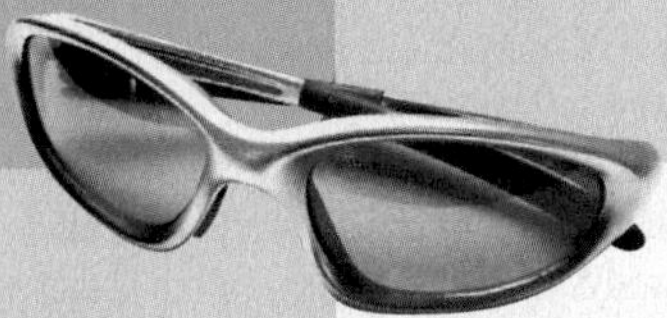

7 Invent something and patent it!

8

9 It's Whitney Houston's birthday. Pray for her today.

10 Pray for the people of the Third World.

11

12

13 It's National Underwear Day. Wear some clean drawers.

14

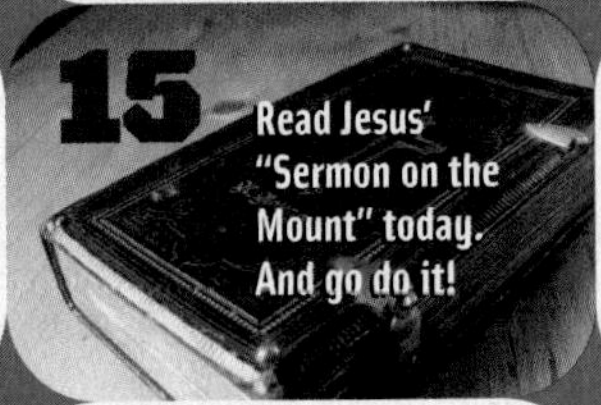

15 Read Jesus' "Sermon on the Mount" today. And go do it!

16 Start preparing for college entrance exams.

17

18 Today is Christian Slater's birthday.

19

20 Pray for the persecuted church.

21

22 Change the oil in the family car.

23

24

25 It's Kiss-and-Make-Up Day. Celebrate with the one you love.

26

27

28 Write down a list of goals you have for the coming school year.

29

30 Today is Andy Roddick's birthday.

31 Pray for the members of Congress.

from slaves. It does not matter that the children own everything. [2]While they are children, they must obey those who are chosen to care for them. But when the children reach the age set by their fathers, they are free. [3]It is the same for us. We were once like children, slaves to the useless rules of this world. [4]But when the right time came, God sent his Son who was born of a woman and lived under the law. [5]God did this so he could buy freedom for those who were under the law and so we could become his children.

[6]Since you are God's children, God sent the Spirit of his Son into your hearts, and the Spirit cries out, "Father."[n] [7]So now you are not a slave; you are God's child, and God will give you the blessing he promised, because you are his child.

PAUL'S LOVE FOR THE CHRISTIANS

[8]In the past you did not know God. You were slaves to gods that were not real. [9]But now you know the true God. Really, it is God who knows you. So why do you turn back to those weak and useless rules you followed before? Do you want to be slaves to those things again? [10]You still follow teachings about special days, months, seasons, and years. [11]I am afraid for you, that my work for you has been wasted.

[12]Brothers and sisters, I became like you, so I beg you to become like me. You were very good to me before. [13]You remember that it was because of an illness that I came to you the first time, preaching the Good News. [14]Though my sickness was a trouble for you, you did not hate me or make me leave. But you welcomed me as an angel from God, as if I were Jesus Christ himself! [15]You were very happy then, but where is that joy now? I am ready to testify that you would have taken out your eyes and given them to me if that were possible. [16]Now am I your enemy because I tell you the truth?

[17]Those people[n] are working hard to persuade you, but this is not good for you. They want to persuade you to turn against us and follow only them. [18]It is good for people to show interest in you, but only if their purpose is good. This is always true, not just when I am with you. [19]My little children, again I feel the pain of childbirth for you until you truly become like Christ. [20]I wish I could be with you now and could change the way I am talking to you, because I do not know what to think about you.

THE EXAMPLE OF HAGAR AND SARAH

[21]Some of you still want to be under the law. Tell me, do you know what the law says? [22]The Scriptures say that Abraham had two sons. The mother of one son was a slave woman, and the mother of the other son was a free woman. [23]Abraham's son from the slave woman was born in the normal human way. But the son from the free woman was born because of the promise God made to Abraham.

[24]This story teaches something else: The two women are like the two agreements between God and his people. One agreement is the law that God made on Mount Sinai,[n] and the people who are under this agreement are like slaves. The mother named Hagar is like that agreement. [25]She is like Mount Sinai in Arabia and is a picture of the earthly city of Jerusalem. This city and its people are slaves to the law. [26]But the heavenly Jerusalem, which is above, is like the free woman. She is our mother. [27]It is written in the Scriptures:

"Be happy, Jerusalem.
You are like a woman who never gave
birth to children.
Start singing and shout for joy.
You never felt the pain of giving birth,
but you will have more children
than the woman who has a husband."

Isaiah 54:1

[28]My brothers and sisters, you are God's children because of his promise, as Isaac was then. [29]The son who was born in the normal way treated the other son badly. It is the same today. [30]But what does the Scripture say? "Throw out the slave woman and her

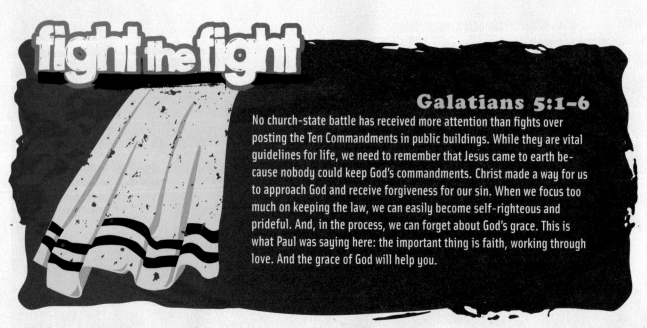

fight the fight

Galatians 5:1–6

No church-state battle has received more attention than fights over posting the Ten Commandments in public buildings. While they are vital guidelines for life, we need to remember that Jesus came to earth because nobody could keep God's commandments. Christ made a way for us to approach God and receive forgiveness for our sin. When we focus too much on keeping the law, we can easily become self-righteous and prideful. And, in the process, we can forget about God's grace. This is what Paul was saying here: the important thing is faith, working through love. And the grace of God will help you.

4:6 **"Father"** Literally, "Abba, Father." Jewish children called their fathers "Abba." 4:17 **Those people** They are the false teachers who were bothering the believers in Galatia (Galatians 1:7). 4:24 **Mount Sinai** Mountain in Arabia where God gave his Law to Moses (Exodus 19 and 20).

DO'S AND Don'ts

DO develop a hobby.

DO study about your hobby.

DO join a club for your hobby.

DO share your hobby with others.

DON'T idolize your hobby.

DON'T overspend on your hobby.

DON'T neglect your hobby.

DON'T allow a hobby to rule you.

son. The son of the slave woman should not inherit anything. The son of the free woman should receive it all."[n] [31]So, my brothers and sisters, we are not children of the slave woman, but of the free woman.

KEEP YOUR FREEDOM

5 We have freedom now, because Christ made us free. So stand strong. Do not change and go back into the slavery of the law. [2]Listen, I Paul tell you that if you go back to the law by being circumcised, Christ does you no good. [3]Again, I warn every man: If you allow yourselves to be circumcised, you must follow all the law. [4]If you try to be made right with God through the law, your life with Christ is over—you have left God's grace. [5]But we have the true hope that comes from being made right with God, and by the Spirit we wait eagerly for this hope. [6]When we are in Christ Jesus, it is not important if we are circumcised or not. The important thing is faith—the kind of faith that works through love.

[7]You were running a good race. Who

stopped you from following the true way? [8]This change did not come from the One who chose you. [9]Be careful! "Just a little yeast makes the whole batch of dough rise." [10]But I trust in the Lord that you will not believe those different ideas. Whoever is confusing you with such ideas will be punished.

[11]My brothers and sisters, I do not teach that a man must be circumcised. If I teach circumcision, why am I still being attacked? If I still taught circumcision, my preaching about the cross would not be a problem. [12]I wish the people who are bothering you would castrate[n] themselves!

[13]My brothers and sisters, God called you to be free, but do not use your freedom as an excuse to do what pleases your sinful self. Serve each other with love. [14]The whole law is made complete in this one command: "Love your neighbor as you love yourself."[n] [15]If you go on hurting each other and tearing each other apart, be careful, or you will completely destroy each other.

THE SPIRIT AND HUMAN NATURE

[16]So I tell you: Live by following the Spirit. Then you will not do what your sinful selves want. [17]Our sinful selves want what is against the Spirit, and the Spirit wants what is against our sinful selves. The two are against each other, so you cannot do just what you please. [18]But if the Spirit is leading you, you are not under the law.

[19]The wrong things the sinful self does are clear: being sexually unfaithful, not being pure, taking part in sexual sins, [20]worshiping gods, doing witchcraft, hating, making trouble, being jealous, being angry, being selfish, making people angry with each other, causing divisions among people, [21]feeling envy, being drunk, having wild and wasteful parties, and doing other things like these. I warn you now as I warned you before: Those who do these things will not inherit God's kingdom. [22]But the Spirit produces the fruit of love, joy, peace, patience, kindness, goodness, faithfulness, [23]gentleness, self-control. There is no law that says these things are wrong. [24]Those who belong to Christ Jesus have crucified their own sinful selves. They have given up their old selfish feelings and the evil things they wanted to do. [25]We get our new life from the Spirit, so we should follow the Spirit. [26]We must not be proud or make trouble with each other or be jealous of each other.

HELP EACH OTHER

6 Brothers and sisters, if someone in your group does something wrong,

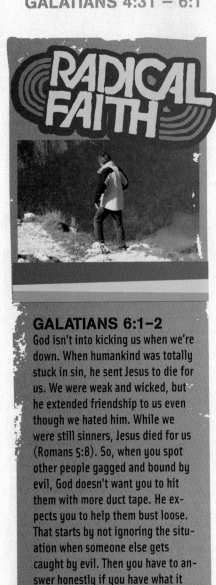

RADICAL FAITH

GALATIANS 6:1–2

God isn't into kicking us when we're down. When humankind was totally stuck in sin, he sent Jesus to die for us. We were weak and wicked, but he extended friendship to us even though we hated him. While we were still sinners, Jesus died for us (Romans 5:8). So, when you spot other people gagged and bound by evil, God doesn't want you to hit them with more duct tape. He expects you to help them bust loose. That starts by not ignoring the situation when someone else gets caught by evil. Then you have to answer honestly if you have what it takes to help. You need to be spiritually mature enough to approach that person and intervene without feeling superior. There's a warning here, too. When you help people stuck in sin, you're walking close to a cliff's edge. You're attempting to rescue someone who has already gone over the lip, and it's easy to get yanked over yourself. So be wise when you help. Consider going in a group. If you're tempted by the same problem, invite someone more mature to go instead.

 4:30 "Throw . . . all." Quotation from Genesis 21:10. 5:12 castrate To cut off part of the male sex organ. Paul uses this word because it is similar to "circumcision." Paul wanted to show that he is very upset with the false teachers. 5:14 "Love . . . yourself." Quotation from Leviticus 19:18.

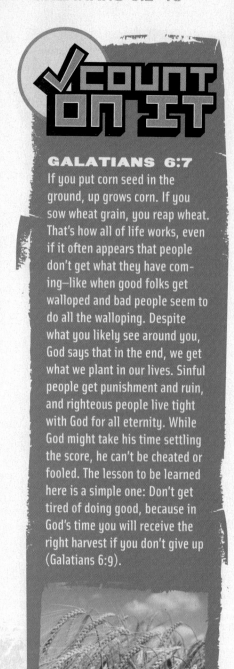

COUNT ON IT

GALATIANS 6:7

If you put corn seed in the ground, up grows corn. If you sow wheat grain, you reap wheat. That's how all of life works, even if it often appears that people don't get what they have coming—like when good folks get walloped and bad people seem to do all the walloping. Despite what you likely see around you, God says that in the end, we get what we plant in our lives. Sinful people get punishment and ruin, and righteous people live tight with God for all eternity. While God might take his time settling the score, he can't be cheated or fooled. The lesson to be learned here is a simple one: Don't get tired of doing good, because in God's time you will receive the right harvest if you don't give up (Galatians 6:9).

you who are spiritual should go to that person and gently help make him right again. But be careful, because you might be tempted to sin, too. [2] By helping each other with your troubles, you truly obey the law of Christ. [3] If anyone thinks he is important when he really is not, he is only fooling himself. [4] Each person should judge his own actions and not compare himself with others. Then he can be proud for what he himself has done. [5] Each person must be responsible for himself.

[6] Anyone who is learning the teaching of God should share all the good things he has with his teacher.

LIFE IS LIKE PLANTING A FIELD

[7] Do not be fooled: You cannot cheat God. People harvest only what they plant. [8] If they plant to satisfy their sinful selves, their sinful selves will bring them ruin. But if they plant to please the Spirit, they will receive eternal life from the Spirit. [9] We must not become tired of doing good. We will receive our harvest of eternal life at the right time if we do not give up. [10] When we have the opportunity to help anyone, we should do it. But we should give special attention to those who are in the family of believers.

PAUL ENDS HIS LETTER

[11] See what large letters I use to write this myself. [12] Some people are trying to force you to be circumcised so the Jews will accept them. They are afraid they will be attacked if they follow only the cross of Christ.[n] [13] Those who are circumcised do not obey the law themselves,

but they want you to be circumcised so they can brag about what they forced you to do. [14] I hope I will never brag about things like that. The cross of our Lord Jesus Christ is my only reason for bragging. Through the cross of Jesus my world was crucified, and I died to the world. [15] It is not important if a man is circumcised or uncircumcised. The important thing is being the new people God has made. [16] Peace and mercy to those who follow this rule—and to all of God's people.

[17] So do not give me any more trouble. I have scars on my body that show[n] I belong to Christ Jesus.

[18] My brothers and sisters, the grace of our Lord Jesus Christ be with your spirit. Amen.

WAYS TO WALK THE WALK

GALATIANS 5:13
WORD: You are free to serve.
WALK IT: Grace isn't a license to sin; it's a license to serve others. Look for a way you can share grace with two other people today as a way of serving them.

GUARD YOUR HEART

Don't go overboard with trying to impress a girl through material things, especially while you're young. Flowers are one thing, but jewelry, perfume, and expensive restaurants should be reserved for serious dating. Instead, impress her with your sincere charm and good heart. She'll like that so much better than "stuff."

6:12 cross of Christ Paul uses the cross as a picture of the Good News, the story of Christ's death and rising from the dead to pay for our sins. The cross, or Christ's death, was God's way to save us. **6:17 that show** Many times Paul was beaten and whipped by people who were against him because he was teaching about Christ. The scars were from these beatings.

*** notes

EPHESIANS

THE GOODNESS OF GOD'S GRACE

It's Friday night and time for a night on the town. Consider what kind of food should kick off the evening. Maybe a plate of ribs drowning in barbecue sauce or a pile of hot wings? What about cheese fries? A breaded onion with dipping sauce? Whatever your favorite delicacy, it can't match the savory news of Ephesians: Through Jesus we are all adopted into God's family. He gives us this grace so freely that it ought to make us sing the praises of the one who cooked all this up.

In fact, Paul says, we should be so grateful for God's love that we act with the same kind of mercy toward others. This means the church should be characterized by loving unity instead of by gossipy arguing. Paul spells out the simple recipe for sweet success: be humble, gentle, patient, and accepting, in good measure.

As anyone who has been part of a church knows, that is a prescription easier spoken than swallowed. Yet, Paul reminds readers that we are all part of the same body of believers, led by the same Holy Spirit. As a result, we are to live a life of love, free from greed and evil. With God's help, that is possible. It's a treat to be savored, indeed.

1 From Paul, an apostle of Christ Jesus. I am an apostle because that is what God wanted.

To God's holy people living in Ephesus,[*] believers in Christ Jesus:

²Grace and peace to you from God our Father and the Lord Jesus Christ.

SPIRITUAL BLESSINGS IN CHRIST

³Praise be to the God and Father of our Lord Jesus Christ. In Christ, God has given us every spiritual blessing in the heavenly world. ⁴That is, in Christ, he chose us before the world was made so that we would be his holy people—people without blame before him. ⁵Because of his love, God had already decided to make us his own children through Jesus Christ. That was what he wanted and what pleased him, ⁶and it brings praise to God because of his wonderful grace. God gave that grace to us freely, in Christ, the One he loves. ⁷In Christ we are set free by the blood of his death, and so we have forgiveness of sins. How rich is God's grace, ⁸which he has given to us so fully and freely. God, with full wisdom and understanding, ⁹let us know his secret purpose. This was what God wanted, and he planned to do it through Christ. ¹⁰His goal was to carry out his plan, when the right time came, that all things in heaven and on earth would be joined together in Christ as the head.

¹¹In Christ we were chosen to be God's people, because from the very beginning God had decided this in keeping with his plan. And he is the One who makes everything agree with what he decides and wants. ¹²We are the first people who hoped in Christ, and we were chosen so that we would bring praise to God's glory. ¹³So it is with you. When you heard the true teaching—the Good News about your salvation—you believed in Christ. And in Christ, God put his special mark of ownership on you by giving you the Holy Spirit that he had promised. ¹⁴That Holy Spirit is the guarantee that we will receive what God promised for his people until God gives full freedom to those who are his—to bring praise to God's glory.

PAUL'S PRAYER

¹⁵That is why since I heard about your faith in the Lord Jesus and your love for all God's people, ¹⁶I have not stopped giving thanks to God for you. I always remember you in my prayers, ¹⁷asking the God of our Lord Jesus Christ, the glorious Father, to give you a spirit of wisdom and revelation so that you will know him better. ¹⁸I pray also that you will have greater understanding in your heart so you will know the hope to which he has called us and that you will know how rich and glorious are the blessings God has promised his holy people. ¹⁹And you will know that God's power is very great for us who believe. That power is the same as the great strength ²⁰God used to raise Christ from the dead and put him at his right side in the heavenly world. ²¹God has put Christ over all rulers, authorities, powers, and kings, not only in this world but also in the next. ²²God put everything under his power and made him the head over everything for the church, ²³which is Christ's body. The church is filled with Christ, and Christ fills everything in every way.

WE NOW HAVE LIFE

2 In the past you were spiritually dead because of your sins and the things you did against God. ²Yes, in the past you lived the way the world lives, following the ruler of the evil powers that are above the earth. That same spirit is now working in those who refuse to obey God. ³In the past all of us lived like them, trying to please our sinful selves and doing all the things our bodies and minds wanted. We should have suffered God's anger because we were sinful by nature. We were the same as all other people.

⁴But God's mercy is great, and he loved us very much. ⁵Though we were spiritually dead because of the things we did against God, he gave us new life with Christ. You have been saved by God's grace. ⁶And he raised us up with Christ and gave us a seat with him in the heavens. He did this for those in Christ Jesus ⁷so that for all future time he could show the very great riches of his grace by being kind to us in Christ Jesus. ⁸I mean that you have been saved by grace through believing. You did not

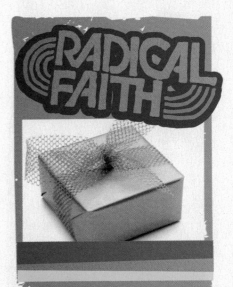

RADICAL FAITH

EPHESIANS 2:8–10

Here's the Good News about Jesus expressed straight ahead, simple enough for anyone to understand: "You have been saved by grace through believing. You did not save yourselves; it was a gift from God. It was not the result of your own efforts, so you cannot brag about it." Getting forgiven for your sins and being set free starts with God's grace, his unearned kindness. Securing a home in heaven isn't something you deserve, rather a gift you accept by believing God's promise. There's nothing in salvation you can brag about, because it's all God's doing. Those profound words from Ephesians are followed by a point that's easy to overlook. When God saved you and made you his friend, he didn't set you on a pedestal, a spiritual trophy to his awesome power. Instead, he made you a new person, specifically designed to do good works. Catch this awesome thought: God has already plotted out what he wants you to do. It's why he saved you. So your top job as long as you live and breathe is learning what pleases God and finding your place in his plans (Ephesians 5:10).

WAYS to WALK the WALK

EPHESIANS 2:19-22

WORD: Consider the foundation of your life.

WALK IT: Think about the foundation of the building you call home. Consider how it supports the building. And remember that Jesus is the foundation of your life.

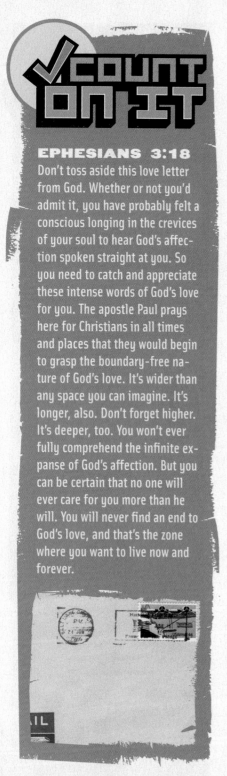

EPHESIANS 3:18

Don't toss aside this love letter from God. Whether or not you'd admit it, you have probably felt a conscious longing in the crevices of your soul to hear God's affection spoken straight at you. So you need to catch and appreciate these intense words of God's love for you. The apostle Paul prays here for Christians in all times and places that they would begin to grasp the boundary-free nature of God's love. It's wider than any space you can imagine. It's longer, also. Don't forget higher. It's deeper, too. You won't ever fully comprehend the infinite expanse of God's affection. But you can be certain that no one will ever care for you more than he will. You will never find an end to God's love, and that's the zone where you want to live now and forever.

save yourselves; it was a gift from God. [9]It was not the result of your own efforts, so you cannot brag about it. [10]God has made us what we are. In Christ Jesus, God made us to do good works, which God planned in advance for us to live our lives doing.

ONE IN CHRIST

[11]You were not born Jewish. You are the people the Jews call "uncircumcised."[n] Those who call you "uncircumcised" call themselves "circumcised." (Their circumcision is only something they themselves do on their bodies.) [12]Remember that in the past you were without Christ. You were not citizens of Israel, and you had no part in the agreements[n] with the promise that God made to his people. You had no hope, and you did not know God. [13]But now in Christ Jesus, you who were far away from God are brought near through the blood of Christ's death. [14]Christ himself is our peace. He made both Jewish people and those who are not Jews one people. They were separated as if there were a wall between them, but Christ broke down that wall of hate by giving his own body. [15]The Jewish law had many commands and rules, but Christ ended that law. His purpose was to make the two groups of people become one new people in him and in this way make peace. [16]It was also Christ's purpose to end the hatred between the two groups, to make them into one body, and to bring them back to God. Christ did all this with his death on the cross. [17]Christ came and preached peace to you who were far away from God, and to those who were near to God. [18]Yes, it is through Christ we all have the right to come to the Father in one Spirit.

[19]Now you who are not Jewish are not foreigners or strangers any longer, but are citizens together with God's holy people. You belong to God's family. [20]You are like a building that was built on the foundation of the apostles and prophets. Christ Jesus himself is the most important stone[n] in that building, [21]and that whole building is joined together in Christ. He makes it grow and become a holy temple in the Lord. [22]And in Christ you, too, are being built together with the Jews into a place where God lives through the Spirit.

PAUL'S WORK IN TELLING THE GOOD NEWS

3 So I, Paul, am a prisoner of Christ Jesus for you who are not Jews. [2]Surely you have heard that God gave me this work to tell you about his grace. [3]He let me know his secret by showing it to me. I have already written a little about this. [4]If you read what I wrote then, you can see that I truly understand the secret about the Christ. [5]People who lived in other times were not told that secret. But now, through the Spirit, God has shown that secret to his holy apostles and prophets. [6]This is that secret: that through the

Good News those who are not Jews will share with the Jews in God's blessing. They belong to the same body, and they share together in the promise that God made in Christ Jesus.

[7]By God's special gift of grace given to me through his power, I became a servant to tell that Good News. [8]I am the least important of all God's people, but God gave me this gift—to tell those who are not Jews the Good News about the riches of Christ, which are too great to understand fully. [9]And God gave me the work of telling all people about the plan for his secret, which has been hidden in him since the beginning of time. He is the One who created everything. [10]His purpose was that through

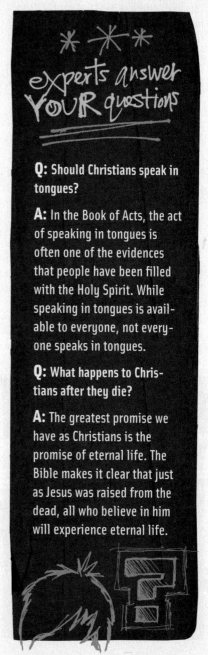

experts answer YOUR questions

Q: Should Christians speak in tongues?

A: In the Book of Acts, the act of speaking in tongues is often one of the evidences that people have been filled with the Holy Spirit. While speaking in tongues is available to everyone, not everyone speaks in tongues.

Q: What happens to Christians after they die?

A: The greatest promise we have as Christians is the promise of eternal life. The Bible makes it clear that just as Jesus was raised from the dead, all who believe in him will experience eternal life.

 2:11 "uncircumcised" People not having the mark of circumcision as the Jews had. **2:12 agreements** The agreements that God gave to his people in the Old Testament. **2:20 most important stone** Literally, "cornerstone." The first and most important stone in a building.

the church all the rulers and powers in the heavenly world will now know God's wisdom, which has so many forms. [11]This agrees with the purpose God had since the beginning of time, and he carried out his plan through Christ Jesus our Lord. [12]In Christ we can come before God with freedom and without fear. We can do this through faith in Christ. [13]So I ask you not to become discouraged because of the sufferings I am having for you. My sufferings are for your glory.

THE LOVE OF CHRIST

[14]So I bow in prayer before the Father [15]from whom every family in heaven and on earth gets its true name. [16]I ask the Father in his great glory to give you the power to be strong inwardly through his Spirit. [17]I pray that Christ will live in your hearts by faith and that your life will be strong in love and be built on love. [18]And I pray that you and all God's holy people will have the power to understand the greatness of Christ's love—how wide and how long and how high and how deep that love is. [19]Christ's love is greater than anyone can ever know, but I pray that you will be able to know that love. Then you can be filled with the fullness of God.

[20]With God's power working in us, God can do much, much more than anything we can ask or imagine. [21]To him be glory in the church and in Christ Jesus for all time, forever and ever. Amen.

THE UNITY OF THE BODY

4 I am in prison because I belong to the Lord. Therefore I urge you who have been chosen by God to live up to the life to which God called you. [2]Always be humble, gentle, and patient, accepting each other in love. [3]You are joined together with peace through the Spirit, so make every effort to continue together in this way. [4]There is one body and one Spirit, and God called you to have one hope. [5]There is one Lord, one faith, and one baptism. [6]There is one God and Father of everything. He rules everything and is everywhere and is in everything.

[7]Christ gave each one of us the special gift of grace, showing how generous he is. [8]That is why it says in the Scriptures,

"When he went up to the heights,
     he led a parade of captives,
     and he gave gifts to people." *Psalm 68:18*

[9]When it says, "He went up," what does it mean? It means that he first came down to the earth. [10]So Jesus came down, and he is the same One who went up above all the heaven. Christ did that to fill everything with his

---

extras:

How to Budget Your Money Wisely

Don't think of a budget as a burden—it's simply a strategy for financial freedom. It is you, deciding in advance, where you want your money to go. Most of the time, budgets are associated with lack (think of the phrase "it isn't in the budget"), but they are really tools that tell you where your money is going. At the beginning of the month, determine how much you're going to earn that month, then decide how much you'll spend on food, transportation, church, entertainment—all of it. Determine how you're going to spend the money you get, and then stick to your strategy. It won't be flawless at first, so give it a few months. You'll soon see how liberating budgets can actually be. Budgets are about being proactive, and the same is true about your relationship with Christ. Jesus works in you, but you must be proactive and work on yourself, too.

---

fight the fight

Ephesians 4:1-3

Patience. It is easy to pretend we have plenty of it. That is, until we are confronted with a slacker at the convenience store, a teacher who doesn't grade fairly, or a curfew that is too early. Yet, Paul was patient even as he sat in prison. Though he didn't necessarily appreciate being jailed for preaching the Good News, he encouraged the church to continue living up to God's calling. In addition to exercising patience, Paul reminded believers to be humble, gentle, and to accept each other. And the same reminder is appropriate for us today. Oh, and don't forget to work together, too.

Relationships

" . . . Speaking the truth with love, we will grow up in every way into Christ, who is the head" (Ephesians 4:15). Paul warned of the dangers of being wishy-washy in your faith, and those dangers extend to the way you interact with others. Be careful of those who might want to take advantage of you or urge you to compromise your faith. Knowing what you believe is a sign of spiritual maturity, and standing your ground against relationship peer pressure will always pay off in the long run. Speak the truth to others, but be sure to do it out of love for them.

until we are all joined together in the same faith and in the same knowledge of the Son of God. We must become like a mature person, growing until we become like Christ and have his perfection.

[14]Then we will no longer be babies. We will not be tossed about like a ship that the waves carry one way and then another. We will not be influenced by every new teaching we hear from people who are trying to fool us. They make plans and try any kind of trick to fool people into following the wrong path. [15]No! Speaking the truth with love, we will grow up in every way into Christ, who is the head. [16]The whole body depends on Christ, and all the parts of the body are joined and held together. Each part does its own work to make the whole body grow and be strong with love.

THE WAY YOU SHOULD LIVE

presence. [11]And Christ gave gifts to people—he made some to be apostles, some to be prophets, some to go and tell the Good News, and some to have the work of caring for and teaching God's people. [12]Christ gave those gifts to prepare God's holy people for the work of serving, to make the body of Christ stronger. [13]This work must continue

[17]In the Lord's name, I tell you this. Do not continue living like those who do not believe. Their thoughts are worth nothing. [18]They do not understand, and they know nothing, because they refuse to listen. So they cannot have the life that God gives. [19]They have lost all feeling of shame, and they use their lives for doing evil. They continually want to do all kinds of evil. [20]But what you learned in Christ was not

*REVIEWS MOVIES

"ONE OF THE GREATEST SPORTS MOVIES EVER MADE"

BILLY BOB THORNTON

FRIDAY NIGHT LIGHTS

FRIDAY NIGHT LIGHTS

Friday Night Lights is the ultimate feel-good movie for almost any red-blooded American male with a liking for sports, sweat, and a good story. Starring Billy Bob Thornton and Tim McGraw, this movie is based on true events and packs a powerful cinematic punch. As with everything in Texas, football is HUGE. So, when a new coach takes over a local county's high school football team, dark issues come to light. This becomes especially true when the championship is on the line. Despite some profanity and sexual situations, the moral of the story is about working hard, being a team player, and becoming totally dedicated to something bigger than one's self.

WHY IT ROCKS:

VALUABLE LIFE LESSONS ARE LEARNED ON THE FIELD.

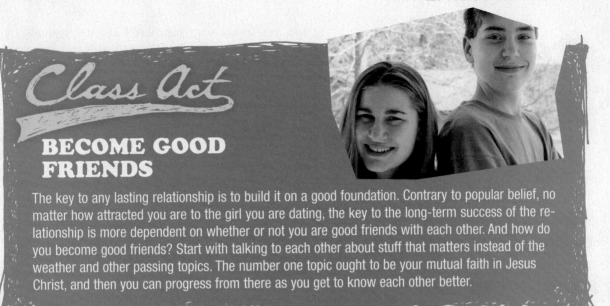

Class Act

BECOME GOOD FRIENDS

The key to any lasting relationship is to build it on a good foundation. Contrary to popular belief, no matter how attracted you are to the girl you are dating, the key to the long-term success of the relationship is more dependent on whether or not you are good friends with each other. And how do you become good friends? Start with talking to each other about stuff that matters instead of the weather and other passing topics. The number one topic ought to be your mutual faith in Jesus Christ, and then you can progress from there as you get to know each other better.

like this. [21] I know that you heard about him, and you are in him, so you were taught the truth that is in Jesus. [22] You were taught to leave your old self—to stop living the evil way you lived before. That old self becomes worse, because people are fooled by the evil things they want to do. [23] But you were taught to be made new in your hearts, [24] to become a new person. That new person is made to be like God—made to be truly good and holy.

[25] So you must stop telling lies. Tell each other the truth, because we all belong to each other in the same body.[n] [26] When you are angry, do not sin, and be sure to stop being angry before the end of the day. [27] Do not give the devil a way to defeat you. [28] Those who are stealing must stop stealing and start working. They should earn an honest living for themselves. Then they will have something to share with those who are poor.

[29] When you talk, do not say harmful things, but say what people need—words that will help others become stronger. Then what you say will do good to those who listen to you. [30] And do not make the Holy Spirit sad. The Spirit is God's proof that you belong to him. God gave you the Spirit to show that God will make you free when the final day comes. [31] Do not be bitter or angry or mad. Never shout angrily or say things to hurt others.

Never do anything evil. [32] Be kind and loving to each other, and forgive each other just as God forgave you in Christ.

LIVING IN THE LIGHT

5 You are God's children whom he loves, so try to be like him. [2] Live a life of love just as Christ loved us and gave himself for us as a sweet-smelling offering and sacrifice to God.

[3] But there must be no sexual sin among you, or any kind of evil or greed. Those things are not right for God's holy people. [4] Also, there must be no evil talk among you, and you must not speak foolishly or tell evil jokes. These

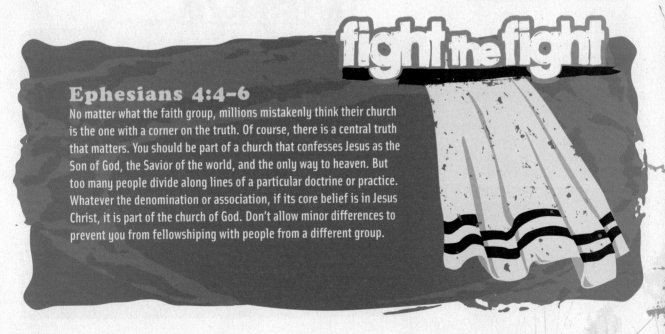

fight the fight

Ephesians 4:4-6

No matter what the faith group, millions mistakenly think their church is the one with a corner on the truth. Of course, there is a central truth that matters. You should be part of a church that confesses Jesus as the Son of God, the Savior of the world, and the only way to heaven. But too many people divide along lines of a particular doctrine or practice. Whatever the denomination or association, if its core belief is in Jesus Christ, it is part of the church of God. Don't allow minor differences to prevent you from fellowshiping with people from a different group.

4:25 Tell . . . body. Quotation from Zechariah 8:16.

EPHESIANS 4:22

There's nothing skimpy about God's forgiveness. The Bible says that when you admit your sins and trust in Jesus' death on your behalf, the Lord flings your sins away from you "as far as the east is from west" (Psalm 103:12). You're forgiven of every sin past, present, and future. But that's no excuse to dart off and sin some more. One of God's main goals in making you his tight friend and follower is to break you free from your sinful past, a life that was bad enough to nail Jesus to the cross. So don't miss the key point of this part of Ephesians: Don't keep living like you don't believe, doing things that dishonor God and cause hurt to you and others. Instead, stick to the truth you know about Jesus. Your aim is to ditch the way you used to live and no longer be duped into thinking evil is fun. God has made you a new person, so live like it. To help you on that path, learn God's plan and purpose for your life, and pursue it with passion.

things are not right for you. Instead, you should be giving thanks to God. [5]You can be sure of this: No one will have a place in the kingdom of Christ and of God who sins sexually, or does evil things, or is greedy. Anyone who is greedy is serving a false god.

[6]Do not let anyone fool you by telling you things that are not true, because these things will bring God's anger on those who do not obey him. [7]So have nothing to do with them. [8]In the past you were full of darkness, but now you are full of light in the Lord. So live like children who belong to the light. [9]Light brings every kind of goodness, right living, and truth. [10]Try to learn what pleases the Lord. [11]Have nothing to do with the things done in darkness, which are not worth anything. But show that they are wrong. [12]It is shameful even to talk about what those people do in secret. [13]But the light makes all things easy to see, [14]and everything that is made easy to see can become light. This is why it is said:

"Wake up, sleeper!
Rise from death,
and Christ will shine on you."

[15]So be very careful how you live. Do not live like those who are not wise, but live wisely. [16]Use every chance you have for doing good, because these are evil times. [17]So do not be foolish but learn what the Lord wants you to do. [18]Do not be drunk with wine, which will ruin you, but be filled with the Spirit. [19]Speak to each other with psalms, hymns, and spiritual songs, singing and making music in your hearts to the Lord. [20]Always give thanks to God the Father for everything, in the name of our Lord Jesus Christ.

WIVES AND HUSBANDS

[21]Yield to obey each other as you would to Christ.

[22]Wives, yield to your husbands, as you do to the Lord, [23]because the husband is the head of the wife, as Christ is the head of the church. And he is the Savior of the body, which is the church. [24]As the church yields to Christ, so you wives should yield to your husbands in everything.

[25]Husbands, love your wives as Christ loved the church and gave himself for it [26]to make it belong to God. Christ used the word to make the church clean by washing it with water. [27]He died so that he could give the church to himself like a bride in all her beauty. He died so that the church could be pure and without fault, with no evil or sin or any other wrong thing in it. [28]In the same way, husbands should love their wives as they love their own bodies. The man who loves his wife loves himself. [29]No one ever hates his own body, but feeds and takes care of it. And that is what Christ does for the church, [30]because we are parts of his body. [31]The Scripture says, "So a man will leave his father and mother and be united with his wife, and the two will become one body."[n] [32]That secret is very important—I am talking about Christ and the church. [33]But each one of you must love his wife as he loves himself, and a wife must respect her husband.

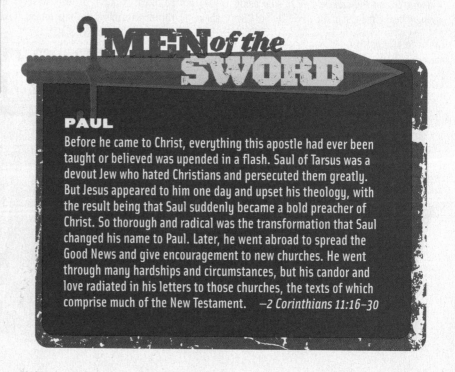

PAUL

Before he came to Christ, everything this apostle had ever been taught or believed was upended in a flash. Saul of Tarsus was a devout Jew who hated Christians and persecuted them greatly. But Jesus appeared to him one day and upset his theology, with the result being that Saul suddenly became a bold preacher of Christ. So thorough and radical was the transformation that Saul changed his name to Paul. Later, he went abroad to spread the Good News and give encouragement to new churches. He went through many hardships and circumstances, but his candor and love radiated in his letters to those churches, the texts of which comprise much of the New Testament. —2 Corinthians 11:16–30

5:31 "So . . . body." Quotation from Genesis 2:24.

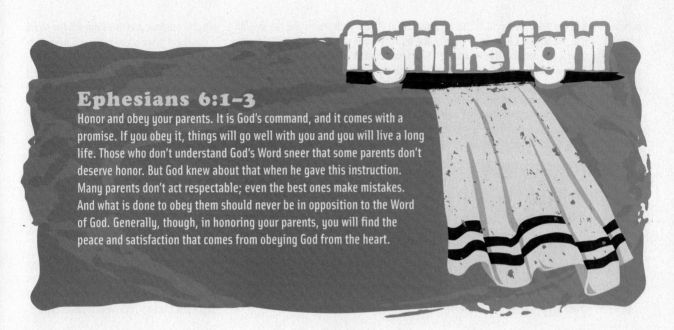

fight the fight

Ephesians 6:1–3

Honor and obey your parents. It is God's command, and it comes with a promise. If you obey it, things will go well with you and you will live a long life. Those who don't understand God's Word sneer that some parents don't deserve honor. But God knew about that when he gave this instruction. Many parents don't act respectable; even the best ones make mistakes. And what is done to obey them should never be in opposition to the Word of God. Generally, though, in honoring your parents, you will find the peace and satisfaction that comes from obeying God from the heart.

CHILDREN AND PARENTS

6 Children, obey your parents as the Lord wants, because this is the right thing to do. [2]The command says, "Honor your father and mother."[n] This is the first command that has a promise with it— [3]"Then everything will be well with you, and you will have a long life on the earth."[n]

[4]Fathers, do not make your children angry, but raise them with the training and teaching of the Lord.

SLAVES AND MASTERS

[5]Slaves, obey your masters here on earth with fear and respect and from a sincere heart, just as you obey Christ. [6]You must do this not only while they are watching you, to please them. With all your heart you must do what God wants as people who are obeying Christ. [7]Do your work with enthusiasm. Work as if you were serving the Lord, not as if you were serving only men and women. [8]Remember that the Lord will give a reward to everyone, slave or free, for doing good.

[9]Masters, in the same way, be good to your slaves. Do not threaten them. Remember that the One who is your Master and their Master is in heaven, and he treats everyone alike.

WEAR THE FULL ARMOR OF GOD

[10]Finally, be strong in the Lord and in his great power. [11]Put on the full armor of God so that you can fight against the devil's evil tricks. [12]Our fight is not against people on earth but against the rulers and authorities and the powers of this world's darkness, against the spiritual

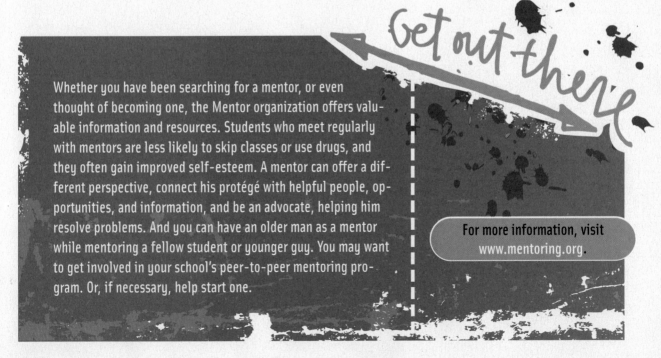

Get out there

Whether you have been searching for a mentor, or even thought of becoming one, the Mentor organization offers valuable information and resources. Students who meet regularly with mentors are less likely to skip classes or use drugs, and they often gain improved self-esteem. A mentor can offer a different perspective, connect his protégé with helpful people, opportunities, and information, and be an advocate, helping him resolve problems. And you can have an older man as a mentor while mentoring a fellow student or younger guy. You may want to get involved in your school's peer-to-peer mentoring program. Or, if necessary, help start one.

For more information, visit www.mentoring.org.

6:2 "Honor . . . mother." Quotation from Exodus 20:12; Deuteronomy 5:16.   6:3 "Then . . . earth." Quotation from Exodus 20:12; Deuteronomy 5:16.

powers of evil in the heavenly world. [13]That is why you need to put on God's full armor. Then on the day of evil you will be able to stand strong. And when you have finished the whole fight, you will still be standing. [14]So stand strong, with the belt of truth tied around your waist and the protection of right living on your chest. [15]On your feet wear the Good News of peace to help you stand strong. [16]And also use the shield of faith with which you can stop all the burning arrows of the Evil One. [17]Accept God's salvation as your helmet, and take the sword of the Spirit, which is the word of God. [18]Pray in the Spirit at all times with all kinds of prayers, asking for everything you need. To do this you must always be ready and never give up. Always pray for all God's people.

[19]Also pray for me that when I speak, God will give me words so that I can tell the secret of the Good News without fear. [20]I have been sent to preach this Good News, and I am doing that now, here in prison. Pray that when I preach the Good News I will speak without fear, as I should.

FINAL GREETINGS

[21]I am sending to you Tychicus, our brother whom we love and a faithful servant of the Lord's work. He will tell you everything that is happening with me. Then you will know how I am and what I am doing. [22]I am sending him to you for this reason—so that you will know how we are, and he can encourage you.

[23]Peace and love with faith to you brothers and sisters from God the Father and the Lord Jesus Christ. [24]Grace to all of you who love our Lord Jesus Christ with love that never ends.

GUARD YOUR HEART

By their teenage years, many guys have made sexual mistakes they aren't proud of. Some find it difficult to maintain purity once sex has already been a part of their lives. If this is you, don't walk into a relationship blindly. Safeguard your relationship with regular prayer, scripture reading, and proper boundaries.

*** notes

PHILIPPIANS

DON'T WORRY; BE HAPPY

Your girlfriend just dumped you, you flunked your math exam, and your computer hard drive crashed. It's humiliation and frustration rolled up into one hunk of bad news. Yet, no matter how terrible life may appear, it's likely not as bad as Paul's circumstances when he wrote this letter.

Paul headed out to be a missionary and got tossed in prison. Yet, in this setting the apostle writes like a man without a care in the world. He is full of joy for the help the church at Philippi gave him when he was preaching. Paul has seen the good work God has done in them and promises it will continue.

There are other reasons Paul is happy. Not only does everyone know he is imprisoned for his faith, this harsh treatment has led other believers to talk boldly about Christ. He is reminded that the Philippians are praying for him and realizes the Holy Spirit is helping him during this trying time. As a result, Paul encourages the believers to make him even happier by accepting Christ's strength for living. He also urges them to do everything without grumbling or complaining. Coming from a man who's writing from a jail cell, these are powerful words.

COUNT ON IT

PHILIPPIANS 1:6

Just when you think you can slide into sin and no one will notice, God tells you he has a bigger plan for your life. The Bible reveals that God aims for you to grow into nothing less than total resemblance to Jesus, so that when people glance at you they will do a double take, thinking they have seen the Lord (2 Corinthians 3:18). Yet, God doesn't just have a plan about where you're going. He knows how you're going to get there. In fact, he's going to take you there himself. From the day you first believed, he has been at work in you, transforming you to look like Jesus. He won't quit the job until he's finished on the day Jesus comes back. So when you feel tempted to give up on yourself, press on. You're destined for God's greatness.

1 From Paul and Timothy, servants of Christ Jesus.

To all of God's holy people in Christ Jesus who live in Philippi, including your overseers and deacons:

²Grace and peace to you from God our Father and the Lord Jesus Christ.

PAUL'S PRAYER

³I thank my God every time I remember you, ⁴always praying with joy for all of you. ⁵I thank God for the help you gave me while I preached the Good News—help you gave from the first day you believed until now. ⁶God began doing a good work in you, and I am sure he will continue it until it is finished when Jesus Christ comes again.

⁷And I know that I am right to think like this about all of you, because I have you in my heart. All of you share in God's grace with me while I am in prison and while I am defending and proving the truth of the Good News. ⁸God knows that I want to see you very much, because I love all of you with the love of Christ Jesus.

⁹This is my prayer for you: that your love will grow more and more; that you will have knowledge and understanding with your love; ¹⁰that you will see the difference between good and bad and will choose the good; that you will be pure and without wrong for the coming of Christ; ¹¹that you will be filled with the good things produced in your life by Christ to bring glory and praise to God.

PAUL'S TROUBLES HELP THE WORK

¹²I want you brothers and sisters to know that what has happened to me has helped to spread the Good News. ¹³All the palace guards and everyone else knows that I am in prison because I am a believer in Christ. ¹⁴Because I am in prison, most of the believers have become more bold in Christ and are not afraid to speak the word of God.

¹⁵It is true that some preach about Christ because they are jealous and ambitious, but others preach about Christ because they want to help. ¹⁶They preach because they have love, and they know that God gave me the work of defending the Good News. ¹⁷But the others preach about Christ for selfish and wrong reasons, wanting to make trouble for me in prison.

¹⁸But it doesn't matter. The important thing is that in every way, whether for right or wrong reasons, they are preaching about Christ. So I am happy, and I will continue to be happy. ¹⁹Because you are praying for me and the Spirit of Jesus Christ is helping me, I know this trouble will bring my freedom. ²⁰I expect and hope that I will not fail Christ in anything but that I will have the courage now, as always, to show the greatness of Christ in my life here on earth, whether I live or die. ²¹To me the

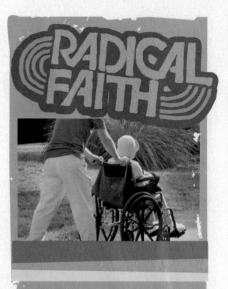

RADICAL FAITH

PHILIPPIANS 2:1–5

As you scan this Bible book you can't help but notice that the believers in Philippi are favorites of the apostle Paul. The book oozes joy, often because of Paul's attachment to these faithful Christians. Yet, everything isn't perfect in that young church. In Philippians 4:2, you even spot a feud between two women. Paul urges the whole group to remember everything Jesus has given them—things like strength, comfort, unity, mercy, and kindness. He says to share those riches, taking deep interest in each other. Then Paul says that the big goal is to think and act like Jesus. Even though Jesus is God, he lowered himself to our level in order to save us from our selfish and sinful selves. He gave up his glory to be born as a man who bled and died for the human race. That's a picture of ultimate humility, giving others more honor than you give yourself. That sort of wild unselfishness sounds unreachable, but it's the same goal God has for you. Be more like Jesus. Become a humble servant. God will reward you (Matthew 23:11).

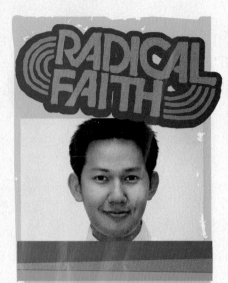

RADICAL FAITH

PHILIPPIANS 3:12–14

Walk into almost any church and you will spot Christians who look amazingly put-together. Whether they're old or young, they look like someone stamped them out with a cookie cutter to look just like Jesus. They seem untroubled and un-tempted, like they live in a different universe from most guys. Don't let appearances bamboozle you. The apostle Paul admitted he wasn't perfect. Even Jesus was tempted to commit sin. No human escapes being tempted, and no human being but Jesus avoids falling into sin (Hebrews 4:15). As Romans 3:23 says, "Everyone has sinned and fallen short of God's glorious stan-dard." Just because some church people are too good to be true, however, doesn't mean believers can't wiggle loose from sin. God doesn't intend for you to be a slave to any evil. Mature followers of Jesus have learned a secret: All be-lievers fall down, but getting up and going on is what matters more. That involves asking God's forgive-ness, then forgetting the past and pushing ahead. Don't give up if you don't look much like Jesus yet. Just press forward, and God will get you to the goal.

only important thing about living is Christ, and dying would be profit for me. ²²If I con-tinue living in my body, I will be able to work for the Lord. I do not know what to choose—living or dying. ²³It is hard to choose between the two. I want to leave this life and be with Christ, which is much better, ²⁴but you need me here in my body. ²⁵Since I am sure of this, I know I will stay with you to help you grow and have joy in your faith. ²⁶You will be very happy in Christ Jesus when I am with you again.

²⁷Only one thing concerns me: Be sure that you live in a way that brings honor to the Good News of Christ. Then whether I come and visit you or am away from you, I will hear that you are standing strong with one purpose, that you work together as one for the faith of the Good News, ²⁸and that you are not afraid of those who are against you. All of this is proof that your enemies will be destroyed but that you will be saved by God. ²⁹God gave you the honor not only of believing in Christ but also of suffering for him, both of which bring glory to Christ. ³⁰When I was with you, you saw the struggles I had, and you hear about the strug-gles I am having now. You yourselves are hav-ing the same kind of struggles.

2 Does your life in Christ give you strength? Does his love comfort you? Do we share together in the spirit? Do you have mercy and kindness? ²If so, make me very happy by having the same thoughts, shar-ing the same love, and having one mind and purpose. ³When you do things, do not let self-ishness or pride be your guide. Instead, be humble and give more honor to others than to yourselves. ⁴Do not be interested only in your own life, but be interested in the lives of oth-ers.

BE UNSELFISH LIKE CHRIST

⁵In your lives you must think and act like Christ Jesus.
⁶Christ himself was like God in everything.
But he did not think that being equal
with God was something to be
used for his own benefit.
⁷But he gave up his place with God and
made himself nothing.
He was born as a man
and became like a servant.
⁸And when he was living as a man,
he humbled himself and was fully
obedient to God,
even when that caused his death—
death on a cross.
⁹So God raised him to the highest place.

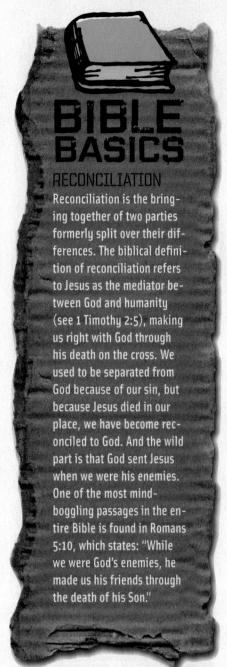

BIBLE BASICS

RECONCILIATION

Reconciliation is the bring-ing together of two parties formerly split over their dif-ferences. The biblical defini-tion of reconciliation refers to Jesus as the mediator be-tween God and humanity (see 1 Timothy 2:5), making us right with God through his death on the cross. We used to be separated from God because of our sin, but because Jesus died in our place, we have become rec-onciled to God. And the wild part is that God sent Jesus when we were his enemies. One of the most mind-boggling passages in the en-tire Bible is found in Romans 5:10, which states: "While we were God's enemies, he made us his friends through the death of his Son."

God made his name greater than every
other name
¹⁰so that every knee will bow to the name of
Jesus—
everyone in heaven, on earth, and under
the earth.
¹¹And everyone will confess that Jesus Christ
is Lord
and bring glory to God the Father.

BE THE PEOPLE GOD WANTS YOU TO BE

¹²My dear friends, you have always obeyed God when I was with you. It is even more im-

portant that you obey now while I am away from you. Keep on working to complete your salvation with fear and trembling, [13]because God is working in you to help you want to do and be able to do what pleases him.

[14]Do everything without complaining or arguing. [15]Then you will be innocent and without any wrong. You will be God's children without fault. But you are living with crooked and mean people all around you, among whom you shine like stars in the dark world. [16]You offer the teaching that gives life. So when Christ comes again, I can be happy because my work was not wasted. I ran the race and won.

[17]Your faith makes you offer your lives as a sacrifice in serving God. If I have to offer my own blood with your sacrifice, I will be happy and full of joy with all of you. [18]You also should be happy and full of joy with me.

TIMOTHY AND EPAPHRODITUS

[19]I hope in the Lord Jesus to send Timothy to you soon. I will be happy to learn how you are. [20]I have no one else like Timothy, who truly cares for you. [21]Other people are interested only in their own lives, not in the work of Jesus Christ. [22]You know the kind of person Timothy is. You know he has served with me in telling the Good News, as a son serves his father. [23]I plan to send him to you quickly when I know what will happen to me. [24]I am sure that the Lord will help me to come to you soon.

[25]Epaphroditus, my brother in Christ, works and serves with me in the army of Christ. When I needed help, you sent him to me. I think now that I must send him back to

you, [26]because he wants very much to see all of you. He is worried because you heard that he was sick. [27]Yes, he was sick, and nearly died, but God had mercy on him and me too so that I would not have more sadness. [28]I want very much to send him to you so that when you see him you can be happy, and I can stop worrying about you. [29]Welcome him in the Lord with much joy. Give honor to people like him, [30]because he almost died for the work of Christ. He risked his life to give me the help you could not give in your service to me.

Extras:

How to Lose Weight Safely

Fad diets come and go, and many of them promise a way to melt off pounds almost instantly. The truth is, rapid weight loss can be dangerous, so it's best to stick to the tried and true method of losing weight, which can be summed up in four words: "eat less, do more." Don't go back for seconds. Walk around the block after a meal. Eat more veggies (raw celery actually burns more calories in your body than the celery contains). Take the stairs at work. You get the picture here. You didn't gain your unnecessary weight in a day, and you certainly won't lose it in one. Give it time, be consistent, and you'll see results. And it helps to have an accountability partner in your corner for encouragement. Take care not to become spiritually flabby, either. Exercise your faith, dine on God's Word, and discuss it with a friend.

THE IMPORTANCE OF CHRIST

3 My brothers and sisters, be full of joy in the Lord. It is no trouble for me to write the same things to you again, and it will help you to be more ready. [2]Watch out for those who do evil, who are like dogs, who demand to cut* the body. [3]We are the ones who are truly circumcised. We worship God through his Spirit, and our pride is in Christ Jesus. We do not put trust in ourselves or anything we can do, [4]although I might be able to

fight the fight

Philippians 4:6-7

Prayer is the subject of thousands of books, seminars, and teachings. It is profound, yet simple. Prayer is talking with God. That means not just listing what you want from him, but listening for his directions. Prayer isn't to be repeated like some formula or used as a mystical mantra. But if you take time to pray—wherever you are, not just at church—you will find peace and direction. Prayer will bring the presence of the Holy Spirit into your life. Instead of grumbling about what all you don't have, you will be thankful for everything God has given you.

 3:2 cut The word in Greek is like the word "circumcise," but it means "to cut completely off."

COUNT ON IT

PHILIPPIANS 4:6-7

You can own a million tanker ships full of crude oil, but you still can't buy peace in the Middle East. You can't single-handedly cure racial hostilities and bring calm to our country's core cities. You might not even be able to mend a dispute between friends. But at least you can find peace in your soul by listening to God's instructions. God knows that humans are always worrying about something, so the Old Testament announced that Jesus would be our "Prince of Peace" (Isaiah 9:6). By talking to Jesus and telling him where and why you're stressed, you can put him in charge of every tough circumstance you face. As you trust in him, he will unleash his peace in you. When you pray about everything, you don't have to worry about anything.

put trust in myself. If anyone thinks he has a reason to trust in himself, he should know that I have greater reason for trusting in myself. [5]I was circumcised eight days after my birth. I am from the people of Israel and the tribe of Benjamin. I am a Hebrew, and my parents were Hebrews. I had a strict view of the law, which is why I became a Pharisee. [6]I was so enthusiastic I tried to hurt the church. No one could find fault with the way I obeyed the law of Moses. [7]Those things were important to me, but now I think they are worth nothing because of Christ. [8]Not only those things, but I think that all things are worth nothing compared with the greatness of knowing Christ Jesus my Lord. Because of him, I have lost all those things, and now I know they are worthless trash. This allows me to have Christ [9]and to belong to him. Now I am right with God, not because I followed the law, but because I believed in Christ. God uses my faith to make me right with him. [10]I want to know Christ and the power that raised him from the dead. I want to share in his sufferings and become like him in his death. [11]Then I have hope that I myself will be raised from the dead.

CONTINUING TOWARD OUR GOAL

[12]I do not mean that I am already as God wants me to be. I have not yet reached that goal, but I continue trying to reach it and to make it mine. Christ wants me to do that, which is the reason he made me his. [13]Brothers and sisters, I know that I have not yet reached that goal, but there is one thing I always do. Forgetting the past and straining toward what is ahead, [14]I keep trying to reach the goal and get the prize for which God called me through Christ to the life above.

[15]All of us who are spiritually mature should think this way, too. And if there are things you do not agree with, God will make them clear to you. [16]But we should continue following the truth we already have.

[17]Brothers and sisters, all of you should try to follow my example and to copy those who live the way we showed you. [18]Many people

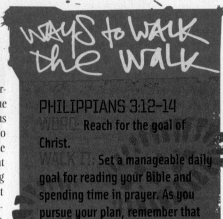

WAYS to WALK the WALK

PHILIPPIANS 3:12-14

WORD: Reach for the goal of Christ.

WALK IT: Set a manageable daily goal for reading your Bible and spending time in prayer. As you pursue your plan, remember that becoming more like Christ is your objective.

live like enemies of the cross of Christ. I have often told you about them, and it makes me cry to tell you about them now. [19]In the end, they will be destroyed. They do whatever their bodies want, they are proud of their shameful acts, and they think only about earthly things. [20]But our homeland is in heaven, and we are waiting for our Savior, the Lord Jesus Christ, to come from heaven. [21]By his power to rule all things, he will change our humble bodies and make them like his own glorious body.

WHAT THE CHRISTIANS ARE TO DO

4 My dear brothers and sisters, I love you and want to see you. You bring me joy and make me proud of you, so stand strong in the Lord as I have told you.

[2]I ask Euodia and Syntyche to agree in the Lord. [3]And I ask you, my faithful friend, to help these women. They served with me in telling the Good News, together with Clement and others who worked with me, whose names are written in the book of life."

[4]Be full of joy in the Lord always. I will say again, be full of joy.

[5]Let everyone see that you are gentle and kind. The Lord is coming soon. [6]Do not worry

GUARD YOUR HEART

Think about what you are looking for in a relationship. In order for you to have a godly relationship with a girl, it's important to know the motives of your own heart. If they aren't pure, you will end up making poor decisions. You will follow your heart, so be sure it is a safe guide.

4:3 **book of life** God's book that has the names of all God's chosen people (Revelation 3:5; 21:27).

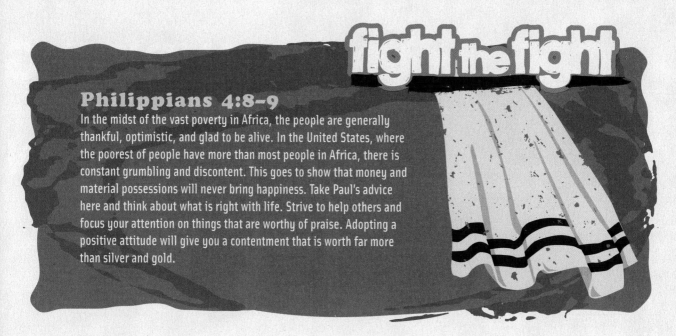

fight the fight

Philippians 4:8–9

In the midst of the vast poverty in Africa, the people are generally thankful, optimistic, and glad to be alive. In the United States, where the poorest of people have more than most people in Africa, there is constant grumbling and discontent. This goes to show that money and material possessions will never bring happiness. Take Paul's advice here and think about what is right with life. Strive to help others and focus your attention on things that are worthy of praise. Adopting a positive attitude will give you a contentment that is worth far more than silver and gold.

about anything, but pray and ask God for everything you need, always giving thanks. [7]And God's peace, which is so great we cannot understand it, will keep your hearts and minds in Christ Jesus.

[8]Brothers and sisters, think about the things that are good and worthy of praise. Think about the things that are true and honorable and right and pure and beautiful and respected. [9]Do what you learned and received from me, what I told you, and what you saw me do. And the God who gives peace will be with you.

PAUL THANKS THE CHRISTIANS

[10]I am very happy in the Lord that you have shown your care for me again. You continued to care about me, but there was no way

for you to show it. [11]I am not telling you this because I need anything. I have learned to be satisfied with the things I have and with everything that happens. [12]I know how to live when I am poor, and I know how to live when I have plenty. I have learned the secret of being happy at any time in everything that happens, when I have enough to eat and when I go hungry, when I have more than I need and when I do not have enough. [13]I can do all things through Christ, because he gives me strength.

[14]But it was good that you helped me when I needed it. [15]You Philippians remember when I first preached the Good News there. When I left Macedonia, you were the only church that gave me help. [16]Several times you sent me things I needed when I was in Thessalonica.

[17]Really, it is not that I want to receive gifts from you, but I want you to have the good that comes from giving. [18]And now I have everything, and more. I have all I need, because Epaphroditus brought your gift to me. It is like a sweet-smelling sacrifice offered to God, who accepts that sacrifice and is pleased with it. [19]My God will use his wonderful riches in Christ Jesus to give you everything you need. [20]Glory to our God and Father forever and ever! Amen.

[21]Greet each of God's people in Christ Jesus. Those who are with me send greetings to you. [22]All of God's people greet you, particularly those from the palace of Caesar.

[23]The grace of the Lord Jesus Christ be with you all.

COLOSSIANS

AVOIDING FALSE RELIGION

Ever hear of "cafeteria faith"? That's where people pick from a variety of beliefs to suit their purposes. Maybe it's some Buddhism, a little Islam, a helping of Hinduism, and a small dose of Jesus thrown in on the side. While many today follow this misguided practice, it started thousands of years ago. Paul even wrote to the church at Colossae to warn it against this very thing. Behind Paul's cheery greeting that opens this letter lies a crisis: False teachers are threatening to draw the people away from loyalty to Christ.

What's interesting is that this threat didn't come from people openly attacking Christianity. Instead, it originated with those who appeared to be religious but who wanted to add a few so-called improvements. To deal with it, Paul tells the Colossians not to follow rules about eating and drinking or festivals and issues a strong warning against the worship of angels.

Paul reminds this group of Christ's followers that they have been set free from worldly spirits and, therefore, should focus their attention on heavenly matters. The bottom line of Colossians is Paul's continuing emphasis on the need for faith in Christ. Paul reminds readers that those who worship God should continue praying and telling others about Jesus. It's a simple command, yet a necessary reminder.

From Paul, an apostle of Christ Jesus. I am an apostle because that is what God wanted. Also from Timothy, our brother.

[2]To the holy and faithful brothers and sisters in Christ that live in Colossae:

Grace and peace to you from God our Father.[n]

[3]In our prayers for you we always thank God, the Father of our Lord Jesus Christ, [4]because we have heard about the faith you have in Christ Jesus and the love you have for all of God's people. [5]You have this faith and love because of your hope, and what you hope for is kept safe for you in heaven. You learned about this hope when you heard the message about the truth, the Good News [6]that was told to you. Everywhere in the world that Good News is bringing blessings and is growing. This has happened with you, too, since you heard the Good News and understood the truth about the grace of God. [7]You learned about God's grace from Epaphras, whom we love. He works together with us and is a faithful servant of Christ for us.[n] [8]He also told us about the love you have from the Holy Spirit.

[9]Because of this, since the day we heard about you, we have continued praying for you, asking God that you will know fully what he wants. We pray that you will also have great wisdom and understanding in spiritual things [10]so that you will live the kind of life that honors and pleases the Lord in every way. You will produce fruit in every good work and grow in the knowledge of God. [11]God will strengthen you with his own great power so that you will not give up when troubles come, but you will be patient.

[12]And you will joyfully give thanks to the Father who has made you[n] able to have a share in all that he has prepared for his people in the kingdom of light. [13]God has freed us from the power of darkness, and he brought us into the kingdom of his dear Son. [14]The Son paid for our sins,[n] and in him we have forgiveness.

THE IMPORTANCE OF CHRIST

[15]No one can see God, but Jesus Christ is exactly like him. He ranks higher than everything that has been made. [16]Through his power all things were made—things in heaven and on earth, things seen and unseen, all powers, authorities, lords, and rulers. All things were made through Christ and for Christ. [17]He was there before anything was made, and all things continue because of him. [18]He is the head of the body, which is the church. Everything comes from him. He is the first one who was raised from the dead. So in all things Jesus has first place. [19]God was pleased for all of himself to live in Christ. [20]And through Christ, God has brought all things back to himself again—things on earth and things in heaven. God made peace through the blood of Christ's death on the cross.

[21]At one time you were separated from God. You were his enemies in your minds, and

* REVIEWS MUSIC

KUTLESS:
STRONG TOWER

These rockers have carved out their own little niche by rearranging older worship songs with a heavier sound and by writing a few rock-influenced worship tunes of their own. It's hard not to compare Kutless to a worshipful Creed—musically and vocally the two bands are very similar. But that doesn't mean Kutless isn't creative. *Strong Tower* contains several dynamic praiseworthy gems that are sure to please those who love to lift their hands and sing something to get excited about. Always ones to let you know where they stand on issues about faith, Kutless's *Strong Tower* might be one of the most spiritually *strong* titles of last year.

WHY IT ROCKS:

JESUS AND ROCK-N-ROLL FIND A NICE HOME TOGETHER.

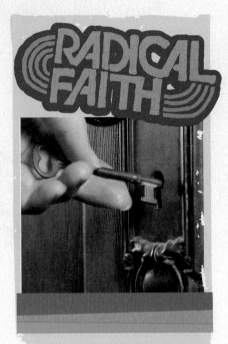

the evil things you did were against God. ²²But now God has made you his friends again. He did this through Christ's death in the body so that he might bring you into God's presence as people who are holy, with no wrong, and with nothing of which God can judge you guilty. ²³This will happen if you continue strong and sure in your faith. You must not be moved away from the hope brought to you by the Good News that you heard. That same Good News has been told to everyone in the world, and I, Paul, help in preaching that Good News.

PAUL'S WORK FOR THE CHURCH

²⁴I am happy in my sufferings for you. There are things that Christ must still suffer through his body, the church. I am accepting, in my body, my part of these things that must be suffered. ²⁵I became a servant of the church because God gave me a special work to do that helps you, and that work is to tell fully the message of God. ²⁶This message is the secret that was hidden from everyone since the beginning of time, but now it is made known to God's holy people. ²⁷God decided to let his people know this rich and glorious secret which he has for all people. This secret is Christ himself, who is in you. He is our only hope for glory. ²⁸So we continue to preach Christ to each person, using all wisdom to warn and to teach everyone, in order to bring each one into God's presence as a mature person in Christ. ²⁹To do this, I work and struggle, using Christ's great strength that works so powerfully in me.

2 I want you to know how hard I work for you, those in Laodicea, and others who have never seen me. ²I want them to be strengthened and joined together with love so that they may be rich in their understanding. This leads to their knowing fully God's secret, that is, Christ himself. ³In him all the treasures of wisdom and knowledge are safely kept.

⁴I say this so that no one can fool you by arguments that seem good, but are false. ⁵Though I am absent from you in my body, my heart is with you, and I am happy to see your good lives and your strong faith in Christ.

CONTINUE TO LIVE IN CHRIST

⁶As you received Christ Jesus the Lord, so continue to live in him. ⁷Keep your roots deep in him and have your lives built on him. Be strong in the faith, just as you were taught, and always be thankful.

⁸Be sure that no one leads you away with false and empty teaching that is only human,

COLOSSIANS 1:20

Sin opened a gaping hole in the friendship between human beings and God. Because of the blood Jesus shed when he died on the cross, you can come back home to God. Even if those facts are old news, you might wonder how Jesus' death can make you right with God. Making sense of that truth starts by grappling with the real size of sin. Your sin against a perfectly pure God is a vast offense, so bad it causes a mammoth separation between you and God. It's so awful that death is the just payment for the crime. But God loved you so much that he didn't want you to die and then be split from him forever in hell. So he sent his Son, Jesus, to pay the penalty you deserve. If you admit that it was your sin that sent Jesus to the cross, he tears up your death sentence and promises you eternal life. Romans 6:23 sums this up: "The payment for sin is death. But God gives us the free gift of life forever in Christ Jesus our Lord."

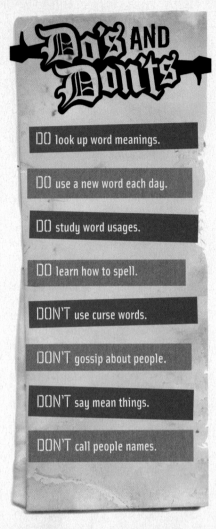

DO look up word meanings.

DO use a new word each day.

DO study word usages.

DO learn how to spell.

DON'T use curse words.

DON'T gossip about people.

DON'T say mean things.

DON'T call people names.

which comes from the ruling spirits of this world, and not from Christ. ⁹All of God lives fully in Christ (even when Christ was on earth), ¹⁰and you have a full and true life in Christ, who is ruler over all rulers and powers.

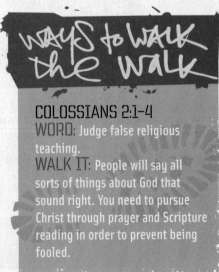

COLOSSIANS 2:1-4
WORD: Judge false religious teaching.
WALK IT: People will say all sorts of things about God that sound right. You need to pursue Christ through prayer and Scripture reading in order to prevent being fooled.

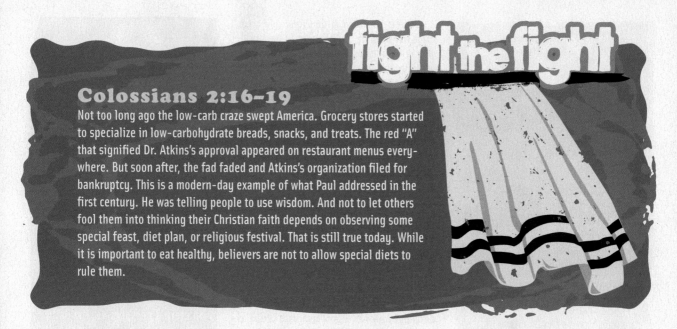

fight the fight

Colossians 2:16-19

Not too long ago the low-carb craze swept America. Grocery stores started to specialize in low-carbohydrate breads, snacks, and treats. The red "A" that signified Dr. Atkins's approval appeared on restaurant menus everywhere. But soon after, the fad faded and Atkins's organization filed for bankruptcy. This is a modern-day example of what Paul addressed in the first century. He was telling people to use wisdom. And not to let others fool them into thinking their Christian faith depends on observing some special feast, diet plan, or religious festival. That is still true today. While it is important to eat healthy, believers are not to allow special diets to rule them.

[11] Also in Christ you had a different kind of circumcision, a circumcision not done by hands. It was through Christ's circumcision, that is, his death, that you were made free from the power of your sinful self. [12] When you were baptized, you were buried with Christ, and you were raised up with him through your faith in God's power that was shown when he raised Christ from the dead. [13] When you were spiritually dead because of your sins and because you were not free from the power of your sinful self, God made you alive with Christ, and he forgave all our sins. [14] He canceled the debt, which listed all the rules we failed to follow. He took away that record with its rules and nailed it to the cross. [15] God stripped the spiritual rulers and powers of their authority. With the cross, he won the victory and showed the world that they were powerless.

DON'T FOLLOW PEOPLE'S RULES

[16] So do not let anyone make rules for you about eating and drinking or about a religious feast, a New Moon Festival, or a Sabbath day. [17] These things were like a shadow of what was to come. But what is true and real has come and is found in Christ. [18] Do not let anyone disqualify you by making you humiliate yourself and worship angels. Such people enter into visions, which fill them with foolish pride because of their human way of thinking. [19] They do not hold tightly to Christ, the head. It is from him that all the parts of the body are cared for and held together. So it grows in the way God wants it to grow.

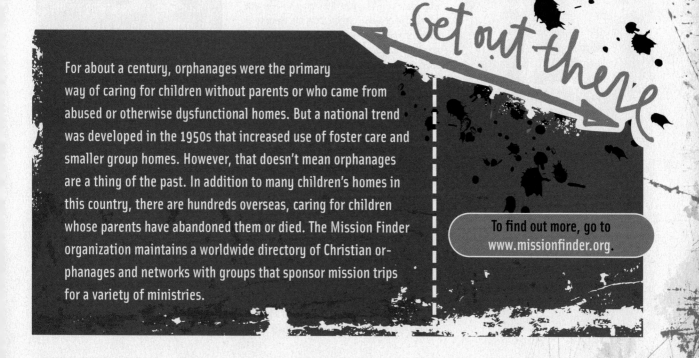

Get out there

For about a century, orphanages were the primary way of caring for children without parents or who came from abused or otherwise dysfunctional homes. But a national trend was developed in the 1950s that increased use of foster care and smaller group homes. However, that doesn't mean orphanages are a thing of the past. In addition to many children's homes in this country, there are hundreds overseas, caring for children whose parents have abandoned them or died. The Mission Finder organization maintains a worldwide directory of Christian orphanages and networks with groups that sponsor mission trips for a variety of ministries.

To find out more, go to www.missionfinder.org.

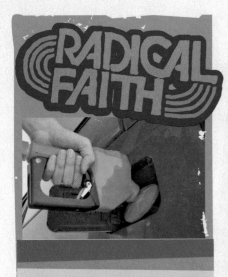

COLOSSIANS 3:12–17

Suppose your parents tell you to top off the gas tank and grab several things from the corner convenience store. Driving down the block, your thoughts drift to the mass of tasks on your own to-do list. Pumping gas, you try hard to remember exactly what mom and pop told you to buy. Standing between the milk and frozen pizzas at the store, you're stalled by indecision. You don't remember the list. And that might not be too far from how you feel when you try to recall everything God wants you to do. Page after page of the Bible is jammed with common commands and instructions, insights and banned behaviors. It's all great stuff, but your brain is already full. Honestly, that's why God put his message to you in written form. Give thanks that you can read, then dive into this Book that teaches you everything you need to know about him. And when you open to a passage like this one, start marking your Bible with notes to yourself. Write down what you want to remember so you won't forget.

²⁰Since you died with Christ and were made free from the ruling spirits of the world, why do you act as if you still belong to this world by following rules like these: ²¹"Don't handle this," "Don't taste that," "Don't even touch that thing"? ²²These rules refer to earthly things that are gone as soon as they are used. They are only human commands and teachings. ²³They seem to be wise, but they are only part of a human religion. They make people pretend not to be proud and make them punish their bodies, but they do not really control the evil desires of the sinful self.

YOUR NEW LIFE IN CHRIST

3 Since you were raised from the dead with Christ, aim at what is in heaven, where Christ is sitting at the right hand of God. ²Think only about the things in heaven, not the things on earth. ³Your old sinful self has died, and your new life is kept with Christ in God. ⁴Christ is your* life, and when he comes again, you will share in his glory.

⁵So put all evil things out of your life: sexual sinning, doing evil, letting evil thoughts control you, wanting things that are evil, and greed. This is really serving a false god. ⁶These things make God angry.* ⁷In your past, evil life you also did these things.

⁸But now also put these things out of your life: anger, bad temper, doing or saying things to hurt others, and using evil words when you talk. ⁹Do not lie to each other. You have left your old sinful life and the things you did before. ¹⁰You have begun to live the new life, in which you are being made new and are becoming like the One who made you. This new life brings you the true knowledge of God. ¹¹In the new life there is no difference between Greeks and Jews, those who are circumcised and those who are not circumcised, or people who are foreigners, or Scythians.* There is no difference between slaves and free people. But Christ is in all believers, and Christ is all that is important.

¹²God has chosen you and made you his holy people. He loves you. So you should always clothe yourselves with mercy, kindness, humility, gentleness, and patience. ¹³Bear with each other, and forgive each other. If someone does wrong to you, forgive that person because the Lord forgave you. ¹⁴Even more than all this, clothe yourself in love. Love is what holds you all together in perfect unity. ¹⁵Let the peace that Christ gives control your thinking, because you were all called together in one body* to have peace. Always be thankful. ¹⁶Let the teaching of Christ live in you richly. Use all wisdom to teach and instruct each other by singing psalms, hymns, and spiritual songs

with thankfulness in your hearts to God. ¹⁷Everything you do or say should be done to obey Jesus your Lord. And in all you do, give thanks to God the Father through Jesus.

YOUR NEW LIFE WITH OTHER PEOPLE

¹⁸Wives, yield to the authority of your husbands, because this is the right thing to do in the Lord.

¹⁹Husbands, love your wives and be gentle with them.

3:4 your Some Greek copies read "our." **3:6 These . . . angry** Some Greek copies continue, "against the people who do not obey God." **3:11 Scythians** The Scythians were known as very wild and cruel people. **3:15 body** The spiritual body of Christ, meaning the church or his people.

[20]Children, obey your parents in all things, because this pleases the Lord.

[21]Fathers, do not nag your children. If you are too hard to please, they may want to stop trying.

[22]Slaves, obey your masters in all things. Do not obey just when they are watching you, to gain their favor, but serve them honestly, because you respect the Lord. [23]In all the work you are doing, work the best you can. Work as if you were doing it for the Lord, not for people. [24]Remember that you will receive your reward from the Lord, which he promised to his people. You are serving the Lord Christ. [25]But remember that anyone who does wrong will be punished for that wrong, and the Lord treats everyone the same.

4 Masters, give what is good and fair to your slaves. Remember that you have a Master in heaven.

WHAT THE CHRISTIANS ARE TO DO

[2]Continue praying, keeping alert, and always thanking God. [3]Also pray for us that God will give us an opportunity to tell people his message. Pray that we can preach the secret that God has made known about Christ. This is why I am in prison. [4]Pray that I can speak in a way that will make it clear, as I should.

[5]Be wise in the way you act with people who are not believers, making the most of every opportunity. [6]When you talk, you should always be kind and pleasant so you will be able to answer everyone in the way you should.

NEWS ABOUT THE PEOPLE WITH PAUL

[7]Tychicus is my dear brother in Christ and a faithful minister and servant with me in the Lord. He will tell you all the things that are happening to me. [8]This is why I am sending him: so you may know how we are[n] and he may encourage you. [9]I send him with Onesimus, a faithful and dear brother in Christ, and one of your group. They will tell you all that has happened here.

[10]Aristarchus, a prisoner with me, and Mark, the cousin of Barnabas, greet you. (I have already told you what to do about Mark. If he comes, welcome him.) [11]Jesus, who is called Justus, also greets you. These are the only Jewish believers who work with me for the kingdom of God, and they have been a comfort to me.

[12]Epaphras, a servant of Jesus Christ, from your group, also greets you. He always prays for you that you will grow to be spiritually mature and have everything God wants for you. [13]I know he has worked hard for you and the people in Laodicea and in Hierapolis. [14]Demas and our dear friend Luke, the doctor, greet you.

[15]Greet the brothers and sisters in Laodicea. And greet Nympha and the church that meets in her house. [16]After this letter is read to you, be sure it is also read to the church in Laodicea. And you read the letter that I wrote to Laodicea. [17]Tell Archippus, "Be sure to finish the work the Lord gave you."

[18]I, Paul, greet you and write this with my own hand. Remember me in prison. Grace be with you.

ways to WALK the WALK

COLOSSIANS 4:5-6

WORD: Act wisely toward nonbelievers.

WALK IT: If you aren't looking for evangelism opportunities, you certainly won't find them. Keep your spiritual eyes open for chances to minister to others and to tell them about the Good News.

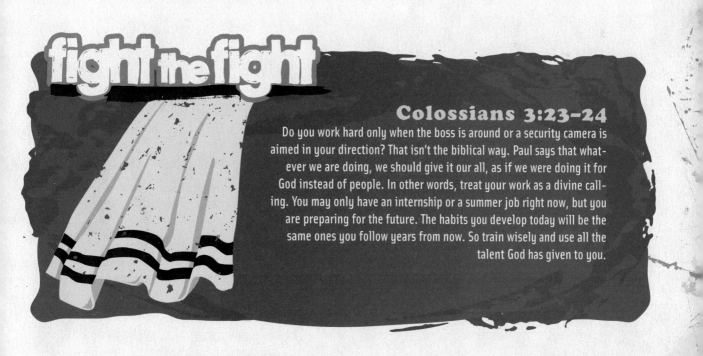

fight the fight

Colossians 3:23-24

Do you work hard only when the boss is around or a security camera is aimed in your direction? That isn't the biblical way. Paul says that whatever we are doing, we should give it our all, as if we were doing it for God instead of people. In other words, treat your work as a divine calling. You may only have an internship or a summer job right now, but you are preparing for the future. The habits you develop today will be the same ones you follow years from now. So train wisely and use all the talent God has given to you.

4:8 so . . . are Some Greek copies read "so he may know how you are."

1 THES SALO NIANS

A CALL FOR PATIENCE

Cardiovascular exercises. Weightlifting routines. People are infatuated with having the perfect physique. But strength isn't just found on the outside. Harassment and other opposition demand reserves of faith and emotional stability. Paul realizes this when he writes to the church at Thessalonica. Although he had visited it earlier, after hearing the members were being persecuted he is unable to return.

So he sends letters telling these believers not to lose hope. Writing on behalf of Silas and Timothy, Paul congratulates them for serving as examples to Christians across Greece and beyond. He tells them their reputation has spread to other places; everywhere he goes people are talking about the Thessalonians' faith.

Yet, this letter is more than a pep talk. It includes a reminder that believers are to live in holy ways. Not only by avoiding sexual immorality, but also by living peacefully, taking care of business, and working diligently to earn the respect of nonbelievers. Paul also touches on the imminence of Christ's return, which Christ guaranteed before going to heaven. Sometimes it takes patience to hold on to promises until we see them fulfilled. Paul reminds these believers that their patience will be rewarded. Likewise for you.

1 From Paul, Silas, and Timothy.

To the church in Thessalonica, the church in God the Father and the Lord Jesus Christ:

Grace and peace to you.

THE FAITH OF THE THESSALONIANS

[2]We always thank God for all of you and mention you when we pray. [3]We continually recall before God our Father the things you have done because of your faith and the work you have done because of your love. And we thank him that you continue to be strong because of your hope in our Lord Jesus Christ.

[4]Brothers and sisters, God loves you, and we know he has chosen you, [5]because the Good News we brought to you came not only with words, but with power, with the Holy Spirit, and with sure knowledge that it is true. Also you know how we lived when we were with you in order to help you. [6]And you became like us and like the Lord. You suffered much, but still you accepted the teaching with the joy that comes from the Holy Spirit. [7]So you became an example to all the believers in Macedonia and Southern Greece. [8]And the Lord's teaching spread from you not only into Macedonia and Southern Greece, but now your faith in God has become known everywhere. So we do not need to say anything about it. [9]People everywhere are telling about the way you accepted us when we were there with you. They tell how you stopped worshiping idols and began serving the living and true God. [10]And you wait for God's Son, whom God raised from the dead, to come from heaven. He is Jesus, who saves us from God's angry judgment that is sure to come.

PAUL'S WORK IN THESSALONICA

2 Brothers and sisters, you know our visit to you was not a failure. [2]Before we came to you, we suffered in Philippi. People there insulted us, as you know, and many people were against us. But our God helped us to be brave and to tell you his Good News. [3]Our appeal does not come from lies or wrong reasons, nor were we trying to trick you. [4]But we speak the Good News because God tested us and trusted us to do it. When we speak, we are not trying to please people, but God, who tests our hearts. [5]You know that we never tried to influence you by saying nice things about you. We were not trying to get your money; we had no selfishness to hide from you. God knows that this is true. [6]We were not looking for human praise, from you or anyone else, [7]even though as apostles of Christ we could have used our authority over you.

But we were very gentle with you,[n] like a mother caring for her little children. [8]Because we loved you, we were happy to share not only God's Good News with you, but even our own lives. You had become so dear to us! [9]Brothers and sisters, I know you remember our hard work and difficulties. We worked night and day so we would not burden any of you while we preached God's Good News to you.

[10]When we were with you, we lived in a holy and honest way, without fault. You know

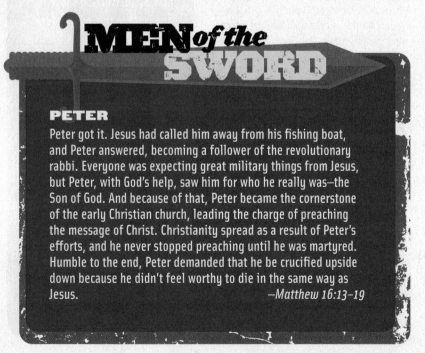

Relationships

"Husbands, love your wives as Christ loved the church and gave himself for it" (Ephesians 5:25). Sacrifice is what being married is all about. On the surface, it may not sound appealing, but looking deeper, you can see all kinds of gain. Christ's death on the cross temporarily looked like the end of the road, but the outcome was the best any of us could ever have hoped for. When you sacrifice yourself for those you love, you wind up coming out on the other side a better person, and you'll see that love returned to you in ways you've never dreamed.

MEN of the SWORD

PETER

Peter got it. Jesus had called him away from his fishing boat, and Peter answered, becoming a follower of the revolutionary rabbi. Everyone was expecting great military things from Jesus, but Peter, with God's help, saw him for who he really was—the Son of God. And because of that, Peter became the cornerstone of the early Christian church, leading the charge of preaching the message of Christ. Christianity spread as a result of Peter's efforts, and he never stopped preaching until he was martyred. Humble to the end, Peter demanded that he be crucified upside down because he didn't feel worthy to die in the same way as Jesus.

—Matthew 16:13-19

✳ 2:7 But . . . you Some Greek copies read "But we were like infants among you."

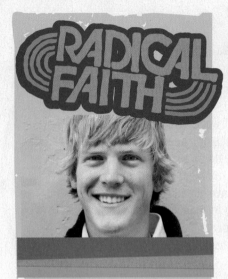

1 THESSALONIANS 4:3–5

There's not a guy alive who isn't interested in experiencing sexual closeness with someone he's attracted to. If that's, indeed, one of your life's greatest desires, you need to study your owner's manual, the instructions bequeathed to you by your Maker. The Bible spills startlingly specific details about how God aims for you to enjoy one of his greatest creations. You can spot his main thoughts in Proverbs 5:15–19: "Be faithful to your own wife. . . . Don't give your love to just any woman. These things are yours alone and shouldn't be shared with strangers. Be happy with the wife you married when you were young. . . . Let her love always make you happy." Hebrews 13:4 says sex between you and your wife-for-life is God's exclusive plan, and a load of passages point out sexual sins to avoid, like adultery (Exodus 20:14), homosexuality (1 Corinthians 6:9–10), incest (Leviticus 18:6), and lust (Matthew 5:28). When you control your body, you maintain the purity God wants you to give as a gift to your future wife. To settle for anything less cheats everyone.

this is true, and so does God. [11]You know that we treated each of you as a father treats his own children. [12]We encouraged you, we urged you, and we insisted that you live good lives for God, who calls you to his glorious kingdom.

[13]Also, we always thank God because when you heard his message from us, you accepted it as the word of God, not the words of humans. And it really is God's message which works in you who believe. [14]Brothers and sisters, your experiences have been like those of God's churches in Christ that are in Judea.[*] You suffered from the people of your own country, as they suffered from the Jews [15]who killed both the Lord Jesus and the prophets and forced us to leave that country. They do not please God and are against all people. [16]They try to stop us from teaching those who are not Jews so they may be saved. By doing this, they are increasing their sins to the limit. The anger of God has come to them at last.

PAUL WANTS TO VISIT THEM AGAIN

[17]Brothers and sisters, though we were separated from you for a short time, our thoughts were still with you. We wanted very much to see you and tried hard to do so. [18]We wanted to come to you. I, Paul, tried to come more than once, but Satan stopped us. [19]You are our hope, our joy, and the crown we will take pride in when our Lord Jesus Christ comes. [20]Truly you are our glory and our joy.

3 When we could not wait any longer, we decided it was best to stay in Athens alone [2]and send Timothy to you. Timothy, our brother, works with us for God and helps us tell people the Good News about Christ. We sent him to strengthen and encourage you in your faith [3]so none of you would be upset by these troubles. You yourselves know that we must face these troubles. [4]Even when we were with you, we told you we all would have to suffer, and you know it has happened. [5]Because of this, when I could wait no longer, I sent Timothy to you so I could learn about your faith. I was afraid the devil had tempted you, and perhaps our hard work would have been wasted.

[6]But Timothy now has come back to us from you and has brought us good news about your faith and love. He told us that you always remember us in a good way and that you want to see us just as much as we want to see you. [7]So, brothers and sisters, while we have much trouble and suffering, we are encouraged about you because of your faith. [8]Our life is really full if you stand strong in the Lord. [9]We

have so much joy before our God because of you. We cannot thank him enough for all the joy we feel. [10]Night and day we continue praying with all our heart that we can see you again and give you all the things you need to make your faith strong.

[11]Now may our God and Father himself and our Lord Jesus prepare the way for us to come to you. [12]May the Lord make your love grow more and multiply for each other and for

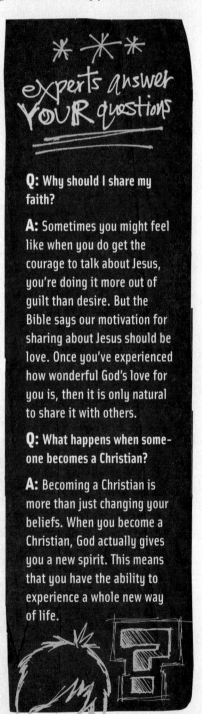

Q: Why should I share my faith?

A: Sometimes you might feel like when you do get the courage to talk about Jesus, you're doing it more out of guilt than desire. But the Bible says our motivation for sharing about Jesus should be love. Once you've experienced how wonderful God's love for you is, then it is only natural to share it with others.

Q: What happens when someone becomes a Christian?

A: Becoming a Christian is more than just changing your beliefs. When you become a Christian, God actually gives you a new spirit. This means that you have the ability to experience a whole new way of life.

2:14 Judea The Jewish land where Jesus lived and taught and where the church first began.

september

NATIONAL SCHOOL SUCCESS MONTH

"It's easy to make a buck. It's a lot tougher to make a difference."
-TOM BROKAW

1 Plan a Labor Day picnic.	**2**	**3** Pray for all of the college students at your church.	**4** Study not only for good grades, but also to learn.
5 Watch a home ball game with your dad.	**6**	**7** Ask your coach how you can pray for him.	**8**
9	**10**	**11** Remember those who lost their lives on this day in 2001.	**12** It's Video Game Day. Enter a local tournament.
13 It's Substitute Teacher Appreciation Week, so be nice to them!	**14**	**15**	**16** It's Alexis Bledel's birthday.
17 Rake some leaves for exercise.	**18**	**19**	**20**
21 Today is Faith Hill's big day.	**22** Clean out the attic for your parents.	**23** It's Bruce Springsteen's birthday.	**24**
25	**26** Today is Jim Caviezel's birthday.	**27** Pray for your church's missionaries.	**28**
29	**30** Read the Book of Romans today.		

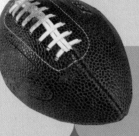

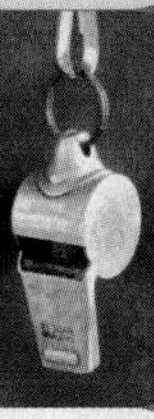

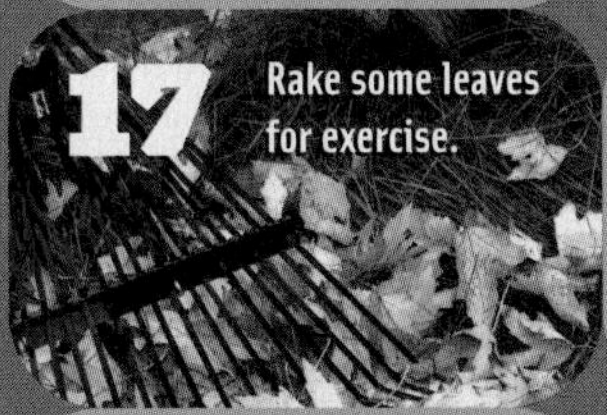

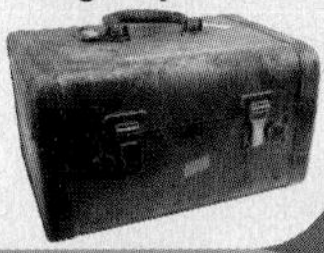

TOP TEN

random life changing inventions

1. Printing press.
2. Microwave oven.
3. Cellular telephone.
4. Cable television.
5. Gasoline automobile.
6. Jet airplane.
7. Lightbulb.
8. Laser technology.
9. Personal computer.
10. Broadband Internet.

all people so that you will love others as we love you. [13]May your hearts be made strong so that you will be holy and without fault before our God and Father when our Lord Jesus comes with all his holy ones.

A LIFE THAT PLEASES GOD

4 Brothers and sisters, we taught you how to live in a way that will please God, and you are living that way. Now we ask and encourage you in the Lord Jesus to live that way even more. [2]You know what we told you to do by the authority of the Lord Jesus. [3]God wants you to be holy and to stay away from sexual sins. [4]He wants each of you to learn to control your own body[n] in a way that is holy and honorable. [5]Don't use your body for sexual sin like the people who do not know God. [6]Also, do not wrong or cheat another Christian in this way. The Lord will punish people who do those things as we have already told you and warned you. [7]God called us to be holy and does not want us to live in sin. [8]So the person who refuses to obey this teaching is disobeying God, not simply a human teaching. And God is the One who gives us his Holy Spirit.

[9]We do not need to write you about having love for your Christian family, because God has already taught you to love each other. [10]And truly you do love the Christians in all of Macedonia. Brothers and sisters, now we encourage you to love them even more.

[11]Do all you can to live a peaceful life. Take care of your own business, and do your own work as we have already told you. [12]If you do, then people who are not believers will respect you, and you will not have to depend on others for what you need.

THE LORD'S COMING

[13]Brothers and sisters, we want you to know about those Christians who have died so you will not be sad, as others who have no hope. [14]We believe that Jesus died and that he rose again. So, because of him, God will raise with Jesus those who have died. [15]What we tell you now is the Lord's own message. We who are living when the Lord comes again will not go before those who have already died. [16]The Lord himself will come down from heaven with a loud command, with the voice of the archangel,[n] and with the trumpet call of God. And those who have died believing in Christ will rise first. [17]After that, we who are still alive will be gathered up with them in the clouds to meet the Lord in the air. And we will be with the Lord forever. [18]So encourage each other with these words.

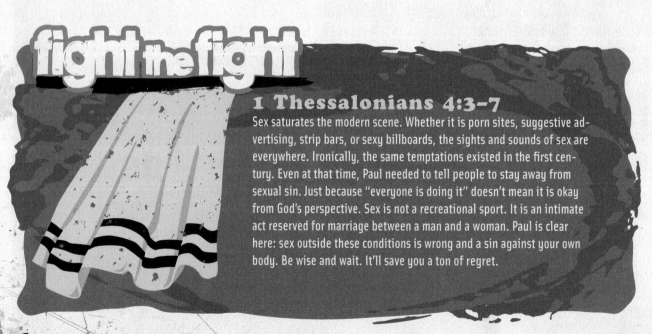

fight the fight

1 Thessalonians 4:3–7

Sex saturates the modern scene. Whether it is porn sites, suggestive advertising, strip bars, or sexy billboards, the sights and sounds of sex are everywhere. Ironically, the same temptations existed in the first century. Even at that time, Paul needed to tell people to stay away from sexual sin. Just because "everyone is doing it" doesn't mean it is okay from God's perspective. Sex is not a recreational sport. It is an intimate act reserved for marriage between a man and a woman. Paul is clear here: sex outside these conditions is wrong and a sin against your own body. Be wise and wait. It'll save you a ton of regret.

4:4 learn . . . body This might also mean "learn to live with your own wife." 4:16 archangel The leader among God's angels or messengers.

ISSUES

FOOD

FAD DIETS COME AND GO LIKE DESIGNER FASHIONS. Even with tons of infomercials, fat camps, and other dietary deterrents, too many teenagers continue to feed their faces like there's no tomorrow, and they have the bulging waistlines to prove it. If you are one who's prone to pack on the pounds, allow God to help you discipline your flesh for your own good. The Bible calls gluttony, which is stuffing your gut, a sinful act. You may be a growing boy, but you can still learn to eat healthy vittles. The habits you form now are the ones you're likely to carry the rest of your life, so travel lightly.

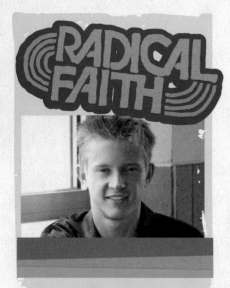

Whether you're watching girls on the beach, at the mall, or even in church, it doesn't take long to realize that baring skin is in. While a part of you may think it's okay, it's important to remember that no matter what, it's not cool to look at women as objects.

1 THESSALONIANS 5:17

Maybe you struggle to put together more than a few prayerful words, flinging thoughts skyward in an attempt to connect with God. Or maybe you often pray on your own, or even regularly get together with Christian friends to talk with God. Whether you pray a little or a lot, this verse might sound way-out. How could anyone ever "pray continually"? Well, you can't talk nonstop at God. That would be like heading through your days with your mouth full. You couldn't do all the other things the Lord commands, and you would never manage more than a mumble at anyone else. You can, however, do life with a prayerful attitude, communing with God during your day. You can make your prayers short and simple, informing God of your needs, your dreams, and your concerns for the world around you. You can say frequent thanks for his gifts and tell him often that he's great. If prayer is about being longwinded, you might never feel up to the task. If prayer is something you only do at a special time and place, you'll miss out on moment-by-moment visits with God.

BE READY FOR THE LORD'S COMING

5 Now, brothers and sisters, we do not need to write you about times and dates. ²You know very well that the day the Lord comes again will be a surprise, like a thief that comes in the night. ³While people are saying, "We have peace and we are safe," they will be destroyed quickly. It is like pains that come quickly to a woman having a baby. Those people will not escape. ⁴But you, brothers and sisters, are not living in darkness, and so that day will not surprise you like a thief. ⁵You are all people who belong to the light and to the day. We do not belong to the night or to darkness. ⁶So we should not be like other people who are sleeping, but we should be alert and have self-control. ⁷Those who sleep, sleep at night. Those who get drunk, get drunk at night. ⁸But we belong to the day, so we should control ourselves. We should wear faith and love to protect us, and the hope of salvation should be our helmet. ⁹God did not choose us to suffer his anger but to have salvation through our Lord Jesus Christ. ¹⁰Jesus died for us so that we can live together with him, whether we are alive or dead when he comes. ¹¹So encourage each other and give each other strength, just as you are doing now.

FINAL INSTRUCTIONS AND GREETINGS

¹²Now, brothers and sisters, we ask you to appreciate those who work hard among you, who lead you in the Lord and teach you. ¹³Respect them with a very special love because of the work they do.

Live in peace with each other. ¹⁴We ask you, brothers and sisters, to warn those who do not work. Encourage the people who are afraid. Help those who are weak. Be patient with everyone. ¹⁵Be sure that no one pays back wrong for wrong, but always try to do what is good for each other and for all people.

¹⁶Always be joyful. ¹⁷Pray continually, ¹⁸and give thanks whatever happens. That is what God wants for you in Christ Jesus.

¹⁹Do not hold back the work of the Holy Spirit. ²⁰Do not treat prophecy as if it were unimportant. ²¹But test everything. Keep what is good, ²²and stay away from everything that is evil.

²³Now may God himself, the God of peace, make you pure, belonging only to him. May your whole self—spirit, soul, and body—be kept safe and without fault when our Lord Jesus Christ comes. ²⁴You can trust the One who calls you to do that for you.

²⁵Brothers and sisters, pray for us.

²⁶Give each other a holy kiss when you meet. ²⁷I tell you by the authority of the Lord to read this letter to all the believers.

²⁸The grace of our Lord Jesus Christ be with you.

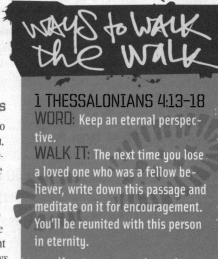

WAYS TO WALK THE WALK

1 THESSALONIANS 4:13–18
WORD: Keep an eternal perspective.
WALK IT: The next time you lose a loved one who was a fellow believer, write down this passage and meditate on it for encouragement. You'll be reunited with this person in eternity.

*** notes

2 THESSALONIANS

TAKING CARE OF BUSINESS

There is nothing wrong with looking forward to the return of Jesus. He promised that one day he would come back to earth. However, it becomes a problem when people want to sit and do nothing while waiting for him to bail them out of their troubles. Paul addresses this exact situation in his second letter to the Thessalonians. Written about six months after the first, in this second letter he feels it necessary to clarify speculation that has cropped up since his original letter to them.

Paul clearly states Christ won't return before a massive turning away from God and the revealing of the Antichrist. Although he reviews some of the terrible things this evil man will do, Paul advises the Thessalonians not to get upset or be afraid when they hear rumors about this event. Then he goes further, commanding them to avoid believers who refuse to work or listen to sound teaching.

Paul isn't saying believers should avoid helping people with legitimate problems. But he is urging them to be quiet and dependable and to continue to do good works. In a world shaking with fear over terrorism and political instability, that is still a good guideline for living a godly life today.

LOVE YOUR FAMILY

One trait that makes a guy stand out from the crowd is a reasonably good relationship with his own family. While there may be extenuating circumstances, the fact remains that a girl usually can tell a lot about a guy from how he interacts with members of his own household. If you are always bothering your brother or mouthing off to your mother, then any thinking girl is bound to have second thoughts about you. On the other hand, if a girl can come to your home for a special meal with the family and feel the genuine love of a welcoming atmosphere, it bodes well for you.

1 From Paul, Silas, and Timothy.

To the church in Thessalonica in God our Father and the Lord Jesus Christ:

²Grace and peace to you from God the Father and the Lord Jesus Christ.

PAUL TALKS ABOUT GOD'S JUDGMENT

³We must always thank God for you, brothers and sisters. This is only right, because your faith is growing more and more, and the love that every one of you has for each other is increasing. ⁴So we brag about you to the other churches of God. We tell them about the way you continue to be strong and have faith even though you are being treated badly and are suffering many troubles.

⁵This is proof that God is right in his judgment. He wants you to be counted worthy of his kingdom for which you are suffering. ⁶God will do what is right. He will give trouble to those who trouble you. ⁷And he will give rest to you who are troubled and to us also when the Lord Jesus appears with burning fire from heaven with his powerful angels. ⁸Then he will punish those who do not know God and who do not obey the Good News about our Lord Jesus Christ. ⁹Those people will be punished

*REVIEWS BOOKS

DAVID CROWDER:
PRAISE HABIT

The David Crowder Band has been rocking houses of worship with its infectious Christ-centered grooves for several years now. And from his musical proclamations, you knew Crowder was capable of greater spiritual depth than the average church-going individual. And he gives it to you here. *Praise Habit* is a funny, honest book that gets down to the nitty-gritty of what it means to worship God in the 21st century. Crowder uses stories and experiences to expound on what he believes to be the most important aspects of praising Jesus. His quirky and humorous nature shines through his writing without overdoing it.

WHY IT ROCKS:

THE AUTHOR IS AS GOOD WITH A PEN AS WITH A GUITAR.

COUNT ON IT

2 THESSALONIANS 2:16-17

You will never find a parent, teacher, coach, or boss who will treat you with the flawless perfection of Christ. While some might picture God as their worst nightmare of a drill sergeant aiming to whip them into shape, he actually takes a totally different approach. He is all about giving you encouragement and strength, from start to finish. He doesn't use words to shred you but to make you whole. He doesn't tell you to dig deep inside to find your own power to win. Instead, he promises you strength as you depend on him. God's love means he will never deviate from that plan. You will never wake up to find out that God is having a bad day—and taking it out on you. He will never change tactics or fall short of this full-of-grace approach to training you.

with a destruction that continues forever. They will be kept away from the Lord and from his great power. [10]This will happen on the day when the Lord Jesus comes to receive glory because of his holy people. And all the people who have believed will be amazed at Jesus.

You will be in that group, because you believed what we told you. [11]That is why we always pray for you, asking our God to help you live the kind of life he called you to live. We pray that with his power God will help you do the good things you want and perform the works that come from your faith. [12]We pray all this so that the name of our Lord Jesus Christ will have glory in you, and you will have glory in him. That glory comes from the grace of our God and the Lord Jesus Christ.

EVIL THINGS WILL HAPPEN

2 Brothers and sisters, we have something to say about the coming of our Lord Jesus Christ and the time when we will meet together with him. [2]Do not become easily upset in your thinking or afraid if you hear that the day of the Lord has already come. Someone may have said this in a prophecy or in a message or in a letter as if it came from us. [3]Do not let anyone fool you in any way. That day of the Lord will not come until the turning away[n] from God happens and the Man of Evil,[n] who is on his way to hell, appears. [4]He will be against and put himself above any so-called god or anything that people worship. And that Man of Evil will even go into God's Temple and sit there and say that he is God.

[5]I told you when I was with you that all this would happen. Do you not remember? [6]And now you know what is stopping that Man of Evil so he will appear at the right time. [7]The secret power of evil is already working in the world, but there is one who is stopping that power. And he will continue to stop it until he is taken out of the way. [8]Then that Man of Evil will appear, and the Lord Jesus will kill him

with the breath that comes from his mouth and will destroy him with the glory of his coming. [9]The Man of Evil will come by the power of Satan. He will have great power, and he will do many different false miracles, signs, and wonders. [10]He will use every kind of evil to trick those who are lost. They will die, because they refused to love the truth. (If they loved the truth, they would be saved.) [11]For this reason God sends them something powerful that

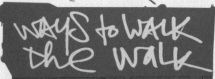

WAYS TO WALK THE WALK

2 THESSALONIANS 1:6
WORD Let God take care of your enemies.
WALK IT It's very tempting to want to get even with people when they wrong you. The next time it happens, just let the incident go, and let God take care of them for you.

leads them away from the truth so they will believe a lie. [12]So all those will be judged guilty who did not believe the truth, but enjoyed doing evil.

YOU ARE CHOSEN FOR SALVATION

[13]Brothers and sisters, whom the Lord loves, God chose you from the beginning[n] to be saved. So we must always thank God for you. You are saved by the Spirit that makes you holy and by your faith in the truth. [14]God used the Good News that we preached to call you to be saved so you can share in the glory of our Lord Jesus Christ. [15]So, brothers and sisters, stand strong and continue to believe the teachings we gave you in our speaking and in our letter.

[16-17]May our Lord Jesus Christ himself and God our Father encourage you and strengthen you in every good thing you do and say. God loved us, and through his grace he gave us a good hope and encouragement that continues forever.

PRAY FOR US

3 And now, brothers and sisters, pray for us that the Lord's teaching will continue to spread quickly and that people will give honor to that teaching, just as happened with you. [2]And pray that we will be protected from stubborn and evil people, because not all people believe.

Fifty-nine percent of teenagers volunteer, as compared to 49 percent of adults.
—Boys & Girls Club of America

stats

 2:3 turning away Or "the rebellion." **2:3 Man of Evil** Some Greek copies read "Man of Sin." **2:13 God . . . beginning** Some Greek copies read "God chose you as the firstfruits of the harvest."

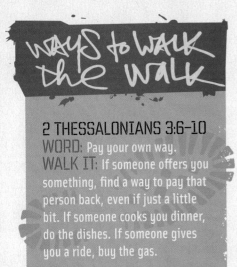

WAYS TO WALK THE WALK

2 THESSALONIANS 3:6–10
WORD: Pay your own way.
WALK IT: If someone offers you something, find a way to pay that person back, even if just a little bit. If someone cooks you dinner, do the dishes. If someone gives you a ride, buy the gas.

3But the Lord is faithful and will give you strength and will protect you from the Evil One. 4The Lord makes us feel sure that you are doing and will continue to do the things we told you. 5May the Lord lead your hearts into God's love and Christ's patience.

THE DUTY TO WORK

6Brothers and sisters, by the authority of our Lord Jesus Christ we command you to stay away from any believer who refuses to work and does not follow the teaching we gave you. 7You yourselves know that you should live as we live. We were not lazy when we were with you. 8And when we ate another person's food, we always paid for it. We worked very hard night and day so we would not be an expense to any of you. 9We had the right to ask you to help us, but we worked to take care of ourselves so we would be an example for you to follow. 10When we were with you, we gave you this rule: "Anyone who refuses to work should not eat."

11We hear that some people in your group refuse to work. They do nothing but busy themselves in other people's lives. 12We command those people and beg them in the Lord Jesus Christ to work quietly and earn their own food. 13But you, brothers and sisters, never become tired of doing good.

14If some people do not obey what we tell you in this letter, then take note of them. Have nothing to do with them so they will feel ashamed. 15But do not treat them as enemies. Warn them as fellow believers.

FINAL WORDS

16Now may the Lord of peace give you peace at all times and in every way. The Lord be with all of you.

17I, Paul, end this letter now in my own handwriting. All my letters have this to show they are from me. This is the way I write.

18The grace of our Lord Jesus Christ be with you all.

How to Be Funny

It's a known fact: girls like guys who can make them laugh. So what do you do if you're humor-impaired? For starters, don't take yourself too seriously; be ready to poke fun at certain traits about yourself that you don't like. Keep your wits about you, and understand that there's a peculiar phoniness to life. See things for what they are, but exaggerate them in a bizarre or random way. Play games to keep your mind occupied; invent back-stories for sales clerks or people in the opposing lanes of traffic. Find the stories in your own life that people can relate to or recognize in themselves. Have confidence in yourself, and remember—timing is everything. Don't rush a joke or you'll ruin the humor. Most of all, just relax and enjoy life. You have a Father who loves you and a future in heaven. You have every reason to enjoy the life you've so graciously been given.

RADICAL FAITH

2 THESSALONIANS 3:7

Some of the Christians in Thessalonica were so convinced that Jesus was coming back to earth at any moment, they quit their jobs to await his return. They quickly ran low on cash, then started mooching off others in the church. When the apostle Paul heard about these lazybones, he pointed to himself as an example of a guy who worked hard to provide for himself, refusing to slyly steal from others. He fired off words that still startle us: "Anyone who refuses to work should not eat" (2 Thessalonians 3:10). His command was short and unsympathetic: Get a job (2 Thessalonians 3:12). While it's not likely that you have quit your job assembling tacos to wait for Jesus to show up, you might still concoct all kinds of reasons not to give it your all at home, school, or work. But hard work is a major sign that you have real faith. Applying yourself builds healthy independence and earns the respect of non-Christians. The Bible sums up your job like this: "In all the work you are doing, work the best you can" (Colossians 3:23).

¹TIMOTHY

GUIDANCE FROM A SPIRITUAL FATHER

Do you have a father at home? If so, you're fortunate. Millions grow up without the influential presence of a man in the house. But even if he's there, that is no guarantee he will provide spiritual guidance. This is the story of Timothy, son of a Jewish mother and a Greek father. His dad gave him little guidance about God, which is why Paul was such a valuable influence on his spiritual protégé.

The relationship of these two men serves as an illustration of the need to seek an older, wiser man who can help you navigate the bewildering puzzle called life. In this first letter to Timothy, Paul ful-

fills the role of wise elder. He encourages Timothy in his role as a pastor, instructs him in the ways of church leadership, and warns him about allowing false doctrine to invade his congregation.

Paul also reminds church members to treat each other with the respect, honor, and care they deserve. And he offers several guidelines for appointing leaders to positions of authority in the church. Thanks to Paul's guidance, Timothy flourished as a leader and lives on as an example of faithfulness, despite his relative youth and inexperience.

From Paul, an apostle of Christ Jesus, by the command of God our Savior and Christ Jesus our hope.

[2]To Timothy, a true child to me because you believe:

Grace, mercy, and peace from God the Father and Christ Jesus our Lord.

WARNING AGAINST FALSE TEACHING

[3]I asked you to stay longer in Ephesus when I went into Macedonia so you could command some people there to stop teaching false things. [4]Tell them not to spend their time on stories that are not true and on long lists of names in family histories. These things only bring arguments; they do not help God's work, which is done in faith. [5]The purpose of this command is for people to have love, a love that comes from a pure heart and a good conscience and a true faith. [6]Some people have missed these things and turned to useless talk. [7]They want to be teachers of the law, but they do not understand either what they are talking about or what they are sure about.

[8]But we know that the law is good if someone uses it lawfully. [9]We also know that the law is not made for good people but for those who are against the law and for those who refuse to follow it. It is for people who are against God and are sinful, who are unholy and ungodly, who kill their fathers and mothers, who murder, [10]who take part in sexual sins, who have sexual relations with people of the same sex, who sell slaves, who tell lies, who speak falsely, and who do anything against the true teaching of God. [11]That teaching is part of the Good News of the blessed God that he gave me to tell.

THANKS FOR GOD'S MERCY

[12]I thank Christ Jesus our Lord, who gave me strength, because he trusted me and gave me this work of serving him. [13]In the past I spoke against Christ and persecuted him and did all kinds of things to hurt him. But God showed me mercy, because I did not know what I was doing. I did not believe. [14]But the grace of our Lord was fully given to me, and with that grace came the faith and love that are in Christ Jesus.

[15]What I say is true, and you should fully accept it: Christ Jesus came into the world to save sinners, of whom I am the worst. [16]But I was given mercy so that in me, the worst of all sinners, Christ Jesus could show that he has patience without limit. His patience with me

MEN of the SWORD

PHILEMON

Not much is known of Philemon, except that he was probably wealthy and that a church group met in his home. From Paul's letter, we find that Philemon was a slave owner who'd had a slave named Onesimus run away from him. Onesimus then somehow met up with Paul in prison, became a Christian, and wanted to return home. Apparently, Onesimus worried that Philemon would punish him for running away, but Paul expressed confidence in Philemon. He encouraged him to welcome Onesimus openly as a fellow believer and to offer him the type of unmerited grace that Christ had offered Philemon.

—Philemon 1

Get out there

Although worldwide hunger is a staggering problem, the situation is improving. About 20 years ago, some 41,000 people died of hunger or related causes daily. That has decreased to 24,000, but it's still a crisis. You may ask, "So what can I do about it?" Well, all it takes is the click of a computer mouse to donate at The Hunger Site, created in 1999 to work on eliminating world hunger. About 220,000 people visit each day to click the "give free food" button, which is paid for by site sponsors and distributed by Mercy Corps and America's Second Harvest.

Check it out at
www.thehungersite.com.

COUNT ON IT

1 TIMOTHY 2:3-6

Jesus gave his followers the job of traveling the whole planet in order to "go and make followers of all people" (Matthew 28:19). So, if you believe in Jesus, you can't shirk the task of telling others about him. But sometimes you might feel jittery in your gut, wondering if speaking up about Jesus is the right thing to do. God wants you to go for it. He wants every human being to grasp this unbending fact: There is only one path for people to get right with him, and that's through the death of Jesus on the cross. God wants everyone to be persuaded to believe that truth so they can spend eternity with him in heaven. So when you tell others about Jesus, you can be sure you're doing what he wants, and he'll even give you the words to share with them.

made me an example for those who would believe in him and have life forever. [17]To the King that rules forever, who will never die, who cannot be seen, the only God, be honor and glory forever and ever. Amen.

[18]Timothy, my child, I am giving you a command that agrees with the prophecies that were given about you in the past. I tell you this so you can follow them and fight the good fight. [19]Continue to have faith and do what you know is right. Some people have rejected this, and their faith has been shipwrecked. [20]Hymenaeus and Alexander have done that, and I have given them to Satan so they will learn not to speak against God.

SOME RULES FOR MEN AND WOMEN

2 First, I tell you to pray for all people, asking God for what they need and being thankful to him. [2]Pray for rulers and for all who have authority so that we can have quiet and peaceful lives full of worship and respect for God. [3]This is good, and it pleases God our Savior, [4]who wants all people to be saved and to know the truth. [5]There is one God and one mediator so that human beings can reach God. That way is through Christ Jesus, who is himself human. [6]He gave himself as a payment to free all people. He is proof that came at the right time. [7]That is why I was chosen to tell the Good News and to be an apostle. (I am telling the truth; I am not lying.) I was chosen to teach those who are not Jews to believe and to know the truth.

[8]So, I want the men everywhere to pray, lifting up their hands in a holy manner, without anger and arguments.

[9]Also, women should wear proper clothes that show respect and self-control, not using braided hair or gold or pearls or expensive clothes. [10]Instead, they should do good deeds, which is right for women who say they worship God.

[11]Let a woman learn by listening quietly and being ready to cooperate in everything. [12]But I do not allow a woman to teach or to have authority over a man, but to listen quietly, [13]because Adam was formed first and then Eve. [14]And Adam was not tricked, but the woman was tricked and became a sinner. [15]But she will be saved through having children if she continues in faith, love, and holiness, with self-control.

ELDERS IN THE CHURCH

3 What I say is true: Anyone wanting to become an overseer desires a good work. [2]An overseer must not give people a reason to criticize him, and he must have only one wife. He must be self-controlled, wise, respected by others, ready to welcome guests, and able to teach. [3]He must not drink too much wine or like to fight, but rather be gentle and peaceable, not loving money. [4]He must be a good family leader, having children who co-operate with full respect. [5](If someone does not know how to lead the family, how can that person take care of God's church?) [6]But an elder must not be a new believer, or he might be too proud of himself and be judged guilty just as the devil was. [7]An elder must also have the respect of people who are not in the church so he will not be criticized by others and caught in the devil's trap.

experts answer YOUR questions

Q: Is it okay for me to date or marry someone who's not a Christian?

A: Paul warns us in 2 Corinthians 6:14 not to be joined together with unbelievers. We are warned against entering any type of relationship where we'd become close with someone who's not a Christian, for our own good.

Q: Should I give money to the church?

A: There's no law that says you have to give money to the church, but there are plenty of good reasons to give. God calls us to share our material goods, including our money, with those who need it, inside and outside of the church.

DEACONS IN THE CHURCH

[8] In the same way, deacons must be respected by others, not saying things they do not mean. They must not drink too much wine or try to get rich by cheating others. [9] With a clear conscience they must follow the secret of the faith that God made known to us. [10] Test them first. Then let them serve as deacons if you find nothing wrong in them. [11] In the same way, women[n] must be respected by others. They must not speak evil of others. They must be self-controlled and trustworthy in everything. [12] Deacons must have only one wife and be good leaders of their children and their own families. [13] Those who serve well as deacons are making an honorable place for themselves, and they will be very bold in their faith in Christ Jesus.

THE SECRET OF OUR LIFE

[14] Although I hope I can come to you soon, I am writing these things to you now. [15] Then, even if I am delayed, you will know how to live in the family of God. That family is the church

Do's and Don'ts

DO go on a mission trip.

DO support mission work.

DO pray for missionaries.

DO send gifts to missionaries.

DON'T ignore home mission fields.

DON'T neglect mission programs.

DON'T forget about missionaries.

DON'T fail to pray for missionaries.

Relationships

"The Scripture says, 'So a man will leave his father and mother and be united with his wife, and the two will become one body'" (Ephesians 5:31). This scripture is a very roundabout way of telling you that when you have sex, you become one with the other person. Sex is a bonding tool, created by God to forge a special relationship between a husband and a wife. It is meant for two people who've committed themselves to each other publicly—that's the "leave your parents" part. Sex is fun, but God means for you to save it for marriage.

of the living God, the support and foundation of the truth. [16] Without doubt, the secret of our life of worship is great:

He[n] was shown to us in a human body,
proved right in spirit,
and seen by angels.
He was proclaimed to the nations,
believed in by the world,
and taken up in glory.

A WARNING ABOUT FALSE TEACHERS

4 Now the Holy Spirit clearly says that in the later times some people will stop believing the faith. They will follow spirits that lie and teachings of demons. [2] Such teachings come from the false words of liars whose consciences are destroyed as if by a hot iron. [3] They forbid people to marry and tell them not to eat certain foods which God created to be eaten with thanks by people who believe and know the truth. [4] Everything God made is good, and nothing should be refused if it is accepted with thanks, [5] because it is made holy by what God has said and by prayer.

BE A GOOD SERVANT OF CHRIST

[6] By telling these things to the brothers and sisters, you will be a good servant of Christ Jesus. You will be made strong by the words of the faith and the good teaching which you have been following. [7] But do not follow foolish stories that disagree with God's truth, but train yourself to serve God. [8] Training your body helps you in some ways, but serving God helps you in every way by bringing you blessings in this life and in the future life, too. [9] What I say is true, and you should fully accept it. [10] This is why we work and struggle:[n] We hope in the living God who is the Savior of all people, especially of those who believe.

[11] Command and teach these things. [12] Do not let anyone treat you as if you are unimportant because you are young. Instead, be an example to the believers with your words, your actions, your love, your faith, and your pure life. [13] Until I come, continue to read the Scriptures to the people, strengthen them, and teach them. [14] Use the gift you have, which was given to you through prophecy when the group of elders laid their hands on[n] you. [15] Continue to do those things; give your life to doing them so your progress may be seen by everyone. [16] Be careful in your life and in your teaching. If you continue to live and teach rightly, you will save both yourself and those who listen to you.

RULES FOR LIVING WITH OTHERS

5 Do not speak angrily to an older man, but plead with him as if he were your father. Treat younger men like brothers, [2] older women like mothers, and younger women like sisters. Always treat them in a pure way.

3:11 women This might mean the wives of the deacons, or it might mean women who serve in the same way as deacons. **3:16 He** Some Greek copies read "God." **4:10 struggle** Some Greek copies read "suffer." **4:14 laid their hands on** The laying on of hands had many purposes, including the giving of a blessing, power, or authority.

How to Build a Wardrobe

You don't have to spend a zillion dollars on clothes to look good—you just have to know where to look. And that would be at the back of the store, on the clearance rack. Most nationwide retailers frequently put their clothes on clearance in order to make room for new stock, so you can often find stylish deals at a fraction of the regular price. And since some basics never go out of style, thrift shops are a good place to find some deals. Also, don't forget about discount and outlet stores that offer factory seconds and last year's apparel (which often resembles the current year's) at sizeable discounts. Shopping all comes down to patience. Waiting to find the best deal more than pays off in the long term. Patience is a trait that works with God, too. Wait on him, trust his timing, and you'll find yourself dressed for success.

³Take care of widows who are truly widows. ⁴But if a widow has children or grandchildren, let them first learn to do their duty to their own family and to repay their parents or grandparents. That pleases God. ⁵The true widow, who is all alone, puts her hope in God and continues to pray night and day for God's help. ⁶But the widow who uses her life to please herself is really dead while she is alive. ⁷Tell the believers to do these things so that no one can criticize them. ⁸Whoever does not care for his own relatives, especially his own family members, has turned against the faith and is worse than someone who does not believe in God.

⁹To be on the list of widows, a woman must be at least sixty years old. She must have been faithful to her husband. ¹⁰She must be known for her good works—works such as raising her children, welcoming strangers, washing the feet of God's people, helping those in trouble, and giving her life to do all kinds of good deeds.

¹¹But do not put younger widows on that list. After they give themselves to Christ, they are pulled away from him by their physical desires, and then they want to marry again. ¹²They will be judged for not doing what they first promised to do. ¹³Besides that, they learn to waste their time, going from house to house. And they not only waste their time but also begin to gossip and busy themselves with other people's lives, saying things they should not say. ¹⁴So I want the younger widows to marry, have children, and manage their homes. Then no enemy will have any reason to criticize them. ¹⁵But some have already turned away to follow Satan.

¹⁶If any woman who is a believer has widows in her family, she should care for them herself. The church should not have to care for them. Then it will be able to take care of those who are truly widows.

¹⁷The elders who lead the church well should receive double honor, especially those who work hard by speaking and teaching, ¹⁸because the Scripture says: "When an ox is working in the grain, do not cover its mouth to keep it from eating,"ⁿ and "A worker should be given his pay."ⁿ

¹⁹Do not listen to someone who accuses an elder, without two or three witnesses. ²⁰Tell those who continue sinning that they are wrong. Do this in front of the whole church so that the others will have a warning.

²¹Before God and Christ Jesus and the chosen angels, I command you to do these things without showing favor of any kind to anyone. ²²Think carefully before you lay your hands onⁿ anyone, and don't share in the sins of others. Keep yourself pure.

fight the fight

1 Timothy 5:1-2

When it comes to how to treat other people, many guys use a pecking order. They will be friendly and outgoing with good-looking girls or popular athletes, but barely bother to speak to shy students or senior citizens. Instead of that approach, take these words from Paul to heart. The apostle mentored the young pastor, Timothy, and advised him to talk with older men as if they were fathers, older women like mothers, and younger men and women like brothers and sisters. In other words, to be gracious and polite with everyone. Seeing each person as God's creation will help you appreciate the value they add to life.

 5:18 "When . . . eating." Quotation from Deuteronomy 25:4.   5:18 "A worker . . . pay." Quotation from Luke 10:7.   5:22 lay your hands on The laying on of hands had many purposes, including the giving of a blessing, power, or authority.

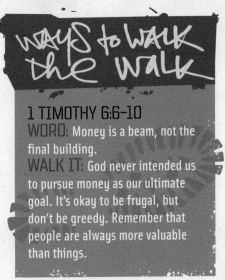

WAYS to WALK the WALK

1 TIMOTHY 6:6-10

WORD: Money is a beam, not the final building.

WALK IT: God never intended us to pursue money as our ultimate goal. It's okay to be frugal, but don't be greedy. Remember that people are always more valuable than things.

23Stop drinking only water, but drink a little wine to help your stomach and your frequent sicknesses.

24The sins of some people are easy to see even before they are judged, but the sins of others are seen only later. 25So also good deeds are easy to see, but even those that are not easily seen cannot stay hidden.

6 All who are slaves under a yoke should show full respect to their masters so no one will speak against God's name and our teaching. 2The slaves whose masters are believers should not show their masters any less respect because they are believers. They should serve their masters even better, because they are helping believers they love. You must teach and preach these things.

FALSE TEACHING AND TRUE RICHES

3Anyone who has a different teaching does not agree with the true teaching of our Lord Jesus Christ and the teaching that shows the true way to serve God. 4This person is full of pride and understands nothing, but is sick with a love for arguing and fighting about words. This brings jealousy, fighting, speaking against others, evil mistrust, 5and constant quarrels from those who have evil minds and have lost the truth. They think that serving God is a way to get rich.

6Serving God does make us very rich, if we are satisfied with what we have. 7We brought nothing into the world, so we can take nothing out. 8But, if we have food and clothes, we will be satisfied with that. 9Those who want to become rich bring temptation to themselves and are caught in a trap. They want many foolish and harmful things that ruin and destroy people. 10The love of money causes all kinds of evil. Some people have left the faith, because they wanted to get more money, but they have caused themselves much sorrow.

SOME THINGS TO REMEMBER

11But you, man of God, run away from all those things. Instead, live in the right way, serve God, have faith, love, patience, and gentleness. 12Fight the good fight of faith, grabbing hold of the life that continues forever. You were called to have that life when you confessed the good confession before many witnesses. 13In the sight of God, who gives life to everything, and of Christ Jesus, I give you a command. Christ Jesus made the good confession when he stood before Pontius Pilate. 14Do what you were commanded to do without wrong or blame until our Lord Jesus Christ comes again. 15God will make that happen at the right time. He is the blessed and only Ruler, the King of all kings and the Lord of all lords. 16He is the only One who never dies. He lives in light so bright no one can go near it. No one has ever seen God, or can see him. May honor and power belong to God forever. Amen.

17Command those who are rich with things of this world not to be proud. Tell them to hope in God, not in their uncertain riches. God richly gives us everything to enjoy. 18Tell the rich people to do good, to be rich in doing good deeds, to be generous and ready to share. 19By doing that, they will be saving a treasure for themselves as a strong foundation for the future. Then they will be able to have the life that is true life.

20Timothy, guard what God has trusted to you. Stay away from foolish, useless talk and from the arguments of what is falsely called "knowledge." 21By saying they have that "knowledge," some have missed the true faith.

Grace be with you.

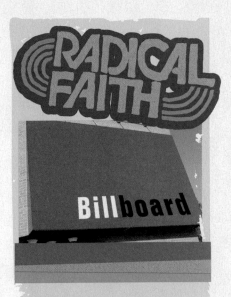

1 TIMOTHY 6:6-11

Hundreds of times a day, advertisers slam your brain with pressure to buy their stuff. They turn your clothes into walking billboards, invade your school by hawking snacks, fill your mailbox with catalogs, and grab your ears and eyes every time you turn on a computer or television. There's one big problem with the stuff they want you to acquire. You can search under the sofa cushions, raid your bank account, even borrow from your parents, and you still won't have enough money to buy it all. What's a guy to do? Learn to be content. The Bible says that people who want to be rich have been sucked into a trap. They're drowning, dragged under by their material desires. But people who choose to be happy with what they have are actually the richest people of all. And while it's not wrong to own stuff you work hard to earn, wanting more than you can reasonably afford is so dangerous that the Bible leaves you only one smart choice, and that's to turn away from greedy advertisements enticing you to sell your soul.

2 TIMOTHY

SOUND ADVICE FOR REMAINING STRONG

Paul's second letter to Timothy is his last and, in some ways, his most moving. To every man who struggles with the lack of a male role model comes the message that Timothy's faith came down from his grandmother and his mother. This faith stems from a spirit of power and love, the apostle says. What powerful words from a man who is writing from jail at the end of his life. Imagine the support Timothy drew from this message of affirmation.

As in his first letter, Paul is training Timothy for ministry here. He reminds Timothy to avoid fruitless arguments and to strive instead to be the kind of honorable person who will find approval from God. Paul also warns that some have already departed from sound teaching, but assures this young pastor that the foundation of God's Word will continue to stand.

These words reverberate in a time when many cast doubt on the accuracy and inspiration of the Bible. Finally, Paul exhorts Timothy to flee from evil desires and embrace faith, love, and peace. That is sound guidance for life today, just as it was when Paul originally wrote those words. They can inspire you to do the same.

From Paul, an apostle of Christ Jesus by the will of God. God sent me to tell about the promise of life that is in Christ Jesus. [2] To Timothy, a dear child to me:

Grace, mercy, and peace to you from God the Father and Christ Jesus our Lord.

ENCOURAGEMENT FOR TIMOTHY

[3] I thank God as I always mention you in my prayers, day and night. I serve him, doing what I know is right as my ancestors did. [4] Remembering that you cried for me, I want very much to see you so I can be filled with joy. [5] I remember your true faith. That faith first lived in your grandmother Lois and in your mother Eunice, and I know you now have that same faith. [6] This is why I remind you to keep using the gift God gave you when I laid my hands on[n] you. Now let it grow, as a small flame grows into a fire. [7] God did not give us a spirit that makes us afraid but a spirit of power and love and self-control.

[8] So do not be ashamed to tell people about our Lord Jesus, and do not be ashamed of me, in prison for the Lord. But suffer with me for the Good News. God, who gives us the strength to do that, [9] saved us and made us his holy people. That was not because of anything we did ourselves but because of God's purpose and grace. That grace was given to us through Christ Jesus before time began, [10] but it is now shown to us by the coming of our Savior Christ Jesus. He destroyed death, and through the Good News he showed us the way to have life that cannot be destroyed. [11] I was chosen to tell that Good News and to be an apostle and a teacher. [12] I am suffering now because I tell the Good News, but I am not ashamed, because I know Jesus, the One in whom I have believed. And I am sure he is able to protect what he has trusted me with until that day.[n] [13] Follow the pattern of true teachings that you heard from me in faith and love, which are in Christ Jesus. [14] Protect the truth that you were given; protect it with the help of the Holy Spirit who lives in us.

[15] You know that everyone in Asia has left me, even Phygelus and Hermogenes. [16] May the Lord show mercy to the family of Onesiphorus, who has often helped me and was not ashamed that I was in prison. [17] When he came to Rome, he looked eagerly for me until he found me. [18] May the Lord allow him to find mercy from the Lord on that day. You know how many ways he helped me in Ephesus.

A LOYAL SOLDIER OF CHRIST JESUS

You then, Timothy, my child, be strong in the grace we have in Christ Jesus. [2] You should teach people whom you can trust the things you and many others have heard me say. Then they will be able to teach others. [3] Share in the troubles we have like a good soldier of Christ Jesus. [4] A soldier wants to please the enlisting officer, so no one serving in the army wastes time with everyday matters. [5] Also an athlete who takes part in a contest must obey all the rules in order to win. [6] The farmer who works hard should be the first person to get some of the food that was grown. [7] Think about what I am saying, because the Lord will give you the ability to understand everything.

WAYS to WALK the WALK

2 TIMOTHY 1:6-7
WORD: Use your gifts with confidence.
WALK IT: God has given you certain gifts, and the more you develop them, the more he is glorified. Ask God to give you confidence to use the gifts he has given you.

[8] Remember Jesus Christ, who was raised from the dead, who is from the family of David. This is the Good News I preach, [9] and I am suffering because of it to the point of being bound with chains like a criminal. But God's teaching is not in chains. [10] So I patiently accept all these troubles so that those whom God has chosen can have the salvation that is in Christ Jesus. With that salvation comes glory that never ends.

[11] This teaching is true:
If we died with him, we will also live with
   him.
[12] If we accept suffering, we will also rule
   with him.
If we say we don't know him, he will say he
   doesn't know us.

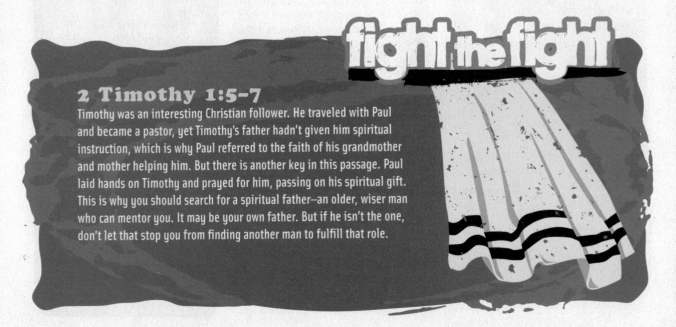

fight the fight

2 Timothy 1:5-7
Timothy was an interesting Christian follower. He traveled with Paul and became a pastor, yet Timothy's father hadn't given him spiritual instruction, which is why Paul referred to the faith of his grandmother and mother helping him. But there is another key in this passage. Paul laid hands on Timothy and prayed for him, passing on his spiritual gift. This is why you should search for a spiritual father—an older, wiser man who can mentor you. It may be your own father. But if he isn't the one, don't let that stop you from finding another man to fulfill that role.

2 TIMOTHY 2:22

Trying to live as a believer all by your lonesome is as smart as taking on a football team by yourself. The odds are seriously stacked against you, and soon you're likely to end up lying in agony on the ground. Okay, there are times when every Christian guy feels alone. You face situations where you have to choose to stand strong for your faith, even when no other human being stands with you. Use those solitary moments to learn to rely on God totally and hang tight with him. Take encouragement from stories of guys who have been where you are. Yet, remember that such lonely moments aren't supposed to be the norm. God tells you to flee evil and try hard to live right, chasing hard after faith, love, and peace. And he doesn't say to go it alone as you do. He wants you to seek out peers and mentors who also trust God with pure hearts. He wants you to live close to other believers, depending on each other like parts put together in a body (1 Corinthians 12:27).

13If we are not faithful, he will still be faithful,
because he must be true to who he is.

A WORKER PLEASING TO GOD

14Continue teaching these things, warning people in God's presence not to argue about words. It does not help anyone, and it ruins those who listen. 15Make every effort to give yourself to God as the kind of person he will approve. Be a worker who is not ashamed and who uses the true teaching in the right way. 16Stay away from foolish, useless talk, because that will lead people further away from God. 17Their evil teaching will spread like a sickness inside the body. Hymenaeus and Philetus are like that. 18They have left the true teaching, saying that the rising from the dead has already taken place, and so they are destroying the faith of some people. 19But God's strong foundation continues to stand. These words are written on the seal: "The Lord knows those who belong to him,"* and "Everyone who wants to belong to the Lord must stop doing wrong."

20In a large house there are not only things made of gold and silver, but also things made of wood and clay. Some things are used for special purposes, and others are made for ordinary jobs. 21All who make themselves clean from evil will be used for special purposes. They will be made holy, useful to the Master, ready to do any good work.

22But run away from the evil desires of youth. Try hard to live right and to have faith, love, and peace, together with those who trust in the Lord from pure hearts. 23Stay away from foolish and stupid arguments, because you know they grow into quarrels. 24And a servant of the Lord must not quarrel but must be kind to everyone, a good teacher, and patient. 25The Lord's servant must gently teach those who disagree. Then maybe God will let them change their minds so they can accept the truth. 26And they may wake up and escape from the trap of the devil, who catches them to do what he wants.

THE LAST DAYS

3 Remember this! In the last days there will be many troubles, 2because people will love themselves, love money, brag, and be proud. They will say evil things against others and will not obey their parents or be thankful or be the kind of people God wants. 3They will not love others, will refuse to forgive, will gossip, and will not control themselves. They will be cruel, will hate what is good, 4will turn against their friends, and will do foolish things without thinking. They will be conceited, will

love pleasure instead of God, 5and will act as if they serve God but will not have his power. Stay away from those people. 6Some of them go into homes and get control of silly women who are full of sin and are led by many evil desires. 7These women are always learning new teachings, but they are never able to understand the truth fully. 8Just as Jannes and Jambres were against Moses, these people are against the truth. Their thinking has been ruined, and they have failed in trying to follow the faith. 9But they will not be successful in what they do, because as with Jannes and Jambres, everyone will see that they are foolish.

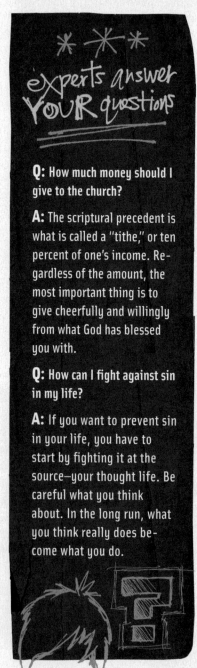

2:19 "The Lord . . . him." Quotation from Numbers 16:5.

SPORTS

SPORTS ARE GOOD FOR YOU, BUT DON'T BECOME OBSESSED WITH THEM TO THE POINT THAT THEY TAKE OVER YOUR LIFE. Some guys play every sport that's in season and then watch other games whenever they're not on the playing field themselves. While physical exercise is definitely good for the physique, any type of activity can be detrimental if overdone. If playing and watching sports consumes so much of your time that you neglect your studies, job, family, friends, or God, then it's time to reevaluate the place that sports occupy in your life. As with all of life, common sense is the key to becoming a champion.

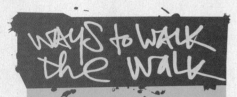

ways to walk the walk

2 TIMOTHY 4:2-5
WORD: Preach the Good News.
WALK IT: Preaching sounds high and holy, but, actually, it simply means proclaiming a message. Proclaim the message of God's love to someone you care about today.

OBEY THE TEACHINGS

[10]But you have followed what I teach, the way I live, my goal, faith, patience, and love. You know I never give up. [11]You know how I have been hurt and have suffered, as in Antioch, Iconium, and Lystra. I have suffered, but the Lord saved me from all those troubles. [12]Everyone who wants to live as God desires, in Christ Jesus, will be persecuted. [13]But people who are evil and cheat others will go from bad to worse. They will fool others, but they will also be fooling themselves.

[14]But you should continue following the teachings you learned. You know they are true, because you trust those who taught you. [15]Since you were a child you have known the Holy Scriptures which are able to make you wise. And that wisdom leads to salvation through faith in Christ Jesus. [16]All Scripture is inspired by God and is useful for teaching, for showing people what is wrong in their lives, for correcting faults, and for teaching how to live right. [17]Using the Scriptures, the person who serves God will be capable, having all that is needed to do every good work.

4 I give you a command in the presence of God and Christ Jesus, the One who will judge the living and the dead, and by his coming and his kingdom: [2]Preach the Good News. Be ready at all times, and tell people what they need to do. Tell them when they are wrong. Encourage them with great patience and careful teaching, [3]because the time will come when people will not listen to the true teaching but will find many more teachers who please them by saying the things they want to hear. [4]They will stop listening to the truth and will begin to follow false stories. [5]But you should control yourself at all times, accept troubles, do the work of telling the Good News, and complete all the duties of a servant of God.

[6]My life is being given as an offering to God, and the time has come for me to leave this life. [7]I have fought the good fight, I have finished the race, I have kept the faith. [8]Now, a

2 Timothy 3:17
"Using the Scriptures, the person who serves God will be capable, having all that is needed to do every good work."

crown is being held for me—a crown for being right with God. The Lord, the judge who judges rightly, will give the crown to me on that day[n]—not only to me but to all those who have waited with love for him to come again.

PERSONAL WORDS

[9]Do your best to come to me as soon as you can, [10]because Demas, who loved this world, left

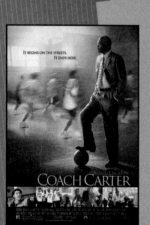

 4:8 day The day Christ will come to judge all people and take his people to live with him.

october

NATIONAL DIVERSITY AWARENESS MONTH

"At the beginning of every act of faith, there is often a seed of fear. For great acts of faith are seldom born out of calm calculation." -MAX LUCADO

1 Pray for your guidance counselor.	**2**	**3** It's Ashlee Simpson's birthday today.	**4**
5 Today is Nikki Hilton's birthday.	**6** Buy lunch for a friend of a different race.	**7** Michael W. Smith celebrates another birthday.	**8**
9 This is fire prevention week, so don't start any.	**10**	**11**	**12** Rent a video for family movie night at home.
13	**14** Change your hairstyle for the fun of it.	**15** Singer Jaci Velasquez turns one year older today.	**16**
17	**18** Take your date out for a nice dinner.	**19**	**20**
21 Return any overdue books to the library.	**22**	**23**	**24** Volunteer to help clean up the dishes after dinner.
25	**26** Pray for the children's ministry at your church.	**27** Study a foreign language.	**28**
29	**30** Practice patience while waiting in lines.	**31** Pray for the safety of neighborhood kids.	

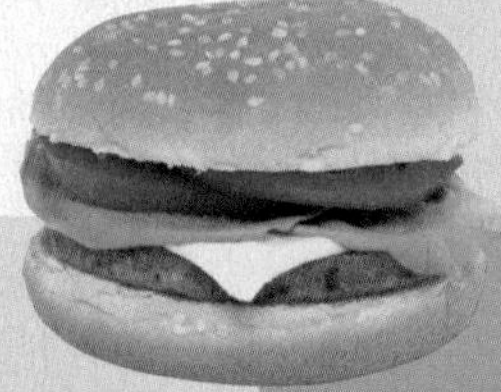

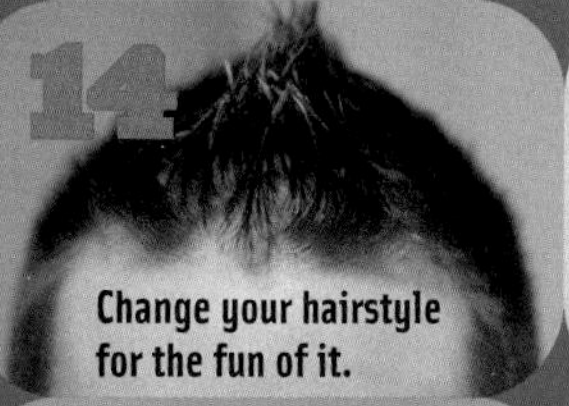

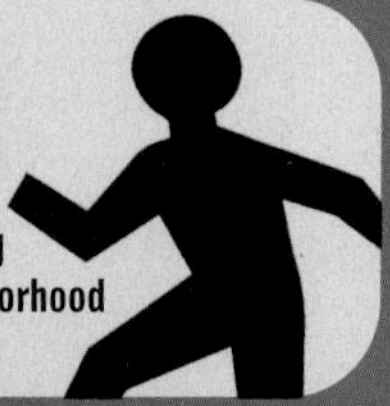

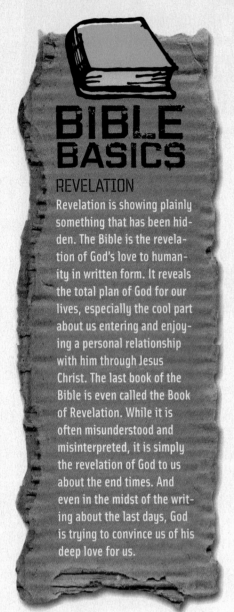

BIBLE BASICS

REVELATION

Revelation is showing plainly something that has been hidden. The Bible is the revelation of God's love to humanity in written form. It reveals the total plan of God for our lives, especially the cool part about us entering and enjoying a personal relationship with him through Jesus Christ. The last book of the Bible is even called the Book of Revelation. While it is often misunderstood and misinterpreted, it is simply the revelation of God to us about the end times. And even in the midst of the writing about the last days, God is trying to convince us of his deep love for us.

me and went to Thessalonica. Crescens went to Galatia, and Titus went to Dalmatia. ¹¹Luke is the only one still with me. Get Mark and bring him with you when you come, because he can help me in my work here. ¹²I sent Tychicus to Ephesus. ¹³When I was in Troas, I left my coat there with Carpus. So when you come, bring it to me, along with my books, particularly the ones written on parchment.*

¹⁴Alexander the metalworker did many harmful things against me. The Lord will punish him for what he did. ¹⁵You also should be careful that he does not hurt you, because he fought strongly against our teaching.

¹⁶The first time I defended myself, no one helped me; everyone left me. May they be forgiven. ¹⁷But the Lord stayed with me and gave me strength so I could fully tell the Good News to all those who are not Jews. So I was saved from the lion's mouth. ¹⁸The Lord will save me when anyone tries to hurt me, and he will bring me safely to his heavenly kingdom. Glory forever and ever be the Lord's. Amen.

FINAL GREETINGS

¹⁹Greet Priscilla and Aquila and the family of Onesiphorus. ²⁰Erastus stayed in Corinth, and I left Trophimus sick in Miletus. ²¹Try as hard as you can to come to me before winter.

Eubulus sends greetings to you. Also Pudens, Linus, Claudia, and all the brothers and sisters in Christ greet you.

²²The Lord be with your spirit. Grace be with you.

TOP 10 TEN

random electronic media uses

1. Recording a motion picture.
2. Customizing a music soundtrack.
3. Organizing a contact list.
4. Reading a downloaded book.
5. Editing a digital picture.
6. Filming a personal documentary.
7. Placing a wireless call.
8. Creating a Web site.
9. Archiving favorite Web pages.
10. Scanning documents for retrieval.

---

* 4:13 parchment A writing paper made from the skins of sheep.

notes

TITUS

INSTRUCTION FOR A ROWDY PLACE

Ever have a coach, teacher, or parent turn to you and say, "Here's what needs to be done, and I know I can count on you"? This is basically what Paul did for Titus, who was one of the apostle's traveling companions. Paul put Titus in charge of organizing churches in Crete. It was a place populated by pirates, thugs, rowdy sailors, and pagan worshipers of the Greek god Zeus. Add to this, religious zealots who insisted believers follow their legalistic rules, and others who liked to argue. Not exactly a plum assignment for Titus.

While anyone might be tempted to cut and run under such circumstances, Paul didn't leave Titus on his own. He wrote to assure Titus that he had left him there to complete the important task of appointing elders to oversee the churches. Such leaders had to be sober, giving, peaceful, and law abiding. And, they must demonstrate faithfulness to God's Word so they could teach others.

Those guidelines helped Titus carry out his job in the toughest of circumstances. Paul's encouraging words also affirmed that following God is still the right thing to do, even if most people around you are acting wild and making lame excuses for their actions.

From Paul, a servant of God and an apostle of Jesus Christ. I was sent to help the faith of God's chosen people and to help them know the truth that shows people how to serve God. ²That faith and that knowledge come from the hope for life forever, which God promised to us before time began. And God cannot lie. ³At the right time God let the world know about that life through preaching. He trusted me with that work, and I preached by the command of God our Savior.

⁴To Titus, my true child in the faith we share:

Grace and peace from God the Father and Christ Jesus our Savior.

TITUS' WORK IN CRETE

⁵I left you in Crete so you could finish doing the things that still needed to be done and so you could appoint elders in every town, as I directed you. ⁶An elder must not be guilty of doing wrong, must have only one wife, and must have believing children. They must not be known as children who are wild and do not cooperate. ⁷As God's managers, overseers must not be guilty of doing wrong, being selfish, or becoming angry quickly. They must not drink too much wine, like to fight, or try to get rich by cheating others. ⁸Overseers must be ready to welcome guests, love what is good, be wise, live right, and be holy and self-controlled. ⁹By holding on to the trustworthy word just as we teach it, overseers can help people by using true teaching, and they can show those who are against the true teaching that they are wrong.

¹⁰There are many people who refuse to cooperate, who talk about worthless things and lead others into the wrong way—mainly those who insist on circumcision to be saved. ¹¹These people must be stopped, because they are upsetting whole families by teaching things they should not teach, which they do to get rich by cheating people. ¹²Even one of their own prophets said, "Cretans are always liars, evil animals, and lazy people who do nothing but eat." ¹³The words that prophet said are true. So firmly tell those people they are wrong so they may become strong in the faith, ¹⁴not accepting Jewish false stories and the commands of people who reject the truth. ¹⁵To those who are pure, all things are pure, but to those who are full of sin and do not believe, nothing is pure. Both their minds and their consciences have been ruined. ¹⁶They say they know God, but their actions show they do not accept him. They are hateful people, they refuse to obey, and they are useless for doing anything good.

FOLLOWING THE TRUE TEACHING

2 But you must tell everyone what to do to follow the true teaching. ²Teach older men to be self-controlled, serious, wise, strong in faith, in love, and in patience.

³In the same way, teach older women to be holy in their behavior, not speaking against

experts answer YOUR questions

Q: Is it ever okay for a Christian to feel proud?

A: All of the abilities we have are a gift from God, so it's not really appropriate to be proud of something that's a gift. The best thing for us to be proud of is not how much we can do for God but how much God can do through us.

Q: Why don't Christians follow all the laws in the Old Testament?

A: The Old Testament laws, while positive and healthy, were given not to save us, but to show us that we could never become good enough to be saved on our own merits. Today, Christians are free to live by grace instead of striving to fulfill the letter of the law.

TITUS 2:14

Imagine living back in the days of the American slave trade. A few of your acquaintances sniff about the evil of captivity and forced human labor, but no one acts to stop it. You, however, heir to an enormous fortune, determine to use your resources to rescue every slave you can. When you uncover a plantation that boasts about its cruelty to countless slaves, you present the slave owner with a deal he can't pass up. You trade him every last cent of your fortune to buy the freedom of every man, woman, and child. That's what Jesus did on the cross. With his blood he paid the price of forgiveness (Ephesians 1:7). By his sacrifice he set you free from slavery to sin, making you one of his pure people, ready to follow him and always do right. If you can begin to grasp that picture, then think of the outrageous tragedy of a slave rejecting freedom and returning to bondage. Every time you give in to sin, you're doing something as crazy as that. Jesus set you free to be a new person. Bask in your freedom. Don't trade it for slavery!

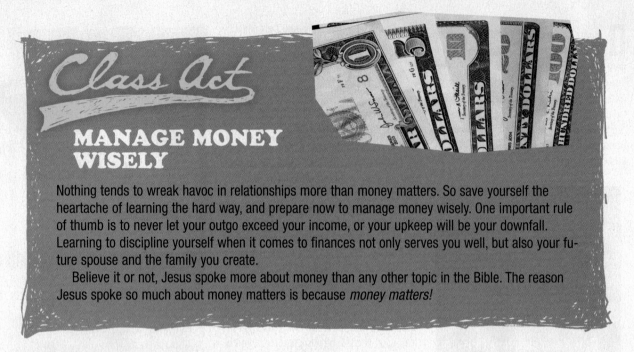

Class Act

MANAGE MONEY WISELY

Nothing tends to wreak havoc in relationships more than money matters. So save yourself the heartache of learning the hard way, and prepare now to manage money wisely. One important rule of thumb is to never let your outgo exceed your income, or your upkeep will be your downfall. Learning to discipline yourself when it comes to finances not only serves you well, but also your future spouse and the family you create.

Believe it or not, Jesus spoke more about money than any other topic in the Bible. The reason Jesus spoke so much about money matters is because *money matters!*

others or enslaved to too much wine, but teaching what is good. ⁴Then they can teach the young women to love their husbands, to love their children, ⁵to be wise and pure, to be good workers at home, to be kind, and to yield to their husbands. Then no one will be able to criticize the teaching God gave us.

⁶In the same way, encourage young men to be wise. ⁷In every way be an example of doing good deeds. When you teach, do it with honesty and seriousness. ⁸Speak the truth so that you cannot be criticized. Then those who are against you will be ashamed because there is nothing bad to say about us.

⁹Slaves should yield to their own masters at all times, trying to please them and not arguing with them. ¹⁰They should not steal from them but should show their masters they can be fully trusted so that in everything they do they will make the teaching of God our Savior attractive.

¹¹That is the way we should live, because God's grace that can save everyone has come. ¹²It teaches us not to live against God nor to do the evil things the world wants to do. Instead, that grace teaches us to live in the present age in a wise and right way and in a way that shows we serve God. ¹³We should live like that while we wait for our great hope and the coming of the glory of our great God and Savior

Jesus Christ. ¹⁴He gave himself for us so he might pay the price to free us from all evil and to make us pure people who belong only to him—people who are always wanting to do good deeds.

¹⁵Say these things and encourage the people and tell them what is wrong in their lives, with all authority. Do not let anyone treat you as if you were unimportant.

THE RIGHT WAY TO LIVE

3 Remind the believers to yield to the authority of rulers and government leaders, to obey them, to be ready to do good, ²to speak no evil about anyone, to live in

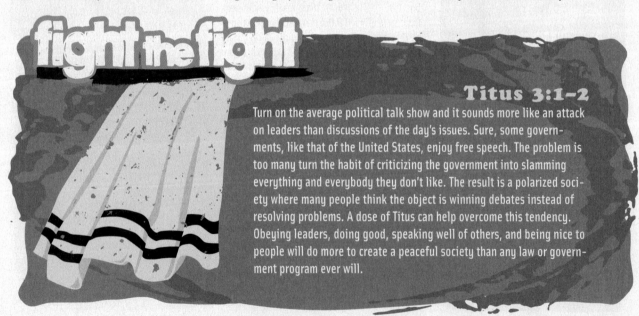

fight the fight

Titus 3:1-2

Turn on the average political talk show and it sounds more like an attack on leaders than discussions of the day's issues. Sure, some governments, like that of the United States, enjoy free speech. The problem is too many turn the habit of criticizing the government into slamming everything and everybody they don't like. The result is a polarized society where many people think the object is winning debates instead of resolving problems. A dose of Titus can help overcome this tendency. Obeying leaders, doing good, speaking well of others, and being nice to people will do more to create a peaceful society than any law or government program ever will.

Do's and Don'ts

DO exercise regularly.

DO get plenty of sleep.

DO brush your teeth.

DO use sunscreen.

DON'T get dehydrated.

DON'T drink alcohol.

DON'T smoke cigarettes.

DON'T do drugs.

peace, and to be gentle and polite to all people. [3]In the past we also were foolish. We did not obey, we were wrong, and we were slaves to many things our bodies wanted and en- joyed. We spent our lives doing evil and being jealous. People hated us, and we hated each other. [4]But when the kindness and love of God our Savior was shown, [5]he saved us because of his mercy. It was not because of good deeds we did to be right with him. He saved us through the washing that made us new people through the Holy Spirit. [6]God poured out richly upon us that Holy Spirit through Jesus Christ our Savior. [7]Being made right with God by his grace, we could have the hope of receiving the life that never ends.

[8]This teaching is true, and I want you to be sure the people understand these things. Then those who believe in God will be careful to use their lives for doing good. These things are good and will help everyone.

[9]But stay away from those who have fool- ish arguments and talk about useless family histories and argue and quarrel about the law. Those things are worth nothing and will not help anyone. [10]After a first and second warn- ing, avoid someone who causes arguments. [11]You can know that such people are evil and sinful; their own sins prove them wrong.

SOME THINGS TO REMEMBER

[12]When I send Artemas or Tychicus to you, make every effort to come to me at Nicopolis, because I have decided to stay there this win- ter. [13]Do all you can to help Zenas the lawyer and Apollos on their journey so that they have everything they need. [14]Our people must learn to use their lives for doing good deeds to pro- vide what is necessary so that their lives will not be useless.

[15]All who are with me greet you. Greet those who love us in the faith.

Grace be with you all.

Ways to Walk the Walk

TITUS 3:9
WORD: Avoid pointless arguments with fools.
WALK IT: Some people are just looking for a fight. Learn to recog- nize these people by their desire to argue, and leave them alone. If you are one of those people, let it go.

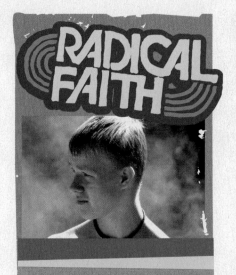

RADICAL FAITH

TITUS 3:3–8
Put on the island of Crete by the apostle Paul to help the young church there, Titus pastored a peo- ple known far and wide as pirates and thugs. But as Paul coached Titus on how to help the church mature, he lumped all of us together as sin- ners. We, too, were foolish like the Cretans. We refused to obey, and we did wrong. We were slaves to our physical desires. We did evil, hating and being hated. Amazingly, God knew what we were like, but he still sent Jesus to save us—not because we earned his approval, but out of grace, his favor we did nothing to deserve. God washed off your sins and made you a new person. Now, you might not have a gruesomely sinful past, no history wild enough to land you on the local news. Even so, whoever you were and whatever sin you were into before you trusted Jesus, you were set against God, living for your own desires. Don't ever forget the bad place God saved you from, because then you will remember the great place God has planned for you.

PHILEMON

CHANGING THE HEARTS OF HUMANITY

Slavery will forever be a stain on America's history. Yet, Paul's letter to Philemon makes it clear that this regrettable practice has been going on for thousands of years. In this case, a runaway slave named Onesimus had converted to Christianity after contacting Paul in prison. As the apostle puts it, "Onesimus became my child."

Now as a father would intervene for a natural son, Paul takes up the cause of this new believer. While noting that he could be bold and order Philemon to do what is right, instead Paul humbly pleads with Philemon to take the man back without punishing him. Indeed, he wants Philemon to accept Onesimus as a brother in Christ, not as a slave.

Though one of the shortest books in the Bible, Philemon delivers one of its most powerful messages. In its verses is a clear pattern of how Christians should act. Instead of using bravado and commands to get his way, Paul models meekness. His humble appeal demonstrates the superiority of forgiveness over revenge. By taking up a slave's cause, Paul shows how we should stand up for the oppressed. And, by using a loving approach, he shows how real change in human hearts comes from God's grace, not laws.

Relationships

"My dear brothers and sisters, always be willing to listen and slow to speak" (James 1:19a). Want to keep your relationships going strong? If so, you need to learn to shut your mouth and open your ears. Listening is vital to maintaining a good relationship, whether it's with friends, family members, or your future wife. Think about it: you don't have relationships just so other people can listen to you talk. Friendship is all about give and take, so tame your tongue and train your ears to hear what others have to say. You can't learn from others unless you're willing to listen.

¹From Paul, a prisoner of Christ Jesus, and from Timothy, our brother.

To Philemon, our dear friend and worker with us; ²to Apphia, our sister; to Archippus, a worker with us; and to the church that meets in your home:

³Grace and peace to you from God our Father and the Lord Jesus Christ.

WAYS to WALK the WALK

PHILEMON 14

WORD: Ask out of respect.

WALK IT: Someone may owe you a favor, or you may have authority over him. Yet, even so, *ask* him to do the task you desire instead of *demanding* that he do it. You'll show him respect, and he'll appreciate you for it.

PHILEMON'S LOVE AND FAITH

⁴I always thank my God when I mention you in my prayers, ⁵because I hear about the love you have for all God's holy people and the faith you have in the Lord Jesus. ⁶I pray that the faith you share may make you understand every blessing we have in Christ. ⁷I have great joy and comfort, my brother, because the love you have shown to God's people has refreshed them.

ACCEPT ONESIMUS AS A BROTHER

⁸So, in Christ, I could be bold and order you to do what is right. ⁹But because I love you, I am pleading with you instead. I, Paul, an old man now and also a prisoner for Christ Jesus, ¹⁰am pleading with you for my child Onesimus, who became my child while I was in prison. ¹¹In the past he was useless to you, but now he has become useful for both you and me. ¹²I am sending him back to you, and with him I am sending my own heart. ¹³I wanted to keep him with me so that in your place he might help me while I am in prison for the Good News. ¹⁴But I did not want to do anything without asking you first so that any good you do for me will be because you want to do it, not because I forced you. ¹⁵Maybe Onesimus was separated from you for a short time so you could have him back forever— ¹⁶no longer as a slave, but better than a slave, as a loved brother. I love him very much, but you will love him even more, both as a person and as a believer in the Lord.

¹⁷So if you consider me your partner, welcome Onesimus as you would welcome me. ¹⁸If he has done anything wrong to you or if he owes you anything, charge that to me. ¹⁹I, Paul, am writing this with my own hand. I will pay it back, and I will say nothing about what you owe me for your own life. ²⁰So, my brother, I ask that you do this for me in the Lord: Refresh my heart in Christ. ²¹I write this letter, knowing that you will do what I ask you and even more.

²²One more thing—prepare a room for me in which to stay, because I hope God will answer your prayers and I will be able to come to you.

FINAL GREETINGS

²³Epaphras, a prisoner with me for Christ Jesus, sends greetings to you. ²⁴And also Mark, Aristarchus, Demas, and Luke, workers together with me, send greetings.

²⁵The grace of our Lord Jesus Christ be with your spirit.

BIBLE BASICS

SALVATION

Salvation is being saved from sin and its punishment, which is eternal separation from God. We experience salvation when we come to God with faith in Jesus Christ as our Savior. Trusting in Christ's death, burial, and resurrection qualifies us to receive all that Jesus came to give us. It not only includes deliverance from the power of sin, but it also guarantees us an eternal home in heaven with Jesus. Romans 10:10 points the way to salvation: "We believe with our hearts, and so we are made right with God. And we declare with our mouths that we believe, and so we are saved."

HEBREWS

HOLDING FAST TO THE FAITH

Ever wonder what a skate park, ballgame, or the mall have in common with ancient history? The temptation you will experience in popular settings to indulge in the fad of the moment is the same kind of pressure Christians encountered nearly 2,000 years ago. While no one knows who wrote the Book of Hebrews, it appears to be written to a group of Jewish believers. Facing persecution, they were tempted to forget about following Christ and retreat to the safety of group conformity. The author comes along to urge them to grow in their faith and increase their dependence on God.

The significance of Hebrews can't be overstated. Its words remind us that God sent his Son to this world to show us how to live. He is greater than any other man who ever lived. Jesus lives as our chief spiritual guide and perfect representative before the heavenly Father.

This is why we should worship him. This is why he is the only way to God. This is why we should have faith even though we can't always see how things will turn out for the best. Jesus is why people endured persecution, suffering, and even death. They knew something better was coming, just as it is for all who believe in Christ.

GOD SPOKE THROUGH HIS SON

1 In the past God spoke to our ancestors through the prophets many times and in many different ways. ²But now in these last days God has spoken to us through his Son. God has chosen his Son to own all things, and through him he made the world. ³The Son reflects the glory of God and shows exactly what God is like. He holds everything together with his powerful word. When the Son made people clean from their sins, he sat down at the right side of God, the Great One in heaven. ⁴The Son became much greater than the angels, and God gave him a name that is much greater than theirs.

⁵This is because God never said to any of the angels,

"You are my Son.
Today I have become your Father."
Psalm 2:7

Nor did God say of any angel,
"I will be his Father,
and he will be my Son." *2 Samuel 7:14*
⁶And when God brings his firstborn Son into the world, he says,
"Let all God's angels worship him."ⁿ
Psalm 97:7
⁷This is what God said about the angels:
"God makes his angels become like winds.
He makes his servants become like
flames of fire." *Psalm 104:4*

⁸But God said this about his Son:
"God, your throne will last forever and ever.
You will rule your kingdom with
fairness.
⁹You love right and hate evil,
so God has chosen you from among
your friends;

he has set you apart with much joy."
Psalm 45:6–7
¹⁰God also says,
"Lord, in the beginning you made the earth,
and your hands made the skies.
¹¹They will be destroyed, but you will
remain.

MEN of the SWORD

PHILIP

When it comes to transportation, there's nothing more tricked-out than what Philip rode. Philip was one of Jesus' original followers, and after Christ's death, Philip became a powerful traveling evangelist. One day he was walking on a desert road when he encountered a man in a chariot reading the Book of Isaiah. The man couldn't understand the prophecies about Jesus, so Philip told him what they meant. The man accepted Christ, and Philip baptized him right there. And then the Spirit of the Lord carried Philip away and caused him to reappear suddenly in a city several miles away. That is cruising! —Acts 8:26–40

 1:6 "Let . . . him." These words are found in Deuteronomy 32:43 in the Septuagint, the Greek version of the Old Testament, and in a Hebrew copy among the Dead Sea Scrolls.

Extras:

How to Jump-start a Car

Start by getting the car with the live battery as close as possible to the car with the dead battery. Turn off the live battery's engine, pop both hoods, and attach the cables in the prescribed order. Connect the positive (usually red handled) to the live battery, positive to the dead battery, negative (usually black handled) to the dead battery, negative to the good battery. Attach the positive clamps to their corresponding posts on the batteries; attach the negative clamps to an unpainted metal part of the car to avoid surges. Start the dead battery, and then remove the clamps in reverse order. If the car still won't start, readjust its positive clamp until it works. Let the car with the formerly dead battery run for a half-hour to recharge the battery. Like your car, you can get run down—so maintain your close connection to God in order to stay charged.

TOP TEN

random family getaway ideas

1. Go to the beach.
2. Check out the mall.
3. Head for the mountains.
4. Hit the local zoo.
5. Go on a cruise.
6. Tour a national landmark.
7. Attend a family reunion.
8. Visit an amusement park.
9. Travel to another state.
10. Go on a picnic.

They will all wear out like clothes.
¹²You will fold them like a coat.
And, like clothes, you will change them.
But you never change,
and your life will never end."

Psalm 102:25–27

¹³And God never said this to an angel:
"Sit by me at my right side
until I put your enemies under your control."ⁿ

Psalm 110:1

¹⁴All the angels are spirits who serve God and are sent to help those who will receive salvation.

OUR SALVATION IS GREAT

2 So we must be more careful to follow what we were taught. Then we will not stray away from the truth. ²The teaching God spoke through angels was shown to be true, and anyone who did not follow it or obey it received the punishment that was earned. ³So surely we also will be punished if we ignore this great salvation. The Lord himself first told about this salvation, and those who heard him testified it was true. ⁴God also testified to the truth of the message by using wonders, great signs, many kinds of miracles, and by giving people gifts through the Holy Spirit, just as he wanted.

CHRIST BECAME LIKE HUMANS

⁵God did not choose angels to be the rulers of the new world that was coming, which is what we have been talking about. ⁶It is written in the Scriptures,
"Why are people even important to you?
Why do you take care of human beings?
⁷You made them a little lower than the angels
and crowned them with glory and honor.ⁿ
⁸You put all things under their control."

Psalm 8:4–6

When God put everything under their control, there was nothing left that they did not rule. Still, we do not yet see them ruling over everything. ⁹But we see Jesus, who for a short time was made lower than the angels. And now he is wearing a crown of glory and honor because he suffered and died. And by God's grace, he died for everyone.

¹⁰God is the One who made all things, and all things are for his glory. He wanted to have many children share his glory, so he made the One who leads people to salvation perfect through suffering.

¹¹Jesus, who makes people holy, and those who are made holy are from the same family. So he is not ashamed to call them his brothers and sisters. ¹²He says,
"Then, I will tell my brothers and sisters about you;
I will praise you in the public meeting."

Psalm 22:22

¹³He also says,
"I will trust in God."   *Isaiah 8:17*
And he also says,
"I am here, and with me are the children God has given me."   *Isaiah 8:18*

¹⁴Since these children are people with physical bodies, Jesus himself became like them. He did this so that, by dying, he could

WAYS to WALK the WALK

HEBREWS 2:1–4
WORD: Follow what you've been taught.
WALK IT: It's all too easy to ignore the lessons of the faith. But don't let your heart become hardened to what you've learned; follow Christ no matter what the cost.

1:13 until . . . control Literally, "until I make your enemies a footstool for your feet." 2:7 You . . . honor. Some Greek copies continue, "You put them in charge of everything you made." See Psalm 8:6.

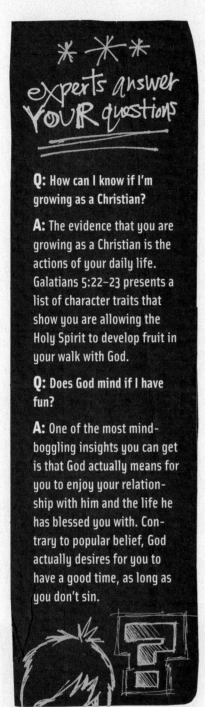

experts answer YOUR questions

Q: How can I know if I'm growing as a Christian?

A: The evidence that you are growing as a Christian is the actions of your daily life. Galatians 5:22–23 presents a list of character traits that show you are allowing the Holy Spirit to develop fruit in your walk with God.

Q: Does God mind if I have fun?

A: One of the most mind-boggling insights you can get is that God actually means for you to enjoy your relationship with him and the life he has blessed you with. Contrary to popular belief, God actually desires for you to have a good time, as long as you don't sin.

destroy the one who has the power of death—the devil— [15]and free those who were like slaves all their lives because of their fear of death. [16]Clearly, it is not angels that Jesus helps, but the people who are from Abraham.[n] [17]For this reason Jesus had to be made like his brothers and sisters in every way so he could be their merciful and faithful high priest in service to God. Then Jesus could die in their place to take away their sins. [18]And now he can

help those who are tempted, because he himself suffered and was tempted.

JESUS IS GREATER THAN MOSES

3 So all of you holy brothers and sisters, who were called by God, think about Jesus, who was sent to us and is the high priest of our faith. [2]Jesus was faithful to God as Moses was in God's family. [3]Jesus has more honor than Moses, just as the builder of a house has more honor than the house itself. [4]Every house is built by someone, but the builder of everything is God himself. [5]Moses was faithful in God's family as a servant, and he told what God would say in the future. [6]But Christ is faithful as a Son over God's house. And we are God's house if we confidently maintain our hope.

WE MUST CONTINUE TO FOLLOW GOD

[7]So it is as the Holy Spirit says:
"Today listen to what he says.
[8]Do not be stubborn as in the past
    when you turned against God,
when you tested God in the desert.
[9]There your ancestors tried me and tested me
    and saw the things I did for forty years.
[10]I was angry with them.
    I said, 'They are not loyal to me
    and have not understood my ways.'
[11]I was angry and made a promise,
    'They will never enter my rest.' "[n]
Psalm 95:7–11

[12]So brothers and sisters, be careful that none of you has an evil, unbelieving heart that will turn you away from the living God. [13]But encourage each other every day while it is "today."[n] Help each other so none of you will become hardened because sin has tricked you. [14]We all share in Christ if we keep till the end the sure faith we had in the beginning. [15]This is what the Scripture says:
"Today listen to what he says.
    Do not be stubborn as in the past
    when you turned against God."
Psalm 95:7–8

[16]Who heard God's voice and was against him? It was all those people Moses led out of Egypt. [17]And with whom was God angry for forty years? He was angry with those who sinned, who died in the desert. [18]And to whom was God talking when he promised that they would never enter his rest? He was talking to those who did not obey him. [19]So we see they were not allowed to enter and have God's rest, because they did not believe.

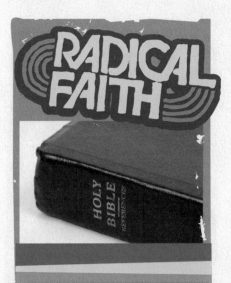

RADICAL FAITH

HEBREWS 4:12–13

Lots of people think of the Bible as a dull black book. Actually, it's razor-sharp, like a double-bladed sword that slices to your core, opening up your innermost thoughts and feelings. Not only does it expose those deep things, but it evaluates whether they are right or wrong. That's something most guys notice when they crack open the Bible, at least when they read the pointed parts. They sense that they're on the right path. Or they feel the tip of the Bible's words and twist away, not wanting to look honestly at the wrong they do. While no one likes to get cut, the truth is that we can't hide anything from God anyway. He knows exactly what we do, think, and say, and one day each of us will explain to him how we lived. Refusing to go under the knife of God's Word is like avoiding surgery you need to save your life. Instead, check into God's waiting room and pray like King David of the Old Testament: "God, examine me and know my heart" (Psalm 139:23).

 2:16 Abraham Most respected ancestor of the Jews. Every Jew hoped to see Abraham. 3:11 rest A place of rest God promised to give his people. 3:13 "today" This word is taken from verse 7. It means that it is important to do these things now.

HEBREWS 4:15

Read this verse about a dozen times until its truth saturates you. The high priest part means that as God the Son, Jesus is both our top spiritual leader and the one who makes us right with God the Father. The rest of the verse is simple, except it contains two radically shocking and life-altering facts: First, Jesus was tempted just like you are. Second, Jesus never yielded to it. The bottom line is that Jesus understands perfectly when you feel weary and tempted, because he has been there, but not done it. Because he triumphed completely over sin, he can show you how to beat evil. So you can confidently go to him for help, knowing he won't rip you to pieces. He will give you both sympathy and strength whenever you need it.

4 Now, since God has left us the promise that we may enter his rest, let us be very careful so none of you will fail to enter. ²The Good News was preached to us just as it was to them. But the teaching they heard did not help them, because they heard it but did not accept it with faith.[n] ³We who have believed are able to enter and have God's rest. As God has said,

"I was angry and made a promise,
'They will never enter my rest.'"
Psalm 95:11

But God's work was finished from the time he made the world. ⁴In the Scriptures he talked about the seventh day of the week: "And on the seventh day God rested from all his works."[n] ⁵And again in the Scripture God said, "They will never enter my rest."

⁶It is still true that some people will enter God's rest, but those who first heard the way to be saved did not enter, because they did not obey. ⁷So God planned another day, called "today." He spoke about that day through David a long time later in the same Scripture used before:

"Today listen to what he says.
Do not be stubborn." *Psalm 95:7–8*

⁸We know that Joshua[n] did not lead the people into that rest, because God spoke later about another day. ⁹This shows that the rest[n] for God's people is still coming. ¹⁰Anyone who enters God's rest will rest from his work as God did. ¹¹Let us try as hard as we can to enter God's rest so that no one will fail by following the example of those who refused to obey.

¹²God's word is alive and working and is sharper than a double-edged sword. It cuts all the way into us, where the soul and the spirit are joined, to the center of our joints and bones. And it judges the thoughts and feelings in our hearts. ¹³Nothing in all the world can be hidden from God. Everything is clear and lies open before him, and to him we must explain the way we have lived.

JESUS IS OUR HIGH PRIEST

¹⁴Since we have a great high priest, Jesus the Son of God, who has gone into heaven, let us hold on to the faith we have. ¹⁵For our high priest is able to understand our weaknesses. He was tempted in every way that we are, but he did not sin. ¹⁶Let us, then, feel very sure that we can come before God's throne where there is grace. There we can receive mercy and grace to help us when we need it.

5 Every high priest is chosen from among other people. He is given the work of going before God for them to offer gifts and sacrifices for sins. ²Since he himself is weak, he is able to be gentle with those who do not understand and who are doing wrong things. ³Because he is weak, the high priest must offer sacrifices for his own sins and also for the sins of the people.

⁴To be a high priest is an honor, but no one chooses himself for this work. He must be called by God as Aaron[n] was. ⁵So also Christ did not choose himself to have the honor of being a high priest, but God chose him. God said to him,

"You are my Son.
Today I have become your Father."
Psalm 2:7

⁶And in another Scripture God says,
"You are a priest forever,
a priest like Melchizedek."[n]
Psalm 110:4

⁷While Jesus lived on earth, he prayed to

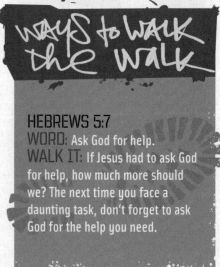

HEBREWS 5:7
WORD: Ask God for help.
WALK IT: If Jesus had to ask God for help, how much more should we? The next time you face a daunting task, don't forget to ask God for the help you need.

4:2 because . . . faith Some Greek copies read "because they did not share the faith of those who heard it." **4:4 "And . . . works."** Quotation from Genesis 2:2. **4:8 Joshua** After Moses died, Joshua became leader of the Jewish people and led them into the land that God promised to give them. **4:9 rest** Literally, "sabbath rest," meaning a sharing in the rest that God began after he created the world. **5:4 Aaron** Moses' brother and the first Jewish high priest. **5:6 Melchizedek** A priest and king who lived in the time of Abraham. (Read Genesis 14:17–24.)

God and asked God for help. He prayed with loud cries and tears to the One who could save him from death, and his prayer was heard because he trusted God. [8]Even though Jesus was the Son of God, he learned obedience by what he suffered. [9]And because his obedience was perfect, he was able to give eternal salvation to all who obey him. [10]In this way God made Jesus a high priest, a priest like Melchizedek.

WARNING AGAINST FALLING AWAY

[11]We have much to say about this, but it is hard to explain because you are so slow to understand. [12]By now you should be teachers, but you need someone to teach you again the first lessons of God's message. You still need the teaching that is like milk. You are not ready for solid food. [13]Anyone who lives on milk is still a baby and knows nothing about right teaching. [14]But solid food is for those who are grown up. They are mature enough to know the difference between good and evil.

DO eat a balanced diet.

DO drink lots of water.

DO take multivitamins.

DO pray over meals.

DON'T eat junk food.

DON'T drink too much soda pop.

DON'T skip breakfast.

DON'T eat just before bed.

[6]So let us go on to grown-up teaching. Let us not go back over the beginning lessons we learned about Christ. We should not again start teaching about faith in God and about turning away from those acts that lead to death. [2]We should not return to the teaching about baptisms,[n] about laying on of hands,[n] about the raising of the dead and eternal judgment. [3]And we will go on to grown-up teaching if God allows.

[4]Some people cannot be brought back again to a changed life. They were once in God's light, and enjoyed heaven's gift, and shared in the Holy Spirit. [5]They found out how good God's word is, and they received the powers of his new world. [6]But they fell away from Christ. It is impossible to bring them back to a changed life again, because they are nailing the Son of God to a cross again and are shaming him in front of others.

[7]Some people are like land that gets plenty of rain. The land produces a good crop for those who work it, and it receives God's blessings. [8]Other people are like land that grows thorns and weeds and is worthless. It is about to be cursed by God and will be destroyed by fire.

[9]Dear friends, we are saying this to you, but we really expect better things from you that will lead to your salvation. [10]God is fair; he will not forget the work you did and the love you showed for him by helping his people. And he will remember that you are still helping them. [11]We want each of you to go on with the same hard work all your lives so you will surely get what you hope for. [12]We do not want you to become lazy. Be like those who through faith and patience will receive what God has promised.

[13]God made a promise to Abraham. And as there is no one greater than God, he used himself when he swore to Abraham, [14]saying, "I will surely bless you and give you many descendants."[n] [15]Abraham waited patiently for this to happen, and he received what God promised.

[16]People always use the name of someone greater than themselves when they swear. The oath proves that what they say is true, and this ends all arguing. [17]God wanted to prove that his promise was true to those who would get what he promised. And he wanted them to understand clearly that his purposes never change, so he made an oath. [18]These two things cannot change: God cannot lie when he makes a promise, and he cannot lie when he makes an oath. These things encourage us who came to God for safety. They give us strength

✓ COUNT ON IT

HEBREWS 6:18

Picture a friend who never lies. You might not like it if your mother asked him what you were doing after school and he felt compelled to spill the real story. But you would relish the fact he'd never yank you around. He would never say one thing and mean another. He wouldn't deceive you, either on purpose or by accident. His opinions wouldn't be mistaken, and he would always deal in reality. Well, you don't have to settle for an imaginary friend, because that's exactly how God acts. He is one hundred percent truth. He cannot lie. Truthfulness is so much a part of his character that he is incapable of lying. Because God is absolutely truthful, he deserves your complete trust. Whatever he says, you can depend on it and live it.

to hold on to the hope we have been given. [19]We have this hope as an anchor for the soul, sure and strong. It enters behind the curtain in the Most Holy Place in heaven, [20]where Jesus has gone ahead of us and for us. He has become the high priest forever, a priest like Melchizedek.[n]

6:2 baptisms The word here may refer to Christian baptism, or it may refer to the Jewish ceremonial washings.   6:2 laying on of hands The laying on of hands had many purposes, including the giving of a blessing, power, or authority.   6:14 "I . . . descendants." Quotation from Genesis 22:17.   6:20 Melchizedek A priest and king who lived in the time of Abraham. (Read Genesis 14:17–24.)

Relationships

"Do you know where your fights and arguments come from? They come from the selfish desires that war within you" (James 4:1). Fights and arguments arise when two people start listening to themselves instead of to each other. So, if you find yourself consistently fighting or arguing with your friends or parents or siblings, check your own heart. It's easy to blame the other person in the midst of a disagreement, and sometimes he or she may be partly at fault. But you can't do anything about that person—you can only take care of yourself. Ask God to help you with your issues, and pray for your loved ones, too.

THE PRIEST MELCHIZEDEK

7 Melchizedek[n] was the king of Salem and a priest for God Most High. He met Abraham when Abraham was coming back after defeating the kings. When they met, Melchizedek blessed Abraham, [2]and Abraham gave him a tenth of everything he had brought back from the battle. First, Melchizedek's name means "king of goodness," and he is king of Salem, which means "king of peace." [3]No one knows who Melchizedek's father or mother was,[n] where he came from, when he was born, or when he died. Melchizedek is like the Son of God; he continues being a priest forever.

[4]You can see how great Melchizedek was. Abraham, the great father, gave him a tenth of everything that he won in battle. [5]Now the law says that those in the tribe of Levi who become priests must collect a tenth from the people—their own people—even though the priests and the people are from the family of Abraham. [6]Melchizedek was not from the tribe of Levi, but he collected a tenth from Abraham. And he blessed Abraham, the man who had God's promises. [7]Now everyone knows that the more important person blesses the less important person. [8]Priests receive a tenth, even though they are only men who live and then die. But Melchizedek, who received a tenth from Abraham, continues living, as the Scripture says. [9]We might even say that Levi, who receives a tenth, also paid it when Abraham paid Melchizedek a tenth. [10]Levi was not yet born, but he was in the body of his ancestor when Melchizedek met Abraham.

[11]The people were given the law[n] concerning the system of priests from the tribe of Levi, but they could not be made perfect through that system. So there was a need for another priest to come, a priest like Melchizedek, not Aaron. [12]And when a different kind of priest comes, the law must be changed, too. [13]We are saying these things about Christ, who belonged to a different tribe. No one from that tribe ever served as a priest at the altar. [14]It is clear that our Lord came from the tribe of Judah, and Moses said nothing about priests belonging to that tribe.

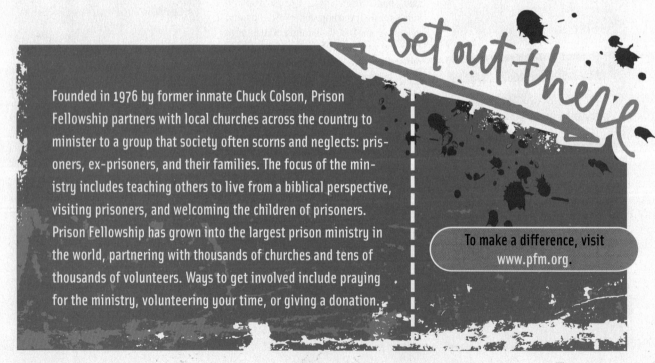

Get out there

Founded in 1976 by former inmate Chuck Colson, Prison Fellowship partners with local churches across the country to minister to a group that society often scorns and neglects: prisoners, ex-prisoners, and their families. The focus of the ministry includes teaching others to live from a biblical perspective, visiting prisoners, and welcoming the children of prisoners. Prison Fellowship has grown into the largest prison ministry in the world, partnering with thousands of churches and tens of thousands of volunteers. Ways to get involved include praying for the ministry, volunteering your time, or giving a donation.

To make a difference, visit www.pfm.org.

 7:1 Melchizedek A priest and king who lived in the time of Abraham. (Read Genesis 14:17–24.) **7:3 No . . . was** Literally, "Melchizedek was without father, without mother, without genealogy." **7:11 The . . . law** This refers to the people of Israel who were given the Law of Moses.

JESUS IS LIKE MELCHIZEDEK

[15]And this becomes even more clear when we see that another priest comes who is like Melchizedek.[n] [16]He was not made a priest by human rules and laws but through the power of his life, which continues forever. [17]It is said about him,

"You are a priest forever,
a priest like Melchizedek." *Psalm 110:4*

[3]Every high priest has the work of offering gifts and sacrifices to God. So our high priest must also offer something to God. [4]If our high priest were now living on earth, he would not be a priest, because there are already priests here who follow the law by offering gifts to God. [5]The work they do as priests is only a copy and a shadow of what is in heaven. This is why God warned Moses when he was ready to

Although teen drivers constitute less than seven percent of all licensed drivers, they are involved in more than 14 percent of fatal motor vehicle-related crashes.
–National Highway Traffic Safety Administration

[18]The old rule is now set aside, because it was weak and useless. [19]The law of Moses could not make anything perfect. But now a better hope has been given to us, and with this hope we can come near to God. [20]It is important that God did this with an oath. Others became priests without an oath, [21]but Christ became a priest with God's oath. God said:

"The Lord has made a promise
and will not change his mind.
'You are a priest forever.'" *Psalm 110:4*

[22]This means that Jesus is the guarantee of a better agreement[n] from God to his people.

[23]When one of the other priests died, he could not continue being a priest. So there were many priests. [24]But because Jesus lives forever, he will never stop serving as priest. [25]So he is able always to save those who come to God through him because he always lives, asking God to help them.

[26]Jesus is the kind of high priest we need. He is holy, sinless, pure, not influenced by sinners, and he is raised above the heavens. [27]He is not like the other priests who had to offer sacrifices every day, first for their own sins, and then for the sins of the people. Christ offered his sacrifice only once and for all time when he offered himself. [28]The law chooses high priests who are people with weaknesses, but the word of God's oath came later than the law. It made God's Son to be the high priest, and that Son has been made perfect forever.

JESUS IS OUR HIGH PRIEST

8 Here is the point of what we are saying: We have a high priest who sits on the right side of God's throne in heaven. [2]Our high priest serves in the Most Holy Place, the true place of worship that was made by God, not by humans.

build the Holy Tent: "Be very careful to make everything by the plan I showed you on the mountain."[n] [6]But the priestly work that has been given to Jesus is much greater than the work that was given to the other priests. In the same way, the new agreement that Jesus brought from God to his people is much greater than the old one. And the new agreement is based on promises of better things.

[7]If there had been nothing wrong with the first agreement,[n] there would have been no need for a second agreement. [8]But God found something wrong with his people. He says:[n]

"Look, the time is coming, says the Lord,
when I will make a new agreement
with the people of Israel
and the people of Judah.
[9]It will not be like the agreement
I made with their ancestors
when I took them by the hand
to bring them out of Egypt.
But they broke that agreement,
and I turned away from them, says the Lord.
[10]This is the agreement I will make
with the people of Israel at that time,
says the Lord.
I will put my teachings in their minds
and write them on their hearts.
I will be their God,
and they will be my people.
[11]People will no longer have to teach their neighbors and relatives
to know the Lord,
because all people will know me,
from the least to the most important.
[12]I will forgive them for the wicked things they did,
and I will not remember their sins anymore." *Jeremiah 31:31–34*

[13]God called this a new agreement, so he has made the first agreement old. And anything that is old and worn out is ready to disappear.

THE OLD AGREEMENT

9 The first agreement[n] had rules for worship and a place on earth for worship. [2]The Holy Tent was set up for this. The first area in the Tent was called the Holy Place. In it were the lamp and the table with the bread that was made holy for God. [3]Behind the second

7:15 Melchizedek A priest and king who lived in the time of Abraham. (Read Genesis 14:17–24.) **7:22 agreement** God gives a contract or agreement to his people. For the Jews, this agreement was the Law of Moses. But now God has given a better agreement to his people through Christ. **8:5 "Be . . . mountain."** Quotation from Exodus 25:40. **8:7; 9:1 first agreement** The contract God gave the Jewish people when he gave them the Law of Moses. **8:8 But . . . says** Some Greek copies read "But God found something wrong and says to his people."

GUARD YOUR HEART

Most guys end up dating girls who are like their moms. So don't be afraid to ask your mom for advice. Since she was your dad's girlfriend, she'll probably be able to give you some good feedback on how to deal with your girlfriend. And your mom will love knowing she can talk to you about it.

curtain was a room called the Most Holy Place. [4]In it was a golden altar for burning incense and the Ark covered with gold that held the old agreement. Inside this Ark was a golden jar of manna, Aaron's rod that once grew leaves, and the stone tablets of the old agreement. [5]Above the Ark were the creatures that showed God's glory, whose wings reached over the lid. But we cannot tell everything about these things now.

[6]When everything in the Tent was made ready in this way, the priests went into the first room every day to worship. [7]But only the high priest could go into the second room, and he did that only once a year. He could never enter the inner room without taking blood with him, which he offered to God for himself and for sins the people did without knowing they did them. [8]The Holy Spirit uses this to show that the way into the Most Holy Place was not open while the system of the old Holy Tent was still being used. [9]This is an example for the present time. It shows that the gifts and sacrifices offered cannot make the conscience of the worshiper perfect. [10]These gifts and sacrifices were only about food and drink and special washings. They were rules for the body, to be followed until the time of God's new way.

THE NEW AGREEMENT

[11]But when Christ came as the high priest of the good things we now have,[n] he entered the greater and more perfect tent. It is not made by humans and does not belong to this world. [12]Christ entered the Most Holy Place only once—and for all time. He did not take with him the blood of goats and calves. His sacrifice was his own blood, and by it he set us free from sin forever. [13]The blood of goats and bulls and the ashes of a cow are sprinkled on the people who are unclean, and this makes their bodies clean again. [14]How much more is done by the blood of Christ. He offered himself through the eternal Spirit[n] as a perfect sacrifice to God. His blood will make our consciences pure from useless acts so we may serve the living God.

[15]For this reason Christ brings a new agreement from God to his people. Those who are called by God can now receive the blessings he has promised, blessings that will last forever. They can have those things because Christ died so that the people who lived under the first agreement could be set free from sin.

[16]When there is a will,[n] it must be proven that the one who wrote that will is dead. [17]A will means nothing while the person is alive; it can be used only after the person dies. [18]This is why even the first agreement could not begin without blood to show death. [19]First, Moses told all the people every command in the law. Next he took the blood of calves and mixed it with water. Then he used red wool and a branch of the hyssop plant to sprinkle it on the book of the law and on all the people. [20]He said, "This is the blood that begins the Agreement that God commanded you to obey."[n] [21]In the same way, Moses sprinkled the blood on

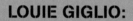

 9:11 good . . . have Some Greek copies read "good things that are to come." 9:14 Spirit This refers to the Holy Spirit, to Christ's own spirit, or to the spiritual and eternal nature of his sacrifice. 9:16 will A legal document that shows how a person's money and property are to be distributed at the time of death. This is the same word in Greek as "agreement" in verse 15. 9:20 "This . . . obey." Quotation from Exodus 24:8.

the Holy Tent and over all the things used in worship. ²²The law says that almost everything must be made clean by blood, and sins cannot be forgiven without blood to show death.

CHRIST'S DEATH TAKES AWAY SINS

²³So the copies of the real things in heaven had to be made clean by animal sacrifices. But the real things in heaven need much better sacrifices. ²⁴Christ did not go into the Most Holy Place made by humans, which is only a copy of the real one. He went into heaven itself and is there now before God to help us. ²⁵The high priest enters the Most Holy Place once every year with blood that is not his own. But Christ did not offer himself many times. ²⁶Then he would have had to suffer many times since the world was made. But Christ came only once and for all time at just the right time to take away all sin by sacrificing himself. ²⁷Just as everyone must die once and then be judged, ²⁸so Christ was offered as a sacrifice one time to take away the sins of many people. And he will come a second time, not to offer himself for sin, but to bring salvation to those who are waiting for him.

10 The law is only an unclear picture of the good things coming in the future; it is not the real thing. The people under the law offer the same sacrifices every year, but these sacrifices can never make perfect those who come near to worship God. ²If the law could make them perfect, the sacrifices would have already stopped. The worshipers would be made clean, and they would no longer have a sense of sin. ³But these sacrifices remind them of their sins every year, ⁴because it is impossible for the blood of bulls and goats to take away sins.

⁵So when Christ came into the world, he said:

"You do not want sacrifices and offerings,
but you have prepared a body for me.
⁶You do not ask for burnt offerings
and offerings to take away sins.
⁷Then I said, 'Look, I have come.
It is written about me in the book.
God, I have come to do what you want.'"

Psalm 40:6–8

⁸In this Scripture he first said, "You do not want sacrifices and offerings. You do not ask for burnt offerings and offerings to take away sins." (These are all sacrifices that the law commands.) ⁹Then he said, "Look, I have come to do what you want." God ends the first system of sacrifices so he can set up the new system. ¹⁰And because of this, we are made holy through the sacrifice Christ made in his body once and for all time.

¹¹Every day the priests stand and do their religious service, often offering the same sacrifices. Those sacrifices can never take away sins. ¹²But after Christ offered one sacrifice for sins, forever, he sat down at the right side of God. ¹³And now Christ waits there for his enemies to be put under his power. ¹⁴With one sacrifice he made perfect forever those who are being made holy.

¹⁵The Holy Spirit also tells us about this. First he says:

¹⁶"This is the agreement*ⁿ* I will make
with them at that time, says the Lord.
I will put my teachings in their hearts
and write them on their minds."

Jeremiah 31:33

¹⁷Then he says:

"Their sins and the evil things they do—
I will not remember anymore."

Jeremiah 31:34

¹⁸Now when these have been forgiven, there is no more need for a sacrifice for sins.

CONTINUE TO TRUST GOD

¹⁹So, brothers and sisters, we are completely free to enter the Most Holy Place without fear because of the blood of Jesus' death. ²⁰We can enter through a new and living way that Jesus opened for us. It leads through the curtain—Christ's body. ²¹And since we have a great priest over God's house, ²²let us come near to God with a sincere heart and a sure faith, because we have been made free from a guilty conscience, and our bodies have been washed with pure water. ²³Let us hold firmly to the hope that we have confessed, because we can trust God to do what he promised.

²⁴Let us think about each other and help each other to show love and do good deeds. ²⁵You should not stay away from the church meetings, as some are doing, but you should meet together and encourage each other. Do this even more as you see the day*ⁿ* coming.

²⁶If we decide to go on sinning after we have learned the truth, there is no longer any sacrifice for sins. ²⁷There is nothing but fear in waiting for the judgment and the terrible fire that will destroy all those who live against God. ²⁸Anyone who refused to obey the law of Moses was found guilty from the proof given by two or three witnesses. He was put to death without mercy. ²⁹So what do you think should be done to those who do not respect the Son of God, who look at the blood of the agreement that made them holy as no different from others' blood, who insult the Spirit of God's grace?

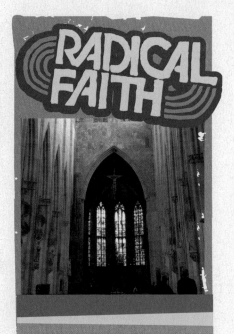

HEBREWS 10:19–22

Back in the Old Testament, there was only one guy who could get close to God's thick presence in the most sacred room of the Temple. Once a year on the Day of Atonement, the high priest of the whole nation carried the blood of a goat into the Most Holy Place, presenting God with an offering for the people's sin. No one else got to get so near God, and on no other day of the year could anyone enter God's holy presence. Jesus, however, opened a new way to God. Because Jesus spilled his blood for you and every believer, you and they can run straight to God. You can get close to him without fear, because Jesus has made you acceptable, forgiven, and scrubbed clean. You can experience a closeness with God that Old Testament believers only dreamed of. When you need help, you can pray to God to get it. When you have troubles, you can give them over to him. You can worship him wildly. And you can simply hang close to the Savior of your life.

10:16 agreement God gives a contract or agreement to his people. For the Jews, this agreement was the Law of Moses. But now God has given a better agreement to his people through Christ.   10:25 day The day Christ will come to judge all people and take his people to live with him.

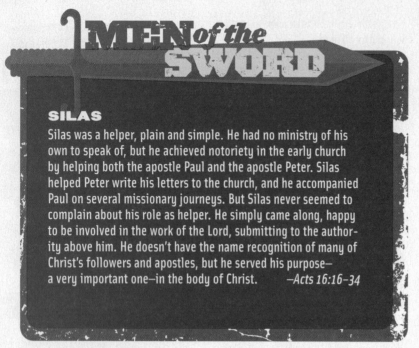

MEN of the SWORD

SILAS

Silas was a helper, plain and simple. He had no ministry of his own to speak of, but he achieved notoriety in the early church by helping both the apostle Paul and the apostle Peter. Silas helped Peter write his letters to the church, and he accompanied Paul on several missionary journeys. But Silas never seemed to complain about his role as helper. He simply came along, happy to be involved in the work of the Lord, submitting to the authority above him. He doesn't have the name recognition of many of Christ's followers and apostles, but he served his purpose— a very important one—in the body of Christ. —*Acts 16:16–34*

Surely they should have a much worse punishment. [30]We know that God said, "I will punish those who do wrong; I will repay them."[n] And he also said, "The Lord will judge his people."[n] [31]It is a terrible thing to fall into the hands of the living God.

[32]Remember those days in the past when you first learned the truth. You had a hard struggle with many sufferings, but you continued strong. [33]Sometimes you were hurt and attacked before crowds of people, and sometimes you shared with those who were being treated that way. [34]You helped the prisoners. You even had joy when all that you owned was taken from you, because you knew you had something better and more lasting.

[35]So do not lose the courage you had in the past, which has a great reward. [36]You must hold on, so you can do what God wants and receive what he has promised. [37]For in a very short time,

"The One who is coming will come
    and will not be delayed.
[38]Those who are right with me
    will live by faith.
But if they turn back with fear,
    I will not be pleased with them."

Habakkuk 2:3–4

[39]But we are not those who turn back and are lost. We are people who have faith and are saved.

WHAT IS FAITH?

11 Faith means being sure of the things we hope for and knowing that something is real even if we do not see it. [2]Faith is the reason we remember great people who lived in the past.

[3]It is by faith we understand that the whole world was made by God's command so what we see was made by something that cannot be seen.

[4]It was by faith that Abel offered God a better sacrifice than Cain did. God said he was pleased with the gifts Abel offered and called Abel a good man because of his faith. Abel died, but through his faith he is still speaking.

[5]It was by faith that Enoch was taken to heaven so he would not die. He could not be found, because God had taken him away. Before he was taken, the Scripture says that he was a man who truly pleased God. [6]Without faith no one can please God. Anyone who comes to God must believe that he is real and that he rewards those who truly want to find him.

[7]It was by faith that Noah heard God's warnings about things he could not yet see. He obeyed God and built a large boat to save his family. By his faith, Noah showed that the world was wrong, and he became one of those who are made right with God through faith.

[8]It was by faith Abraham obeyed God's call to go to another place God promised to give him. He left his own country, not knowing

fight the fight

Hebrews 10:24-25

One survey recently showed 88 percent of young people leave church after graduating from high school. Many reasons were given, such as busy schedules, failing to connect with a new church after going to college, and student uncertainty over whether their parents' faith would become their own. While it is true each person must decide whether to follow Christ, this dropout trend rejects the advice in Hebrews. The writer here told Christians to meet together regularly and to encourage each other. As you will discover in years to come, life can be difficult to manage. You will need the kind of help and spiritual support you can find in church.

10:30 "I . . . them." Quotation from Deuteronomy 32:35. 10:30 "The Lord . . . people." Quotation from Deuteronomy 32:36; Psalm 135:14.

where he was to go. [9]It was by faith that he lived like a foreigner in the country God promised to give him. He lived in tents with Isaac and Jacob, who had received that same promise from God. [10]Abraham was waiting for the city[n] that has real foundations—the city planned and built by God.

[11]He was too old to have children, and Sarah could not have children. It was by faith that Abraham was made able to become a father, because he trusted God to do what he had promised.[n] [12]This man was so old he was almost dead, but from him came as many descendants as there are stars in the sky. Like the sand on the seashore, they could not be counted.

[13]All these great people died in faith. They did not get the things that God promised his people, but they saw them coming far in the future and were glad. They said they were like visitors and strangers on earth. [14]When people say such things, they show they are looking for a country that will be their own. [15]If they had been thinking about the country they had left, they could have gone back. [16]But they were waiting for a better country—a heavenly country. So God is not ashamed to be called their God, because he has prepared a city for them.

[17]It was by faith that Abraham, when God tested him, offered his son Isaac as a sacrifice. God made the promises to Abraham, but Abraham was ready to offer his own son as a sacrifice. [18]God had said, "The descendants I promised you will be from Isaac."[n] [19]Abraham believed that God could raise the dead, and really, it was as if Abraham got Isaac back from death.

[20]It was by faith that Isaac blessed the future of Jacob and Esau. [21]It was by faith that Jacob, as he was dying, blessed each one of Joseph's sons. Then he worshiped as he leaned on the top of his walking stick.

[22]It was by faith that Joseph, while he was dying, spoke about the Israelites leaving Egypt and gave instructions about what to do with his body.

[23]It was by faith that Moses' parents hid him for three months after he was born. They saw that Moses was a beautiful baby, and they were not afraid to disobey the king's order.

[24]It was by faith that Moses, when he grew up, refused to be called the son of the king of Egypt's daughter. [25]He chose to suffer with God's people instead of enjoying sin for a short time. [26]He thought it was better to suffer for the Christ than to have all the treasures of Egypt, because he was looking for God's reward. [27]It was by faith that Moses left Egypt and was not afraid of the king's anger. Moses continued strong as if he could see the God that no one can see. [28]It was by faith that Moses prepared the Passover and spread the blood on the doors so the one who brings death would not kill the firstborn sons of Israel.

[29]It was by faith that the people crossed the Red Sea as if it were dry land. But when the Egyptians tried it, they were drowned.

[30]It was by faith that the walls of Jericho fell after the people had marched around them for seven days.

[31]It was by faith that Rahab, the prostitute, welcomed the spies and was not killed with those who refused to obey God.

[32]Do I need to give more examples? I do not have time to tell you about Gideon, Barak, Samson, Jephthah, David, Samuel, and the prophets. [33]Through their faith they defeated kingdoms. They did what was right, received God's promises, and shut the mouths of lions. [34]They stopped great fires and were saved from being killed with swords. They were weak, and yet were made strong. They were powerful in battle and defeated other armies. [35]Women received their dead relatives raised back to life. Others were tortured and refused to accept their freedom so they could be raised from the dead to a better life. [36]Some were laughed at and beaten. Others were put in chains and thrown into prison. [37]They were stoned to death, they were cut in half,[n] and they were killed with swords. Some wore the skins of sheep and goats. They were poor, abused, and treated badly. [38]The world was not good enough for them! They wandered in deserts and mountains, living in caves and holes in the earth.

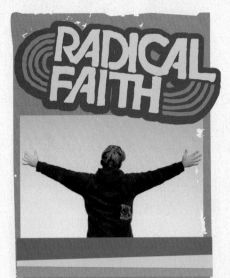

RADICAL FAITH

HEBREWS 11:6

So what exactly is radical faith? This verse says it straight: It starts with believing that God actually exists—and trusting that the one real God will reward you if you truly want to find him. The verse comes at the start of a whole chapter of the Bible that illustrates what radical faith is all about. Faith means being sure of God even if you can't see him (Hebrews 11:1). That's nothing like accepting the existence of God with no evidence. After all, you are surrounded by evidence for him. Like Romans 1:20 says, "There are things about him that people cannot see—his eternal power and all the things that make him God. But since the beginning of the world those things have been easy to understand by what God has made." But radical faith doesn't stop with the mere fact that God is real. It trusts that he is good, so perfect and awesome that he is worth living and dying for, a fact seen in the stories of believers reeled off in this chapter. Read this whole chapter to see what radical faith looks like in real life, and model it.

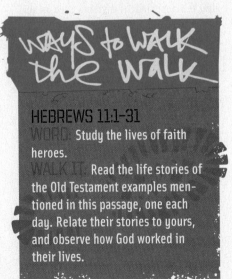

WAYS to WALK the WALK

HEBREWS 11:1–31

WORD: Study the lives of faith heroes.
WALK IT: Read the life stories of the Old Testament examples mentioned in this passage, one each day. Relate their stories to yours, and observe how God worked in their lives.

11:10 city The spiritual "city" where God's people live with him. Also called "the heavenly Jerusalem." (See Hebrews 12:22.) **11:11 It . . . promised.** Some Greek copies refer to Sarah's faith, rather than Abraham's. **11:18 "The descendants . . . Isaac."** Quotation from Genesis 21:12. **11:37 they were cut in half** Some Greek copies also include, "they were tested."

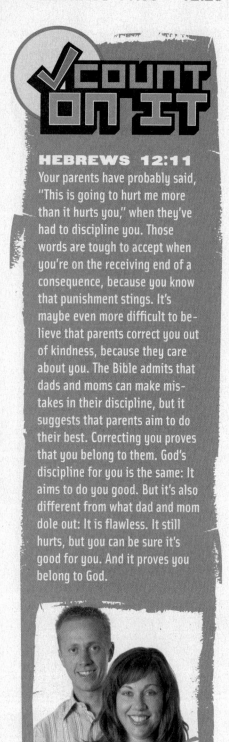

✓ COUNT ON IT

HEBREWS 12:11

Your parents have probably said, "This is going to hurt me more than it hurts you," when they've had to discipline you. Those words are tough to accept when you're on the receiving end of a consequence, because you know that punishment stings. It's maybe even more difficult to believe that parents correct you out of kindness, because they care about you. The Bible admits that dads and moms can make mistakes in their discipline, but it suggests that parents aim to do their best. Correcting you proves that you belong to them. God's discipline for you is the same: It aims to do you good. But it's also different from what dad and mom dole out: It is flawless. It still hurts, but you can be sure it's good for you. And it proves you belong to God.

GUARD YOUR HEART

Guys and girls are as different as night and day, and that's okay. Celebrate those differences. If your girl likes to see plays and watch chick flicks, then swallow your pride and do those things with her once in a while. It might even make her more willing to try playing your extreme sports.

39All these people are known for their faith, but none of them received what God had promised. 40God planned to give us something better so that they would be made perfect, but only together with us.

FOLLOW JESUS' EXAMPLE

12 We are surrounded by a great cloud of people whose lives tell us what faith means. So let us run the race that is before us and never give up. We should remove from our lives anything that would get in the way and the sin that so easily holds us back. 2Let us look only to Jesus, the One who began our faith and who makes it perfect. He suffered death on the cross. But he accepted the shame as if it were nothing because of the joy that God put before him. And now he is sitting at the right side of God's throne. 3Think about Jesus' example. He held on while wicked people were doing evil things to him. So do not get tired and stop trying.

GOD IS LIKE A FATHER

4You are struggling against sin, but your struggles have not yet caused you to be killed. 5You have forgotten the encouraging words that call you his children:

"My child, don't think the Lord's discipline
    is worth nothing,
and don't stop trying when he corrects
    you.
6The Lord disciplines those he loves,
    and he punishes everyone he accepts as
        his child."   *Proverbs 3:11–12*

7So hold on through your sufferings, because they are like a father's discipline. God is treating you as children. All children are disciplined by their fathers. 8If you are never disciplined (and every child must be disciplined), you are not true children. 9We have all had fathers here on earth who disciplined us, and we respected them. So it is even more important that we accept discipline from the Father of our spirits so we will have life. 10Our fathers on earth disciplined us for a short time in the way they thought was best. But God disciplines us to help us, so we can become holy as he is. 11We do not enjoy being disciplined. It is painful at the time, but later, after we have learned from it, we have peace, because we start living in the right way.

BE CAREFUL HOW YOU LIVE

12You have become weak, so make yourselves strong again. 13Keep on the right path, so the weak will not stumble but rather be strengthened.

14Try to live in peace with all people, and try to live free from sin. Anyone whose life is not holy will never see the Lord. 15Be careful that no one fails to receive God's grace and begins to cause trouble among you. A person like that can ruin many of you. 16Be careful that no one takes part in sexual sin or is like Esau and never thinks about God. As the oldest son, Esau would have received everything from his father, but he sold all that for a single meal. 17You remember that after Esau did this, he wanted to get his father's blessing, but his father refused. Esau could find no way to change what he had done, even though he wanted the blessing so much that he cried.

18You have not come to a mountain that can be touched and that is burning with fire. You have not come to darkness, sadness, and storms. 19You have not come to the noise of a trumpet or to the sound of a voice like the one the people of Israel heard and begged not to hear another word. 20They did not want to hear the command: "If anything, even an animal, touches the mountain, it must be put to death with stones."[n] 21What they saw was so terrible that Moses said, "I am shaking with fear."[n]

22But you have come to Mount Zion,[n] to the city of the living God, the heavenly Jerusalem. You have come to thousands of angels gathered together with joy. 23You have come to the meeting of God's firstborn[n] children whose names are written in heaven. You have come to God, the judge of all people, and to the spirits of good people who have been made perfect. 24You have come to Jesus, the One who brought the new agreement from God to his people, and you have come to the sprinkled blood[n] that has a better message than the blood of Abel.[n]

25So be careful and do not refuse to listen

 12:20 **"If . . . stones."** Quotation from Exodus 19:12–13.   12:21 **"I . . . fear."** Quotation from Deuteronomy 9:19.   12:22 **Mount Zion** Another name for Jerusalem, here meaning the spiritual city of God's people.   12:23 **firstborn** The first son born in a Jewish family was given the most important place in the family and received special blessings. All of God's children are like that.   12:24 **sprinkled blood** The blood of Jesus' death.   12:24 **Abel** The son of Adam and Eve, who was killed by his brother Cain (Genesis 4:8).

when God speaks. Others refused to listen to him when he warned them on earth, and they did not escape. So it will be worse for us if we refuse to listen to God who warns us from heaven. [26]When he spoke before, his voice shook the earth, but now he has promised, "Once again I will shake not only the earth but also the heavens."[n] [27]The words "once again" clearly show us that everything that was made—things that can be shaken—will be destroyed. Only the things that cannot be shaken will remain.

[28]So let us be thankful, because we have a kingdom that cannot be shaken. We should worship God in a way that pleases him with respect and fear, [29]because our God is like a fire that burns things up.

13 Keep on loving each other as brothers and sisters. [2]Remember to welcome strangers, because some who have done this have welcomed angels without knowing it. [3]Remember those who are in prison as if you were in prison with them. Remember those who are suffering as if you were suffering with them.

[4]Marriage should be honored by everyone, and husband and wife should keep their marriage pure. God will judge as guilty those who take part in sexual sins. [5]Keep your lives free from the love of money, and be satisfied with what you have. God has said,

"I will never leave you;
I will never abandon you."

Deuteronomy 31:6

[6]So we can be sure when we say,

"I will not be afraid, because the Lord is my
helper.
People can't do anything to me."

Psalm 118:6

[7]Remember your leaders who taught God's message to you. Remember how they lived and died, and copy their faith. [8]Jesus Christ is the same yesterday, today, and forever.

[9]Do not let all kinds of strange teachings lead you into the wrong way. Your hearts should be strengthened by God's grace, not by obeying rules about foods, which do not help those who obey them.

[10]We have a sacrifice, but the priests who serve in the Holy Tent cannot eat from it. [11]The high priest carries the blood of animals into the Most Holy Place where he offers this blood for sins. But the bodies of the animals are burned outside the camp. [12]So Jesus also suffered outside the city to make his people holy with his own blood. [13]So let us go to Jesus outside the camp, holding on as he did when we are abused.

[14]Here on earth we do not have a city that lasts forever, but we are looking for the city that we will have in the future. [15]So through

Jesus let us always offer to God our sacrifice of praise, coming from lips that speak his name. [16]Do not forget to do good to others, and share with them, because such sacrifices please God.

[17]Obey your leaders and act under their authority. They are watching over you, because

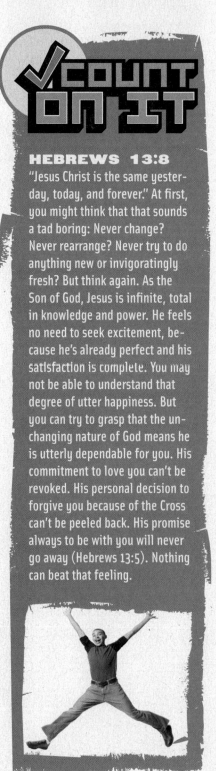

COUNT ON IT

HEBREWS 13:8

"Jesus Christ is the same yesterday, today, and forever." At first, you might think that that sounds a tad boring: Never change? Never rearrange? Never try to do anything new or invigoratingly fresh? But think again. As the Son of God, Jesus is infinite, total in knowledge and power. He feels no need to seek excitement, because he's already perfect and his satisfaction is complete. You may not be able to understand that degree of utter happiness. But you can try to grasp that the unchanging nature of God means he is utterly dependable for you. His commitment to love you can't be revoked. His personal decision to forgive you because of the Cross can't be peeled back. His promise always to be with you will never go away (Hebrews 13:5). Nothing can beat that feeling.

Extras:

How to Get People to Read Your Blog

Thanks to Weblogs, or blogs for short, you can post your innermost thoughts (or random musings) for anyone to read. But online availability doesn't equal eyeballs in front of the screen, so how do you get people to read what you've written? First, write things people want to read. It doesn't have to be generic—you can write for a specific audience—but it does need to be coherent and worth someone's time. Also, link to as many sources as possible, such as other blogs, pages you find interesting, etc. Chances are, they'll link back to you. And it doesn't hurt to advertise. Tell everyone you know about your blog, and make up some inexpensive cards with your Web address. Hopefully, you'll be able to get some valuable word-of-mouth advertising and create a buzz. There's power in numbers—just as in prayer. Don't shoulder your prayer burdens alone. Instead, get a few trusted friends to agree with you in prayer.

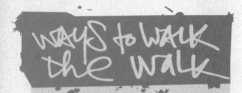

HEBREWS 13:1-2

WORD: Remember to welcome strangers.

WALK IT: Welcome the new kids in school. Introduce yourself to them. You may not wind up being best friends, but you'll at least be sharing the love of Christ with them.

they are responsible for your souls. Obey them so that they will do this work with joy, not sadness. It will not help you to make their work hard.

[18]Pray for us. We are sure that we have a clear conscience, because we always want to do the right thing. [19]I especially beg you to pray so that God will send me back to you soon.

[20-21]I pray that the God of peace will give you every good thing you need so you can do what he wants. God raised from the dead our Lord Jesus, the Great Shepherd of the sheep, because of the blood of his death. His blood began the eternal agreement that God made with his people. I pray that God will do in us what pleases him, through Jesus Christ, and to him be glory forever and ever. Amen.

[22]My brothers and sisters, I beg you to listen patiently to this message I have written to encourage you, because it is not very long. [23]I want you to know that our brother Timothy has been let out of prison. If he arrives soon, we will both come to see you.

[24]Greet all your leaders and all of God's people. Those from Italy send greetings to you.

[25]Grace be with you all.

*** notes

JA
ME
S

DIRECTIONS
FOR
LIFE

Several years ago, when computers had no hard drives, software came with a manual. Now, all the CDs and DVDs contain help menus and links to the company's Web site. But the idea is the same: We need instructions on how to use the programs on our computers. Think of the Book of James as a practical, how-to manual for life.

In just five chapters the half brother of Jesus spells out numerous directions for living. He emphasizes that Christ's followers live with integrity. They don't say one thing and then do something else. They also are moved to action. Not because they're trying to earn "bonus points" from God, but because their faith inspires them to do so.

If you want to live as an authentic follower of Christ, you can learn how to do so from this book. It shows how to quit giving in to temptation and trying to blame it on God. It also gives instructions on loving all types of people instead of just flattering the rich and famous in hopes of getting something in return. And it demonstrates the awesome power of prayer. James is a simple set of guidelines that will yield rich dividends if we follow them.

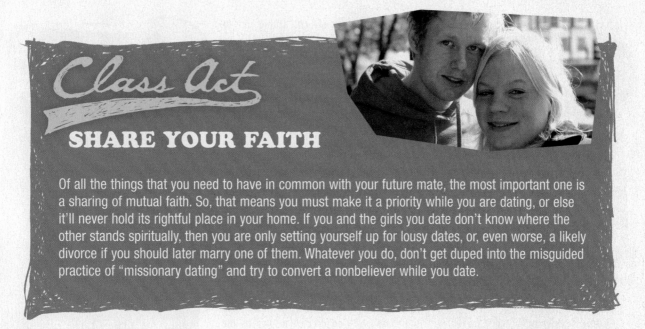

Class Act

SHARE YOUR FAITH

Of all the things that you need to have in common with your future mate, the most important one is a sharing of mutual faith. So, that means you must make it a priority while you are dating, or else it'll never hold its rightful place in your home. If you and the girls you date don't know where the other stands spiritually, then you are only setting yourself up for lousy dates, or, even worse, a likely divorce if you should later marry one of them. Whatever you do, don't get duped into the misguided practice of "missionary dating" and try to convert a nonbeliever while you date.

1 From James, a servant of God and of the Lord Jesus Christ.

To all of God's people who are scattered everywhere in the world:

Greetings.

FAITH AND WISDOM

2 My brothers and sisters, when you have many kinds of troubles, you should be full of joy, 3 because you know that these troubles test your faith, and this will give you patience. 4 Let your patience show itself perfectly in what you do. Then you will be perfect and complete and will have everything you need. 5 But if any of you needs wisdom, you should ask God for it. He is generous to everyone and will give you wisdom without criticizing you. 6 But when you ask God, you must believe and not doubt. Anyone who doubts is like a wave in the sea, blown up and down by the wind. 7-8 Such doubters are thinking two different things at the same time, and they cannot decide about anything they do. They should not think they will receive anything from the Lord.

TRUE RICHES

9 Believers who are poor should take pride that God has made them spiritually rich. 10 Those who are rich should take pride that God has shown them that they are spiritually poor. The rich will die like a wild flower in the grass. 11 The sun rises with burning heat and dries up the plants. The flower falls off, and its beauty is gone. In the same way the rich

Get out there

Each year, 3 million child abuse reports are filed, an average of one every 10 seconds. And what's more, the incidence of abuse is estimated to be three times greater than the number reported. Abuse can take many forms, whether physical, sexual, emotional, or abuse through neglect. Childhelp USA seeks to help children in crisis by maintaining a national abuse hotline (800-4-A-CHILD), working to prevent abuse, and sponsoring the annual National Day of Hope to raise public awareness. The organization relies upon individuals, corporations, and foundations to provide donations of time, products, services, and money.

For more details, visit
www.childhelpusa.org.

RADICAL FAITH

JAMES 1:22-24

Clearly, being a fool in the Bible is uncool. Fools think to themselves, "There is no God" (Psalm 53:1). Foolish people ignore and disobey God's words, constructing their lives on the equivalent of shifting sand. The Book of James spills yet another dumb thing fools do: They think that merely listening to God's instructions is as good as carrying out his commands. Those who hear the Bible's teaching but do nothing about it are like crazy people who study their faces in a mirror but forget what they look like moments after they walk away. So God's goal is for you both to listen and obey. You know that hearing your dad tell you to take out the trash isn't the same thing as getting the garbage to the curb. Listening to a teacher give an assignment doesn't count for anything; only handing in your homework does. Thus, don't deceive yourself into thinking that showing up at church or even cracking open your Bible is all that matters. Those are huge first steps. But the next step is to act on what you know.

will die while they are still taking care of business.

TEMPTATION IS NOT FROM GOD

[12]When people are tempted and still continue strong, they should be happy. After they have proved their faith, God will reward them with life forever. God promised this to all those who love him. [13]When people are tempted, they should not say, "God is tempting me." Evil cannot tempt God, and God himself does not tempt anyone. [14]But people are tempted when their own evil desire leads them away and traps them. [15]This desire leads to sin, and then the sin grows and brings death.

[16]My dear brothers and sisters, do not be fooled about this. [17]Every good action and every perfect gift is from God. These good gifts come down from the Creator of the sun, moon, and stars, who does not change like their shifting shadows. [18]God decided to give us life through the word of truth so we might be the most important of all the things he made.

LISTENING AND OBEYING

[19]My dear brothers and sisters, always be willing to listen and slow to speak. Do not become angry easily, [20]because anger will not help you live the right kind of life God wants. [21]So put out of your life every evil thing and every kind of wrong. Then in gentleness accept God's teaching that is planted in your hearts, which can save you.

[22]Do what God's teaching says; when you only listen and do nothing, you are fooling yourselves. [23]Those who hear God's teaching and do nothing are like people who look at themselves in a mirror. [24]They see their faces and then go away and quickly forget what they looked like. [25]But the truly happy people are those who carefully study God's perfect law that makes people free, and they continue to study it. They do not forget what they heard, but they obey what God's teaching says. Those who do this will be made happy.

THE TRUE WAY TO WORSHIP GOD

[26]People who think they are religious but say things they should not say are just fooling themselves. Their "religion" is worth nothing. [27]Religion that God accepts as pure and without fault is this: caring for orphans or widows who need help, and keeping yourself free from the world's evil influence.

LOVE ALL PEOPLE

2 My dear brothers and sisters, as believers in our glorious Lord Jesus Christ,

COUNT ON IT

JAMES 1:2-4

You can pump iron and still not get the girl. You can study until your brain hurts and still not ace the test. You can do everything right at work and still miss out on a pay raise. But the trials you suffer can improve your patience if you allow them to. Life's difficulties alone don't benefit you. But God working within you during tough times helps you to grow (Romans 8:28). When you see troubles ahead, steer clear if you can. But if you can't, rest in God. As you trust God, he will teach and strengthen you, perfecting your trust in him. You will walk out on the far side of the trial as a more patient and mature believer. So hang on to this promise: Trials will perfect your faith if you maintain a good attitude.

never think some people are more important than others. [2]Suppose someone comes into your church meeting wearing nice clothes and a gold ring. At the same time a poor person comes in wearing old, dirty clothes. [3]You show special attention to the one wearing nice clothes and say, "Please, sit here in this good seat." But you say to the poor person, "Stand over there," or, "Sit on the floor by my feet." [4]What are you

ISSUES

TOBACCO

DESPITE ALL THE WARNING LABELS AND CAUTIONARY ADVERTISEMENTS, SOME TEENAGERS CONTINUE TO TURN TO TOBACCO IN A TWISTED ATTEMPT TO LOOK COOL. The only thing more tragic than that is the number of teens getting addicted to the habit, many for the rest of what likely will become much-abbreviated lives. What your so-called friends who want you to smoke won't tell you is the highly addictive nature of nicotine, the ingredient in tobacco that makes it so difficult to quit. Play it smart and realize that NOT smoking is the coolest move you could make. Not only will you live healthier and longer, but you'll actually be able to breathe.

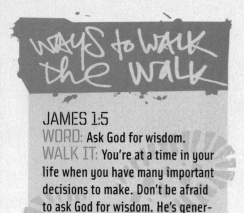

ways to WALK the WALK

JAMES 1:5

WORD: Ask God for wisdom.

WALK IT: You're at a time in your life when you have many important decisions to make. Don't be afraid to ask God for wisdom. He's generous and loving and will give you wisdom without criticizing your questions.

doing? You are making some people more important than others, and with evil thoughts you are deciding that one person is better.

⁵Listen, my dear brothers and sisters! God

Do's AND Don'ts

DO wash your own clothes.

DO separate lights and darks.

DO bleach white clothes.

DO clean the lint filter.

DON'T overload the washer.

DON'T leave clothes in the dryer.

DON'T forget to use fabric softener.

DON'T use too much detergent.

chose the poor in the world to be rich with faith and to receive the kingdom God promised to those who love him. ⁶But you show no respect to the poor. The rich are always trying to control your lives. They are the ones who take you to court. ⁷And they are the ones who speak against Jesus, who owns you.

⁸This royal law is found in the Scriptures: "Love your neighbor as you love yourself."ⁿ If you obey this law, you are doing right. ⁹But if you treat one person as being more important than another, you are sinning. You are guilty of breaking God's law. ¹⁰A person who follows all of God's law but fails to obey even one command is guilty of breaking all the commands in that law. ¹¹The same God who said, "You must not be guilty of adultery,"ⁿ also said, "You must not murder anyone."ⁿ So if you do not take part in adultery but you murder someone, you are guilty of breaking all of God's law. ¹²In everything you say and do, remember that you will be judged by the law that makes people free. ¹³So you must show mercy to others, or God will not show mercy to you when he judges you. But the person who shows mercy can stand without fear at the judgment.

FAITH AND GOOD WORKS

¹⁴My brothers and sisters, if people say they have faith, but do nothing, their faith is worth nothing. Can faith like that save them? ¹⁵A brother or sister in Christ might need clothes or food. ¹⁶If you say to that person, "God be with you! I hope you stay warm and get plenty to eat," but you do not give what that person needs, your words are worth nothing. ¹⁷In the same way, faith by itself—that does nothing—is dead.

¹⁸Someone might say, "You have faith, but I have deeds." Show me your faith without doing anything, and I will show you my faith by what I do. ¹⁹You believe there is one God. Good! But the demons believe that, too, and they tremble with fear.

²⁰You foolish person! Must you be shown that faith that does nothing is worth nothing? ²¹Abraham, our ancestor, was made right with God by what he did when he offered his son Isaac on the altar. ²²So you see that Abraham's faith and the things he did worked together. His faith was made perfect by what he did. ²³This shows the full meaning of the Scripture that says: "Abraham believed God, and God accepted Abraham's faith, and that faith made him right with God."ⁿ And Abraham was called God's friend.ⁿ ²⁴So you see that people are made right with God by what they do, not by faith only.

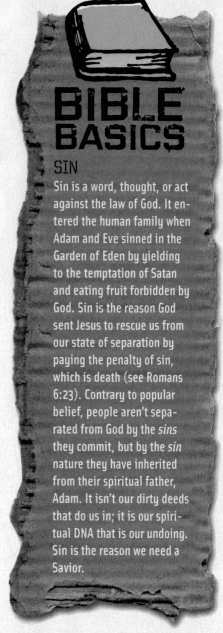

BIBLE BASICS

SIN

Sin is a word, thought, or act against the law of God. It entered the human family when Adam and Eve sinned in the Garden of Eden by yielding to the temptation of Satan and eating fruit forbidden by God. Sin is the reason God sent Jesus to rescue us from our state of separation by paying the penalty of sin, which is death (see Romans 6:23). Contrary to popular belief, people aren't separated from God by the *sins* they commit, but by the *sin* nature they have inherited from their spiritual father, Adam. It isn't our dirty deeds that do us in; it is our spiritual DNA that is our undoing. Sin is the reason we need a Savior.

²⁵Another example is Rahab, a prostitute, who was made right with God by something she did. She welcomed the spies into her home and helped them escape by a different road.

²⁶Just as a person's body that does not have a spirit is dead, so faith that does nothing is dead!

CONTROLLING THE THINGS WE SAY

3 My brothers and sisters, not many of you should become teachers, because you know that we who teach will be judged more strictly. ²We all make many mistakes. If people never said anything wrong, they would be perfect and able to control their entire

november

NATIONAL HUNGER AWARENESS MONTH

"Let God be as original with other people as he is with you
-OSWALD CHAMBERS

1 Ask God to give you wisdom throughout this month.	**2**	**3**	**4** Pray for the pastors of your church.
5 Fast today and pray for an end to world hunger.	**6**	**7** Billy Graham's birthday is today.	**8** Start thinking about Christmas shopping.
9	**10**	**11** It's Veteran's Day. Thank a veteran for his or her sacrifice.	**12**
13	**14** Joy Williams gets a year older today.	**15** Schedule a visit to the family doctor.	**16**
17	**18** Give thanks to God for our leaders.	**19**	**20** Plan a big flag-football game with your friends on the day after Thanksgiving.
21 Steven Curtis Chapman's birthday is today.	**22** Make a list of all that you are thankful for.	**23**	**24**
25 Singer Amy Grant turns another year older today.	**26**	**27**	**28** Read the Book of Hebrews.
29	**30** Praise God for his goodness.		

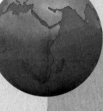

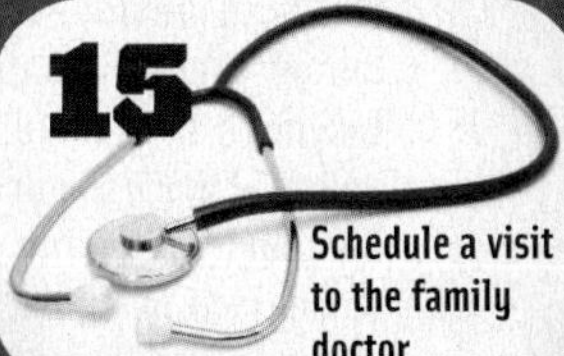

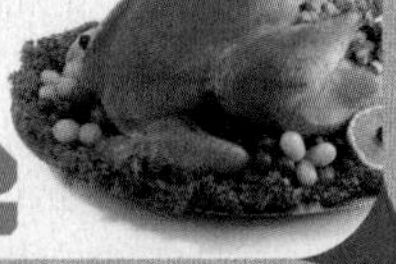

JAMES 3:2–9

The Bible doesn't accuse all guys of being pyromaniacs, but it comes sort of close. The apostle James says that the human tongue is like a fire and a blazing beast at that. Your mouth's superheated words start with a spark from hell, which, in turn, ignites an inferno that roasts all of life. The tongue is like a tiny lighter with the potential to kindle gigantic forest fires. Of course, your tongue can do good, uttering uplifting words like praises to God. But, it's way too easy to zig-zag from telling God you think he's awesome to torching your neighbor with your verbal flamethrower. You might think you can tame your tongue, but that's a job so difficult that if you can do it, you are, indeed, the boss of your whole body, as well. If you want to obey God with your tongue, you need more than a sock stuffed in your mouth. Ask God for his help in changing the thoughts and feelings of your heart, because that's the spot where all of your words actually start (Matthew 12:34).

selves, too. [3] When we put bits into the mouths of horses to make them obey us, we can control their whole bodies. [4] Also a ship is very big, and it is pushed by strong winds. But a very small rudder controls that big ship, making it go wherever the pilot wants. [5] It is the same with the tongue. It is a small part of the body, but it brags about great things.

A big forest fire can be started with only a little flame. [6] And the tongue is like a fire. It is a whole world of evil among the parts of our bodies. The tongue spreads its evil through the whole body. The tongue is set on fire by hell, and it starts a fire that influences all of life. [7] People can tame every kind of wild animal, bird, reptile, and fish, and they have tamed them, [8] but no one can tame the tongue. It is wild and evil and full of deadly poison. [9] We use our tongues to praise our Lord and Father, but then we curse people, whom God made like himself. [10] Praises and curses come from the same mouth! My brothers and sisters, this should not happen. [11] Do good and bad water flow from the same spring? [12] My brothers and sisters, can a fig tree make olives, or can a grapevine make figs? No! And a well full of salty water cannot give good water.

TRUE WISDOM

[13] Are there those among you who are truly wise and understanding? Then they should show it by living right and doing good things with a gentleness that comes from wisdom. [14] But if you are selfish and have bitter jealousy in your hearts, do not brag. Your bragging is a lie that hides the truth. [15] That kind of "wisdom" does not come from God but from the world. It is not spiritual; it is from the devil. [16] Where jealousy and selfishness are, there will be confusion and every kind of evil. [17] But the wisdom that comes from God is first of all pure, then peaceful, gentle, and easy to please. This wisdom is always ready to help those who are troubled and to do good for others. It is always fair and honest. [18] People who work for peace in a peaceful way plant a good crop of right-living.

GIVE YOURSELVES TO GOD

4 Do you know where your fights and arguments come from? They come from the selfish desires that war within you. [2] You want things, but you do not have them. So you are ready to kill and are jealous of other people, but you still cannot get what you want. So you argue and fight. You do not get what you want, because you do not ask God. [3] Or when you ask, you do not receive because the reason you ask is wrong. You want things so you can use them for your own pleasures.

[4] So, you are not loyal to God! You should know that loving the world is the same as hating God. Anyone who wants to be a friend of the world becomes God's enemy. [5] Do you think the Scripture means nothing that says, "The Spirit that God made to live in us wants us for himself alone"?[n] [6] But God gives us even more grace, as the Scripture says,

"God is against the proud,
    but he gives grace to the humble."

Proverbs 3:34

[7] So give yourselves completely to God. Stand against the devil, and the devil will run

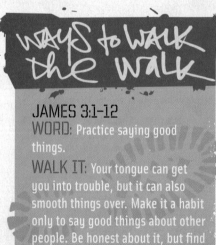

JAMES 3:1-12
WORD: Practice saying good things.
WALK IT: Your tongue can get you into trouble, but it can also smooth things over. Make it a habit only to say good things about other people. Be honest about it, but find something good to say.

4:5 "The Spirit . . . alone." These words may be from Exodus 20:5.

from you. [8]Come near to God, and God will come near to you. You sinners, clean sin out of your lives. You who are trying to follow God and the world at the same time, make your thinking pure. [9]Be sad, cry, and weep! Change your laughter into crying and your joy into sadness. [10]Humble yourself in the Lord's presence, and he will honor you.

YOU ARE NOT THE JUDGE

[11]Brothers and sisters, do not tell evil lies about each other. If you speak against your fellow believers or judge them, you are judging and speaking against the law they follow. And when you are judging the law, you are no longer a follower of the law. You have become a judge. [12]God is the only Lawmaker and Judge. He is the only One who can save and destroy. So it is not right for you to judge your neighbor.

LET GOD PLAN YOUR LIFE

[13]Some of you say, "Today or tomorrow we will go to some city. We will stay there a year, do business, and make money." [14]But you do not know what will happen tomorrow! Your life is like a mist. You can see it for a short time, but then it goes away. [15]So you should say, "If the Lord wants, we will live and do this or that." [16]But now you are proud and you brag. All of this bragging is wrong. [17]Anyone who knows the right thing to do, but does not do it, is sinning.

A WARNING TO THE RICH

5 You rich people, listen! Cry and be very sad because of the troubles that are coming to you. [2]Your riches have rotted, and your clothes have been eaten by moths. [3]Your gold and silver have rusted, and that rust will be a proof that you were wrong. It will eat your bodies like fire. You saved your treasure for the last days. [4]The pay you did not give the workers who mowed your fields cries out against you, and the cries of the workers have been heard by the Lord All-Powerful. [5]Your life on earth was full of rich living and pleasing yourselves with everything you wanted. You made yourselves fat, like an animal ready to be killed. [6]You have judged guilty and then murdered innocent people, who were not against you.

BE PATIENT

[7]Brothers and sisters, be patient until the Lord comes again. A farmer patiently waits for his valuable crop to grow from the earth and for it to receive the autumn and spring rains. [8]You, too, must be patient. Do not give up hope, because the Lord is coming soon. [9]Brothers and sisters, do not complain against each other or you will be judged guilty. And the Judge is ready to come! [10]Brothers and sisters, follow the example of the prophets who spoke for the Lord. They suffered many hard things, but they were patient. [11]We say they are happy because they did not give up. You have heard about Job's patience, and you know the Lord's purpose for him in the end. You know the Lord is full of mercy and is kind.

BE CAREFUL WHAT YOU SAY

[12]My brothers and sisters, above all, do not use an oath when you make a promise. Don't use the name of heaven, earth, or anything else to prove what you say. When you mean yes, say only yes, and when you mean no, say only no so you will not be judged guilty.

TOP 10 TEN

random qualities of friendship

1. Lending a listening ear.
2. Spending time with each other.
3. Speaking the truth in love.
4. Giving each other space.
5. Learning to forgive offenses.
6. Praying for each other.
7. Holding each other accountable.
8. Being there for each other.
9. Challenging each other to grow.
10. Defending each other to outsiders.

fight the fight

James 3:5-8

Whether it's a relatively unknown event, like who asked who to the prom, or as highly publicized as a Hollywood star's marriage breaking up, people love to gossip. Church members are often guilty of it, under the guise of sharing prayer requests. Yet, James warns against this habit. He compares the damage done by our tongues to a forest fire started by a small flame. The next time you are tempted to pass along a story about someone, ask yourself whether it is flattering or damaging to that person's reputation. Most of the time, it's the latter. If so, stop the tale in its tracks and don't repeat it.

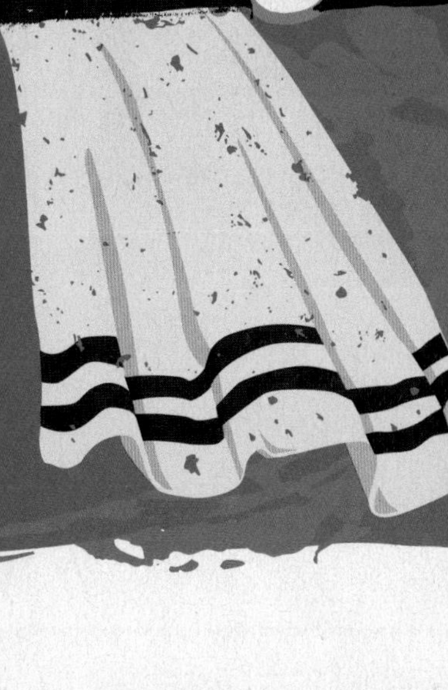

311

COUNT ON IT

JAMES 4:7

While pop culture pictures Satan as a guy with horns and a pitchfork, the Bible reveals him as he truly is. He is a spirit being, a fallen angel who rebelled against God and was tossed from heaven (Luke 10:18). He seeks to destroy believers, including you, but he will spend eternity in hell for his dastardly deeds. In your own strength, you don't stand a chance against the devil, but Jesus defeated Satan at the cross for you (Colossians 2:15). You make that victory real in your own life when you do exactly what this verse says. You start by submitting to God, trusting his great heart toward you and choosing to obey his commands completely. Then you say "no" to whatever evil Satan offers you. And the result is that Satan will bolt like lightning.

THE POWER OF PRAYER

¹³Anyone who is having troubles should pray. Anyone who is happy should sing praises. ¹⁴Anyone who is sick should call the church's elders. They should pray for and pour oil on the person[n] in the name of the Lord. ¹⁵And the prayer that is said with faith will make the sick person well; the Lord will heal that person. And if the person has sinned, the sins will be forgiven. ¹⁶Confess your sins to each other and pray for each other so God can heal you. When a believing person prays, great things happen. ¹⁷Elijah was a human being just like us. He prayed that it would not rain, and it did not rain on the land for three and a half years! ¹⁸Then Elijah prayed again, and the rain came down from the sky, and the land produced crops again.

SAVING A SOUL

¹⁹My brothers and sisters, if one of you wanders away from the truth, and someone helps that person come back, ²⁰remember this: Anyone who brings a sinner back from the wrong way will save that sinner's soul from death and will cause many sins to be forgiven.

✱ 5:14 pour oil on the person Oil was used in the name of the Lord as a sign that the person was now set apart for God's special attention and care.

*** notes

¹PETER

WORDS OF ENCOURAGEMENT

If you've ever blown a test and wished for a make-up exam or dropped mustard on your shirt while trying to impress a girl, you can relate to Peter. Except his mistake was one of historical proportions. The good news is that although Peter denied knowing Christ before the Crucifixion, God turned to him when the first-century church needed encouragement.

As a result of God's belief in him, Peter grew from a reckless follower of Christ into a rock-solid example of faith. Scholars say this letter may have been addressed to converts Peter led to Christ as a missionary. No matter who read it, though, they received encouragement to stand fast despite persecution.

Peter starts by reminding his readers they have a living hope in Jesus, which brings blessings no matter how bad conditions seem. He encourages them to accept Christ and follow his example, living lives of obedience that may include suffering for doing the right thing. The apostle also reminds readers they should treat each other with decency and respect while using their gifts to serve each other. The lesson to be learned from the life of Peter is that God never gives up on us, no matter how we might miss fulfilling his plan for us.

From Peter, an apostle of Jesus Christ. To God's chosen people who are away from their homes and are scattered all around Pontus, Galatia, Cappadocia, Asia, and Bithynia. [2]God planned long ago to choose you by making you his holy people, which is the Spirit's work. God wanted you to obey him and to be made clean by the blood of the death of Jesus Christ.

Grace and peace be yours more and more.

WE HAVE A LIVING HOPE

[3]Praise be to the God and Father of our Lord Jesus Christ. In God's great mercy he has caused us to be born again into a living hope, because Jesus Christ rose from the dead. [4]Now we hope for the blessings God has for his children. These blessings, which cannot be destroyed or be spoiled or lose their beauty, are kept in heaven for you. [5]God's power protects you through your faith until salvation is shown to you at the end of time. [6]This makes you very happy, even though now for a short time different kinds of troubles may make you sad. [7]These troubles come to prove that your faith is pure. This purity of faith is worth more than gold, which can be proved to be pure by fire but will ruin. But the purity of your faith will bring you praise and glory and honor

when Jesus Christ is shown to you. [8]You have not seen Christ, but still you love him. You cannot see him now, but you believe in him. So you are filled with a joy that cannot be explained, a joy full of glory. [9]And you are receiving the goal of your faith—the salvation of your souls.

Relationships

"Confess your sins to each other and pray for each other so God can heal you" (James 5:16a). God never intended for you to stumble along on your faith journey by yourself. He wants you to have real, honest relationships with other people; people who can help you in your faith walk, and whom you can help, also. Face the facts, friend: you're going to miss it from time to time, just like everyone else. The way to handle it is to share your shortcomings with someone you have a strong relationship with. This can be humbling, but it's healthy, too.

*REVIEWS MOVIES

MADAGASCAR

A few zoo animals learn a hard lesson about what life is like in the wild in this computer-generated cartoon. The writing is sleek, funny, and VERY entertaining. More movies should be this clean. In the same way *Finding Nemo* and *The Incredibles* use a great story with good writing to capture the imaginations of kids of all ages, *Madagascar* is the perfect flick to watch when you're simply wanting some uplifting entertainment. The voices of the animals are enthusiastically recorded by some of Hollywood's most famous actors. Although the main characters are great, it's the penguins that steal the show.

WHY IT ROCKS:

THE GOOD CLEAN FUN HAS REDEEMING VALUE.

RADICAL FAITH

1 PETER 1:14–21

Put it at the top of your to-do list: God says you have to be holy just like he is. No, authentic holiness doesn't mean you put on a monk's robe and head off to the monastery. The word "holy" simply means "set apart" or "separate." To be holy means you live so totally devoted to God that you completely cut yourself off from sin. You ditch what you used to do when you didn't understand God. Because you are growing in obedience to God, your mind makes an inner decision that you no longer want anything to do with rebellion against your Lord. You dedicate yourself to staying close to Jesus, obeying him not only in small ways, but in everything you do or don't do. Holiness doesn't happen overnight. It's a process that starts now and continues until heaven. Your motivation comes from realizing what Jesus did to bust you loose from sin. He bought you with his blood, so he deserves all of the honor you can give him. And, with his help, you can live a holy life.

[10]The prophets searched carefully and tried to learn about this salvation. They prophesied about the grace that was coming to you. [11]The Spirit of Christ was in the prophets, telling in advance about the sufferings of Christ and about the glory that would follow those sufferings. The prophets tried to learn about what the Spirit was showing them, when those things would happen, and what the world would be like at that time. [12]It was shown them that their service was not for themselves but for you, when they told about the truths you have now heard. Those who preached the Good News to you told you those things with the help of the Holy Spirit who was sent from heaven—things into which angels desire to look.

A CALL TO HOLY LIVING

[13]So prepare your minds for service and have self-control. All your hope should be for the gift of grace that will be yours when Jesus Christ is shown to you. [14]Now that you are obedient children of God do not live as you did in the past. You did not understand, so you did the evil things you wanted. [15]But be holy in all you do, just as God, the One who called you, is holy. [16]It is written in the Scriptures: "You must be holy, because I am holy."[n]

[17]You pray to God and call him Father, and he judges each person's work equally. So while you are here on earth, you should live with respect for God. [18]You know that in the past you were living in a worthless way, a way passed down from the people who lived before you. But you were saved from that useless life. You were bought, not with something that ruins like gold or silver, [19]but with the precious blood of Christ, who was like a pure and perfect lamb. [20]Christ was chosen before the world was made, but he was shown to the world in these last times for your sake. [21]Through Christ you believe in God, who raised Christ from the dead and gave him glory. So your faith and your hope are in God.

[22]Now that your obedience to the truth has purified your souls, you can have true love for your Christian brothers and sisters. So love each other deeply with all your heart.[n] [23]You have been born again, and this new life did not come from something that dies, but from something that cannot die. You were born again through God's living message that continues forever. [24]The Scripture says,

"All people are like the grass,
and all their glory is like the flowers of the field.
The grass dies and the flowers fall,

[25] but the word of the Lord will live forever."   *Isaiah 40:6–8*
And this is the word that was preached to you.

JESUS IS THE LIVING STONE

2 So then, rid yourselves of all evil, all lying, hypocrisy, jealousy, and evil speech. [2]As newborn babies want milk, you should want the pure and simple teaching. By it you can mature in your salvation, [3]because you have already examined and seen how good the Lord is.

[4]Come to the Lord Jesus, the "stone"[n] that lives. The people of the world did not want this stone, but he was the stone God chose, and he was precious. [5]You also are like living stones, so let yourselves be used to build a spiritual temple—to be holy priests who offer spiritual sacrifices to God. He will accept those sacrifices through Jesus Christ. [6]The Scripture says:

"I will put a stone in the ground in Jerusalem.
Everything will be built on this important and precious rock.
Anyone who trusts in him will never be disappointed."
            Isaiah 28:16

[7]This stone is worth much to you who believe. But to the people who do not believe,

"the stone that the builders rejected has become the cornerstone."
            Psalm 118:22

[8]Also, he is

"a stone that causes people to stumble, a rock that makes them fall."   *Isaiah 8:14*
They stumble because they do not obey what God says, which is what God planned to happen to them.

[9]But you are a chosen people, royal priests,

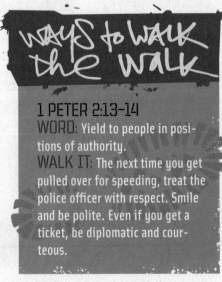

WAYS TO WALK THE WALK

1 PETER 2:13–14

WORD: Yield to people in positions of authority.

WALK IT: The next time you get pulled over for speeding, treat the police officer with respect. Smile and be polite. Even if you get a ticket, be diplomatic and courteous.

1:16 "You must be . . . holy." Quotation from Leviticus 11:45; 19:2; 20:7.   1:22 with all your heart Some Greek copies read "with a pure heart."   2:4 "stone" The most important stone in God's spiritual temple or house (his people).

316

GUARD YOUR HEART

Don't be afraid to end a bad relationship. If your relationship is causing you to sin or feel weighed down, don't try to force it. It's okay to call it quits. And sometimes it's the healthiest decision for both of you. Better to end it before it derails your destiny.

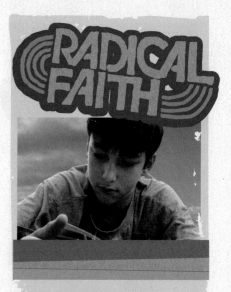

RADICAL FAITH

a holy nation, a people for God's own possession. You were chosen to tell about the wonderful acts of God, who called you out of darkness into his wonderful light. [10]At one time you were not a people, but now you are God's people. In the past you had never received mercy, but now you have received God's mercy.

LIVE FOR GOD

[11]Dear friends, you are like foreigners and strangers in this world. I beg you to avoid the evil things your bodies want to do that fight against your soul. [12]People who do not believe are living all around you and might say that you are doing wrong. Live such good lives that they will see the good things you do and will give glory to God on the day when Christ comes again.

YIELD TO EVERY HUMAN AUTHORITY

[13]For the Lord's sake, yield to the people who have authority in this world: the king, who is the highest authority, [14]and the leaders who are sent by him to punish those who do wrong and to praise those who do right. [15]It is God's desire that by doing good you should stop foolish people from saying stupid things about you. [16]Live as free people, but do not use your freedom as an excuse to do evil. Live as servants of God. [17]Show respect for all people: Love the brothers and sisters of God's family, respect God, honor the king.

FOLLOW CHRIST'S EXAMPLE

[18]Slaves, yield to the authority of your masters with all respect, not only those who are good and kind, but also those who are dishonest. [19]A person might have to suffer even when it is unfair, but if he thinks of God and can stand the pain, God is pleased. [20]If you are beaten for doing wrong, there is no reason to praise you for being patient in your punishment. But if you suffer for doing good, and you are patient, then God is pleased. [21]This is what you were called to do, because Christ suffered

for you and gave you an example to follow. So you should do as he did.

[22]"He had never sinned,
    and he had never lied."   *Isaiah 53:9*

[23]People insulted Christ, but he did not insult them in return. Christ suffered, but he did not threaten. He let God, the One who judges rightly, take care of him. [24]Christ carried our sins in his body on the cross so we would stop living for sin and start living for what is right. And you are healed because of his wounds. [25]You were like sheep that wandered away, but now you have come back to the Shepherd and Overseer of your souls.

WIVES AND HUSBANDS

3 In the same way, you wives should yield to your husbands. Then, if some husbands do not obey God's teaching, they will be persuaded to believe without anyone's saying a word to them. They will be persuaded by the way their wives live. [2]Your husbands will see the pure lives you live with your respect for God. [3]It is not fancy hair, gold jewelry, or fine clothes that should make you beautiful. [4]No, your beauty should come from within you—the beauty of a gentle and quiet spirit that will never be destroyed and is very precious to God. [5]In this same way the holy women who lived long ago and followed God made themselves beautiful, yielding to their own husbands. [6]Sarah obeyed Abraham, her husband, and called him her master. And you women are true children of Sarah if you always do what is right and are not afraid.

[7]In the same way, you husbands should live with your wives in an understanding way, since they are weaker than you. But show them respect, because God gives them the same blessing he gives you—the grace that gives true life. Do this so that nothing will stop your prayers.

SUFFERING FOR DOING RIGHT

[8]Finally, all of you should be in agreement, understanding each other, loving each other as family, being kind and humble. [9]Do not do

1 PETER 3:15–16

The Lord commanded all believers to spread the Good News about him to the whole earth, making followers of "all people in the world" (Matthew 28:19). He's looking for willing coworkers to help minister to people ripe to meet him. He's not afraid of using systematic training to help his followers master wise tactics for introducing people to him. He even promised us the power of the Holy Spirit to boldly get the task done (Acts 1:8). That's a full-court-press kind of plan. But don't get the idea that your job is to get pushy with people who don't know God. Instead, focus on persuasion. While you can't know the answer to every question someone could ask about your faith, be ready to explain what you believe and why. Know where to turn for help. Speak with gentleness and respect, the way you want to be talked to. Don't live a wild lifestyle, giving anyone ammunition to discredit your faith. Keep in mind that none of this matters if Jesus isn't really Lord of your life, because you can't give away what you don't possess.

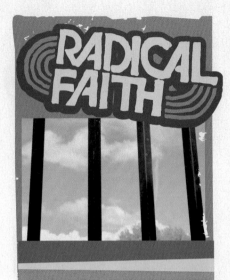

RADICAL FAITH

1 PETER 4:15–16

One of Jesus' key followers, the apostle Peter, was so brash that he swore he was willing to die for Jesus. Yet, when the Lord went to the cross, Peter wouldn't even admit that he knew him. He later cried huge tears of regret, and Jesus restored him as a friend and follower (John 21:19). Not long after Jesus headed back to heaven, Peter stood up and preached the church's first sermon (Acts 2:14). He soon was seized and thrown in jail, and Jesus even predicted that Peter would, indeed, one day die for being his friend. Tradition suggests the apostle died in Rome, hung upside down on a cross. So, when Peter says something about suffering for your faith, you can trust that he knows what he's talking about. He offers two nuggets of wisdom here. First, don't suffer for something stupid, like getting a punishment you deserve for doing wrong. Second, take it to heart when you pay the painful price for knowing Jesus. It is a sure sign of your connection to him and shows that you are his true friend forever.

wrong to repay a wrong, and do not insult to repay an insult. But repay with a blessing, because you yourselves were called to do this so that you might receive a blessing. ¹⁰The Scripture says,

"A person must do these things
to enjoy life and have many happy days.
He must not say evil things,
and he must not tell lies.
¹¹He must stop doing evil and do good.
He must look for peace and work for it.
¹²The Lord sees the good people
and listens to their prayers.
But the Lord is against
those who do evil."   *Psalm 34:12–16*

¹³If you are trying hard to do good, no one can really hurt you. ¹⁴But even if you suffer for doing right, you are blessed.

"Don't be afraid of what they fear;
do not dread those things."
     Isaiah 8:12–13

¹⁵But respect Christ as the holy Lord in your hearts. Always be ready to answer everyone who asks you to explain about the hope you have, ¹⁶but answer in a gentle way and with respect. Keep a clear conscience so that those who speak evil of your good life in Christ will be made ashamed. ¹⁷It is better to suffer for doing good than for doing wrong if that is what God wants. ¹⁸Christ himself suffered for sins once. He was not guilty, but he suffered for those who are guilty to bring you to God. His body was killed, but he was made alive in the spirit. ¹⁹And in the spirit he went and preached to the spirits in prison ²⁰who refused to obey God long ago in the time of Noah. God was waiting patiently for

the same way of thinking Christ had. The person who has suffered in the body is finished with sin. ²Strengthen yourselves so that you will live here on earth doing what God wants, not the evil things people want. ³In the past you wasted too much time doing what nonbelievers enjoy. You were guilty of sexual sins, evil desires, drunkenness, wild and drunken parties, and hateful idol worship. ⁴Nonbelievers think it is strange that you do not do the many wild and wasteful things they do, so they insult you. ⁵But they will have to explain this to God, who is ready to judge the living and the dead. ⁶For this reason the Good News was preached to those who are now dead. Even though they were judged like all people, the Good News was preached to them so they could live in the spirit as God lives.

USE GOD'S GIFTS WISELY

⁷The time is near when all things will end. So think clearly and control yourselves so you will be able to pray. ⁸Most importantly, love each other deeply, because love will cause people to forgive each other for many sins. ⁹Open your homes to each other, without complaining. ¹⁰Each of you has received a gift to use to serve others. Be good servants of God's various gifts of grace. ¹¹Anyone who speaks should speak words from God. Anyone who serves should serve with the strength God gives so that in everything God will be praised through Jesus Christ. Power and glory belong to him forever and ever. Amen.

them while Noah was building the boat. Only a few people—eight in all—were saved by water. ²¹And that water is like baptism that now saves you—not the washing of dirt from the body, but the promise made to God from a good conscience. And this is because Jesus Christ was raised from the dead. ²²Now Jesus has gone into heaven and is at God's right side ruling over angels, authorities, and powers.

CHANGE YOUR LIVES

 Since Christ suffered while he was in his body, strengthen yourselves with

SUFFERING AS A CHRISTIAN

¹²My friends, do not be surprised at the terrible trouble which now comes to test you. Do not think that something strange is happening to you. ¹³But be happy that you are sharing in Christ's sufferings so that you will be happy and full of joy when Christ comes again in glory. ¹⁴When people insult you because you follow Christ, you are blessed, because the glorious Spirit, the Spirit of God, is with you. ¹⁵Do not suffer for murder, theft, or any other crime, nor because you trouble other people. ¹⁶But if you

WAYS to WALK the WALK

1 PETER 5:5-6

WORD: Show respect to your elders.

WALK IT: If you have a disagreement with a parent or teacher, give your opinion once, and then submit to their opinion. Trust God to show everyone involved the right way of thinking.

suffer because you are a Christian, do not be ashamed. Praise God because you wear that name. [17] It is time for judgment to begin with God's family. And if that judging begins with us, what will happen to those people who do not obey the Good News of God?

[18] "If it is very hard for a good person to be saved,
the wicked person and the sinner will surely be lost!"[n]

[19] So those who suffer as God wants should trust their souls to the faithful Creator as they continue to do what is right.

THE FLOCK OF GOD

5 Now I have something to say to the elders in your group. I also am an elder. I have seen Christ's sufferings, and I will share in the glory that will be shown to us. I beg you to [2] shepherd God's flock, for whom you are responsible. Watch over them because you want to, not because you are forced. That is how God wants it. Do it because you are happy to serve, not because you want money. [3] Do not be like a ruler over people you are responsible for, but be good examples to them. [4] Then when Christ, the Chief Shepherd, comes, you will get a glorious crown that will never lose its beauty.

[5] In the same way, younger people should be willing to be under older people. And all of you should be very humble with each other.
"God is against the proud,
but he gives grace to the humble."
Proverbs 3:34

[6] Be humble under God's powerful hand so he will lift you up when the right time comes. [7] Give all your worries to him, because he cares about you.

[8] Control yourselves and be careful! The devil, your enemy, goes around like a roaring lion looking for someone to eat. [9] Refuse to give in to him, by standing strong in your faith. You know that your Christian family all over the world is having the same kinds of suffering.

[10] And after you suffer for a short time, God, who gives all grace, will make everything right. He will make you strong and support you and keep you from falling. He called you to share in his glory in Christ, a glory that will continue forever. [11] All power is his forever and ever. Amen.

FINAL GREETINGS

[12] I wrote this short letter with the help of Silas, who I know is a faithful brother in Christ. I wrote to encourage you and to tell you that this is the true grace of God. Stand strong in that grace.

[13] The church in Babylon, who was chosen like you, sends you greetings. Mark, my son in Christ, also greets you. [14] Give each other a kiss of Christian love when you meet.

Peace to all of you who are in Christ.

experts answer YOUR questions

Q: Is there such a thing as spiritual warfare?

A: Spiritual warfare is very real, yet the good news is that Jesus has defeated the enemy for us and we simply need to enforce his victory. Colossians 2:15 reminds us that, through Christ, God stripped the spiritual rulers and powers of their authority and showed the whole world that they were powerless.

Q: How can I fight against evil spiritual powers?

A: Ephesians 6:10–18 gives us a list of the weapons God has given us to fight against the spiritual powers of darkness. The most powerful weapon we have is the Bible, and the more we read it and study it, the more prepared we'll be to fight against spiritual enemies.

In the wilderness, Jesus rebuffed Satan by quoting scripture verses to him.

4:18 "If . . . lost!" Quotation from Proverbs 11:31 in the Septuagint, the Greek version of the Old Testament.

319

²PE TER

AVOIDING FALSE TEACHERS

Ever have a friend on a sports team or a class project who dogged it instead of giving his best effort? If so, you probably felt like giving him an earful about it! That's how the apostle Peter felt when he wrote this letter. Following his first letter of gentle encouragement, he delivers a tongue lashing here.

Most of the letter is a warning to watch out for false teachers. Just as there were phony ones in the past, Peter advises there will be deceitful teachers who will even refuse to accept Jesus as the Messiah. Thanks to Peter's writings, we know that someone whose lifestyle demonstrates greed and immorality isn't of God, no matter what that person proclaims.

Together with its words of correction, this letter also contains a word of encouragement: to hold fast to the promise of Christ's return. Although people may mock God's children about the return of Jesus, Peter reminds believers not to give in to the critics. His words are a stirring reminder that God is not bound by time or other human limitations. Peter's words are full of hope that help us maintain our focus on Christ, no matter how much time passes before Jesus' second coming.

MEN of the SWORD

1 From Simon Peter, a servant and apostle of Jesus Christ.

To you who have received a faith as valuable as ours, because our God and Savior Jesus Christ does what is right.

²Grace and peace be given to you more and more, because you truly know God and Jesus our Lord.

GOD HAS GIVEN US BLESSINGS

³Jesus has the power of God, by which he has given us everything we need to live and to serve God. We have these things because we know him. Jesus called us by his glory and goodness. ⁴Through these he gave us the very great and precious promises. With these gifts you can share in God's nature, and the world will not ruin you with its evil desires.

⁵Because you have these blessings, do your best to add these things to your lives: to your faith, add goodness; and to your goodness, add knowledge; ⁶and to your knowledge, add self-control; and to your self-control, add patience; and to your patience, add service for God; ⁷and to your service for God, add kindness for your brothers and sisters in Christ; and to this kindness, add love. ⁸If all these things are in you and are growing, they will help you to be useful and productive in your knowledge of our Lord Jesus Christ. ⁹But anyone who does not have these things cannot see clearly. He is blind and has forgotten that he was made clean from his past sins.

¹⁰My brothers and sisters, try hard to be certain that you really are called and chosen by God. If you do all these things, you will never fall. ¹¹And you will be given a very great welcome into the eternal kingdom of our Lord and Savior Jesus Christ.

¹²You know these things, and you are very strong in the truth, but I will always help you remember them. ¹³I think it is right for me to help you remember as long as I am in this body. ¹⁴I know I must soon leave this body, as our Lord Jesus Christ has shown me. ¹⁵I will try my best so that you may be able to remember these things even after I am gone.

WE SAW CHRIST'S GLORY

¹⁶When we told you about the powerful coming of our Lord Jesus Christ, we were not telling just clever stories that someone invented. But we saw the greatness of Jesus with our own eyes. ¹⁷Jesus heard the voice of God, the Greatest Glory, when he received honor and glory from God the Father. The voice said,

STEPHEN

How would you like to be described this way: "His words were so strong that they could not argue with him." Such was the case with Stephen, a powerful servant of God who spoke with the authority of the Holy Spirit. He ruffled a lot of feathers and, like Jesus, was accused by Jewish leaders of things he didn't do. Stephen gave an eloquent speech that infuriated the leaders, who immediately had him killed by stoning. Through it all, though, Stephen retained an immense love for Jesus, and was full of forgiveness up to the very moment of his death.

—Acts 6:8–14, 7:54–60

Get out there

Samaritan's Purse is a nondenominational evangelical Christian organization providing spiritual and physical aid to hurting people around the world. Since 1970, Samaritan's Purse has helped meet the needs of people who are victims of war, poverty, natural disasters, disease, and famine, with the purpose of sharing God's love. Founded by former Youth for Christ journalist Bob Pierce, the organization has been led for more than 20 years by Franklin Graham, son of famed evangelist Billy Graham. The ministry gets its name from the biblical story of the Good Samaritan and seeks to help needy people regardless of religious affiliation.

For more information, visit
www.samaritanspurse.org.

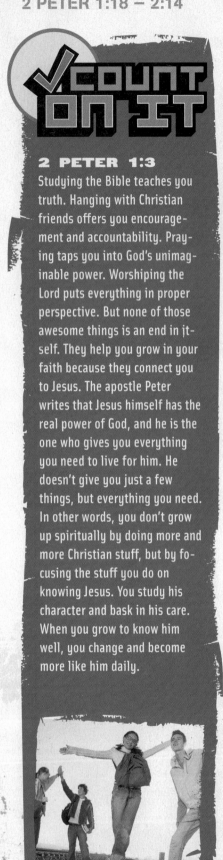

COUNT ON IT

2 PETER 1:3

Studying the Bible teaches you truth. Hanging with Christian friends offers you encouragement and accountability. Praying taps you into God's unimaginable power. Worshiping the Lord puts everything in proper perspective. But none of those awesome things is an end in itself. They help you grow in your faith because they connect you to Jesus. The apostle Peter writes that Jesus himself has the real power of God, and he is the one who gives you everything you need to live for him. He doesn't give you just a few things, but everything you need. In other words, you don't grow up spiritually by doing more and more Christian stuff, but by focusing the stuff you do on knowing Jesus. You study his character and bask in his care. When you grow to know him well, you change and become more like him daily.

GUARD YOUR HEART

Jesus desires our first and foremost attention. No relationship with a girl should come between you and Jesus. If your relationship is pulling you away from God, either fix it or get out of it. There are no other remedies. Any girl who would distract you from God doesn't love you anyhow.

"This is my Son, whom I love, and I am very pleased with him." [18] We heard that voice from heaven while we were with Jesus on the holy mountain.

[19] This makes us more sure about the message the prophets gave. It is good for you to follow closely what they said as you would follow a light shining in a dark place, until the day begins and the morning star rises in your hearts. [20] Most of all, you must understand this: No prophecy in the Scriptures ever comes from the prophet's own interpretation. [21] No prophecy ever came from what a person wanted to say, but people led by the Holy Spirit spoke words from God.

FALSE TEACHERS

2 There used to be false prophets among God's people, just as you will have some false teachers in your group. They will secretly teach things that are wrong—teachings that will cause people to be lost. They will even refuse to accept the Master, Jesus, who bought their freedom. So they will bring quick ruin on themselves. [2] Many will follow their evil ways and say evil things about the way of truth. [3] Those false teachers only want your money, so they will use you by telling you lies. Their judgment spoken against them long ago is still coming, and their ruin is certain.

[4] When angels sinned, God did not let them go free without punishment. He sent them to hell and put them in caves[n] of darkness where they are being held for judgment. [5] And God punished the world long ago when he brought a flood to the world that was full of people who were against him. But God saved Noah, who preached about being right with God, and seven other people with him. [6] And God also destroyed the evil cities of Sodom and Gomorrah[n] by burning them until they were ashes. He made those cities an example of what will happen to those who are against God. [7] But he saved Lot from those cities. Lot, a good man, was troubled because of the filthy lives of evil people. [8] (Lot was a good man, but

because he lived with evil people every day, his good heart was hurt by the evil things he saw and heard.) [9] So the Lord knows how to save those who serve him when troubles come. He will hold evil people and punish them, while waiting for the Judgment Day. [10] That punishment is especially for those who live by doing the evil things their sinful selves want and who hate authority.

These false teachers are bold and do anything they want. They are not afraid to speak against the angels. [11] But even the angels, who are much stronger and more powerful than false teachers, do not accuse them with insults before[n] the Lord. [12] But these people speak against things they do not understand. They are like animals that act without thinking, animals born to be caught and killed. And, like animals, these false teachers will be destroyed. [13] They have caused many people to suffer, so they themselves will suffer. That is their pay for what they have done. They take pleasure in openly doing evil, so they are like dirty spots and stains among you. They delight in deceiving you while eating meals with you. [14] Every time they look at a woman they want her, and their desire for sin is never satisfied. They lead

WAYS to WALK the WALK

2 PETER 1:5-8

WORD: Grow in the things of God.
WALK IT: Don't wander through your faith journey; study the important topics in this passage. Get a concordance, search them out, and find ways to apply them in your life.

2:4 caves Some Greek copies read "chains." **2:6 Sodom and Gomorrah** Two cities God destroyed because the people were so evil. **2:11 before** Some Greek copies read "from."

weak people into the trap of sin, and they have taught their hearts to be greedy. God will punish them! [15]These false teachers left the right road and lost their way, following the way Balaam went. Balaam was the son of Beor, who loved being paid for doing wrong. [16]But a donkey, which cannot talk, told Balaam he was sinning. It spoke with a man's voice and stopped the prophet's crazy thinking.

[17]Those false teachers are like springs without water and clouds blown by a storm. A place in the blackest darkness has been kept for them. [18]They brag with words that mean nothing. By their evil desires they lead people into the trap of sin—people who are just beginning to escape from others who live in error. [19]They promise them freedom, but they themselves are not free. They are slaves of things that will be destroyed. For people are slaves of anything that controls them. [20]They were made free from the evil in the world by knowing our Lord and Savior Jesus Christ. But if they return to evil things and those things control them, then it is worse for them than it was before. [21]Yes, it would be better for them to have never known the right way than to know it and to turn away from the holy teaching that was given to them. [22]What they did is like this true saying: "A dog goes back to what it has thrown up,"[n] and, "After a pig is washed, it goes back and rolls in the mud."

JESUS WILL COME AGAIN

3 My friends, this is the second letter I have written you to help your honest minds remember. [2]I want you to think about the words the holy prophets spoke in the past, and remember the command our Lord and Savior gave us through your apostles. [3]It is most important for you to understand what will happen in the last days. People will laugh at you. They will live doing the evil things they want to do. [4]They will say, "Jesus promised to come again. Where is he? Our fathers have died, but the world continues the way it has been since it was made." [5]But they do not want to remember what happened long ago. By the word of God heaven was made, and the earth was made from water and with water. [6]Then the world was flooded and destroyed with water. [7]And that same word of God is keeping heaven and earth that we now have in order to be destroyed by fire. They are being kept for the Judgment Day and the destruction of all who are against God.

[8]But do not forget this one thing, dear friends: To the Lord one day is as a thousand years, and a thousand years is as one day. [9]The Lord is not slow in doing what he promised—the way some people understand slowness. But God is being patient with you. He does not want anyone to be lost, but he wants all people to change their hearts and lives.

[10]But the day of the Lord will come like a thief. The skies will disappear with a loud

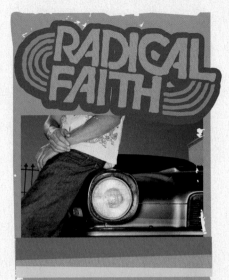

RADICAL FAITH

2 PETER 2:9

Drug dealers drive sweet rides. Homework thieves graduate with high grades. Guys who grope girls never lack dates. When you see evil people succeed, it makes you wonder if God is paying attention. Where is he when bad guys win? Well, God really wants you to understand the score. Back in the apostle Peter's day, plenty of people questioned where Jesus was. He had promised to come back to earth, but years later he hadn't shown up. Peter said that God isn't slow in keeping that promise. But Jesus won't return until the right time, and for good reason. He's being patient, giving more and more people time to turn back to him (2 Peter 3:9). But there's more to that promise. His return is the decisive time when he will deal with evil without holding back. Therefore, when you see evil people succeed, you can be sure that God takes note. When his judgment comes, he will spare you because you serve him. He will punish people who have spent their lives rebelling against him. Live totally for him, because he notices if you don't.

Extras:

How to Deal with Road Rage

The streets are full of rude drivers, and it seems like there are more of them getting a driver's license all the time. So, if traffic is making you mad, it's time to stop for a moment (your rampaging thoughts, not the vehicle you're driving). Like it or not, those are real people driving those cars, and, more than likely, they are usually nice individuals who don't even realize they've been unfriendly to you. But even if they have, getting even with them isn't part of God's plan. He created those people, he loves them, and he alone is responsible for judging them (well, maybe the police are, too). You are only responsible for you, and, if you'll admit it, sometimes you can be a handful, also. Jesus plainly said that you are in need of forgiveness, and if you won't forgive others, God can't forgive you. Temper your road rage with forgiveness, and you'll travel lightly.

 2:22 "A dog . . . up." Quotation from Proverbs 26:11.

DO develop a sense of humor.

DO smile at other people.

DO laugh at yourself.

DO learn to tell a good story.

DON'T make fun of others.

DON'T humiliate people.

DON'T play practical jokes.

DON'T forget the punch line.

noise. Everything in them will be destroyed by fire, and the earth and everything in it will be exposed.″ [11]In that way everything will be destroyed. So what kind of people should you be? You should live holy lives and serve God, [12]as you wait for and look forward to the coming of the day of God. When that day comes, the skies will be destroyed with fire, and everything in them will melt with heat. [13]But God made a promise to us, and we are waiting for a new heaven and a new earth where goodness lives.

[14]Dear friends, since you are waiting for this to happen, do your best to be without sin and without fault. Try to be at peace with God. [15]Remember that we are saved because our Lord is patient. Our dear brother Paul told you the same thing when he wrote to you with the wisdom that God gave him. [16]He writes about this in all his letters. Some things in Paul's letters are hard to understand, and people who are ignorant and weak in faith explain these things falsely. They also falsely explain the other Scriptures, but they are destroying themselves by doing this.

[17]Dear friends, since you already know about this, be careful. Do not let those evil people lead you away by the wrong they do. Be careful so you will not fall from your strong faith. [18]But grow in the grace and knowledge of our Lord and Savior Jesus Christ. Glory be to him now and forever! Amen.

3:10 and . . . exposed Some Greek copies read "and everything in it will be burned up."

***

notes

HOW TO LOVE ONE ANOTHER

Contrary to Western practice, Eastern cultures typically treat the elderly with honor and respect. People there value the wisdom their elders have accumulated across many years. Taking a page from their playbook, listen to John's words here with similar respect, since they were written near the end of his long life in service to God.

If one word were to leap off the pages, it would be "love." John wants God's children to understand it and show it to each other. He points out that someone can't proclaim to know God's love yet hate another person, whether because of something that individual does, how he looks, or the color of his skin.

This book can appear confusing at first glance. On the one hand, John says if we continuing living in darkness, we can't have fellowship with God. Then he turns around and says if we claim not to sin, we are fooling ourselves. So which is it? The answer is clear: Those who are God's children will not make a practice of sinning. In other words, we will make mistakes, but we won't eagerly pursue the wrong lifestyle. As John says, "To be like Christ a person must do what is right."

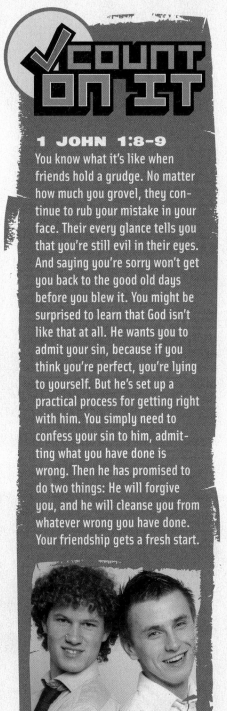

1 We write you now about what has always existed, which we have heard, we have seen with our own eyes, we have looked at, and we have touched with our hands. We write to you about the Word[n] that gives life. [2]He who gives life was shown to us. We saw him and can give proof about it. And now we announce to you that he has life that continues forever. He was with God the Father and was shown to us. [3]We announce to you what we have seen and heard, because we want you also to have fellowship with us. Our fellowship is with God the Father and with his Son, Jesus Christ. [4]We write this to you so we may be full of joy.[n]

GOD FORGIVES OUR SINS

[5]Here is the message we have heard from Christ and now announce to you: God is light,[n] and in him there is no darkness at all. [6]So if we say we have fellowship with God, but we continue living in darkness, we are liars and do not follow the truth. [7]But if we live in the light, as God is in the light, we can share fellowship with each other. Then the blood of Jesus, God's Son, cleanses us from every sin.

[8]If we say we have no sin, we are fooling ourselves, and the truth is not in us. [9]But if we confess our sins, he will forgive our sins, because we can trust God to do what is right. He will cleanse us from all the wrongs we have done. [10]If we say we have not sinned, we make God a liar, and we do not accept God's teaching.

JESUS IS OUR HELPER

2 My dear children, I write this letter to you so you will not sin. But if anyone does sin, we have a helper in the presence of the Father—Jesus Christ, the One who does what is right. [2]He died in our place to take away our sins, and not only our sins but the sins of all people.

[3]We can be sure that we know God if we obey his commands. [4]Anyone who says, "I know God," but does not obey God's commands is a liar, and the truth is not in that person. [5]But if someone obeys God's teaching, then in that person God's love has truly reached its goal. This is how we can be sure we are living in God: [6]Whoever says that he lives in God must live as Jesus lived.

THE COMMAND TO LOVE OTHERS

[7]My dear friends, I am not writing a new command to you but an old command you have had from the beginning. It is the teaching you have already heard. [8]But also I am writing a new command to you, and you can see its truth in Jesus and in you, because the darkness is passing away, and the true light is already shining.

[9]Anyone who says, "I am in the light,"[n] but hates a brother or sister, is still in the darkness. [10]Whoever loves a brother or sister lives in the light and will not cause anyone to stumble in his faith. [11]But whoever hates a brother or sister is in darkness, lives in darkness, and does not know where to go, because the darkness has made that person blind.

[12]I write to you, dear children,
because your sins are forgiven through Christ.

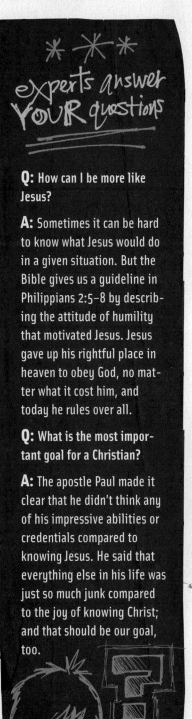

1:1 **Word** The Greek word is "logos," meaning any kind of communication. Here, it means Christ, who was the way God told people about himself. 1:4 **so . . . joy** Some Greek copies read "so you may be full of joy." 1:5; 2:9 **light** Here, it is used as a symbol of God's goodness or truth.

Relationships

"Show respect for all people: Love the brothers and sisters of God's family, respect God, honor the king" (1 Peter 2:17). It's easy to show respect to people you like: people such as your girlfriend or the rest of your friends. But how are you at showing other types of people the respect they're due? Here's the deal: God wants you to be respectful to people, no matter what you may think of them. It's the cornerstone of your relationships with others. And it's the only way you'll get the respect you crave from other people. You've got to give it to get it.

[13] I write to you, fathers,
because you know the One who existed from the beginning.
I write to you, young people,
because you have defeated the Evil One.
[14] I write to you, children,
because you know the Father.

I write to you, fathers,
because you know the One who existed from the beginning.
I write to you, young people,
because you are strong;
the teaching of God lives in you,
and you have defeated the Evil One.
[15] Do not love the world or the things in the world. If you love the world, the love of the Father is not in you. [16] These are the ways of the world: wanting to please our sinful selves, wanting the sinful things we see, and being too proud of what we have. None of these come from the Father, but all of them come from the world. [17] The world and everything that people want in it are passing away, but the person who does what God wants lives forever.

REJECT THE ENEMIES OF CHRIST

[18] My dear children, these are the last days. You have heard that the enemy of Christ is coming, and now many enemies of Christ are already here. This is how we know that these are the last days. [19] These enemies of Christ were in our fellowship, but they left us. They never really belonged to us; if they had been a part of us, they would have stayed with us. But they left, and this shows that none of them really belonged to us. [20] You have the gift[n] that the Holy One gave you, so you all know the truth.[n] [21] I do not

*REVIEWS MUSIC

MAT KEARNEY:
BULLET

Mat Kearney humorously describes his musical style as a cross between Tupac Shakur and Bob Dylan. Although it's a funny combination, there is some truth to it. On *Bullet*, Kearney pulls out some old-school rapping skills and places the vocals atop a layered acoustic/hip-hop track. Surprisingly, the combo works and the result is a musical delight. The title track might be one of the best Christian tunes of the last few years. Its chorus is catchy and simple; its verses are poignant and convicting. Altogether, this album is a thought-provoking, spiritual essay put to rap and acoustic guitar for adventurous types.

WHY IT ROCKS:

WHY IT ROCKS: THE RAPPING PUTS THE HIP IN HIP-HOP.

 2:20 **gift** This might mean the Holy Spirit, or it might mean teaching or truth as in verse 24. 2:20 **you . . . truth** Some Greek copies read "so you know all things."

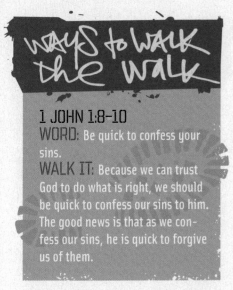

ways to walk the walk

1 JOHN 1:8-10

WORD: Be quick to confess your sins.

WALK IT: Because we can trust God to do what is right, we should be quick to confess our sins to him. The good news is that as we confess our sins, he is quick to forgive us of them.

write to you because you do not know the truth but because you do know the truth. And you know that no lie comes from the truth. 22Who is the liar? It is the person who does not accept Jesus as the Christ. This is the enemy of Christ: the person who does not accept the Father and his Son. 23Whoever does not accept the Son does not have the Father. But whoever confesses the Son has the Father, too.

24Be sure you continue to follow the teaching you heard from the beginning. If you continue to follow what you heard from the beginning, you will stay in the Son and in the Father. 25And this is what the Son promised to us—life forever.

26I am writing this letter about those people who are trying to lead you the wrong way. 27Christ gave you a special gift that is still in you, so you do not need any other teacher. His gift teaches you about everything, and it is true, not false. So continue to live in Christ, as his gift taught you. 28Yes, my dear children, live in him so that when Christ comes back, we can be without fear and not be ashamed in his presence. 29Since you know that Christ is righteous, you know that all who do right are God's children.

WE ARE GOD'S CHILDREN

3 The Father has loved us so much that we are called children of God. And we really are his children. The reason the people in the world do not know us is that they have not known him. 2Dear friends, now we are children of God, and we have not yet been shown what we will be in the future. But we know that when Christ comes again, we will be like him, because we will see him as he really is.

3Christ is pure, and all who have this hope in Christ keep themselves pure like Christ.

4The person who sins breaks God's law. Yes, sin is living against God's law. 5You know that Christ came to take away sins and that there is no sin in Christ. 6So anyone who lives in Christ does not go on sinning. Anyone who goes on sinning has never really understood Christ and has never known him.

7Dear children, do not let anyone lead you the wrong way. Christ is righteous. So to be like Christ a person must do what is right. 8The devil has been sinning since the beginning, so anyone who continues to sin belongs to the devil. The Son of God came for this purpose: to destroy the devil's work.

9Those who are God's children do not continue sinning, because the new life from God remains in them. They are not able to go on sinning, because they have become children of God. 10So we can see who God's children are and who the devil's children are: Those who do not do what is right are not God's children, and those who do not love their brothers and sisters are not God's children.

WE MUST LOVE EACH OTHER

11This is the teaching you have heard from the beginning: We must love each other. 12Do not be like Cain who belonged to the Evil One and killed his brother. And why did he kill him? Because the things Cain did were evil, and the things his brother did were good.

13Brothers and sisters, do not be surprised when the people of the world hate you. 14We know we have left death and have come into life because we love each other. Whoever does not love is still dead. 15Everyone who hates a brother or sister is a murderer,[n] and you know that no murderers have eternal life in them. 16This is how we know what real love is: Jesus gave his life for us. So we should give our lives for our brothers and sisters. 17Suppose someone has enough to live and sees a brother or sister in need, but does not help. Then God's love is not living in that person. 18My children, we should love people not only with words and talk, but by our actions and true caring.

19-20This is the way we know that we belong to the way of truth. When our hearts make us feel guilty, we can still have peace before God. God is greater than our hearts, and he knows everything. 21My dear friends, if our hearts do not make us feel guilty, we can come without fear into God's presence. 22And God gives us what we ask for because we obey God's commands and do what pleases him. 23This is what God commands: that we believe in his Son, Jesus Christ, and that we love each

1 JOHN 3:16

Clueless girls measure love by the buckets of syrupy ooze they see in chick flicks, romance novels, and soap operas. Spineless guys gauge love by the distorted images of airbrushed models featured in centerfolds. The Bible shouts that real love is defined by one act: the death of Jesus on the cross. The greatest-ever picture of authentic love is Jesus sacrificing his life for the whole human race, arms stretched wide as he dies for human sin. That love is infinitely costly. It is absolutely unselfish. It completely submits to God's will. Believe it or not, it's the same love God wants us to show other believers. As this verse states, "Jesus gave his life for us. So we should give our lives for our brothers and sisters." You won't be going to a literal cross anytime soon. But you love like Jesus any time you put others' interests before your own, thinking more about meeting their needs than yours. When people argue that love looks like this or that, test their shaky definition: Does it look anything like the true love of Jesus?

3:15 Everyone . . . murderer If one person hates a brother or sister, then in the heart that person has killed that brother or sister. Jesus taught about this sin to his followers (Matthew 5:21–26).

RADICAL FAITH

1 JOHN 4:19

The Bible commands us to love as Jesus loves, spilling our lives out for others just as the Lord gave himself for us (1 John 3:16). But ponder this: No human being ever has the ability to accomplish that on his own. Figuring that you can love others in your own strength is like expecting a car to disappear down a dragstrip without gas in the tank. You need to be tanked up from the right fuel source in order to love. And there's only one place to get that power. Like the apostle John wrote, "We love because God first loved us." If you really want to love others—whether friends, parents, siblings, or others—you have to grasp how God has loved you. That's partly an education thing, studying what the Bible says about God's character and his loving plan for the world (John 3:16). And it's partly an experience thing, getting with other Christians so you can feel his love in real life (1 John 4:11). The more of God's love you get, the more you've got to love others with.

other, just as he commanded. [24] The people who obey God's commands live in God, and God lives in them. We know that God lives in us because of the Spirit God gave us.

WARNING AGAINST FALSE TEACHERS

4 My dear friends, many false prophets have gone out into the world. So do not believe every spirit, but test the spirits to see if they are from God. [2] This is how you can know God's Spirit: Every spirit who confesses that Jesus Christ came to earth as a human is from God. [3] And every spirit who refuses to say this about Jesus is not from God. It is the spirit of the enemy of Christ, which you have heard is coming, and now he is already in the world.

[4] My dear children, you belong to God and have defeated them; because God's Spirit, who is in you, is greater than the devil, who is in the world. [5] And they belong to the world, so what they say is from the world, and the world listens to them. [6] But we belong to God, and those who know God listen to us. But those who are not from God do not listen to us. That is how we know the Spirit that is true and the spirit that is false.

LOVE COMES FROM GOD

[7] Dear friends, we should love each other, because love comes from God. Everyone who loves has become God's child and knows God. [8] Whoever does not love does not know God, because God is love. [9] This is how God showed his love to us: He sent his one and only Son into the world so that we could have life through him. [10] This is what real love is: It is not our love for God; it is God's love for us. He sent his Son to die in our place to take away our sins.

[11] Dear friends, if God loved us that much we also should love each other. [12] No one has ever seen God, but if we love each other, God lives in us, and his love is made perfect in us.

[13] We know that we live in God and he lives in us, because he gave us his Spirit. [14] We have seen and can testify that the Father sent his Son to be the Savior of the world. [15] Whoever confesses that Jesus is the Son of God has God living inside, and that person lives in God. [16] And so we know the love that God has for us, and we trust that love.

God is love. Those who live in love live in God, and God lives in them. [17] This is how love is made perfect in us: that we can be without fear on the day God judges us, because in this world we are like him. [18] Where God's love is, there is no fear, because God's

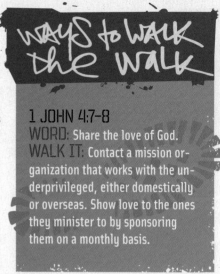

ways to walk the walk

1 JOHN 4:7-8
WORD: Share the love of God.
WALK IT: Contact a mission organization that works with the underprivileged, either domestically or overseas. Show love to the ones they minister to by sponsoring them on a monthly basis.

perfect love drives out fear. It is punishment that makes a person fear, so love is not made perfect in the person who fears.

[19] We love because God first loved us. [20] If people say, "I love God," but hate their brothers or sisters, they are liars. Those who do not love their brothers and sisters, whom they

TOP TEN

random rainy day activities

1. Read a book.
2. Listen to music.
3. Play a game.
4. Call a friend.
5. Surf the Internet.
6. View a movie.
7. Write a letter.
8. Take a nap.
9. Pray for others.
10. Watch television.

have seen, cannot love God, whom they have never seen. [21]And God gave us this command: Those who love God must also love their brothers and sisters.

FAITH IN THE SON OF GOD

5 Everyone who believes that Jesus is the Christ is God's child, and who-ever loves the Father also loves the Father's children. [2]This is how we know we love God's children: when we love God and obey his commands. [3]Loving God means obeying his commands. And God's commands are not too hard for us, [4]because everyone who is a child of God conquers the world. And this is the victory that conquers the world—our faith. [5]So the one who conquers the world is the person who believes that Jesus is the Son of God.

[6]Jesus Christ is the One who came by water[n] and blood.[n] He did not come by water only, but by water and blood. And the Spirit says that this is true, because the Spirit is the truth. [7]So there are three witnesses:[n] [8]the Spirit, the water, and the blood; and these three witnesses agree. [9]We believe people when they say something is true. But what God says is more important, and he has told us the truth about his own Son. [10]Anyone who believes in the Son of God has the truth that God told us. Anyone who does not believe makes God a liar, because that person does not believe what God told us about his Son. [11]This is what God told us: God has given us eternal life, and this life is in his Son. [12]Whoever has the Son has life, but whoever does not have the Son of God does not have life.

WE HAVE ETERNAL LIFE NOW

[13]I write this letter to you who believe in the Son of God so you will know you have eternal life. [14]And this is the boldness we have in God's presence: that if we ask God for anything that agrees with what he wants, he hears us. [15]If we know he hears us every time we ask him, we know we have what we ask from him.

[16]If anyone sees a brother or sister sinning (sin that does not lead to eternal death), that person should pray, and God will give the sinner life. I am talking about people whose sin does not lead to eternal death. There is sin that leads to death. I do not mean that a person should pray about that sin. [17]Doing wrong is always sin, but there is sin that does not lead to eternal death.

[18]We know that those who are God's children do not continue to sin. The Son of God keeps them safe, and the Evil One cannot touch them. [19]We know that we belong to God, but the Evil One controls the whole world. [20]We also know that the Son of God has come and has given us understanding so that we can know the True One. And our lives are in the True One and in his Son, Jesus Christ. He is the true God and the eternal life.

[21]So, dear children, keep yourselves away from false gods.

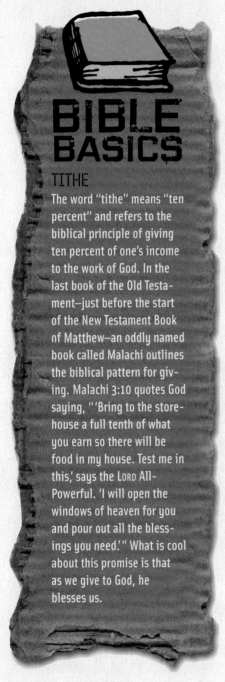

BIBLE BASICS

TITHE

The word "tithe" means "ten percent" and refers to the biblical principle of giving ten percent of one's income to the work of God. In the last book of the Old Testament—just before the start of the New Testament Book of Matthew—an oddly named book called Malachi outlines the biblical pattern for giving. Malachi 3:10 quotes God saying, "'Bring to the storehouse a full tenth of what you earn so there will be food in my house. Test me in this,' says the Lord All-Powerful. 'I will open the windows of heaven for you and pour out all the blessings you need.'" What is cool about this promise is that as we give to God, he blesses us.

2 JOHN

LOVE EXERCISES WISDOM

You probably know what it's like to walk into a room and see someone else's face light up, welcoming you into the circle. Such a greeting conveys many things, including friendship and acceptance, especially if it's a party you are attending and the host is the one greeting you. It is natural to extend such hospitality to guests.

However, John closes that door in this letter, warning God's children not to show hospitality to false teachers. Who is a false teacher? John spells it out: Anyone who does not confess that Jesus Christ came to earth as a human. Those who deny this are the Lord's enemies. This is why John tells the church to avoid following non-Christian leaders. Doing so is like giving comfort and aid to the enemy.

In addition to this warning, John continues to emphasize the message of love that characterized his earlier letter. He also defines love, which means living the way God commanded us to live. Also implied in John's letter is the fact that love includes human contact. Near the end of this message, he notes that he has many things he wants to say, but he prefers not to use paper. Instead, he wants to communicate face-to-face. That is worth remembering in a world where instant messaging passes for intimate communication.

[1] From the Elder.[n]

To the chosen lady[n] and her children:

I love all of you in the truth,[n] and all those who know the truth love you. [2] We love you because of the truth that lives in us and will be with us forever.

[3] Grace, mercy, and peace from God the Father and his Son, Jesus Christ, will be with us in truth and love.

[4] I was very happy to learn that some of your children are following the way of truth, as the Father commanded us. [5] And now, dear lady, this is not a new command but is the same command we have had from the beginning. I ask you that we all love each other. [6] And love means living the way God commanded us to live. As you have heard from the beginning, his command is this: Live a life of love.

[7] Many false teachers are in the world now who do not confess that Jesus Christ came to earth as a human. Anyone who does not confess this is a false teacher and an enemy of Christ. [8] Be careful yourselves that you do not lose everything you[n] have worked for, but that you receive your full reward.

[9] Anyone who goes beyond Christ's teaching and does not continue to follow only his teaching does not have God. But whoever continues to follow the teaching of Christ has both the Father and the Son. [10] If someone comes to you and does not bring this teaching, do not welcome or accept that person into your house. [11] If you welcome such a person, you share in the evil work.

[12] I have many things to write to you, but I do not want to use paper and ink. Instead, I hope to come to you and talk face to face so we can be full of joy. [13] The children of your chosen sister[n] greet you.

ways to WALK the WALK

2 JOHN 7–8

WORD: Study the teaching of Scripture.

WALK IT: The only way you'll recognize unscriptural counterfeit teaching is if you study the authentic teaching of Scripture. Internalize what the Bible has to say, and you'll identify anything that is contrary to it.

Get out there

World Relief works with local evangelical churches to bring relief to suffering people in the name of Christ. Together, World Relief and partner churches save lives and restore hope through ministries that address poverty, disease, hunger, persecution, and the effects of war and disasters. World Relief states its first priority as meeting the physical, emotional, and spiritual needs of the more than 800 million poorest of the poor and the displaced refugees, orphans, and homeless of the world. Through community banks, disaster response, agricultural ministries, refugee care, and immigrant assistance, the group is making a difference around the world.

For specifics, visit www.wr.org.

3 JOHN

EXERCISING DISCERNMENT

Imagine welcoming a guy into your home, only to have him cuss you out, eat all your food, trash your computer, and play wild music until dawn. You probably wouldn't invite him to return. In the same spirit, John warns in this letter that similar troublemakers will find their way into the church. No, they may not be so blatant as a loud-mouthed houseguest. But they will cause problems, spread confusion, and oppose sound teaching. John doesn't want God's children to be misled by such people.

However, he does want them to show hospitality toward fellow believers who also teach that Christ is Savior and Lord. John addresses this letter to a good friend who has been bragged about by others in the church for his good deeds. John also rejoices over hearing that converts—he calls them all "my children"—are following the truth.

And he commends the church for showing hospitality to missionaries. Just as he warned against helping false teachers in his second letter, John reminds here that helping Christians is sharing in their work. John concludes with encouragement to greet other believers by name, underscoring the value of genuine Christian friendship.

GUARD YOUR HEART

Consider what your girlfriend is passionate about. If she talks more about satisfying her own selfish desires than helping other people, you'd be smart to reevaluate your relationship. Pursue a girl who is interested in more than just partying and having fun. Make sure she's passionate about things that matter.

[1]From the Elder.[n]

To my dear friend Gaius, whom I love in the truth:[n]

[2]My dear friend, I know your soul is doing fine, and I pray that you are doing well in every way and that your health is good. [3]I was very happy when some brothers and sisters came and told me about the truth in your life and how you are following the way of truth. [4]Nothing gives me greater joy than to hear that my children are following the way of truth.

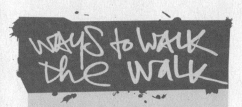

ways to WALK the WALK

3 JOHN 5-8

WORD: Help out where you can.

WALK IT: It's good to help those who are teaching the truth. Volunteer to fill vacancies in your church, and, in so doing, you'll be helping the pastoral staff to fulfill its calling of ministering the Good News.

[5]My dear friend, it is good that you help the brothers and sisters, even those you do not know. [6]They told the church about your love. Please help them to continue their trip in a way worthy of God. [7]They started out in service to Christ, and they have been accepting nothing from nonbelievers. [8]So we should help such people; when we do, we share in their work for the truth.

[9]I wrote something to the church, but Diotrephes, who loves to be their leader, will not listen to us. [10]So if I come, I will talk about what Diotrephes is doing, about how he lies and says evil things about us. But more than that, he refuses to accept the other brothers and sisters; he even stops those who do want to accept them and puts them out of the church.

[11]My dear friend, do not follow what is bad; follow what is good. The one who does good belongs to God. But the one who does evil has never known God.

[12]Everyone says good things about Demetrius, and the truth agrees with what they say. We also speak well of him, and you know what we say is true.

[13]I have many things I want to write you, but I do not want to use pen and ink. [14]I hope to see you soon and talk face to face. [15]Peace to you. The friends here greet you. Please greet each friend there by name.

experts answer YOUR questions

Q: Why should I read the Bible?

A: The Bible is much more than a book that teaches about God. The Bible is inspired by God, which means that everything in it is profoundly useful for growing in our Christian lives. The Bible is a manual for living that teaches us how to think about life and death.

Q: Can I always come to God, even when I've sinned?

A: No matter whether you've sinned or not, your best move is always to run to God and never from him. You don't have to be sinless to approach God. When you commit sin, all you need to do is confess it, and then go to God with confidence, trusting in the power of his mercy to forgive you.

 1 Elder "Elder" means an older person. It can also mean a special leader in the church (as in Titus 1:5).   1 truth The truth or "Good News" about Jesus Christ that joins all believers together.

JUDE

GRACE ISN'T CHEAP

Cohabitation, or living together outside of marriage, increased dramatically between 1960 and 2000, from an estimated 500,000 couples to 5.5 million. Sex without the responsibilities of marriage isn't a new idea, however. It is what Jude confronts here during the early days of the church. False teachers were turning God's grace into an excuse for indulging in sexual sin. They also refused to accept Jesus as Lord. Such rebellion carries a serious price, and Jude reminds readers that doubt and unbelief are no laughing matter to God.

The interesting thing to note about this book is that these teachers were inside the church, or "people who have en-tered your group," as Jude says. Such people rejected God's authority, had given up their souls for money, and had become consumed by self-centeredness.

They bragged about themselves and flattered others to get what they wanted. Yet, despite his obvious dis-pleasure with such false teachers, Jude reminds the church to remember God's grace. He wants them to show mercy to those who may have doubts and to rescue those are have wandered away. This teaches us to be cautious about judging others, yet not to be so "loving" that we overlook obvious wrongdoing in our midst.

[1]From Jude, a servant of Jesus Christ and a brother of James.

To all who have been called by God. God the Father loves you, and you have been kept safe in Jesus Christ:

[2]Mercy, peace, and love be yours richly.

GOD WILL PUNISH SINNERS

[3]Dear friends, I wanted very much to write you about the salvation we all share. But I felt the need to write you about something else: I want to encourage you to fight hard for the faith that was given the holy people of God once and for all time. [4]Some people have secretly entered your group. Long ago the prophets wrote about these people who will be judged guilty. They are against God and have changed the grace of our God into a reason for sexual sin. They also refuse to accept Jesus Christ, our only Master and Lord.

[5]I want to remind you of some things you already know: Remember that the Lord[n] saved his people by bringing them out of the land of Egypt. But later he destroyed all those who did not believe. [6]And remember the angels who did not keep their place of power but left their proper home. The Lord has kept these angels in darkness, bound with everlasting chains, to be judged on the great day. [7]Also remember the cities of Sodom and Gomorrah[n] and the other towns around them. In the same way they were full of sexual sin and people who desired sexual relations that God does not allow. They suffer the punishment of eternal fire, as an example for all to see.

[8]It is the same with these people who have entered your group. They are guided by dreams and make themselves filthy with sin. They reject God's authority and speak against the angels. [9]Not even the archangel[n] Michael, when he argued with the devil about who would have the body of Moses, dared to judge the devil guilty. Instead, he said, "The Lord punish you." [10]But these people speak against things they do not understand. And what they do know, by feeling, as dumb animals know things, are the very things that destroy them. [11]It will be terrible for them. They have followed the way of Cain, and for money they have given themselves to doing the wrong that Balaam did. They have fought against God as Korah did, and like Korah, they surely will be destroyed. [12]They are like dirty spots in your special Christian meals you share. They eat with you and have no fear, caring only for themselves. They are clouds without rain, which the wind blows around. They are autumn trees without fruit that are pulled out of the ground. So they are twice dead. [13]They are like wild waves of the sea, tossing up their own shameful actions like foam. They are like stars that wander in the sky. A place in the blackest darkness has been kept for them forever.

[14]Enoch, the seventh descendant from Adam, said about these people: "Look, the Lord is coming with many thousands of his holy angels to [15]judge every person. He is coming to punish all who are against God for all the evil they have done against him. And he will

RADICAL FAITH

JUDE 3–4
Jude wanted to write a much longer letter about the awesome stuff God had done by saving believers; but, instead, he needed to write a short, sharp dispatch. He urged his readers to "fight hard for the faith that was given the holy people of God once and for all time." The back part of that phrase asserts that the faith we hold to as Christians is something that the Lord has delivered to us complete. There's plenty to learn, but there's no more to add. At no time will someone be able to add a secret book to the Bible, and no one is free to change the commands of God's Word or its teaching about God. As Jude's letter shows, spiritual fakes were trying to rewrite God's rules about sex, and they rejected Jesus as their supreme Master. The front part of that phrase says that real faith is worth fighting for. It's not an excuse to bash people with the Bible. Rather, like the end of this little letter says, your job is to show mercy, rescuing people from destruction (Jude 23).

MEN of the SWORD

THOMAS
Thomas's biggest distinction has entered the public vocabulary: doubting. It's where we get the descriptive term "doubting Thomas." What people forget is that Thomas was a loyal follower of Jesus. When Jesus and his followers were going back to Judea, Thomas anticipated they would be stoned, but he wanted to go anyway so that he could die with Jesus. After Jesus died and rose again, all the other followers except Thomas got to see him. They told Thomas the story, but he didn't believe them—he wanted physical proof. A week later, Jesus appeared again to give Thomas the proof he needed to believe. —John 20:24–29

JUDE 3

WORD: Adjust to God's leading.
WALK IT: Jude wanted to write about something, but changed his mind according to God's leading. Be attentive to the Holy Spirit, and change direction if he asks you to do so.

punish the sinners who are against God for all the evil they have said against him."

[16]These people complain and blame others, doing the evil things they want to do. They brag about themselves, and they flatter others to get what they want.

A WARNING AND THINGS TO DO

[17]Dear friends, remember what the apostles of our Lord Jesus Christ said before. [18]They said to you, "In the last times there will be people who laugh about God, following their own evil desires which are against God." [19]These are the people who divide you, people whose thoughts are only of this world, who do not have the Spirit.

[20]But dear friends, use your most holy faith to build yourselves up, praying in the Holy Spirit. [21]Keep yourselves in God's love as you wait for the Lord Jesus Christ with his mercy to give you life forever.

[22]Show mercy to some people who have doubts. [23]Take others out of the fire, and save them. Show mercy mixed with fear to others, hating even their clothes which are dirty from sin.

PRAISE GOD

[24]God is strong and can help you not to fall. He can bring you before his glory without any wrong in you and can give you great joy. [25]He is the only God, the One who saves us. To him be glory, greatness, power, and authority through Jesus Christ our Lord for all time past, now, and forever. Amen.

notes

REVELATION?

MAKING SENSE OF END TIMES

If Revelation were a modern film, it might be titled "*The Matrix Meets The Lord of the Rings*." Weird? So are many of the images in the Bible's final book: locusts that sting like scorpions, hail and fire mixed with blood, a burning mountain wiping out a third of everything in the sea, and a seven-headed beast so powerful people worship it. What does it all mean?

Nearly 2,000 years after John wrote these words, scholars still disagree. Some believe he was encouraging the first-century church and that all its prophecies have been fulfilled. Others see Revelation as a prophetic vision of the end of the earth, right before Christ's return. There are all kinds of twists in the dozens of interpretations about this book.

In the end, what matters most is what Revelation reveals about God's plan for humanity. There will be a final judgment, at which every person will stand before God and account for his or her actions while on earth. Satan will face damnation for rebelling against God and leading so many people astray. And the only way to join God in paradise will be to believe in his Son, Jesus. That is the most important lesson to be learned from reading Revelation.

JOHN TELLS ABOUT THIS BOOK

This is the revelation[n] of Jesus Christ, which God gave to him, to show his servants what must soon happen. And Jesus sent his angel to show it to his servant John, [2] who has told everything he has seen. It is the word of God; it is the message from Jesus Christ. [3] Blessed is the one who reads the words of God's message, and blessed are the people who hear this message and do what is written in it. The time is near when all of this will happen.

JESUS' MESSAGE TO THE CHURCHES

[4] From John.

To the seven churches in Asia:

Grace and peace to you from the One who is and was and is coming, and from the seven spirits before his throne, [5] and from Jesus Christ. Jesus is the faithful witness, the first among those raised from the dead. He is the ruler of the kings of the earth.

He is the One who loves us, who made us free from our sins with the blood of his death.

[6] He made us to be a kingdom of priests who serve God his Father. To Jesus Christ be glory and power forever and ever! Amen.

[7] Look, Jesus is coming with the clouds, and everyone will see him, even those who stabbed him. And all peoples of the earth will cry loudly because of him. Yes, this will happen! Amen.

[8] The Lord God says, "I am the Alpha and the Omega.[n] I am the One who is and was and is coming. I am the Almighty."

[9] I, John, am your brother. All of us share with Christ in suffering, in the kingdom, and in patience to continue. I was on the island of Patmos,[n] because I had preached the word of God and the message about Jesus. [10] On the Lord's day I was in the Spirit, and I heard a loud voice behind me that sounded like a trumpet. [11] The voice said, "Write what you see in a book and send it to the seven churches: to Ephesus, Smyrna, Pergamum, Thyatira, Sardis, Philadelphia, and Laodicea."

[12] I turned to see who was talking to me. When I turned, I saw seven golden lampstands [13] and someone among the lampstands who was "like a Son of Man."[n] He was dressed in a long robe and had a gold band around his chest. [14] His head and hair were white like wool, as white as snow, and his eyes were like flames of fire. [15] His feet were like bronze that glows hot in a furnace, and his voice was like the noise of flooding water. [16] He held seven stars in his right hand, and a sharp double-edged sword came out of his mouth. He looked like the sun shining at its brightest time.

[17] When I saw him, I fell down at his feet like a dead man. He put his right hand on me and said, "Do not be afraid. I am the First and the Last. [18] I am the One who lives; I was dead, but look, I am alive forever and ever! And I hold the keys to death and to the place of the dead. [19] So write the things you see, what is now and what will happen later. [20] Here is the secret of the seven stars that you saw in my right hand and the seven golden lampstands: The seven lampstands are the seven churches, and the seven stars are the angels of the seven churches.

TO THE CHURCH IN EPHESUS

2 "Write this to the angel of the church in Ephesus:

"The One who holds the seven stars in his right hand and walks among the seven golden lampstands says this: [2] I know what you do, how you work hard and never give up. I know you do not put up with the false teachings of evil people. You have tested those who say they are apostles but really are not, and you

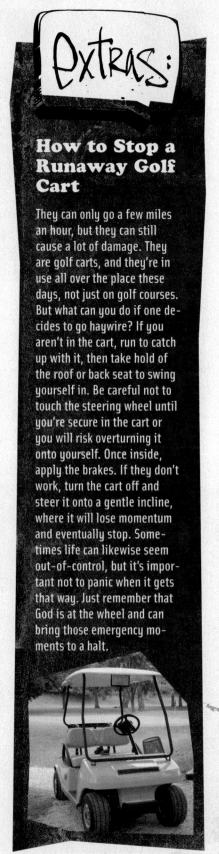

Do's AND Don'ts

- **DO** travel to other places.
- **DO** make reservations.
- **DO** use travelers' checks.
- **DO** take lots of pictures.
- **DON'T** carry too much cash.
- **DON'T** act like a tourist.
- **DON'T** drink the tap water.
- **DON'T** forget your passport.

extras:

How to Stop a Runaway Golf Cart

They can only go a few miles an hour, but they can still cause a lot of damage. They are golf carts, and they're in use all over the place these days, not just on golf courses. But what can you do if one decides to go haywire? If you aren't in the cart, run to catch up with it, then take hold of the roof or back seat to swing yourself in. Be careful not to touch the steering wheel until you're secure in the cart or you will risk overturning it onto yourself. Once inside, apply the brakes. If they don't work, turn the cart off and steer it onto a gentle incline, where it will lose momentum and eventually stop. Sometimes life can likewise seem out-of-control, but it's important not to panic when it gets that way. Just remember that God is at the wheel and can bring those emergency moments to a halt.

1:1 **revelation** Making known truth that has been hidden.   1:8 **Alpha and the Omega** The first and last letters of the Greek alphabet. This means "the beginning and the end."   1:9 **Patmos** A small island in the Aegean Sea, near the coast of Asia Minor (modern Turkey).   1:13 **"like . . . Man"** "Son of Man" is a name Jesus called himself.

341

Class Act

SAVE THE SEX

The myth of "safe sex" is finally getting exposed for the lie it is. People are realizing that condoms not only can't promise safe sex, but they practically condone promiscuity. As many people are learning after the fact, the only safe sex is "saved sex," which is sex that is saved for the sacred relationship of marriage. Your hormones might be raging now, but practicing abstinence will pay off handsomely on your honeymoon. Think of saving sex for marriage as the gift that keeps on giving. You and your future spouse will thank yourselves for waiting on each other, and you'll skip the regret of trying it in your timing.

found they are liars. [3]You have patience and have suffered troubles for my name and have not given up.

[4]"But I have this against you: You have left the love you had in the beginning. [5]So remember where you were before you fell. Change your hearts and do what you did at first. If you do not change, I will come to you and will take away your lampstand from its place. [6]But there is something you do that is right:

You hate what the Nicolaitans[n] do, as much as I.

[7]"Every person who has ears should listen to what the Spirit says to the churches. To those who win the victory I will give the right to eat the fruit from the tree of life, which is in the garden of God.

TO THE CHURCH IN SMYRNA

[8]"Write this to the angel of the church in Smyrna:

"The One who is the First and the Last, who died and came to life again, says this: [9]I know your troubles and that you are poor, but really you are rich! I know the bad things some people say about you. They say they are Jews, but they are not true Jews. They are a synagogue that belongs to Satan. [10]Do not be afraid of what you are about to suffer. I tell you, the devil will put some of you in prison to test you, and you will suffer for ten days. But be

*REVIEWS BOOKS

ERWIN RAPHAEL MCMANUS:
THE BARBARIAN WAY

Like most books by Erwin Raphael McManus, the title of his latest is dramatic and grandiose. But the great thing about this author is that he always backs up his big titles with meaty, interesting, and relevant content. *The Barbarian Way* is not necessarily a book for guys only, but it certainly seems to speak right to the masculine spirit in us. The call in this book is for Christians to live an "original, powerful, untamed" existence for Christ. It's the way McManus has striven to live his life. For guys who like John Eldredge's *Wild at Heart*, this book is for you.

WHY IT ROCKS:

A ROUGH AND RUGGED LOOK AT JESUS IS COOL.

 2:6 Nicolaitans This is the name of a religious group that followed false beliefs and ideas.

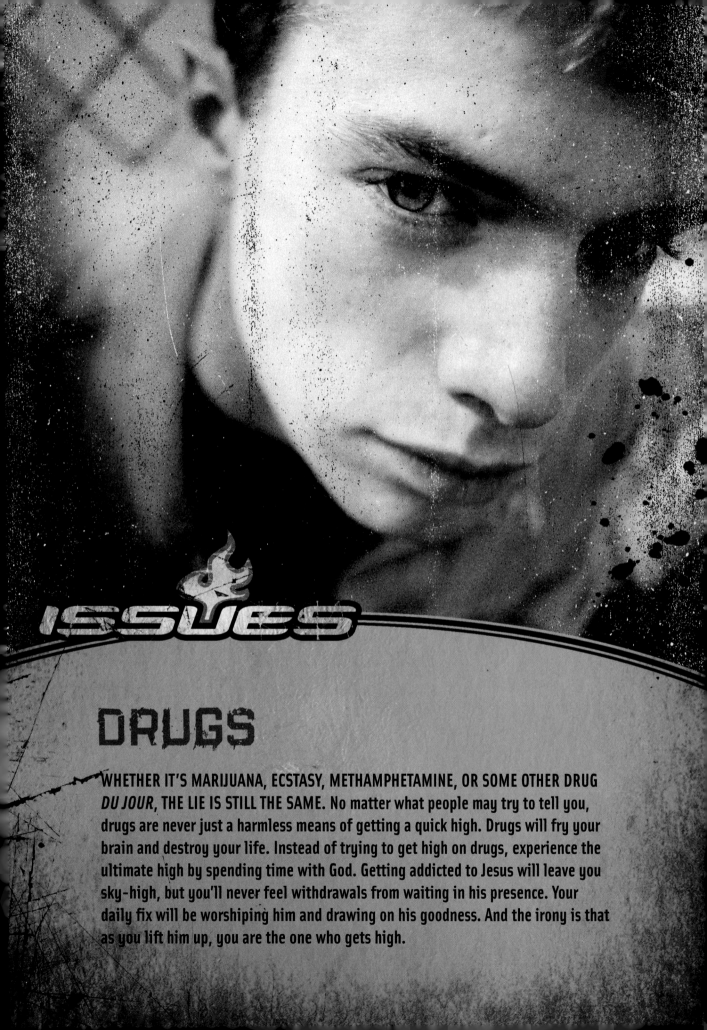

DRUGS

WHETHER IT'S MARIJUANA, ECSTASY, METHAMPHETAMINE, OR SOME OTHER DRUG *DU JOUR*, THE LIE IS STILL THE SAME. No matter what people may try to tell you, drugs are never just a harmless means of getting a quick high. Drugs will fry your brain and destroy your life. Instead of trying to get high on drugs, experience the ultimate high by spending time with God. Getting addicted to Jesus will leave you sky-high, but you'll never feel withdrawals from waiting in his presence. Your daily fix will be worshiping him and drawing on his goodness. And the irony is that as you lift him up, you are the one who gets high.

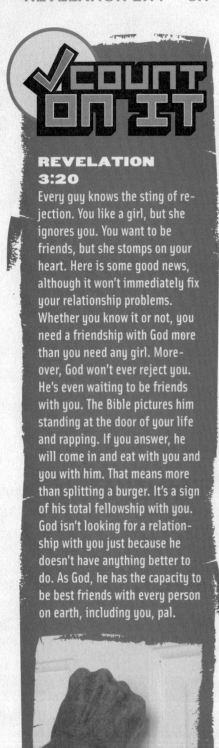

COUNT ON IT

REVELATION 3:20

Every guy knows the sting of rejection. You like a girl, but she ignores you. You want to be friends, but she stomps on your heart. Here is some good news, although it won't immediately fix your relationship problems. Whether you know it or not, you need a friendship with God more than you need any girl. Moreover, God won't ever reject you. He's even waiting to be friends with you. The Bible pictures him standing at the door of your life and rapping. If you answer, he will come in and eat with you and you with him. That means more than splitting a burger. It's a sign of his total fellowship with you. God isn't looking for a relationship with you just because he doesn't have anything better to do. As God, he has the capacity to be best friends with every person on earth, including you, pal.

who win the victory will not be hurt by the second death.

TO THE CHURCH IN PERGAMUM

¹²"Write this to the angel of the church in Pergamum:

"The One who has the sharp, double-edged sword says this: ¹³I know where you live. It is where Satan has his throne. But you are true to me. You did not refuse to tell about your faith in me even during the time of Antipas, my faithful witness who was killed in your city, where Satan lives.

¹⁴"But I have a few things against you: You have some there who follow the teaching of Balaam. He taught Balak how to cause the people of Israel to sin by eating food offered to idols and by taking part in sexual sins. ¹⁵You also have some who follow the teaching of the Nicolaitans.ⁿ ¹⁶So change your hearts and lives. If you do not, I will come to you quickly and fight against them with the sword that comes out of my mouth.

¹⁷"Everyone who has ears should listen to what the Spirit says to the churches.

"I will give some of the hidden manna to everyone who wins the victory. I will also give to each one who wins the victory a white stone with a new name written on it. No one knows this new name except the one who receives it.

TO THE CHURCH IN THYATIRA

¹⁸"Write this to the angel of the church in Thyatira:

"The Son of God, who has eyes that blaze like fire and feet like shining bronze, says this: ¹⁹I know what you do. I know about your love, your faith, your service, and your patience. I know that you are doing more now than you did at first.

²⁰"But I have this against you: You let that woman Jezebel spread false teachings. She says she is a prophetess, but by her teaching she leads my people to take part in sexual sins and to eat food that is offered to idols. ²¹I have given her time to change her heart and turn away from her sin, but she does not want to change. ²²So I will throw her on a bed of suffer-

ing. And all those who take part in adultery with her will suffer greatly if they do not turn away from the wrongs she does. ²³I will also kill her followers. Then all the churches will know I am the One who searches hearts and minds, and I will repay each of you for what you have done.

²⁴"But others of you in Thyatira have not followed her teaching and have not learned

what some call Satan's deep secrets. I say to you that I will not put any other load on you. ²⁵Only continue in your loyalty until I come.

²⁶"I will give power over the nations to everyone who wins the victory and continues to be obedient to me until the end.

²⁷'You will rule over them with an iron rod, as when pottery is broken into pieces.'

Psalm 2:9

²⁸This is the same power I received from my Father. I will also give him the morning star. ²⁹Everyone who has ears should listen to what the Spirit says to the churches.

TO THE CHURCH IN SARDIS

3 "Write this to the angel of the church in Sardis:

"The One who has the seven spirits and the seven stars says this: I know what you do. People say that you are alive, but really you are

WAYS to WALK the WALK

REVELATION 3:15-16

WORD: Be extreme for Jesus.
WALK IT: Heat and cold are at extreme ends of the temperature scale, but lukewarm is in no-man's-land. Be extreme in your faith, and forget lukewarm living that pleases no one.

faithful, even if you have to die, and I will give you the crown of life.

¹¹"Everyone who has ears should listen to what the Spirit says to the churches. Those

 2:15 Nicolaitans This is the name of a religious group that followed false beliefs and ideas.

december

NATIONAL SPIRITUAL LITERACY MONTH

> "To what greater inspiration and counsel can we turn than to the imperishable truth to be found in this treasure house, the Bible?"
> —QUEEN ELIZABETH

1 Mercy Me's Bart Millard celebrates a birthday today.

2

3

4 Read the Christmas story as a family.

5

6 Pray for the kids around the world who can't afford to celebrate Christmas.

7 Today is Aaron Carter's birthday. Pray for his family.

8 Go caroling with your church youth group.

9

10 It's Human Rights Day. Pray for those who are suffering around the world.

11

12

13 It's National Cliché Day. Use a "ton" of them!

14

15 Pray for all of your Jewish friends.

16

17

18 Katie Holmes is another year older today.

19

20 Finish your Christmas shopping.

21

22 Open a savings account for your cash from Christmas.

23

24 It's Ryan Seacrest's birthday.

25 Celebrate Christmas Day with family and friends.

26

27 Enjoy the time off from school!

28

29

30 Ask God what he wants you to change for the coming year.

31 It's New Year's Eve. Learn the words to "Auld Lang Syne."

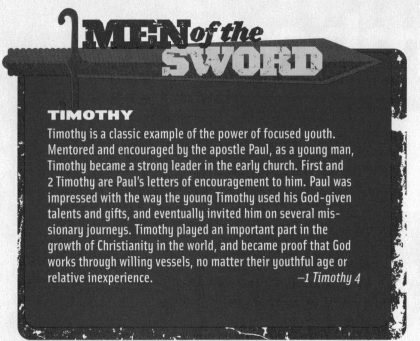

MEN of the SWORD

TIMOTHY

Timothy is a classic example of the power of focused youth. Mentored and encouraged by the apostle Paul, as a young man, Timothy became a strong leader in the early church. First and 2 Timothy are Paul's letters of encouragement to him. Paul was impressed with the way the young Timothy used his God-given talents and gifts, and eventually invited him on several missionary journeys. Timothy played an important part in the growth of Christianity in the world, and became proof that God works through willing vessels, no matter their youthful age or relative inexperience.　　　　　　　　　—1 Timothy 4

dead. [2] Wake up! Strengthen what you have left before it dies completely. I have found that what you are doing is less than what my God wants. [3] So do not forget what you have received and heard. Obey it, and change your hearts and lives. So you must wake up, or I will come like a thief, and you will not know when I will come to you. [4] But you have a few there in Sardis who have kept their clothes unstained, so they will walk with me and will wear white clothes, because they are worthy.

[5] Those who win the victory will be dressed in white clothes like them. And I will not erase their names from the book of life, but I will say they belong to me before my Father and before his angels. [6] Everyone who has ears should listen to what the Spirit says to the churches.

TO THE CHURCH IN PHILADELPHIA

[7] "Write this to the angel of the church in Philadelphia:

"This is what the One who is holy and true, who holds the key of David, says. When he opens a door, no one can close it. And when he closes it, no one can open it. [8] I know what you do. I have put an open door before you, which no one can close. I know you have little strength, but you have obeyed my teaching and were not afraid to speak my name. [9] Those in the synagogue that belongs to Satan say they are Jews, but they are not true Jews; they are liars. I will make them come before you and bow at your feet, and they will know that I have loved you. [10] You have obeyed my teaching about not giving up your faith. So I will keep you from the time of trouble that will come to the whole world to test those who live on earth.

[11] "I am coming soon. Continue strong in your faith so no one will take away your crown. [12] I will make those who win the victory pillars in the temple of my God, and they will never have to leave it. I will write on them the name of my God and the name of the city of my God, the new Jerusalem,[n] that comes down out of heaven from my God. I will also write on them my new name. [13] Everyone who has ears should listen to what the Spirit says to the churches.

TO THE CHURCH IN LAODICEA

[14] "Write this to the angel of the church in Laodicea:

"The Amen,[n] the faithful and true witness, the ruler of all God has made, says this: [15] I know what you do, that you are not hot or

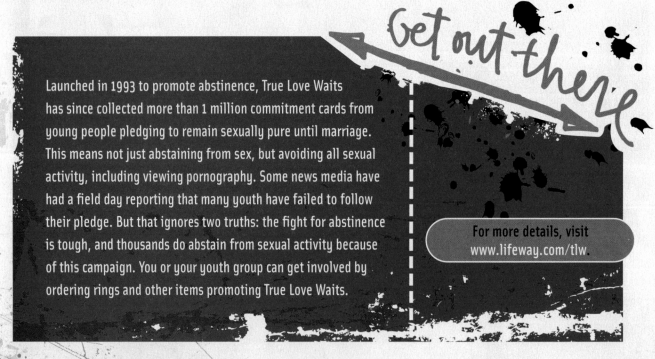

Get out there

Launched in 1993 to promote abstinence, True Love Waits has since collected more than 1 million commitment cards from young people pledging to remain sexually pure until marriage. This means not just abstaining from sex, but avoiding all sexual activity, including viewing pornography. Some news media have had a field day reporting that many youth have failed to follow their pledge. But that ignores two truths: the fight for abstinence is tough, and thousands do abstain from sexual activity because of this campaign. You or your youth group can get involved by ordering rings and other items promoting True Love Waits.

For more details, visit
www.lifeway.com/tlw.

3:12 Jerusalem This name is used to mean the spiritual city God built for his people. See Revelation 21-22.　　3:14 Amen Used here as a name for Jesus; it means to agree fully that something is true.

cold. I wish that you were hot or cold! ¹⁶But because you are lukewarm—neither hot, nor cold—I am ready to spit you out of my mouth. ¹⁷You say, 'I am rich, and I have become wealthy and do not need anything.' But you do not know that you are really miserable, pitiful, poor, blind, and naked. ¹⁸I advise you to buy from me gold made pure in fire so you can be truly rich. Buy from me white clothes so you can be clothed and so you can cover your shameful nakedness. Buy from me medicine to put on your eyes so you can truly see.

¹⁹"I correct and punish those whom I love. So be eager to do right, and change your hearts and lives. ²⁰Here I am! I stand at the door and knock. If you hear my voice and open the door, I will come in and eat with you, and you will eat with me.

²¹"Those who win the victory will sit with me on my throne in the same way that I won the victory and sat down with my Father on his throne. ²²Everyone who has ears should listen to what the Spirit says to the churches."

JOHN SEES HEAVEN

4 After the vision of these things I looked, and there before me was an open door in heaven. And the same voice that spoke to me before, that sounded like a trumpet, said, "Come up here, and I will show you what must happen after this." ²Immediately I was in the Spirit, and before me was a throne in heaven, and someone was sitting on it. ³The One who sat on the throne looked like precious stones, like jasper and carnelian. All around the throne was a rainbow the color of an emerald. ⁴Around the throne there were twenty-four other thrones with twenty-four elders sitting on them. They were dressed in white and had golden crowns on their heads. ⁵Lightning flashes and noises and thunder came from the throne. Before the throne seven lamps were burning, which are the seven spirits of God. ⁶Also before the throne there was something that looked like a sea of glass, clear like crystal.

In the center and around the throne were four living creatures with eyes all over them, in front and in back. ⁷The first living creature was like a lion. The second was like a calf. The third had a face like a man. The fourth was like a flying eagle. ⁸Each of these four living creatures had six wings and was covered all over with eyes, inside and out. Day and night they never stop saying:

"Holy, holy, holy is the Lord God Almighty.

He was, he is, and he is coming."

⁹These living creatures give glory, honor, and thanks to the One who sits on the throne, who lives forever and ever. ¹⁰Then the twenty-four elders bow down before the One who sits on the throne, and they worship him who lives forever and ever. They put their crowns down before the throne and say:

¹¹"You are worthy, our Lord and God,

to receive glory and honor and power,

because you made all things.

Everything existed and was made,

because you wanted it."

5 Then I saw a scroll in the right hand of the One sitting on the throne. The scroll had writing on both sides and was kept closed with seven seals. ²And I saw a powerful angel calling in a loud voice, "Who is worthy to break the seals and open the scroll?" ³But there

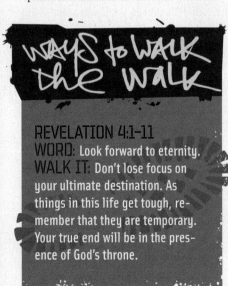

6 Then I saw a Lamb standing in the center of the throne and in the middle of the four living creatures and the elders. The Lamb looked as if he had been killed. He had seven horns and seven eyes, which are the seven spirits of God that were sent into all the world. 7 The Lamb came and took the scroll from the right hand of the One sitting on the throne. 8 When

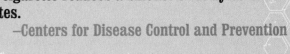

he took the scroll, the four living creatures and the twenty-four elders bowed down before the Lamb. Each one of them had a harp and golden bowls full of incense, which are the prayers of God's holy people. 9 And they all sang a new song to the Lamb:

"You are worthy to take the scroll
  and to open its seals,
because you were killed,
  and with the blood of your death you
    bought people for God
  from every tribe, language, people, and
    nation.
10 You made them to be a kingdom of priests
    for our God,
  and they will rule on the earth."

11 Then I looked, and I heard the voices of many angels around the throne, and the four living creatures, and the elders. There were thousands and thousands of angels, 12 saying in a loud voice:

"The Lamb who was killed is worthy
  to receive power, wealth, wisdom, and
    strength,
  honor, glory, and praise!"

13 Then I heard all creatures in heaven and on earth and under the earth and in the sea saying:

"To the One who sits on the throne
  and to the Lamb
be praise and honor and glory and power
  forever and ever."

14 The four living creatures said, "Amen," and the elders bowed down and worshiped.

6 Then I watched while the Lamb opened the first of the seven seals. I heard one of the four living creatures say with a voice like thunder, "Come!" 2 I looked, and there before me was a white horse. The rider on the horse held a bow, and he was given a

crown, and he rode out, determined to win the victory.

3 When the Lamb opened the second seal, I heard the second living creature say, "Come!" 4 Then another horse came out, a red one. Its rider was given power to take away peace from the earth and to make people kill each other, and he was given a big sword.

5 When the Lamb opened the third seal, I heard the third living creature say, "Come!" I looked, and there before me was a black horse, and its rider held a pair of scales in his hand. 6 Then I heard something that sounded like a voice coming from the middle of the four living creatures. The voice said, "A quart of wheat for a day's pay, and three quarts of barley for a day's pay, and do not damage the olive oil and wine!"

7 When the Lamb opened the fourth seal, I heard the voice of the fourth living creature say, "Come!" 8 I looked, and there before me was a pale horse. Its rider was named death, and Hades[n] was following close behind him. They were given power over a fourth of the earth to kill people by war, by starvation, by disease, and by the wild animals of the earth.

9 When the Lamb opened the fifth seal, I saw under the altar the souls of those who had been killed because they were faithful to the word of God and to the message they had received. 10 These souls shouted in a loud voice, "Holy and true Lord, how long until you judge the people of the earth and punish them for killing us?" 11 Then each one of them was given a white robe and was told to wait a short time longer. There were still some of their fellow servants and brothers and sisters in the service of Christ who must be killed as they were. They had to wait until all of this was finished.

12 Then I watched while the Lamb opened the sixth seal, and there was a great earthquake. The sun became black like rough black cloth, and the whole moon became red like blood. 13 And the stars in the sky fell to the earth like figs falling from a fig tree when the wind blows. 14 The sky disappeared as a scroll when it is rolled up, and every mountain and island was moved from its place.

15 Then the kings of the earth, the rulers,

was no one in heaven or on earth or under the earth who could open the scroll or look inside it. 4 I cried bitterly because there was no one who was worthy to open the scroll or look inside. 5 But one of the elders said to me, "Do not cry! The Lion[n] from the tribe of Judah, David's descendant, has won the victory so that he is able to open the scroll and its seven seals."

 5:5 Lion Here refers to Christ. **6:8 Hades** The unseen world of the dead.

the generals, the rich people, the powerful people, the slaves, and the free people hid themselves in caves and in the rocks on the mountains. [16] They called to the mountains and the rocks, "Fall on us. Hide us from the face of the One who sits on the throne and from the anger of the Lamb! [17] The great day for their anger has come, and who can stand against it?"

THE 144,000 PEOPLE OF ISRAEL

7 After the vision of these things I saw four angels standing at the four corners of the earth. The angels were holding the four winds of the earth to keep them from blowing on the land or on the sea or on any tree. [2] Then I saw another angel coming up from the east who had the seal of the living God. And he called out in a loud voice to the four angels to whom God had given power to harm the earth and the sea. [3] He said to them, "Do not harm the land or the sea or the trees until we mark with a sign the foreheads of the people who serve our God." [4] Then I heard how many people were marked with the sign. There were one hundred forty-four thousand from every tribe of the people of Israel.

[5] From the tribe of Judah twelve thousand were marked with the sign, from the tribe of Reuben twelve thousand, from the tribe of Gad twelve thousand, [6] from the tribe of Asher twelve thousand, from the tribe of Naphtali twelve thousand, from the tribe of Manasseh twelve thousand, [7] from the tribe of Simeon twelve thousand, from the tribe of Levi twelve thousand, from the tribe of Issachar twelve thousand, [8] from the tribe of Zebulun twelve thousand, from the tribe of Joseph twelve thousand, and from the tribe of Benjamin twelve thousand were marked with the sign.

THE GREAT CROWD WORSHIPS GOD

[9] After the vision of these things I looked, and there was a great number of people, so many that no one could count them. They were from every nation, tribe, people, and language of the earth. They were all standing before the throne and before the Lamb, wearing white robes and holding palm branches in their hands. [10] They were shouting in a loud voice, "Salvation belongs to our God, who sits on the throne, and to the Lamb." [11] All the angels were standing around the throne and the elders and the four living creatures. They all bowed down on their faces before the throne and worshiped God, [12] saying, "Amen! Praise, glory, wisdom, thanks, honor, power, and strength belong to our God forever and ever. Amen!"

[13] Then one of the elders asked me, "Who are these people dressed in white robes? Where did they come from?"

[14] I answered, "You know, sir."

And the elder said to me, "These are the people who have come out of the great distress. They have washed their robes" and made them white in the blood of the Lamb. [15] Because of this, they are before the throne of God. They worship him day and night in his temple. And the One who sits on the throne will be present with them. [16] Those people will never be hungry again, and they will never be thirsty again. The sun will not hurt them, and no heat will burn them, [17] because the Lamb at the center of the throne will be their shepherd. He will lead them to springs of water that give life. And God will wipe away every tear from their eyes."

THE SEVENTH SEAL

8 When the Lamb opened the seventh seal, there was silence in heaven for about half an hour. [2] And I saw the seven angels

who stand before God and to whom were given seven trumpets.

[3] Another angel came and stood at the altar, holding a golden pan for incense. He was given

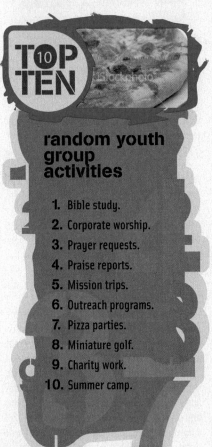

TOP 10 TEN

random youth group activities

1. Bible study.
2. Corporate worship.
3. Prayer requests.
4. Praise reports.
5. Mission trips.
6. Outreach programs.
7. Pizza parties.
8. Miniature golf.
9. Charity work.
10. Summer camp.

* * *
experts answer YOUR questions

Q: What can I do when I'm discouraged in my Christian walk?

A: Throughout the trials of our faith journey, we can be encouraged by remembering that Jesus understands our struggles. He went through a bigger challenge than any of us will ever face, and he overcame it. Remembering that can give us the courage to persevere.

Q: What should I do when I struggle with issues?

A: It can be hard to continue trusting God when you're going through difficult times in your life. But the Bible says that trials, although they're painful, aren't always a bad thing. In fact, we're encouraged to rejoice in our trials, because we know that God is working through them to strengthen our faith and to give us patience.

✱ **7:14 washed their robes** This means they believed in Jesus so that their sins could be forgiven by Christ's blood.

much incense to offer with the prayers of all God's holy people. The angel put this offering on the golden altar before the throne. [4] The smoke from the incense went up from the angel's hand to God with the prayers of God's people. [5] Then the angel filled the incense pan with fire from the altar and threw it on the earth, and there were flashes of lightning, thunder and loud noises, and an earthquake.

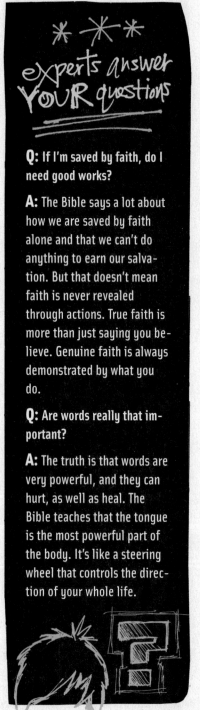

experts answer YOUR questions

Q: If I'm saved by faith, do I need good works?

A: The Bible says a lot about how we are saved by faith alone and that we can't do anything to earn our salvation. But that doesn't mean faith is never revealed through actions. True faith is more than just saying you believe. Genuine faith is always demonstrated by what you do.

Q: Are words really that important?

A: The truth is that words are very powerful, and they can hurt, as well as heal. The Bible teaches that the tongue is the most powerful part of the body. It's like a steering wheel that controls the direction of your whole life.

THE SEVEN ANGELS AND TRUMPETS

[6] Then the seven angels who had the seven trumpets prepared to blow them.

[7] The first angel blew his trumpet, and hail and fire mixed with blood were poured down on the earth. And a third of the earth, and all the green grass, and a third of the trees were burned up.

[8] Then the second angel blew his trumpet, and something that looked like a big mountain, burning with fire, was thrown into the sea. And a third of the sea became blood, [9] a third of the living things in the sea died, and a third of the ships were destroyed.

[10] Then the third angel blew his trumpet, and a large star, burning like a torch, fell from the sky. It fell on a third of the rivers and on the springs of water. [11] The name of the star is Wormwood.[n] And a third of all the water became bitter, and many people died from drinking the water that was bitter.

[12] Then the fourth angel blew his trumpet, and a third of the sun, and a third of the moon, and a third of the stars were struck. So a third of them became dark, and a third of the day was without light, and also the night.

[13] While I watched, I heard an eagle that was flying high in the air cry out in a loud voice, "Trouble! Trouble! Trouble for those who live on the earth because of the remaining sounds of the trumpets that the other three angels are about to blow!"

9 Then the fifth angel blew his trumpet, and I saw a star fall from the sky to the earth. The star was given the key to the deep hole that leads to the bottomless pit. [2] Then it opened up the hole that leads to the bottomless pit, and smoke came up from the hole like smoke from a big furnace. Then the sun and sky became dark because of the smoke from the hole. [3] Then locusts came down to the earth out of the smoke, and they were given the power to sting like scorpions.[n] [4] They were told not to harm the grass on the earth or any plant or tree. They could harm only the people who did not have the sign of God on their foreheads. [5] These locusts were not given the power to kill anyone, but to cause pain to the people for five months. And the pain they felt was like the pain a scorpion gives when it stings someone. [6] During those days people will look for a way to die, but they will not find it. They will want to die, but death will run away from them.

[7] The locusts looked like horses prepared for battle. On their heads they wore what looked like crowns of gold, and their faces looked like human faces. [8] Their hair was like

DO's AND Don'ts

DO study language.

DO write for fun.

DO collect quotes.

DO start a blog.

DON'T plagiarize others.

DON'T misuse words.

DON'T mix metaphors.

DON'T make typing errors.

women's hair, and their teeth were like lions' teeth. [9] Their chests looked like iron breastplates, and the sound of their wings was like the noise of many horses and chariots hurrying into battle. [10] The locusts had tails with stingers like scorpions, and in their tails was their power to hurt people for five months. [11] The locusts had a king who was the angel of the bottomless pit. His name in the Hebrew language is Abaddon and in the Greek language is Apollyon.[n]

[12] The first trouble is past; there are still two other troubles that will come.

[13] Then the sixth angel blew his trumpet, and I heard a voice coming from the horns on the golden altar that is before God. [14] The voice said to the sixth angel who had the trumpet, "Free the four angels who are tied at the great river Euphrates." [15] And they let loose the four angels who had been kept ready for this hour and day and month and year so they could kill a third of all people on the earth. [16] I heard how many troops on horses were in their army— two hundred million.

 8:11 Wormwood Name of a very bitter plant; used here to give the idea of bitter sorrow. **9:3 scorpions** A scorpion is an insect that stings with a bad poison. **9:11 Abaddon, Apollyon** Both names mean "Destroyer."

[17]The horses and their riders I saw in the vision looked like this: They had breastplates that were fiery red, dark blue, and yellow like sulfur. The heads of the horses looked like heads of lions, with fire, smoke, and sulfur coming out of their mouths. [18]A third of all the people on earth were killed by these three terrible disasters coming out of the horses' mouths: the fire, the smoke, and the sulfur. [19]The horses' power was in their mouths and in their tails; their tails were like snakes with heads, and with them they hurt people.

[20]The other people who were not killed by these terrible disasters still did not change their hearts and turn away from what they had made with their own hands. They did not stop worshiping demons and idols made of gold, silver, bronze, stone, and wood—things that cannot see or hear or walk. [21]These people did not change their hearts and turn away from murder or evil magic, from their sexual sins or stealing.

THE ANGEL AND THE SMALL SCROLL

10 Then I saw another powerful angel coming down from heaven dressed in a cloud with a rainbow over his head. His face was like the sun, and his legs were like pillars of fire. [2]The angel was holding a small scroll open in his hand. He put his right foot on the sea and his left foot on the land. [3]Then he shouted loudly like the roaring of a lion. And when he shouted, the voices of seven thunders spoke. [4]When the seven thunders spoke, I started to write. But I heard a voice from heaven say, "Keep hidden what the seven thunders said, and do not write them down."

[5]Then the angel I saw standing on the sea and on the land raised his right hand to heaven, [6]and he made a promise by the power of the One who lives forever and ever. He is the One who made the skies and all that is in them, the earth and all that is in it, and the sea and all that is in it. The angel promised, "There will be no more waiting! [7]In the days when the seventh angel is ready to blow his trumpet, God's secret will be finished. This secret is the Good News God told to his servants, the prophets."

[8]Then I heard the same voice from heaven

Relationships

"He must look for peace and work for it" (1 Peter 3:11b). This passage of Scripture is talking about what people must do to be happy and enjoy their lives. Sorry to say, but you're going to have to work for peace—especially when it comes to your relationships with others. You can't expect it to come easy. You're going to hit some snags, and, when you do, you will have to look for peace in that relationship, and then work for it. It may be work, but it'll be worth it; peace comes at a price, but it pays.

Get out there

Artists Helping Children seeks to comfort children in hospitals, clinics, and shelters by brightening their environment. Because so many institutions have bleak, white walls, this non-profit agency tries to bring color and fun into children's lives with murals and other art. The group has also been raising money to send thousands of teddy bears overseas to victims of the tsunami in Southeast Asia. Teens can help this cause by making pictures or cards to send to hospitalized children, painting tote bags that will later be filled with gifts, or by organizing a stuffed animal drive for charity.

To find out more, surf over to www.artistshelpingchildren.org.

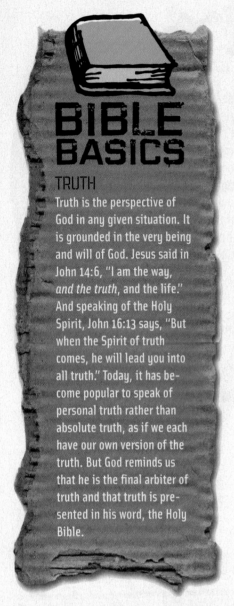

people worshiping there. ²But do not measure the yard outside the temple. Leave it alone, because it has been given to those who are not God's people. And they will trample on the holy city for forty-two months. ³And I will give power to my two witnesses to prophesy for one thousand two hundred sixty days, and they will be dressed in rough cloth to show their sadness."

⁴These two witnesses are the two olive trees and the two lampstands that stand before the Lord of the earth. ⁵And if anyone tries to hurt them, fire comes from their mouths and kills their enemies. And if anyone tries to hurt them in whatever way, in that same way that person will die. ⁶These witnesses have the power to stop the sky from raining during the time they are prophesying. And they have power to make the waters become blood, and they have power to send every kind of trouble to the earth as many times as they want.

⁷When the two witnesses have finished telling their message, the beast that comes up from the bottomless pit will fight a war against them. He will defeat them and kill them. ⁸The bodies of the two witnesses will lie in the street of the great city where the Lord was killed. This city is named Sodom" and Egypt, which has a spiritual meaning. ⁹Those from every race of people, tribe, language, and nation will look at the bodies of the two witnesses for three and one-half days, and they will refuse to bury them. ¹⁰People who live on the earth will rejoice and be happy because these two are dead. They will send each other gifts, because these two prophets brought much suffering to those who live on the earth.

¹¹But after three and one-half days, God put the breath of life into the two prophets again. They stood on their feet, and everyone who saw them became very afraid. ¹²Then the two prophets heard a loud voice from heaven saying, "Come up here!" And they went up into heaven in a cloud as their enemies watched.

¹³In the same hour there was a great earthquake, and a tenth of the city was destroyed. Seven thousand people were killed in the earthquake, and those who did not die were very afraid and gave glory to the God of heaven.

¹⁴The second trouble is finished. Pay attention: The third trouble is coming soon.

THE SEVENTH TRUMPET

¹⁵Then the seventh angel blew his trumpet. And there were loud voices in heaven, saying:

"The power to rule the world now belongs
   to our Lord and his Christ,
   and he will rule forever and ever."

¹⁶Then the twenty-four elders, who sit on their thrones before God, bowed down on their faces and worshiped God. ¹⁷They said:

"We give thanks to you, Lord God
   Almighty,
   who is and who was,
because you have used your great power
   and have begun to rule!

again, saying to me: "Go and take the open scroll that is in the hand of the angel that is standing on the sea and on the land."

⁹So I went to the angel and told him to give me the small scroll. And he said to me, "Take the scroll and eat it. It will be sour in your stomach, but in your mouth it will be sweet as honey." ¹⁰So I took the small scroll from the angel's hand and ate it. In my mouth it tasted sweet as honey, but after I ate it, it was sour in my stomach. ¹¹Then I was told, "You must prophesy again about many peoples, nations, languages, and kings."

THE TWO WITNESSES

11 I was given a measuring stick like a rod, and I was told, "Go and measure the temple of God and the altar, and count the

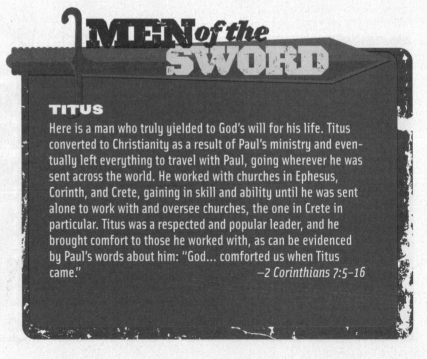

 11:8 Sodom City that God destroyed because the people were so evil.

GUARD YOUR HEART

Your teenage years should be some of the happiest and most fruitful moments of your life. Don't counterfeit something as important as love. Enter relationships cautiously and carry what you learn to be true about love into your marriage. The less baggage you carry into it, the better it will be for you.

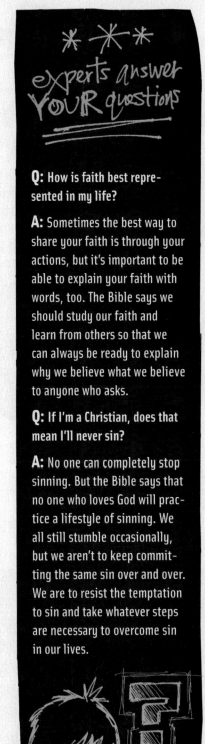

[18] The people of the world were angry,
but your anger has come.
The time has come to judge the dead,
and to reward your servants the
prophets
and your holy people,
all who respect you, great and small.
The time has come to destroy those who
destroy the earth!"

[19] Then God's temple in heaven was opened. The Ark that holds the agreement God gave to his people could be seen in his temple. Then there were flashes of lightning, noises, thunder, an earthquake, and a great hailstorm.

THE WOMAN AND THE DRAGON

12 And then a great wonder appeared in heaven: A woman was clothed with the sun, and the moon was under her feet, and a crown of twelve stars was on her head. [2] She was pregnant and cried out with pain, because she was about to give birth. [3] Then another wonder appeared in heaven: There was a giant red dragon with seven heads and seven crowns on each head. He also had ten horns. [4] His tail swept a third of the stars out of the sky and threw them down to the earth. He stood in front of the woman who was ready to give birth so he could eat her baby as soon as it was born. [5] Then the woman gave birth to a son who will rule all the nations with an iron rod. And her child was taken up to God and to his throne. [6] The woman ran away into the desert to a place God prepared for her where she would be taken care of for one thousand two hundred sixty days.

[7] Then there was a war in heaven. Michael[n] and his angels fought against the dragon, and the dragon and his angels fought back. [8] But the dragon was not strong enough, and he and his angels lost their place in heaven. [9] The giant dragon was thrown down out of heaven. (He is that old snake called the devil or Satan, who tricks the whole world.) The dragon with his angels was thrown down to the earth.

[10] Then I heard a loud voice in heaven saying:

"The salvation and the power and the
kingdom of our God
and the authority of his Christ have now
come.
The accuser of our brothers and sisters,
who accused them day and night before
our God,
has been thrown down.
[11] And our brothers and sisters defeated him
by the blood of the Lamb's death
and by the message they preached.
They did not love their lives so much
that they were afraid of death.
[12] So rejoice, you heavens
and all who live there!
But it will be terrible for the earth and the
sea,
because the devil has come down to
you!
He is filled with anger,
because he knows he does not have
much time."

[13] When the dragon saw he had been thrown down to the earth, he hunted for the woman who had given birth to the son. [14] But the woman was given the two wings of a great eagle so she could fly to the place prepared for her in the desert. There she would be taken care of for three and one-half years, away from the snake. [15] Then the snake poured water out of its mouth like a river toward the woman so the flood would carry her away. [16] But the earth helped the woman by opening its mouth and swallowing the river that came from the mouth of the dragon. [17] Then the dragon was very angry at the woman, and he went off to make war against all her other children—those who obey God's commands and who have the message Jesus taught.

[18] And the dragon[n] stood on the seashore.

THE TWO BEASTS

13 Then I saw a beast coming up out of the sea. It had ten horns and seven heads, and there was a crown on each horn. A name against God was written on each head. [2] This beast looked like a leopard, with feet like a bear's feet and a mouth like a lion's mouth. And the dragon gave the beast all of his power and his throne and great authority. [3] One of the heads of the beast looked as if it had been

12:7 **Michael** The archangel—leader among God's angels or messengers (Jude 9).   12:18 **the dragon** Some Greek copies read "I."

Relationships

"My children, we should love people not only with words and talk, but by our actions and true caring" (1 John 3:18). Love shouldn't be all talk; it requires some action. Show your parents that you love them by keeping your room clean. Maybe even do some dishes or take out the trash. Show your siblings that you love them by letting them take the first shower in the morning. Prove to your friends that you love them by volunteering your car (and gas) for a group outing. Do things for the ones you love, and you'll tell them how you feel without saying a word.

killed by a wound, but this death wound was healed. Then the whole world was amazed and followed the beast. [4]People worshiped the dragon because he had given his power to the beast. And they also worshiped the beast, asking, "Who is like the beast? Who can make war against it?"

[5]The beast was allowed to say proud words and words against God, and it was allowed to use its power for forty-two months. [6]It used its mouth to speak against God, against God's name, against the place where God lives, and against all those who live in heaven. [7]It was given power to make war against God's holy people and to defeat them. It was given power over every tribe, people, language, and nation. [8]And all who live on earth will worship the beast—all the people since the beginning of the world whose names are not written in the Lamb's book of life. The Lamb is the One who was killed.

[9]Anyone who has ears should listen:
[10]If you are to be a prisoner,
    then you will be a prisoner.
If you are to be killed with the sword,
    then you will be killed with the sword.
This means that God's holy people must have patience and faith.

[11]Then I saw another beast coming up out of the earth. It had two horns like a lamb, but it spoke like a dragon. [12]This beast stands before the first beast and uses the same power the first beast has. By this power it makes everyone living on earth worship the first beast, who had the death wound that was healed. [13]And the second beast does great miracles so that it even makes fire come down from heaven to earth while people are watching. [14]It fools those who live on earth by the miracles it has been given the power to do. It does these miracles to serve the first beast. The second beast orders people to make an idol to honor the first beast, the one that was wounded by the deadly sword but sprang to life again. [15]The second beast was given power to give life to the idol of the first one so that the idol could speak. And the second beast was given power to command all who will not worship the image of the beast to be killed. [16]The second beast also forced all people, small and great,

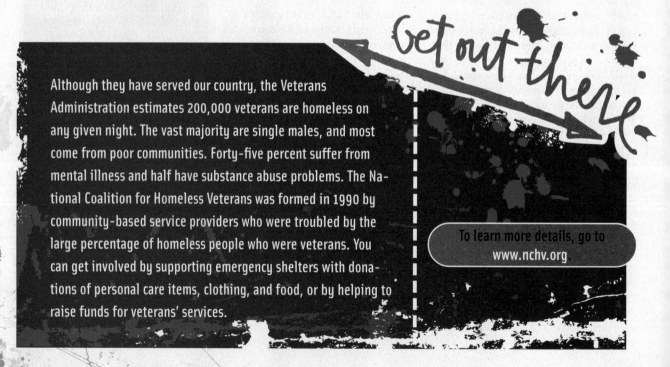

Get out there

Although they have served our country, the Veterans Administration estimates 200,000 veterans are homeless on any given night. The vast majority are single males, and most come from poor communities. Forty-five percent suffer from mental illness and half have substance abuse problems. The National Coalition for Homeless Veterans was formed in 1990 by community-based service providers who were troubled by the large percentage of homeless people who were veterans. You can get involved by supporting emergency shelters with donations of personal care items, clothing, and food, or by helping to raise funds for veterans' services.

To learn more details, go to
www.nchv.org

rich and poor, free and slave, to have a mark on their right hand or on their forehead. [17]No one could buy or sell without this mark, which is the name of the beast or the number of its name. [18]This takes wisdom. Let the one who has understanding find the meaning of the number, which is the number of a person. Its number is 666.[n]

THE SONG OF THE SAVED

14 Then I looked, and there before me was the Lamb standing on Mount Zion.[n] With him were one hundred forty-four thousand people who had his name and his Father's name written on their foreheads. [2]And I heard a sound from heaven like the noise of flooding water and like the sound of loud thunder. The sound I heard was like people playing harps. [3]And they sang a new song before the throne and before the four living creatures and the elders. No one could learn the new song except the one hundred forty-four thousand who had been bought from the earth. [4]These are the ones who did not do sinful things with women, because they kept themselves pure. They follow the Lamb every place he goes. These one hundred forty-four thousand were bought from among the people of the earth as people to be offered to God and the Lamb. [5]They were not guilty of telling lies; they are without fault.

How to Put Out an Oven Fire

Believe it or not, it happens. That frozen pizza gets a little too cooked and, when you open the door to the oven, it catches on fire. So what now? The temptation is to throw something on it, like water or whatever you have available, but that can spread the fire and cause it to flame out of control. Believe it or not, your best course of action is simply to close the door, turn the oven off, and wait. Give it five minutes or so, then crack the oven door to see if the fire's extinguished. If there's a lot of smoke, be sure to open as many windows as you can, and turn on the vent-hood to get rid of it. Sometimes outside influences can inflame temptation in you. The best way to handle them is to cut them off and close the door on the situation altogether.

THE THREE ANGELS

[6]Then I saw another angel flying high in the air. He had the eternal Good News to preach to those who live on earth—to every nation, tribe, language, and people. [7]He preached in a loud voice, "Fear God and give him praise, because the time has come for God to judge all people. So worship God who made the heavens, and the earth, and the sea, and the springs of water."

CHARLIE AND THE CHOCOLATE FACTORY

Director Tim Burton is a movie genius, as his ability to bring a set and story to life is magical. That's certainly true in his updated version of this classic tale. With Johnny Depp starring as the stranger-than-strange candy maker, Burton adds his own spin to Willy Wonka's story by giving us a glimpse of his childhood, which is meant to explain why this eccentric guy lives as he does. No doubt, this new movie will become a classic, much like its predecessor. While it's not necessarily for guys who like tons of action and suspense, it makes a good date movie.

WHY IT ROCKS:

A TIMELESS STORY GETS RETOLD WITH BIG COLOR.

 13:18 666 Some Greek copies read "616." 14:1 Mount Zion Another name for Jerusalem; here meaning the spiritual city of God's people.

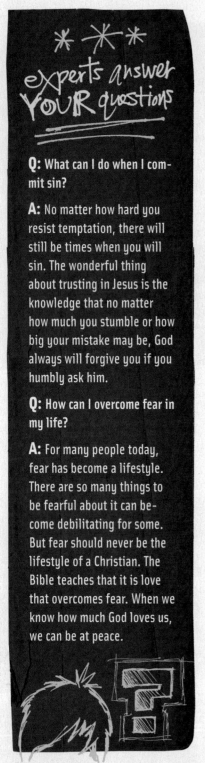

experts answer
YOUR questions

Q: What can I do when I commit sin?

A: No matter how hard you resist temptation, there will still be times when you will sin. The wonderful thing about trusting in Jesus is the knowledge that no matter how much you stumble or how big your mistake may be, God always will forgive you if you humbly ask him.

Q: How can I overcome fear in my life?

A: For many people today, fear has become a lifestyle. There are so many things to be fearful about it can become debilitating for some. But fear should never be the lifestyle of a Christian. The Bible teaches that it is love that overcomes fear. When we know how much God loves us, we can be at peace.

ships the beast and his idol and gets the beast's mark on the forehead or on the hand, [10]that one also will drink the wine of God's anger, which is prepared with all its strength in the cup of his anger. And that person will be put in pain with burning sulfur before the holy angels and the Lamb. [11]And the smoke from their burning pain will rise forever and ever. There will be no rest, day or night, for those who worship the beast and his idol or who get the mark of his name." [12]This means God's holy people must be patient. They must obey God's commands and keep their faith in Jesus.

[13]Then I heard a voice from heaven saying, "Write this: Blessed are the dead who die from now on in the Lord."

The Spirit says, "Yes, they will rest from their hard work, and the reward of all they have done stays with them."

THE EARTH IS HARVESTED

[14]Then I looked, and there before me was a white cloud, and sitting on the white cloud was One who looked like a Son of Man.[n] He had a gold crown on his head and a sharp sickle[n] in his hand. [15]Then another angel came out of the temple and called out in a loud voice to the One who was sitting on the cloud, "Take your sickle and harvest from the earth, because the time to harvest has come, and the fruit of the earth is ripe." [16]So the One who was sitting on the cloud swung his sickle over the earth, and the earth was harvested.

[17]Then another angel came out of the temple in heaven, and he also had a sharp sickle. [18]And then another angel, who has power over the fire, came from the altar. This angel called to the angel with the sharp sickle, saying, "Take your sharp sickle and gather the bunches of grapes from the earth's vine, because its grapes are ripe." [19]Then the angel swung his sickle over the earth. He gathered the earth's grapes and threw them into the great winepress of God's anger. [20]They were trampled in the winepress outside the city, and blood flowed out of the winepress as high as horses' bridles for a distance of about one hundred eighty miles.

THE LAST TROUBLES

15 Then I saw another wonder in heaven that was great and amazing. There were seven angels bringing seven disasters. These are the last disasters, because after them, God's anger is finished.

[2]I saw what looked like a sea of glass mixed with fire. All of those who had won the victory over the beast and his idol and over the number of his name were standing by the sea of glass. They had harps that God had given them. [3]They sang the song of Moses, the servant of God, and the song of the Lamb:

"You do great and wonderful things,
Psalm 111:2
Lord God Almighty. *Amos 3:13*
Everything the Lord does is right and true,
Psalm 145:17
King of the nations.[n]
[4]Everyone will respect you, Lord,
Jeremiah 10:7
and will honor you.
Only you are holy.
All the nations will come
and worship you, *Psalm 86:9–10*
because the right things you have done
are now made known."
Deuteronomy 32:4

[5]After this I saw that the temple (the Tent of the Agreement) in heaven was opened. [6]And the seven angels bringing the seven disasters came out of the temple. They were dressed in clean, shining linen and wore golden bands tied around their chests. [7]Then one of the four living creatures gave to the seven angels seven golden bowls filled with the anger of God, who

random money-making ideas

1. Collect cans.
2. Wash cars.
3. Mow lawns.
4. Rake yards.
5. Flip hamburgers.
6. Bag groceries.
7. Run errands.
8. Wait tables.
9. Fix computers.
10. Baby-sit siblings.

[8]Then the second angel followed the first angel and said, "Ruined, ruined is the great city of Babylon! She made all the nations drink the wine of the anger of her adultery."

[9]Then a third angel followed the first two angels, saying in a loud voice: "If anyone wor-

14:14 Son of Man "Son of Man" is a name Jesus called himself. **14:14 sickle** A farming tool with a curved blade. It was used to harvest grain. **15:3 King . . . nations** Some Greek copies read "King of the ages."

356

lives forever and ever. [8]The temple was filled with smoke from the glory and the power of God, and no one could enter the temple until the seven disasters of the seven angels were finished.

THE BOWLS OF GOD'S ANGER

16 Then I heard a loud voice from the temple saying to the seven angels, "Go and pour out the seven bowls of God's anger on the earth."

[2]The first angel left and poured out his bowl on the land. Then ugly and painful sores came upon all those who had the mark of the beast and who worshiped his idol.

[3]The second angel poured out his bowl on the sea, and it became blood like that of a dead man, and every living thing in the sea died.

[4]The third angel poured out his bowl on the rivers and the springs of water, and they became blood. [5]Then I heard the angel of the waters saying:

"Holy One, you are the One who is and
who was.
You are right to decide to punish these
evil people.
[6]They have poured out the blood of your
holy people and your prophets.
So now you have given them blood to
drink as they deserve."
[7]And I heard a voice coming from the altar saying:

"Yes, Lord God Almighty,
the way you punish evil people is right
and fair."

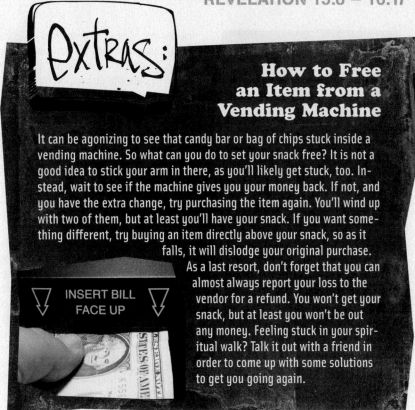

Extras:

How to Free an Item from a Vending Machine

It can be agonizing to see that candy bar or bag of chips stuck inside a vending machine. So what can you do to set your snack free? It is not a good idea to stick your arm in there, as you'll likely get stuck, too. Instead, wait to see if the machine gives you your money back. If not, and you have the extra change, try purchasing the item again. You'll wind up with two of them, but at least you'll have your snack. If you want something different, try buying an item directly above your snack, so as it falls, it will dislodge your original purchase. As a last resort, don't forget that you can almost always report your loss to the vendor for a refund. You won't get your snack, but at least you won't be out any money. Feeling stuck in your spiritual walk? Talk it out with a friend in order to come up with some solutions to get you going again.

INSERT BILL FACE UP

[8]The fourth angel poured out his bowl on the sun, and he was given power to burn the people with fire. [9]They were burned by the great heat, and they cursed the name of God, who had control over these disasters. But the people refused to change their hearts and lives and give glory to God.

[10]The fifth angel poured out his bowl on the throne of the beast, and darkness covered its kingdom. People gnawed their tongues because of the pain. [11]They also cursed the God of heaven because of their pain and the sores they had, but they refused to change their hearts and turn away from the evil things they did.

[12]The sixth angel poured out his bowl on the great river Euphrates so that the water in the river was dried up to prepare the way for the kings from the east to come. [13]Then I saw three evil spirits that looked like frogs coming out of the mouth of the dragon, out of the mouth of the beast, and out of the mouth of the false prophet. [14]These evil spirits are the spirits of demons, which have power to do miracles. They go out to the kings of the whole world to gather them together for the battle on the great day of God Almighty.

[15]"Listen! I will come as a thief comes! Blessed are those who stay awake and keep their clothes on so that they will not walk around naked and have people see their shame."

[16]Then the evil spirits gathered the kings together to the place that is called Armageddon in the Hebrew language.

[17]The seventh angel poured out his bowl into the air. Then a loud voice came out of the temple from the throne, saying, "It is finished!"

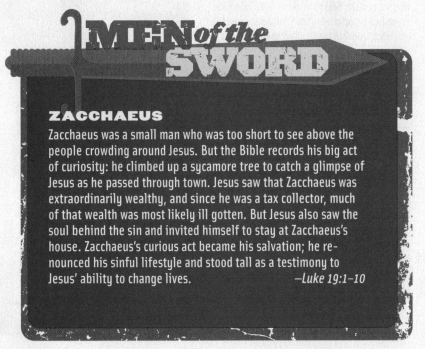

MEN of the SWORD

ZACCHAEUS

Zacchaeus was a small man who was too short to see above the people crowding around Jesus. But the Bible records his big act of curiosity: he climbed up a sycamore tree to catch a glimpse of Jesus as he passed through town. Jesus saw that Zacchaeus was extraordinarily wealthy, and since he was a tax collector, much of that wealth was most likely ill gotten. But Jesus also saw the soul behind the sin and invited himself to stay at Zacchaeus's house. Zacchaeus's curious act became his salvation; he renounced his sinful lifestyle and stood tall as a testimony to Jesus' ability to change lives.
                                                                  —Luke 19:1–10

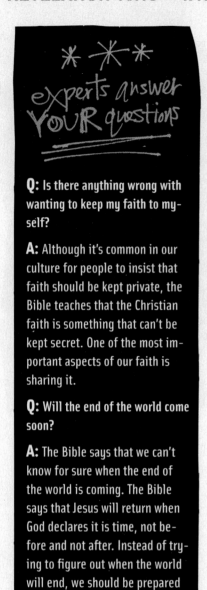

experts answer YOUR questions

Q: Is there anything wrong with wanting to keep my faith to myself?

A: Although it's common in our culture for people to insist that faith should be kept private, the Bible teaches that the Christian faith is something that can't be kept secret. One of the most important aspects of our faith is sharing it.

Q: Will the end of the world come soon?

A: The Bible says that we can't know for sure when the end of the world is coming. The Bible says that Jesus will return when God declares it is time, not before and not after. Instead of trying to figure out when the world will end, we should be prepared for Jesus to return at any time.

[18] Then there were flashes of lightning, noises, thunder, and a big earthquake—the worst earthquake that has ever happened since people have been on earth. [19] The great city split into three parts, and the cities of the nations were destroyed. And God remembered the sins of Babylon the Great, so he gave that city the cup filled with the wine of his terrible anger. [20] Then every island ran away, and mountains disappeared. [21] Giant hailstones, each weighing about a hundred pounds, fell from the sky upon people. People cursed God for the disaster of the hail, because this disaster was so terrible.

THE WOMAN ON THE ANIMAL

17 Then one of the seven angels who had the seven bowls came and spoke to me. He said, "Come, and I will show you the punishment that will be given to the great prostitute, the one sitting over many waters. [2] The kings of the earth sinned sexually with her, and the people of the earth became drunk from the wine of her sexual sin."

[3] Then the angel carried me away by the Spirit to the desert. There I saw a woman sitting on a red beast. It was covered with names against God written on it, and it had seven heads and ten horns. [4] The woman was dressed in purple and red and was shining with the gold, precious jewels, and pearls she was wearing. She had a golden cup in her hand, a cup filled with evil things and the uncleanness of her sexual sin. [5] On her forehead a title was written that was secret. This is what was written:

THE GREAT BABYLON
MOTHER OF PROSTITUTES
AND OF THE EVIL THINGS OF THE EARTH

[6] Then I saw that the woman was drunk with the blood of God's holy people and with the blood of those who were killed because of their faith in Jesus.

When I saw the woman, I was very amazed. [7] Then the angel said to me, "Why are you amazed? I will tell you the secret of this woman and the beast she rides—the one with seven heads and ten horns. [8] The beast you saw was once alive but is not alive now. But soon it will come up out of the bottomless pit and go away to be destroyed. There are people who live on earth whose names have not been written in the book of life since the beginning of the world. They will be amazed when they see the beast, because he was once alive, is not alive now, but will come again.

[9] "You need a wise mind to understand this. The seven heads on the beast are seven mountains where the woman sits. [10] And they are seven kings. Five of the kings have already been destroyed, one of the kings lives now, and another has not yet come. When he comes, he must stay a short time. [11] The beast that was once alive, but is not alive now, is also an eighth king. He belongs to the first seven kings, and he will go away to be destroyed.

[12] "The ten horns you saw are ten kings who have not yet begun to rule, but they will receive power to rule with the beast for one hour. [13] All ten of these kings have the same purpose, and they will give their power and authority to the beast. [14] They will make war against the Lamb, but the Lamb will defeat them, because he is Lord of lords and King of kings. He will defeat them with his called, chosen, and faithful followers."

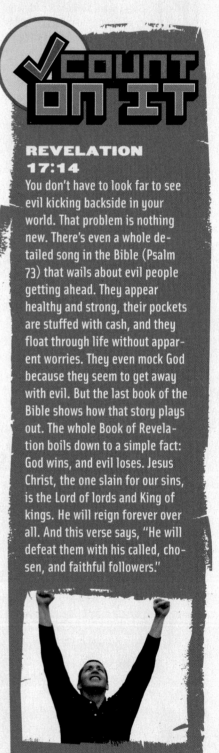

COUNT ON IT

REVELATION 17:14

You don't have to look far to see evil kicking backside in your world. That problem is nothing new. There's even a whole detailed song in the Bible (Psalm 73) that wails about evil people getting ahead. They appear healthy and strong, their pockets are stuffed with cash, and they float through life without apparent worries. They even mock God because they seem to get away with evil. But the last book of the Bible shows how that story plays out. The whole Book of Revelation boils down to a simple fact: God wins, and evil loses. Jesus Christ, the one slain for our sins, is the Lord of lords and King of kings. He will reign forever over all. And this verse says, "He will defeat them with his called, chosen, and faithful followers."

¹⁵Then the angel said to me, "The waters that you saw, where the prostitute sits, are peoples, races, nations, and languages. ¹⁶The ten horns and the beast you saw will hate the prostitute. They will take everything she has and leave her naked. They will eat her body and burn her with fire. ¹⁷God made the ten horns want to carry out his purpose by agreeing to give the beast their power to rule, until what God has said comes about. ¹⁸The woman you saw is the great city that rules over the kings of the earth."

BABYLON IS DESTROYED

18 After the vision of these things, I saw another angel coming down from heaven. This angel had great power, and his glory made the earth bright. ²He shouted in a powerful voice:

"Ruined, ruined is the great city of
    Babylon!
  She has become a home for demons
and a prison for every evil spirit,
    and a prison for every unclean bird and
        unclean beast.
³She has been ruined, because all the
        peoples of the earth
  have drunk the wine of the desire of her
        sexual sin.
She has been ruined also because the kings
        of the earth
  have sinned sexually with her,
and the merchants of the earth
  have grown rich from the great wealth of
        her luxury."

⁷She gave herself much glory and rich
        living.
  Give her that much suffering and
        sadness.
She says to herself, 'I am a queen sitting on
        my throne.
  I am not a widow; I will never be sad.'
⁸So these disasters will come to her in one
        day:
  death, and crying, and great hunger,
and she will be destroyed by fire,
  because the Lord God who judges her is
        powerful."

⁹The kings of the earth who sinned sexually with her and shared her wealth will see the smoke from her burning. Then they will cry and be sad because of her death. ¹⁰They will be afraid of her suffering and stand far away and say:

"Terrible! How terrible for you, great city,
        powerful city of Babylon,
  because your punishment has come in one
        hour!"

¹¹And the merchants of the earth will cry and be sad about her, because now there is no one to buy their cargoes— ¹²cargoes of gold, silver, jewels, pearls, fine linen, purple cloth, silk, red cloth; all kinds of citron wood and all kinds of things made from ivory, expensive wood, bronze, iron, and marble; ¹³cinnamon, spice, incense, myrrh, frankincense, wine, olive oil, fine flour, wheat, cattle, sheep, horses, carriages, slaves, and human lives.

¹⁴The merchants will say,

"Babylon, the good things you wanted are
        gone from you.

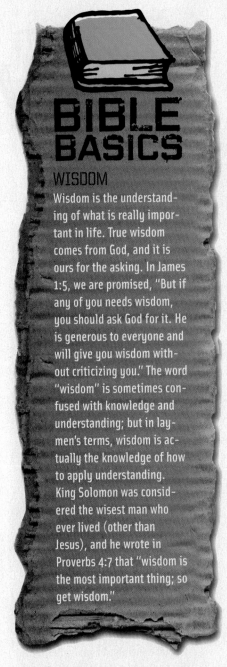

⁴Then I heard another voice from heaven saying:

"Come out of that city, my people,
  so that you will not share in her sins,
  so that you will not receive the disasters
        that will come to her.
⁵Her sins have piled up as high as the sky,
  and God has not forgotten the wrongs
        she has done.
⁶Give that city the same as she gave to others.
  Pay her back twice as much as she did.
  Prepare wine for her that is twice as strong
        as the wine she prepared for others.

All your rich and fancy things have
        disappeared.
  You will never have them again."

¹⁵The merchants who became rich from selling to her will be afraid of her suffering and will stand far away. They will cry and be sad ¹⁶and say:

"Terrible! How terrible for the great
        city!
  She was dressed in fine linen, purple
        and red cloth,
  and she was shining with gold, precious
        jewels, and pearls!

¹⁷All these riches have been destroyed in one
        hour!"

Every sea captain, every passenger, the sailors, and all those who earn their living from the sea stood far away from Babylon. ¹⁸As they saw the smoke from her burning, they cried out loudly, "There was never a city like this great city!" ¹⁹And they threw dust on their heads and cried out, weeping and being sad. They said:

"Terrible! How terrible for the great city!
  All the people who had ships on the sea
        became rich because of her wealth!
But she has been destroyed in one hour!

RADICAL FAITH

REVELATION 19:11–16

Don't mess with Jesus. Sure, some guys think he's not all that. He placed his hands on children's heads and blessed them. He let a woman cry all over his feet and pour perfume on his toes, then mop up the dampness with her hair. He wept deeply when a close friend died (John 11:35). He allowed his enemies to mock, strip, and beat him, then died when they spiked him to a cross. But anyone who thinks Jesus was weak is missing the strength in his character. They're also ignorant of the rest of the story. Jesus spoke to a deadly storm and the waves went still. He cried for his dead friend, then raised him to life from the tomb (John 11:43). He exercised total control over a mob of demons. He vaulted from the grave. And one day he will return as King of kings to reign over all creation, stomping out his enemies and rewarding those who seek him. That's not at all wimpy. Radical faith means living all-out for this almighty Lord of all.

[20]Be happy because of this, heaven!
Be happy, God's holy people and apostles and prophets!
God has punished her because of what she did to you."

[21]Then a powerful angel picked up a large stone, like one used for grinding grain, and threw it into the sea. He said:
"In the same way, the great city of Babylon will be thrown down,
and it will never be found again.
[22]The music of people playing harps and other instruments, flutes, and trumpets,
will never be heard in you again.
No workman doing any job
will ever be found in you again.
The sound of grinding grain
will never be heard in you again.
[23]The light of a lamp
will never shine in you again,
and the voices of a bridegroom and bride will never be heard in you again.
Your merchants were the world's great people,
and all the nations were tricked by your magic.
[24]You are guilty of the death of the prophets and God's holy people
and all who have been killed on earth."

PEOPLE IN HEAVEN PRAISE GOD

19 After this vision and announcement I heard what sounded like a great many people in heaven saying:
"Hallelujah!"[n]
Salvation, glory, and power belong to our God,
[2] because his judgments are true and right. He has punished the prostitute
who made the earth evil with her sexual sin.
He has paid her back for the death of his servants."
[3]Again they said:
"Hallelujah!
She is burning, and her smoke will rise forever and ever."
[4]Then the twenty-four elders and the four living creatures bowed down and worshiped God, who sits on the throne. They said:
"Amen, Hallelujah!"
[5]Then a voice came from the throne, saying:
"Praise our God, all you who serve him
and all you who honor him, both small and great!"
[6]Then I heard what sounded like a great many people, like the noise of flooding water,

and like the noise of loud thunder. The people were saying:
"Hallelujah!
Our Lord God, the Almighty, rules.
[7]Let us rejoice and be happy
and give God glory,

experts answer YOUR questions

Q: What kind of bodies will we have in heaven?

A: Although the Bible promises that all Christians who die will be raised to eternal life, Paul says that the bodies we'll have in heaven will be different from our bodies on earth. They will be spiritual bodies, rather than physical ones. God is going to give us eternal life in new bodies that won't decay or die.

Q: How can I get more faith?

A: Jesus often praised people for their faith, saying that it was because of their faith that God was able to do miracles in their lives. By remembering all God has done for us in the past, we can have more faith for the future. And the Bible also says that faith comes from studying the Word of God, so we need to feed our spirits with it daily.

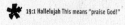
19:1 Hallelujah This means "praise God!"

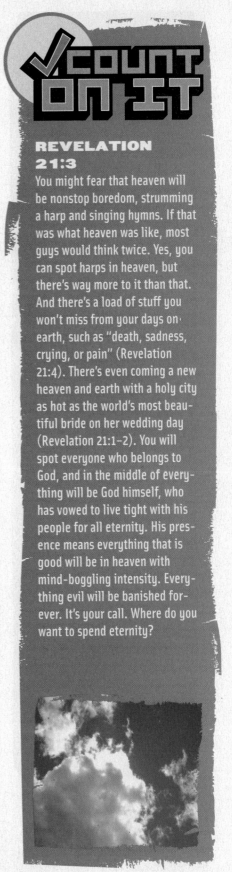

because the wedding of the Lamb has
  come,
  and the Lamb's bride has made herself
  ready.
⁸Fine linen, bright and clean, was given to
  her to wear."
(The fine linen means the good things done by
God's holy people.)

⁹And the angel said to me, "Write this: Blessed are those who have been invited to the wedding meal of the Lamb!" And the angel said, "These are the true words of God."

¹⁰Then I bowed down at the angel's feet to worship him, but he said to me, "Do not worship me! I am a servant like you and your brothers and sisters who have the message of Jesus. Worship God, because the message about Jesus is the spirit that gives all prophecy."

THE RIDER ON THE WHITE HORSE

¹¹Then I saw heaven opened, and there before me was a white horse. The rider on the horse is called Faithful and True, and he is right when he judges and makes war. ¹²His eyes are like burning fire, and on his head are many crowns. He has a name written on him, which no one but himself knows. ¹³He is dressed in a robe dipped in blood, and his name is the Word of God. ¹⁴The armies of heaven, dressed in fine linen, white and clean, were following him on white horses. ¹⁵Out of the rider's mouth comes a sharp sword that he will use to defeat the nations, and he will rule them with a rod of iron. He will crush out the wine in the winepress of the terrible anger of God the Almighty. ¹⁶On his robe and on his upper leg was written this name: KING OF KINGS AND LORD OF LORDS.

¹⁷Then I saw an angel standing in the sun, and he called with a loud voice to all the birds flying in the sky: "Come and gather together for the great feast of God ¹⁸so that you can eat the bodies of kings, generals, mighty people, horses and their riders, and the bodies of all people—free, slave, small, and great."

¹⁹Then I saw the beast and the kings of the earth. Their armies were gathered together to make war against the rider on the horse and his army. ²⁰But the beast was captured and with him the false prophet who did the miracles for the beast. The false prophet had used these miracles to trick those who had the mark of the beast and worshiped his idol. The false prophet and the beast were thrown alive into the lake of fire that burns with sulfur. ²¹And their armies were killed with the sword that came out of the mouth of the rider on the horse, and all the birds ate the bodies until they were full.

THE THOUSAND YEARS

20 I saw an angel coming down from heaven. He had the key to the bottomless pit and a large chain in his hand. ²The angel grabbed the dragon, that old snake who is the devil and Satan, and tied him up for a thousand years. ³Then he threw him into the bottomless pit, closed it, and locked it over him. The angel did this so he could not trick the people of the earth anymore until the thousand years were ended. After a thousand years he must be set free for a short time.

⁴Then I saw some thrones and people sitting on them who had been given the power to judge. And I saw the souls of those who had been killed because they were faithful to the message of Jesus and the message from God. They had not worshiped the beast or his idol, and they had not received the mark of the beast on their foreheads or on their hands. They came back to life and ruled with Christ for a thousand years. ⁵(The others that were dead did not live again until the thousand years were ended.) This is the first raising of the dead. ⁶Blessed and holy are those who share in this first raising of the dead. The second death has no power over them. They will be priests for God and for Christ and will rule with him for a thousand years.

⁷When the thousand years are over, Satan will be set free from his prison. ⁸Then he will go out to trick the nations in all the earth—

REVELATION 21:3

You might fear that heaven will be nonstop boredom, strumming a harp and singing hymns. If that was what heaven was like, most guys would think twice. Yes, you can spot harps in heaven, but there's way more to it than that. And there's a load of stuff you won't miss from your days on earth, such as "death, sadness, crying, or pain" (Revelation 21:4). There's even coming a new heaven and earth with a holy city as hot as the world's most beautiful bride on her wedding day (Revelation 21:1–2). You will spot everyone who belongs to God, and in the middle of everything will be God himself, who has vowed to live tight with his people for all eternity. His presence means everything that is good will be in heaven with mind-boggling intensity. Everything evil will be banished forever. It's your call. Where do you want to spend eternity?

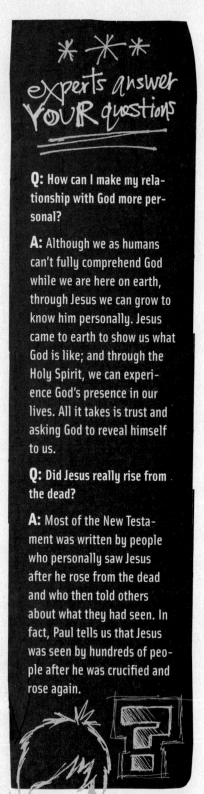

the camp of God's people and the city God loves. But fire came down from heaven and burned them up. [10]And Satan, who tricked them, was thrown into the lake of burning sulfur with the beast and the false prophet. There they will be punished day and night forever and ever.

PEOPLE OF THE WORLD ARE JUDGED

[11]Then I saw a great white throne and the One who was sitting on it. Earth and sky ran away from him and disappeared. [12]And I saw the dead, great and small, standing before the throne. Then books were opened, and the book of life was opened. The dead were judged by what they had done, which was written in the books. [13]The sea gave up the dead who were in it, and Death and Hades[n] gave up the dead who were in them. Each person was judged by what he had done. [14]And Death and Hades were thrown into the lake of fire. The lake of fire is the second death. [15]And anyone whose name was not found written in the book of life was thrown into the lake of fire.

THE NEW JERUSALEM

21 Then I saw a new heaven and a new earth. The first heaven and the first earth had disappeared, and there was no sea anymore. [2]And I saw the holy city, the new Jerusalem,[n] coming down out of heaven from God. It was prepared like a bride dressed for her husband. [3]And I heard a loud voice from the throne, saying, "Now God's presence is with people, and he will live with them, and they will be his people. God himself will be with them and will be their God.[n] [4]He will wipe away every tear from their eyes, and there will be no more death, sadness, crying, or pain, because all the old ways are gone."

[5]The One who was sitting on the throne said, "Look! I am making everything new!" Then he said, "Write this, because these words are true and can be trusted."

[6]The One on the throne said to me, "It is finished. I am the Alpha and the Omega,[n] the Beginning and the End. I will give free water from the spring of the water of life to anyone who is thirsty. [7]Those who win the victory will receive this, and I will be their God, and they will be my children. [8]But cowards, those who refuse to believe, who do evil things, who kill, who sin sexually, who do evil magic, who worship idols, and who tell lies—all these will have a place in the lake of burning sulfur. This is the second death."

[9]Then one of the seven angels who had the seven bowls full of the seven last troubles came to me, saying, "Come with me, and I will show you the bride, the wife of the Lamb." [10]And the angel carried me away by the Spirit to a very large and high mountain. He showed me the holy city, Jerusalem, coming down out of heaven from God. [11]It was shining with the glory of God and was bright like a very expensive jewel, like a jasper, clear as crystal. [12]The city had a great high wall with twelve gates with twelve angels at the gates, and on each gate was written the name of one of the twelve tribes of Israel. [13]There were three gates on the east, three on the north, three on the south, and three on the west. [14]The walls of the city were built on twelve foundation stones, and on the stones were written the names of the twelve apostles of the Lamb.

[15]The angel who talked with me had a measuring rod made of gold to measure the city, its gates, and its wall. [16]The city was built in a square, and its length was equal to its width. The angel measured the city with the rod. The city was 1,500 miles long, 1,500 miles wide, and 1,500 miles high. [17]The angel also measured the wall. It was 216 feet high, by human measurements, which the angel was using. [18]The wall was made of jasper, and the city was made of pure gold, as pure as glass. [19]The foundation stones of the city walls were decorated with every kind of jewel. The first foundation was jasper, the second was sapphire, the third was chalcedony, the fourth was emerald, [20]the fifth was onyx, the sixth was carnelian, the seventh was chrysolite, the eighth was beryl, the ninth was topaz, the tenth was chrysoprase, the eleventh was jacinth, and the twelfth was amethyst. [21]The twelve gates were twelve pearls, each gate having been made from a sin-

Gog and Magog—to gather them for battle. There are so many people they will be like sand on the seashore. [9]And Satan's army marched across the earth and gathered around

 20:13 Hades The place of the dead. **21:2 new Jerusalem** The spiritual city where God's people live with him. **21:3 and . . . God** Some Greek copies do not have this phrase. **21:6 Alpha and the Omega** The first and last letters of the Greek alphabet. This means "the beginning and the end."

362

gle pearl. And the street of the city was made of pure gold as clear as glass.

²²I did not see a temple in the city, because the Lord God Almighty and the Lamb are the city's temple. ²³The city does not need the sun or the moon to shine on it, because the glory of God is its light, and the Lamb is the city's lamp. ²⁴By its light the people of the world will walk, and the kings of the earth will bring their glory into it. ²⁵The city's gates will never be shut on any day, because there is no night there. ²⁶The glory and the honor of the nations will be brought into it. ²⁷Nothing unclean and no one who does shameful things or tells lies will ever go into it. Only those whose names are written in the Lamb's book of life will enter the city.

22 Then the angel showed me the river of the water of life. It was shining like crystal and was flowing from the throne of God and of the Lamb ²down the middle of the street of the city. The tree of life was on each side of the river. It produces fruit twelve times a year, once each month. The leaves of the tree are for the healing of all the nations. ³Nothing that God judges guilty will be in that city. The throne of God and of the Lamb will be there, and God's servants will worship him. ⁴They will see his face, and his name will be written on their foreheads. ⁵There will never be night again. They will not need the light of a lamp or the light of the sun, because the Lord God will give them light. And they will rule as kings forever and ever.

⁶The angel said to me, "These words can be trusted and are true." The Lord, the God of the spirits of the prophets, sent his angel to show his servants the things that must happen soon.

⁷"Listen! I am coming soon! Blessed is the one who obeys the words of prophecy in this book."

⁸I, John, am the one who heard and saw these things. When I heard and saw them, I bowed down to worship at the feet of the angel

Revelation 22:17 "The Spirit and the bride say, 'Come!' Let the one who hears this say, 'Come!' Let whoever is thirsty come; whoever wishes may have the water of life as a free gift."

who showed these things to me. ⁹But the angel said to me, "Do not worship me! I am a servant like you, your brothers the prophets, and all those who obey the words in this book. Worship God!"

¹⁰Then the angel told me, "Do not keep secret the words of prophecy in this book, because the time is near for all this to happen. ¹¹Let whoever is doing evil continue to do evil. Let whoever is unclean continue to be unclean. Let whoever is doing right continue to do right. Let whoever is holy continue to be holy."

¹²"Listen! I am coming soon! I will bring my reward with me, and I will repay each one of you for what you have done. ¹³I am the Alpha and the Omega,ⁿ the First and the Last, the Beginning and the End.

¹⁴"Blessed are those who wash their robesⁿ so that they will receive the right to eat the fruit from the tree of life and may go through the gates into the city. ¹⁵Outside the city are the evil people, those who do evil magic, who sin sexually, who murder, who worship idols, and who love lies and tell lies.

¹⁶"I, Jesus, have sent my angel to tell you these things for the churches. I am the descendant from the family of David, and I am the bright morning star."

¹⁷The Spirit and the bride say, "Come!" Let the one who hears this say, "Come!" Let whoever is thirsty come; whoever wishes may have the water of life as a free gift.

¹⁸I warn everyone who hears the words of the prophecy of this book: If anyone adds anything to these words, God will add to that person the disasters written about in this book. ¹⁹And if anyone takes away from the words of this book of prophecy, God will take away that one's share of the tree of life and of the holy city, which are written about in this book.

²⁰Jesus, the One who says these things are true, says, "Yes, I am coming soon."

Amen. Come, Lord Jesus!

²¹The grace of the Lord Jesus be with all. Amen.

22:13 Alpha and the Omega The first and last letters of the Greek alphabet. This means "the beginning and the end." **22:14 wash their robes** This means they believed and obeyed Jesus so that their sins could be forgiven by Christ's blood. The "washing" may refer to baptism (Acts 22:16).

30 DAYS WITH JESUS

60 DAYS
WITH PAUL

MIRACLES of Jesus Christ

MIRACLE	MATTHEW	MARK	LUKE	JOHN
1. HEALING A MAN WITH SKIN DISEASE	8:2	1:40	5:12	
2. HEALING AN ARMY OFFICER'S SERVANT (OF PARALYSIS)	8:5		7:1	
3. HEALING PETER'S MOTHER-IN-LAW	8:14	1:30	4:38	
4. HEALING THE SICK AT EVENING	8:16	1:32	4:40	
5. CALMING THE STORM	8:23	4:35	8:22	
6. DEMONS ENTERING A HERD OF PIGS	8:28	5:1	8:26	
7. HEALING A PARALYZED MAN	9:2	2:3	5:18	
8. RAISING THE SYNAGOGUE LEADER'S DAUGHTER	9:18, 23	5:22, 35	8:40, 49	
9. HEALING THE HEMORRHAGING WOMAN	9:20	5:25	8:43	
10. HEALING TWO BLIND MEN	9:27			
11. CURING A DEMON-POSSESSED, MUTE MAN	9:32			
12. HEALING A MAN'S CRIPPLED HAND	12:9	3:1	6:6	
13. CURING A DEMON-POSSESSED, BLIND, AND MUTE MAN	12:22		11:14	
14. FEEDING THE FIVE THOUSAND	14:13	6:30	9:10	6:1
15. WALKING ON THE LAKE	14:25	6:48		6:19
16. HEALING THE NON-JEWISH WOMAN'S DAUGHTER	15:21	7:24		
17. FEEDING THE FOUR THOUSAND	15:32	8:1		
18. HEALING THE EPILEPTIC BOY	17:14	9:17	9:38	
19. TEMPLE TAX IN THE FISH'S MOUTH	17:24			
20. HEALING TWO BLIND MEN	20:30	10:46	18:35	

STORIES [PARABLES]

PARABLE	MATTHEW	MARK	LUKE
YOU ARE LIKE LIGHT	5:14-16	4:21-22	8:16-17
			11:33-36
TWO KINDS OF PEOPLE	7:24-27		6:47-49
UNSHRUNK CLOTH ON AN OLD COAT	9:16	2:21	5:36
NEW WINE INTO OLD LEATHER BAGS	9:17	2:22	5:37-38
A STORY ABOUT PLANTING SEED	13:3-23	4:2-20	8:4-15
A STORY ABOUT WHEAT AND WEEDS	13:24-30		
A STORY OF A MUSTARD SEED	13:31-32	4:30-32	13:18-19
A STORY OF YEAST	13:33		13:20-21
A STORY OF A TREASURE	13:44		
A STORY OF A PEARL	13:45-46		
A STORY OF A FISHING NET	13:47-50		
A LOST SHEEP	18:12-14		15:3-7
AN UNFORGIVING SERVANT	18:23-35		
A STORY ABOUT WORKERS	20:1-16		
A STORY ABOUT TWO SONS	21:28-32		
A STORY ABOUT GOD'S SON	21:33-46	12:1-12	20:9-19
A STORY ABOUT A WEDDING FEAST	22:2-14		
A STORY ABOUT A FIG TREE	24:29-44	13:28-32	21:29-33
A STORY ABOUT TEN BRIDESMAIDS	25:1-13		

PARABLE	MATTHEW	MARK	LUKE
A STORY ABOUT THREE SERVANTS	25:14–30		
A STORY ABOUT A SEED		4:26–29	
A MAN WHO GOES ON A TRIP		13:33–37	
THE BANKER AND TWO PEOPLE IN DEBT			7:41–43
THE GOOD SAMARITAN			10:30 37
A FRIEND IN NEED			11:5–13
THE RICH FOOL			12:16–21
THE READY SERVANTS			12:35–40
THE WISE SERVANT			12:42–44
THE USELESS TREE			13:6–9
A STORY ABOUT A BIG BANQUET			14:16–24
THE COST OF BEING JESUS' FOLLOWER			14:25–33
A LOST COIN			15:8–10
THE SON WHO LEFT HOME			15:11–32
THE DISHONEST MANAGER			16:1–13
THE RICH MAN AND LAZARUS			16:19–31
BE GOOD SERVANTS			17:7–10
THE PERSISTENT WIDOW			18:1–8
A STORY OF A PHARISEE AND A TAX COLLECTOR			18:9–14
A STORY ABOUT THREE SERVANTS			19:11–27

points
along the way

Map your faith journey with
significant happenings in your life
and meaningful directions from God's Word.

Your word is like a lamp for my feet
and a light for my path.

—Psalm 119:105